More information about this series at http://www.springer.com/series/7409

Lecture Notes in Computer Science 12205

Panayiotis Zaphiris · Andri Ioannou (Eds.)

Learning and Collaboration Technologies

Designing, Developing and Deploying Learning Experiences

7th International Conference, LCT 2020
Held as Part of the 22nd HCI International Conference, HCII 2020
Copenhagen, Denmark, July 19–24, 2020
Proceedings, Part I

Springer

Editors
Panayiotis Zaphiris
Cyprus University of Technology
Limassol, Cyprus

Andri Ioannou ⓘ
Cyprus University of Technology
Limassol, Cyprus

Research Center on Interactive Media,
Smart Systems and Emerging
Technologies (RISE)
Limassol, Cyprus

ISSN 0302-9743   ISSN 1611-3349 (electronic)
Lecture Notes in Computer Science
ISBN 978-3-030-50512-7   ISBN 978-3-030-50513-4 (eBook)
https://doi.org/10.1007/978-3-030-50513-4

LNCS Sublibrary: SL3 – Information Systems and Applications, incl. Internet/Web, and HCI

This Springer imprint is published by the registered company Springer Nature Switzerland AG
The registered company address is: Gewerbestrasse 11, 6330 Cham, Switzerland

Foreword

The 22nd International Conference on Human-Computer Interaction, HCI International 2020 (HCII 2020), was planned to be held at the AC Bella Sky Hotel and Bella Center, Copenhagen, Denmark, during July 19–24, 2020. Due to the COVID-19 coronavirus pandemic and the resolution of the Danish government not to allow events larger than 500 people to be hosted until September 1, 2020, HCII 2020 had to be held virtually. It incorporated the 21 thematic areas and affiliated conferences listed on the following page.

A total of 6,326 individuals from academia, research institutes, industry, and governmental agencies from 97 countries submitted contributions, and 1,439 papers and 238 posters were included in the conference proceedings. These contributions address the latest research and development efforts and highlight the human aspects of design and use of computing systems. The contributions thoroughly cover the entire field of human-computer interaction, addressing major advances in knowledge and effective use of computers in a variety of application areas. The volumes constituting the full set of the conference proceedings are listed in the following pages.

The HCI International (HCII) conference also offers the option of "late-breaking work" which applies both for papers and posters and the corresponding volume(s) of the proceedings will be published just after the conference. Full papers will be included in the "HCII 2020 - Late Breaking Papers" volume of the proceedings to be published in the Springer LNCS series, while poster extended abstracts will be included as short papers in the "HCII 2020 - Late Breaking Posters" volume to be published in the Springer CCIS series.

I would like to thank the program board chairs and the members of the program boards of all thematic areas and affiliated conferences for their contribution to the highest scientific quality and the overall success of the HCI International 2020 conference.

This conference would not have been possible without the continuous and unwavering support and advice of the founder, Conference General Chair Emeritus and Conference Scientific Advisor Prof. Gavriel Salvendy. For his outstanding efforts, I would like to express my appreciation to the communications chair and editor of HCI International News, Dr. Abbas Moallem.

July 2020   Constantine Stephanidis

HCI International 2020 Thematic Areas and Affiliated Conferences

Thematic areas:

- HCI 2020: Human-Computer Interaction
- HIMI 2020: Human Interface and the Management of Information

Affiliated conferences:

- EPCE: 17th International Conference on Engineering Psychology and Cognitive Ergonomics
- UAHCI: 14th International Conference on Universal Access in Human-Computer Interaction
- VAMR: 12th International Conference on Virtual, Augmented and Mixed Reality
- CCD: 12th International Conference on Cross-Cultural Design
- SCSM: 12th International Conference on Social Computing and Social Media
- AC: 14th International Conference on Augmented Cognition
- DHM: 11th International Conference on Digital Human Modeling and Applications in Health, Safety, Ergonomics and Risk Management
- DUXU: 9th International Conference on Design, User Experience and Usability
- DAPI: 8th International Conference on Distributed, Ambient and Pervasive Interactions
- HCIBGO: 7th International Conference on HCI in Business, Government and Organizations
- LCT: 7th International Conference on Learning and Collaboration Technologies
- ITAP: 6th International Conference on Human Aspects of IT for the Aged Population
- HCI-CPT: Second International Conference on HCI for Cybersecurity, Privacy and Trust
- HCI-Games: Second International Conference on HCI in Games
- MobiTAS: Second International Conference on HCI in Mobility, Transport and Automotive Systems
- AIS: Second International Conference on Adaptive Instructional Systems
- C&C: 8th International Conference on Culture and Computing
- MOBILE: First International Conference on Design, Operation and Evaluation of Mobile Communications
- AI-HCI: First International Conference on Artificial Intelligence in HCI

Conference Proceedings Volumes Full List

1. LNCS 12181, Human-Computer Interaction: Design and User Experience (Part I), edited by Masaaki Kurosu
2. LNCS 12182, Human-Computer Interaction: Multimodal and Natural Interaction (Part II), edited by Masaaki Kurosu
3. LNCS 12183, Human-Computer Interaction: Human Values and Quality of Life (Part III), edited by Masaaki Kurosu
4. LNCS 12184, Human Interface and the Management of Information: Designing Information (Part I), edited by Sakae Yamamoto and Hirohiko Mori
5. LNCS 12185, Human Interface and the Management of Information: Interacting with Information (Part II), edited by Sakae Yamamoto and Hirohiko Mori
6. LNAI 12186, Engineering Psychology and Cognitive Ergonomics: Mental Workload, Human Physiology, and Human Energy (Part I), edited by Don Harris and Wen-Chin Li
7. LNAI 12187, Engineering Psychology and Cognitive Ergonomics: Cognition and Design (Part II), edited by Don Harris and Wen-Chin Li
8. LNCS 12188, Universal Access in Human-Computer Interaction: Design Approaches and Supporting Technologies (Part I), edited by Margherita Antona and Constantine Stephanidis
9. LNCS 12189, Universal Access in Human-Computer Interaction: Applications and Practice (Part II), edited by Margherita Antona and Constantine Stephanidis
10. LNCS 12190, Virtual, Augmented and Mixed Reality: Design and Interaction (Part I), edited by Jessie Y. C. Chen and Gino Fragomeni
11. LNCS 12191, Virtual, Augmented and Mixed Reality: Industrial and Everyday Life Applications (Part II), edited by Jessie Y. C. Chen and Gino Fragomeni
12. LNCS 12192, Cross-Cultural Design: User Experience of Products, Services, and Intelligent Environments (Part I), edited by P. L. Patrick Rau
13. LNCS 12193, Cross-Cultural Design: Applications in Health, Learning, Communication, and Creativity (Part II), edited by P. L. Patrick Rau
14. LNCS 12194, Social Computing and Social Media: Design, Ethics, User Behavior, and Social Network Analysis (Part I), edited by Gabriele Meiselwitz
15. LNCS 12195, Social Computing and Social Media: Participation, User Experience, Consumer Experience, and Applications of Social Computing (Part II), edited by Gabriele Meiselwitz
16. LNAI 12196, Augmented Cognition: Theoretical and Technological Approaches (Part I), edited by Dylan D. Schmorrow and Cali M. Fidopiastis
17. LNAI 12197, Augmented Cognition: Human Cognition and Behaviour (Part II), edited by Dylan D. Schmorrow and Cali M. Fidopiastis

38. CCIS 1224, HCI International 2020 Posters - Part I, edited by Constantine Stephanidis and Margherita Antona
39. CCIS 1225, HCI International 2020 Posters - Part II, edited by Constantine Stephanidis and Margherita Antona
40. CCIS 1226, HCI International 2020 Posters - Part III, edited by Constantine Stephanidis and Margherita Antona

http://2020.hci.international/proceedings

7th International Conference on Learning and Collaboration Technologies (LCT 2020)

Program Board Chairs: **Panayiotis Zaphiris, Cyprus University of Technology, Cyprus, and Andri Ioannou, Cyprus University of Technology and RISE, Cyprus**

- Ruthi Aladjem, Israel
- Kaushal Kumar Bhagat, India
- Fisnik Dalipi, Sweden
- Camille Dickson-Deane, Australia
- Daphne Economou, UK
- Maka Eradze, Italy
- David Fonseca, Spain
- Yiannis Georgiou, Cyprus
- Preben Hansen, Sweden
- Tomaž Klobučar, Slovenia
- Birgy Lorenz, Estonia
- Ana Loureiro, Portugal
- Alejandra Martínez-Monés, Spain
- Markos Mentzelopoulos, UK
- Antigoni Parmaxi, Cyprus
- Marcos Román González, Spain

The full list with the Program Board Chairs and the members of the Program Boards of all thematic areas and affiliated conferences is available online at:

http://www.hci.international/board-members-2020.php

HCI International 2021

The 23rd International Conference on Human-Computer Interaction, HCI International 2021 (HCII 2021), will be held jointly with the affiliated conferences in Washington DC, USA, at the Washington Hilton Hotel, July 24–29, 2021. It will cover a broad spectrum of themes related to Human-Computer Interaction (HCI), including theoretical issues, methods, tools, processes, and case studies in HCI design, as well as novel interaction techniques, interfaces, and applications. The proceedings will be published by Springer. More information will be available on the conference website: http://2021.hci.international/.

General Chair
Prof. Constantine Stephanidis
University of Crete and ICS-FORTH
Heraklion, Crete, Greece
Email: general_chair@hcii2021.org

http://2021.hci.international/

Contents – Part I

Language Learning and Teaching

Technology in Education: Policies and Practice

Contents – Part II

Cognition, Emotions and Learning

Games and Gamification in Learning

Collaboration Technology and Collaborative Learning

Designing and Evaluating Learning Experiences

A Comparative Usability Study of Blackboard and Desire2Learn: Students' Perspective

Obead Alhadreti[(✉)]

Al-Qunfudhah Computing College, Umm Al-Qura University,
Mecca, Kingdom of Saudi Arabia
oghadreti@uqu.edu.sa

Abstract. Educational institutions currently favor the adoption and use of modern information and communication technology for teaching and learning. As a result, many Learning Management Systems (LMS), which are online, content-management systems specifically designed to fulfil this function, have been developed over the few years and established in education systems. This paper reports the results of a study that experimentally compared the usability of two LMSs: Blackboard (BB) and Desire2Learn (D2L), at Umm Al-Qura University in the Kingdom of Saudi Arabia. The comparison involved four points: the quantity and quality of usability problems discovered, effectiveness of the targeted systems, their efficiency, and users' satisfaction. The results of the study revealed that there are significant differences between the two systems. The evaluation discovered a higher number of major usability problems on BB. Participants were also significantly faster in completing their tasks on D2L, made fewer errors and mouse clicks, and visited fewer pages to achieve the task on D2L than on BB. However, interestingly no difference was found between the two systems in terms of users' satisfaction. Taken together, the findings suggest that appropriate customization of Blackboard should be considered in order to enhance its usability and meet the specific requirements of its end users at the current institution.

Keywords: Learning Management Systems · Usability testing

1 Introduction

The Internet has become an increasingly important means of communication between educational establishments and their students, as information and communications technology (ICT) has swiftly spread around the globe. E-learning is therefore becoming an essential teaching and learning tool for schools, colleges and universities, and it is crucial that access to pedagogical resources is both efficient and valuable. Consequently, the theoretical and methodological aspects of this rapidly growing learning mode are also increasing in significance. E-learning has many obvious advantages over traditional learning forms, not least its applicability at any time and in any place. Furthermore, it presents a wealth of opportunities for novel educational approaches and establishes settings which allow students to be active participants in their learning, to achieve independence, to become self-reflective and work collaboratively with others.

© Springer Nature Switzerland AG 2020
P. Zaphiris and A. Ioannou (Eds.): HCII 2020, LNCS 12205, pp. 3–19, 2020.
https://doi.org/10.1007/978-3-030-50513-4_1

Moreover, e-learning facilitates the management of online teaching programs and provides teachers with opportunities to design new courses, to revise, adjust or reuse existing material and tailor the digital content to the needs of their students and their learning objectives [2].

Learning Management Systems (LMS) have developed in response to these improvements in online technology. LMS are powerful software systems, designed to manage educational activities, whose aim is to aid teachers as they impart knowledge to their students and expediate learning processes. Learning establishments can utilize LMS to store educational content, to manage it and to share it as appropriate [7]. An LMS would normally be comprised of numerous features which are well-integrated to assist both teachers and students in achieving their teaching and learning goals. It thus allows a wide range of diverse activities to be carried out. These might typically include, uploading and downloading digital content, uploading student work and assignments, facilitating teacher-student, student-teacher and student-student contact, allowing easy online course registration, managing courses, administering examinations and assessing students' progress. LMS fosters a culture of collaboration amongst students and teachers through the means of ICT, and allows educational establishments to run blended learning courses as well as those which are delivered entirely online. Furthermore, LMS specifications are also designed to enable the use of e-libraries and wikis [2].

Recent years have seen the emergence of a number of LMS platforms, which differ in their functionalities and in the opportunities they offer their users. Certain contemporary versions of LMS use cloud computing. In such cases it is not necessary for the system administrator to be experienced in either the installation or the support of the software. However, for some systems, it is essential that the administrator is well versed in such web programming languages as JavaScript and PHP, and has an in-depth understanding of databases which are used for management and administration, for example, MySQL and Microsoft SQL Server [26]. Examples of LMS include Blackboard (BB), Desire2Learn (D2L), and Moodle which their global market was valued at $3 billion in 2016. By 2020, this is predicted to increase by 24% [14]. However, there is a growing acknowledgement that if the adoption and application of LMS are to be successful, they must have high levels of usability.

The rest of this paper is structured into the following sections. Firstly, a review of the current literature in the field of the importance of usability to LMS will be presented. This section also considers various methods for evaluating usability and sets out the aims and research questions for the current study. The chosen methodological approach is then discussed; the data analysis is examined and the results presented. A brief conclusion is given, along with suggestions for future work.

1.1 Usability and LMS

In the 1990s, the term "usability" was introduced to replace the term "user-friendly" [10]. The International Standard ISO 9241-11 [24] defines usability as "the extent to which a product can be used by specified users to achieve specified goals with effectiveness, efficiency and satisfaction in a specified context of use". "Effectiveness" here refers to the accuracy and completeness with which users achieve specified goals.

"Efficiency" means the amount of resources expended in relation to the product's effectiveness. User satisfaction refers to their comfort levels while carrying out their tasks and whether their experience of the product was a positive one. The "context" in terms of usability, encompasses the users, the type of task they are undertaking, their aims and the equipment. The concept also takes into account the environment, both physical and social, in which the product is being used. This is illustrated in the Fig. 1 below. The usability of a product is thus taken to mean far more than the product itself and includes how product use is affected by context. A product may be found to be highly usable in one context but far less so in another. It is therefore essential that all evaluations of products and their design should take into account the context in which they are intended to be used [24].

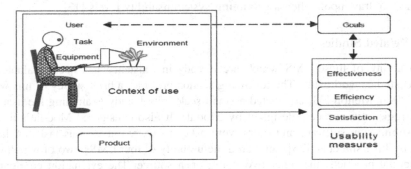

Fig. 1. Usability framework [24]

A usable LMS is time-efficient for teachers because they can design and deliver their courses more quickly and effectively. The learning experience is also enhanced as tutors and students can concentrate on course content rather than struggling to cope with problematic technologies. Nevertheless, some research has indicated that inadequate emphasis has been placed on the design of LMS, to the extent that serious problems with usability can arise [6]. Therefore, institutions considering implementing an LMS must carefully evaluate its usability before putting it to use with a student population. To examine the usability of LMS systems various methods can be employed.

1.2 Usability Evaluation

Usability evaluation has been defined by [25] as the assessment of the interface between a specific application, input device or interaction method and its user. The purpose of such an evaluation is to establish the actual or potential usability of the product in question. The process of designing a product necessitates usability evaluations being conducted at a number of stages during its development. The earlier such evaluations are conducted the better because, once decisions about exact design and functionality have been made, it can be very costly to implement changes [4].

Usability evaluation methods can be classified in numerous ways. The most common approach is to divide them into expert-based methods, model-based methods, and user-based methods. User-based evaluation necessitates the involvement of the users themselves: those people the system has been designed to serve. One of the most commonly used approaches of the former is concurrent think-aloud usability testing method. During the think-aloud process, participants are given tasks to carry out and are requested to speak about their thinking process while they are conducting the tasks. These verbalisations are usually recorded. Participant behavior is also taken into consideration and a test evaluator will normally watch participants and assess them while they work at the tasks. Usability practitioners thus have both verbal and visual evidence to draw upon when ascertaining system usability levels [13].

1.3   Related Studies

The usability of those LMS which are already in existence has been evaluated in various studies worldwide. The following section provides a brief survey of this work.

In 2006, Melton [33] conducted a small-scale initial study examining the usability of the registration process designed by Moodle. It also considered Moodle's assignment submission software and users were asked to carry out various tasks. A larger study, by Inversini et al. [23], compared the usability of four LMSs, two of which were commercial products, the other two being open source. The evaluation employed a technique known as "MiLE+", which combines task-based methods with heuristic assessment. A survey study of graduate and undergraduate students was conducted to compare usability levels of Blackboard and Desire2Learn [12]. Meanwhile, in India, Agariya and Singh [3] sought to create measurement scales for e-learning which were high quality, valid and reliable and took into account the views of both learners and faculty staff. Taking, the perspective of administrative staff, a study by Lalande and Grewal evaluated the comparative usability of BB and D2L by setting tasks for users [27]. In another study [11], a "User perception based web site usability scale", with a construct of four factors including of 25 items was developed and applied to 239 e-learners in order to determine the usability level of the LMS web site.

1.4   Aims and Research Questions

In Saudi Arabia, most of the research into LMS applications used in higher education have focused on technical issues, with very few considering matters of usability [6]. The aim of the current study is to experimentally evaluate and compare the usability of the two learning management systems: BB and Desire2Learn D2L at Umm Al-Qura University (UQU) in the Kingdom of Saudi Arabia. In the spring of 2019, UQU began the transition of the current LMS, D2L, to BB. BB was designed and produced by the BB Corporation, an IMS Global Learning Consortium consultant, first established in 1997. BB is currently in use in 90 countries worldwide; it has 16,000 clients and 100 million users [1]. Meanwhile, D2L was the first LMS to use responsive web design to allow its full use on any mobile device. The D2L company was established in 1999 by

John Baker M.Sc., while he was still in his third year at the University of Waterloo, studying Systems Design Engineering. Baker is now both CEO and president of the company and D2L is used internationally by numerous educational establishments and businesses [32].

This study addresses the following research questions:

- **Research Question 1 (RQ1):** Are there differences between the two systems in terms of the quantity and quality of usability problems identified?
- **Research Question 2 (RQ2):** Are there differences between the two systems in terms of their effectiveness?
- **Research Question 3 (RQ3):** Are there differences between the two systems in terms of their efficiency?
- **Research Question 4 (RQ4):** Are there differences between the two systems in terms of users' satisfaction?

2　Methodology

This section covers firstly the methodology employed to address the research questions, and secondly the analytical strategies considered for evaluating the data.

2.1　Study Design

The independent variable scrutinized in this study is the type of the LMS system used. There are two levels to this variable: 1. BB and 2. D2L. An experimental approach, and within-group design, with three data collection techniques, namely, observation, concurrent think-aloud protocol, and questionnaires were used to achieve the aim of the study. A between-group study design was not considered suitable for the current research due to such individual differences between participants as demographic details, which could have had a considerable influence on how well participants managed the task [29]. However, the use of repeated measures raises the issue of participants potentially using the experience gained in one test to help them with the second test. To mitigate against the possibility, a cross-over design, or Latin Square was applied [36]. This enabled me to control the experience participants had of the systems. Participants were divided into two groups, one of which began with BB while the other started with D2L. Allowing one week's break between protocols reduced the risk of transfer, and was sufficient time to guarantee that participants had forgotten the minutiae of the experimental session. However, it meant that the second test was close enough to the first that participants remained willing to return for the follow-up session.

2.2　Tasks and Participants

I carried out a context of use analysis for each site for the purpose of, firstly, identifying the representative user characteristics and secondly, to consider the tasks [31]. There were five tasks constructed for each website. Tasks, which existed for both LMSs were chosen. The constructed tasks each focused on a different area of the site to avoid the learning effect and were designed to be completely independent of each other so that failure in one task did not affect the overall process. Tasks were carefully designed to avoid biasing language and task-related cues. All tasks were piloted with two representative participants prior to testing.

Twenty students who had never used the evaluated websites before (first-time users) were recruited from UQU and were asked to perform the tasks on each website. Participants were all native speakers of Arabic, male, aged between 18 and 22. This gave a mean age of 20 years. All participants used the internet frequently. 96% had been using the Internet several times a day. None of the participants had ever participated in a usability test. No incentives were offered for taking part in the study.

2.3   Measures and Instruments

The dependent variables are the following four evaluation criteria: 1) usability problems discovered, 2) effectiveness of the tested systems, 3) their efficiency, and 4) users' satisfaction. These four themes have been identified as being typical of those used to evaluate the usability of software products [4].

Usability Problems. The main reason for conducting a usability assessment is to identify the maximum number of usability issues. For the purposes of the current study, the following definition, written by Lavery, Cockton and Atkinson [28] has been used:

"An aspect of the system and/or a demand on the user which makes it unpleasant, inefficient, onerous or impossible for the user to achieve their goals in typical usage situations".

The above definition is frequently used in the related literature and in usability studies in particular. The method for identifying usability problems used in the present study was that that set out by [5]. The most commonly used technique for evaluating usability is to calculate the number of problems which arise [4]. This may be limiting, however, and a number of researchers posit that it is important to take into account the qualitative variations between the problems in addition to just the number of them [8, 21]. The current research follows these recommendations by taking into consideration the quality of the problems, assessing them according to type and severity.

Severity of Usability Problems. Usability issues vary considerably. Some are merely irritating or frustrating to the user while others may lead to incorrect decisions or even the loss of data. Those problems which are severe are more likely to be identified by designers and dealt with than those whose effect is less significant [34]. Table 1 set out the four categories of severity level used in the current research. This classification was established by Dumas and Reddish [15]. These usability problems are evaluated by according to participant task performance and the frequency of their occurrence.

Table 1. Coding scheme for problem severity levels.

	Problem severity level	Definition
1	Prevent task	The usability problem prevented the task completion
2	Significant delay	The usability problem led to significantly delayed or hindered task completion
3	Minor	The usability problem had minor effect on usability, several seconds of delay and minor frustration
4	Enhancement	Participants made suggestions or indicated a preference, although performance was unaffected

Types of Usability Problems. This study also classified usability problems by type. All the problems identified in the two websites were grouped into four different problem categories by two independent experts in usability. The four categories, which are set out in Table 2, are navigation, layout, content and functionality. These classifications were developed in accordance with the literature on website usability problem classification [4, 38]. Nevertheless, the independent experts were given the freedom to code problems into a new category if they felt it was necessary to do so.

Table 2. Coding scheme for problem types.

	Problem type	Definition
1	Navigation	Participants have problems navigating between pages or identifying suitable links for information/functions
2	Layout	Participants encounter difficulties due to web elements, display problems, visibility issues, inconsistency, and problematic structure and form design
3	Content	Participants think certain information is unnecessary or is absent; Participants have problems understanding the information including terminology and dialogue
4	Functionality	Participants encounter difficulties due to the absence of certain functions or the presence of problematic functions

Effectiveness. Effectiveness were measured by 1) success rate, 2) number or errors. Success rate is a widely used performance measure which quantifies the percentage of tasks completed correctly during testing [4]. The scheme used for categorizing task completion, presented in Table 3, was constructed based on Tullis and Albert's [4] coding scheme. Another measurement of effectiveness involves counting the number of errors the participant makes when attempting to complete a task. Errors are the possible outcome of a usability issues. They are incorrect actions that may lead to task failure.

Table 3. Categorization scheme for task completion.

Category	Definition
Completed	Completed successfully
Failed	Participant gave up
	Participant performed the task incorrectly
	Participant believed that the task was complete even though it was not

Efficiency. Efficiency were measured by 1) time on task, 2) number of pages browsed, and 3) number of mouse clicks. Such data can offer greater insights into the user behavior, and assist in understanding the efficiency of a particular website or application [19].

User' Satisfaction. The System Usability Scale (SUS) questionnaire was used in this research to gauge participants' satisfaction with the tested websites. The questionnaire contains ten items, all items are evaluated on a 5-point Likert scale, ranging from 1 = strongly disagree to 5 = strongly agree. It is widely accepted across the industry as a reliable tool for measuring the usability of computing products. However, the scores for individual items are not meaningful on their own; instead, these are compiled to yield a single score representing a composite measure of the overall usability of the system being studied. Each question has a contribution score between 0 and 4. For each of the odd-numbered questions (1, 3, 5, 7 and 9) the contribution score is calculated by subtracting 1 from the participant's Likert scale rating. For each of the even-numbered items (2, 4, 6, 8 and 10), the contribution score is calculated by subtracting the participant's Likert scale rating from 5. The sum of the contribution scores is then multiplied by 2.5 to obtain the overall SUS score. SUS scores have a range of 0 to 100, with a higher score reflecting greater participant satisfaction with a site [9]. For this experiment, the standard SUS questionnaire was slightly modified by replacing the term "system" with "website" (e.g. 'I thought the website was easy to use'). To automatically calculate the SUS score for the study's multiple participants, Thomas's [22] spreadsheet was used.

2.4 Setting and Equipment

The venue for all the experimental sessions was the same UQU laboratory. Good experimental practice was guaranteed by controlling the environment and thus minimizing the risk of bias which could have arisen had the sessions been carried out in different settings. The ambient temperature in the laboratory was kept at a normal level, the lighting levels were appropriate and noise distraction was avoided as far as possible.

The test venue had both a waiting room and an experimental laboratory. Participants were provided with a suitable table and chair and a personal computer. The surroundings were designed to mirror a typical office environment, with shelves, books, posters, pinboards and potted plants. The privacy of participants was guaranteed since the only other person present was myself, in my capacity as evaluator. I played the role of the evaluator in the current study. Since I did not wish participants to feel too strongly that they were under observation, I sat behind them, on their right-hand side. This also avoided the risk of distraction. However, it was believed that having an evaluator physically present in the test laboratory facilitates the think-aloud process and helps participants feel more relaxed about it and more comfortable about verbalizing their thoughts.

All the usability tests used the same computer to avoid any bias resulting from differing performance levels which could have arisen had a variety of machines been used. The computer ran a Windows 10 Workstation (64 bit operating system) and used Google Chrome via high-speed connection. The selection of this browser was based on its popularity in the KSA, where it is widely used [35]. Indeed, 92% of the research participants reported themselves to be users of Google Chrome. The browser had the website under evaluation set as its default homepage. The computer was fitted with a mouse, an external dual headset and a microphone.

2.5 Experimental Procedure

Participants were warmly welcomed on their arrival at the facility, and every effort was made to ensure that they felt comfortable before they were given information about the study, how their data would be stored and how confidently would be assured. They were then asked sign the form giving informed consent to participation. The information and form were expressed clearly in straightforward language so that none of them would feel disheartened [37]. In order for the mouse to be correctly placed, participants were asked whether they were right- or left-handed. They were then given a short time (no more than two minutes) to become acquainted with the test machine so they would be able to interact with it at their normal speed. I then familiarized the participants with the think aloud protocol. The instructions given were those developed by [17]. Participants were asked to verbalise their thoughts while carrying out the test and not to seek assistance from the evaluator. They were also told that if they stopped verbalizing their thoughts at any point, they would be reminded to resume thinking aloud. A short session was then conducted to give participants the opportunity to practice thinking aloud, in line with Ericsson and Simon's [17] recommendations. Participants were given an easy task with no connection to the websites under evaluation. They were asked to consult an online dictionary to find the meaning of the word "chord".

Once the think aloud practice had been completed, participants received an instruction sheet which explained the required tasks. They were asked to read it and ensure that they fully understood what was required of them before embarking on the tasks themselves, which were to be carried out in the order given in the instructions. Since it was essential that participants understood precisely what the tasks involved, prior to commencing each individual task, they were asked to describe in their own words what they needed to do. Participants were not made aware that they would be timed while carrying out the task because I wished to avoid putting them under pressure or giving them an impression that this was an examination. It is important that the order of the tasks should not have an impact on the results [36], so the tasks were set out in a counterbalanced sequence. No clues were given to the participants as to whether or not they had managed the task successfully.

The guidance given by Ericsson and Simon [17] was adhered to while participants were carrying out the tasks. There was no interaction between the evaluator and the participants except in cases where participants failed to verbalize their thoughts for 15 s. In such cases, I gave them a simple instruction to continue speaking. I also endeavored to avoid giving any body language clues. At the end of the set of tasks participants were asked to complete a post-test questionnaire, the online SUS. The purpose of the question was to ascertain how satisfied participants were with the level of usability for each website they had tested. The order effect was minimized by randomizing the order in which the statements were presented.

3   Results and Discussion

This section presents and discusses the results obtained from the evaluation of the two LMSs targeted in the study.

3.1   Usability Problems

This subsection presents problem-based data at the level of individual usability problems and the final problem set.

Individual Usability Problems. The differences between the two systems are explored using statistical analysis for individual problem data. As the data is not normally distributed, non- parametric tests were used.

Number of Individual Usability Problems. Table 4 presents the number of problems discovered during interaction with the websites. A Wilcoxon Signed Rank test revealed that a higher number of individual problems were significantly found on BB than on D2L.

Table 4. Number of individual problems identified.

	BB		D2L		p-value
	Mean	SD	Mean	SD	
No. of problems*	8.15	4.24	5.50	2.74	.041

*p < 0.05 significance obtained

Severity of Individual Usability Problems. A Wilcoxon Signed Rank test found a significant difference between the systems regarding the number of individual problems whose severity was rated as "major". The evaluation produced significantly more individual major problems on BB than on D2L (see Table 5). The assignation of levels of severity to particular issues takes into account how frequently they affect the test participant, in terms of the number of occasions the problem arises for that person [20]. Thus, a problem which arises on more than three occasions is deemed to be major regardless of the fact that its effect each time may only have been minimal, due to the cumulative effect of its recurrence [4].

Table 5. Severity levels of individual problem.

	BB		D2L		p-value
	Mean	SD	Mean	SD	
Critical	0.55	0.68	0.40	0.82	.454
Major*	3.60	1.39	1.70	1.45	.003
Minor	3.95	2.03	3.30	1.89	.109
Enhancement	0.05	0.22	0.10	0.30	.546

*$p < 0.05$ significance obtained

Types of Individual Usability Problems. Table 6 shows the number of different types of individual problems identified. A Wilcoxon Signed Rank test revealed the evaluation produced significantly more individual problems on BB compared to D2L relating to navigation and content problems. Indeed, it was observed during the evaluation sessions that participants struggled particularly with understanding the terminology of BB and in identifying suitable links for functions.

Table 6. Types of individual problem.

	BB		D2L		p-value
	Mean	SD	Mean	SD	
Navigation*	2.75	1.48	2.00	1.02	.038
Layout	1.05	0.99	1.30	0.97	.475
Content*	3.10	1.77	1.20	1.19	.003
Functionality	1.25	1.16	1.00	0.85	0.578

*$p < 0.05$ significance obtained

Final Usability Problems. Descriptive data is presented for the final problem set.

Number of Final Usability Problems. After analysing all of the usability problems found, the number of problems encountered by all participants were collected, excluding any repeated problems, to arrive at a total number of final usability problems found on each website. In total, 64 final usability problems were extracted from the tested websites. 38 problems on BB; and 26 problems on D2L. Accordingly, a higher number of final problems were detected on BB than on D2L.

Severity of Final Usability Problems. When determining levels of severity, differences in how participants experience and deal with that issue must be taken into consideration. It may, for instance, be the case that one participant rapidly finds a solution to the problem, while another may struggle for a considerable time to resolve it. In order to avoid any possible disagreements about severity levels, assignation was decided on a majority basis [30]. If the same number of participants experienced the problem at differing levels of severity, the problem was classified at the highest severity level [16].

The results show that 26% (10 problems) of the final problems from the BB were high impact problems (with critical and major effects), and 74% (28 problems) were low impact problems (with minor and enhancement effects), whereas, for the D2L, 19% (5 problems) of final problems were high impact, and 81% (21 problems) were low impact problems (see Table 7).

Table 7. Severity levels of final problem.

	BB	D2L
Critical	1	1
Major	9	4
Minor	24	19
Enhancement	4	2

Types of Final Usability Problems. The final problems discovered on the tested websites in this study were classified by the usability experts into four types as stated earlier: navigational problems, layout problems, content problems, and functional problems. Table 8 shows the number of final usability problems by their type for both systems. Compared with the D2L, more problems of each type were found on BB apart from layout problems.

Table 8. Types of final problem.

	BB	D2L
Navigation	11	9
Layout	6	10
Content	13	4
Functionality	8	3

Figures 2, and 3 depict the final problems detected according to their types and severity levels in each system. As shown here, all of the critical problems found in the two websites related to navigation.

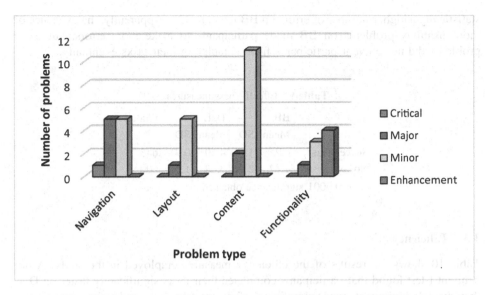

Fig. 2. Types and severity levels for the final problems in BB

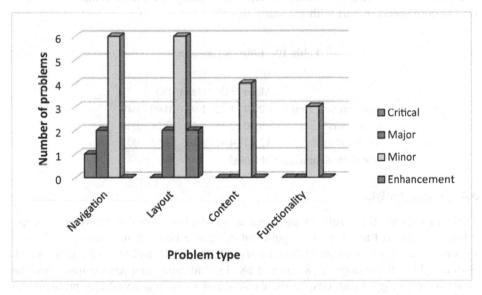

Fig. 3. Types and severity levels for the final problems in D2L

3.2 Effectiveness

Table 9 shows the results of the task performance measures employed in the study.

The results revealed that participants performed their tasks on BB neither better nor worse than on D2L. However, a paired-sample t-test found that participants committed statistically a higher number of errors on BB than on D2L. Apparently, the existence of more usability problems on BB made participants to make more errors, but those problems did not prevent participants from completing their tasks eventually.

Table 9. Effectiveness measures.

	BB		D2L		p-value
	Mean	SD	Mean	SD	
Success rate	4.25	1.04	4.40	0.91	.643
No. of errors*	7.17	2.07	3.68	1.64	.000

* p < 0.0001 significance obtained

3.3   Efficiency

Table 10 shows the results of the efficiency measures employed in the study. A dependent t-test found that participants completed their tasks significantly faster on D2L than on BB; participants made significantly fewer mouse clicks and visited fewer pages to achieve the task on D2L than on BB. These results could be attributed to the existence of more major problems on BB which delayed the task completion. These results correspond in part with the study of [27].

Table 10. Efficiency measures.

	BB		D2L		p-value
	Mean	SD	Mean	SD	
Time on task (min)*	2.67	1.12	1.93	0.90	.049
Page visits*	8.30	2.45	5.45	2.21	.008
Mouse clicks*	12.41	4.41	8.80	2.52	.002

*p < 0.05 significance obtained

3.4   Users' Satisfaction

Table 11 presents the results of participants' satisfaction with the two systems. Interestingly, a paired t-test fond no significant difference between the ratings of the two systems. The overall average SUS score was 83.20 for BB, and 86.60 for D2L, which both are above the average SUS score of 68 [23], indicating that participants found the systems very easy to use, despite the existence of more major usability problems on BB, which adversely influence the effectiveness and efficiency of the interface, as discussed earlier. This may be slightly attributed to the concern of people from collectivistic cultures such as Saudi culture for the "other-face", as suggested by [18]. In other words, an individual from such culture focuses on how other people view them. As a result, they might tend not to openly criticize a website during a usability evaluation. These results are in line with [12] who found no significant difference between the students' rating of the usability of the two systems.

Table 11. Users' satisfaction with the two systems.

	BB		D2L		p-value
	Mean	SD	Mean	SD	
SUS	83.20	8.27	86.60	13.49	.360

4 Conclusions and Future Work

The aim of this study was to evaluate and compare the usability of two learning management systems namely; Blackboard and Desire to Learn from the perspectives of students at Umm Al-Qura University in the Kingdom of Saudi Arabia. This aim was investigated by carrying out a series of usability tests using the traditional concurrent think aloud usability testing method. The results indicate that Blackboard has numerous severe usability issues. Task completion was much slower on BB than on D2L, required more mouse clicks and more pages visited. Participants also made more mistakes. It was, however, interesting to note that levels of user satisfaction were the same for both systems. These findings indicate that it would be worthwhile customizing Blackboard to meet the needs of its users at Umm Al-Qura University and to improve its usability.

The study presented in this paper has some limitations that could be improved in future work. First, while a range of task performance measures were reported, further behavioral differences during task performance were not pinpointed. Other researchers have used eye tracking to explore differences in users' attention resources during tasks [19]. Second, the usability test sessions were performed in a formal laboratory-based setting, an important aspect for observation and analysis of results in a scientific setting. However, this sort of setting is not reflective of the environments in which people typically access the web, and therefore might not have completely captured the normal web browsing behavior of the participants.

Acknowledgements. The author would like to thank all those people who took time to take part in the experiments. Thanks also to the anonymous reviewers for their helpful comments.

References

1. About Us. https://www.blackboard.com/about-us. Accessed 10 July 2019
2. Adelsberger, H.H., Collis, B., Pawlowski, J.M.: Handbook on Information Technologies for Education and Training. Springer, Heidelberg (2013). https://doi.org/10.1007/978-3-540-74155-8
3. Agariya, A.K., Singh, D.: E-learning quality: scale development and validation in Indian context, knowledge management & e-learning. Int. J. (KM&EL) **4**(4), 500–517 (2012)
4. Albert, W., Tullis, T.: Measuring the User Experience: Collecting, Analyzing, and Presenting Usability Metrics. Newnes, Oxford (2013)
5. Alhadreti, O., Mayhew, P.: To intervene or not to intervene: an investigation of three think-aloud protocols in usability testing. J. Usability Stud. **12**(3), 111–132 (2017)

6. Alturki, U.T., Aldraiweesh, A.: Evaluating the usability and accessibility of LMS "Blackboard" at King Saud University. Contemp. Issues Educ. Res. (CIER) **9**(1), 33–44 (2016)
7. Aydin, B., Darwish, M.M., Selvi, E.: The state-of-the-art matrix analysis for usability of learning management systems. ASEE Comput. Educ. (CoED) J. **7**(4), 48 (2016)
8. Blandford, A., Hyde, J., Green, T., Connell, I.: Scoping analytical usability evaluation methods: a case study. Hum.-Comput. Interact. **23**(3), 278–327 (2008)
9. Brooke, J.: SUS - a quick and dirty usability scale. Usability Eval. Ind. **189**(194), 4–7 (1996)
10. Brown, M.: Evaluating computer game usability: developing heuristics based on user experience. In: Proceedings of IHCI Conference, pp. 16–21 (2008)
11. Cakmak, E.K., Gunes, E., Ciftci, S., Ustundag, M.T.: Developing a web site usability scale. The validity and reliability analysis & implementation results. Pegem Eğitim Ve Öğreti **I**(II), 31–40 (2011)
12. Chawdhry, A., Paullet, K., Benjamin, D.: Assessing blackboard: improving online instructional delivery. Inf. Syst. Educ. J. **9**(4), 20 (2011)
13. Dillon, A.: The Evaluation of Software Usability. Taylor and Francis, London (2001)
14. Docebo. https://eclass.teicrete.gr/modules/document/file.php/TP271/Additional%20material/docebo-elearning-trends-report-2017.pdf. Accessed 11 Sept 2019 and 21 Aug 2019
15. Dumas, J.S., Redish, J.: A Practical Guide to Usability Testing. Intellect, Bristol (1999)
16. Ebling, M.R., John, B.E.: On the contributions of different empirical data in usability testing. In: Proceedings of the 3rd Conference on Designing Interactive Systems: Processes, Practices, Methods, and Techniques, pp. 289–296. ACM, New York (2000)
17. Ericsson, K.A., Simon, H.A.: Protocol Analysis: Verbal Reports as Data. Revised edn. MIT Press, Cambridge (1993)
18. Hall, M., De Jong, M., Steehouder, M.: Cultural differences and usability evaluation: individualistic and collectivistic participants compared. Tech. Commun. **51**(4), 489–503 (2004)
19. Hertzum, M., Hansen, K.D., Andersen, H.H.K.: Scrutinising usability evaluation: does thinking aloud affect behaviour and mental workload? Behav. Inf. Technol. **28**(2), 165–181 (2009)
20. Hertzum, M.: Problem prioritization in usability evaluation: from severity assessments toward impact on design. Int. J. Hum. Comput. Interact. **21**(2), 125–146 (2006)
21. Hornbaek, K.: Dogmas in the assessment of usability evaluation methods. Behav. Inf. Technol. **29**(1), 97–111 (2010)
22. How to Use the System Usability Scale (SUS) to Evaluate the Usability of Your Website. http://usabilitygeek.com/how-to-use-the-system-usability-scale-sus-to-evaluate-theusability. Accessed 11 June 2019
23. Inversini, A., Botturi, L., Triacca, L.: Evaluating LMS usability for enhanced e-learning experience. In: Inedmedia + Innovate Learning Association for the Advancement of Computing in Education (AACE), pp. 595–601 (2006)
24. ISO W. 9241-11: Ergonomic Requirements for Office Work with Visual Display Terminals (VDTs). The International Organization for Standardization (1998)
25. Koutsabasis, P., Spyrou, T., Darzentas, J.: Evaluating usability evaluation methods: criteria, method and a case study. In: Jacko, J.A. (ed.) HCI 2007. LNCS, vol. 4550, pp. 569–578. Springer, Heidelberg (2007). https://doi.org/10.1007/978-3-540-73105-4_63
26. Kraleva, R., Sabani, M., Kralev, V.: An analysis of some learning management systems. Int. J. Adv. Sci. Eng. Inf. Technol. **9**(4), 1190–1198 (2019)
27. Lalande, N., Grewal, R.: Blackboard vs. Desire2Learn: a system administrator's perspective on usability. In: International Conference on Education and E-Learning Innovations, pp. 1–4. IEEE (2012)

28. Lavery, D., Cockton, G., Atkinson, M.P.: Comparison of evaluation methods using structured usability problem reports. Behav. Inf. Technol. **16**(4–5), 246–266 (1997)
29. Lazar, J., Feng, J.H., Hochheiser, H.: Research Methods in Human-Computer Interaction. Wiley, Hoboken (2010)
30. Lindgaard, G., Chattratichart, J.: Usability testing: what have we overlooked? In: Proceedings of the SIGCHI Conference on Human Factors in Computing Systems, pp. 1415–1424. ACM, New York (2007)
31. Maguire, M.: Context of use within usability activities. Int. J. Hum. Comput. Stud. **55**(4), 453–483 (2001)
32. Mea. https://www.d2l.com/en-mea/. Accessed 23 Aug 2019
33. Melton, J.: The LMS moodle: a usability evaluation. Lang. Issues **11/12**(1), 1–24 (2006)
34. Molich, R., Dumas, J.: Comparative usability evaluation (CUE 4). Behav. Inf. Technol. **27** (3), 263–281 (2008)
35. Saudi Arabia. https://gs.statcounter.com/browser-market-share/all/saudi-arabia/2019. Accessed 06 Oct 2019
36. Sauro, J.: A Practical Guide to Measuring Usability: 72 Answers to the Most Common Questions About Quantifying the Usability of Websites and Software. A Measuring Usability, LLC (2010)
37. Tips and Tricks for Recruiting Users. http://www.nngroup.com/reports/tips/recruiting/234_recruiting_tips. Accessed 17 Feb 2019
38. Zhao, T., Mcdonald, S., Edwards, H.M.: The impact of two different think aloud instructions in a usability test: a case of just following orders? Behav. Inf. Technol. **33**(2), 163–183 (2012)

Evaluation of the Virtual Mobility Learning Hub

Diana Andone$^{(\boxtimes)}$ ⓘ, Silviu Vert ⓘ, Vlad Mihaescu ⓘ,
Daniela Stoica ⓘ, and Andrei Ternauciuc ⓘ

Politehnica University of Timisoara, Timisoara, Romania
{diana.andone, silviu.vert, vlad.mihaescu,
andrei.ternauciuc}@upt.ro,
daniela.stoica@student.upt.ro

Abstract. We live in a fast-paced world where the most valuable of all commodities is time. All of us dream of having enough time to live, work, learn and enjoy life. Higher Education is transformed by these aspirations, as in today's society students are also working adults. Therefore, online courses especially under the form of MOOCs, virtual learning environments, offers them access to virtual learning and working. The OpenVMLH (Virtual Mobility Learning Hub) is an innovative multilingual environment which was created as part of the Open Virtual Mobility, a European-funded project, with the purpose to promote collaborative learning, social connectivism and networking as an instructional method, OERs as the main content and open digital credentials. This paper presents the analysis of the OpenVMLH. By harmonizing the qualitative and quantitative evaluation performed on 139 participants, using several usability testing methods in an extended period of time (8 months), we draw our conclusions on how a MOOC platform dedicated to virtual mobility should perform. Some of the issues are related to the usability of the OpenVMLH, others pertained to the actual creation and formatting of the learning materials but very few are of high severity. The improved version of the learning hub is now used by students and professors in 5 universities.

Keywords: Learning Management System · Massive Open Online Course · Open education · Virtual mobility · Usability · Focus group · User observation · Error testing · Survey · Expert review

1 Introduction

We live in a world where the most valuable of all commodities is time. Many people urge to have more than 24 h each day, in order to be able to solve all their issues and fulfill all of their desires. This is affecting and transforming all areas of the society, including education. Higher Education in particular is more affected, mainly because students are also working adults. Fewer and fewer students have the chance of the time to participate in a three months mobility, exchange program. Mobilities in higher education are amongst the main topics with which the European Commission is concerned according to [1] and [2]. Mobility is considered an important part of higher

© Springer Nature Switzerland AG 2020
P. Zaphiris and A. Ioannou (Eds.): HCII 2020, LNCS 12205, pp. 20–33, 2020.
https://doi.org/10.1007/978-3-030-50513-4_2

education as it supports personal development and employability, fosters respect for diversity and a capacity to deal with other cultures, encourages linguistic pluralism underpinning the multilingual tradition of Europe and increases cooperation and competition between higher education institutions [1] and [2].

The Virtual Mobility Learning Hub is an innovative multilingual (in seven languages) ICT-based environment (as a directory of virtual mobility attributes) with the main plan to promote collaborative learning, connectivism social networking as an instructional method, open educational resources OERs as the main content, open digital credentials as recognition and validation of VM skills which can be applied to all ages and levels of digital education. It was created to help students living in different parts of the world to learn and collaborate together and also to have free access to some relevant Massive Open Online Courses (MOOCs). Therefore, online courses especially under the form of MOOCs, virtual learning environments, teacher mobilities have become solutions to the pressing problem of lack of time. Moreover, these solutions address other problems regarding mobilities, such as lack of resources and various disabilities.

The VMLH initial requirements were: to be built on a user-friendly interface, as well as a mobile interface, to encourage everyone to access it, engage in different open learning activities, connect with others and develop their VM competencies.

The experience of users is one of the most important things to consider when measuring the quality of a system, especially when evaluating a MOOC.

Usability is defined in the context of Human Computer Interaction as a "quality attribute that assesses how easy user interfaces are to use" [3]. In the context of MOOCs and LMSs (Learning Management Systems), usability defines the measure in which students can do the purposed tasks with efficiency, effectiveness and satisfaction [4].

Usability evaluations are comprised of several techniques which combine engineering, psychology and user research in order to determine the positive and negative usability aspects of a software, in order to improve it [5]. Five quality components define usability and can be measured: learnability, efficiency, memorability, errors and satisfaction [3].

Heuristic evaluation, cognitive walkthroughs, interviews, focus groups, surveys, user observation sessions and eye tracking are among the most used methods and techniques for measuring the usability of software systems [4].

The current paper describes the methods used to test the usability of VMLH, the results and conclusions that occurred.

2 Related Work

To the best of our knowledge, very few studies have been made on assessing the usability of MOOCs.

In [6], the authors develop a list of usability guidelines in the form of an adaptable usability checklist for evaluating the user interface of MOOCs. In [7], the authors propose and test a methodology for assessing user satisfaction of MOOCs, using techniques such as UMUX Lite, SUS questionnaires, Testbirds Company's approach, and the ISO standards. In [8], the authors describe a usability evaluation of three popular MOOC platforms: edX, Coursera and Udacity. The methodology combined the user testing and questionnaires methods and involved 31 participants, its focus being more on the comparative side of the evaluation.

A lot more usability tests have been performed on LMSs, the basis for MOOCs.

The authors in [9] analyzed all the activity tools (Lesson, HTML page, Glossary etc) and blocks (People, Calendar, Online Users etc) present in the default installation of Moodle. The methodology consisted in an experience-based evaluation for web apps that combines heuristic evaluation, questionnaires and task-driven techniques. The study had 84 students, 8 teachers and 2 system administrators as participants. While the results indicated a good usability rating, some modules came clearly as limited, which is explainable because of the limited development of Moodle in the year of the study, 2008 (first version released in 2002, current version 3.8.0 released in 2019).

Another research [10] done in our department in 2012 focuses on the usability evaluation of the mobile display of a LMS platform. The tested platform is also Moodle, whose mobile application was in its infancy. The authors propose an evaluation framework which approaches usability from four perspectives: pedagogical usability (how an educational app supports students in their learning process), usability of the device (software and hardware issues that influence usability testing on mobile devices), usability of the content (the format and structuring of the learning content and how adapted they are to mobile displays) and usability of the mobile web interface (the elements and structure of the web interface, such as navigation). The authors mention several metrics, methods and guideline for usability testing of mobile LMS apps that need to be further tested and validated.

Other studies focus on specific aspects of evaluation of usability of LMS, such as on navigational aspects [11], or on specific universities or regions, such as [12, 13].

A systematic review of usability and user experience evaluations of LMS was published in 2019 [14]. The study analyzes 23 selected papers as relevant for the research and extracts overall aspects, identified by the authors of the original research, related to general usability and user experience, characteristics of LMS, activities/characteristics of the usability evaluation models and guidelines considered in other domains to evaluate usability. While the research is valuable in the sense that it provides a checklist-type of usability evaluation framework for LMS, it needs to be further refined through testing and validation.

3   Usability Testing of the Virtual Learning Mobility Hub

3.1   Methodology

To validate the Virtual Mobility Learning Hub, we identified three main research questions:

Q1. Can a Moodle LMS sustain fully open, online, not tutorized courses?

Q2. What are the experiences that real students might have as learners in the VMLH?

Q3. Are the OpenVM MOOCs error-free and ready to become available for the HEI market?

To be able to answer these questions and to deploy the OpenVM MOOCs in the HEI market, we decided to run a usability test with real users i.e. university students. They are among the HEI stakeholders, so they are a valid target group for the courses (Fig. 1).

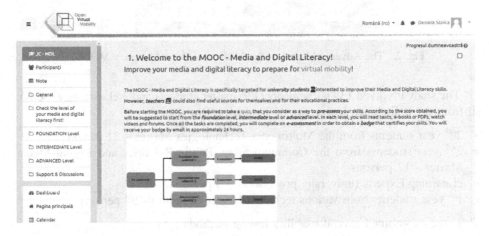

Fig. 1. Introduction to the Media and Digital Literacy MOOC.

The VMLH started with 8 mini MOOCs, each composed of 3 courses for Foundation Level, Intermediate Level and Advanced Level. Seven of them, which are finalized, were analyzed and evaluated from a pedagogical and usability point of view. These courses are Media and Digital Literacy, Intercultural skills, Autonomy-driven Learning, Active Self-regulated Learning, Collaborative Learning, Networked Learning Course and Open mindedness. In total there were 21 courses evaluated. Figure 2 and Fig. 2 show some typical parts of the MOOCs that were evaluated.

The usability evaluation extended from April 2019 until November 2019. Some usability methods, such as the focus group, was done in one day, in the usability lab that was set up at the university, while others, such as the error testing, was done over a period of 2 months, from the participants' home or office.

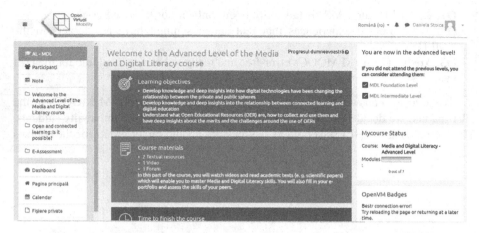

Fig. 2. The Advanced Level of the Media and Digital Literacy MOOC.

The study involved 139 participants (136 master students and 3 eLearning experts), all from the Politehnica University of Timisoara, Romania:

- 2nd year students from the Multimedia Technologies Master – 21 persons
- 2nd year students from the Communication, Public Relations and Digital Media Master – 17 persons
- eLearning Experts (university professors) – 3 persons
- 1st year students from various technical Master Programs - 98 persons

This study combined several usability testing methods [15]:

1. Focus Group – to answer Q1 and Q2
2. User Observation Sessions (as a combination of direct observation, think-aloud protocol, video-recorded observation, screen-logging observation and questionnaires) – to answer Q2 and Q3
3. Error Testing– to answer Q3
4. Survey (together with a written report) – to answer Q1, Q2 and Q3
5. Expert Review– to answer Q1 and Q3

Each of the usability methods is described below, together with who took part in it, when and where it took place and how it unfolded, concluding with the usability problems that it revealed.

3.2 Focus Group

A focus group is an informal method to assess the features of a user interface. Usually, focus groups lasts for approximately 2 h and are run by a moderator that conducts a discussion about the issues and concerns that the participants have after they tested the user interface of a product [16].

The authors organized a focus group with their students to see how they actually use the platform, by assigning key tasks to users and analyzing their performance and experience. They also had some discussions, following the tasks completion, using the focus group in order to discuss their feelings, attitudes and thoughts on the website and to reveal their motivations and preferences.

The students were told that the platform was developed to offer the possibility for users to have free access to some open educational resources such as MOOCs related to different topics. Testing of the platform was planned with the help of the master students, because they represent a target category of the focus group of this website.

The testing took place at the Multimedia Center which is part of the Politehnica University of Timisoara. The participants were 21 master students, aged between 23 and 26, most of them working on the IT industry, and using the computer multiple times a day (Fig. 3).

Fig. 3. The setup of the focus group

All of them were already familiar with MOOC platforms such as Coursera, Edx, Udacity and so on. Furthermore, some of them studied or worked in virtual teams or virtual mobilities.

As part of the focus group, the students had the task to try and create an account on the platform. The authors had some questions prepared in advance, mostly referring to how the students felt about the process and their perception about the UI of the platform.

At first glance they said that the User Interface design was good, the colors were chosen right, but they did not have a pleasant experience while using the platform.

Some negative remarks that the students mentioned:

- Platform flow is not user friendly and intuitive;
- Links are not intuitive and hardly visible;

- The header on the pages was too big;
- Social media accounts login is hardly visible.

3.3 User Observation Session

User observations implies the experts observing users performing some tasks they had been given to test how they interact with the user interface. The experts will be taking notes about "user performance and timing sequences of actions" [17].

This testing session also took place at the Multimedia Center inside the university, with 5 master students.

For the observation sessions, the authors prepared in advance the required materials for proper usability testing: video recording and confidentiality agreement, prequestionnaire, postquestionnaire, list of participant tasks, facilitator guideline, observer guideline, tables for registering participant comments, participant notes, times, steps and errors sheets.

On this testing session the participants, master students, had to complete the following tasks:

1. *Access the Active Self-regulated learning MOOC that is related to your actual knowledge.* The users made several errors during the process such as choosing the wrong course and thinking that they finished the task without actually enrolling in the course. Some major issues were that the pre-assessment activity was not checked automatically, the course link is not clear and the results are not complete for every grade, representing the knowledge level.
2. *Change your profile picture.* The users did not had any issues in completing this task and all of them completed it without making errors.
3. *Run partially the activities on the chosen course and complete the final test.* The users had several issues trying to find out what course level they should pick because the grades of the pre-assessment did not offer them any information about the course level they should pick. Besides that, some of the final test's answers were wrong. Also, an issue remarked by the users was that the videos weren't integrated properly and they had some issues trying to play them. Another negative remark was that the links were really hard to observe, for example the course link was hard to find and the final test was also hardly visible.

The participants' activity was recorded with a mirrorless Panasonic Lumix GH4 video camera placed at an appropriate height above the desk, so that the participant would still feel comfortable. The recording was projected in real-time on a wall, behind the user, so the observers could follow the participants' activity on the laptop (Fig. 4). Another video camera, this time a DSLR Canon 6D, paired with a Sennheiser microphone, recorded the mimics of the participant face and what they said during the process. The facilitator kept encouraging the participant to think aloud whenever possible. Both recordings were later correlated with the observers' notes.

Fig. 4. The setup of the user observation method

3.4   Error Testing Method

An error testing method involves that the participants try to perform some actions on the platform that's being tested and, thus, discover the errors that show up in the process.

For this testing session the users, 98 master students, had to enroll into one MOOC course and complete all the activities associated with it. They reported the errors that they experienced using an online form.

The students identified two major categories of errors: issues related to the platform's functionality and issues regarding the content of the courses.

The most important errors where the following:

- After completing some of the courses, the students did not received the badges.
- There were major issues regarding the quizzes they had to complete at the end of the courses because, on some of them, there were missing questions and, without those questions, they could not complete the quiz.
- Some of them said that they could not check their progress because the progress bar did not update.
- On some courses, they could not post anything in the forum section.
- The students also had problems when they tried to upload a file in some of the courses' sections.

3.5   Questionnaire Method

Using the questionnaire method, experts collect data using a survey that can have both open and closed questions [17].

The authors prepared for this session a questionnaire for the students that are enrolled in the Communication, Public Relations and Digital Media Master so they can express their opinion about the experience they had with the platform.

There was a number of 17 students that completed it and overall they appreciated the platform, even though they also said that it needed to be improved. They also had to realize a written report about their interaction with the platform. The survey's results are presented below.

When the students were asked about the quality and the quantity of the activities that they had to explore, most of them appreciated that the activities had a high quality (Fig. 5) and the quantity was just perfect (Fig. 6).

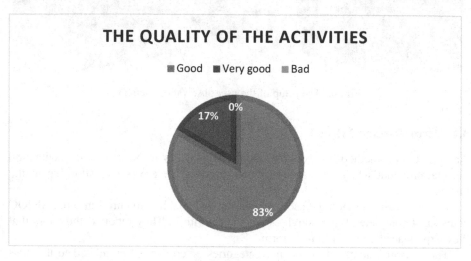

Fig. 5. Student answers regarding the quality of the MOOC activities

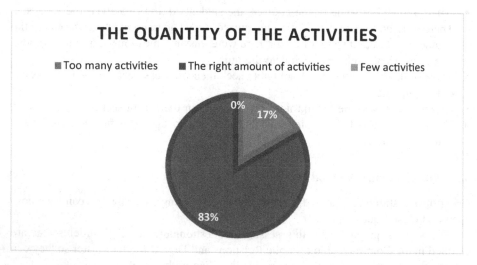

Fig. 6. Student answers regarding the quantity of the MOOC activities

When they were asked how they would compare the MOOCs from OpenVM platform with the faculty courses, more than half of them said that they consider the MOOCs more interesting (Fig. 7).

Fig. 7. Student answers regarding OpenVM MOOCs vs faculty courses

The students also had to say what they liked and what they disliked most about the platform and the courses. They said that they liked the fact that the courses are free and can be accessed anytime, anywhere, from any device connected to the Internet. They also thought that the video materials were good. What they did not like about the courses was that they did not have the chance to communicate with their colleagues during this courses and also the fact that they had issues when accessing the quizzes.

3.6   E-learning Experts' Evaluation

The eLearning experts who evaluated the platform helped reveal some general "neuralgic points" of the MOOCs. Firstly, they pointed that the students need to better understand what the role of the pre-assessment test is.

The experts noticed that some courses have too many questions, some have extremely complicated questions, and some have non-sense or duplicate questions. Another issue related to the course flow is that each course should have a clear pathway of content and activities; at the moment of the evaluation, everything was put there together and it was difficult to understand by students.

Some other issues that they found were that the videos integrated using H5P do not work as they are supposed to and their suggestion was that the videos should be embedded in an alternative technical manner.

Besides, the experts added that the insertion of images in the main page of a course is not beneficial, as students need to scroll down too much until they reach the content, and from the mobile phone this is even more frustrating. Another issue might be that the courses which allow students to self-check their progress will easily offer fake badges to students.

Finally, they concluded saying that the students need to have a better understanding of what they have to do in each course. Also, that they should understand that they can receive a badge and what they need to do in order to receive it.

3.7   Identified Usability Problems and Their Severity Ratings

The authors used severity ratings to prioritize the issues that were affecting the most the users' experience. According to [18] we consider three factors when analyzing a usability problem: frequency ("is it common or rare?"), impact ("will it be easy or difficult for the users to overcome?") and persistence ("is it a one-time problem that users can overcome once they know about it or will users repeatedly be bothered by the problem?").

Jakob Nielsen also proposed a four-step scale to rate the severity of usability problems, as it follows [18]:

0 = The problem is not an usability issue.
1 = "Cosmetic problem only": it doesn't have to be fixed unless extra time is available on project.
2 = "Minor usability problem": as the issue is not severe it should be solved only after major problems are solved.
3 = "Major usability problem": fixing this kind of issue should be a high priority because it affects the user experience.
4 = "Usability catastrophe": the product should not be released until this kind of issue is resolved (Table 1).

Table 1. List of identified usability problems and their severity ratings

Usability problem	Severity rating
The header on the page was too big	1
Social media accounts login are hardly visible	2
Some activities and tests could be checked even if the users did not complete them	3
The integration of some YouTube videos and PDF documents is defective	3
Some links are hardly visible	2
Not everything is written in English	2
Some test answers are wrong	4
The courses' names are confusing and not specific	3
The tasks and activities weren't displayed correctly	3
Platform flow is not user friendly and intuitive	3

4   Results and Recommendations

The usability testing of the Virtual Mobility Learning Hub had the role of helping the authors find out if the Moodle LMS can sustain fully open, online, not tutorized courses, what are the experiences of the students in the platform and if the MOOCs are ready to become available for the HEI market.

Most of the participants consider that MOOCs could easily replace some of the faculty courses and it's easier for them to learn from MOOCs because they can have access anytime, using a device that has Internet connection.

On the other hand, the students were not so pleased of the experience they had using the platform because they encountered many issues that had a negative impact on their journey trying to get the badges for the courses. Some of them did not receive the badges even if they finished the course, and other students could not finish the courses because some of the quizzes were not implemented right and many of the "correct" answers were in fact wrong.

The participants proposed some improvements for both platform and courses. They believe that the experience of using the platform would improve if the videos and PDF documents would be integrated better because, at the moment of the evaluation, their implementation was defective. Also, the links should be more readable, visible and clear, and the quizzes should be revised and corrected, especially the checkboxes functionality. Another important aspect they mentioned is about the tasks and activities of each course, because they need to be revised and displayed correctly. The participants believe that for some of the courses, the structure should be modified in order to be more user friendly because they had some issues understanding exactly what they are supposed to do.

5   Conclusions

This paper reports on a usability evaluation of a MOOC platform, namely the Virtual Mobility Learning Hub, which is an innovative multilingual ICT-based environment to support virtual mobilities between universities. A mix of usability evaluation methods was used, namely focus groups, user observation sessions, error testing, surveys and expert reviews. A number of 139 participants took part in the study, most of them students enrolled in Master Studies in Communication and various technical fields, and some eLearning Experts. The paper reported on each usability method used and how, when and where it was applied, concluding each chapter with the usability problems that were identified.

At the end, we summarized the major categories of usability problems that came out of the process. Some problems pertained to the platform itself (social media accounts login is hardly visible, platform flow is not user friendly and intuitive, links are not intuitive and hardly visible, the integration of YouTube videos and PDF documents is defective etc.) while others pertained to the actual creation and formatting of the learning materials (not everything is written in English/ translated, some test answers are wrong, the courses' names are confusing and not specific, the tasks and activities weren't displayed correctly etc.).

A lot of suggestions for improvements were derived from the applied usability methods and some suggestions have already started to be implemented.

The usability evaluation allowed us to answer the three main research questions as follows:

A1. The evaluation showed that, indeed, a Moodle-based Learning Management System has all the functionalities required and offers the right user experience for sustaining fully open, online, not tutorized courses. However, this also depends on the actual content of the courses and how the teachers set up the learning environment.

A2. The students generally reported that their experience in the VMLH was a good one. They rated the courses as better than their faculty ones and they found the VMLH courses to have the right amount of activities and that these activities are of good quality. However, they often stumbled upon small to medium annoyances, such as hidden social media login, page headers too big, defective integration of some multimedia learning materials etc.

A3. The OpenVM MOOCs are not error-free and many - thought small - improvements need to be done in order for the courses to be made available to the HEI market. Most of the improvements are in the area of the content of the courses, so the tutors should be in charge with implementing them.

The major contribution of the paper is in using a mix of 5 usability evaluation methods, with a large group of participants (139 persons), in an extended period of time (8 months), to derive usability issues pertaining to a MOOC platform. Also, the study shows how this mixed usability testing can be done in a university environment, with a practical outcome but also with a pedagogical purpose. The improved version of the learning hub is now used by students and professors in 5 universities.

Acknowledgments. The current study has been carried out in the framework of the Erasmus+ Project *Open Virtual Mobility*, key action Cooperation for Innovation and the Exchange of Good Practices, Strategic Partnerships for higher education, (partially) founded by the European Union, Project Number 2017-1-DE01-KA203-003494. Thanks are also due to PhD student Rafael Leucuța for video recording all the usability evaluation sessions and processing the recordings so that they could be used afterwards in reviewing the tests.

References

1. Buchem, I., et al.: Designing a collaborative learning hub for virtual mobility skills - insights from the European project *Open Virtual Mobility*. In: Zaphiris, P., Ioannou, A. (eds.) LCT 2018. LNCS, vol. 10924, pp. 350–375. Springer, Cham (2018). https://doi.org/10.1007/978-3-319-91743-6_27
2. Communiqué, L.: The Bologna process 2020-the european higher education area in the new decade. In: Communiqué of the Conference of European Ministers Responsible for Higher Education (2009)
3. Nielsen, J.: Usability 101: Introduction to Usability. Jakob Nielsen's Alertbox (2003). http://www.useit.com/alertbox/20030825.html. Accessed 25 Mar 2015

4. Ramakrisnan, P., Jaafar, A., Razak, F.H.A., Ramba, D.A.: Evaluation of user interface design for Learning Management System (LMS): investigating student's eye tracking pattern and experiences. Procedia – Soc. Behav. Sci. **67**, 527–537 (2012). https://doi.org/10.1016/j.sbspro.2012.11.357

5. Issa, T., Isaias, P.: Usability and human computer interaction (HCI). In: Issa, T., Isaias, P. (eds.) Sustainable Design, pp. 19–36. Springer, London (2015). https://doi.org/10.1007/978-1-4471-6753-2_2

6. Johansson, S., Frolov, I.: An adaptable usability checklist for MOOCs: a usability evaluation instrument for massive open online courses (2014)

7. Korableva, O., Durand, T., Kalimullina, O., Stepanova, I.: Usability testing of MOOC: identifying user interface problems. In: Proceedings of the 21st International Conference on Enterprise Information Systems, ICEIS 2019, pp. 468–475. SciTePress (2019)

8. Tsironis, A., Katsanos, C., Xenos, M.: Comparative usability evaluation of three popular MOOC platforms. In: 2016 IEEE Global Engineering Education Conference (EDUCON), pp. 608–612. IEEE (2016)

9. Kakasevski, G., Mihajlov, M., Arsenovski, S., Chungurski, S.: Evaluating usability in learning management system moodle. In: 30th International Conference on Information Technology Interfaces, ITI 2008, pp. 613–618 (2008). https://doi.org/10.1109/ITI.2008.4588480

10. Ivanc, D., Vasiu, R., Onita, M.: Usability evaluation of a LMS mobile web interface. In: Skersys, T., Butleris, R., Butkiene, R. (eds.) ICIST 2012. CCIS, vol. 319, pp. 348–361. Springer, Heidelberg (2012). https://doi.org/10.1007/978-3-642-33308-8_29

11. Arshad, R., Majeed, A., Afzal, H., Muzammal, M., ur Rahman, A.: Evaluation of navigational aspects of moodle. Int. J. Adv. Comput. Sci. Appl. **7**, 287–298 (2016). https://doi.org/10.14569/IJACSA.2016.070342

12. Vertesi, A., Dogan, H., Stefanidis, A., Ashton, G., Drake, W.: Usability evaluation of a virtual learning environment: a university case study. Presented at the 15th International Conference on Cognition and Exploratory Learning in Digital Age (CELDA), Budapest, Hungary, 21 October (2018)

13. Hasan, L.: The usefulness and usability of moodle LMS as employed by Zarqa University in Jordan. JISTEM – J. Inf. Syst. Technol. Manag. **16** (2019)

14. Salas, J., et al.: Guidelines to evaluate the usability and user experience of learning support platforms: a systematic review. In: Ruiz, P.H., Agredo-Delgado, V. (eds.) HCI-COLLAB 2019. CCIS, vol. 1114, pp. 238–254. Springer, Cham (2019). https://doi.org/10.1007/978-3-030-37386-3_18

15. Razeghi, R.: Usability of eye tracking as a user research technique in geo-information processing and dissemination. University of Twente Faculty of Geo-Information and Earth Observation (ITC) (2010)

16. Nielsen, J.: Focus Groups in UX Research. https://www.nngroup.com/articles/focus-groups/. Accessed 23 Jan 2020

17. Carvalho, A.A.A.: Usability testing of educational software: methods, techniques and evaluators. In: Actas do 3° Simpósio Internacional de Informática Educativa, pp. 139–148 (2006)

18. Nielsen, J.: Severity Ratings for Usability Problems. https://www.nngroup.com/articles/how-to-rate-the-severity-of-usability-problems/. Accessed 23 Jan 2020

Case Studies of Developing and Using Learning Systems in a Department of Engineering

Sachiko Deguchi[(⊠)]

Kindai University, Higashi-Hiroshima, Hiroshima 739-2116, Japan
deguchi@hiro.kindai.ac.jp

Abstract. Sequential circuits are difficult for 1st year university students to understand because of the concept of state. In this research, learning systems were developed for education of FF circuits and counter circuits, and the systems have been used in experiment classes. This paper describes the development and usage of a FF circuits learning system in 2012, and describes the development and usage of a new learning system in 2019. This paper also describes the development and usage of a counter circuits learning system in 2012, and describes the new usage of the same learning system and the development of a new learning system in 2019. Students answered the questionnaire after using the systems. The evaluation of usefulness of the system is relatively high. This result indicates that the basic framework of learning part and quiz part of our system is necessary and the contents are adequate. Also, displaying multiple materials (diagram, chart, table and text) on the same page is effective for counter learning system. The results also indicate that usefulness and contentedness are related if students use the system individually, but that some students are not contented if they use the learning system with members. The evaluation of "motivated" is relatively lower than the evaluations of "useful" or "contented". Therefore, we have to develop a new system to encourage students to study with members and to improve the motivation for study.

Keywords: Flip-Flop circuits · Counter circuits · Learning system · Group work · Motivation · Experiment class

1 Introduction

This paper describes learning systems for sequential circuits education. Simulation systems have been commonly used for the education of sequential circuits in university [1–3], however, it is difficult for 1st year students to use simulation systems. In recent years, several systems are proposed for beginners [4–6], but we need a system suitable for our experiment course. In the experiment class of Flip-Flop (FF) circuits, the experiment is easy, but it is difficult to understand the concept of "state" and "state transition". Therefore, we developed a system for students to study FFs after the experiment by changing states on the system [7, 8]. In the experiment class of counter circuits, explanation before experiment is difficult, and students have to design a counter circuit in the experiment. Therefore, we developed a system to understand

© Springer Nature Switzerland AG 2020
P. Zaphiris and A. Ioannou (Eds.): HCII 2020, LNCS 12205, pp. 34–48, 2020.
https://doi.org/10.1007/978-3-030-50513-4_3

counter circuits before the experiment so that students can design a circuit [9]. Also, our systems provide quizzes to check whether students understood the circuit, and students can proceed to learn next circuit if they pass the quiz. The framework of learning part and quiz part is necessary for learning system.

These years, the importance of active learning and group work in the education of university has been discussed [10–12] and PBL has commonly been carried out in engineering education [13, 14], while the difficulty of group work is also discussed [15]. In an experiment class, students work with members, but usually some students are active and some students are not so active. We started using the learning system partially because students should study by themselves (individually) even in an experiment class. However, we tried another approach in 2019.

This paper describes the development and usage of a FF circuits learning system in 2012, and describes the development and usage of a new learning system in 2019. This paper also describes the development and usage of a counter circuits learning system in 2012, and describes the new usage of the same learning system and the development of a new learning system in 2019.

2 Learning Systems for Flip-Flop Circuits Education

We developed a Flip-Flop (FF) circuits learning system in 2011 and had been using the system in the class of experiment of FF until 2017. Section 2.1 describes the development of the system and Sect. 2.2 describes the using experience of the system. We decided to stop using the system in 2018, and tried another approach in 2019, which is described in Sect. 2.3 and 2.4.

2.1 Development of FF Circuits Learning System

We developed a FF circuits learning system [7, 8] and had been using the system after the experiment of FF because FF circuits were difficult for 1st year students to understand by using textbooks or doing experiments. This system consists of learning part and quiz part. It takes around 60 min to study all the contents of the system.

The system was developed on Windows by using Visual C++2010 and Windows Forms Application. This system explains Inverter pair, RS-FF, Synchronous RS-FF, D-FF, JK-FF and master-slave JK-FF. For each circuit, students study the circuit and answer quiz questions about the knowledge of circuit. Students have to study the circuit again if correct ratio of the answer is less than 60%. If students pass the quiz of knowledge, they can proceed to the quiz of circuit diagram. After finishing the quiz of circuit diagram, students can study next circuit.

Figure 1 shows a UI of learning part of RS-FF. A circuit diagram, timing chart, state transition diagram, truth table and explanatory text are displayed on the same page. The left circuit diagram of RS-FF shows the previous state and the right diagram shows the current state. The red numbers in the diagram show the changed values. The red parts in the timing chart, state transition diagram and truth table show the current state. Students can change a state by pushing a button in the page. A recorded speech (reading the text) is played, and the students cannot proceed until the end of the speech.

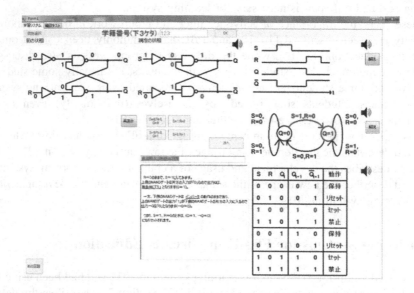

Fig. 1. UI of learning part of RS-FF. (Color figure online)

In the quiz part about knowledge, students choose one from four choices in each question. Each quiz of FF has five questions. If correct ratio is less than 60%, students have to answer the questions after they study the same FF again. On the other hand, in the quiz part about circuit diagram, students input 1 or 0 in the diagram and push "answer button". They can correct errors and confirm the answer again.

2.2   Usage of FF Circuits Learning System

Method. The learning system described above had been used from 2011 to 2017 in a class of experiments for 1st year university students [16]. This course teaches 6 subjects and each subject uses 2 weeks (3 h in 1 week). "Sequential Circuit" is one of the subjects and this subject teaches "FF circuits" for 3 h and "Counter circuits" for 3 h. This system was used in "FF circuits". Around 80 students are divided into 6 groups, therefor, around 14 students study one subject at the same time.

In a class of "FF circuits", a faculty member explained RS-FF, Synchronous RS-FF, D-FF and master-slave JK-FF. Next, students made an experiment on these four FF circuits (2 students worked together). After the experiment, students studied Inverter pair and RS-FF by using the learning system in the class to understand the basis of FF circuits (each student used one PC). It takes around 30 min to study these contents. The system has contents of other FF circuits, so students could study them as extracurricular activities.

After using the system in a class, students answered the following questions by rating 4, 3, 2 or 1 (4: positive, 3: mildly positive, 2: mildly negative, 1: negative).

- Questions (F1-1)–(F1-7) ask about the ease of use of following items:
    (F1-1) the learning part
    (F1-2) buttons in the learning part
    (F1-3) the tab
    (F1-4) the quiz part about knowledge
    (F1-5) buttons in the quiz part about knowledge
    (F1-6) buttons in the quiz part about circuit diagram
    (F1-7) to input numbers in the circuit diagram quiz
- Questions (F2-1)–(F2-2) ask about the comprehensibility of "explanatory text" of followings:
    (F2-1) Inverter pair
    (F2-2) RS-FF
- Question (F3-1) asks about the usefulness of "displaying multiple materials" (diagrams, chart, table and text) on the same page.
- Questions (F4-1)–(F4-2) ask about speech:
    (F4-1) usefulness of using speech for explanatory text
    (F4-2) adequacy of the speech rate
- Questions (F5-1)–(F5-2) ask about readability:
    (F5-1) UI
    (F5-2) the letters
- Questions (F6-1)–(F6-2) ask about the easiness of quizzes about followings:
    (F6-1) knowledge
    (F6-2) circuit diagram
- Questions (F7-1)–(F7-3) are total evaluations:
    (F7-1) Are the contents of the system easy?
    (F7-2) Is the system useful?
    (F7-3) Are you content with the system?

Result and Discussion. In 2012, 81 students enrolled in the class. The result of the questionnaire in 2012 [16] is shown in Table 1. The average of the mean values of all questions is 3.32. The values higher than 3.6 are (F1-5), (F1-6) and (F1-7), which are about operability. The values lower than 3.0 are (F6-1), (F6-2) and (F7-1), which are about easiness of quizzes and contents. This result indicates that the operability of the system is relatively easy and that the quizzes and contents of the system are relatively difficult.

The correlation coefficients of values of (F7-2: useful) and other questions are calculated. The correlation coefficients that are higher than 0.4 are as follows. The correlation coefficients of (F7-2) and ((F2-1), (F2-2), (F7-3)) are (0.43, 0.42, 0.42). This result indicates that students would think the system is useful if they can understand the explanation. Also, students would be content with the system if they think the system is useful.

Table 1. The mean values of evaluation of FF learning system, 2012

Question	Value	Question	Value	Question	Value
(F1-1)	3.30	(F2-1)	3.17	(F5-1)	3.33
(F1-2)	3.57	(F2-2)	3.02	(F5-2)	3.43
(F1-3)	3.41	(F3-1)	3.10	(F6-1)	2.81
(F1-4)	3.51	(F4-1)	3.35	(F6-2)	2.77
(F1-5)	3.65	(F4-2)	3.56	(F7-1)	2.60
(F1-6)	3.70			(F7-2)	3.58
(F1-7)	3.79			(F7-3)	3.33

2.3   Developing New Learning System

We decided to stop using the learning system in 2018 because students could understand well by using the system but they would not study further by themselves. We gave an assignment about RS-FF to students instead of using the system. Then, they studied by themselves, but some students had difficulty dealing with the assignment. Therefore, we tried another approach. The aim of this trial is to improve students' motivation as well as knowledge.

It is said that a peer support by students is effective. We are trying to make a cycle of teaching and learning by using the system which has been developed by students. In 2019, 3rd year students developed learning systems in Problem Based Learning (PBL) class, and one of the systems was used by 1st year students in a class of experiments. The students were informed that one of their systems would be used in the class of experiment of FF circuits for 1st year students.

The PBL class has 8 subjects. Students choose 2 subjects and work on each subject for 7 weeks (21 h). "Development of sequential circuits learning system" is one of the subjects. The course plan of 2019 (spring term: Apr. to July) is as follows.

1st class (3 h): (1) Understanding sequential circuits learning system. (2) Exercise of HTML, CSS and JavaScript. (3) Grouping (3 students X 4 groups).
2nd–6th classes (15 h): Design and development of learning system.
7th class (3 h): Presentation and evaluation of the systems.
8th–14th classes: same as 1st–7th classes for other 12 students.

Some features of UI programming such as quick feedback or interactive programming are effective to study how to design software. Most students were working actively and designed adequate learning system. But a few students were interested in building UI rather than understanding the design or purpose of the system. We have chosen one system to use in a class of experiment for 1st year students in autumn term, 2019. The reasons why this system was chosen are as follows:

(1) The operation of the system is simple and easy.
(2) It takes around 10 min to use this system. The aim of using a system is to improve motivation for study, so a small system is suitable for our purpose.

(3) This system is teaching D-FF, while the assignment which is given to 1st year students after using the system is about RS-FF. It would be good for 1st year students to study RS-FF by themselves.
(4) This system explains circuit diagram, timing chart and truth table, so these explanations would help 1st year students to do their assignment.
(5) This system explains state transition but does not show "state transition diagram", so it would be good for 1st year students to study it by themselves.

2.4   Using New Learning System

Method. In 2019, the learning system developed by 3rd year students was used in the class of experiment (in "FF circuits"). Students are divided into A groups (3 groups) and B groups (3 groups). In this class, faculty member explained four FFs as described above, then, students made an experiment on these four FF circuits. After the experiment, students studied D-FF by using the new learning system developed by 3rd year students. They were informed that the system was developed by 3rd year students. After using the system, students answered the following questions by rating 4, 3, 2 or 1 (4: positive, 3: mildly positive, 2: mildly negative, 1: negative).

(Fn7-1) Are the contents of the system easy? (Same as (F7-1) described above)
(Fn7-2) Is the system useful? (Same as (F7-2))
(Fn7-3) Are you content with the system? (Same as (F7-3))
(Fn7-4) Are you motivated by the system? (New question)

After the questionnaire, students did their assignment about RF-FF.

Result and Discussion. In 2019, 83 students enrolled in the class (A groups: 42, B groups: 41). The result of the questionnaire in 2019 is shown in Table 2. The mean values of A groups' Fn7-* and B groups' Fn7-* (* = 1, 2, 3, 4) are compared using Welch's t-test, and the analysis cannot show any difference, i.e., the mean values of A groups and B groups for the same question are almost the same. The mean value of (Fn7-4: motivated) is slightly smaller than the mean values of (Fn7-2: useful) or (Fn7-3: contented) in both A groups and B groups, therefore, these values are compared using paired sample t-test. In A groups, the degrees of freedom is 41, the critical value for significance level of 0.05 (two-tailed test) is 2.020, and t-ratios are 3.420 (Fn7-2 vs. Fn7-4) and 4.407 (Fn7-3 vs. Fn7-4), therefore, there are significant differences. In B groups, the degrees of freedom is 40, the critical value for significance level of 0.05 (two-tailed test) is 2.021, and t-ratios are 3.955 (Fn7-2 vs. Fn7-4) and 3.592 (Fn7-3 vs. Fn7-4), therefore, there are also significant differences. This result indicates that students' evaluations of "useful" and "motivated" are different, and "contented" and "motivated" are also different.

The correlation coefficients of values of "(Fn7-2: useful) and other questions" and those of "(Fn7-4: motivated) and other questions" are calculated. The correlation coefficients that are higher than 0.4 are as follows. In A groups, the correlation coefficient of (Fn7-2) and (Fn7-3) is 0.59. In B groups, the correlation coefficient of (Fn7-2) and (Fn7-3) is 0.64. This result indicates that students would be content with the system if they think the system is useful. While, in A groups, the correlation coefficient of (Fn7-4) and (Fn7-3) is 0.53, but in B groups, the coefficients of (Fn7-4) and other questions are lower than 0.4. This result indicates that the factors to motivate students are complicated, and some students would think "contented" and "motivated" differently.

Students used the learning system earnestly. Since students studied circuit diagram, timing chart and truth table of D-FF, they could do their assignment of RS-FF by themselves.

Table 2. The mean values of evaluation of FF learning system, 2019.

A groups		B groups	
Question	Value	Question	Value
(Fn7-1)	2.67	(Fn7-1)	2.68
(Fn7-2)	3.40	(Fn7-2)	3.51
(Fn7-3)	3.43	(Fn7-3)	3.46
(Fn7-4)	3.00	(Fn7-4)	2.98

3   Learning Systems for Counter Circuits Education

We developed a counter circuits learning system in 2012 and have been using the system in the class of experiment of counter circuits. Section 3.1 describes the development of the system and Sect. 3.2 describes the using experience of the system. In 2019, we changed the usage of the system, which is described in Sect. 3.3. We are now developing a new counter circuits learning system which can be used by members of experiment together. The concept of this system is described in Sect. 3.4.

3.1   Development of Counter Circuits Learning System

We developed a counter circuits learning system [9] and have been using the system before the experiment, because counter circuits were difficult for an instructor to explain using whiteboard or PowerPoint and also difficult for students to understand. This system consists of learning part and quiz part. It takes around 50 min to use the system for each student.

The system was developed on Windows by using Visual C++2010 and Windows Forms Application. This system explains MOD-16 counter, MOD-5 counter, and MOD-10 counter. For each counter, students study the counter and answer quiz questions about the counter. Students have to study the counter again if correct ratio of the answer is less than 60%. If students pass the quiz, they can study next counter.

Figure 2 shows a UI of learning part of MOD-16 counter. A circuit diagram, timing chart, truth table and explanatory text are displayed on the same page. The red numbers in the diagram show the changed values. The red parts in the timing chart and truth table show the current state. Students can proceed to the next state by pushing a "clock input button" in the page. A recorded speech (reading the text) is played, and the students cannot proceed until the end of the speech.

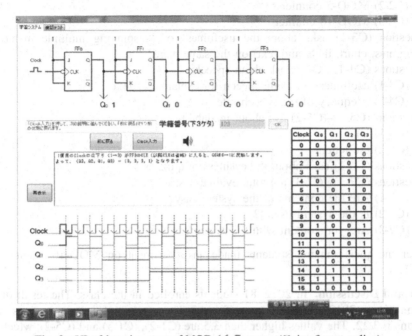

Fig. 2. UI of learning part of MOD-16 Counter. (Color figure online)

In the quiz part, students choose one from three choices in each question. Each quiz of counter circuit has four or five questions. If correct ratio is less than 60%, students have to answer the questions after they study the same counter circuit again.

3.2 Usage of Counter Circuits Learning System

Method. The learning system described in Sect. 3.1 had been used from 2012 [16] to 2018 in the same course of experiments as described in Sects. 2.2. This system was used in "Counter circuits" of "Sequential circuits".

In this class, students first studied MOD-16 counter, MOD-5 counter and MOD-10 counter by using the learning system. After using the system, students answered the following questions by rating 4, 3, 2 or 1 (4: positive, 3: mildly positive, 2: mildly negative, 1: negative).

– Questions (C1-1)–(C1-5) ask about the ease of use of following items:
  (C1-1) the learning part
  (C1-2) buttons in the learning part
  (C1-3) the tab
  (C1-4) the quiz part
  (C1-5) buttons in the quiz part

- Questions (C2-1)–(C2-3) ask about the comprehensibility of "explanatory text" of followings:
    (C2-1) MOD-16 counter
    (C2-2) MOD-5 counter
    (C2-3) MOD-10 counter
- Question (C3-1) asks about the usefulness of "displaying multiple materials" (diagrams, chart, table and text) on the same page.
- Questions (C4-1)–(C4-2) ask about speech:
    (C4-1) usefulness of using speech for explanatory text
    (C4-2) adequacy of the speech rate
- Questions (C5-1)–(C5-2) ask about readability:
    (C5-1) UI
    (C5-2) the letters
- Questions (C6-1) asks about the easiness of quizzes.
- Questions (C7-1)–(C7-3) are total evaluations:
    (C7-1) Are the contents of the system easy?
    (C7-2) Is the system useful?
    (C7-3) Are you content with the system?

After the questionnaire, students made an experiment on MOD-10 counter and MOD-12 counter.

Result and Discussion. In 2012, 81 students enrolled in the class. The result of the questionnaire in 2012 [16] is shown in Table 3. The average of the mean values of all questions is 3.22. The values higher than 3.5 are (C1-2), (C1-5) and (C5-2), which are about operability and readability. The values lower than 2.9 are (C2-2), (C6-1) and (C7-1), which are about easiness of explanation, quizzes and contents. This result indicates that the operability of the system is relatively easy and that the quizzes and contents of the system are relatively difficult. This result is similar to the result of FF learning system.

The correlation coefficients of values of (C7-2: useful) and other questions are calculated. The correlation coefficients that are higher than 0.4 are as follows. The correlation coefficients of (C7-2) and ((C1-1), (C2-3), (C3-1), (C7-3)) are (0.45, 0.45, 0.42, 0.60). This result indicates that students would think the system is useful if they can easily use the system and understand the explanation, diagram and chart. Also, students would be content with the system if they think the system is useful.

Paired sample t-test was used for the comparison of the mean values of evaluations of FF system and counter system. (F3-1) and (C3-1) (usefulness of "displaying multiple materials") are compared. The mean value of (F3-1) is 3.10 and the mean value of (C3-1) is 3.36. In this analysis, the degrees of freedom is 80, the critical value for significance level of 0.05 (two-tailed test) is 1.990, and t-ratio is -2.578, therefore, there is a significant difference between the mean values of (F3-1) and (C3-1). This result indicates that "displaying multiple materials" is more effective for counter learning system than for FF learning system. In counter learning system, the explanation refers both circuit diagram and timing chart at the same time, while in FF learning system, the explanation refers diagram and chart sequentially. This would be the reason of the difference between the mean values of (F3-1) and (C3-1).

Table 3. The mean values of evaluation of Counter learning system, 2012.

Question	Value	Question	Value	Question	Value
(C1-1)	3.36	(C2-1)	3.23	(C5-1)	3.46
(C1-2)	3.57	(C2-2)	2.86	(C5-2)	3.54
(C1-3)	3.40	(C2-3)	2.95	(C6-1)	2.68
(C1-4)	3.47	(C3-1)	3.36	(C7-1)	2.68
(C1-5)	3.52	(C4-1)	3.06	(C7-2)	3.33
		(C4-2)	3.14	(C7-3)	3.19

The students used the system seriously because they had to finish the system to start the experiment. This type of learning system is effective for acquiring knowledge. Student could easily make an experiment on MOD-10 counter and MOD-12 counter. In the learning system, MOD-12 counter was not mentioned, however, students easily designed MOD-12 counter as "MOD-2 and MOD-6" counter, because they studied MOD-10 counter as "MOD-2 and MOD-5" counter. Also, students easily designed MOD-6 counter because they studied how to reset MOD-5 counter.

3.3 Using Learning System with Members of Experiment

Method. In this experiment class, around 80 students are divided into A groups (3 groups) and B groups (3 groups). This year, we changed the usage of the system as follows.

A groups: Students used the counter learning system with members of experiment (usually 2 students work together).

B groups: Students used the counter learning system individually as before.

The reasons for this trial are as follows.

(1) Students had been using the counter learning system individually until 2018. A student made an experiment with another student who had finished the learning system at about the same time. Usually, a student work with another student whom he/she didn't work with in FF experiment.

(2) For some students, it took a long time to finish the learning system, so it was sometimes difficult to manage the experiment class.

(3) It was effective to use the learning system individually; however, we would like to provide the system which can increase motivation as well as knowledge for the students.

After using the system, students answered the following questions by rating 4, 3, 2 or 1 (4: positive, 3: mildly positive, 2: mildly negative, 1: negative).

- Question (Cn1) asks about the ease of use of the system. (Corresponding to (C1-1)–(C1-5) described above)
- Question (Cn2) asks about the comprehensibility of "explanatory text". (Corresponding to (C2-1)–(C2-3))

– Question (Cn3) asks about the usefulness of "displaying multiple materials" on the same page. (Same as (C3-1))
– Question (Cn4) asks about the usefulness of using speech. (Same as (C4-1))
– Question (Cn6) asks about the easiness of quiz. (Same as (C6-1))
– Questions (Cn7-1)–(Cn7-4) are as follows:
    (Cn7-1) Are the contents of the system easy? (Same as (C7-1))
    (Cn7-2) Is the system useful? (Same as (C7-2))
    (Cn7-3) Are you content with the system? (Same as (C7-3))
    (Cn7-4) Are you motivated by the system? (New question)

In the following question, students chose one symbol (a, b, c or d).

– Questions (Cn7-5): Which do you prefer?
    a: I prefer using the system individually, b: I might prefer using the system individually, c: I might prefer using the system with members d: I prefer using the system with members

After the questionnaire, students made an experiment on MOD-10 counter and MOD-12 counter.

Result and Discussion. In 2019, 83 students enrolled in the class (A groups: 42, B groups: 41). The result of the questionnaire in 2019 is shown in Table 4. The mean values of A groups' Cn* and B groups' Cn* (* = 1, 2, 3, 4, 6, 7-1, 7-2, 7-3, 7-4) are compared using Welch's t-test, and the analysis cannot show any difference, i.e., the mean values of A groups and B groups for the same question are almost the same. The mean value of (Cn7-4: motivated) is slightly smaller than the mean values of (Cn7-2: useful) or (Cn7-3: contented) in both A groups and B groups, therefore, these values are compared using paired sample t-test. In A groups, the critical value for significance level of 0.05 is 2.020, and t-ratios are 4.156 (Cn7-2 vs. Cn7-4) and 2.152 (Cn7-3 vs. Cn7-4), therefore, there are significant differences. In B groups, the critical value for significance level of 0.05 is 2.021, and t-ratios are 4.866 (Cn7-2 vs. Cn7-4) and 3.534 (Cn7-3 vs. Cn7-4), therefore, there are significant differences. This result indicates that students' evaluations of "useful" and "motivated" are different, and "contented" and "motivated" are also different as described in the discussion of FF learning system.

The correlation coefficients of values of "(Cn7-2: useful) and other questions" and those of "(Cn7-4: motivated) and other questions" are calculated. The correlation coefficients that are higher than 0.4 are as follows. In A groups, the correlation coefficients of (Cn7-2) and ((Cn3), (Cn7-1)) are (0.49, 0.49), but in B groups, the correlation coefficients of (Cn7-2) and ((Cn1), (Cn2), (Cn7-3)) are (0.55, 0.51, 0.47). While, in A groups, the correlation coefficient of (Cn7-4) and ((Cn1), (Cn2), (Cn3)) are (0.52, 0.43, 0.47), but in B groups, all coefficients of (Cn7-4) and other questions are lower than 0.4. The tendencies of A groups and B groups are different. In A groups, students studied using the system with members. This method might have affected the result.

In A groups, the mean value of (Cn7-3: contented, in counter system) is slightly smaller than that of (Fn7-3: contented, in FF system), therefore, these values are compared by using paired sample t-test. The critical value for significance level of 0.05 is 2.020, and t-ratio is 2.033 (Fn7-3 vs. Cn7-3), therefore, there is a significant difference. While, in B groups, the critical value for significance level of 0.05 is 2.021, and t-ratio is 0.781 (Fn7-3 vs. Cn7-3), therefore, there is not a significant difference. Also, the mean value of (Cn7-3) and (Cn7-2: useful) in A groups are compared by using paired sample t-test, and it is shown that there is a significant difference. But, in B groups, there is not a significant difference between the mean values of (Cn7-3) and (Cn7-2). This result indicates that some students in A groups might not be contented because they studied with members. Some students wrote in a free text field that they felt difficulty in using the system with members.

The average of mean values of all questions is 3.11 in A groups and it is 3.11 in B groups. Therefore, the mean value of (Cn7-2: useful) is relatively high in both groups. This result indicates that the basic framework of learning part and quiz part of our system is necessary and the contents are adequate.

The values of (Cn3: multiple materials) is the highest in both A and B groups. While, the values of (Cn4: speech) is low in both groups. The values of (Cn4) and (Cn7-2) are compared using t-test, and there are significant differences in both groups. This result indicates that "displaying multiple materials" is effective but "using speech" is not so effective.

Table 4. The mean values of evaluation of Counter learning system, 2019.

A groups				B groups			
Question	Value	Question	Value	Question	Value	Question	Value
(Cn1)	3.29	(Cn7-1)	2.71	(Cn1)	3.20	(Cn7-1)	2.63
(Cn2)	3.17	(Cn7-2)	3.43	(Cn2)	3.32	(Cn7-2)	3.51
(Cn3)	3.50	(Cn7-3)	3.19	(Cn3)	3.56	(Cn7-3)	3.37
(Cn4)	2.93	(Cn7-4)	2.98	(Cn4)	2.73	(Cn7-4)	2.90
(Cn6)	2.98			(Cn6)	2.80		

The result of the last question (Cn7-5) is as follows. The numbers of students who chose a, b, c or d are shown below.

A groups	a: 2	b: 10	c: 15	d: 15
B groups	a: 14	b: 9	c: 12	d: 6

The number of students who chose c (I might prefer using the system with members) and d (I prefer using the system with members) is 30 in A groups and it is 18 in B groups. This result indicates that students would understand the merit of studying with members if they work together.

3.4 Developing New Learning System

We analyzed the results of questionnaires and designed a new counter circuits learning system. The summary of discussions is as follows.

- The operability of previous system is appropriate.
- Displaying multiple materials (diagram, chart, table and text) on the same page is effective for counter learning system.

- Using speech is not so effective. Therefore, we decided to delete this function from the new system.
- The contents and quizzes are not so easy for the students. Therefore, we do not have to provide more difficult contents or quizzes.
- The evaluation of usefulness of the system is relatively high. Therefore, we do not have to change the contents and basic framework (learning part and quiz part).
- Usefulness and contentedness are related if students use the system individually.
- Some students are not contented if they use the learning system with members.
- The evaluation of "motivated" is relatively lower than "useful" or "contented".

We designed a new learning system based on these discussions. The aim of the new system is as follows.

- To encourage students to study with members.
- To improve the motivation for study.

The new system is developed by using HTML, CSS and JavaScript. This system can be used by one, two or three students. At the first page of the system, users should input their names, then, the system prompts each student to do next operation in turn. A student uses each mouse, and clicks the button when the prompt is displayed on the UI. In the quiz part, a student also answers in turn. A student sometimes is discontent with a member if he/she does not work well, therefore, this system ask students to do operations and to answer quizzes fairly.

"To improve the motivation" is difficult. "Motivated" is different from "contented" or "useful". "The system developed by 3rd year students" was not so effective to motivate students to study, and "using the system with members" were not so effective for motivation either. We might have to add some example of applications of the counter circuits to the system, so that students understand the importance of counter circuits.

Our previous systems also took logs of students' usage of the systems. These logs were not analyzed precisely, but they were checked to know how students use the system, and this knowledge was used for the design of new system. Our new system is under development. We have implemented the basic functions of the system and made learning contents and quizzes of MOD-16 counter. We will finish developing the system and will evaluate the system next year.

4   Conclusions and Future Work

FF Circuits Learning System. We developed a FF circuits learning system, which explains Inverter pair and five FF circuits. This system consists of learning part and quiz part, and students can proceed to learn next circuit if they pass the quiz. This learning system had been used from 2011 to 2017 in a class of experiments for 1st year university students. After the experiment of four FFs, students studied Inverter pair and RS-FF by using the learning system. After using the system, students answered the questionnaire. The results indicate as follows.

(a) Students would think the system is useful if they can understand the explanation.
(b) Students would be content with the system if they think the system is useful.

We stopped using the learning system in 2018 and we tried another approach. In 2019, 3rd year students developed FF circuits learning systems in PBL class. One of the learning systems developed by 3rd year students was used in the class of experiments of 1st year students. After using the system, students answered the questionnaire. The results indicate as follows.

(c) Students' evaluation of "motivated" is lower than the evaluations of "useful" or "contented". The factors to motivate students are complicated, and some students would think "contented" and "motivated" differently.

After the questionnaire, students did their assignment by themselves.

Counter Circuits Learning System. On the other hand, we developed a counter circuits learning system, which explains three counter circuits. This system also consists of learning part and quiz part, and students can proceed to learn next circuit if they pass the quiz. This learning system had been used individually by 1st year students before the experiment of counter circuits from 2012 to 2018. After using the system, students answered the questionnaire. The results indicate the same findings as (a) and (b) which were described in the discussion of FF learning system.
After the questionnaire, students made an experiment on two counter circuits.

In 2019, students used the same counter circuits learning system with members in A groups, and individually in B groups. After using the system, students answered the questionnaire. The results indicate the same finding as (c) described in the discussion of the new FF learning system. The results also indicate as follows.

(d) Some students in A groups might not be contented because they studied with members. However, the majority of students would understand the merit of studying with members if they work together.
(e) The evaluation of "useful" is relatively high. Therefore, we think that the basic framework of the system (learning part and quiz part) is necessary and the contents are adequate.
(f) "Displaying multiple materials" is effective but "using speech" is not so effective.

We designed a new counter circuits learning system based on the discussions. The aim of the new system is to encourage students to study with members and to improve the motivation for study. This system is under development and will be evaluated next year.

Future Work. Future work includes following problems. We have to finish the development of new system of counter circuits. We have to consider adding some contents to motivate students to study. In these years, new approaches have been proposed for higher education, e.g. using games [17, 18]. We might have to add some characteristics of these approaches. Also, we have to reconsider the cycle of teaching and learning by using the system developed by students.

Acknowledgments. The author would like to thank M. Matsumoto and S. Miyano for their contribution to the development of the new system of counter circuits. The author would also like to thank Professor Sasaki for the discussion about the usage of counter circuits learning system.

References

1. Kishimoto, M., Kaneko, K.: Implementation of logic circuit simulator for educational use. IEICE Tech. Rep. **101**(609), 61–67 (2002). (in Japanese)
2. Donzellini, G., Ponta, D.: A simulation environment for e-learning in digital design. IEEE Trans. Industr. Electron. **54**(6), 3078–3085 (2007)
3. Yang, O., Shiping, Y., Yabo, D., Miaoliang, Z.: Web-based interactive virtual laboratory system for digital circuit experiment. In: Iskander, M. (ed.) Innovations in E-learning, Instruction Technology, Assessment, and Engineering Education, pp. 305–309. Springer, Dordrecht (2007). 10.1007/978-1-4020-6262-9_53
4. Japan Science and Technology Agency: e-learning, Digital Circuits Course. https://jrecin.jst. go.jp/seek/html/e-learning/701/index_701.html. Accessed 18 Jan 2020
5. Ishihata, H.: Support tool for logic circuit course. IEICE Tech. Rep. **114**(513), 65–69 (2015). (in Japanese)
6. Arase, K.: SimcirJS. https://kazuhikoarase.github.io/simcirjs/. Accessed 18 Jan 2020
7. Deguchi, S., Ueki, D., Takagi, A.: Research on learning system for sequential circuits. In: Proceedings of the Annual Conference of JSiSE 2011, pp. 428–429 (2011). (in Japanese)
8. Deguchi, S., Takagi, A.: Development and evaluation of the learning system for sequential circuits. IEICE Tech. Rep. **112**(66), 1–6 (2012). (in Japanese)
9. Deguchi, S., Takagi, A.: Development, utilization and evaluation of the learning system for counter circuits. IEICE Tech. Rep. **113**(67), 11–16 (2013). (in Japanese)
10. Keats, D.W., Boughey, J.: Task-based small group learning in large classes: design and implementation in a second year university botany course. High. Educ. **27**(1), 59–73 (1994)
11. Hammar Chiriac, E.: A scheme for understanding group processes in problem-based learning. High. Educ. **55**(5), 505–518 (2008)
12. Bovill, C.: Co-creation in learning and teaching: the case for a whole-class approach. High. Educ. (2019). https://doi.org/10.1007/s10734-019-00453-w
13. O'Connell, R.M.: Adapting team-based learning for application in the basic electric circuit theory sequence. IEEE Trans. Educ. **58**(2), 90–97 (2015)
14. Martinez-Rodrigo, F., et al.: Using PBL to improve educational outcomes and student satisfaction in the teaching of DC/DC and DC/AC converters. IEEE Trans. Educ. **60**(3), 229–237 (2017)
15. Lavy, S.: Who benefits from group work in higher education? An attachment theory perspective. High. Educ. **73**(2), 175–187 (2017)
16. Deguchi, S.: Development of the learning system for sequential circuits and introduction of the system to classes. Trans. JSiSE **31**(2), 214–219 (2014). (in Japanese)
17. Vahed, A., McKenna, S., Singh, S.: Linking the 'know-that' and 'know-how' knowledge through games: a quest to evolve the future for science and engineering education. High. Educ. **71**, 781–790 (2016)
18. Coleman, T.E., Money, A.G.: Student-centred digital game-based learning: a conceptual framework and survey of the state of the art. High. Educ. (2019). https://doi.org/10.1007/s10734-019-00417-0

Designing a Mobile Platform for Developing Scholar Physical Education Activities: A WebQuest Based Approach

Carlos Alexandre Gustavo de Souza[1], Ferrucio de Franco Rosa[1,2], and Rodrigo Bonacin[1,2(✉)]

[1] UNIFACCAMP, Campo Limpo Paulista, Brazil
prof.allexandre@gmail.com
[2] Renato Archer Information Technology Center - CTI, Campinas, SP, Brazil
{ferrucio.rosa,rodrigo.bonacin}@cti.gov.br

Abstract. Due to the advance of the use and capabilities of the Web, the educational institutions increasingly look for effective learning methods that explore it as an educational resource, including those methods related to physical education. WebQuest (WQ) is a Web based and inquire-oriented learning method. We identified studies about the use of WQ in class activities and autonomous learning activities. Some studies report the use of WQ lessons in educational activities with mobile devices. However, existing works do not address how to use the WQ methodology with mobile technologies aiming to promote advanced teaching activities for scholar physical education. This work contributes to the research about how the WQ can be used in conjunction with mobile and tangible technologies for the improvement of learning in scholar physical education. A design of a mobile platform model is proposed, and it is implemented in a prototype of a WQ-based tool for supporting physical education teaching, which integrates theory and practical activities. We present preliminary results with 15 students of Physical Education and Dance disciplines of 7th grade of elementary school level.

Keywords: WebQuest · Mobile learning · Scholar physical education

1 Introduction

The increasing popularity of the Internet turned it into an important mean for information sharing, knowledge construction and learning. Educational institutions increasingly look for effective learning methods that use mobile technologies on the Web. Mobile technologies are used to support learning activities of various disciplines and domains, including those activities focused on physical education.

Nowadays, there is a large content in the realm of physical education available on the Web, including practices, methods, and theories. It is a rich source of

© Springer Nature Switzerland AG 2020
P. Zaphiris and A. Ioannou (Eds.): HCII 2020, LNCS 12205, pp. 49–63, 2020.
https://doi.org/10.1007/978-3-030-50513-4_4

information to be explored during scholar physical education learning activities. Besides, mobile and tangible technologies are needed to provide flexible solutions, to develop practical physical activities as well as to integrate theoretical and practical activities.

WebQuest (WQ) is a Web-based and inquiry-oriented learning technique [6], which we propose be used to support the improvements in scholar physical education. Some studies report the use of WQ in educational activities with mobile devices outside the classrooms (*e.g.*, [4]) and positive results arise from studies about the use of WQ in class-based learning activities (*e.g.*, [2]). However, existing works do not address how to use the WQ method with mobile technologies and tangible objects to provide advanced teaching activities in the scholar physical education domain, as well as professional physical activities, whether they are related to sports or not.

In this context, this paper focuses on the use of WQ in conjunction with mobile and tangible technologies aiming at improving scholar physical education activities. WQ lessons are used for structuring mobile learning theoretical and practical activities supported by Web resources. To this end, we propose a design solution and the WQC_MOBILE platform, which includes the following components:

- *A responsive interface (Web and mobile) for the specification of physical education activities.* It includes the development of WQ lessons and the specification of markers (*e.g.*, using QR code or RFID) to be used in physical objects during the practical activities, which are linked to the WQ lessons. The specification of those activities is guided by physical education methods (global, partial and mixed).
- *A mobile application.* It is used by the students to explore Web resources, develop theoretical activities, as well as to interact with physical objects (with markers) during the development of practical activities.

The WQC_MOBILE was evaluated by two teachers and fifteen students (from 12 to 13 years old) of a school situated in São Paulo, Brazil.

Our main contributions are: (1) an design solution for conducting physical education practices with WQ, mobile and tangible artifacts; (2) a software platform (WQC_MOBILE) to support and exercise the proposal, including an authoring tool and a mobile application; and (3) a case study with students in a school to analyze the implications of applying our proposal.

This paper is structured as follows: Sect. 2 describes the background and related work on the use of WebQuest and collaborative learning. Section 3 details the proposed design and application. Section 4 presents the case study and reports on the obtained results. Section 5 concludes the paper and proposes future work.

2   Background and Related Work

Firstly, this section presents the theoretical framework used in the proposed approach, with a focus on the WQ methodology (Subsect. 2.1) and the practice of school physical education and mobile computing (Subsect. 2.2). In Subsect. 2.3, we present studies (related work) on the use of the WQ in collaborative activities.

2.1 WebQuest Learning

Currently, there are thousands (or millions) of schools connected to the Internet and the number of new connections has been growing. Despite the large quantity of learning objects available on the Web, many educational institutions do not show significant changes in the teaching process [6].

New training strategies have been developed by educators and institutions with the objective of train teachers about the usefulness and value of Web content and resources. The concept of WQ was proposed by Bernie Dodge and Tom March in [6], and it means an oriented investigation in which some (or all) information with which the learners interact comes from Web sources.

WQ improves students' abilities to solve problems, by asking them to expand and improve their knowledge and skills, interacting to perform an authentic learning task, *i.e.*, something that provides relevant learning [8]. WQ offers learning tasks for students, as well as resources and processes for carrying out these tasks. There is no single correct way to complete a task with WQ, *i.e.*, there is no definitive guide to apply WQ. Students must find their own path based on their learning experiences and preferences, with individual goals and differences to succeed. The challenges provided by WQ can become opportunities for problem solving and for the development of critical thinking and creativity.

WQ can be used as a research and application tool aimed at improving educational performance. We can use it in two moments: Short term (*Short WQ*), aiming to appropriate and interact with knowledge; and Long term (*Long WQ*), aiming to promote the understanding of the application and the development of knowledge. A Long WQ can last for days, whereas a Short WQ can only last a few hours. Both (Long and Short) have to be planned (or re-planned) during the execution to obtain better results.

A WQ requires a clear task, optimizing the time spent browsing the Web. This task must be interesting and pleasant, in order to induce the student to investigate, interact and sharpen his/her will to proceed from beginning to end of the task. To achieve this goal, it will be necessary to include in the WQ the following attributes [6]:

- The "*Stage*", which needs to be prepared with a short introduction that provides basic information.
- An *interesting topic* that should attract the learner's attention and mobilization.
- *Web searches*, obtaining specific content for the development of tasks.
- *Clear description of the task performance*, in order to have continuity and a satisfactory result.
- *Guidance* on how to organize the results.
- *Feedback*, in order to show the acquired knowledge.

The WQ should be motivating and interesting, involving the basic structure of an investigation, giving the learner the role of scientist, reporter or detective. It must lead learners to think, imagine and dare, giving them the audacity to create and criticize. WQ can be planned for a single discipline, or it can be multidisciplinary. It is possible to compare, classify, induce, deduce, build support, abstract and analyze personal perspectives about the investigation [15].

WebQuest consists of 6 components [6], namely:

- *Introduction.* A motivating theme should be presented and the research information highlighted to the learner.
- *Task.* The proposed task must be challenging and feasible. We need to dialogue and write with the learner what they should elaborate to solve it, making them think, write and contextualize until reaching the end, as well as producing a satisfactory solution, with the participation of all involved.
- *Process.* Learners should be guided during the dialogue and context, with a step-by-step approach to solving tasks, encouraging them to think and rethink.
- *Resource.* An inventory of resources must be available on the Web to systematize learning in thinking and rethinking, and especially to ease research and investigation. These resources must create paths for success and motivate them to perform the task.
- *Conclusion.* Generate tracks for future searches. When the task is finished, the teacher should give feedback, presenting what has been learned and giving the learner the opportunity to report what the experience was like for everyone involved in the task.
- *Evaluation.* It can be both quantitative and qualitative. A systematic process for recording and evaluating results should be used. The evaluation can be continuous, and should be performed during the process. It can be done through writing, oral or test; it cannot be conducted in a punitive way, but enlightening.

Regarding the planning activities, when developing a WQ lesson, we start with a simple process, then we move on to the most complex and, with that we arrive at the innovative process. Strategy example: start with a single theme, with a short WQ, and gradually move on to longer and interdisciplinary activities [6].

The use of WQ can be conciliated with other learning objectives such as Universal Design for Learning (UDL) [20]. In this context, the role of the teacher must go much further, changing his practices. Collaborative learning can be used as a tool to promote new activities with learners and to share knowledge with teachers.

2.2   School Physical Education and Mobile Computing

School physical education approaches experienced several paradigms over time, due to their relation to economic, social and political issues. These approaches and proposals for teaching Physical Education are essential to form a critical and reflective teacher. We need to provide a physical education with quality in the context of its reality of pedagogical practice, extracting from each phase what it has of educational potential [1].

Nowadays, we have to think about the current physical education, by considering the influence of technology and the constant changes in society. However, it is also necessary to look to the past to bring what has already been built. Physical education is characterized by body experimentation and body culture, and is applied in sports, games, fights, health, etc. In this perspective, thinking about the body in movement and its education supported by digital technologies arises as a great challenge both for the field of physical education at school and for the design of solutions for this context. We need to understand the educational context (*e.g.*, available resources, assessment objectives, methodology), *i.e.*, the main aspects of the pedagogical process must be considered when introducing technology in conjunction with physical education.

"Teaching method" is an important concept to our research, since mobile computing and tangible interfaces in educational environments are applied according to it. Teaching method can be understood as the teacher's action when directing and stimulating the teaching process according to the students' learning. A set of actions, steps, external conditions, and procedures is considered in the teaching method [13].

We use the Partial, Global and Mixed methods to define WQ lessons for scholar physical education. The application of mobile computing and tangible interfaces supports and differentiates our proposal. The Partial method consists of teaching a movement skill in parts to join later these parts with each other. This skill can be subdivided. The Global method analyzes a movement skill and presents its whole. The Mixed method consists of synchronizing the Global and Partial methods and it is executed in the following order: first, the execution of the gesture as a whole occurs; then the movement is divided to correct the previous movement; and finally we return to the complete practice of movements.

2.3   WebQuest and Colaboration

We present studies from the following scientific research databases and indexes: Google Scholar, ScienceDirect, IEEE Xplore, ACM Digital Library, and Springer link. We analyzed articles and experiments related to the best practices for better student learning that uses WQ and mobile and tangible physical education learning in English and Portuguese languages.

WQs and blogs can be used as tools to promote collaborative writing in interdisciplinary activities in elementary school. The insertion of the Internet and research in pedagogical practice is analyzed in [19]. The authors point out that the use of guided and accompanied research goes beyond instruction and training activities, especially when it encourage the autonomy of learners. The authors developed a collective blog. The combination of WQ with the blog proved to be effective for educational practice. This research highlighted the importance of WQ as a study method and the relevance of blogs as a collaborative learning tool.

A WQ editor to be used as an educational technique is proposed in [3]. The study aims to reduce the learner's distraction during the pedagogical activity. The WebQuest Editor (WQE) generates content in HTML format. This editor works with the IMS Learning Design (IMSLD) metalanguage, which is a standard for building learning units independent of teaching methods [10]. IMSLD allows the development of learning activities, such as the creation of different roles and access to services. The article details the use of WQE, including its structure, architecture and the relationship between WQ and the IMSLD standard.

A Collaborative WQ editor based on the theoretical framework of Dodge [6] is presented in [17] to explore information that is easy and quick to access. It also aims to highlight the need for reflection in relation to the use of web resources by learners. According to the authors, WQ can assist in the development of activities based on constructionist theory, which presents the computer as a mediating tool for the construction of knowledge.

An application of WQ in conjunction with Mobile Learning (M-Learning) is presented in [2] aiming to create mechanisms that enable students to continue to learn, even outside the classroom. The paper explores how a WQ can be applied in an educational context supported by mobile devices (this is also proposed in our work). A WQ named "Learning from Plants" was developed. It is a research task, which consists of checking the types of plants, leaves, stems, fruits and flowers that are found in nature. According to the authors, mobility made students work collaboratively. Teachers assisted the group in search, image capture and poster organization.

The collaborative work using WQ aims to change the individual use of the computer to more participatory applications, where everyone collaborates to solve the problem of each task. An approach to explore Web resources in higher education is presented in [5]. A WQ activity was carried out with students from the Accounting Sciences undergraduate course. According to the authors, students had the opportunity to improve their skills in presenting tasks, in work as a team, and in their creativity.

Building WQ with student participation is the focus of Leahy & Twomey [12], who use reflective creativity to create a WQ lesson. This activity includes cooperation, planning and decision making. According to the authors, each student had a different learning experience; the collaborative construction of WQ is related to the generation of critical thinking skills.

WQ is applied where information exchange takes place (chats and discussion forums) in [7]. The main purpose is learning together, investigating together, i.e., evolving the group in a heterogeneous manner.

Learning by young people for whom digital technologies (DT) are natural (digital natives) is studied by Mostmans, Vleugels & Bannier [16]. According to the authors, young people apply DTs to improve their creative skills, social processes and collaborative creativity.

WQ has a problem-solving approach and has a clear structure, which guides the learning and interaction processes, and can be used in various domains. The WQ preparation promotes the teachers' interests to interact with each other and explore the technology [21].

A study on how to implement WQ as a tool for improving learning in teacher preparation programs is carried out in [18]. The study depicts the teacher training by using programming. Many teachers expressed their intention to use more technological resources in teaching, and also to use WQ. From the bibliographic survey, we identified the relevance of using WQ as an instrument to improve the educational process, making the student the core of learning.

The analyzed studies confirm the importance of the theme and point to the need for works aiming to include or increase the use of information technologies in the school environment. We aim to provide a pedagogical platform (WQC_MOBILE) for the scholar physical education, which helps teachers to be prepared to work with collaborative teaching methods, renewing his practices inside and outside the classroom. Our focus is on allowing significant actions to be taken in order to make students interested, responsible and committed to their own learning in a context of collective Web research.

Our approach presents a research contribution by merging lessons from the WQ technique with mobile and tangible computing, in addition to applying it to physical education teaching activities.

3   Design Solution and Application

We detail our design solution for the proposed WQ based platform for scholar physical education in Subsect. 3.1. In Subsect. 3.2, we present how this design solution was implemented in WQC_MOBILE.

3.1   Design Solution

Initially, teachers can use a Web tool in a desktop (or mobile) to create WQ lessons to be used by students on the mobile platform. This tool provides a set of features to support teachers in design, execution, evaluation and management of WQ lessons. Besides, they can share content and experiences with other teachers. To this end, we modeled the following steps for the teachers:

- **Step 1**: *Login/Register.*
- **Step 2**: *Search for content* aiming at stimulating the collaboration between teachers in the design of WQ lessons. This step provides a search engine, where teachers can reuse existing WQ lessons or individual media shared by others.
- **Step 3**: *Select the results.* In this step, the teacher can individually visualize and analyze each shared file, and select them for reuse.
- **Step 4**: *Develop the introduction of a WQ lesson.* If the teacher selected to reuse the introduction (or an entire lesson) it is automatically loaded in an editable field; otherwise a blank field is presented. The teacher can also return to Step 3.

- **Step 5**: *Develop the tasks of a WQ lesson.* There are two types of task to be created (or reused). The first task type is related to theoretical content (*e.g.*, links and forms with multiple choice questions). The second task type is related to practical activities. The teacher can reuse both types of tasks. The use of mixed teaching method (*cf.*, Sect. 2.2) and the combination of theory and practice are supported in this stage. For the practical tasks, the tangible object markers (*e.g.*, QR code) are generated and linked to the task description. These markers can also be linked to theoretical concepts or Web resources. For group tasks, the teacher may require to share the markers (or content) in using social network services.
- **Step 6**: *Develop the process of a WQ lesson.* This step aims to guide students in the actions to be followed during the activities. The global teaching method (*cf.*, Sect. 2.2) can be used in this step to provide an overview of the situation and to guide the teacher in the construction of the WQ lesson.
- **Step 7**: *Develop the resources of a WQ lesson.* The goal of this step is to provide for students the resources to be used during theoretical and practical tasks. To this end, resources are available for the 3 types of methods (Global, Partial, and Mixed). Resources can be tagged (using these types) to be shared and reused, as described in Step 2.
- **Step 8**: *Develop the conclusion of a WQ lesson.* The teacher is guided to develop the conclusion of the WQ, including best practices and shared content by others.
- **Step 9**: *Develop the evaluation of a WQ lesson.* This step defines the evaluation of both theoretical and practical tasks. Automatic evaluation features for multiple choice questions can be used for theoretical tasks.
- **Step 10**: *Review and publish a WQ lesson.* In this step the teacher can review a lesson (visualizing it in the student's view) and publish it.

The students have access to the WQ lessons and makers in a mobile interface. They can use mobile resources, such as a camera, to access the markers as well as to achieve goals in practical activities (*e.g.*, using the accelerometer and step counters). They also have access to collaborative tools (*e.g.*, chats and forum), where they can share their experiences with other students.

3.2   The WQC_MOBILE Platform

We present how the proposed steps and functionalities presented above were implemented by the WQC_MOBILE platform. The development of the application was carried out in three prototyping cycles described as follows:

1. *Non-functional prototypes* - We developed non-functional prototypes, including low-fidelity and high-fidelity ones, aiming to evaluate design alternatives and to collect the feedback from a physical education teacher.
2. *First functional prototype* - This prototype consists of all the user interfaces, including those designed for teachers and students. This prototype was limited in terms of storage (database), authoring tools, communication and content sharing features. This prototype was presented to a physical education

teacher. The feedback and bugs were collected and corrected in the next version.

3. *Complete Functional Prototype* - This is the first fully functional version of the system, which is presented in this section. This version was used in the preliminary study presented in Sect. 4.

We choose to use free hosting technologies and services. Thus, we used HTML, CSS, Javascript and PHP languages, the CodeIgniter[1] and Bootstrap[2] frameworks, and the MySQL[3] database. A version of the WQC_MOBILE is hosted at GearHost cloud service[4].

WQC_MOBILE has 2 interface color palettes; the blue one is used by teachers (left side of Fig. 1), and the orange one is used by students (right side of Fig. 1). This distinction was elicited during the first prototyping cycle, as teachers want to visualize the students' interface without getting confused.

Figure 1 presents the menu options of teachers and students mobile interfaces. Both can access the shared WQ lessons and visualize usage instructions in the home interface. Teachers can also update their profiles, create QR code and images (or GIFs) animations. They can also collaborate by using chats or forums.

Fig. 1. Teachers and students menu options.

---

[1] https://codeigniter.com/.

[2] https://getbootstrap.com/.

[3] https://www.mysql.com/.

[4] http://cmseawqs.gear.host/.

Teachers and students can search and visualize the WQ lessons, as shown in Fig. 2. Teachers are allowed to visualize, edit and reuse their own lessons as well as those shared by other teachers. They can also create a new lesson from an initial sketch (*i.e.*, without reuse an existing one) or exclude their lessons. Students are allowed to visualize and execute WQ addressed to them as a school activity or those shared for everyone (as extra class activities).

Fig. 2. WQ lessons list interface.

Figure 3 presents two teachers' interfaces used to create a new WQ lesson using the mobile platform. The first (left side of Fig. 3) includes options with the lesson identification, a brief summary of the lesson, and the students (class/grade) that will execute the lesson. The second (right side of Fig. 3) shows the reuse of the introduction of a WQ lesson (see Step 4 - Subsect. 3.1) in a text editor interface. This interface can be used to edit all the 6 WQ components, including 2 types of the task component (see Step 5 - Subsect. 3.1). This interface also allows to include links to QR codes, images, animated GIFs and videos from an internal database, as well as links to external resources. At the end, the WQ lessons, their components and individual resources can be shared to be reused by other teachers.

4   Preliminary Study

A preliminary study was carried out to assess the potential use of WQC_MOBILE in practice. Subsection 4.1 presents a brief description of the

Fig. 3. Interface for developing a new WQ lesson.

study, including the procedures adopted in its execution and analysis. Subsection 4.2 presents the preliminary results, including the quantitative and qualitative ones. Subsection 4.3 discusses the obtained results, limitations and research challenges.

4.1 Study Description and Procedures

Two (2) teachers and 15 students of "Physical Education and Dance" discipline of 7th grade (from 12 to 13 years old) of a private primary school situated in São Paulo, Brazil, participated in the evaluation of the proposal. The school has computer labs with Internet access and the students often use them. All the students declared to use often smartphones with Internet access.

Both teachers have large experience with physical education (18 and 9 years), as well as they have basic skills in informatics and never developed WQ lessons before. Thus, the researchers firstly prepared a WQ tutorial for the teachers. Afterwards, they were asked to create three lessons on the theme "physical activities based on exercise physiology".

The students were randomly divided in three groups of the same size. Each group attended one lesson as follows:

- The *Group 1* had classes as usual, *i.e.*, the theory in a classroom, and practical lessons at the school sports court. A pre-test (pre-exam) was applied before the explanations and theoretical orientations, referring to the topic "Physical Activity and Physical Exercise". The pre-test was applied to obtain the basic knowledge levels of the students and their understanding of the afore-mentioned theme. In sequence, the students received a text with explanations about this topic, and the teachers addressed it in theory at the classroom and practices at the school sports court. A post-test (post-exam) was applied, in order to measure their score after the classes.

- The *Group 2* had the theoretical WQ lessons in computer labs (elaborated by the teachers) and the practical ones at school sports court. These WQ lessons follow the format recommended by Dodge [6], but they do not make use of physical education methods (global, partial and mixed) and they do not explore mobile and QR code technologies. As described above, a pre-test and a post-test was also applied to this group.
- The *Group 3* used the school sports court to perform both theoretical and practical lessons using the WQC_MOBILE. The WQ lessons were created by the teachers, using the global, partial and mixed methods and the mobile tool; as well as they make use of QR code markers. As described above, a pre-test and a post-test was also applied to this group.

The study was carried out during 5 days in May 2019. At the end of the study, 2 qualitative open questions were addressed in discussions with teachers and students after the activities. They were about the experience of using WQC_MOBILE; we also asked for suggestions for improvements. The quantitative and qualitative results are presented in the next subsection.

4.2   Preliminary Results

Table 1 presents the individual score and the average score of students of the three groups on post-test. The group 3 has the highest average, however, our pre-test also pointed out differences between the groups. The three groups got around 3 more points in their score after the lessons. These are inconclusive results (also due to the group size) in terms of score (quantitative).

Table 1. Groups final scores

Student #	Group 1	Group 2	Group 3
1	7	9	10
2	8	9	10
3	9	6	9
4	10	9	8
5	8	10	9
Average	**8.4**	**8.6**	**9.2**

The qualitative results show the viability of the proposal as well as difficulties in terms of infrastructure and technology. Teachers and students agreed about the positive effect of technology on student motivation, and reported positive results and situations. The teachers stated that the students evolved more quickly with the use of the mobile tool. However, they also reported difficulties involving the infrastructure needs, such as the velocity of the WiFi network at the sports court, restrictions of using mobile in certain parts of the school, and the size of the place dedicated to activities with QR code markers.

4.3   Discussion

Technology is increasingly present in the development of physical activities, such as those related to scholar physical education. In our study, WQ aligned with mobile technology and markers (QR code) on physical objects proved to be a valuable alternative for physical education lessons. Teachers reported the feasibility of the application in carrying out physical education practices.

Particularly, the WQC_MOBILLE contributed by giving the opportunity of presenting the theoretical content and other Web resources articulated with practical activities. This was enabled by the use of mobile devices, which can be used when the practical activity is performed, as well as markers (QR codes) enable to elaborate lessons including interaction with physical objects. Therefore, the theoretical content is related to physical artifacts, which might facilitate the assimilation of the content by the students. The groups' scores also show positive final results for Group 3 as compared with Group 1 and 2.

The practical study is limited in terms of size (only 5 students per group) and coverage (a small number of lessons were developed). These results were not conclusive in statistical terms, besides the Groups 1 and 2 were also slightly worse in the pre test results. New studies must be carried out in order to statically evaluate the proposal and to propose improvements in WQC_MOBILLE based on empirical results. However, we point out the preliminary study indicates the feasibility of our proposal. Complementary studies also include long term analysis of WQC_MOBILLE in use.

Other technologies can be integrated with WQC_MOBILLE to improve its functionalities, such as wearable artifacts [11,14], computer vision [9], and other mobile features (e.g., record videos and take photos). Despite technological difficulties involved in this extension, a key challenge is how to develop WQ models capable of taking advantage of these technologies in a way that it can integrate theoretical and practical content of scholar physical education.

5   Conclusion

The Web has extensive content on physical education, such as theoretical texts, animations and videos. WQ aims to explore Web content in inquiry-oriented lessons. New mobile and tangible technologies can be applied in practical scholar physical education activities. We presented a design solution and a platform, which integrate theoretical content on the Web with practical lessons. Preliminary results point out the feasibility of the proposal in practical activities with students of 7th grade (from 12 to 13 years old). The next steps of this research include integrate new technologies in WQC-MOBILLE platform, and conduct comprehensive and long-term studies.

References

1. Betti, M.: Educação física escolar: ensino e pesquisa-ação. Unijuí (2009)
2. Bottenttuit, J.B., Coutinho, C., Sternaldt, D.: M-learning and Webquests: the new technologies as pedagogical resource. In: Current Developments in Technology-Assisted Education, pp. 931–935 (2006)
3. Camargo, E.Z., Fernandes, C.T.: WQE: um editor de webquests versátil. In: Brazilian Symposium on Computers in Education (Simpósio Brasileiro de Informática na Educação-SBIE), vol. 1 (2010)
4. Chang, C.S., Chen, T.S., Hsu, W.H.: The study on integrating webquest with mobile learning for environmental education. Comput. Educ. **57**(1), 1228–1239 (2011). https://doi.org/10.1016/j.compedu.2010.12.005. https://www.sciencedirect.com/science/article/abs/pii/S0360131510003544
5. Coutinho, C.P., Junior, B., Batista, J.: Blog e wiki: os futuros professores e as ferramentas da web 2.0. In: SIIE 2007: actas do Simpósio Internacional de Informática Educativa, pp. 199–204 (2007)
6. Dodge, B.: Webquests: a technique for internet-based learning. Distance Educ. **1**(2), 10–13 (1995)
7. Ellis, T., Hafner, W.: Building a framework to support project-based collaborative learning experiences in an asynchronous learning network. Interdiscip. J. E-Learn. Learn. Objects **4**(1), 167–190 (2008)
8. Gohagan, D.: Computer-facilitated instructional strategies for education: designing webquests. J. Technol. Hum. Serv. **16**(2–3), 145–159 (2000)
9. Kim, S.J., Jang, M.S., Kuc, T.Y.: An interactive user interface for computer-based education: the laser shot system±. In: EdMedia+ Innovate Learning, pp. 4174–4178. Association for the Advancement of Computing in Education (AACE) (2004)
10. Koper, R., Tattersall, C.: Learning Design: A Handbook on Modelling and Delivering Networked Education and Training. Springer, Heidelberg (2005). https://doi.org/10.1007/b138966
11. Labus, A., Milutinovic, M., Stepanic, D., Stevanovic, M., Milinovic, S.: Wearable computing in e-education. RUO. Revija za Univerzalno Odličnost **4**(1), A39 (2015)
12. Leahy, M., Twomey, D.: Using web design with pre-service teachers as a means of creating a collaborative learning environment. Educ. Media Int. **42**(2), 143–151 (2005)
13. Libâneo, J.C.: Reflexividade e formação de professores: outra oscilação do pensamento pedagógico brasileiro. Professor reflexivo no Brasil: gênese e crítica de um conceito. Cortez, São Paulo, pp. 53–79 (2002)
14. Lindberg, R., Seo, J., Laine, T.H.: Enhancing physical education with exergames and wearable technology. IEEE Trans. Learn. Technol. **9**(4), 328–341 (2016)
15. Marzano, R.J.: A different kind of classroom. Teaching with Dimension of Learning, Alexandria, Association for Supervision and Curriculum Development (1992)
16. Mostmans, L., Vleugels, C., Bannier, S.: Raise your hands or hands-on? The role of computer-supported collaborative learning in stimulating intercreativity in education. J. Educ. Technol. Soc. **15**(4), 104–113 (2012)

17. Nunes, E., Ramires, L.: WQC um editor de webquest colaborativo. In: Brazilian Symposium on Computers in Education (Simpósio Brasileiro de Informática na Educação-SBIE), vol. 27, p. 70 (2016)
18. Pereira, R.: Webquest: ferramenta pedagógica para o professor. Portal Dia-a-dia Educação, Paraná, Programa de desenvolvimento educacional (PDE), pp. 1–52 (2008)
19. Reis, F.d.C.S., dos Santos, F.E.P., Nascimento, V.A.: Pesquisa e escrita colaborativa no ensino fundamental: a webquest e o blog em atividades interdisciplinares. In: Brazilian Symposium on Computers in Education (Simpósio Brasileiro de Informática na Educação-SBIE), vol. 1 (2010)
20. Rose, D.H., Gravel, J.W.: Universal design for learning (2010)
21. Yang, C.H., Tzuo, P.W., Komara, C.: Using webquest as a universal design for learning tool to enhance teaching and learning in teacher preparation programs. J. Coll. Teach. Learn. (TLC) 8(3), 21–30 (2011)

Supporting Online Video e-Learning with Semi-automatic Concept-Map Generation

Tessai Hayama[✉] and Shuma Sato

Nagaoka University of Technology,
1603-1, Kamitomioka, Nagaoka, Niigata, Japan
t-hayama@kjs.nagaokaut.ac.jp, s151047@stn.nagaokaut.ac.jp
https://kmlab.nagaokaut.ac.jp/

Abstract. E-learning, which can be used anywhere and at any time, is very convenient and has been introduced to improve learning efficiency. However, securing a completion rate has been a major problem. Recently, the learning forms of e-learning require learners to be introspective, deliberate, and logical and have proven to be incompatible with many learners of low completion rates. In this paper, we propose an e-learning system that allows learners to deepen their understanding by creating a concept-map while watching a video. This system supports the presentation of candidate components such as concept-labels and related words from lecture speech texts when creating a concept map, which is difficult to create from scratch within a short time the learner is playing a video. Then, by interactively creating the proper concept-map of learning content aids the learner to learn the learning content in reflective and active thinking ways. Further, we conducted an experiment to compare a simple concept-map creation interface and a non-concept-map interface to confirm the effectiveness of our proposed system.

Keywords: e-Learning support · Visual thinking tool · Concept-map mining

1 Introduction

Generally, providing learners with a step-by-step understanding of learning content in online video courses prevents a lot of the learners from dropping out. Specifically, this paper proposes an e-learning system that provides video-based learning content with a visual thinking tool for promoting learners f understanding of content in real-time.

In online video-based learning, a learner usually does not have to be in direct contact with the class at the same time, which has significant advantages. It supports learning anywhere and anytime via a mobile phone or a computer and enables learning access that has never been available before. Recently, although online learning courses are increasingly marketed to adults as well as students, the high dropout rate from the courses remain a concern to educational institutions and organizations. Much research has shown a high dropout percentage rate

© Springer Nature Switzerland AG 2020
P. Zaphiris and A. Ioannou (Eds.): HCII 2020, LNCS 12205, pp. 64–76, 2020.
https://doi.org/10.1007/978-3-030-50513-4_5

of learners participating in online courses compared to learners in a face-to-face classroom. For example, it was recorded that more than 95% rate dropped out from MOOC [1,8] and approximately 78% dropped out from Open University [18,19].

According to a survey report [20], learners who dropped out of the online learning courses are classified into two major categories: learners' procrastination and incompatible learning style to e-learning. The problem with the first category is that some learners cannot well-manage the time and learning progress of e-learning by themselves, which makes it hard to complete the e-learning courses. To address the issue for the first category, some e-learning institutions introduced online tutoring and mentoring to provide individual support to such learners [7]. Others identified learners that are likely to drop out by analyzing their learning activities from the system logs [15]. These approaches are effective ways to keep the retention rate of e-learning courses [5]. On another note, the issue for the second category is that multimedia content that an e-learning system provides generates cognitive load effects for a learner compared to the face-to-face learning in the classroom [4]. The cognitive load effects in the e-learning reduce the learning performance of the learners, so learners tend to drop out. To address the issue for the second category, some researchers have designed e-learning systems with functions to match the learning style of the e-learning; e.g., designing a web-based course with consideration of content and learning style [2] and effective multimedia presentations [6,9,12]. Despite creating a better approach than normal e-learning style, many recent e-learning systems still adopt a simple form with a video in the center of the interface.

Moreover, some researchers investigated the learning style of the e-learning and demonstrated that both reflective and active learning styles were relevant to enhance the e-learning progress and sensory learner is likely to be adaptive to the learning style of e-learning [3,7,14]. Therefore, it is required for a learner to perform learning with metacognitive skills and the step-by-step thinking way during e-learning. However, it is difficult for many learners to fulfill their meta-cognitive skills because the current video-based learning affords passive learning, and it is challenging for the learners to leave the concepts of learning content while watching the video. Furthermore, learners who have drop-out tendencies cannot effectively understand the learning content from the beginning of the e-learning course [19]. If the e-learning system has supports to match learner's thinking way in e-learning and the learning style, which the e-learning requires, the dropout rates in each e-learning course will reduce.

Therefore, in this paper, we propose an online video learning interface that provides a concept-map creation support tool. A Concept-map is an effective way to provide complex concepts with graph representation; hence, it is often used in educational institutions to provide the learners with an enhanced understanding of the learning content [16]. The proposed system provides the components of a concept-map generated from the automated transcription of the lecture video while watching the video using speech recognition and our developed heuristic algorithm. By creating a concept-map, the user can interactively expand the current concept-map in the area of concept-map creation by selecting concepts and links with a mouse. Thus, such visualization and interaction aid the user to actively and reflectively understand the video lecture content. Also, we performed an experiment to compare a simple concept-map creation interface with a non-concept-map interface. The result demonstrated that the developed system supports learners in understanding lecture content in video-based learning.

2   Approach

In this section, first, we analyze some problems of scenarios where a learner tries to create a concept-map on learning content while watching a lecture video. Next, we present the system design policy for supporting the concept-map creation in the e-learning.

2.1   Problems in Case of Creating Concept-Map in E-Learning

Creating a concept-map for learning content is an effective way for a learner to understand the learning content [16]. However, creating the concept-map in the process of watching a lecture video would be difficult for a learner to effectively understand the learning content.

The conventional e-learning systems contain various types of multimedia data, such as text, image, movie, and voice, to teach learning content. So, the learners in e-learning have been given more cognitive load effects than face-to-face learning in the classroom [11]. Although learning styles of e-learning styles (i.e., reflective and active thinking ways) are required for learners to concentrate on the learning, it is difficult for a lot of learners that are not used to such ways of learning during a lecture. Almost all of the learners who dropped out of the e-learning course cannot effectively understand the learning content of the course from the beginning [19]. Therefore, it is one of the significant approaches for mitigating the drop-out rate of each e-learning course to make learners while having the e-learning keep in reflective and active thinking ways.

Then, to make a learner hold the appropriate learning style of e-learning, we try to introduce concept-map creation of learning content into video-based learning. Concept-map consists of some concept-labels and links showing relationships between the pairs of the concept-labels, as shown in Fig. 1. Interactively creating and overviewing the concept-map of learning content is useful for a learner to think of learning content in e-learning logically. However, creating the concept-map while watching a lecture video is likely to interrupt the understanding of the learning content. In concept-map creation process for learning [17], the first step is extracting topic terms from learning content to make concept-labels, and next is assigning terms meaning the relationship between pairs of the concept-labels into between the pairs of the concept-labels. In the case of e-learning, it is more difficult to achieve the concept-map creation process since the learning content consists of multimedia information, including unfamiliar technical terms. Further, it is difficult for a learner who doesn't get used to concept-map to create a suitable concept-map of learning content without delay of understanding the lecture video.

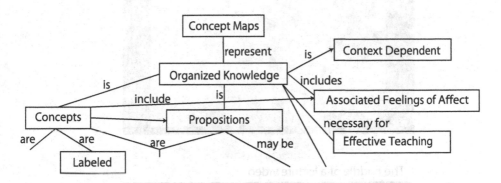

Fig. 1. Concept-map explaining concept-map [17].

As mentioned earlier, the problems of creating the concept-map of learning content in e-learning are as follows: 1) creating concept-map of learning content in real-time and 2) creating a suitable concept-map from the learning content which includes multimedia information.

2.2   System Design Policy

To provide solutions to the problems as stated in the previous section, a design policy of implementing the e-learning system is as follows:

- Supporting the process of creating an appropriate concept-map of the learning content,
- Supporting system operation to create an interactive and real-time based concept-map.

3   Implementation

3.1   Overview

We proposed an online video-based e-learning support system that provides a concept-map support tool, which is based on the design policy (see Sect. 2.2). The proposed system comprised of three kinds of display areas: lecture video area, concept-map-component provision area, and concept-map creation area, as shown in Fig. 2.

A user of the proposed system learns the learning content while watching a lecture video and creates a concept-map of the learning content by selecting components from the concept-map-component provision area using mouse

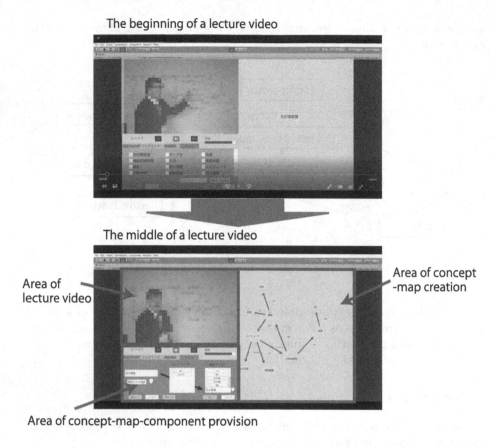

Fig. 2. The interface of the proposed system.

operation. In the concept-map-component area, some of the candidate components of the concept-label and link-label are provided based on the concept-label being clicked in the concept-map creation area. Further, the user selects a pair of concept-label and link-label among the displayed candidate components, and the selected pair is added into the concept-map being created in the concept-map creation area. The user completes the concept-map of the learning content by repeatedly selecting pairs of the concept-label and link-label in the concept-map-component provision area. The candidate components in the concept-map-component provision area are automatically generated in the preprocessing, as described in Sect. 3.2.

Moreover, in the other functions being implemented on the currently proposed system, the user directly makes the concept-label and link-label with the keyboard and then add them to the concept-map. The system stores logs of the user's operations in the concept-map creation process and displays the process of the user's operations from the logs. Then, the user replays the lecture video to check the learning content at a time when each of the concept-label and link-label was created. These functions help the user to reflectively think and understand the learning content and context in which the concept-map was created.

3.2   Concept-Map Component Generation

The candidates of the concept-label pairs and their link-labels are provided as a concept-map component in the concept-map-component provision area of the proposed system. To obtain the candidates of each of them, they are extracted from each learning video. In this section, the candidate extraction of the concept-label pair and link-label are, respectively, described below.

Concept-Label-Pair Candidate Extraction. Some candidates of the concept-label-pairs with high potential are extracted through the following steps:

1) transcribing from speech within lecture video via speech recognition technique,
2) decomposing the speech text into morphemes via morphological analyzer,
3) extracting noun terms from the morphemes and removing general terms by using the stop-word list,
4) setting a tf-idf weight into each of the extracted terms,
5) adding more weight into the technical terms by using the technical term dictionary of the learning content, and
6) judging pairs of the terms within one sentence in the speech recognition result as concept-label-pair candidates if the pairs of the terms are assigned with higher weight than the threshold.

Here, each sentence included in the speech recognition result indicates a unit divided by filler and pause in the process of the speech recognition.

According to the study [21], more than 80% of the concept-labels being included in the human-made concept-maps are nouns, and more than 92.1% pairs of all the concept-labels are within the same sentence. So, the concept-label-pair candidate extraction outputs the pairs of noun words/phrases within the same sentence.

Link-Label Candidate Extraction. The candidates of the link-labels with high potential are extracted from the speech text of lecture video.

In [21], more than 80% of the link-labels being included in the human-made concept-maps are one of the following parts of speech: verb, noun, sentence question, adverb, and adjective. Also, 92.1% of the human-made link-labels are included within the same sentence, as the concept-label pairs. So, the link-label candidate extraction outputs the word/phrase of verb, noun, sentence question, adverb, or adjective being included in the same sentence as the related concept-label pair.

Examples of the Generated Concept-Map Components. The examples of the concept-map components generated from a lecture video about "bookkeeping and accounting" by the above extraction procedures, and each of the items represents an after-arrow concept-label, a link label, and a before-arrow concept-label, respectively, as shown below.

– [finantial condition] - [summary] → [loan balance sheet]
– [business performance] - [summary] → [profit/loss statement]
– [loan] - [good] → [assets]
– [loan] - [postpay] → [debt]
– [net assets] - [-] → [capital]
– [profit] - [increase] → [extraneous income]
– [cost] - [decrease] → [advertisement]
– [debt] - [-] → [loan balance sheet]

3.3 Expected Effects

Using the proposed system enables a learner to easily create the concept-map of the learning content by utilizing the concept-map components, which are given on the interface of the system. Thus, the learner can create a similar concept-map to a human-made concept-map; however, it may not be perfect concept-map since the concept-map components are given based on the limited parts of speech and the partial misrecognized speech. The expected effects of using the proposed system are as follows:

– Enabling a learner to interactively create a concept-map of the learning content while watching a lecture video by providing the concept-map creation with simple mouse operation.
– Enabling a learner to easily create a suitable concept-map of the learning content by providing the concept-labels and link-labels similar to the human-made concept-map.

Creating the concept-map of the learning content in e-learning supports the learner to perform the e-learning with reflective and logical thinking ways. Therefore, the environment of using the proposed e-learning system is well-adapted to the learning style of e-learning.

4 Experiment

4.1 Overview

In this section, we experimented to confirm the effectiveness of our proposed e-learning support system. During the experiment, the proposed system was compared with the understanding and satisfaction of learners to two learning methods: a video-based learning interface with concept-map creation and a simple video-based e-learning interface. Further, we recruited nine college students who have studied in the department of engineering for the experiment.

The e-learning contents were chosen with three lecture videos about "book-keeping and accounting" since none of the subjects knows about it. In each of the lecture videos, a lecturer explained the learning content with a whiteboard lecture-style within an hour. For each of the participants, each of the lecture contents was assigned with one of the learning methods for order effects of the methods with counter balance of them. We adopted 15 questions from each learning content to check the understanding of the lecture content. Also, we adopted five Likert-scale questionnaires to measure the satisfaction and cognitive load effect in each of the learning method.

In the procedure of the experiment, the subjects firstly were given the pre-questionnaire about e-learning experiments and knowledge about the learning contents. Also, they were given instructions about how to use the e-learning system and how to make concept-map. Then, they had three lectures with the different methods and the examination and questionnaire after each of the lectures; The time given between the lectures interval is 10 min.

4.2   Results

Tables 1 and 2 show the results of the comprehension test and post-questionnaire for each of the learning methods, respectively. The result of the test includes the comprehension scores for each of the subjects and their deviation values for each of the learning contents. The deviation values were used for comparing the comprehension degrees of the subjects among the learning methods to make different difficulties between the learning contents insignificant.

Table 1. Result of the comprehension test for three kinds of learning methods: the comprehension scores and their deviation values.

Subject	VBL+CMAP+CPF	VBL+CMAP	VBL
A	76(58.29)	72(52.25)	80(57.21)
B	48(41.45)	84(59.84)	68(45.76)
C	48(41.45)	72(52.25)	88(64.85)
D	52(39.60)	76(53.39)	76(55.88)
E	72(52.25)	64(41.94)	64(46.26)
F	92(64.90)	84(61.03)	84(63.10)
G	72(49.58)	84(63.10)	72(52.25)
E	56(34.31)	48(41.45)	56(44.66)
F	64(41.94)	44(39.04)	64(32.00)
Average	62(47.08)	68(51.59)	72(51.33)

The VBL+CMAP+CPF, VBL+CMAP, and VBL represent video-based learning with concept-map creation of using the component provision function, video-based learning with concept-map creation, and video-based learning, respectively. The numbers in parentheses represent the comprehension score variation values.

Table 2. Result of questionnaires with 5 Likert scale (with '5' indicating strongly agree, with '1' indicating strongly disagree).

Questionnaire item	VBL+CMAP+CPF	VBL+CMAP	VBL
Satisfaction score to his/her own learning	3.67(1.12)	3.33(0.71)	2.44(0.88)
Concentration score to his/her own learning	3.89(0.93)	3.44(0.88)	2.33(1.22)
Satisfaction score to his/her created concept-map	2.67(1.00)	2.78(0.97)	–
Appropriateness of the system-provided components	3.33(0.87)	–	–

The VBL+CMAP+CPF, VBL+CMAP, and VBL represent video-based learning with concept-map creation of using the component provision function, video-based learning with concept-map creation, and video-based learning, respectively. The numbers in parentheses represent the comprehension score variation values.

In the result of the comprehension test, although there are the largest numbers of the subjects who obtained the best score by using the proposed system among using the three learning methods, there is no statistically significant difference between them, $F(2,8)$, $p > 0.05$. However, there is a statistically significant difference between comprehension degree in cases of using better video-based learning with concept-map creation and using video-based learning, $F(1,8)$, $p < 0.05$. This suggests that creating concept-map of learning content while watching a lecture video is useful to improve the understanding of the learning content. However, the concept-map component provision of the proposed system did not perform well in creating the concept-map.

In the result of the post-questionnaire, using the proposed system outperformed the other two to achieve the most satisfaction and concentration on the learner's learning. There is a statistically significant difference between them, $F(2,8)$, $p < 0.05$. However, there is no statistically significant difference in (satisfaction score to his/her own created concept-map) between VBL+CMAP+CPF and VBL+CMAP. The appropriateness of the proposed-system-provided components is 3.00 on average. Thus, the concept-map-component provision function of the proposed system has no advantage in creating a concept-map of learning content while watching a lecture video.

4.3 Discussions

From the experimental results, adapting concept-map creation to video-based learning is useful for the understanding of the learning content and the satisfaction to the learner's learning, compared with traditional video-based learning. However, the concept-map component provision of the proposed system did not affect their usefulness much. Therefore, we analyzed the concept-maps created by the subjects (A-E, G, and E in Table 1) who got more than 5 points difference between the deviation values of comprehension scores in using the two kinds of the learning methods with concept-map creation. Then, we checked the differences of the created concept-maps between in the cases of better and worse comprehension of the learning content. Table 3 shows the concept-map properties.

Table 3. Concept-map properties created by the subjects who got more than 5 point differences between in cases of better and worse comprehension to learning content in the experiment.

Subject	Better comprehension to learning content				Worse comprehension to learning content			
	Link-label	Concept-label	Cluster	Crossing of links	Link-label	Concept-label label	Cluster	Crossing links
A	6	29	23	0	8	25	17	2
B	23	24	3	0	19	13	2	4
C	26	23	1	4	39	32	2	13
D	12	12	1	0	19	16	1	2
E	16	19	4	0	11	14	4	0
G	9	11	3	0	1	8	7	0
E	16	16	1	0	20	22	1	2

There are no statistically significant differences in the numbers of nodes, links, and clusters between the concept-maps in the cases of better and worse comprehension of the learning contents. However, there is a statistically significant difference in the numbers of link-crossings between the concept-maps. Five out of the seven subjects created the concept-maps with fewer link-crossings in the case of better comprehension to the learning content than in the case of worse comprehension to the learning content, and the rest of the subjects created the concept-maps with no link-crossing in both cases. Figure 3 shows an example of the concept-maps created by the subject 'B' in the experience. This suggests that a concept-map created with a good comprehension of the learning content while watching a lecture video may have good visibility.

5   Related Studies

In the human-computer interaction domain, there exists a few numbers research on the concept-map interface for e-learning. Meng et al. [13] proposed a note-taking system that supports to create concept-map by turning the user's key-inputted sentences into a concept-map. They showed that the use of their system led to a superior understanding of video-based lectures compared with the use of text-editor applications. Moreover, Liu et al. [10] proposed a collaborative concept-map creation method to provide a concept-map of the lecture content in video-based learning. The system engages crowd workers to collectively generate a concept-map by prompting them to externalized reflections on the video. They

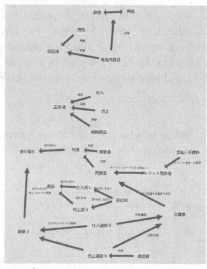 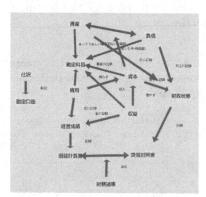

In case of better comprehension to learnig content   In case of worse comprehension to learning content

Fig. 3. Example of the concept-maps which the subject 'B' created in the experience.

showed that concept-maps generated by their system match the quality of those generated by experts. However, our approach is different from these two because our method aids a single user to quickly build their concept-map with good quality suitable for video-based learning.

6   Conclusion

Although e-learning is very convenient and has been introduced to improve learning efficiency, securing the completion rate has been a major problem. Recently, learning forms of e-learning require learners to be introspective, deliberate, and logical and have proven to be incompatible with many learners with low completion rates. In this paper, we proposed an e-learning system that allows learners to deepen their understanding of creating a concept-map while watching a video. This system supports the presentation of candidate components such as concept labels and related words from lecture speech texts when creating a concept map. Further, we experimented and confirmed that video-based e-learning with concept-map creation is useful for the understanding of the learning content and the satisfaction of the learner's learning. However, the evaluation results also showed that concept-maps that were created with a better understanding of learning content included fewer link-crossings.

In the future, we hope to improve the support function of creating the concept-map since the component provision function of our proposed system failed to provide the usefulness for creating the concept-map of learning content in the experiment. Also, we will conduct more experiments and analyze the relationships between the learning performance and concept-map of learning content in detail.

Acknowledgement. This work was supported by JSPS KAKENHI Grant Number 19K12264.

References

1. Alraimi, K.M., Zo, H., Ciganek, A.P.: Understanding the MOOCs continuance: the role of openness and reputation. Comput. Educ. **80**, 28–38 (2015)
2. Combs, L.: The design, assessment, and implementation of a web-based course. Assoc. Adv. Comput. Educ. **12**(1), 27–37 (2004)
3. Dalmolin, A.C., Mackeivicz, G.A.O., Pochapski, M.T., Pilatti, G.L., Santos, F.A.: Learning styles preferences and e-learning experience of undergraduate dental students. Revista de Odontologia da UNESP **47**(3), 175–182 (2018)
4. DeLeeuw, K., Mayer, R.E.: A comparison of these measures of cognitive load: evidence for separable measures of intrinsic, extraneous, and germane load. J. Educ. Psychol. **100**, 223–234 (2008)
5. Grau, J., Minguillon, J.: When procrastination leads to dropping out: analysing students at risk. eLC Res. Paper Ser. **6**, 63–74 (2013)
6. Guo, P.J., Kim, J., Rubin, R.: How video production affects student engagement: an empirical study of MOOC videos. In: Proceedings of the first ACM Learning@ Scale Conference, pp. 41–50 (2014)
7. Huang, E., Lin, S., Huang, T.: What type of learning style leads to online participation in the mixed mode e-learning environment? A study of software usage instruction. Comput. Educ. **58**(1), 338–349 (2012)
8. Khalil, H., Ebner, M.: MOOCs completion rates and possible methods to improve retention - a literature review. In: 2014 Proceedings of World Conference on Educational Multimedia, Hypermedia and Telecommunications, pp. 1236–1244 (2014)
9. Kizilcec, R.F., Papadopulolos, K., Sritanyaratana, L.: Showing face in video instruction: effects on information retention, visual attention, and affect. In: Proceedings of the Annual SIGCHI Conference on Human Factors in Computing Systems, pp. 2095–2102 (2014)
10. Liu, C., Kim, J., Wang, H.: ConceptScape: collaborative concept mapping for video learning. In: Proceedings of the 2018 CHI Conference on Human Factors in Computing Systems. Paper no. 387, pp. 1–12 (2018)
11. Mayer, R.: Learning environments: the case for evidence-based practice and issue-driven research. Educ. Psychol. Rev. **15**, 359–373 (2003)
12. Mayer, R.E.: Principles of multimedia learning based on social cues: personalization, voice, and image principles. In: Mayer, R.E. (ed.) The Cambridge Handbook of Multimedia Learning, pp. 201–212. Cambridge University Press (2005)
13. Meng, X., Zhao, S., Edge, D., HyNote: integrated concept mapping and notetaking. In: Proceedings of the International Working Conference on Advanced Visual Interfaces, pp. 236–239 (2016)
14. Morita, Y., Koen, B., Ma, G., Wu, Z., Johendran, A.: Pilot study of the relationships between learning progress and learning style in a web-based PSI course. Proc. E-Learn **2005**, 2243–2248 (2005)

15. Mduma, N., Kalegele, K., Machuve, D.: A survey of machine learning approaches and techniques for student dropout prediction. Data Sci. J. **8**(14), 1–10 (2019)
16. Novak, J.D.: Concept mapping: a useful tool for science education. J. Res. Sci. Teach. **27**(10), 937–949 (1990)
17. Novak, J.D., Canas, A.J.: The theory underlying concept maps and how to construct and use them. Technical Report IHMC CmapTools, Florida Institute for Human and Machine Cognition (2008)
18. Simpson, O.: 22% - can we do better? CWP Retention Liter. Rev. **47** (2010)
19. Simpson, O.: Student retention in distance education: are we failing our students. Open Learn.: J. Open Distance e-Learn. **28**(2), 105–119 (2013)
20. Tominaga, A., Kogo, C.: Developments and issues in practical studies of e-learning. Annu. Rep. Educ. Psychol. Jpn. **53**, 156–165 (2014). (in Japanese)
21. Villalon. J., Calvo. R.A., Montenegro. R.: Analysis of a gold standard for concept map mining? How humans summarize text using concept maps. In: Proceedings of the 4th International Conference on Concept Mapping, pp. 14–22 (2010)

User Experience Evaluation of an e-Assessment System

Sidra Iftikhar[1(✉)], Ana-Elena Guerrero-Roldán[1,2(✉)], Enric Mor[1(✉)], and David Bañeres[1,2(✉)]

[1] Computer Science, Multimedia and Telecommunication Studies,
Universitat Oberta de Catalunya, Barcelona, Spain
{siftikhari, aguerreror, emor, dbaneres}@uoc.edu
[2] eLearn Center, Universitat Oberta de Catalunya, Barcelona, Spain

Abstract. In order to attain a good user experience in e-assessment systems, learners should be aware of how they are progressing in the courses and they should feel motivated and engaged. The goal of this paper is to propose an e-assessment system, that aims to increase the self-awareness of learners about the courses' progress that they are taking, and also to improve the learner's motivation and engagement. While designing the system, two major design challenges have been identified and addressed. The design challenges include, informing the learners about their progress and making the learners feel motivated to work harder and enhance their learning of the course contents and learning activities. The proposed system informs the learners about their progress and aims to keep them motivated by providing them with minimum grade predictions for the next learning activity they would perform, during the semester of an online course. The learners are also informed of their risk of failing the course throughout the semester. Also, to keep the learners motivated and engaged personalized suggestions are provided by the teachers to enhance the learning of the course. The user experience evaluation of LIS highlights that it has helped the learners to enhance their learning experiences.

Keywords: E-assessment system · User experience design · User experience evaluation

1 Introduction

Technology Enhanced Learning (TEL), when applied to higher education has provided the opportunity to attain higher education to many students who couldn't attend the university physically. E-learning, learning through electronic means, in online higher education has been made possible through e-learning systems that deliver courses online. In addition to providing the opportunity to learn, there are specific e-learning systems, known as the e-assessment systems that assess learners electronically and provide them with feedback. Over the period of time the e-learning and e-assessment systems have evolved drastically from being able to evaluate the learned content, students have been facilitated in many ways. One such important contribution of

© Springer Nature Switzerland AG 2020
P. Zaphiris and A. Ioannou (Eds.): HCII 2020, LNCS 12205, pp. 77–91, 2020.
https://doi.org/10.1007/978-3-030-50513-4_6

e-learning and e-assessment systems have been providing the students with feedback and informing them about the way they are progressing while learning.

However, apart from the fact that there are numerous advantages of e-learning and e-assessment, there is a significant dropout rate from online higher education. The possible reasons for dropouts are, poor learner satisfaction, low motivation levels of the learners, little learner-teacher interaction, timing constraints and also the e-learning and e-assessment systems not meeting the student's expectations. Due to these reasons the learners usually encounter an unfavorable user experience. As for any other system, to ensure continued usage and to reduce the dropout rate in online higher education, e-learning and e-assessment systems should be designed to provide a good user experience [1].

User experience (UX), the way users feel when interacting with a system, product or service is extremely important as it helps to determine the continued usage of the systems [2]. User experience evaluation typically considers the pragmatic and hedonic qualities of the system [3]. The pragmatic qualities deal with the usability aspects that are the "do goals" of the system. In addition to the hedonic aspects deal with what the system should "be like" e.g. the system should be unique in its nature. In addition to the pragmatic and hedonic aspects, it is also essential to evaluate what the users feel when using the system [4]. Along with considering the user feelings and the pragmatic and hedonic characteristics of the system it is essential to consider the domain specific characteristics for which the user experience is evaluated [5]. For example, in case of an online shopping system, the goal is to provide a great shopping experience to the customer. Thus, it is necessary to evaluate the shopping experience along with the evaluation of pragmatic and hedonic characteristics. Similarly, in the domain of e-learning and e-assessment an important characteristic is the learning experience of the systems, because they are set in an educational context and the goal is to enhance student learning by making them feel motivated and engaged. A worthwhile user and learner experience in e-learning and e-assessment systems should fulfil the learner goals by keeping them motivated and engaged in the courses they are learning. As evident, taking into account the parameters of user experience in e-assessment systems is essential for a good user experience. When considering the user experience the way the systems are designed cannot be neglected [6]. It is essential to design the systems keeping in view the experience that the system would deliver to the users of the system. A system designed for experience would be closer to the users' expectation and would lead to a good experience [7].

Keeping in consideration the significance of a good user experience in e-assessment, that would help students learn better, this paper presents an e-assessment system. The goal of this e-assessment system is to enhance the learning and user experience of learners, by making them self-aware of the way they are progressing in the courses. Furthermore, the proposed e-assessment system has also been evaluated for user experiences.

The rest of the paper is divided into the following sections: Sect. 2 discusses the related work for this study, Sect. 3 discusses the design of the proposed system, Sect. 4 describes the pilot study design and data collection, Sect. 5 presents the evaluation results for the pilot study and the last section presents the conclusion and future work.

2 Related Work

Numerous studies have been proposed to evaluate the user experience in the context of e-learning and e-assessment systems. Walker et al. [8] evaluate the staff and student experience that use the Moodle system. The results highlight that the learners are satisfied but the instructors are not satisfied with the Moodle learning management system (LMS). In another study, Majors et al. [9] present user experience evaluation that uses mixed methods for a blended learning environment. A questionnaire is used to identify the usability problems that the students face. The results of the study highlight that for e-learning systems to be effective, it is essential to ask the users about their point of view before designing a system. Similarly, for another e-learning system, Blackboard, Alturki et al. [10] evaluate the accessibility and usability of the system. Zaitseva [11] performs an evaluation of usability and user friendliness of a German online course delivered through a LMS. The instructors of the course conclude that learners did not find the course motivating. In another study for the evaluation of user experience, Scholl [12] proposes a technique that implements the Taylors value added (TEDs) model to Moodle. The results highlight that the system artefacts should be made simpler and easy to use and the system should be designed to provide feedback to the users. One of the studies conducted by Ternauciuc and Vasiu [3] suggests the importance of usability testing for e-learning systems and proposes a technique that is used to test the e-learning platforms. Apart from evaluating the usability and user experiences for e-learning systems, few of the studies also perform comparison of the user experiences for different e-learning systems, but the systems have not been compared for assessment features. One such study conducted by Machado and Tao [13] compares the user experience and usability of Moodle and Blackboard. The results of the study highlight that the functionality of both systems is similar, and users are satisfied with both systems when it comes to functionality. However, 75% of the students concluded that Moodle is easy to use. Few studies also evaluate the user experiences for mobile versions of the e-learning systems, but the assessment process has not been considered. Beltran et al. [14] evaluate the usability for e-learning mobile application. The results of the evaluation highlight some issues with the user interface. Similarly, Hasan [15] conducts a study to identify usability problems in desktop and mobile platforms of the LMS. Several usability problems were highlighted as a part of this study for e-learning systems.

Apart from the questionnaire-based approaches, some studies use other techniques to evaluate user experiences and usability of e-learning systems, but without considering the assessment aspects. One such study, conducted by Bee [16] claims to use a data mining technique, to evaluate the user experience of a LMS. Similarly, Fenu et al. [17] use learning analytics to automatically evaluate the usability and user experience of an online learning tool.

User interface for e-learning systems is also evaluated, as part of user experience in a few studies. Arshad et al. [18] present a study for evaluating the navigational aspects of an LMS and proposes a framework for navigation of LMS. The results of the study highlight that some navigational features are not present in the system. Similarly, Luo et al. [19] propose a framework for design and evaluation of user interface of synchronous e-learning systems. However, Arshad et al. and Luo et al. have focused on the navigational features for e-learning systems but the assessment part of the mobile e-learning systems has not been considered.

Few studies also evaluate the user experience for e-learning systems that have been custom designed. Santoso [20] performs a study that helps to evaluate the user experience and usability of a Student-Centred e-Learning Environment (SCELE). Similarly, Green et al. [21] discuss the need for personalization in virtual learning environments. In another study, Sahid et al. [22] evaluate the user experience of a LMS. The users of the system have been asked various questions concerning the user experience. The metrics used for evaluation are, likeness, ease of learning, fast, pleasant, clear and user friendliness of the system. Similarly, Wang and Wang [23] conduct a study to evaluate the usability and user experience of an e-learning system. The study uses usability scale and user experience questionnaire for evaluation. The results of the study highlight that the system has good usability. Ardito et al. [24] conduct a study to evaluate the usability of an e-learning system. The results of the study highlight that it is important to consider the educational experiences of the students when evaluating usability for e-learning systems. Similarly, a study conducted by Zaharias [25] proposes a framework for the usability evaluation of e-learning systems that emphasizes the need to consider the educational usability and learner's perspective when designing e-learning systems. In another study for usability evaluation, Zaharias and Poylymenakou [26] propose a questionnaire-based approach to evaluate usability of e-learning systems. The need for special usability metrics for e-learning systems is discussed in the study, these metrics include motivation and learning experience. Later Zaharias [27] also proposes a framework for quality in e-learning that emphasizes on motivation of the learners.

In the literature, usability evaluation criteria for e-learning systems is provided. These criteria are related to general usability of e-learning systems, but the design of the system has not been considered by these studies. A study conducted by Costabile et al. [28] propose a usability evaluation criterion for e-learning systems. The various dimensions for the system include presentation, hypermediality (excess use of hyperlinks), application proactivity and user activity. Similarly, Davids et al. [29] perform a study to evaluate the usability of a multimedia e-learning system that is specific for clinics. The heuristics from Nielsen are used to evaluate the system. The results of the study highlight some problems with the usability of the system. Sim and Read [30] propose usability heuristics that are specific for computer assisted assessments. An example of the proposed heuristics is that the user should be allowed to navigate and terminate the exams when it is required. In general, the usability criteria specific for assessment features of the system have not been defined. However, Luca and McLoughlin [31] discuss the learner centered features for e-assessment systems and highlight how learners can be in control of these features. An example for these features is online discussion of learners.

The literature comprises of the studies that evaluate user experience of e-learning systems, however, fewer studies focus on the evaluation of the user experience of the assessment aspects of the systems. The assessment aspects include, learning activities, informing learners about progress, feedback and evaluation features of the systems. However, several studies emphasize on evaluating e-learning systems for motivation and engagement [25–27] but these studies have not evaluated the assessment features of the systems, for motivating and engaging user and learning experiences. This paper focuses on the design and evaluation of an e-assessment system that aims to enhance the user and learning experience of the online courses the learners are taking. A good user and learning experience would facilitate the learners to learn and perform better in the online courses.

3 Design of the Learning Intelligent System (LIS)

To achieve their learning goals, the learners who are enrolled in the online courses expect to have good learning experiences of the courses. To provide a good learning experience to the learners, it is essential that the systems delivering these courses are designed and developed with the perspective to enhance learning. This paper proposes an e-assessment system that aims to enhance the user and learning experience of the online courses. Learning Intelligent System (LIS), the proposed system is being developed at the Universitat Oberta de Catalunya (UOC). UOC, established in 1994, is a fully online university based in Barcelona (Spain) with over 70,000 students and with more than 4,500 teaching and research staff. The university aims to provide the learners with quality personalized learning in online higher education. UOC educational model is based on breaking space and time barriers through asynchronous distance education based on TEL.

For an online educational institution like UOC, that has a large number of online learners, discovering ways to enhance their learning experiences is essential. A significant way to enhance learning is by keeping the learners informed of their progress in online courses. Informing learners about their progress can facilitate the learners to be self-aware and self-regulate, who can take measures to perform better. Also, a way of improving the learning experience is to identify early during the course learners who are at-risk of failure or dropping out. The at-risk learners can take advantage of early detection and work harder and pass the course. Self-aware learners, who know how they are progressing would feel empowered, as they can take control of their learning. This empowerment of the learners can help them to achieve their learning goals better and attain better grades by working towards enhanced progress [32] With a satisfactory learning experience, learners would prefer to continue their education, which would consequently reduce the dropout rate.

LIS as an e-assessment system, enlightens the learners with their risk of failing the course and also provides the learners with personalized feedback to attain better marks in the learning activities. When designing LIS, among the solutions and functionalities it should provide, two major design challenges were identified and addressed. These challenges are: 1) learners should be informed about their progress to facilitate the learning process, and 2) the design of the system should motivate the learners to work harder, learn better and improve their user experience and engagement.

3.1 Learners Being Informed About Their Progress

Learners should be aware of how they are progressing in the courses. Having information about the progress helps the learners to identify how much more effort they need put in order to receive good grades and achieve their learning goals. Also, the information about learner progress and feedback, should be provided in a continuous manner [33]. This can be achieved by making sure that the learners first, receive the evaluations and feedback for a learning activity before they receive the next activity to be performed. It is important that the learners are made aware of their progress because otherwise it leads to frustration and results in a bad user experience [34]. When designing the system, keeping the learners informed about their progress was especially considered as a main goal is to enhance the learner and user experience.

In the first design challenge, learners being informed about their progress, was addressed by providing grade predictions during a semester of an online course. As a result of the grade predictions, early detection of learners who might be "at-risk" of failing the course is also made possible. Not only the predicted grades are provided to the learners but the suggestions in the form of personalized feedback are also provided to each learner, so that they can take measures to avoid failure and enhance their grades. The grade predictions are made by building prediction models that are based on data mining techniques [35]. The learner data is obtained automatically from the UOC data mart [36]. The UOC data mart collects and aggregates data that are transferred from the different operational data sources from the custom UOC LMS using ETL (extract-transform-load) processes. During the ETL processes, sensitive data are anonymized. This process of anonymity consists of obfuscating all the personal data and changing all the internal identifiers to a new one. The UOC data mart includes data from two main types of data sources: 1) those related to the LMS and other learning spaces (e.g., data about navigation, interaction, communication, etc.); and 2) data from institutional warehouse systems (CRM, ERP, etc.), which includes data about enrolment, accreditation, assessment, student curriculum, among others. The prediction models are trained for each course with the help of the historical data and predictions are made by using the daily data produced daily by the learners enrolled in the courses. This makes the predictions independent of the nature of course and the types of learning activities used in the courses.

As for the representation of the predicted grades the system has the learners' dashboard that provides information about the chances to pass one specific course based on his or her graded assessment activities. The information on the dashboard is presented in two ways. Firstly, a prediction is given for each graded assessment activity by giving the minimum grade that the learner should get in the next assessment activity to pass the course (see Fig. 1). This is done before the submission of the activity takes place to inform the learner about the likelihood to pass the course. The second one is a general warning level for the course that also helps to determine the risk level of the learner (see Fig. 2). This warning level is computed after the activity is graded and based on the new information about the grade a new prediction is performed for the next activity.

As we can observe, for the first part of information on the dashboard, there are progress bars for each activity. Each progress bar has two options, pass and fail, depending on the grades obtained (N, D, C−, C+, B or A) by the learner in an assessment activity and the grade limit between both options is the minimum grade that a student should get to pass the course. Note that, the activities are graded in qualitative marks at UOC being D the lowest mark and A the higher one. The C+ grade is considered as the mark that specifies that the student has passed the activity and the N grade is reserved for non-submitted activities. For the second part, the progress bar for an activity that has been graded has triangles for representation of the grade that was attained and the general warning level on the dashboard is shown by a colored warning level indicator. The colors that are used for indication are green-amber-red. The green-amber-red colored indication has been adapted by the concept of traffic lights. Based on the grades attained for each activity during the semester, a warning level is indicated, green color representing the least risk and red representing the most. In addition to the information presented on the dashboard of each learner, personalized feedback addressing the learners, that includes measures to help them to mitigate low performance is also provided via email.

3.2   Learners Feeling Motivated

Motivation refers to the internal process that derives the user behavior and could be intrinsic or extrinsic [37]. This definition of motivation also applies to the context of learners and is an integral part of learning [27]. On the other hand, engagement is the desire and willingness to learn, and is dependent on motivation, learners need to be motivated in order to be engaged [38]. Motivation and engagement have been discussed since the early time periods of online learning and even now many studies are being conducted to evaluate the learner engagement [39]. Also, user engagement is an integral part of user experience, the more the user is engaged the better experience of the product they are likely to attain [40].

Learner motivation and engagement is one of the important factors that help to learn and ensure continued usage [41]. Thereby, for the design of an e-assessment system like LIS it is essential to design experiences that motivate the learners and keep them engaged. In terms of designing LIS, a major aim was to make the experiences motivating and engaging. Learner motivation and engagement was addressed by providing the learners with features that would keep them involved towards the courses. The minimum grade predictions that are provided for the next learning activity aims to enhance the learners' desire to increase the effort so that they can avoid failure or achieve a better grade.

Moreover, warning level indicator aims to help the learners to be engaged towards the course. The learners attaining the green color, through the warning level indicator, would be motivated to maintain that color and the low risk throughout the semester. Learners at low risk would be involved in the course and keep engaged. On the other hand, for the learners attaining the other two colors, i.e. amber and red, that depicts moderate to high risk of failing, would have the desire to work harder and consequently pass the course by increasing efforts for the next learning activities.

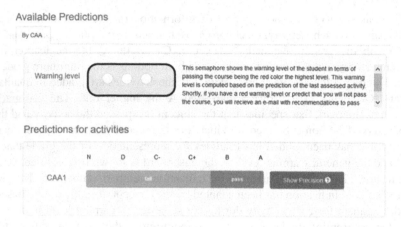

Fig. 1. Dashboard before submitting the activity (Color figure online)

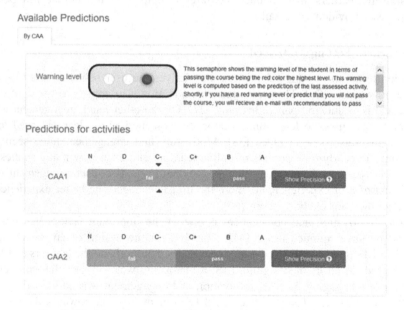

Fig. 2. Dashboard after submitting the activity (Color figure online)

The functionality of LIS providing the learners with personalized feedback, motivates the learners in two ways. Firstly, the messages provided to the learners are motivating in nature, i.e. they are addressed to the learners with motivating words. For example, learners are told that they did a good job and have the capability to perform even better. Motivating words are expected to have a strong impact on the motivation and engagement level of the learners. Secondly, without a doubt personalization enhances engagement of the learners [42]. When the learners would be addressed personally to deal with specific measures that are unique to their situations it is expected that they would be engaged in the course and motivated to learn.

After the design, the system was developed during a time span of 6 months. The main features and components were tested for functionality and usability. Apart from testing, the system was also evaluated in its real settings at UOC, during an academic semester. The evaluation took into account the functionalities and solutions the system should offer and also the learning experience that learners had from using the system.

4 Pilot Study Design and Data Collection

In this section, the study design for the evaluation of user experience in LIS is discussed. LIS has been tested in three different courses at UOC. These three courses are, Databases, Fundamentals of Computer Sciences and Human Computer Interaction and are a part of the Bachelor Computer Science degree program at UOC. The medium of instruction for these courses was Spanish and Catalan languages. The courses covered learners from different semesters of the degree program that helped to have a variety of users for the system, with a variable number of years of experience of taking online courses. The courses were carried fully online with a time span of around 14 weeks, one fall semester. The number of learners in these courses who signed the consent form to participate in the case study was 242. The courses, Databases and Human Computer Interaction used LIS on5 learning activities. Whereas, for Fundamentals of Computer Science course it was used for 3 learning activities. For each course, the learners were provided with the minimum predicted grade required to pass the course and also with the level of risk of failing the course throughout the semester.

The first pilot data capture included quantitative and qualitative approach. The system collected quantitative data in order to improve system interface, the accuracy of the prediction models, number of at-risk learners and potential dropout learners. However, the qualitative data was captured with a survey conducted in Spanish and Catalan language. The questionnaires for the survey consisted of 29 questions and took into account the parameters of the user experience, in e-assessment systems, that are discussed above, 1) pragmatic qualities of the system, 2) user feelings and 3) learning experiences. 138 learners choose to answer the questionnaire. Around 121 of the learners answered in Spanish language, whereas, 17 chose to answer in Catalan language. The survey took place almost at the end of the semester once the learners have received the minimum grade that was required to pass the last course activity. Conducting the survey at this point in the semester helped to capture the user and learning experience that learners had for all of the learning activities during the semester. Learners from the three courses who consented to participate were asked by email to answer the questionnaires, on a voluntary basis.

However, as per the scope of this paper, only the questions that are related closely to the design challenges that are described in Sect. 3, i.e. learners being informed about their progress and learners feeling motivated. That is a total of 12 questions were considered. A final question that directly inquired the learners about the overall user experience they had using the system was also considered.

For the first design challenge, informing learners about their progress, the evaluation has been divided into further two parts: Evaluation of the representation features of the progress and evaluation of feedback procedures. In the case of LIS, the learners' dashboard that contains the progress bars and colored warning level indicator are the representation features of progress. For the feedback procedures, in terms of LIS are the suggestions or measures provided as feedback by the teacher to enhance grades through a personalized email message. Progress bars on the dashboard represent all the learning activities that have been graded. However, the last progress bar on the dashboard represents the minimum grade for the next activity that is required to pass the course. Another representation feature on the learner's dashboard is the colored warning level indicator that indicates the risk level of the learner. Similarly, for the second design challenge, that is making the learners feel motivated, 6 questions were used from the questionnaire.

5 Case Study Evaluation Results

In this section, the evaluation results of the case study are presented. The overall user experience encountered by the learners is presented first and later results specific to the design challenges are highlighted. When the learners were asked about their experience of using LIS, 1.7% of the learners had a very bad experience, 10.7% had a bad one, 27.3% answered that the experience was alright, 43% had a good experience and 17.4% of the learners had a very good experience (see Fig. 3). It can be considered that around 87% of the learners would like to continue using the course but the rest might not want to use the LIS again, since they did not encounter a good user experience the first time. The designers of the system need to explore aspects of the LIS that can be improved to provide a good experience.

The answer for the first design challenge, depends on 6 questions, for the first question, that asked about the progress bars, 76.9% of the learners believed that the progress bar is interesting, 14.9% were not sure if it is interesting or not and around 8.3% did not find it interesting. Even though a large number of learners are satisfied with the progress bar, with the mean and mode value of 1, that is "satisfied" and having a low standard deviation (see Table 1), emphasizes that progress bar should be designed to appeal to all learners. When the learners were asked, that should be another graphical representation for the predicted grades (question 2), 41.3% learners preferred to say no, 43.8% learners were not sure, and 14.9% believed that there should be another graphical representation. With a mode value of 3, representing 'not sure', and a low standard deviation, these results highlight the fact that it's important that the representation features of the predicted grades should be re-evaluated by the system designers. In case of the third question, about sufficient information provided by progress bar, 90.9% of the learners answered that the information represented by the progress bar is enough whereas, 9.1% believe that more information is required. The learners preferring the negative answer, suggested that teacher's notes could be added, the probability percentages need to be more explained and more feedback should be given about which topics are more critical in the course. On inquiring about the learners' point of view for color representation, in question 4, 90.1 learners liked this idea, 9.1% learners were neutral as they were not sure that the colored representation is appealing or not and 0.8% answered no, they don't like this idea. Even though the mean and mode value highlight the first answer, these suggestions need to be taken into account. On asking the learners about the usefulness of the suggestions provided by the teachers to enhance their grades, in question 5, 62% answered positively whereas, 38% answered negatively. Even though the mean value is inclined toward the positive answer but 38% is a large number of learners, it needs to be considered why the suggestions are not useful for the learners and what needs to be improved while addressing them personally. Similarly, when inquired that the suggestions enhanced their learning of the course, question number 6, 52.1% of the learners answered yes, 21.5% were not sure about it and 26.4% answered no. Overall, considering the results for the evaluation of first design challenge, that is, informing learners about their progress, for the representation features, the progress bars need to have more information for the learners. As for the feedback procedures, that in case of LIS are the measures and suggestions sent to the learners personally, also need to be enhanced so that all the learners find them useful and effective.

For the evaluation of the second design challenge, learners feeling motivated, questions 7 to 12 that address motivation are considered. For the seventh question, that inquired that the learners wanted to quit the course after receiving their predicted grade. 6.6% of the learners wanted to quit the course, 7.4% were confused about continuing the course whereas, 86% wanted to continue the course. 14% seems like a small number of learners but this means that there is a significant percentage that did not feel motivated and have a very good user and learner experience that is why either they were not sure, or they were certain that they wanted to quit. When investigating the time period for motivation, question 8, that were the learners motivated when they saw the first-grade predictions, 50.4% answered yes, 40.5% answered neutral whereas, 9.1% learners were clearly demotivated. This signifies that the system design needs to be considered to design for motivating experience, throughout the time span of course being delivered. Further the learners were asked if they contacted and asked the teacher for help if they were at-risk, in question 9. This particular course question addressed the motivation level of the learners once their risk level was identified. 93.4% did not contact the teacher and only 6.6% did. The learners who were at-risk felt a low level of motivation and engagement to learn the course better or to improve their grades. The suggestions that are provided to the learners that are at-risk need to be improved in a way that they provide motivation to the learners to continue learning rather than giving up when they are at-risk. About performing the tasks that were suggested by the teacher in the 10th question, 52.1% learners took the measures to improve their grades, which means that at least this number of learners were engaged and were having a worthwhile experience with the LIS. 21.5% were not sure about performing the tasks and 26.4% did not want to take the measures, the last category sounds small, but it points out that the measures and tasks suggested as feedback to enhance grades needs to be re-evaluated in order to be engaging for the learners. For question 11, 81.8% of the learners did not want to discontinue the course when the predicted grades were not up to their expectations. However, 10.7% of the learners were not sure and 7.4% wanted to quit the course. On inquiring about consulting the learning resources after receiving the predicted grade, 68.8% consulted the learning resources, which shows that they were keen to enhance their learning, consequently highlighting the fact that they were engaged. However, there is still a significant number of learners, 31.4% who did not consult any learning resources that could help them enhance their grades. On the whole, for the evaluation of the second design challenge in the LIS, making the learners feel motivated, the motivation level of learners was average.

Table 1. Analysis of questions related to design challenges. The values for mean, median and mode range from 1-3. 1 represents the positive answer whereas 3 is negative

Question/Analysis	1	2	3	4	5	6	7	8	9	10	11	12
Mean	1.38	2.29	1.09	1.19	1.38	1.69	2.00	2.31	1.93	1.69	2.03	1.31
Median	1.00	2.00	1.00	1.00	1.00	1.00	2.00	2.00	2.00	1.00	2.00	1.00
Mode	1.00	3.00	1.00	1.00	1.00	1.00	2.00	2.00	2.00	1.00	2.00	1.00
Std. deviation	0.73	0.71	0.29	0.58	0.48	0.80	0.38	0.63	0.25	0.80	0.43	0.47

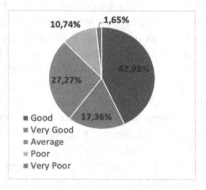

Fig. 3. User experience of learners

6   Conclusion and Future Work

This paper proposes an e-assessment system, Learning Intelligent System (LIS), that aims to enhance the user and learner experience of online courses. While designing the system, two major design challenges have been identified and addressed. The design challenges that have been identified include, informing the learners about their progress and the learners feeling motivated when taking online courses. The system informs the learners about their progress during the semester of an online course and aims to motivate them to learn. This has been achieved by providing the learners with grade predictions, also, the at-risk learners were identified in order to motivate them to learn by providing them suggestions to pass the course.

Furthermore, the evaluation of the LIS highlighted some important factors. Providing the learners with predicted grades have helped them attain worthwhile and motivating learning experiences. As highlighted by the results and according to the learner's point of view, the system has facilitated to enhance the learning experience and increased their motivation and engagement towards the courses. Majority of the learners had a good experience and would prefer to use the LIS again for other courses.

However, the results highlight clearly that the motivation level for different categories of learners had fluctuated. These categories of learners were determined by their level of risk defined by the colored semaphore warning level indicator present on the individuals' dashboard. The learners who were not at-risk or were at moderate risk of failing were motivated to continue the courses. On the contrary, the learners who were at-risk of failing the course, mostly did not contact the teachers after knowing that they are at-risk. Therefore, there was a lack of motivation for the learners who were at-risk of failing the courses. A low level of motivation and engagement of the at-risk learners emphasizes on the need to identify and address the design challenges that are specific for different categories of learners. As the goal is not just to enhance the learning experiences of the learners who are performing well but to also motivate those who are at-risk, encourage them to work harder and consequently enhance their learning.

Acknowledgments. This work was funded by the eLearn Center at Universitat Oberta de Catalunya through the project: New Goals 2018NG001 "LIS: Learning Intelligent System".

References

1. Rostaminezhad, M.A., Mozayani, N., Norozi, D., Iziy, M.: Factors related to e-learner dropout: case study of IUST e-learning center. Procedia - Soc. Behav. Sci. **83**, 522–527 (2013). https://doi.org/10.1016/j.sbspro.2013.06.100
2. Bevan, N.: What is the difference between the purpose of usability and user experience evaluation methods. In: Proceedings of the Workshop UXEM 2009 (Interact 2009), pp. 1–4 (2009)
3. Ternauciuc, A., Vasiu, R.: Testing usability in Moodle: when and how to do it. In: Proceedings of the IEEE 13th International Symposium Intelligent System Informatics, SISY 2015, pp. 263–268 (2015). https://doi.org/10.1109/SISY.2015.7325391
4. Law, E.L., Leicester, L.E., Hassenzahl, M.: Understanding, scoping and defining user experience: a survey approach, pp. 719–728 (2009)
5. Hoonhout, J., Law, E.L.-C., Väänänen-Vainio-Mattila, K., Vermeeren, A.P.O.S., Roto, V., Obrist, M.: User experience evaluation methods, p. 521 (2010). https://doi.org/10.1145/1868914.1868973
6. Hassenzahl, M.: User experience and experience design. Encycl. Hum.-Comput. Interact. 1–35 (2005). https://doi.org/10.1111/j.1654-1103.2012.01452.x
7. Hassenzahl, M.: A personal journey through user experience the beauty and the cognitive. J. Usability Stud. **13**, 168–176 (2018)
8. Walker, S., Prytherch, D., Turner, J.: The pivotal role of staff user experiences in Moodle and the potential impact on student learning. In: 2013 2nd International Conference on E-Learning E-Technologies Education, ICEEE 2013, pp. 192–197 (2013). https://doi.org/10.1109/ICeLeTE.2013.6644372
9. Majors, J., Bengs, A., Granlund, S., Ylitalo, A., Byholm, M.: Moodle moods?: a user experience study of a small private online course for higher teacher education. In: Proceedings of the 22nd International Academic Mindtrek Conference, pp. 228–235 (2018). https://doi.org/10.1145/3275116.3275146
10. Alturki, U.T., Aldraiweesh, A., Kinshuck, D.: Evaluating the usability and accessibility of LMS "Blackboard" at King Saud University. Contemp. Issues Educ. Res. **9**, 33 (2016). https://doi.org/10.19030/cier.v9i1.9548

11. Zaitseva, N.: Usability and user friendliness estimation. **811**, 2015–2016 (2016)
12. Scholl, M.: An implementation of user-experience-based evaluation to achieve transparency in the usage and design of information artifacts. In: Proceedings of the Annual Hawaii International Conference on System Sciences, 21–32 March 2015 (2015). https://doi.org/10.1109/HICSS.2015.14
13. Machado, M., Tao, E.: Blackboard vs. Moodle: comparing user experience of learning management systems, pp. 7–12 (2007)
14. Beltrán, B.A.G., López, L.G., Ortíz, A.R.: User-centered design in Moodle redesign for mobile use, pp. 1212–1224 (2016)
15. Hasan, L.: Usability problems on desktop and mobile interfaces of the Moodle Learning Management System (LMS), pp. 69–73 (2018). https://doi.org/10.1145/3194188.3194192
16. Sheshasaayee, A., Bee, M.N.: Evaluating user experience in moodle learning management systems. In: Proceedings of the IEEE International Conference on Innovative Mechanisms for Industry Applications, ICIMIA 2017, pp. 735–738 (2017). https://doi.org/10.1109/ICIMIA.2017.7975562
17. Fenu, G., Marras, M., Meles, M.: A learning analytics tool for usability assessment in Moodle environments. J. E-Learn. Knowl. Soc. **13**, 23–34 (2017). https://doi.org/10.20368/1971-8829/1388
18. Arshad, R., Majeed, A., Afzal, H., Muzammal, M., ur Rahman, A.: Evaluation of navigational aspects of Moodle. Int. J. Adv. Comput. Sci. Appl. **7** (2016). https://doi.org/10.14569/ijacsa.2016.070342
19. Luo, M., Zheng, S., Zhang, Y.: Design and implementation of efficient user interface in a synchronous e-learning system. In: Proceedings of the 2016 8th International Conference on Information Technology in Medicine and Education, ITME 2016, pp. 490–494 (2017). https://doi.org/10.1109/ITME.2016.0117
20. Santoso, H.B., Isal, R.Y.K., Basaruddin, T., Sadira, L., Schrepp, M.: Research-in-progress: user experience evaluation of Student Centered E-Learning Environment for computer science program. In: Proceedings of the 2014 3rd International Conference on User Science and Engineering. Experience Engineer Engage, i-USEr 2014, pp. 52–55 (2015). https://doi.org/10.1109/IUSER.2014.7002676
21. Green, S., Nacheva-Skopalik, L., Pearson, E.: An adaptable personal learning environment for e-learning and e-assessment. IV.5 (2009). https://doi.org/10.1145/1500879.1500939
22. Sahid, D.S.S., Santosa, P.I., Ferdiana, R., Lukito, E.N.: Evaluation and measurement of Learning Management System based on user experience. In: Proceedings of the 2016 6th International Annual Engineering Seminar, InAES 2016, pp. 72–77 (2017). https://doi.org/10.1109/INAES.2016.7821910
23. Wang, C.H., Wang, T.Y.: E-learning platform of STEAM aesthetic course materials based on user experience. In: Proceedings of the 2018 1st International Cognitive Cities Conference, IC3 2018, pp. 123–128 (2018). https://doi.org/10.1109/IC3.2018.00-46
24. Ardito, C., et al.: Usability of E-learning tools. 80 (2004). https://doi.org/10.1145/989863.989873
25. Zaharias, P.: Usability in the Context of e-Learning: A Framework Augmenting 'Traditional' Usability Constructs with Instructional Design and Motivation to Learn. https://doi.org/10.4018/jthi.2009062503
26. Zaharias, P., Poylymenakou, A.: Developing a usability evaluation method for e-learning applications: beyond functional usability for e-learning applications, 7318 (2009). https://doi.org/10.1080/10447310802546716
27. Zaharias, P., Pappas, C.: Quality management of learning management systems: a user experience perspective. Curr. Issues Emerg. eLearn. **3**, 60–83 (2016)
28. Costabile, M.F., et al.: On the usability evaluation of e-learning applications, pp. 1–10 (2005)

29. Davids, M.R., Chikte, U.M.E., Halperin, M.L.: An efficient approach to improve the usability of e-learning resources: the role of heuristic evaluation. 242–248 (2019). https://doi.org/10.1152/advan.00043.2013
30. Sim, G., Read, J.C.: Using computer-assisted assessment heuristics for usability evaluations. Br. J. Educ. Technol. **47**, 694–709 (2016). https://doi.org/10.1111/bjet.12255
31. McLoughlin, C., Luca, J.: Beyond marks and measurement: developing dynamic and authentic forms of e-assessment. In: Australasian Society for Computers in Learning in Tertiary Education, ASCILITE 2006, vol. 2, pp. 559–562 (2006)
32. Longstaff, E.: How MOOCs can empower learners: a comparison of provider goals and user experiences. J. Furth. High. Educ. **41**, 314–327 (2017)
33. Carless, D., Boud, D.: The development of student feedback literacy: enabling uptake of feedback. Assess. Eval. High. Educ. **43**, 1315–1325 (2018). https://doi.org/10.1080/02602938.2018.1463354
34. Stödberg, U.: A research review of e-assessment. Assess. Eval. High. Educ. **37**, 591–604 (2012). https://doi.org/10.1080/02602938.2011.557496
35. Baneres, D., Rodríguez-Gonzalez, M.E., Serra, M.: An early feedback prediction system for learners at-risk within a first-year higher education course. IEEE Trans. Learn. Technol. **12**, 249–263 (2019). https://doi.org/10.1109/TLT.2019.2912167
36. Minguillón, J., Conesa, J., Rodríguez, M.E., Santanach, F.: Learning analytics in practice: providing e-learning researchers and practitioners with activity data. In: Spector, J., et al. (eds.) Frontiers of Cyberlearning. LNET, pp. 145–167. Springer, Singapore (2018). https://doi.org/10.1007/978-981-13-0650-1_8
37. Reeve, J.: Motivating Others: Nurturing Inner Motivational Resources. Allyn & Bacon (1996)
38. Yoo, S.J., Huang, W.D.: Engaging online adult learners in higher education: motivational factors impacted by gender, age, and prior experiences. J. Contin. High. Educ. **61**, 151–164 (2013). https://doi.org/10.1080/07377363.2013.836823
39. Henrie, C.R., Halverson, L.R., Graham, C.R.: Measuring student engagement in technology-mediated learning: a review. Comput. Educ. **90**, 36–53 (2015). https://doi.org/10.1016/j.compedu.2015.09.005
40. Doherty, K., Doherty, G.: Engagement in HCI: conception, theory and measurement. ACM Comput. Surv. **51**, 99:1–99:39 (2018). https://doi.org/10.1145/3234149
41. Gray, J.A., DiLoreto, M.: The effects of student engagement, student satisfaction, and perceived learning in online learning environments. NCPEA Int. J. Educ. Leadersh. Prep. **11**, 98–119 (2016)
42. Assami, S., Daoudi, N., Ajhoun, R.: Personalization criteria for enhancing learner engagement in MOOC platforms. In: 2018 IEEE Global Engineering Education Conference (EDUCON), pp. 1265–1272. IEEE (2018)

Investigating Mobile Device-Based Interaction Techniques for Collocated Merging

Romina Kühn[1]([envelope]), Mandy Korzetz[1]([envelope]), Felix Kallenbach[1], Karl Kegel[1],
Uwe Aßmann[1]([envelope]), and Thomas Schlegel[2]([envelope])

[1] Institute of Software and Multimedia Technology, TU Dresden, Dresden, Germany
{romina.kuehn,mandy.korzetz,uwe.assmann}@tu-dresden.de
[2] Institute for Ubiquitous Mobility Systems,
Karlsruhe University of Applied Science, Karlsruhe, Germany
thomas.schlegel@hs-karlsruhe.de

Abstract. In mixed-focus collaboration, group members create content both individually as a kind of groundwork for discussion and further processing as well as directly together in group work sessions. In case of individual creation, separate documents and contents need to be merged to receive an overall solution. In our work, we focus on mixed-focus collaboration using mobile devices, especially smartphones, to create and merge content. Instead of using emails or messenger services to share content within a group, we describe three different mobile device-based interaction techniques for merging that use built-in sensors to enable ad-hoc collaboration and that are easy and eyes-free to perform. We conducted a user study to investigate these merging interactions. Overall, 21 participants tested the interactions and evaluated task load and User Experience (UX) of the proposed device-based interactions. Furthermore, they compared the interactions with a common way to share content, namely writing an email to send attached content. Participants gave valuable user feedback and stated that our merging interaction techniques were much easier to perform. Furthermore, we found that they were much faster, less demanding, and had a greater UX than email.

Keywords: Collocated interaction · Device-based interaction · Merging · Mixed-focus collaboration · Mobile phone

1 Introduction

In collocated mixed-focus collaboration, as proposed by Gutwin and Saulberg [6], group members move back and forth between individual and shared tasks to reach a common goal in terms of fulfilling their collaborative task. While working individually, group members typically perform collaboration activities [13] such as creating or editing content as partial solution of an overall collaborative solution. Then, after the individual tasks are completed the results need to be shared completely or merged in parts for further processing within the group.

© Springer Nature Switzerland AG 2020
P. Zaphiris and A. Ioannou (Eds.): HCII 2020, LNCS 12205, pp. 92–108, 2020.
https://doi.org/10.1007/978-3-030-50513-4_7

Fig. 1. Collocated collaboration scenario with merging interactions. Group members apply our proposed interaction techniques with their mobile devices to merge content.

A common way to share content across mobile phones is to send an email with attached documents or using a messaging service, e.g., WhatsApp[1]. For more enhanced sharing, people also use cloud services such as Dropbox[2] or similar tools that work as file hosting services. However, there are different issues with using these techniques, e.g., limited storage space or higher complexity of selecting files when switching between several applications. Switching leads to media breaks, which can be awkward. There are several ways and tools that enable group members to work simultaneously, which would eliminate the need of sharing files explicitly. For example, Google Docs[3] facilitates collaborative text writing and Git[4] can be used for collaborative software development. However, these tools do not support switching between individual and collaborative work and the resulting communicative merging between group members in terms of face-to-face communication, which would be beneficial for collocated collaboration [4]. We focus on mobile devices especially smartphones as ubiquitous devices [1,2] and their usage in collocated mixed-focus collaboration. As stated by Lucero et al. [17] and Dong et al. [5] the main issue with applying smartphones in collaboration is a lack of intuitive and easy-to-perform interactions. To address this issue, we utilize mobile device-based interaction techniques that were presented by Korzetz et al. [11]. Such interactions aim at facilitating unobtrusive interactions in collocated multi-user tasks and enabling quick access to various device functions. Furthermore, they focus on their spatial and tangible behavior by using the built-in sensors instead of the display's representations and, therefore, do not need much user attention. By applying mobile device-based interactions, we aim at integrating mobile devices in collocated collaborative merging in an easy and intuitive way without affecting communication adversely. We investigate three specific mobile device-based interaction techniques for merging results in collocated mixed-focus collaboration (see Fig. 1).

---

[1] https://www.whatsapp.com/
[2] https://www.dropbox.com/
[3] https://docs.google.com
[4] https://git-scm.com/

To present the results of our investigations, we structured the paper as follows: First, we give an overview on related work that describes approaches on merging and sharing content with mobile devices. Then we describe our proposed interaction techniques that aim at merging content more easily compared to common merging strategies. This aim was investigated in a user study we performed by means of an interactive prototype. We present the results and conclude with recommendations and future work.

2   Related Work

Using mobile devices as physical interfaces enables users to interact efficiently in certain situations and to provide fast and easy-to-use input possibilities [15,23]. Korzetz et al. [11] proposed the *mobile spaces* model (MSM) to facilitate the design of such mobile device-based interaction techniques to support individual as well as collaborative usage scenarios. As device-based interaction techniques are lightweight and additionally have been investigated and assessed as effective possibility to support collaboration activities [13,18], we utilize the concepts of the MSM for our merging interactions. Exchanging and sharing information and media with other devices is very important in general, e.g., for creating joint results in collaboration. In this context, we identified two main areas of related work that have influenced the development of our merging interactions, namely (1) sharing interactions with a mobile device in general and (2) sharing interactions between two or more mobile devices.

MobiSurf [24] integrates various personal mobile devices and one shared interactive surface in a home setting to support solving collocated collaborative tasks. Content that should be discussed, e.g., a web page, is transferred by touching the interactive surface with the mobile device, then the browser of the interactive surface loads the page. Ubi-Jector [16] is a system that provides a shared information screen utilizing the users' personal mobile devices in a casual meeting environment. The system provides a visual interface to provide file access to the attendees automatically when connecting to the system. To move information between a mobile device and a large display, several interaction techniques were proposed. The idea of cross-device sharing can be traced back to the work of Rekimoto [22] who proposed the concept of pick-and-drop to use direct manipulation techniques to transfer data between displays using a pen. Shoot-and-copy is an interaction technique to transfer information from public displays to mobile phones by using the built-in camera [3]. The user captures an arbitrary region of the large display and then the corresponding data is sent to the users' device. The interaction techniques pinch, swipe, throw and tilt were investigated to move information vice versa to a large display, e.g., by Paay et al. [21]. Although these techniques were rated as effective and easy-to-learn device-based interactions, they do not support ad-hoc collaboration because an additional and mostly bigger device is required. Our merging interactions are designed to support spontaneous collaboration by solely utilizing mobile devices.

Some research already investigates interaction techniques for sharing between multiple mobile devices. Whereas Ohta [19] proposed a pinch gesture across the borders of two mobile devices to establish a network connection between them and thereby enable moving a photograph over the device boundaries, Hinckley explored bumping devices [7] and stitching gestures [8] for tiling together displays. These approaches use devices as physical interface but concentrate on establishing a device connection and providing a joint viewing area instead of sharing information among a group. However, our interaction approach aims at sharing and especially merging parts of content to enable further processing.

3   Merging Interaction Techniques

To merge individually created content there are several aspects and challenges to address. First, the type of data and media can influence the way of merging. Content can include text, several kinds of illustrations, e.g., images, photos, and diagrams, or videos as well as combinations of different kinds of media. Whereas text can be merged in small units, e.g., sentences or even phrases, visuals are usually merged either completely or not at all. This aspect mainly influences the selection of content that needs to be merged, e.g., a number of images or concrete text phrases, but also the merging itself, e.g., the location within a given text where the phrases need to be added. Depending on the way of working individually in mixed-focus collaboration, single tasks can be performed as alternatives or subtasks to complete a group work more efficiently. Hence, solutions or partial solutions can overlap in different ways and need to be merged before they are further edited. For example, five members of a student group have to prepare a mind map with three subtopics. Whereas one member can work on one subtopic, two members work on the second subtopic and two other members on the third subtopic. Thus, they create alternatives of the subtopics. Alternatives often need to be discussed first within the subgroup before they can be further edited by the whole group. This leads to the need to share content within subgroups bidirectionally so that each subgroup member has a joint solution. Consequently, the direction is also important for merging. Finally, the user roles in collaboration can affect the way of merging content. In case, there is one concrete person using one specific mobile device that collects all parts of an overall solution, content is merged on that specific device. This can be useful for editing together on one device before sharing within the whole group. In the other case, merged content can be provided for each group member immediately. Figure 2 illustrates these aspects for the merging activity.

For our proposed interaction techniques, we focus on the direction of merging content, namely bidirectional and unidirectional merging. We also add the option that content is not merged at all and instead excluded from the merging process. We further refer to the way of merging that is derived from the direction as merging style. In case (partial) solutions do not overlap they can be united easily by adding one solution to another solution and vice versa (bidirectional merging). Composing is necessary in case of partial overlapping as content can be complemented partially in one direction from one device to another device. Content of several devices that overlaps completely can be excluded. The proposed merging interactions were introduced by Korzetz et al. [9] and are shown

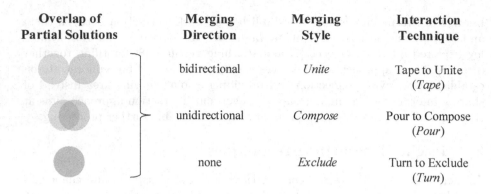

Overlap of Partial Solutions	Merging Direction	Merging Style	Interaction Technique
	bidirectional	*Unite*	Tape to Unite (*Tape*)
	unidirectional	*Compose*	Pour to Compose (*Pour*)
	none	*Exclude*	Turn to Exclude (*Turn*)

Fig. 2. Overview of relevant merging aspects.

in Fig. 3. They are inspired by everyday actions and address the mixed-focus collaboration activity *sharing results* by setting in after group members compared several interim results and want to generate an overall solution [13]. They are designed to be easy and eyes-free to perform without further equipment. Furthermore, they address the concepts of the *mobile spaces* model (MSM) [11].

Tape to Unite (Fig. 3a) enables users to directly add a part to an overall solution, e.g., one part of a bigger mind map or a text section of a chapter. The interaction is performed as follows: First, the devices are placed next to each other. Second, the user performs a swipe gesture on the screens of the involved devices simultaneously (see Fig. 3a). Depending on the position where the devices are placed next to each other, the content is merged. For example, text can be added at the end of a continuous text by placing devices on the short sides of the smartphones and performing the tape gesture along those sides. While the devices "stick together" the content can be presented on each involved device to enlarge the presentation area as described, e.g., by Ohta and Tanaka [20]. When the devices are detached a united solution remains on both devices. We further refer to this interaction technique as *Tape*.

The *Pour to Compose* (or *Pour*) interaction is more versatile in terms of the merging options. This interaction can be used in case users want to put together several pieces for an overall solution. For example, to create a joint text several text blocks of different group members can be merged with this interaction technique on one or several devices. *Pour* is performed by pouring the content from one device out into another device as shown in Fig. 3b. The sending device (left) is tilted above the receiving device (right) and the content flows into the receiving device. Varying the tilt angle increases or decreases the speed of transferring the data. For selecting the content of the sending device and specifying the position to merge the content on the receiving device, additional pick and point gestures can be used. For example, a touch-based lasso gesture can be used to pick content and a finger tap can be used for pointing. In contrast to the *Tape* interaction, *Pour* is unidirectional, which means that the pouring device only receives content when it changes roles and becomes a receiving device.

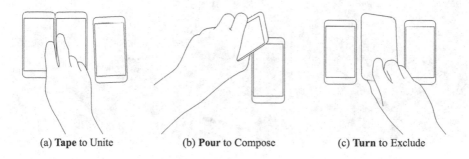

(a) **Tape** to Unite   (b) **Pour** to Compose   (c) **Turn** to Exclude

Fig. 3. Device-based interactions for collocated merging

The *Turn to Exclude* (or *Turn*) interaction (see Fig. 3c) enables users to exclude a solution from further discussions by turning the device [12]. This interaction technique focuses on the digital content of the other devices and excludes content successively if necessary. Excluding can be useful in case a proposed partial solution is not suitable for further processing.

4   User Study

We conducted a user study to examine the proposed interaction techniques concerning their task load and UX using the standardized NASA Task Load Index[5] (NASA-TLX) and the User Experience Questionnaire[6] (UEQ). Furthermore, we compared the proposed merging interactions with a commonly used technique for sharing content, namely attaching files to an email and sending it to another device. In the following section, we describe the setup and design of our user study, participants, and our interactive prototype in detail.

4.1   Participants

We recruited 21 unpaid participants (5 female) from age 24 to 42 ($M = 32.2$, $SD = 5.3$) via email or personally. Participants assessed their smartphone experience on a 5-point Likert scale ranging from 1 (little experience) to 5 (expert). Participants had an overall high prior experience in using smartphones ($M = 4.2$, $SD = 1.0$). They stated that they mainly use their smartphones for messaging and communication services (20), browsing the internet (14), and entertainment purposes (12), e.g., watching videos or gaming. The majority of participants (16) use smartphones with Android as operating system. Furthermore, they stated that they mainly use messaging services (15), cloud services (12), and email (6) for merging content depending on their individual goal.

---

[5] https://humansystems.arc.nasa.gov/groups/TLX/
[6] https://www.ueq-online.org/

98   R. Kühn et al.

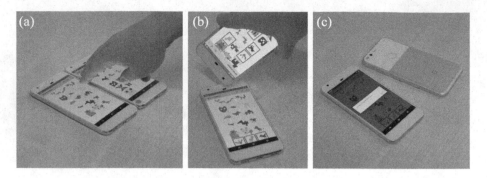

Fig. 4. Interactive prototype. (a) *Tape* interaction to unite content. (b) *Pour* for composing content. (c) *Turn* to exclude content.

4.2 Interactive Prototype

We implemented the above-mentioned interaction techniques using the *Milky-Way* toolbox [10], a toolbox to facilitate fast and easy development of mobile device-based interactions. The toolbox provides a simple connection establishment between devices using Wi-Fi direct and a gesture editor that combines several movements and gestures to create one joint gesture set. To conduct each interaction properly all devices that were used for the user study had to provide an accelerometer, a gyroscope, and a proximity sensor as well as a touch display. The participants used two Google Pixel smartphones with Android version 10.0, which we provided for the user study to guarantee the availability of the necessary sensors and to control the setting. The *Tape* interaction used the touch screen and recognized the touch gesture within a predefined area. For *Pour* the sending device recognized the changing orientation using the accelerometer. Additionally, the receiving device recognized the other device using the proximity sensor. Finally, for *Turn* the gyroscope and the proximity sensor detected the turning of the device. As soon as a merging interaction was recognized the respective merging style was triggered.

Our interactive prototype was built as an image sharing application (see Fig. 4). We provided several simple pixel graphics for merging into one gallery for further processing, e.g., starting a joint exhibition in an art class. The application presented the provided images. The action bar contained a button to select all images at once, a sharing button for sending pictures via email, and a shortcut for resetting the gallery. Within the gallery, images could be selected or deselected by touching the respective image. Each merging interaction technique was implemented as described in Sect. 3. We merged images by adding them to the end of the gallery. As soon as users performed an interaction, they received visual feedback either as added images or textual information. Furthermore, the device vibrated in order to give haptic feedback. To compare the interaction techniques, we implemented a common alternative way to share content. A sharing button enabled the user to open the Gmail application and to attach the selected images to an email for sending it. The other device received the email, downloaded the image manually, and added it to the gallery automatically. We decided to use email as alternative because it is (still) a very common way to share data between several devices, data is not compressed automatically as it is the case when using messaging services, and it is also used by people who do not use cloud services.

4.3 Procedure

To investigate the interaction techniques accordingly, participants performed the user study as follows. It started with an explanation of the global procedure and the goal of the user study. The participants were asked to describe their usual way of merging content. Then, the study leader presented the three merging interactions by demonstration and described the email interaction as well as the study application itself. The participants were asked to merge either all images, several selected images, or no images with our proposed interaction techniques and via email. After each performed interaction technique, participants completed the NASA-TLX questionnaire as well as the UEQ. Afterwards, the study leader reset the gallery for the next merging task. This procedure was repeated with the other interactions. Overall, the participants were asked to perform each merging style task (*Unite, Compose*, and *Exclude*) twice using email and our merging interactions. To address the order bias, we permuted the order of interactions. A session concluded with an interview concerning final comments about the interactions and their potential usage in collaborative scenarios as well as a short questionnaire to collect demographic data. During a session the study leader took additional notes regarding a participant's performance and remarks. A session took about 35 min ($M = 35.2$, $SD = 6.6$).

4.4 Design

We realized a within-subject design with the merging style as independent variable. We had two conditions: common email merging and using our device-based merging interactions *Tape, Pour*, and *Turn*. The dependent variable was the task completion time. To avoid learning effects, we counterbalanced the testing order of all interactions.

5 Results

We examined the task load as well as the UX of each interaction technique using the NASA-TLX questionnaire respectively the User Experience Questionnaire (UEQ) [14]. The NASA-TLX assesses task load on a scale from 1 (least demanding) to 100 (very demanding). The UEQ includes three main scales: attractiveness, pragmatic quality (measuring perspicuity, efficiency, and dependability) and hedonic quality (measuring stimulation and novelty). These three dimensions help us to evaluate UX aspects. User Experience was assessed on a 7-point Likert scale. In the following section, we describe the results of our user study.

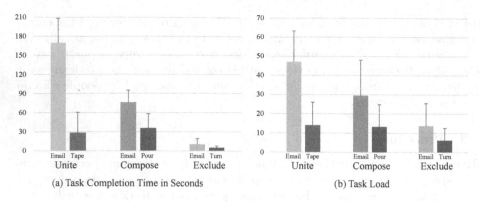

(a) Task Completion Time in Seconds   (b) Task Load

Fig. 5. Means and standard deviations of (a) task completion time in seconds and (b) task load per merging style and condition.

5.1 Task Completion Time

We compared the task completion time per merging style using either email or our merging interactions. Figure 5a illustrates the results from the task completion times by displaying the mean values (M) and standard deviations (SD). Measuring the task completion time started after we described the particular task and stopped after participants received the feedback of a successful merging. Uniting content on both devices took the participants between 90 and 222 s (M = 169.8, SD = 38.5) using email and between 6 and 157 s (M = 28.5, SD = 32.0) applying the *Tape* interaction. Whereas for sending emails the standard deviation is relatively low, *Tape* performed one time much worse in contrast to the other sessions because of technical issues. Eliminating the session with a task completion time of 157 s, using *Tape* took between 6 and 53 s (M = 22.1, SD = 12.8), which shows better results.

Composing content on one device took between 50 and 118 s (M = 76.0, SD = 19.0) using email and between 12 and 86 s (M = 35.7, SD = 22.4) applying the *Pour* interaction both including the selection of the content first. For excluding the content, participants took between 2 and 38 s (M = 10.5, SD = 8.9) using email and between 2 and 11 s (M = 5.2, SD = 2.6) applying the *Turn* interaction. Using email for excluding ranged from doing nothing to writing a short text via email that the participant won't send any images. We performed an analysis of variance (ANOVA) to investigate effects of the merging style conditions on task completion time. The analysis shows that for all merging styles the results are statistical significant: *Unite* ($F_{1,20} = 233.298, p < .0001$), *Compose* ($F_{1,20} = 89.657, p < .0001$), and *Exclude* ($F_{1,20} = 9.355, p < .01$). The results show a significantly longer task completion time for sending emails than using our proposed merging interactions. Although, the participants were all used to send images via email, the process of selecting images, attaching them to an email, waiting for the email to arrive at the other device, downloading the images and pasting them into the gallery was quite cumbersome and more

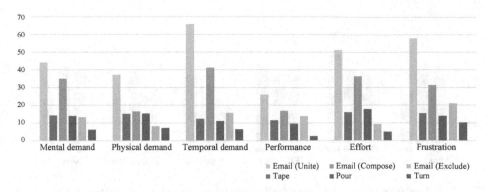

Fig. 6. Comparison of TLX means per criteria for all interactions after usage.

complex in contrast to the merging interactions, especially for uniting content. There are less differences in the task completion times between email and *Pour* due to the lower complexity of the task. Overall, the standard deviation values of the task completion time were relatively high for the merging interactions because the interactions were all new to the participants and were performed for the first time during the user study. Consequently, some participants had to try the merging interactions several times. However, the merging interactions still performed significantly better than sending an email.

5.2 Comparison of Task Load

After completing each task using either email or a merging interaction, participants were asked to fill out the NASA-TLX to assess the perceived individual task load. Figure 6 presents a comparison of the TLX means of all criteria for all interactions. We used ANOVA to investigate the statistical significance for the overall task load of each interaction. The results show that the effect of the interaction (email vs. merging interaction) on the task load was statistically significant for all merging styles: *Unite* ($F_{1,20} = 52.880, p < .0001$), *Compose* ($F_{1,20} = 36.994, p < .0001$), and *Exclude* ($F_{1,20} = 7.500, p < .05$). However, as shown in Fig. 6 the differences for the merging style *Exclude* are lower than for the other merging styles. As shown in Fig. 5b the overall task load for sending emails was much higher than for the respective merging interaction. For *Unite*, we found very high temporal demand due to the complexity of sending an email in both directions, which correlates with the measured task completion time and which we assume also led to high frustration. We found a similar valuation for sending emails for *Compose* where especially temporal demand and effort are high. The proposed merging interactions perform better for every single criteria.

5.3 User Experience of Merging Interaction Techniques

Additionally to the task load evaluation, we asked the participants to fill out the standardized User Experience Questionnaire (UEQ). The UEQ includes 26 word

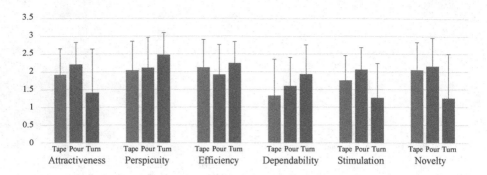

Fig. 7. UX ratings (means and standard deviation) of merging interaction techniques.

pairs that can characterize a product. These pairs are assessed by the participants on a 7-point Likert scale and are mapped to attractiveness, perspicuity, efficiency, dependability, stimulation, and novelty. Figure 7 shows the means and standard deviations of the merging interaction techniques *Tape*, *Pour*, and *Turn* in terms of the UX ratings. Values >0.8 represent a positive rating, which shows an overall positive evaluation for all three merging interaction techniques. However, we wanted to have a closer look at the particular ratings.

Whereas for *Tape*, the single values of perspicuity, efficiency, and novelty culminate in relatively high means, the mean value of dependability is significantly lower with a high standard deviation (SD = 1.03). From that, we derive that performing the interaction did not work flawlessly all the time. This correlates with our observation that some participants had to perform the *Tape* gesture several times before it was recognized. However, in general *Tape* was evaluated positively with a high attractiveness, pragmatic, and hedonic quality. For *Pour*, especially attractiveness and hedonic factors (stimulation and novelty) were rated high with lower standard deviations. Some participants also mentioned that they enjoyed performing the interaction very much. However, pragmatic quality aspects, especially efficiency and dependability, need to be improved to guarantee a high usability. We observed that some participants also had to perform the *Pour* interaction several times and in different ways. We assume that this led to devaluation. In contrast, the *Turn* interaction was rated best concerning pragmatic quality aspects which we interpret as *Turn* is a very explicit and comprehensible interaction technique. However, aspects in terms of attractiveness and hedonic quality were rated worse with high values of the standard deviation in contrast to *Tape* and *Pour*. We trace these ratings to a very easy and short interaction which is already known from muting an incoming call[7] and consequently not new to some participants. Overall, from the UEQ we can derive that our merging interaction techniques were rated positively.

---

[7] https://www.samsung.com/ca/support/mobile-devices/what-are-the-advanced-feat ures-available-on-my-galaxy-note8/

Table 1. Results from the t-test with an alpha level $\alpha = 0.01$ comparing merging interaction technique and email.

UX aspect	Unite	Compose	Exclude
Attractiveness	$p < .0001$	$p < .0001$	$p < .01$
Perspicuity	$p < .0001$	$p < .0001$	$p < .01$
Efficiency	$p < .0001$	$p < .0001$	$p < .01$
Dependability	$p < .01$	$p > .01$	$p > .01$
Stimulation	$p < .0001$	$p < .0001$	$p < .0001$
Novelty	$p < .0001$	$p < .0001$	$p < .0001$

5.4 Comparison of User Experience

To assess the results from the UEQ better, we compared the participants' UX evaluation of the merging interactions with one common alternative for sharing content: sending an email with attached files. The results show very strong differences in rating the various UX aspects of the merging interactions compared to sending an email. Figure 8 illustrates the means and standard deviations of all interactions. Beside the partially much worse rating for email concerning attractiveness and hedonic quality in general, which we explain with the fact that sending emails is a very common concept, email also performed worse for pragmatic quality. Especially for *Tape*, the email condition performed much worse concerning perspicuity and efficiency. This rating correlates with the overall TLX rating of the *Unite* email interaction. Especially, the TLX showed higher temporal demands, effort, and frustration comparing email and *Tape*. For *Pour*, our analysis of the UX questionnaire showed a similar but mitigated effect in terms of pragmatic quality. We assume that the higher temporal demand and the more process steps for selecting the images, sending an email, and downloading the images led to devalued efficiency. This observation would also explain, why *Exclude* was rated more similar in both conditions.

We performed a t-test with an alpha level of $\alpha = 0.01$ to check if the scale means differ significantly. Table 1 shows the results in detail. For *Unite*, the means for all scales differ significantly. For *Compose* as well as *Exclude* we also found significant differences for nearly all scales except dependability with $p = .0303$ for *Compose* and $p = .0194$ for *Exclude*.

5.5 Usage in Multi-user Scenarios and Final Feedback

After participants completed all tasks and questionnaires, we asked some questions concerning the usage of our merging interaction techniques in collaborative multi-user scenarios and invited the participants to give final feedback. Overall, they mainly stated that the proposed merging interaction techniques will be useful in multi-user settings because they stimulate to talk to each other. One participant said, "I think it was a lot of fun [using the merging interaction techniques] and it is much more collaborative and easier than email. Furthermore,

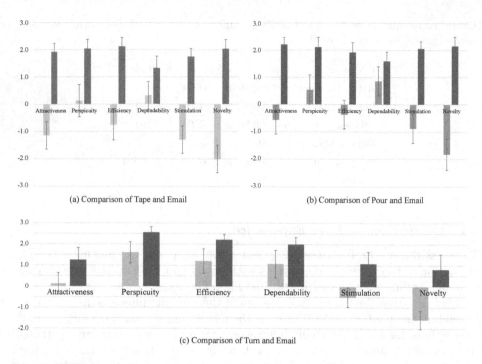

Fig. 8. Comparison of means and standard deviations of (a) *Tape* and email, (b) *Pour* and email as well as (c) *Turn* and email concerning the different UX aspects.

[the merging interaction techniques] are connecting.". Furthermore, another participant said that the interaction techniques would be "a relief in contrast to other interactions" and people would be less distracted compared to emails. For *Tape*, the main comments comprised that this interaction technique is very easy and fast, especially compared to sending an email. However, participants wondered how this interaction technique will be performed in a larger group: "I think [Tape] can be confusing with many people in terms of space problems [when devices need to be placed next to each other].". Although, participants were not sure how this will work, they think *Tape* is useful in social situations when you can talk to each other, e.g., to coordinate the merging. *Pour* received a lot of positive comments, e.g., "[Pour] was fun." and "It feels very intuitive.". Since it is a "playful" interaction technique, two participants said the interaction technique would "spice up collaborating". However, it is necessary to avoid accidental pouring or dropping the phone while pouring. The excluding interaction *Turn* was mentioned least and comments ranged from "can be seen as unfriendly" to "useful in terms of giving feedback". Participants suggested additional oral communication with other people within the group when performing the *Turn* interaction. Some participants had concerns touching another persons smartphone, e.g., for hygienic, data protection, or private property reasons. They stated that it is important to trust each other and to talk to each other while using the merging interaction techniques. Furthermore, one participant said that it would be useful to have an undo option in case content was sent accidental.

Some participants mentioned that they especially liked that the merging interaction techniques were performed within one mobile application in contrast to sending an email. For email, the participants had to switch to the mail application and back to our study application. An in-app solution seems to increase the assessment in general. As a side effect, during the study conduct we observed that sending email took some time because of bad Wi-Fi connection. Because the proposed interaction techniques are built on the *MilkyWay* toolbox by Korzetz et al. [10] that provides a Wi-Fi direct connection between the applied devices, the data exchange was very fast.

6 Findings and Recommendations

From the results, we derived suggestions for improving the tested merging interaction techniques as well as some further ideas and impressions for merging content in mixed-focus collaboration. The focus of the user study was to investigate our proposed merging interaction techniques regarding their task load and user experience and compare them with a common alternative.

First of all, the user study showed that our proposed merging interaction techniques are suitable for collocated merging scenarios because they are fast to perform, easy to learn and to use. Furthermore, participants stated that these interaction techniques will affect communication and social interaction positively. To improve task completion times of *Tape* and *Pour* and increase the rating of dependability, the implementation of the interactions should be revised. As mentioned by some participants, a visual marking would be beneficial for *Tape* to know where exactly to swipe. We will improve this in further revisions. For *Pour* additional alternatives of performing the interaction would be beneficial because participants varied the way of pouring the content from one device to another one. For example, some tried to "shake" the content out of one device, which impeded the detection of the interaction. At the same time, it is important that the interactions remain explicit to avoid accidental detection. This leads us to the necessity to reconsider the learning phase because we observed that participants sometimes took a while to perform an interaction technique correctly. Additionally, we interpret the higher values of standard deviation concerning the task completion time that sometimes the interaction techniques worked immediately and sometimes after several trials. We applied a learning-by-demonstration approach by the study leader to present the interaction techniques. From our observations we found that participants sometimes still had difficulties with execution speed (*Tape*), tilt angle (*Pour*), exact steps (email), and positioning (*Pour*). We hypothesize that improved feedback mechanisms during performing the interactions would lead to better results and less errors. As a starting point, we will apply visual feedback when the device recognized, for example, a movement but without detecting the concrete interaction technique. With corresponding help functions, we aim at supporting the user.

6.1 Limitations and Future Work

In this work, we compared the merging interaction techniques to common email interaction. Participants also mentioned quite often that they would also use messaging services, e.g., WhatsApp. Such services normally compress data, which is one reason why we used email instead. However, a comparison between our proposed interaction techniques and messaging services would be interesting, too, and could substantiate our findings. Nevertheless, for messaging services a good Wi-Fi connection is also necessary. Our merging interactions do not need an external Wi-Fi connection due to the usage of the smartphone sensors.

Whereas we could proof that our proposed merging interaction techniques are usable, attractive, and overall stimulating, we did not investigate in depth how they would be evaluated in multi-user settings. Consequently, applying them in a mixed-focus collaboration scenario would be beneficial to consolidate our findings. However, from the user feedback and the tailoring to merging activities [13], we hypothesize that the merging interaction techniques will be useful in mixed-focus collaboration. Hence, we plan a combined user study that investigates several mobile device-based interaction techniques in collaboration scenarios to receive extensive user feedback.

7 Conclusion

In our work, we presented and investigated three merging interaction techniques for mobile devices, namely *Tape*, *Pour*, and *Turn*. The interaction techniques' main aim is to provide an easy and fast way to merge content either bidirectional, unidirectional, or not at all. We developed an Android prototype that was utilized in order to evaluate task load and UX aspects within a user study. We collected data from time measurements, standardized questionnaires (NASA-TLX and UEQ), and observations. Furthermore, we compared our interactions with a common way to share content, i.e., sending email with attached content.

The results show that especially *Tape* and *Pour* performed well in terms of their attractiveness and hedonic quality. Furthermore, the results concerning the task load prove a positive effect. Compared to sending an email, all three mobile device-based interactions for merging performed better. With the collected feedback, we will revise our merging interactions and apply them to collaborative multi-user scenarios. With our approach and investigation, we contribute to the field of collaboration technology in terms of mobile device-based interaction techniques for mixed-focus collaboration and provide easy to use interaction techniques for collocated merging.

Acknowledgements. The European Social Fund (ESF) and the German Federal State of Saxony have funded this work within the project CyPhyMan (100268299). This work is also funded by the German Research Foundation (DFG, Deutsche Forschungsgemeinschaft) as part of Germany's Excellence Strategy - EXC 2050/1 - Project ID 390696704 - Cluster of Excellence "Centre for Tactile Internet with Human-in-the-Loop" (CeTI) of Technische Universität Dresden.

References

1. Abowd, G.D., Iftode, L., Mitchell, H.: The smart phone: a first platform for pervasive computing. IEEE Pervasive Comput. **4**(2), 18–19 (2005). https://doi.org/10.1016/j.bjps.2009.11.010
2. Ballagas, R., Borchers, J., Rohs, M., Sheridan, J.G.: The smart phone: a ubiquitous input device. IEEE Pervasive Comput. **5**(1), 70–77 (2006). https://doi.org/10.1109/MPRV.2006.18
3. Boring, S., Altendorfer, M., Broll, G., Hilliges, O., Butz, A.: Shoot & copy: phonecam-based information transfer from public displays onto mobile phones. In: Proceedings of the 4th International Conference on Mobile Technology, Applications, and Systems and the 1st International Symposium on Computer Human Interaction in Mobile Technology, Mobility 2007, pp. 24–31. Association for Computing Machinery, New York (2007). https://doi.org/10.1145/1378063.1378068
4. Diehl, M., Stroebe, W.: Productivity loss in brainstorming groups: toward the solution of a riddle. J. Pers. Soc. Psychol. **53**, 497–509 (1987). https://doi.org/10.1037/0022-3514.53.3.497
5. Dong, T., Churchill, E.F., Nichols, J.: Understanding the challenges of designing and developing multi-device experiences. In: Proceedings of the 2016 ACM Conference on Designing Interactive Systems, DIS 2016, pp. 62–72 (2016)
6. Gutwin, C., Greenberg, S.: Design for individuals, design for groups: tradeoffs between power and workspace awareness. In: Proceedings of the 1998 ACM Conference on Computer Supported Cooperative Work (CSCW 1998), pp. 207–216 (1998). https://doi.org/10.1145/289444.289495
7. Hinckley, K.: Synchronous gestures for multiple persons and computers. In: Proceedings of the 16th Annual ACM Symposium on User Interface Software and Technology, UIST 2003, pp. 149–158. Association for Computing Machinery, New York (2003). https://doi.org/10.1145/964696.964713
8. Hinckley, K., Ramos, G., Guimbretiere, F., Baudisch, P., Smith, M.: Stitching: pen gestures that span multiple displays. In: Proceedings of the Working Conference on Advanced Visual Interfaces, AVI 2004, pp. 23–31. Association for Computing Machinery, New York (2004). https://doi.org/10.1145/989863.989866
9. Korzetz, M., Kühn, R., Heisig, P., Schlegel, T.: Natural collocated interactions for merging results with mobile devices. In: Proceedings of the 18th International Conference on Human-Computer Interaction with Mobile Devices and Services, MobileHCI 2016, pp. 746–752 (2016). https://doi.org/10.1145/2957265.2961839
10. Korzetz, M., Kühn, R., Kegel, K., Georgi, L., Schumann, F.-W., Schlegel, T.: *MilkyWay*: a toolbox for prototyping collaborative mobile-based interaction techniques. In: Antona, M., Stephanidis, C. (eds.) HCII 2019. LNCS, vol. 11573, pp. 477–490. Springer, Cham (2019). https://doi.org/10.1007/978-3-030-23563-5_38
11. Korzetz, M., Kühn, R., Schlegel, T.: Turn it, pour it, twist it: a model for designing mobile device-based interactions. In: Proceedings of the 5th International ACM In-cooperation HCI and UX Conference, CHIuXiD 2019, pp. 20–23. ACM, New York (2019). https://doi.org/10.1145/3328243.3328246
12. Kühn, R., Korzetz, M., Büschel, L., Korger, C., Manja, P., Schlegel, T.: Natural voting interactions for collaborative work with mobile devices. In: Proceedings of the 34th of the International Conference Extended Abstracts on Human Factors in Computing Systems, CHI 2016, pp. 2570–2575 (2016). https://doi.org/10.1145/2851581.2892300

13. Kühn, R., Schlegel, T.: Mixed-focus collaboration activities for designing mobile interactions. In: Proceedings of the 20th International Conference on Human-Computer Interaction with Mobile Devices and Services, MobileHCI 2018, pp. 71–78 (2018). https://doi.org/10.1145/3236112.3236122
14. Laugwitz, B., Held, T., Schrepp, M.: Construction and evaluation of a user experience questionnaire. In: Holzinger, A. (ed.) USAB 2008. LNCS, vol. 5298, pp. 63–76. Springer, Heidelberg (2008). https://doi.org/10.1007/978-3-540-89350-9_6
15. Leigh, S.W., Schoessler, P., Heibeck, F., Maes, P., Ishii, H.: THAW: tangible interaction with see-through augmentation for smartphones on computer screens. In: Proceedings of the 9th International Conference on Tangible, Embedded, and Embodied Interaction, TEI 2015, pp. 89–96 (2015)
16. Lim, H., Ahn, H., Kang, J., Suh, B., Lee, J.: Ubi-jector: an information-sharing workspace in casual places using mobile devices. In: Proceedings of the 16th International Conference on Human-Computer Interaction with Mobile Devices & Services (MobileHCI 2014), pp. 379–388 (2014)
17. Lucero, A., Jones, M., Jokela, T., Robinson, S.: Mobile collocated interactions: taking an offline break together. Interactions 20(2), 26–32 (2013)
18. Lucero, A., Keränen, J., Jokela, T.: Social and spatial interactions: shared co-located mobile phone use. In: Proceedings of the 28th of the International Conference Extended Abstracts on Human Factors in Computing Systems, CHI EA 2010, pp. 3223–3228. ACM Press (2010)
19. Ohta, T.: Intuitive gesture set on touch screen for ad-hoc file sharing among multiple mobile devices. In: 2014 IEEE 3rd Global Conference on Consumer Electronics (GCCE), pp. 751–752 (2014). https://doi.org/10.1109/GCCE.2014.7031188
20. Ohta, T., Tanaka, J.: MovieTile: interactively adjustable free shape multi-display of mobile devices. In: SIGGRAPH Asia 2015 Mobile Graphics and Interactive Applications, SA 2015. Association for Computing Machinery, New York (2015). https://doi.org/10.1145/2818427.2818436
21. Paay, J., et al.: A comparison of techniques for cross-device interaction from mobile devices to large displays. In: Proceedings of the 14th International Conference on Advances in Mobile Computing and Multi Media, MoMM 2016, pp. 137–146. ACM (2016). https://doi.org/10.1145/3007120.3007140
22. Rekimoto, J.: Pick-and-drop: a direct manipulation technique for multiple computer environments. In: Proceedings of the 10th Annual ACM Symposium on User Interface Software and Technology, UIST 1997, pp. 31–39. Association for Computing Machinery, New York (1997). https://doi.org/10.1145/263407.263505
23. Rico, J., Brewster, S.: Usable gestures for mobile interfaces: evaluating social acceptability. In: Proceedings of the 28th International Conference on Human Factors in Computing Systems, CHI 2010, pp. 887–896 (2010)
24. Seifert, J., et al.: MobiSurf: improving co-located collaboration through integrating mobile devices and interactive surfaces. In: Proceedings of the 2012 ACM International Conference on Interactive Tabletops and Surfaces, ITS 2012, pp. 51–60. ACM Press (2012)

The Influence of Simulation Tool Usage on Architecture Student Design: Shifting from a Technical Perspective to a Design-Focused Perspective

Camilla Maia[1] , Jaewan Park[1] , Sungeun Lee[1] ,
Bokgiu Choi[2] , Suji Choi[1] , and Sangwon Lee[1(✉)]

[1] Department of Human Environment and Design, Yonsei University,
Seodaemun-gu, Seoul 03722, Republic of Korea
sangwon.lee@yonsei.ac.kr
[2] Department of Cognitive Science, Yonsei University,
Seodaemun-gu, Seoul 03722, Republic of Korea

Abstract. In this paper, we describe the influence that simulation tools can potentially have on architecture students' design process. In order to understand the simulation usage in the educational context, we first reviewed the previous uses of technological tools in architectural design. In the experiment, students of South Korea performed design tasks guided by either a simulation tool or a studio instructor. The given task also differed by its nature, optimization- vs. concept-driven. As a result, we found that the simulation provided a creative-prone environment to the students and increased their attention to detail.

Keywords: Agent-based modeling · Simulation · Architecture education

1 Introduction

Historically, there has been a constant development of technological tools to aid the students in their learning process and the development of their design proposals. Fonseca et al. [5] explain that spatial information, for example, can be demonstrated in several ways, extending from traditional methods, such as printed designs and physical models, to contemporary methods, such as digital plans and tridimensional models, or even further to include the new information-based modeling methodologies.

Those tools allow designers to navigate the project in different scales and update the design seamlessly according to the architect's decisions. While specialists and researchers have been analyzing and creating more powerful tools, professionals and professors have started to incorporate their usage into the design process [13]. Bilda and Demirkan [1], for example, found out that Computer Assisted Design promotes more frequent modification actions from the designer than traditional media-based design. Thus, it has been described as a useful resource to improve student learning effectiveness and satisfaction with the learning process [7]. The application of technology resources to help the design process has been expanded and, recently, the agent-

© Springer Nature Switzerland AG 2020
P. Zaphiris and A. Ioannou (Eds.): HCII 2020, LNCS 12205, pp. 109–120, 2020.
https://doi.org/10.1007/978-3-030-50513-4_8

based modeling technology was also identified as one suitable solution to help designers understand the architecture constraints. Therefore, recent studies investigated the possibility of using virtual humans to simulate the behavior of people in existing or yet to be built environments [6]. However, the interest and urgency of incorporating technological solutions within the educational context, particularly university classes, is new, and its effects are still not completely understood [12]. Specifically, in the design fields, Dickson et al. [3] concluded that it is crucial to consider the introduction of such tools to promote and facilitate the process of creating design solutions.

2   Statement of the Problem

Architecture students are expected to be able to modify and adapt a proposal according to different perspectives aiming to conceptualize a suitable solution for the architecture complex design problems. In order to achieve this goal, the design studio setup within the university context helps the novice professionals to acquire the necessary skills to conceptualize, explore, and accomplish appropriate architectural design notions. However, especially in the early years of architecture studies, the learners often lack the experience to understand the professors' feedback thoroughly and often are not able to evaluate how much their solutions are adequate to the several task requirements as a result of limited experience in the field [16]. Therefore, Dickson et al. [3] point out that new teaching strategies are necessary in order to aid the student in getting design information anytime and anywhere while endorsing the establishment of innovative solutions during the design process. For example, building performance simulation has become a popular research topic in the architecture education field [13].

However, there are still difficulties with the implementation and usage of techno-logical tools within the architectural design context. Several researchers point out the limitations of the tool application within the learning process [1, 15]. Studies have also questioned the degree of influence that such technology tools should ideally have in the design process [13]. There seems to be a separation between the simulation tool uti-lization and the design process itself. This gap leads to studies that are mainly focused on the scientific justification of the simulation usage with little or no emphasis on the simulation integration within the creative design process [16]. Hong and Lee [7], for example, describes that the effect of human behavior simulation on architects and designers' decision making and solution experimentation remains unknown. Accord-ingly, Østergård, Jensen, and Maagaard [16] also discuss the current limitations of using simulations to produce architectural proposals. The author mentions the general excessive focus on the technical aspects of the tool instead of its potential to improve the design itself. Therefore, regardless of the development of technological solutions to aid novice and experienced designers within practice and education contexts, there has not been a systematic way for the designer to control the simulation environment and explore further interferences that each simulation variable can have on the overall outcome.

The present research aims to examine the influence of agent behavior simulation utilization over the architecture students' design process. First, it was assessed if and how students change or adapt their design process according to the simulation aid. In this case, we assumed that the simulation utilization would increase the number of iterations in the design process. Also, we investigated if the influence of simulation differs between context-based design and performance-based design. We anticipated that the simulation application would have a more profound influence on performance-based design solutions. The hypothesis described above aims to produce a broader understanding of how students use simulation tools and to what extent the simulation influences their design and process and their design proposals within an architecture-based education environment.

3 Background

3.1   Agent-Based Modeling Simulation as a Design Tool

According to Sciences and Jun (2011) definition, design problems are unique, highly dependable on the problem formulation itself, and they usually do not carry one specific optimal solution. For that reason, according to Rittel [11], regarding the design practice environment, a systematic way to analyze the interactions between the design variables is needed. Among the possible solutions to evaluate design variables and their influence over the general design adequacy to requirements, simulation has been implemented at a university environment as a useful and secure tool [7]. Thus, simulation allows the learner to experiment with the dynamic relations among variables to understand and anticipate the behavior of the system [9]. Such tools facilitate consecutive examination of a system behavior aiming to prove or refute a specific predicted performance [6]. According to Dickson et al. [3], the act of creating and evaluating simulation results facilitates the novice professionals' process of generating ideas to produce design products suitable for specific requirements.

Dickson et al. [3] also complement that simulation has become a standard teaching resource amongst educators from different fields. Regarding the architecture field, the computer simulation's main advantage is to assess the quality of student's proposals seamlessly. Among the currently available simulations, the agent-based simulations are increasingly gaining space within education environments [13]. Agent simulation can be summarized as simulations of autonomous, usually goal-oriented agents, which aim at representing the prospective user's behavior in a specific environment [6]. Therefore, agent-based modeling simulations can be described as tools to experiment with the relationships between a proposed building floor plan and user expected behavior pattern [7]. The referred simulation setups support the exploration of a wide range of users and consideration of the complexity of user scope in detail [6]. However, there is a lack of research about the influence of agent simulation tools on the students' design process [10].

3.2 Design Process Enhanced Through Technology

The architectural design often starts with the conceptual phase to resolve a design problem until a solution is achieved through a design product [16]. Hong, Schaumann, and Kalay [6] describe the process as a set of iterations that students and professionals perform in order to accomplish a specific goal by continuous refinement. Technology can be used to increase the amount of information that the architects have while designing, improving their overall design process.

Technology solutions present several advantages to architectural professionals. For example, it aids them to search a broader range of solutions [4]; switch more frequently the focus between small scale and big scale [15]; while reducing the designing process complexity [3]. Similarly, simulations are also considered a valuable design resource for architects [6]. Furthermore, it has been discussed by previous research that simulations provide opportunities for students to handle 'trial-and-error' analysis and assess relations between the agents' properties and the environmental conditions [8]. Nevertheless, the simulation tools usage and its influence on the student design process still require further inquiry.

Østergård, Jensen, and Maagaard [16], for example, argues that it is still not entirely understood by practitioners and educators how simulation usage affects the standard architecture design process. The author adds that while simulation tools are widely used during the late design stages, there is a lack of simulation resources to aid early design phases, even though the initial design stage's central role on the entire proposal development is well known. The limitation of the simulation tools and its negative influence on the design assessment is also discussed by Lu et al. [10]. Also, the authors comment on the negative influence of the lack of standards for both simulation setups and results assessment.

3.3 Performance-Based Versus Aesthetic-Based Design

Architects must resolve complex design problems. Therefore, they are continually facing a complicated impasse about making decisions focusing on performance-based or aesthetic-based approaches to reach the optimal design solution [14]. As stated by Rittel [11], a professional architect should have the ability to systematically frame structural problems and iteratively test solutions until achieving satisfactory results. Iterations aim to modify the design goal or solution to maximize the consistency of the two design objectives. According to Shi and Yang [13], this match can be defined by a wide range of standards, for example, the building performance.

The architectural process focused on performance achievement has been increasingly engaging architects, engineers, and researchers. The performance-driven architectural design focus on the unified and extensive optimization of several measurable performances of buildings [13]. There is currently a rise in architectural modeling capacity and design-related software, prompting the architect's rational thinking. As a result, the process is focused on quantifying and evaluating how well solutions resolve the design constraints [13]. However, architects want to express their creativity in the projects they produce. Architects tend to reuse, explore, and enhance the technics and methods they are familiar with, leading to a specific pattern production spread over their project portfolio. Personal style and process also help to guide the design decisions throughout the architecture practice, having a relevant impact on the project essence and its result [16]. Therefore, designers use their artistic skills to help them experiment, create, and evaluate solutions as a process of returning to the central concept of the proposal, that is, it's essence [16].

Therefore, it is possible to identify two complementary facets of design production. One being performance-based [13] and the other being aesthetic based [3]. Usually, architects are expected to find the equilibrium between both aspects while designing [13]. Each design solution should embrace the designer's creative expression while being able to resolve and fulfill the design requirements and user needs, based on building performance.

Following the gradual introduction of simulation implementation on professional design practice and, especially, design education, there has been an increasing discussion about what is the simulation usage influence over the student design process and how does it affect the performance-based and aesthetic-based decisions [7, 10, 16]. The impact of tool usage on creative cognitive processes is an essential topic of study for cognitive science, design research, and design education [15]. According to Shi and Yang [13], simulations tend to focus on the technical aspects of the project. Therefore, better tools and methodologies of usage should be implemented, so the technological resources work in favor of architects' aesthetics decisions as well [3]. Following the previous results, this research will evaluate the influence of simulation usage within architecture students' design process, considering both the performance and aesthetic aspects of the design process.

4   Research Design

4.1   Methodology

We designed the experiment to assess to what extent architecture student's design strategies differ when using agent-based simulation tools or their usual architectural design tools. Twelve architecture design students, studying in South Korea and with corresponding background, participated in this research. The sample was made up of students who had been formally taught at least three years of architecture design at the university. The students were randomly divided into two groups, and each student participated in a two-session workshop when they were asked to fulfill a design task according to their assigned group for up to two and a half hours per session. The group division is based on the performance-based and aesthetic-based design process. Students in group 1 were asked to fulfill both of their design tasks focusing only on building optimal circulation performance, not their own insights as architects, while students in group 2 were given a chance to explore personal insights and develop a concept-based proposal (see Fig. 1). Similarly, to Stones and Cassidy [15], each group was expected to fulfill two design tasks.

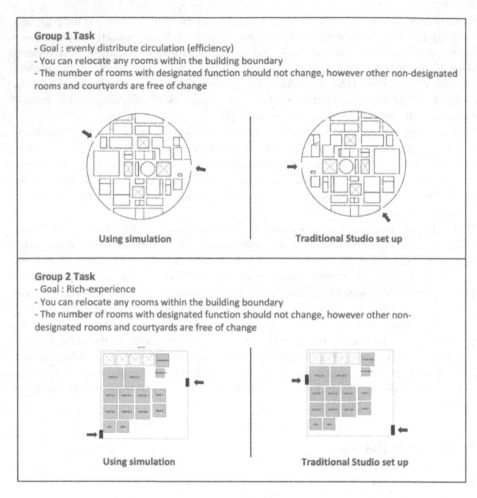

Fig. 1. A Floor plan according to each group

The tasks were designed to allow the authors to contrast results while reducing the external variables' influence on the analysis and limit as much as possible the learning effect from the first session to the second (see Fig. 1). The task sessions setups were divided according to the Stones and Cassidy [15] paper aiming to reduce the learning effect while maintaining the most similar context to promote reliable comparisons. Regardless of group or task, students were expected to redesign of the 21st-century museum of contemporary art, located in Kanazawa, Japan. The main goal of the task and group set up was analyzing how the simulation usage and performance focus constrains influenced the student design process. The main difference between the task sessions was the floor plan the students were given. During one of the workshop sessions, the learners only used the agent-based modeling simulation software to design and, on the other session, students did not use the agent-based modeling simulation tool, using their preferred design tools and receiving feedback from an Architecture Professor, refer to Stones and Cassidy [15].

The simulation tool chosen for this research is called Anylogic. Among all analyzed agent-based modeling tools, Anylogic provided the simpler editing methods with the best robustness for student usage while making it possible for the authors to maintain control over the agent's behavior set up, (see Fig. 2). The agents' movement patterns were defined together with the Architecture Professor who evaluated the students' design during the traditional studio setup.

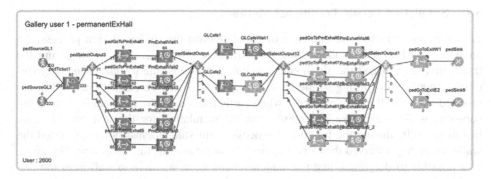

Fig. 2. User behavior design using Analogic software

Workshop. Before the workshop, students took a pretest questionnaire to assess their background. Following, they were randomly assigned to groups 1 and 2. After that, a two-session workshop was carried out. In the first session, they asked to fulfill a design task by using their preferred design tool and received feedback from the professor or using the simulation tool only. In the case of simulation usage, during the first 45 min of the session, the students were given orientations about their respective tasks as well as the Anylogic software features, followed by a 15 min practice using a sample Anylogic file designed by the research team. After that, students started recording their screens and produced their own proposals, according to their group designation, either circulation-focused design or concept-based design. In the case of the traditional studio setup, the architecture professor was always available to assist the students. All participants fulfilled both methods, simulation usage, and professor feedback, on either the first or second session, according to a random assignment. Finally, all students answered a post-test questionnaire regarding their perspective about the simulation software and their general experience with the workshop. Afterward, the screen recordings were briefly analyzed, aiming to identify relevant individual design process features or further insights that would be discussed over the individual interview section carried out with all research participants. Each interview lasted up to 60 min. The interview covered the student perspective about their design processes on both workshop scenarios, using the simulation tool, and not using it.

The data collection was done by recording each subjects' computer screen, done during both workshop sessions. Also, the interview transcripts were assessed. Research subjects were asked to fill out a questionnaire after the experiment. The questions were based on previously described usability scales to identify the software usability limitations, in addition to the assessment of perceived usefulness, and perceived ease of use, variables that influence user acceptance [2].

5   Results

5.1   Simulation versus Traditional Methods

In order to understand the influence of simulation on the student design process, the analysis was focused on identifying the differences in student processes during the traditional session and the simulation session. It was possible to find changes in students' approach according to the session (see Figs. 3 and 4). Firstly, the walls were inserted earlier in the design process when participants used the simulation. Among the subjects, while only three individuals ran the simulation for the first time without inserting walls, during the traditional process, eight students had not yet inserted the walls when they received their first feedback from the architecture professor. Therefore, it is possible to determine that the students were more attentive to wall insertion and positioning during the session that included the simulation tool. The action for including walls is marked as the light-yellow color, and the action of wall transformation is signed as dark yellow (see Figs. 3 and 4). It is possible to notice that most students in the traditional process performed those two actions at the very end of their design process, and one student did not insert walls. As a result, there was very little time for walls consideration, and fewer wall transformations were made. On the other hand, observing the simulation session result, it is possible to see that most wall insertions and transformations were done earlier in the process. For this reason, students had more wall transformation actions in this session.

Simulations were a useful tool to promote more design interactions on a student's process if compared to professor feedback. Simulations were carried out several times, while professor feedback happened mostly one time during the entire session. During the simulation usage scenario, after visualizing the simulation results, students would proceed to design changes and a new simulation run. Hong, Schaumann, and Kalay [6] also indicated that human behavior simulation was useful for iterating solutions to develop prototypes to masterplans and specify master plans to details. However, during the traditional process, the professor's feedback would lead to similar design changes, the major difference is that students did not proactively seek a following up design evaluation from the professor after the first changes. Therefore, during the entire session, most students had their design evaluated only once, when the professor approached them.

Task type	Subject	Design Action											
Task 01 - Circulation	Subject 01				Copy existing design	Insert space	Change position	Change shape	Prof Feedback	After feedback change position	After feedback change shape	Add wall	Transf wall
	Subject 02			Insert space	Change shape	Change position	Insert courtyard	Group according to functions / symmetry	Prof Feedback	After feedback change position	After feedback change shape	Hand sketching	
	Subject 03					Insert space	Copy existing design	Prof Feedback	After feedback change position	After feedback change shape	Add wall	Transf wall	
	Subject 04	Copy existing design	Insert space	Change position	Change space	Insert courtyard	Add wall	Transf wall	Prof Feedback	After feedback change position	After feedback change shape	Group according to functions / symmetry	
	Subject 09	Copy existing design	Group according to functions / symmetry	Hand sketching	Insert space	Change position	Change shape	Add wall	Prof Feedback	After feedback change position	After feedback change shape	Transf wall	Insert courtyard
	Subject 10		Insert space	Change position	Change shape	Insert courtyard	Group according to functions / symmetry	Prof Feedback	After feedback change position	After feedback change shape	Add wall	Transf wall	After feedback start over
Task 02 - Rich Design	Subject 05		Insert space	Change position	Group according to functions / symmetry	Insert courtyard	Add wall	Start over	Prof Feedback	After feedback change position	After feedback change shape	After feedback start over	
	Subject 06		Insert space	Change position	Change shape	Copy existing design	Insert courtyard	Prof Feedback	After feedback change position	After feedback change shape	Add wall	Transf wall	
	Subject 07	Insert space	Insert courtyard	Delete space	Change position	Change shape	Add wall	Group according to functions / symmetry	Prof Feedback	After feedback change position	Transf wall	After feedback change shape	
	Subject 08		Change position	Insert courtyard	Change shape	Insert space	Start over	Group according to functions / symmetry	Prof Feedback	Hand sketching	After feedback change position	Add wall	Transf wall	After feedback change shape
	Subject 11	Insert space	Change positon	Change shape	Start over	Hand sketching	Insert courtyard	Copy existing deisng	Prof Feedback	After feedback change position	After feedback change shape	Add wall	Transf wall
	Subject 12		Insert space	Change position	Insert courtyard	Group according to functions / symmetry	Change shape	After feedback change position	After feedback change shape	Add wall			

Fig. 3. Student design pattern while using traditional design methods (Color figure online)

Task type	Subject	Design Action											
Task 01 - Circulation	Subject 01		Insert space	Add wall	Transf wall	Change position	Change Shape	Insert courtyard	Run Simu 13x	Technical Issues	After Simu Change position	After Simu Change shape	
	Subject 02					Insert space	Change position	Change shape	Add wall	Run Simu 4x	After Simu Change position	After Simu Change shape	Insert courtyard	Transf wall
	Subject 03	Insert space	Change position	Insert courtyard	Change Shape	Group according to functions / symmetry	Add wall	Transf wall	Run Simu 6x	After Simu Change position	After Simu Change shape	Technical issues	
	Subject 04	Insert space	Change position	Delete space	Group according to functions / symmetry	Change Shap	Technical issues	Insert courtyard	Run Simu 7x	After Simu Change position	Add wall	After Simu Change shape	
	Subject 09		Insert space	Add wall	Transf wall	Change position	Change Shape	Insert courtyard	Run Simu 11x	Technical issues	After Simu Change position	After Simu Change shape	
	Subject 10					Insert space	Insert courtyard	Change position	Run Simu 6x	After Simu Change position	After Simu Change shape	Add wall	Transf wall
Task 02 - Rich Design	Subject 05		Insert space	Change position	Insert courtyard	Change Shape	Add wall	Transf wall	Run Simu 2x	After Simu Change position	After Simu Change shape		
	Subject 06			Insert space	Change position	Change Shape	Insert courtyard	Technical issues	Run Simu 14x	After Simu Change position	After Simu Change shape	Add wall	Group according to functions / symmetry
	Subject 07		Insert space	Change position	Insert courtyard	Change Shape	Add wall	Transf wall	Run Simu 5x	After Simu Change shap			
	Subject 08	Insert space	Group according to functions / symmetry	Change position	Insert courtyard	Change Shape	Add wall	Transf wall	Run Simu 3x	Technical issues	After Simu Change position	After Simu Change shape	
	Subject 11		Insert space	Change position	Change Shape	Insert courtyard	Add wall	Transf wall	Run Simu 1x	Technical issues			

Fig. 4. Student design patter while using simulation tool (Color figure online)

Finally, while using the traditional method, the students constantly referred to the original museum design reference material, and half of the participants replicated parts of the existing design without any changes. Contrarily, during the simulation session, students developed their solutions, including those who replicated during the traditional setup. Demonstrating that the simulation tool was effective in increasing student's careful consideration of design development and increased their creativity to develop original proposals. In other words, simulation increased student creativity and the ability to analyze the task and propose an appropriate original solution critically.

5.2   Individual Design Process

From the students' design process individual analysis, it was possible to reach two main results. Students claimed in interviews that often, the user circulation is not considered in the early design or not considered at all during their architectural proposals design. During their usual design process, students can only guess how the relationship between the design and the user behavior will occur. For this reason, they could visualize previously unexpected user behavior and possible pain points through the simulation result, leading to more accurate identification of user circulation patterns and their proposal suitability. The second identified result is that students would benefit better from the simulation result if the tool was introduced after the design concept establishment. The lack of experience the students have with such a tool that leads them to consider the simulation suited for assessing the performance of design proposals rather than a conceptual design improvement tool. Students from the performance-based group were more willing to change their design according to a performance result, while the concept based group of students were more conservative with their changes after seeing the simulation results. Therefore, the simulation results will help students improve their proposals in terms of performance after the main concepts have already been established. The reason for research subjects to consider that simulation is more appropriate as a proof tool than a design improvement tool is caused mainly by the fear that the simulation result will affect or modify their design proposals' concept. Several research subjects described that they feared the final proposal would lose their conceived concept or idea due to adjustments to the simulation result. The fear of excessive influence from the simulation tool on design causes the students to have resistance towards the tool, especially within the early design phases.

5.3   Performance-Focused versus Aesthetic-Focused Design

It was possible to identify some differences in the design process aspects of the research subjects on group 1, whose design process was focused specifically on circulation and research subjects on group 2, focused on a strong individual design concept. According to the results, students doing task 1, did major changes in design after the simulation results. As a result, their design ideas were different from the beginning of the process until the final proposal. On the other hand, the students assigned to task 2 tried to maintain their major design concept throughout the simulation results, leading them to adjust the design according to the simulation results avoiding making substantial changes to the design. The students considered the simulation tool excessively focused on performance, making them feel protective over their design because they feared that the results would become too different if they focused only on the simulation result.

6 Discussion

The simulation usage has changed the student design process. Therefore, the experiment result provided interesting insights on how that change occurred and the reasons for it. The first relevant difference is the fact that students did fewer design explorations on the traditional session than on simulation sessions. During the simulation usage method, there was no replica action identified, while we found several copying actions during the traditional setup method. During the simulation method, the students carried out a diverse range of design analysis. The student seemed more flexible to experiment design major changes. For that reason, it is possible to assume that the simulation stimulated creativity in students and opened them to design explorations further if compared to the traditional process. The second aspect highlighted in the results was the fact that simulation stimulated students to explore detailed design, especially the location of walls and doors, early in the design process. During the traditional session, students would insert doors and walls at the very end of the design process. The late insertion left little or no time to modify doors and walls during the process before the proposal submission. During the simulation session, the students inserted walls and doors before running the first simulation, usually during the middle of the session scheduled timeline. For this reason, during the simulation session, research subjects did more explorations with walls and door positioning.

7 Conclusion

It was already called out from researches the need to improve the students' creative process when designing [3]. While most research focused on student usage of currently widely available computer-aided design [6] or architects' universal design process [16]. In this research, the focus was mainly on how agent-based modeling simulation usage would influence the architecture students' design process. The simulation usage changed the student process, and the experiment result provided interesting insights on how that changed occurred and the reasons behind it. There were three main aspects highlighted in the results. The first one is the fact that while using a simulation tool, the students tend to explore more design ideas if compared to the traditional setup. Besides, simulation appears to influence early consideration of small-scale design, mainly wall and door positioning. Finally, students' fear the excessive influence from simulation results, and the usage resistance consequently was also visualized through the results.

The Agent-based simulations should be introduced in the architecture design degree curriculum as a potent tool to support the design process. At first, it should be introduced as a verification tool for design proposals. After the technology is adapted into the design process, its introduction should be moved to earlier usage. In other words, from a performance verification tool to a design improvement tool. It is also critical to increase the integration between platforms to avoid unnecessary repetitions within the design process. That is, agent simulation assessment tools should be available for the students in a seamless way. This solution is expected to reduce the student burden when running the simulations, increase the cycles within the design process, and reduce design process interruptions. Following the increase in usability and ease of use, the cycles of the simulation run and design adjustments should increase, leading to more suitable overall design solutions.

Acknowledgments. This research was supported by Basic Science Research Program through the National Research Foundation of Korea (NRF) funded by the Ministry of Education (NRF-2017M3C1A6075018).

References

1. Bilda, Z., Demirkan, H.: An insight on designers' sketching activities in traditional versus digital media. Des. Stud. **24**(1), 27–50 (2003)
2. Davis, F.D.: Perceived usefulness, perceived ease of use, and user acceptance of information technology. MIS Q. **13**(3), 319–340 (2019)
3. Dickson, P.P., Pendidikan, F., Malysia, U.K., Perguruan, U., Idris, S.: The effects of integrating mobile and cad technology in teaching design process for Malaysian polytechnic. Turk. Online J. Educ. Technol. **9**(4), 162–173 (2010)
4. Dong, W., Gibson, K.R.: Computer Visualization: An Integrated Approach for Interior Design and Architecture, 1st edn. McGraw-Hill Education Group, New York (1998)
5. Fonseca, D., Martí, N., Redondo, E., Navarro, I., Sánchez, A.: Relationship between student profile, tool use, participation, and academic performance with the use of Augmented Reality technology for visualized architecture models. Comput. Hum. Behav. **31**(1), 434–445 (2014)
6. Hong, S.W., Schaumann, D., Kalay, Y.E.: Human behavior simulation in architectural design projects: an observational study in an academic course. Comput. Environ. Urban Syst. **60**, 1–11 (2016)
7. Hong, S.W., Lee, Y.G.: The effects of human behavior simulation on architecture major students' fire egress planning. J. Asian Archit. Build. Eng. **17**(1), 125–132 (2018)
8. Kalay, Y.E., Irazàbal, C.E.: Virtual users (VUsers): auto animated human-forms for representation and evaluation of behavior in designed environment. Technical report, Berkeley: University of California (1995)
9. Liang, Y., Yuan, Z.: Assignment performance at Beijing South Railway Station based on Anylogic simulation. Adv. Mater. Res. **989–994**, 2283–2287 (2014)
10. Lu, Y., Wu, Z., Chang, R., Li, Y.: Automation in construction Building Information Modeling (BIM) for green buildings: a critical review and future directions. Autom. Constr. **83**, 134–148 (2017)
11. Rittel, H.: Some principles for the design of an educational system for design. J. Archit. Educ. **25**(1–2), 16–27 (1971)
12. Rogers, D.: A paradigm shift: technology integration for higher education in the new millennium. Educ. Technol. Rev. **1**(13), 19–33 (2000)
13. Shi, X., Yang, W.: Performance-driven architectural design and optimization technique from a perspective of architects. Autom. Constr. **32**, 125–135 (2013)
14. Rittel, H.W.J., Webber, M.M.: Dilemmas in a general theory of planning. Policy Sci. **4**, 155–169 (1973)
15. Stones, C., Cassidy, T.: Comparing synthesis strategies of novice graphic designers using digital and traditional design tools. Des. Stud. **28**(1), 59–72 (2007)
16. Østergård, T., Jensen, R.L., Maagaard, S.E.: Building simulations supporting decision making in early design – a review. Des. Stud. **61**, 187–201 (2016)

Proposal of a Training Method for Beat Count Ability

Kazuhiro Minami[1]([⊠]), Takayoshi Kitamura[2], Tomoko Izumi[2],
and Yoshio Nakatani[3]

[1] Graduate School of Information Science and Technology,
Ritsumeikan University, 1-1-1 Noji-Higashi, Kusatsu, Shiga 525-8577, Japan
kzuw5133@gmail.com
[2] Collage of Information and Science and Technology,
1-1-1 Noji-Higashi, Kusatsu, Shiga 525-8577, Japan
{ktmr, izumi-t}@fc.ritsumei.ac.jp
[3] Ritsumeikan Trust, 1 Nishinokyo-Suzaku-cho,
Nakagyo-ku, Kyoto 604-8520, Japan
nakatani@is.ritsumei.ac.jp

Abstract. There are several different musical abilities, and previous researchers have developed various tests to measure them. For disc jockeys (DJs), the ability to find changing points in phrases and melodies while listening to music is essential because they need to find these points for mixing two songs. Herein, we have defined this ability as "beat count ability." Beat count ability is not well known, and no proper training methods exist. Therefore, we propose a training method for the improvement of the beat count ability to enhance basic mixing skills of beginner DJs. There are three training steps in the method, and the users learn about beat count ability by watching learning videos and answering confirmation questions. We conducted an experiment with five participants who had no prior musical experience. As a result, our proposed training method was shown to improve their beat count ability.

Keywords: Music · Disc jockey · Beat count ability

1 Introduction

Disc Jockeys (DJs) usually select and mix songs by using two or more devices to keep a good mood in a night club. They always count beats and bars of songs and find the changing points of the melody and the phrase to achieve a smooth transition between two songs during their performances. Therefore, the ability to find the changing points of melodies and grasp the structure of songs by counting beats and bars correctly is important for DJs. Most released songs follow the 4/4-time signature and change their melody only every even bar. In most cases, songs change their melody in 8 bar spans. DJs can predict the next changing point by finding previous ones while listening to the music.

We defined the ability to predict changing points as "beat count ability," and developed a measurement test which can measure whether people have this ability and the extent of their ability [1]. In some of the experiments we conducted, we found that

© Springer Nature Switzerland AG 2020
P. Zaphiris and A. Ioannou (Eds.): HCII 2020, LNCS 12205, pp. 121–131, 2020.
https://doi.org/10.1007/978-3-030-50513-4_9

participants who have musical experience do not always have a high beat count ability. In addition, participants who have musical experience in performing according to beats, such as DJs or dancers, tend to have a higher beat count ability than participants with other musical experiences. Considering these results, beat count ability differs significantly from other musical abilities. Furthermore, it is difficult to acquire beat count ability, unless one repeatedly listens to music while paying attention to beats and changing melodies. However, most beginner DJs need to teach themselves because of the low number of DJs. Additionally, beat count ability is not generally counted as a musical ability, and there is no proper training method.

In this paper, we propose a training method to improve personal beat count ability. We extract the elements which are considered to be effective for training from popular DJ software. Based on them, we produce learning videos and implement three steps into our training method. We taught the training method to five participants who had no prior musical experience and evaluated the results by using beat count ability measurement tests developed in our previous work. In this study, we show the possibility that the proposed training method can improve a user's beat count ability, thereby making it possible to find the changing points of melodies even in complex songs, and that the improvements in this ability are sustained.

2   Related Research

There are various musical abilities, such as an ability to distinguish pitch, sound strength and rhythms, and an ability to memorize sounds. Several tests have been developed to measure these abilities [2], and there have been numerous attempts to improve those abilities using information technology. Goto determined various kinds of approaches using Music Information Processing [3], and he mentioned that the following two classifications are especially important [4].

- "for professionals" and "for amateurs"
- "fully automatic" and "semi-automatic"

The following section details these approaches.

2.1   Research on Ability Acquisition for Beginners and Experts in Music

One of the attempts of "for amateurs" is to support training to acquire some musical abilities. Rizqyawan et al. [5] proposed a training system for a child to achieve relative pitch and learn the pitch of a piece of music correctly. They mentioned that one of the problems with learning music theory is boredom; therefore, they developed a system which allows children to enjoy the learning process by introducing challenge elements, such as in a game. It could improve a user's musical abilities in terms of pitch. This result shows that it may be effective to integrate some gaming elements, so to present learning material but also promote the correct answers to questions in a training system for the improvement of musical ability.

Furthermore, regarding an attempt "for professionals", Tomibayashi et al. [6] proposed a new style of DJing connecting gesture movements by using wearable sensors so as to improve DJing, when there is only a small space available and therefore make it more flexible. In the case of DJs, any attempt to assist beginners in acquiring specific skills are not found; however, research and product development for professionals has been conducted. This differs to attempts for the development of teaching systems for popular instruments such as guitar and the piano, which also exist for beginners.

Our research supports beginner DJs in acquiring beat count abilities. This goal is different from existing studies which are aimed at supporting expert DJs. This is contrary to other musical abilities, as there are numerous attempts to support users in acquiring basic musical abilities, yet no one supports the training of beat count ability.

2.2   Research to Fully Automate Professional Performances

Automatic track making and performance are common examples of attempts of "fully automatic" and "semi-automatic" music information processing. Ishisaki et al. [7] proposed a DJ mixing system which automatically matches the tempo and timing of the beats of two songs to connect them continuously. They defined individual indices of listener discomfort and used it to evaluate the results of their experiments. As a result, the automatic DJ mixing system is more comfortable for listeners than any other existing system. There have been several attempts to reproduce professional performances using systems similar to the one aforedescribed; however, there have been no attempts to provide assistance to beginner DJs in acquiring the basic skills necessary for DJ mixing.

Attempts to support skill training and those to automate the performances of professionals are completely different; one enables users "to become able to play the instrument", and the other enables users to "experience the situation wherein they can play the instrument like professional". For acquiring basic DJ mixing skills, it is essential to support users in acquiring beat count ability. Further, a large amount of the existing research investigates major musical abilities such as pitch and rhythm. Moreover, attempts to improve musical abilities are important, especially in the period from early childhood to the lower grades of elementary school, and several attempts set their targets to those age groups [2]. We propose that beat count ability can be acquired at any age because there are cases of people who did not originally have any musical experience and subsequently learned the skills necessary for being a DJ. This study aims at acquiring beat count ability and proposes a training method which incorporates challenging elements such as requiring that users answer some questions after learning.

3   Training Method for Beat Count Ability

As mentioned in Sect. 1, we confirmed that musical experience such as that of DJs and dancers may be related to a high beat count ability. It is thought that listening to music while paying attention to beats and bars is related to acquiring beat count ability. Therefore, we introduce three steps to our training process and confirmation questions, and users work on only one process per day. As the user progresses through the steps, we try to improve a user's ability by gradually reducing the information which was given initially to help them answer questions.

3.1   Information to Help Users Learn Beat Count Ability

Information which helps users to accurately understand the relationship between counting beats and changes in melody are waveform, counts of beats and bars, and the sound source. In our proposed training method, this information is presented to users. Several DJ software recently available have implemented the waveform of songs and display the bars by numbers [8]. That shows these elements are effective to help DJ mixing, so we decided to use these elements in our training method.

3.2   Training Procedure

Our training method consists of three training steps: Step 1, Step 2, and Step 3. Users work on only one step per day. For all steps a web system is used, and we explain the outline of the system and the training contents in this section.

Each training step contains five learning videos and five confirmation questions. Figure 1 shows the form of the confirmation questions. A song is played starting in the middle of a song at the time a user presses the "PLAY" button; subsequently, the user answers the question by pressing the "HIT" button at the time of the change in melody of the song. The user answers the confirmation questions after watching several learning videos. He/she proceeds to the next step on the next day if he/she can correctly answer a certain number of questions but has to repeat the same step the next day if they cannot.

Furthermore, learning videos and confirmation questions use one song from each of the five patterns shown in Table 1. These patterns are chosen based on the results of our previous work on developing a beat count ability measurement test. The results show that the difficulty in finding the changing points of songs differs depending on these music patterns. While the five songs used in the videos and confirmation questions of one step use the same pattern, the songs are different for each step. In a conformation question phase in each step, users listen to the same songs from the same start positions as to the ones they listen to in the learning video phase, i.e., the correct positions to be answered are the same in the both phases.

Figure 2 shows examples of learning videos of each step. The details of the learning videos used in each step are described below:

Fig. 1. The page of confirmation questions.

Table 1. The 5 track patterns of the beat count ability measurement test

	Pattern description
1	Big change from phrase to phrase
2	Low correct answer rate in previous cycle
3	Small change, complicated phrases
4	Small change, instruments with vocal
5	Low BPM (stands for Beat Par Minutes)

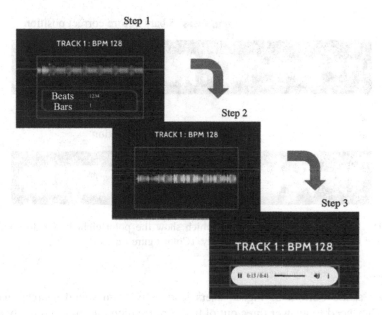

Fig. 2. The learning videos of each step

- Step 1

The top picture shown in Fig. 2 shows the learning videos in Step 1, which are composed of waveforms, count of beats and bars and sound sources. As shown in Fig. 3, a blue mark marks the point eight bars before the correct position and a yellow mark shows the correct position. Users understand the relation between the number of bars and the change of melody by referring to these marks. Step 1 is the most basic step of our training method; therefore, users need to give correct answers to all five confirmation questions to proceed to Step 2.

- Step 2

As shown the middle of Fig. 2, the learning videos in Step 2 are composed waveforms and sound sources without a display of the counts of beats and bars. Users need to predict the next changing point from these elements. The procedure of training is the same as in Step 1, users answer confirmation questions after watching a sufficient number of learning videos. In addition, the waveform contains a blue mark and a yellow mark, same as in Step 1. In Step 2, users need to answer three out of five confirmation questions correctly to proceed to Step 3. In an experiment we conducted in a previous study about developing tests, 19 participants, who have no prior musical experience answered five questions which were the same as the confirmation questions in this experiment, and the average number of their correct answers was two. So, considering the training effect of our method, we decided to set three correct answers as the criteria to proceed to the next step.

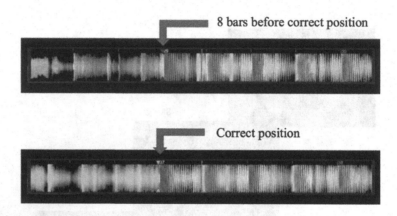

Fig. 3. The blue mark and yellow mark which show the point eight bars before the correct position and the correct position, respectively. (Color figure online)

- Step 3

As shown at the bottom of Fig. 2, users learn only from sound sources instead of videos. They need to answer three out of five confirmation questions correctly to finish the training.

4   Experiment

We conducted an experiment to confirm the extent of the improvement of the beat count ability of the participants due to our training. The results are described in this section.

4.1   Evaluation of the Training Effect

We divided the 40 questions of the beat count ability measurement test in half and defined each set as a "pre-test" (i.e., test before training) and an "after-test" (i.e., test after training), dependent on the participant group. Participants took these tests, and we evaluated the training method by confirming a change in the scores of each test of a participant. Both tests were conducted on another day to the training in the experiment.

To produce two tests with the same level of difficulty, we referred to the results of the experiments we conducted on 44 participants [1], when we developed the beat count ability measurement test. In addition, the patterns of songs used in both tests are the same as the five patterns used in the beat count ability measurement test. The same number of songs of each pattern are used in both tests. The details of these two tests are described below.

- Pre-test

Participants took a test composed of 20 questions to measure their beat count ability before participating in our training. The pre-test was composed of five songs of the categories "big change from phrase to phrase", five songs of "low correct answer rate in previous experiment", two songs of "small change, complicated phrase", three songs of "small change, instruments with vocal" and five songs of "low BPM", as listed in Table 1. The form of the questions and answers are the same for both the confirmation questions and the training steps.

- After-test

Participants took a test consisting of another 20 questions after training. The after-test is composed of five songs of the categories of "big change from phrase to phrase", five songs of "low correct answer rate in previous experiment", three songs of "small change, complicated phrase", two songs of "small change, instruments with vocal" and five songs of "low BPM", as listed in Table 1.

4.2   Participants and Experimental Procedure

Five participants with no prior musical experience used our training method in this experiment, and we evaluated its training effect. We define those who have no musical experience other than a school education as inexperienced participants. The participants worked on the training starting with the pre-test to the after-test by themselves, each day. At the end of Steps 1, 2, and 3, we conducted confirmation questions and judge whether they fulfilled the requirements of each step and could proceed to the next step. Then we conducted an interview to ask them the five items described below.

- On which points did the participant place emphasis when watching a learning video?
- How many times did a participant watch each video?
- How often did a participant listen to music between training steps?
- Did the participant try to count beats and bars when listening to music in their daily lives?
- Which patterns of songs did the participant find difficult?

We conducted the after-test again three weeks after the end of the training to check whether the training effect was temporary (referred to as "three weeks later test" hereafter).

4.3   Results

Figure 4 shows the results of the experiment to gauge the effects of our training method. All five participants could answer between three to ten more questions correctly than in the pre-test. This shows that our training method can improve a participant's beat count ability, and the effect remains until at least one day after. Here, we describe the results of the three weeks later test, which was conducted to gauge whether any changes in their ability were temporary. Comparing the test scores of the after-test and the three weeks later test, the difference in correct answers of each participant is within 2, so we can confirm almost the same results even three weeks after completion of our training. In addition, we check the number of questions, to which the answer given did not change between the after-test and the three weeks later test in order to accurately grasp the number of answers given based on ability of the participants, and discount answers given by intuition. As a result, we can confirm 70% or more answers remain the same in both tests for all participants. The correct answers extracted from the results are shown as "fixed" in Fig. 4. It shows that four out of five participants can answer more questions correctly than in the pre-test, and one participant answered the same number of questions correctly as in the pre-test. That shows the possibility that our training method can improve a participant's beat count ability and that the improvement in ability is sustained for a certain period of time.

Here, we describe the results from the viewpoint of the number of correct answers given to difficult questions. We define the questions which less than half of the participants could answer correctly in our previous experiment [1] as "difficult questions". There are nine difficult questions in the pre-test, and eight in the after-test. Table 2 shows the number of participants who answered the difficult questions correctly in the pre-test and the after-test. As a result of our training, four out of five participants could correctly answer three or four more difficult questions as compared with the pre-test. That confirms the possibility that participants who have no prior musical experience can learn to count beats and listen to the changing points of melodies of complicated songs by participating in our training.

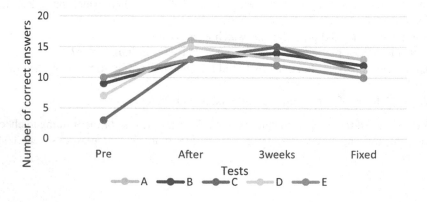

Fig. 4. The number of correct answers of each participant of each test

Table 2. The change of the number of correct answers to difficult questions of each participant

	A	B	C	D	E
Pre-test	2	3	1	1	3
After-test	5	6	4	5	3

4.4   Consideration

From the results of the pre-test and the after-test, we could confirm that our training method can improve a participant's beat count ability and that this improvement is sustained for a certain period of time. In addition, since the number of correct answers to difficult questions increased, our training method teaches participants to count beats and listen to the changes in melodies even of complicated songs. Subsequently, we considered which factors in the training improve a participant's ability based on the interview responses.

As a result of the interview, we found that although all participants listened to music during the training for an average of 30 min to one hour a day, no participant tried to count beats and bars during their daily listening. This shows that the possibility of improving of a participant's beat count ability is influenced only by the effects of our training.

Table 3 shows the number of viewings of learning videos and sound sources at each step of each participant. No relationship was found between this result and a change in the number of correct answers in the pre-test and after-test of each participant. We assume that each participant originally has a different sense of music and attitude toward learning something; hence, the viewing activities are not related with the test scores of a participant. Hence, we consider the difference between participant C with the highest increase in the number of correct answers and participant E with the least increase between pre-test and after-test by focusing on the points which each participant placed emphasis on when watching the learning video.

First, in Step 1, participant C watched the point at eight bars before the correct position carefully (blue mark, the point participants have to start counting) in the learning videos. C responded to the question we asked about them trying to count beats and bars by grasping the point participants have to start counting, and confirmed whether the counting was correct by referring to the count of the beats and bars displayed in the learning videos. C correctly answered all five confirmation questions the first time. In contrast, participant E tried to remember the point of the correct position (yellow mark, the point participants have to press the "HIT" button). As a result, E answered correctly only two out of five questions, so E took the same step the next day again. In Step 2, C could correctly answer four questions and E could correctly answer three questions. The point both participants placed emphasis on is the point participants need to start counting. In Step 3, C could correctly answer four questions and E could correctly answer three questions. C tried to adjust the rhythm of counting by comparing the speed between a song C likes and the song used in the questions. E used the sound sources just for preparation for answering the confirmation questions. As a result, C could correctly answer ten more questions in the after-test

Table 3. The number of viewing activities of each step of the participants

	A	B	C	D	E
Step 1	28	17	16	15	20
Step 2	37	6	10	7	21
Step 3	31	5	9	5	23

compared to the pre-test, while E could correctly answer only three more questions. Considering the points made above, in case of the participants C and E, their way of learning in Step 2 and 3 is almost the same, so the most important difference is the way of learning in Step 1. E tried to remember the correct position, while C tried to count by oneself. We assume that was the reason for the difference in results of both participants.

Furthermore, in another case, participant A watched the learning videos as many times as participant E; however, A could correctly answer six more questions in the after-test compared with the pre-test. Many songs have a feature which was in before changes melody. For example, drum patterns change slightly from simple 8 beats and so on. A grasped the feature when A learned in Step 1 and 2. We assume that this way of learning was the cause of the improvement in A's ability.

5   Conclusion

We conducted this experiment to evaluate and proposed a training method to improve beat count ability. Five participants used our training method, and we evaluated the effects of our training method by using the beat count ability measurement test. In addition, we conducted the test again three weeks after their training to confirm whether the effect of our training method was temporary. As a result, four out of five participants could correctly answer more questions in the after-test as compared with the pre-test. This shows that our training method can improve a user's beat count ability and the improvement is sustained for at least three weeks.

In the future, we will investigate whether people can improve their DJ mixing if they can improve their beat count ability. The research on whether improving the beat count ability is effective in improving the playing of instruments is also a possible future work.

References

1. Minami, K., Kitamura, T., Izumi, T., Nakatani, Y.: Proposal of a beat count ability measurement for learning DJ mixing. In: IEEE 8th Global Conference on Consumer Electronics, pp. 35–39 (2019)
2. Hasegawa, K.: A point of view on teaching materials for early childhood care and education: developing a sense of pitch and harmony in children on the basis of the results of musical ability diagnostic test. Bull. Jr. Coll. Shutoku **48**, 137–153 (2009)
3. Goto, M.: Music informatics. Jouhoushori (IPSJ Mag.) **51**(6), 661–668 (2010). (in Japanese)

4. Goto, M.: Future music informatics. IPSJ SIG Tech. Rep. **2013-MUS-99**(33), 1–9 (2013). (in Japanese)
5. Rizqyawan, M., Hemawan, G.: Adventure game as learning media for introducing music interval and ear training to kids. In: 2015 International Conference on Automation, Cognitive Science, Optics, Micro Electro-Mechanical System, and Information Technology (ICACO-MIT) (2015)
6. Tomibayashi, Y., Takekawa, Y., Terada, T., Tsukamoto, M.: Development and actual use of a wearable DJ system using wearable sensors. IPSJ SIG Techn. Rep. **76**, 39–44 (2008)
7. Ishisaki, H., Hotate, K., Takishima, Y.: Automatic DJ mixing system based on measurement function of user discomfort on music. IPSJ Trans. **52**(2), 890–900 (2011)
8. Serato: Serato DJ Pro. https://serato.com/dj. Accessed 20 Dec 2019

A Real-Time Remote Courses Model for the Improvement of the Overall Learning Experience

Martha Elena Nuñez[1]([⊠]) [iD] and Miguel X. Rodriguez-Paz[2] [iD]

[1] Escuela de Arquitectura, Arte y Diseño, Tecnologico de Monterrey,
72453 Puebla, Mexico
martha.nunez@tec.mx
[2] Escuela de Ingeniería y Ciencias, Tecnologico de Monterrey,
72453 Puebla, Mexico
rodriguez.miguel@tec.mx

Abstract. The presence of International professors in any faculty enriches the overall experience of the students and provides students different point of views in the subjects they learn. Sometimes it is not possible for a university to have more international faculty members because of many factors, including financial resources. In this work we present a model that introduces students to international professors in real-time via video conference. This model has proven to be very useful in our university as professors are able to teach a group of students in a campus located in the Southern Region of Mexico while being in their own countries. Professors from Japan, Europe and North America have taken part of this implementation in the last few semesters and the results on student satisfaction are shown in this work. The model presented in this work uses a real-time remote teaching scheme, supported by on-campus IT resources that are available in any lecture room of our university so no investment was needed for new hardware, in order to implement our model. The model allows students to develop and strengthen their digital and communication competencies as the courses taught in this model uses technology as a learning tool.

Keywords: Educational innovation · Higher education · Remote teaching · Student satisfaction · International professors · Competency-based education

1 Introduction

Remote teaching is an alternative to traditional teaching where communication between the students and the professor is direct in real time [1]. This paper is a sequel of a previous work, which takes as reference our University's PEV program that was implemented in recent years in order to be able to invite foreign visitor professors to Mexico for one year. In the previous work, it was established that one way to get more benefits from the program is to invite them to give distance classes once their presence year in Mexico has ended [2]. The current work adds the measurement of transversal competencies that are part of the university's new educational model.

Tecnologico de Monterrey has recently implemented a new Educational Model, established as a key foundation of the university's strategic plan 2030. A process of

© Springer Nature Switzerland AG 2020
P. Zaphiris and A. Ioannou (Eds.): HCII 2020, LNCS 12205, pp. 132–143, 2020.
https://doi.org/10.1007/978-3-030-50513-4_10

renewing the curriculum began in 2014 and in 2017 a team of professors from different campuses was formed in order to design the 2019 study plan, with the premise that acquiring knowledge is not enough, but to learn experientially and master the competencies demanded by the 21st century [3].

One of the main differences between the new curriculum and previous curricula, lies in the new curriculum's use of methods of learning and evaluation based on competencies. In the new educational model there are two types of skills to be developed by the students:

1. Disciplines (typical of each professional area).
2. Transversals (common and equally valuable for all professions): 1. Self-knowledge and management. 2. Innovative Entrepreneurship. 3. Social intelligence. 4. Ethics and citizenship. 5. Reasoning for complexity. 6. Communication. 7. Digital transformation [3].

The new curricula started to be offered in August 2019, but the students that are currently coursing the third to the nineth semester are still enrolled in the previous curricula. The model presented in this work takes advantage of the previously described PEV program and introduces the measurement of two transversal competencies from the new educational model into courses that belong to the previous curricula. The aim is to develop the communication competences of students in the use of digital skills as the courses taught in this model uses technology as a learning tool.

The two transversal competencies that where measured in these courses are for the purpose of this study are:

- Communication: Using native language well orally and in writing. In addition to being efficient in presenting an idea and mastering other languages.
- Digital transformation: Using technology to potentiate and make processes more efficient [3].

This study proposes that competency-based education can contribute in providing an important teaching and learning strategy in the context of the new educational model, as competency-based education permits greater emphasis on the individual student's personal learning journey, including motivations and attitudes in respect to real-world problems. The study also proposes that quality education can benefit of digital educational resources [4, 5].

The results continue to confirm that real-time remote classes can be a valuable complement to presence learning by bringing students to recognized leaders from other countries who provide them with a global perspective and external vision of their profession [2].

'This is an alternative to those students who do not have the means to study abroad: being part of a course group where they live a bicultural experience' [2].

2 Aim

The main objective of this paper is to present the results on student satisfaction and the main points to consider when designing courses taught using a real-time remote model. The model presented in this work has been implemented at our university and the results show that student satisfaction has been maintained and in some cases exceeds the level obtained by courses taught using a traditional model with the professor present on campus. All the professors that have taken part of this model are located in a different country and for most of the cases, English is not their first language. Another objective of this model is to develop the communication competences of students in use of digital skills as the courses taught in this model uses technology as a learning tool.

3   Context of the Study

According to Guzman, professor at the Department of Educational Psychology, School of Psychology, National Autonomous University of Mexico, in the definition of CBE in the educational field, the most accepted position is to consider competencies from the labour point of view [6].

"The CBE is an educational modality that allows educating the learner based on labour or professional competency standards obtained from the requirements of the productive sector and services. Its teaching methodology emphasises know-how and uses an organisation and infrastructure similar to those in the workplace to deploy these skills" [6].

An advantage of the application of a competency-based education (CBE) model is that it prevents the contents of curricula from "responding to ... disciplinary whims or is the result of pressure from the institution's power groups" [6]. A whim, in this context, could arguably be thought of as a potentially constructive starting point for innovation. However, the key point with respect to the current study's focus on digital and communication skills in is that, as Guzman goes on to state, competencies enable "'the development of a set knowledge, skills and attitudes" that "allows the learner to acquire integral and relevant skills for their professional work" [6]'.

The European Commission supported the development of key competences in European countries (European Commission/EACEA/Eurydice, 2012). England, Canada, Australia, the United States of America and the European Union were pioneers in the implementation of competency-based education to improve the efficiency and quality of education [7]. As for the EBC in Latin America, an important project was the Latin American Tuning (2004–2007) and the 6 × 4 UEALC project (2003–2007) [7].

In Mexico, an official policy related to the EBC emerged in 1994 with the Project for the Modernisation of Technical Education and Training (PMETYC), focused on vocational training in charge of the institutions of the Technological Education Sub-system, such as CONALEP and the National Polytechnic Institute. In 1995, the Council for Standardisation and Certification of Labor Competence (CONOCER) emerged based on a model from England and with representatives of the public, private and social sectors. In 2004, the educational model of the Technological Universities was implemented, in order to respond to the needs of the different productive sectors and society [8].

CBE focuses on learning rather than teaching, as in the traditional didactic approach [9]. The competency model also has the advantage that it is related to practical learning experiences associated with knowledge and that together they produce an observable, measurable result, which can be shown physically or as a behavior associated with the activities of a profession [10].

Regarding the changes in the student's role, the "Permanent Training Center" of the University of Seville explains that the role of the student changes from being passive (listening, reading and memorizing) to becoming active, a role that implies practice, problem solving, analysis of situations, search for explanations, among other activities [11].

For the purposes of this study, competency-based education is considered as a way of enabling students to develop their ability to deal more efficiently with an uncertain and globalised world where everything is constantly changing and at an accelerated pace. Within this environment of uncertainty, professionals with new skills and capable of adapting with flexibility to new times are required [12].

As identified above, one of the aims of the study, is to analyse and evaluate student development of digital and communication competencies aligned with the university's new educational model. Here, a brief summary of the education contexts that have led to this development is relevant to understanding the relationship between competencies, the university's education goals and within this scope, the measurement of digital and communication competencies. In our university's digital magazine, periodic reports are presented on educational developments that demonstrate the greatest potential for impact in higher education. The report published in February 2015, was dedicated to CBE and it commences by explaining that the concept of competency in education appeared in the 1970s, in response to the inadequate relationship that existed at that time between education programs and the needs of the labour market [13].

In Mexico, an official policy related to CBE emerged in 1994 through the Project for the Modernization of Technical Education and Training (PMETYC). It focused on vocational training in charge of the institutions of the Technological Education Sub system, such as CONALEP and the National Polytechnic Institute. In 1995, the Council for Standardization and Certification of Labor Competence (CONOCER) emerged. Based on a model from England, it included representatives of private and social sectors and members of the public. In 2004, the educational model of the Technological Universities was implemented, in order to respond to the needs of the different productive sectors and society.

Our university has decided to use this pedagogical model for the 2019 curricula because of its closer connection to and emphasis on professional competencies and its alignment to the trends of higher education worldwide. In our new educational model 'the evaluation focuses on the development of student competencies that make up their graduation profile' and the achievement of these 'at key moments of their academic life' is observed [13].

The university's new educational model proposes a change in the curriculum which has led to redefining the learning assessment process consistently with the competency-based approach [13]. Among the advantages of CBE, is that this model represents an alternative to the current model, which articulates learning objectives: that is, students no longer focus only on passing the course (know-how), but must demonstrate the acquisition of a set of skills, values and attitudes (know how to be). Another advantage is that CBE is active, functional and comprehensive; and brings the students to real challenges where they must act in ways that enable the practical application of the knowledge they have acquired. The advantage of the university's development and use of competency-based education is that it makes it possible to construct and articulate competencies across a range of skills, areas of knowledge and attitudes - and importantly with regard to integrating digital and communication skills into the curriculum, through the use of competencies.

4 Method

A. Situating the Case

At our university, we have always encouraged the use of technology in the classroom. Our new education model makes extensive use of the latest technologies including remote courses, MOOCs and even courses that make use of telepresence [14–17]. Another aspect that the university is interested in improving is the number of international professors. With this model, we invite professors that have already visited our university and know our education model so that the adaptation time is minimized.

B. Methodology

This work analyzes the data obtained in the previous consecutive semesters through a survey that was answered by a group of 42 students (33% women, 66% men).

The survey was answered by students who are enrolled in the following courses during the Fall 2019 semester: Urban theories, History of Architecture and the city III and Language and Meaning of Objects.

Several questions relate to the perception of students regarding the model itself as well as their perception on the development of digital and communication competencies and another set of questions have to do with the perception of students on the professor-student interaction.

5 Analysis

The answers from the survey use a Likert-type scale with values from one to five (1 = low and 5 = high). As mentioned in the previous section, the first part of the analysis has to do with the interaction of students and the professor. The second analysis has to do with the several factors of the model including its flexibility and how students perceive the impact of the model in their curricula by having an international professor teaching them those courses. It is important to mention that all students have at least one year of experience in our university taking courses in our traditional model, so they are able to answer questions that compare the traditional model with this real-time remote course.

6 Results

The analysis of the answers by the students show that, in general, student satisfaction is high and they appreciate the flexibility of the model and its novelty when compared to traditional courses they have already taken on campus. On the other hand, the implementation of the model has been in a straightforward manner as most lecture room are equipped with projectors or screens connected to a personal computer with good internet connection. More than eighty percent of students responded that they would take another course using the same model and nearly ninety percent of students consider that the professors chosen for this model are "inspiring professors". Several graphs are included that show the different aspects of the perception of the students regarding the implementation of the model. Some suggestions are also given that can be considered guidelines when designing semesters or courses that will be taught in real-time by a professor at a remote location.

The key elements were asked in the next questions in a yes/no format:

1. Do you like the contents of the course?
2. Do you feel that there is adequate quality of contact between professor and student?
3. Does the professor inspire you during the delivery of the course?
4. Would you choose to take a course in the real-time distance format again?
5. Would you recommend this type of course to other students?
6. Do you think that this course helped you to develop the competence of Communication? (Using native language well orally and in writing/be efficient when presenting an idea)
7. Do you think that this course helped you to develop the competence of Digital Transformation? (Using technology to potentiate and make processes more efficient).

   The next three questions measured the perception of factors that describe the remote course impact using Likert-type a scale from one to five, where one is the low and five the high:
8. How do you evaluate the flexibility of the course model?
9. How do you evaluate the innovation on having a distance expert professor as part of the course model?
10. How do you evaluate the utility of the course model?

This paper took information from three courses taught in Architecture and Industrial Design bachelor programs. 42 students (14 women and 28 men) experienced a real-time distance course during the Spring 2019 semester and the Fall 2018 semester.

The results can be reviewed in the next table and figures. The quality of contact between the professor and the students as well as the inspiration perceived by the students are positive, however, there seems to be a small discrepancy in taking a similar course and the recommendation of the course to other students. Of the total of participating students, 89.65% perceived an adequate quality of contact between professor and student. 88.40% of them affirmed that the professor was inspiring during the delivery of the course. 81.75% would choose to take a course in this format again and 80.55% would recommend this course format to other students (Figs. 1, 2, 3 and 4).

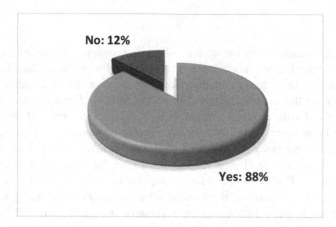

Fig. 1. Do you feel that there is an adequate quality of contact between professor and student?

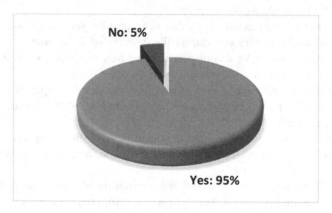

Fig. 2. Does the professor inspire you during the delivery of the course?

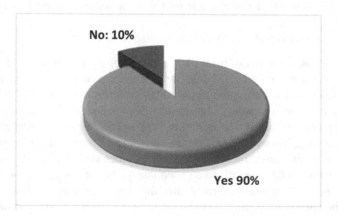

Fig. 3. Would you choose to take a course in the real-time distance format again?

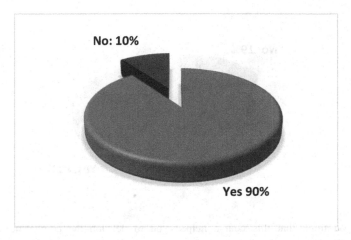

Fig. 4. Would you recommend this type of course to other students?

The second analysis is the observation of the perceived development of the digital and communication competencies. In the Fig. 5 and 6, it is observable how the perceived development of these transversal competencies (that pertains to our university's new educational model) is positive. Of the total of participating students, 88% believe that the course helped them to develop the competence of Communication and 81% of them believe that the course helped them to develop the competence of Digital Transformation (Figs. 5 and 6).

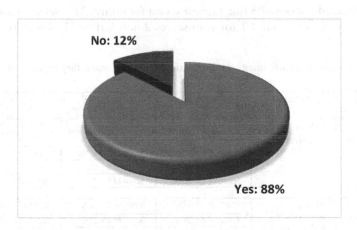

Fig. 5. Do you think that this course helped you to develop the competence of Communication?

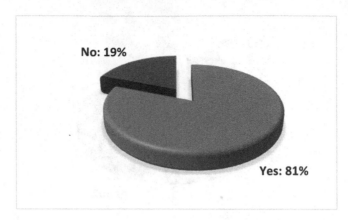

Fig. 6. Do you think that this course helped you to develop the competence of Digital Transformation?

The third analysis is the observation of the experience in the course regarding three characteristics: the perceived flexibility, innovation and utility of the course (see Table 1). In the Fig. 7, 8 and 9, it is observable how the perceived flexibility of the model is positive, however, there seems to be a small discrepancy in the perceived novelty and the perceived utility. Of the total of participating students, 55% selected a score of 5 (the highest score) for flexibility, 31% a score of 4 on this regard, 10% a score of 3 and 2% for both scores 2 and 1. 62% chose a score of 5 (the highest score) for novelty and 19% a score of 4 on this characteristic, 17% a score of 3 and 2% a score of 1. 57% selected a score of 5 (the highest score) for utility, 24% selected a score of 4 on it, 9.6% a score of 3 and 4.7 for both scores 2 and 1 (Figs. 7, 8 and 9).

Table 1. Opinion of the participants on the flexibility, novelty and utility of the studied courses.

Period	Subject	Flexibility	Innovation	Utility
August–December 2019	Urban Theories	Score of 5 = 69%	Score of 5 = 69%	Score of 5 = 54%
		Score of 4 = 7.7%	Score of 4 = 15%	Score of 4 = 23%
		Score of 3 = 7.7%	Score of 3 = 7.7%	Score of 3 = 7.7%
		Score of 2 = 7.7%	Score of 2 = 0%	Score of 2 = 7.7%
		Score of 1 = 7.7%	Score of 1 = 7.7%	Score of 1 = 7.7%
August–December 2019	History of Architecture and the city III	Score of 5 = 67%	Score of 5 = 72%	Score of 5 = 78%
		Score of 4 = 28%	Score of 4 = 22%	Score of 4 = 17%
		Score of 3 = 5%	Score of 3 = 5%	Score of 3 = 5%
August–December 2019	Language and Meaning of Objects	Score of 5 = 18%	Score of 5 = 36%	Score of 5 = 36%
		Score of 4 = 64%	Score of 4 = 18%	Score of 4 = 36%
		Score of 3 = 18%	Score of 3 = 45%	Score of 3 = 18%
		Score of 2 = 0%	Score of 2 = 0%	Score of 2 = 9%

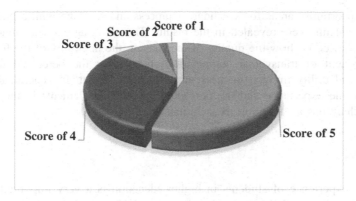

Fig. 7. How do you evaluate the flexibility of the model? (the highest score is 5)

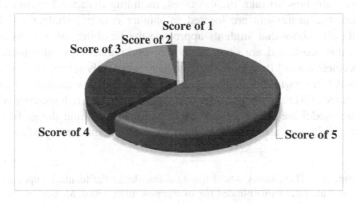

Fig. 8. How do you evaluate the innovation of the model? (the highest score is 5)

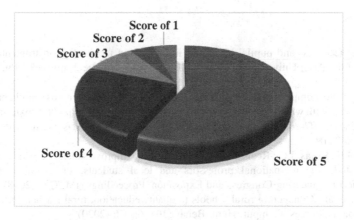

Fig. 9. How do you evaluate the utility of the model? (the highest score is 5)

Some opportunity areas for a validation process and redesign with a much larger sample of students were revealed in the results. The study agrees with much of the literature reviewed on how the quality of the content, the flexibility of the format and the development of transversal competencies determines the perceived flexibility, innovation and utility implied in the remote teaching format. In general, this study reveals how the experience and the perception of relevant elements in the real-time remote teaching has a validation in its format.

7 Results

The overall experience of students in higher education is a very important topic as universities attract new talent that is looking not only for an education of high quality but to have a memorable experience [18, 19]. We consider that by offering students several options on how to take their courses, including distance learning courses or courses where the professors are located in another country, student satisfaction is improved. Results show that students appreciate the flexibility of models as the one presented in this work and are open to try new approaches that offer more than the traditional lectures model that most students have previously taken. One of the bonus that students get in this model is the chance to improve their communication skills in another language. Overall, we consider that the benefits of implementing a real-time remote course model are worth all the required efforts, including the global search of experts in the field that are willing to participate as international professors for our students.

Acknowledgement.   The authors would like to acknowledge the financial support of our university's Writing Lab, (real name blinded for anonymous submission), Mexico, in the production of this work.

References

1. Exploring teachers' and pupils' behaviour in online and face-to face instrumental lessons. School of the Arts, University of Hull, Hull, UK, vol. 21, issue 2, pp. 197–209, 15 March 2019
2. Conecta: Siete competencias con las que el Tec busca preparar a sus estudiantes. Seven competencies with which Tec seeks to prepare its students (2019). https://tec.mx/es/noticias/nacional/educacion/7-competencias-con-las-que-el-tec-busca-preparar-sus-estudiantes. Accessed 21 Oct 2019
3. Nuñez, M.E., Rojas, J.C.: Real-time distance courses to improve satisfaction and competence: a case study of international professors and local students. In: ASME International Mechanical Engineering Congress and Exposition, Proceedings (IMECE) (2018)
4. Wang, J., et al.: Connecting rural schools to quality education: rural teachers' use of digital educational resources. Comput. Hum. Behav. **101**, 68–76 (2020)
5. Xie, Z.: Modelling the dropout patterns of MOOC learners. Tsinghua Sci. Tecnhol. **25**(3), 313–324 (2020). https://doi.org/10.26599/tst.2019.9010011. ISSN ll 1007-0214 01/11

6. Guzmán, J.: Los claroscuros de la educación basada en Competencias. The chiaroscuros of Competency-based education Nueva Antropología, vol. XIX, núm. 62, abril, 2003, pp. 143–162. Asociación Nueva Antropología A.C. Distrito Federal, México (2003). http://www.redalyc.org/pdf/159/15906208.pdf. Accessed 6 Nov 2019

7. Argudin, Y.: Educación basada en competencias. Competency-based Education (2006). https://www.uv.mx/dgdaie/files/2013/09/Argudin-Educacion_basada_en_competencias.pdf. Accessed 07 Dec 2019

8. Ochoa, C., et al.: Continuum, the Continuing Education (2015). https://ac.els-cdn.com/S2341287916000272/1-s2.0-S2341287916000272-main.pdf?_tid=e24fc40a-a7bb-48fa-9167-4c4a61b87fca&acdnat=1521770027_7240f51fd43ad860969dd342a44c1753. Accessed 06 Nov 2019

9. Turcio, D., Palacios, J.: Experiencias en la enseñanza experimental basada en competencias. Experiences in experimental teaching based on competencies (2015). https://www.sciencedirect.com/science/article/pii/S0187893X15720963. Accessed 06 Nov 2019

10. García, J.: Modelo educativo basadao en competencias: Importancia y necesidad. Competency-based education model: Importance and need, Revista Electrónica Actualidades Investigativas en Educación, pp. 1–24 (2011). https://www.redalyc.org/articulo.oa?id=44722178014

11. Centro de Formación Permanente: El alumno en e-Learning: Rol y Características. The student in e-Learning: Role and Characteristics. http://www.cfp.us.es/area-de-alumnos/e-learning/el-alumno-en-e-learning-rol-y-caracteristicas. Accessed 06 Nov 2019

12. Harvard Business Review: Educating the next generation of leaders (2019). https://hbr.org/2019/03/educating-the-next-generation-of-leaders. Accessed 20 Nov 2019

13. Edutrends: Educación basada en Competencias (EBC). Competency-based Educaton. Observatorio de Innovación Educativa, Tecnologico de Monterrey (2015). https://observatorio.tec.mx/edutrendsradar2015. Accessed 22 Nov 2019

14. Rodríguez-Paz, M.X., Gonzalez-Mendivil, J.A., Zarate-Garcia, J.A., Peña-Ortega, L.O.: The positive effects of using social networks in courses of applied mechanics on students' performance. In: Proceedings of the ASME 2018 International Mechanical Engineering Congress and Exposition (IMECE), ASME (2018). https://doi.org/10.1115/IMECE2018-87217

15. Rodríguez-Paz, M.X., Gonzalez-Mendivil, J.A., Rojas, J.-C., Núñez, M.E.: Use of an offline video repository as a tool to improve students' performance in Engineering courses versus real-time long distance courses. In: Proceedings of the 2019 IEEE Global Engineering Education Conference (EDUCON), pp. 574–581 (2019). https://doi.org/10.1109/EDUCON.2019.8725105

16. Rojas, J.-C., Núñez, M.E., Rodríguez-Paz, M.X.: Real-time distance courses to improve satisfaction and competence - a case study on the performance of students observing their grades. In: Proceedings of the 2019 IEEE Global Engineering Education Conference (EDUCON), pp. 549–555 (2019). https://doi.org/10.1109/EDUCON.2019.8725235

17. Luévano, E., López de Lara, E., Castro, J.E.: Use of telepresence and holographic projection mobile device for college degree level. Procedia Comput. Sci. **75**, 339–347 (2015). https://doi.org/10.1016/j.procs.2015.12.256

18. Núñez, M.: Las clases a distancia en tiempo real como apoyo al Modelo Tec 21. The real-time distance classes in support of the Tec 21 Model. Vislumbra Revista de Divulgación del Tecnológico de Monterrey, pp. 45–54 (2015)

19. Wei, W., Yu, X., Qianying, W., Kang, Z.: School and enterprise remote interactive visualization approach in environmental art design teaching. In: Eighth International Conference on Measuring Technology and Mechatronics Automation, p. 3 (2016). Accessed 21 Nov 2016

Reflective Journaling: A Theoretical Model and Digital Prototype for Developing Resilience and Creativity

Ana Rivera[1]([✉]), Alwin de Rooij[2], and Sara Jones[1]

[1] City, University of London, London EC1Y 8TZ, UK
ana.rivera@cass.city.ac.uk, s.v.jones@city.ac.uk
[2] Tilburg University, Warandelaan 2, 5037 AB Tilburg, The Netherlands
alwinderooij@tilburguniversity.edu

Abstract. Reflection is commonly discussed as a tool for personal and professional development that is becoming increasingly important in today's global and digital world. In this paper, we propose a model that suggests ways in which reflection, in the form of Reflective Journaling, can support the development of creativity and resilience, which are needed to enable individuals to function effectively in a fast-changing environment. In addition, the model proposes ways in which external support and progress monitoring can be used in conjunction with skills in adaptive resilience and structured creativity, to support the maintenance of reflective journaling as a habit, in the longer term, thus creating virtuous cycles of skills and behaviours that can reinforce each other. Based on our model, and additional user research, we describe the design of a first digital prototype that aims to support the use of Reflective Journaling and to develop creativity and resilience through suggested mechanisms. Initial evaluations of our prototype are positive. It has been well-received by early test users, and has the potential to address all the connections defined. We therefore suggest that the theoretical model can be used to develop digital tools, such as the one included, to help those who wish to develop the habit of reflective journaling, and through that a range of other skills associated with resilience and creative thinking. We see this as a starting point for investigating this potential in more depth.

Keywords: Reflective Journaling · Learning · Digital prototype · Creativity · Resilience · Emerging technologies

1 Introduction

We are increasingly finding ourselves overwhelmed and under-equipped to deal with global and digital disruption, where data travels fast, in bulk, and in every direction [30]. An important component of the lifelong learning that may help us to manage this situation, by learning how to adapt to each new circumstance in which we find ourselves, is reflection, or reflective practice.

Reflective practice is a crucial activity for learning from experience, and adapting to new circumstances [2]. Its most popular form is Reflective Journaling, which we define as a structured writing process with the purposes of acquiring a set of abilities and

© Springer Nature Switzerland AG 2020
P. Zaphiris and A. Ioannou (Eds.): HCII 2020, LNCS 12205, pp. 144–158, 2020.
https://doi.org/10.1007/978-3-030-50513-4_11

skills; thinking in a critical inquisitive way; and solving problems within a professional context. Reflective practice through journaling, also known as Reflective Journaling, allows us to externalize important thoughts and feelings in academic, personal, and professional contexts [21, 33]. Unfortunately, while the benefits of journaling are noteworthy, O'Connell and Dyment [32] remind us that striking issues and challenges remain, not least in understanding how best to employ Reflective Journaling to support learning in a range of different contexts.

In this paper, we first present the results of a literature review that illustrate the links between Reflective Journaling, creativity and resilience, to better understand each of the concepts, and what may be needed to build strong habits, and monitor ongoing progress in each area. The links are shown in a model, as a series of virtuous cycles, in which Reflective Journaling supports the development of creativity and resilience, and vice-versa. This is important, since both creative thinking i.e. the development of original and effective solutions, and resilience, i.e. the ability to recover quickly from encountered difficulties are also key to helping us overcome new challenges and think of new ways forward in today's uncertain and ever-changing circumstances [24, 37].

Based on our model, and some additional user research, we then describe the design of a first digital prototype to help reflective practitioners develop their creativity, resilience and reflective journaling habits through mechanisms suggested by our model. This prototype is digital to exploit the advantages of e-learning in enhancing self-monitoring skills and supplying online support. Initial evaluations of our prototype are positive, and we end with some discussion and suggestions for further work.

2 Theoretical Model

Reflection as a learning method was first introduced with Gregory Bateson's levels of learning in 1972 [35]. However, better known is the concept of single and double loop learning by Argyris and Schön from 1978, which achieved great relevance in organisational learning and evolved into Schön's reflection in and on-action model [31].

Reflection is a common approach to engaging in structured, self-directed learning and integrates theory with real world practice, due to the ease with which it can be implemented, the potential depth of feedback it provides, and the variety of structures that can be used to support it [31, 36, 38]. Reflection in the context of practice, reflective practice, originated in the professions of nursing, but has broadened across many industries over the years [10]. There is little consensus on a definition for reflective practice. Moon [31] listed some of them, which define reflection as a: set of abilities and skills [6], critical thinking process [36, 38], state of mind [8, 35], problem solving process [7, 16, 25], intuition and cognition trait [26], behaviour pattern [41], practice within professional context [22], or a maturation process [15].

Reflective practice can be exercised in an infinite number of ways as long as individuals can learn from their personal experiences and theory [4]. However, the most popular form is journaling, which allows to display thoughts and feelings of the academic and professional pursuits [21, 27]. For the purpose of this paper, reflective practice through journaling, or Reflective Journaling, is defined as a combination of the above: a structured writing process to acquire a set of abilities, skills, and wisdom; think in a critical inquisitive way; and solve problems within a professional context.

Below we introduce each component of our model of Reflective Journaling based on this definition.

2.1 Reflective Journaling and Adaptive Resilience

An appropriate level of self-doubt allows individuals to acquire a stronger mindset – to be more resilient – while simultaneously becoming more flexible and sensitive – or more adaptable. De Haan [9] refers to this process as becoming both thicker and thinner skinned, or having both backbone and heart. To face adversity, practitioners must develop their resilience, and to retain a beginner's openness, they must develop their flexibility [6]. So far, little research has focused on resilience in the workplace: in other areas of study, sleep, exercise, and diet have been identified as health factors that help build resilience [24]. In the same way, Reflective Journaling can be seen as a healthy habit, that can contribute to acquiring resilience.

On the other hand, too little self-criticism can hinder our learning abilities by mistakenly focusing on the external environment instead of ourselves [2]. Freire [12] defines this negative perception of commitment to critical reflection as the "banking model" of education. Individuals need to constantly work on their weaknesses by staying open to feedback, however uncomfortable it may be, and Reflective Journaling can provide a mechanism for doing this [11].

Skinner [39] pioneered one of the first models to understand patterns of behaviour and broke the process into three steps: antecedent, behaviour, and consequence. Many models of reflection are based on this structure and aim to help individuals focus on their own actions and behaviours, instead of external factors, by reframing attitudes to re-evaluate events. In this context, Reflective Journaling can help to build an open attitude to understand and evaluate how behaviours shape triggers into outcomes.

In summary, an appropriate level of self-doubt, developed through Reflective Journaling, allows individuals to acquire a stronger mindset – to be more resilient – while simultaneously becoming more sensitive and flexible – or more adaptable (Fig. 1).

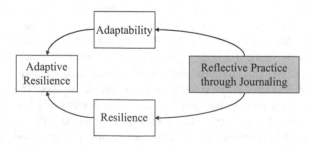

Fig. 1. Reflective Journaling, Resilience and Adaptability

2.2   Reflective Journaling and Structured Creativity

To achieve optimal learning for long periods, reflective practitioners must be organised, and to maintain interest and motivation, they must apply variation to their practice [28].

Multiple studies demonstrate the obvious lifestyle improvements of implementing orderly activities and behaviours, such as self-control or positive discipline [3]. In a similar way, there are many ways in which a process of reflection can be structured: for example, there are many levels of reflection that can be engaged in, from basic observation, to integrating theory with practice, to connecting experiences [23]. Many authors have observed that the majority of reflective practitioners mainly describe events without reflecting on them [32]. However, Reflective Journaling can be used to develop critical, reasoned and rational thinking [30, 38], thereby enhancing structured thought processes that help improve our healthy behaviours.

Additionally, Reflective Journaling provides a space to promote creativity and provides individuals with the opportunity for self-expression [17, 18], and the variety of forms in which reflection can be practiced allows individuals to express themselves in their own way [32].

Thus, an appropriate level of structured thinking, developed through Reflective Journaling, allows individuals to acquire an organised mindset – to be more structured - while simultaneously becoming more self-expressive – or more creative (Fig. 2).

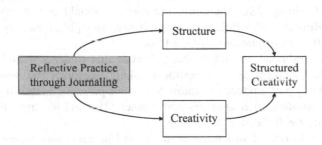

Fig. 2. Reflective Journaling, Structure and Creativity

2.3   Reflective Journaling and External Support

Integrating Reflective Practice in a routine requires an important behaviour change in the sense that reflective practitioners must learn to maintain their practice over time [32]. Reflective practitioners should be aware that relapses, or periods when little reflection is undertaken, are unavoidable, and should therefore, prepare themselves with appropriate tools, or support, to bounce back into practice [19].

This support can take several forms, such as training or financial incentives [32]. It may also take the form of emotional support from a social network of the kind that is known to contribute to an individual's personal resilience, if, for example, an individual is willing to share entries in their reflective journal with others.

Reflective Journaling is a very personal activity and many authors have raised issues in regard to sharing reflective journal entries with others, considering ethics and psychological safety and the effects on the quality of the reflection [14]. If reflection is to be shared, the risks it involves must be addressed: accepting feedback from others and giving deep reflections.

There is still much to be learnt about how best to use external support as part of a reflective journaling process, but certainly a combination of adaptive resilience and external support can be helpful in generating momentum in the reflective journaling process (Fig. 3).

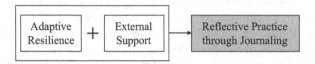

Fig. 3. Adaptive Resilience and External Support facilitate Reflective Journaling

2.4   Reflective Journaling and Progress Monitoring

As mentioned above, a certain level of originality and novelty is necessary to maintain motivation in learning [28]. Therefore, practitioners should use diverse structured approaches to Reflective Practice, such as remix exercises [28], creativity triggers [1], serious play [40], or Socratic questioning [13].

Additionally, Edmondson and Saxber [11] state that students should think about learning and development as an investment, asking questions and setting frequent follow-ups and key performance indicators to monitor progress. Measuring progress is key in certain activities, such as sports performance [19], and we argue that the same may well be true for Reflective Journaling.

Thus, a combination of structured creativity and progress monitoring can support the practice of Reflective Journaling in the long-term (Fig. 4).

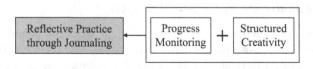

Fig. 4. Structured Creativity and Progress Monitoring enhance Reflective Journaling

Bringing together all of the above, the developed theoretical model (Fig. 5) shows the virtuous cycles, through which Reflective Journaling supports the development of creativity and resilience, and vice-versa.

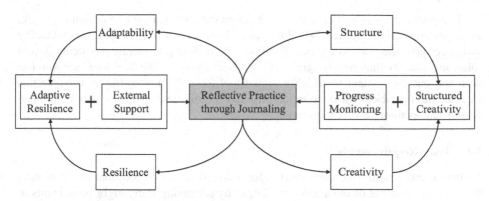

Fig. 5. Theoretical model of Reflective Practice through Journaling

This model can serve as a basis for developing applications that use emerging technologies with the aim of supporting lifelong learning through Reflective Journaling, as described in the following section.

3 Digital Prototype

To provide some insight into the utility of our model, a digital prototype was designed, developed, and evaluated. Inspired by applications used for habit building in other areas, such as exercise or meditation, and by other attempts to use mobile technologies to support reflective learning in the workplace [34], we first assumed that our prototype should include features corresponding to each of the concepts in the model of reflective practice discussed above, as shown in Fig. 6.

Features proposed on this basis included support for adaptive resilience through plan setting (2), support for creative structure through reflection models (3ab), provision of external support through a social club (4), and progress monitoring through statistics and insights (5).

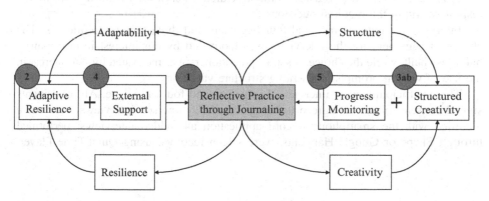

Fig. 6. Links between the Theoretical model of Reflective Practice through Journaling and the Five Main Screens on the Prototype

The prototype was further designed by following a human-centred design approach, as characterised by Maguire [29]. This approach involves 4 main stages: understanding and specifying the context of use, specifying the user requirements, producing design solutions and evaluating designs against requirements. The previous section has sketched out the context in which a digital tool for reflection would be used. In this section, we describe work done to identify user requirements for such a tool, and then design and evaluate a first prototype.

3.1   User Requirements

To better understand user requirements for a digital reflection tool that could support the various elements of our model, we began by surveying thirty-eight participants to analyse their journaling preferences and strategies. Participants included master's students with previous professional experience, researchers, and professors (Males = 17, Females = 20, Prefer not say = 1, Majority aged 26–35, Participant ages ranging from 26–35 to 46–55).

The survey was broadcasted through social media, shared with researchers through email, and included in email newsletters, such as the one circulated by the Boosting Resilience project [5]. All participants signed consent forms before completing the survey. The survey included four screening questions to ensure the participants were fit for the study as current reflective practitioners.

The survey was used to understand current reflective practitioner's preferences including: journaling frequency (daily, almost daily, weekly, almost weekly, monthly, almost monthly, or barely), seniority (a few months, 6 months, 1 year, 2 years, or more than 5 years), writing prompts or guided questions (Structured Creativity), and shared reflections with trustees or community of friends (External Support). The responses were analysed using statistical analyses, extracts of which are shown below.

From the pool of thirty-eight respondents to the survey, seven participants (Males = 4, Females = 3, Majority aged 26–35, Participant ages ranging from 26–35 to Over 66) that practiced Reflective Journaling and showed some level of dissatisfaction with at least one aspect of their practice were selected to understand their preferences in more depth using semi-structured interviews to allow unrestricted responses within the required questions.

Interview participants included four beginners and three senior practitioners. The choice of beginners for the interviews was motivated by our interest in observing a habit less built, while the choice of senior practitioners was motivated by our interest in the use of writing prompts and writing structure variation.

Three participants were interviewed in-person and four via Skype. All participants signed consent forms and agreed to being recorded. In-person interviews were voice recorded with the smartphone Record application and video interviews, performed through Skype or Google Hangouts, were screen recorded using QuickTime Player.

The interviews had five main sections and lasted about 30 min: thoughts on key aspects to practice reflective journaling, preferred format and style, use of progress evaluations in their practice, and preference in using prompted questions or reflective models to journal.

Interviews were used to further understand the more personal elements of the model, which would have been difficult to explore through questions in the survey: the use of plans in reflection for self-evaluation, Adaptive Resilience, (for example, by asking "Is there anything you currently do to keep track of your personal evolution in reflective journaling? How is this working for you?") and use of goal setting and personal evolution, Progress Monitoring, (for example, by asking "It is my understanding that you have not used pre-filled journals before, why is this?"). The responses were transcribed and analysed with a thematic analysis.

The findings are examined below.

Adaptive Resilience. Regarding the development of a healthy reflective journaling habit to support resilience, all interviewees agreed that making time to journal and having a journaling routine is key. Participant 1 (P1) stated: "I struggle to keep it going on a regular basis". The minimum viable product, required by all, is the ability to set journaling reminders and record activities to develop a journaling habit.

Participants also had different views on goal setting. P2 stated: "I've grown up in a world of SMART goal setting in business and while this applies to my career, I am not interested in applying it to journaling", while P6 showed high interest in applying goals and development planning to their practice, saying: "I personally love personal development apps of any kind". Given the variety of preferences among the participants, setting of reminders and goals was optional in our prototype.

Structured Creativity. Regarding structured creativity, 58% of survey respondents. said that they already used prompts to structure their journaling. Favourite prompts were questions, quotes and pictures, with the most common sources of prompts being cited as a participant's own notes, online searches and books. 42% of the participants had never used prompts to journal.

Of these, the most common reasons for lack of prompt usage were lack of interest (44%) or lack of awareness (37%) (Fig. 7). Additionally, some interviewees had said they found the use of prompts restrictive, P3 stated: "I would find a pre-formatted journal restrictive but I'm sure other people would like that extra layer".

In our prototype, we therefore offered practitioners the opportunity to search for prompts of different forms (visual, audio or video), but did not mandate their use.

External Support. The survey suggested that although most people (74%) had attended a workshop or programme on reflective learning, not so many (58%) had received feedback on shared reflections, and 21% of respondents had not shared their reflections at all. Those who did share reflections, would share them with a friend, a partner or spouse, a colleague or a teacher/mentor (Fig. 8).

Participants had very different perspectives on their journaling preferences regarding a potential community with which to share reflections. P5, for example, was nervous of sharing their reflections, saying: "when I journal, with real unfiltered comments that could be not politically correct and maybe very exposed"; In P6's view, however:

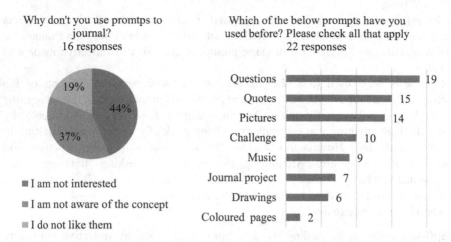

Fig. 7. Survey responses regarding Structured Creativity

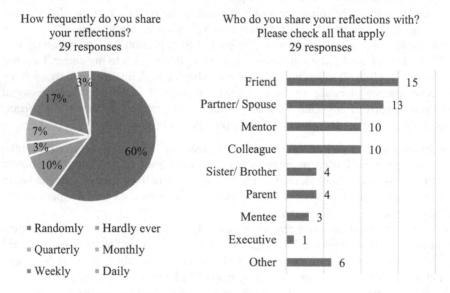

Fig. 8. Survey responses regarding External Support

"Reflective responses as feedback would make a lot more sense because it's actually engaging rather than simply saying your point of view is awesome or maybe not that good".

In our prototype, we therefore implemented use of an optional closed community, for people who wanted to share and receive feedback on their reflections, which enabled practitioners to share or not share any individual reflection.

Progress Monitoring. While the literature suggests that monitoring of progress is important to maintain practice over time, none of the interviewed reflective practitioners actually applied any sort of progress monitoring or showed interest when proposed, suggesting that users may be wary of this. It was therefore decided that the this should only be implemented in the prototype as a background feature that participants could access if they wished to.

3.2 Prototype Design and Evaluation

Based on the above, an initial prototype was designed to serve as a mock-up to discuss the proposed system with users. The prototype was developed with Indigo Studio [20], a wireframe service that supports interaction design prototyping.

A controlled evaluation was carried out, working closely with two participants (P1 and P6) from the initial user research interviews to evaluate how successful they were in using the system (Male = 1, Female = 1, Ages 26–35). Participants were chosen by their availability to test the prototype in an in-person study.

The Indigo platform offered a usability test feature that worked perfectly for the evaluation purpose. However, any modifications to the prototype would not be updated live on the usability test and, therefore, this feature was discarded. However, its design inspired the structure for feedback collection and the tasks were introduced by the researcher manually, using the Wizard of Oz protocol [29]. This allowed think-aloud interaction with the prototype to be observed and to guide participants through emerging interactions. The test included a structured set of activities with each of the prototype's main features, allowing consistent forms of data generation and researcher-participant interactions.

The tasks performed by the two users included: 1) upload a reflection piece, 2) check a reflective response from a friend, 3) upload a reflective response to a friend, 4) review activity progress and recommendations, and 5) create a journaling plan with a set of preferences.

The variables tested were: efficiency, measured as the time it took to complete each task; effectiveness, measured as the number of participants who completed the task successfully, struggled with certain steps, or got lost in the task; and satisfaction, assessed based on the feedback compiled through the think-aloud protocol [51] and post-experience interviews on the user's favourite features to evaluate their satisfaction. Each research-participant session lasted approximately 10 min in total, after which, a post-study open discussion was carried out. This unstructured talk allowed the users to express their overall experience and provide us with critical feedback on our design and further design opportunities.

From these insights, a set of changes were prioritized and applied onto a second, and third version of the prototype. The final version of the prototype had five sections (Fig. 7) that linked to each of the components of the theoretical model (Fig. 9, Fig. 10):

1. Journal (Main screen): allowed practitioners to record activities, log reflections, and reply to others' reflections.
2. My Plan (Adaptive Resilience): allowed users to set journaling goals and create journaling plans based on a series of preferences, including their main goal, experience, level of instruction, and activity preference.
3. Activities (Structured Creativity): practitioners were able to search reflection models, articles and prompts by a series of filters, including goals (creativity,

Fig. 9. Five Main Screens in Prototype of a digital tool to support Reflective Practice through Journaling.

resilience, learning), prompts (visual, audio, video), and themes (work, life, travel). Additionally, users were able to filter with what level of detail they wished to receive the exercises: from very detailed to barely.

4. Club (External Support): practitioners were able to add community, read others' reflective pages and notes, and share their own journals and reflective responses.
5. Stats (Progress Monitoring): allowed users to view their journaling stats and insights using a series of simple charts and graphs.

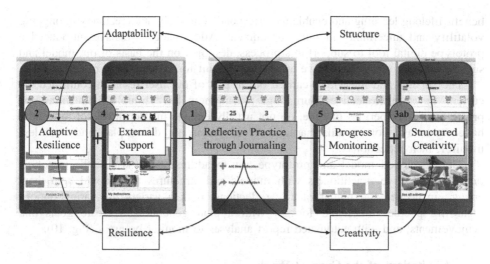

Fig. 10. Five Main Screens in Prototype within the Theoretical model of Reflective Practice through Journaling

With the final prototype version, additional interviews were carried out to set future expectations and design recommendations. Two coaches (Male = 1, Female = 1, Ages Over 66) were identified from the initial survey pool and recruited to gather feedback on the prototype and identify design improvements. Both participants signed consent forms and agreed to be recorded. The first participant was interviewed via phone and recorded through the laptop using Quick Time Player voice recording, the second was interviewed via Skype and was recorded using Quick Time Player screen recording. Similar to the user research interviews, the conversations were recorded and transcribed for thematic analysis.

These coaches were interviewed with a semi-structured approach for 20 min each, similarly to the previous interviews. Interviews had three sections: first, about their experience of using digital tools, helping students build Reflective Practice, the combination of digital and physical platforms, and the relationship between reflection, creativity and resilience. Second, their thoughts on the application of prompts, prefilled journals, and evolution tracking in Reflective Practice. Finally, their view on the developed solution and proposed features, gathering feedback for changes to be applied if it were to be used within teaching programmes, either within the prototype, as a follow-up tool, or both.

4 Discussion

4.1 Summary and Integration with Previous Work

In this paper we have summarised a new theoretical model that characterizes important relationships between Reflective Practice through Journaling and the development of adaptive resilience and structured creativity. This has been done with the aim of providing a theoretical basis for future design research on how emerging technologies can benefit lifelong learning and enable us to respond adaptively and creatively to ongoing volatility and uncertainty in our environment. Additionally, we have introduced a prototype digital tool to support this process, designed on the basis of our model and subsequent user research to serve as a starting point for future design research.

The surveys and interviews carried out as part of our user research confirmed the current flaws in Reflective Journaling: practitioners have trouble maintaining the practice for long periods of time, do not usually engage in deep levels of reflection, have a great aversion towards sharing their reflections, and do not plan, and much less monitor, their reflections.

The developed model and prototype aim to address these issues: the prototype provides reflective practitioners with models and structures that should help them engage in deeper and higher quality reflections, with a variety of sharing options regarding people, time, and format; with a plan generator to create goals and achievements; and with automated report analyses to monitor progress (Fig. 10).

4.2 Limitations of the Current Work

The data gathered is not sufficient to prove that a Reflective Journaling digital tool can help develop resilience and creativity. Efforts made to gather a more diverse sample of participants for this study met with limited success. Most of the participants belonged to the researchers' network and therefore had a similar educational background.

The survey results show an indicative perspective of 38 reflective practitioners. For the results of our research to be more accurate, more participants' perspectives would be needed to understand the apparently emerging trends better. However, although the results of our research are not sufficient for statistical purposes, they do offer a good basis for initial system development. Our prototype incorporated all identified user requirements and the final product was well-received, suggesting high desirability.

Based on inputs from users who evaluated our prototype, some later stage changes were noted, to perhaps be included in future versions of our prototype:

- Support the digital tool with a physical notebook with prompts, following P8's comment that: "Everybody does reflection both digital and analogue";
- Integrate computer learning and tracking to scan journal entries for progress monitoring, following P8's observation that: "The two main options are creating content digitally or create your content on paper. So, you scan it or photograph it and upload it";
- Sync with other apps, such as Facebook or Meetup, for community simplification, following P8's statement that: "the history of sharing platforms is that there will be popular platforms at any one point in time, but people always use a diversity of platforms".

4.3 Future Work

In more general terms, the "soft" skills that were the focus of this study were creativity and resilience. Further research could further explore the links between reflective journaling and each of these concepts, as well as considering links with other characteristics and skills required to thrive in the workplace, such as empathy or collaboration [18]. Regarding resilience, research could examine the effects of different levels of reflection, on resilience and professional development. Additionally, it could explore the diverse points of view on sharing reflections and receiving feedback.

Considering what is shared with others and what is received in exchange will provide insights to improve depth of reflection. Regarding creativity, research could analyse the unpopularity of prompts in Reflective Practice. It is crucial to understand if resistance originates in a specific prompt range or format, or if there is a natural resistance to using structure in Reflective Journaling. This could be carried out by examining the effects of different levels of structured reflection, from free writing to reflective models, on creativity and professional development.

Acknowledgements.   We acknowledge reviewers for their valuable feedback that greatly improved the quality of this paper. Second, we thank all participants who shared their time and thoughts. Finally, we thank Eric McNulty and Clive Holtham, who offered great help and insight.

References

1. Amabile, T., Kramer, S.J.: The power of small wins. Harvard Bus. Rev. **89**(5), 70–80 (2011)
2. Argyris, A.: Teaching Smart People How to Learn. Harvard Business Review, Brighton (1991)
3. Baumeister, R., Vohs, K., Tice, D.: The strength model of self-control. Curr. Dir. Psychol. Sci. **16**, 351–355 (2007)
4. Bolton, G.: Reflective Practice: Writing and Professional Development, 2nd edn. SAGE Publications, London (2005)
5. Boosting Resilience. http://www.boostingresilience.net. Accessed 18 Jan 2020
6. Calderhead, J., Gates, P..: Conceptualising Reflection in Teacher Development. Falmer Press, London (1993)
7. Copeland, W.D., Birmingham, C., de la Cruz, E., Lewin, B.: The reflective practitioner in teaching: towards a research agenda. Teach. Teach. Educ. **9**(4), 247–259 (1993)
8. Dewey, J.: How We Think: A Restatement of the Relation of Reflective Thinking to the Educative Process. D. C. Heath and Company, Boston (1933)
9. De Haan, E.: Becoming simultaneously thicker and thinner skinned: the inherent conflicts arising in the professional development of coaches. Pers. Rev. **37**(5), 526–542 (2008)
10. Done, E., Knowler, H., Murphy, M., Rea, T., Gale, Y.: (Re)writing CPD: creative analytical practices and the 'continuing professional development' of teachers. Reflective Pract. **12**, 389–399 (2011)
11. Edmondson, A., Saxberg, B.: Putting Lifelong Learning on the CEO Agenda. McKinsey (2017)
12. Freire, P.: Pedagogy of the Oppressed, 2nd edn. Continuum, New York (1993)
13. Freydberg, B.: The Play of the Platonic Dialogues. Peter Lang, Oxford (1997)
14. Ghaye, T.: Is reflective practice ethical? (The case of the reflective portfolio). Reflective Pract. **8**(2), 151–162 (2007)
15. Gregorc, A.F.: Developing plans for professional growth. NASSP Bull. **57**(377), 1–8 (1973)
16. Grimmett, P.P., Erikson, G.L.: Reflective Practice in Teacher Education. Teachers College Press, New York (1988)

17. Hettich, P.: Journal writing: old fare or nouvelle cuisine. Teach. Psychol. **17**(1), 36–39 (1990)
18. Hiemstra, R.: Uses and benefits of journal writing. New Dir. Adult Continuing Educ. **90**, 19–26 (2001)
19. Holli, B., Beto, J.A.: Nutrition Counseling and Education Skills for Dietetics Professionals, 6th edn. Lippincott Williams & Wilkins, Philadelphia (2014)
20. Indigo. https://cloud.indigo.design/. Accessed 18 Jan 2020
21. Jefferson, J.K., Martin, I.H., Owens, J.: Leader development through reading and reflection. J. Leadersh. Stud. **8**(2), 67–75 (2014)
22. Jones, S., Joss, R.: Models of professionalism. In: Yelloly, M., Henkel, M. (eds.) Learning and Teaching in Social Work. Jessica Kingsley, London (1995)
23. Kember, D., McKay, J., Sinclair, K., Wong, F.K.Y.: A four-category scheme for coding and assessing the level of reflection in written work. Assess. Eval. High. Educ. **33**(4), 369–379 (2008)
24. King, D.D., Newman, A., Luthans, F.: Not if, but when we need resilience in the workplace. J. Organ. Behav. **37**(5), 782–786 (2016)
25. Kirby, P.C., Teddlie, C.: Development of the reflective teaching instrument. J. Res. Dev. Educ. **22**(4), 45–51 (1989)
26. Korthagen, F.A.J.: Two models of reflection. Teach. Teach. Educ. **9**(3), 317–326 (1993)
27. Krogstie, B.R., Prilla, M., Pammer, V.: Understanding and supporting reflective learning processes in the workplace: the CSRL model. In: Hernández-Leo, D., Ley, T., Klamma, R., Harrer, A. (eds.) EC-TEL 2013. LNCS, vol. 8095, pp. 151–164. Springer, Heidelberg (2013). https://doi.org/10.1007/978-3-642-40814-4_13
28. Liu, C., Chen, W., Lin, H., Huang, Y.: A remix-oriented approach to promoting student engagement in a long-term participatory learning program. Comput. Educ. **110**, 1–15 (2017)
29. Maguire, M.: Methods to support human-centred design. Int. J. Hum. – Comput. Stud. **55**(4), 587–634 (2001)
30. McNulty, E.J.: Journaling Can Boost Your Leadership Skills. Strategy + Business (2018)
31. Moon, J.A.: Reflection in Learning and Professional Development. Routledge, London (1999)
32. O'Connell, T.S., Dyment, J.E.: The case of reflective journals: is the jury still out? Reflective Pract. **12**(1), 47–59 (2011)
33. Pammer, V., Krogstie, B., Prilla, M.: Let's talk about reflection at work. Int. J. Tech. Enhanc. Learn. **9**(2–3), 151–168 (2017)
34. Pitts, K., et al.: Using mobile devices and apps to support reflective learning about older people with dementia. Behav. Inf. Technol. **34**(6), 613–631 (2015)
35. Reynolds, M.: Critical reflection and management education: rehabilitating less hierarchical approaches. J. Manag. Educ. **23**(5), 537–553 (1999)
36. Roberts, C.: Developing future leaders: the role of reflection in the classroom. J. Leadersh. Educ. **7**(1), 116–130 (2008)
37. Robinson, K.: Do schools kill creativity?. TED (2006)
38. Schön, D.A.: The Reflective Practitioner: How Professionals Think in Action. Ashgate Publishing, USA (1991)
39. Skinner, B.: Science and Human Behavior. Macmillan, New York (1953)
40. Statler, M., Heracleous, L., Jacobs, C.D.: Serious play as a practice of paradox. J. Appl. Behav. Sci. **47**(2), 236–256 (2011)
41. van Manen, M.: The Tact of Teaching: The Meaning of Pedagogical Thoughtfulness. SUNY Press, New York (1991)

Prototyping a Touch-Optimized Modeling Tool for Co-located and Inverted Classroom Group Modeling Scenarios

Marcel Schmittchen[1]([⊠]) [iD], Arlind Avdullahu[1] [iD],
and Robin Beermann[2]

[1] Department for Information and Technology Management,
Ruhr-University Bochum, Bochum, Germany
{marcel.schmittchen,
arlind.avdullahu}@ruhr-uni-bochum.de
[2] Ruhr-University Bochum, Bochum, Germany
robin.beermann@rub.de

Abstract. To support the mastery of necessary skills and knowledge for modeling, manifold approaches and concepts are present. Ranging from theoretical backgrounds, over video tutorials to coached pieces of training and seminars. But the learning from collaborative group work has proven benefits, especially in modeling tasks. During our experiments with touch-based portable projectors in our higher education software engineering courses, we explored and iteratively improved concepts and exercises for collaborative group work. Encountering many grievances with the used software modeling tools we identified the need for a special concept and tool to not only support group modeling itself but also our research and evaluation efforts. In this paper, we will describe the profits of collaborative modeling and present our concept. Afterward, we will present the first prototype we implemented that focuses on automatically placed elements and a minimalistic interaction scheme tailored but not limited to the use with touch projectors. Finally, we will describe our plans for further development and related research.

Keywords: Business process modeling · Process modeling · UML · Co-located group work · Digital education · Inverted classroom · Flipped classroom

1 Introduction

The use of models and formal modeling notations as a means to design, communicate, comprehend and coordinate complex systems and processes never lost its importance. In times of more and more complex systems and agile development methods, the mastery of creating and understanding models is vital as ever.

In the last years, we taught a multitude of modeling techniques and notations to students of the applied computer sciences studies in Bochum in courses ranging from bachelor courses of software engineering and project management to master courses of groupware and knowledge management and sociotechnical design. The modeling

© Springer Nature Switzerland AG 2020
P. Zaphiris and A. Ioannou (Eds.): HCII 2020, LNCS 12205, pp. 159–168, 2020.
https://doi.org/10.1007/978-3-030-50513-4_12

notations include but are not limited to business process modeling [1], UML based techniques [2, 3] like activity charts, critical path analysis, and sociotechnical process modeling. The latter is presented by a modeling notation created by our chair of information and technology management [4].

Within the digitization of education, we tried to incorporate digital means of teaching and using modeling processes in our courses while also optimizing our methods of practical exercises. The use of touch-based systems such as semi-public displays, tablets, touch projectors, etc. all shared a common problem in educational settings: A lot of time is used for mundane aesthetic tasks like positioning elements and connections in evenly distributed positions. Since most educational settings have a lot of time and attention constraints, this time is lost for more productive tasks and less focus is laid on reflecting the created model and the modeling process itself.

In order to support this modeling process, based on our previous studies, we designed a concept for a modeling tool that supports parallel modeling, merging tasks and evaluation of the above and started by developing a touch-based modeling software with a simplified interaction scheme that places and resizes elements automatically allowing the students to focus more on the models contents and implications.

2   Co-located Group Modeling

Knutas [5] showed that in higher education software engineering courses student motivation, productivity, and critical thinking improved with the use of computer-supported collaborative learning. But group work needs special care considering the group sizes and experience levels of its members [6, 7]. Differences in experience are often handled by having seasoned modelers in charge of the modeling process in the role of chauffeur or moderator[1]. Renger [7] describes the struggle between the positive effects of productivity by having a modeler or chauffeur present versus the challenges posed by taking direct access and influence away from individual group members. This could potentially lead to less direct interaction between the group members as well as the feeling of less ownership or contribution to the final model. Another way to deal with the problem of different expertise is the integration of parallel modeling.

> A critical enabler of full group participation is the ability to work in parallel. In all cases where the model was built in parallel, the group divided into subgroups, and subgroups were assigned parts of the model corresponding to the subgroups' expertise [7].

Another benefit of parallel modeling is that it is much faster and efficient [7]. While designing parallel modeling distinct and overlapping tasks and areas of responsibility are important to keep interactions going in group work scenarios. Positive effects are lost when group members don't participate or work for themselves in silence [10]. Thus more focus must be laid on finding consensus and a shared understanding of the final model during the merging phases [7]. Also, instructions need to be as specified as possible. The learning success is much higher when the strategies for collaboration are established beforehand [10].

---

[1] e.g. social-technical-walkthrough/SeeMe Walkthrough [8, 9].

Nolte [11] suggests three distinct modes of parallel modeling processes for groups (see Fig. 1):

1. Every participant works on their own device and can change the whole model. Optionally an overview of the complete model is also viewable for everyone involved e.g. on a big screen.
2. Parts of the model are divided into submodels that are worked on by subgroups that can share a single device. In this mode, the subgroups may develop different styles of collaboration [12].
3. The group works collaboratively on one screen or device. Here different modes could be used: Using a split surface that allows different participants to work on different parts of the model or have a single overview of the whole model with which everyone interacts.

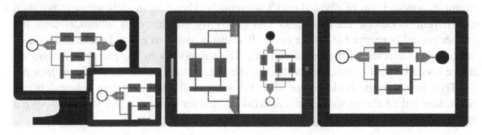

Fig. 1. Concept of different usages of parallel modeling. Individual devices (left), split mode on one device (middle), multiuser on one device (right)

To enable these scenarios different setups can be used. E.g. large, high-resolution interactive screens [13], combined with smartphones [11] or touchscreen tables [12, 14, 15]. These multi-screen environments are getting more common and systems like Touch Projector by Boring [16] work on seamless interactions with tabletop systems, wall projections or laptops via mobile phone as input devices. We tried to incorporate portable touch projectors[2] in our group modeling sessions.

We also structured our courses after the inverted classroom model to have more time for practical exercises and group work tasks. Studies by Mason [18] suggest that in Inverted Classroom scenarios students tend to report spending less time studying outside of class while doing actually more, because the learning via video, quizzes, etc. is not perceived as regular "studying" while leading to better or equal results in terms of educational goals.

It is known that especially in software engineering education the need for good supporting software tools is high [5] but especially in collaborative and parallel model building more research and literature is needed [7]. Thus an optimal tool should not only focus on supporting the learning and modeling process but also allow for more in-depth evaluation.

---

[2] Sony Xperia Touch (see [17]).

3 Concept

In the following, we will present the three main concept ideas that developed during our previous studies and our experiences in teaching software engineering and i.e. modeling notations in tutorial groups of up to 30 students.

3.1 Parallel Display Modes

In terms of display modes, we differentiate three cases. The first being a simple "one user - one screen" setup. Secondly a continuous display of the model on one screen, but it should be possible to edit it in parallel at several places at the same time. Thirdly, it should be possible to divide the screen into several areas that scroll and edit parts of the model independently from each other.

When used for parallel modeling, these modes can be mixed and expanded. For example, a model can be divided into 3 submodels. Those submodels are now assigned to different modelers. Each modeler can now only edit his own submodel until the greater model is merged at a later point. It's also possible to expand these concepts to more than one screen (or type of screen). The submodels in the example mentioned above could be sent to three individual devices (e.g. smartphones or touch projectors).

To summarize the basic design idea: We want to allow that certain submodels can be broken out of the model for detail work in smaller groups, while still keeping the main model, all connections and dependencies intact (see Fig. 2).

Fig. 2. Sketch of the "on-the-fly" separation of submodels for group work tasks

3.2 Easy Point of Entry

To allow an easy point of entry we follow several design ideas. For co-located group work in educational settings, we want to minimize time wasted on less productive parts of the modeling process that tend to get annoying for students or tedious with certain hardware. For example, in our experiments, a lot of time and motivation was lost while placing relation arrows or elements at the exact right place or creating an aesthetic overall look. At other times modeling tools are filled with many options and functions that can easily intimidate inexperienced users.

Based on the assumption that it will be easier for users to understand the principles of modeling when they can focus more on the content we want to allow the software to take care of the aesthetics and placement. Especially in simple process scenarios, such as are used in early training exercises, will benefit.

As the user improves their skill and knowledge, we want the tool to gradually give the user more and more control over parts of the modeling process and the interactions possible with the model. This could even be used to level the playing field when confronted with groups of different experiences and skills concerning modeling tasks and allow for more complex and productive exercises.

Still, modeling languages and notations are learned primarily from text, videos or pictures when not practiced in co-located exercises. Once the tool will be able to switch between different levels of control for the users depending on their current skillset, it will also become useful for inverted or flipped classroom and blended learning scenarios with emphasis on self-learning and preparation. Combined with prompts and predefined tasks the tool could be used to train basic modeling rules for a single user as well.

3.3 Evaluation Support

The tool is designed with the teaching and evaluation of the modeling process in mind. It, therefore, should be able to store and reconstruct the complete interactions including all deletions and changes made during the modeling process. While often the quality of the modeling process is measured in the time needed and the quality of the final model a lot of interesting factors are harder to reconstruct and evaluate.

This is why we want the tool to gather more information during the modeling process (e.g. how many mistakes were made, how many changes were made or undone later, etc.). By saving the modeling process (i.e. every iteration of the model instead of the final version) we want to integrate a "timeline" mode allowing us to reconstruct and review the iterations of the modeling process (see Fig. 3). This could also be used to support the reflection process in group work sessions by replaying certain situations of the modeling process for the users.

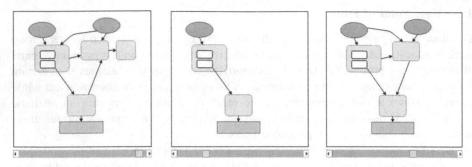

Fig. 3. Mockup of the timeline mode used to analyze model iterations.

4   Touch-Optimized Prototype and First Evaluation

Based on the concept presented in Sect. 3 we started developing the first prototype. This early prototype focused on the *Easy Point of Entry* (see Sect. 3.2) design idea while laying the groundwork for the future implementation of the *Parallel Display Modes* (see Sect. 3.1) and the *Evaluation Support* (see Sect. 3.3).

4.1   Flow-Notation

When inexperienced persons are tasked to document processes over 90% start to structure them graphically and more than two thirds intuitively use flowcharts as a means of modeling [19]. This could prove the ideal starting point for teaching more and more complex modeling notations and tasks. Thus we started with a notation based on the concept of flowcharts with a mandatory start and end element and the option to create divergently and joining paths.

The start element is represented by an open circle while the end element is represented by a filled circle. Both elements are connected from the start. The process can be modeled using rectangle shaped activity elements lined along paths between the start and end that can be labeled. Binary branching is structured as two corresponding elements called IF (diverging) and FI (merging). These can also be labeled with a certain question or test condition leading to different paths. For this early version, we set the rule that the upper path represents the positive and the lower path the negative condition.

With this set of elements, simple first models can be created. In order to step by step, increase the complexity of the tasks and models, a number of additional elements are planned but not yet implemented. Among others are *parallel branching elements* allowing for any number of paths running in parallel lanes. Also using corresponding start and end elements for parallel processes similar to their counterparts in activity diagrams. *Subprocesses* that themselves consist of their own start and end elements and can be collapsed and expanded for better structuring and overview. Leading up to the inclusion of *events*, *jump labels*, *roles*, and *objects*.

4.2   Automated Placement and Saving

The original inspiration for the automated placement of the process model is based on Graphviz [20]. With this tool, models of graphs can be written in a source code style that is then parsed into a graphical output.

All paths and elements are automatically created and placed in the most symmetric and clear way possible. When elements are removed from the model, the remaining elements and paths are also adjusted accordingly. The position of all elements are calculated in a virtual coordinate grid. The reading direction of the model is from left to right along the X-axis, so that successive elements are next to each other in the direction of the right side. Consequently, the Y-axis becomes relevant as soon as more paths and lanes are created. After calculating the virtual positions, the sizes of all elements are determined and assigned to the respective cells. This allows for calculating the final screen coordinates and expansions for all elements. Afterward, the appropriate graphics and texts can be drawn. Finally, the connections are calculated and drawn on the basis of the coordinates of the associated elements.

Internally, the model is stored as a set of components. Thereby each component references its direct predecessors and successors. Arbitrary many predecessors or successors are possible. The corresponding references are stored in sorted lists so that there is a clear order. Related elements have sorted lists corresponding to their paths so that the first connection leading out of the splitting element also the first connection is the one that leads into the merging elements (and so on). This allows the entire model can be run through in linear form. The graphic representation is statically calculated by the software by adding all elements that can be arranged in a grid. This ensures an efficient runtime of the algorithm (O(n)) and no components can overlap. Even when models get bigger, the performance and the clarity are not compromised (see Fig. 4).

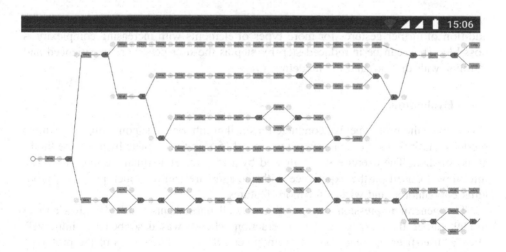

Fig. 4. Example of a bigger model created with the prototype

The way in which the model data is stored allows for the future implementation of many of the concepts presented in Sect. 3, e.g. separation and merging of submodels or the recreation of the modeling process.

4.3   Interaction Scheme

Since the development was focused on touch-based systems (tablets, touch projectors) the prototype was created for Android 8 and with a minimalistic approach concerning inputs. Instead of menus, symbols or bars the user just tabs the diagram with one or two fingers. To create a new element, the user taps the green area on the path, were they want to place the element (see Fig. 5) with one finger. To create an IF symbol the user taps the green area on the path with two fingers. Tapping on an already existing element with one finger lets the user edit the element while tapping an element with two fingers removes the element from the model.

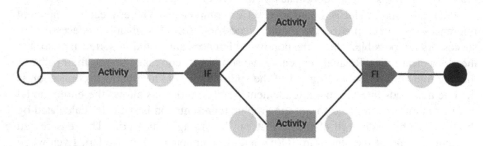

Fig. 5. The prototype flow model with round interaction zones between elements

Since modern touch devices allow for ten or more touchpoints simultaneous the addition of further gestures for more types of elements with increasing complexity is possible. They can be introduced step by step as the user gets more experienced and familiar with the tool and the modeling process.

4.4   Evaluation

To evaluate the prototype, we conducted a small number of tests consisting of a simple modeling task that took the participants around 15 min to complete by using the think-aloud method. The exercise was followed by a 15-min semi-structured interview. The interview focused on the experience with the software and the touch projector, problems encountered and wishes for more features.

The general impression was positive and all participants finished with a correct model earlier than expected. The interaction scheme was described as "intuitive", "fast", "user-friendly" and "easy to remember". Several weaknesses of the prototype were also revealed. E.g. the zoom and centering of the model did not work as expected in all cases. The most frequently mentioned wishes were for an undo & redo function and the ability to drag & drop created elements into different lanes or positions.

Another mentioned wish was that a newly created element should start in focus allowing the user to name the new element without having to select it first.

A factor not previously considered was brought to our attention during the tests. Up to this point, we used the standard Android onscreen keyboard and paid it not much mind during our exercises and tests. But in the interactions, we noticed huge differences in style the participants used to type on the touch projector. From one finger to ten-finger typing, usage of one or two hands and even swipe typing was used leading to many different results in the time used to finish the model with swipe typing being the fastest.

5   Conclusion and Future Works

We identified three key concepts and requirements for supporting collaborative modeling processes and their evaluation from our former studies. Based on these concepts we developed the first prototype that completely takes over the graphic design of the process model so that the users can concentrate on the actual modeling. The graphical position of an element is calculated from its connections to the other elements. In addition, the interaction is greatly simplified for the user. Instead of menu structures, the most important functions can be used directly as touch gestures. The relational storage of the model enables future developments to incorporate the separation of submodels and reconstruction of the modeling process for evaluation and reflection purposes.

Finally, the prototype was tested with a small number of users that helped us identify minor bugs and showed potential points to improve the usability of the prototype and opened up the additional factor of the typing tool and mode used.

We developed the first prototype with touch devices such as touch projectors or tablets in mind. Since parallel work should utilize more than one medium [11] a future use of and combination with VR, AR, keyboards and other forms of inputs and devices should be considered. Also implementing server synchronization allowing for more than one device to edit the same model is our next step.

The current prototype and concept will be improved and expanded through more end-user tests and experiments in the coming semesters and with the help of experts from pedagogical and psychological backgrounds.

References

1. Benedict, T.: BPM CBOK: Business process management common body of knowledge (BPM CBOK R). ABPMP, Lexington, KY (2013)
2. Fowler, M.: UML Distilled: A Brief Guide to the Standard Object Modeling Language. Addison-Wesley, Boston (2010)
3. Mandl, P.: Grundkurs Betriebssysteme: Architekturen, Betriebsmittelverwaltung, Synchronisation, Prozesskommunikation, Virtualisierung (2014). https://doi.org/10.1007/978-3-658-06218-7

4. Herrmann, T.: SeeMe in a Nutshell. The Semi-structured Socio-Technical Modeling Method (2006). https://www.imtm-iaw.ruhr-uni-bochum.de/imperia/md/content/seeme/seeme_in_a_nutshell.pdf. Accessed 17 Feb 2020
5. Knutas, A., Ikonen, J., Porras, J.: Computer-supported collaborative learning in software engineering education: a systematic mapping study. J. Inf. Technol. Secur. **7**, 4 (2015)
6. Becker, F.: Teamarbeit, Teampsychologie, Teamentwicklung: So führen Sie Teams! (2016). https://doi.org/10.1007/978-3-662-49427-1
7. Renger, M., Kolfschoten, G.L., Vreede, G.J.D.: Challenges in collaborative modelling: a literature review and research agenda. Int. J. Simul. Process Model. **4**, 248 (2008). https://doi.org/10.1504/IJSPM.2008.023686
8. Herrmann, T.: Systems design with the socio-technical walkthrough. In: Handbook of Research on Socio-Technical Design and Social Networking Systems, pp. 336–351 (2009)
9. SeeMe Walktrough. https://seeme.iaw.ruhr-uni-bochum.de/?locale=en. Accessed 17 Feb 2020
10. Schneider, M., Mustafić, M. (eds.): Gute Hochschullehre: Eine evidenzbasierte Orientierungshilfe, pp. 41–43. Springer, Heidelberg (2015). https://doi.org/10.1007/978-3-662-45062-8
11. Nolte, A., Brown, R., Anslow, C., Wiechers, M., Polyvyanyy, A., Herrmann, T.: Collaborative business process modeling in multi-surface environments. In: Anslow, C., Campos, P., Jorge, J. (eds.) Collaboration Meets Interactive Spaces, pp. 259–286. Springer, Cham (2016). https://doi.org/10.1007/978-3-319-45853-3_12
12. Isenberg, P., Fisher, D., Morris, M.R., Inkpen, K., Czerwinski, M.: An exploratory study of co-located collaborative visual analytics around a tabletop display, pp. 179–186 (2010). https://doi.org/10.1109/VAST.2010.5652880
13. Turnwald, M., Nolte, A., Ksoll, M.: Easy collaboration on interactive wall-size displays in a user distinction environment. In: Workshop "Designing Collaborative Interactive Spaces for e-Creativity, e-Science and e-Learning. Citeseer (2012)
14. Hornecker, E., Marshall, P., Dalton, N.S., Rogers, Y.: Collaboration and Interference: Awareness with Mice or Touch Input. University of Strathclyde, Glasgow (2008)
15. Marshall, P., Hornecker, E., Morris, R., Dalton, N.S., Rogers, Y.: When the Fingers do the Talking: A Study of Group Participation with Varying Constraints to a Tabletop Interface. University of Strathclyde, Glasgow (2008)
16. Boring, S., Baur, D., Butz, A., Gustafson, S., Baudisch, P.: Touch projector: mobile interaction through video. In: Proceedings of the 28th International Conference on Human Factors in Computing Systems - CHI 2010, p. 2287. ACM Press, Atlanta (2010). https://doi.org/10.1145/1753326.1753671
17. Techradar Review of the Sony Xperia Touch. https://www.techradar.com/reviews/sony-xperia-touch. Accessed 18 Feb 2020
18. Mason, G.S., Shuman, T.R., Cook, K.E.: Comparing the effectiveness of an inverted classroom to a traditional classroom in an upper-division engineering course. IEEE Trans. Educ. **56**, 430–435 (2013). https://doi.org/10.1109/TE.2013.2249066
19. Recker, J., Safrudin, N., Rosemann, M.: How novices design business processes. Inf. Syst. **37**(6), 557–573 (2012)
20. Graphviz. https://www.graphviz.org/. Accessed 17 Feb 2020

Evaluating Portable Touch Projectors in the Context of Digital Education

Marcel Schmittchen[(⊠)] and Arlind Avdullahu

Department for Information and Technology Management,
Ruhr-University Bochum, Bochum, Germany
{marcel.schmittchen,
arlind.avdullahu}@ruhr-uni-bochum.de

Abstract. In digital education, it is becoming increasingly important to provide devices that lower the entry point and motivate high levels of participation, especially during group work scenarios. Within the context of digitization of education projects at Ruhr-University Bochum, we conducted studies in multiple courses using touch-based portable projectors. Teaching collaborative and creative modeling was the setting of these experiments. The experiments were conducted and evaluated in three different phases. Finally, the gathered data was used to improve the method and the software requirements for the following phases iteratively and also to assess whether the use of the touch projector improves the collaborative learning of the modeling process. During the evaluation, we found out that the participants using the touch projector always ranked their level of participation in the modeling process much higher than it was actually observable.

Keywords: Digital education · Computer-supported collaborative learning · Group awareness · Participation · Inverted Classroom

1 Introduction

Research shows that collaborative learning is an effective method not only in terms of learning success but also in the learning process. It helps the students among other things to form productive strategies for problem-solving [1]. Also, it is considered positively for student motivation and improved critical thinking [2]. To focus on this in our higher education courses we started to implement the Inverted Classroom method. Studies show that the Inverted Classroom method can improve higher education settings in many ways. Mason [3] found that more course material could be covered while student results were better (i.e. at problem-solving tasks) or equal to classic classroom settings. It also allowed us to have more time that could be used for practical exercises, discussion, and reflection. While students need some time to adjust to the Inverted Classroom format, they tend to learn to take more responsibility for their learning progress [3] which can be seen as another positive side effect.

© Springer Nature Switzerland AG 2020
P. Zaphiris and A. Ioannou (Eds.): HCII 2020, LNCS 12205, pp. 169–178, 2020.
https://doi.org/10.1007/978-3-030-50513-4_13

While many formats and methods (as well as tools) are constantly developed and tested, the definite elements or guidelines for successful Computer-Supported Cooperative Learning environments are still not clear [2]. Renger [4] assessed the need for more identification, codification, and documentation of best practices and methods for collaborative modeling with an emphasis on a shared understanding of the final result and the participants' evaluation of the resulting model as well the efficiency of the process. To that goal, we tried to iteratively explore and improve group work exercises in our courses utilizing a set of portable touch projectors[1] for creative collaborative modeling with focus on participation, group awareness and flexibility of the touch-based input devices. Touch surfaces provide support for co-located collaboration and provide a higher level of awareness and fluidity of interaction [6]. Studies with multi-user touch systems even showed that they allow for more equity in group work since it eliminates the possibility of the dominance of some group members when the medium has limited access points or resources (e.g. a pen or a computer mouse) [7].

For the final phase of our experiments, we integrated parallel modeling tasks which offer a much faster and efficient way of modeling but raises new challenges for the process by demanding more focus on finding consensus and a shared understanding of the final model during the merging phase [4].

2 Methods and Approach

The experiments were performed at the Ruhr-University Bochum in multiple 4th-semester courses of applied computer science studies over a period of one year. The experiments and their respective evaluation were divided into three phases that will be explained in detail in the following subcsections. In order to be able to make qualitative and quantitative statements, the experiments were filmed, interviews with the students were conducted and questionnaires were distributed among the participants in each phase.

During the first phase, three different input devices (flipchart, tablet pc, touch projector) were compared against each other (see Sect. 2.1). In the following second phase, the participants were tasked to create a model using the portable touch projector. In contrast to the first phase, an experimental multitouch mode was used, which could process several different user inputs simultaneously (see Sect. 2.2). In the last phase, we used an existing online modeling tool (draw.io [8]) with prepared elements and a more complex modeling task that demanded the merging of the groups models into one joint model during the exercise (see Sect. 2.3).

All experiments were conducted in our moderation lab (modlab) utilizing a large interactive touch screen (4.80 m × 1.20 m; 4200 × 1050 px) used for many years as an interactive workspace for studying amongst other things collaborative and creative processes [9], as well as a set of cameras and microphones connected to a separate

---

[1] Sony Xperia Touch (see [5]).

control room to observe and capture all activities. Also, each experiment benefited from being included in the regular course/tutorial schedule of the students, allowing us to discover the pains and gains of using the methods and technology in real higher education settings for students as well as for tutors and lecturers.

2.1   Phase One – Comparison of Different Input Devices

Phase one was carried out in several tutorials of a software engineering course. The experiment was conducted on three different days with different groups of students. In total 33 students participated in the experiment. Of these, 6 were female and 27 were male. The persons were aged between 18 and 28 years. The participants were divided randomly into three groups with variable sizes at each experiment. In total there were nine groups of sizes two to six.

In this experiment, the test persons were asked to identify digital tools to improve the university's cafeteria visit and create mind maps of their findings. For this purpose, three mind maps were to be created at different stations in the room, each dealing with one of the three categories "Before the cafeteria visit", "During the cafeteria visit" and "After the cafeteria visit". Each mind map was modeled on a different medium. In addition to the touch projector, the participants also worked on a tablet pc and an analog flipchart. For the modeling of the mind maps on the touch projector and the tablet pc, the SeeMe[2] web editor developed by the Chair of Information and Technology Management was used. The topics were distributed to different stations for each session. This was done to ensure that each topic was worked on each medium. Thus, it can be determined afterward whether the topic had an influence on the quality of the final model that would otherwise be attributed to the used medium. The exercise itself was based on the World Café method. Each group rotated to a different station after five minutes of brainstorming (see Fig. 1). This way each team used each medium once in a mixed order. Finally, after every group completed all stations, they had to present the mind map they had last worked on to the entire course.

Each run of the experiment was recorded with three cameras. Each camera was directed at one station. The participants filled out a questionnaire focused on the usability factors of all three mediums. Also, the recordings were later coded and analyzed using the qualitative content analysis by Mayring [11].

One problem that emerged soon in the process was that the interactions on the portable touch projector were usually only initiated by one person per group. Since the used software allowed no parallel working or multitouch functionality we decided to try an experimental prototype plugin for phase two. Since the literature indicates that the multitouch functionality would increase the participation significantly [7].

---

[2] Semi-structured, socio-technical modelling method [10].

Fig. 1. Experiment set-up and illustration of the "World Café" method using a tablet (left), flipchart (right) and portable touch projector (middle)

2.2   Phase Two – Multitouch Mode

The second phase took place during the summer project management seminar. A total of ten students aged between 21 and 25 years participated. One of them was female and nine were male. In this experiment, the participants were randomly divided into two groups of five. Both groups worked simultaneously on the same task. The participants' task was to create a process model using a modeling software on a touch projector. The model should represent the procedure of an ideal student research project, based on the learning content the participants had acquired during the course so far.

Again, the modeling was done using the SeeMe web editor. The notation and the functions the participants needed to create the model were explained to them. Then they had 30 min to perform the given modeling task. In this phase, we introduced a prototype multi-touch plugin in the hope to increase the participation of all group members. The modeling activities were also recorded by cameras, with each camera pointing at a group table. This video material was later used to analyze participation and group awareness. Also, a questionnaire was handed out and interviews with each participant were conducted. In section three, the results of the analysis are discussed in detail. After the time was up, one person from each group presented the results on a large display in the room to the other group.

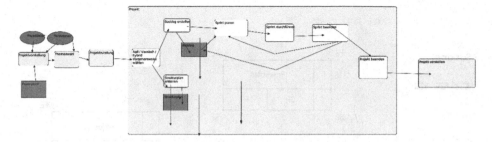

Fig. 2. Example process model created by students during phase two

The same modeling software was used in phases one and two. In both experiments problems with the modeling occurred that were connected to the used software. E.g. because the placement of elements (especially the relation arrows) was a big challenge for the participants (see Fig. 2) that took a lot of time and motivation away from the task. Also, the prototype plugin had several bugs that hindered the experiment. E.g. the multi-touch mode randomly switched itself off and a non-functional undo feature led to much frustration when elements were deleted by accident and could not be restored. For this reason, a different more stable and established modeling tool (draw.io) was used in phase three in order to avoid software problems and to focus more on already available collaborative modeling features. The method was made more complex and integrated more switching between group work and presentation/merging segments.

2.3   Phase Three – Merging Task with a Collaborative Modeling Tool

In the final phase 19 students participated, 3 of them were female and 16 were male. It was conducted in the winter project management seminar. The participants were divided into three groups with 6 to 7 group members. Each group's table represented the department of a fictional company. The students took on the role of members of the marketing department, development department and general management. At each group's table, a portable touch projector was prepared with an empty canvas in draw.io shared with a lecturers account on the big modlab screen. Also, the basic elements were created in advance by the lecturers so that the students could create the more complex network plan elements with one click and could focus more on the task at hand (see Fig. 3).

Each group was given an individual task sheet. In this sheet, work packages were defined for their department complete with dependencies and workloads. The task was to model a critical path analysis for their respective departments. The students modeled their submodels for 20 min (see Fig. 4). After these three models were completed, one student from each group was sent to the large display in front of the room to merge the three sub-models together into the final diagram. Afterward, the three groups analyzed the final refined model to determine strategies to optimize the workflow of the projects. This experiment was also captured on video and questionnaires were handed out.

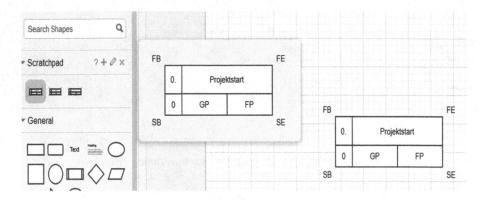

Fig. 3. Prepared network planning elements in draw.io's Scratchpad

Fig. 4. Experiment setup at the beginning of phase three

By using this modeling software, a small improvement in the group interaction with the portable touch projector could be observed, but the problem described in the previous section, the placement of the elements i.e. of the connecting arrows between two elements, remained. During the merging task students not directly involved at the big screen tended to switch their focus on their mobile phones and private conversations and did not use the offered option to follow their colleagues' progress via the big screen or the mirrored model on their groups projectors. This can be attributed to the too big group sizes (leaving behind 5–6 people waiting for one group member to work out the solution) and the lecturer's failure to explain the need to follow the merging process for further tasks as well as the failure to point out the option to see the merging process on their groups own devices.

3 Results

In the first experiment, (and in stark contrast to our expectations) the interaction with the touch-based portable projector was performed almost exclusively by one person per group in phase one. The percentage of interactions by one group member was on average 92%. The compared tablet was also used primarily by one person to a large extent (83%), but the tablet was passed around more casually, which led to minimal more active interactions of the other team members.

The introduction of the multi-touch mode was intended to increase participation and group awareness. Regarding participation, a small improvement was seen. The two groups had one person dominating the interactions with the touch projector with a share of 87% and 62%. In the third and last phase (again without multi-touch functionality) a similar picture was seen. In one of the three groups, the device interaction was performed by one person exclusively. In another group, the device interaction was performed by two team members having shared the interactions evenly with 50% each. The last group had a 50/30/20 split of the interaction between three team members. However, the group size in this final phase was six to seven persons and on average four to five team members did not interact with the touch projector at all. Our group composition was mostly homogenous in terms of skill and knowledge, but it was again proven that when group size increases productivity decreases [4].

The questionnaires delivered another surprising result in terms of participation. In the first phase, 12 persons were observed interacting with the touch projector, but 15 persons stated that they had interacted with it. The result was similar in the other two phases. In phase three, 6 of 19 people were observed interacting with the devices. However, 11 people in the questionnaire stated that they had interacted with it. In all other categories like group awareness, communication and conflicts the results of the questionnaires matched with the analyzed video material.

In terms of communication, the results are positive. In all three phases, all team members communicated actively about the model and provided input for the problem-solving process. The analysis of the video material and questionnaires showed that group awareness was also increased when the portable touch projector was used. Each team member observed the person interacting with the touch-based portable projector closely. With the exception of the merging task in phase three in which the large groups lost interest in their teammates working in a smaller group on the large screen.

Conflicts between team members were not apparent. Conflicts between the participants and the projectors were more common in all phases. Although a more stable software was used in the last phase, conflicts with the precise placement of elements were still observed.

The model quality was low in all three phases. Due to the operating problems with the software used, the focus on the modeling task was quickly lost and resulted in the models not being of good quality in phases one and two with a slight improvement in phase three.

Besides these difficulties the participants stated that interacting with the touch projector was easy to learn and fun to use.

4   Conclusion and Future Work

The aim of this paper was to investigate the potential of touch-based portable projectors for collaborative education. Here, the focus was laid on increasing the participation of group members in modeling activities. Analyzing the video material showed that the interaction with the portable touch projector was used by a maximum of three persons per group. Using the multi-touch mode did not increase participation in this context very much. Large groups in phase three proved contra-productive. Thus, we recommend group sizes of three persons for this device. In terms of tasks, it is much more important to give each team member distinct tasks and defined areas of responsibility in order to keep the participation levels high for the whole group [1]. This will be incorporated in further exercises.

In comparison, the tablet and flipchart were easier to engage (considering every participant has interacted with similar devices before) but the smaller screen of the tablet led to more conflicts in sharing the interaction screen while the flipchart lacked (of course) editing functions the digital devices provided.

Similar to Marshall [7] we measured participation disconnected from the actual quality of the participation or the learning progress made. We plan to shift our focus to a more comprehensive evaluation of the method and its results. Also, during the execution of the three phases, it became clear that most participants stated they had interacted with the touch projector. However, the video analysis of the three phases showed a different result, namely that the interaction was mainly carried out by one person. This perceived active participation should be investigated more closely in the future eliminating the chance of misunderstandings between interaction, participation and the quality of each.

E.g. a future phase could incorporate the following scenario. In a course groups of more than three students are formed. Since we observed that in such large groups a big share of participants does not interact with the touch projector. Every participant will have a button placed in close range or given to them and they are asked to press the button whenever they feel like they have participated in a meaningful way to the final model (see Fig. 5). Later the timecodes given by the pushed buttons could be used to be compared to the video material as well be used to reflect the interaction or participation with an individual group member or even the whole group.

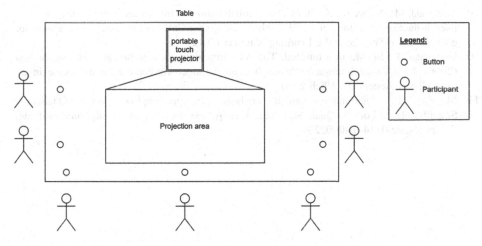

Fig. 5. Possible setting of phase four

Finally, a major problem in all three phases were flaws and annoyances with the used software. For this reason, problems encountered in all three phases were reflected and used to identify requirements, which will provide a basis for implementing a suitable software for collaborative learning modeling activities with touch projectors in the future.

Acknowledgments. The authors would like to thank Kevin Hermann for his support and work on the experiments and the evaluation that provided the basis for this paper.

References

1. Schneider, M., Mustafić, M. (eds.): Gute Hochschullehre: Eine evidenzbasierte Orientierungshilfe. Springer, Heidelberg (2015). https://doi.org/10.1007/978-3-662-45062-8
2. Knutas, A., Ikonen, J., Porras, J.: Computer-supported collaborative learning in software engineering education: a systematic mapping study. J. Inf. Technol. Secur. **7**, 4 (2015)
3. Mason, G.S., Shuman, T.R., Cook, K.E.: Comparing the effectiveness of an inverted classroom to a traditional classroom in an upper-division engineering course. IEEE Trans. Educ. **56**, 430–435 (2013). https://doi.org/10.1109/TE.2013.2249066
4. Renger, M., Kolfschoten, G.L., Vreede, G.J.D.: Challenges in collaborative modelling: a literature review and research agenda. Int. J. Simul. Process Model. **4**, 248 (2008). https://doi.org/10.1504/IJSPM.2008.023686
5. Techradar Review of the Sony Xperia Touch. https://www.techradar.com/reviews/sony-xperia-touch. Accessed 18 Feb 2020
6. Hornecker, E., Marshall, P., Dalton, N.S., Rogers, Y.: Collaboration and Interference: Awareness with Mice or Touch Input. University of Strathclyde, Glasgow (2008)
7. Marshall, P., Hornecker, E., Morris, R., Dalton, N.S., Rogers, Y.: When the fingers do the talking: a study of group participation with varying constraints to a tabletop interface. University of Strathclyde, Glasgow (2008)
8. draw.io: https://www.draw.io/. Accessed 17 Feb 2020

9. Turnwald, M., Nolte, A., Ksoll, M.: Easy collaboration on interactive wall-size displays in a user distinction environment. In: Workshop "Designing Collaborative Interactive Spaces for e-Creativity, e-Science and e-Learning. Citeseer (2012)

10. Herrmann, T.: SeeMe in a nutshell. The semi-structured socio-technical modeling method (2006). https://www.imtm-iaw.ruhr-uni-bochum.de/imperia/md/content/seeme/seeme_in_a_nutshell.pdf. Accessed 17 Feb 2020

11. Mayring, P.: Qualitative content analysis (28 paragraphs). Forum Qualitative Sozialforschung/Forum: Qual. Soc. Res. 1(2), Article no. 20 (2000). http://nbnresolving.de/urn:nbn:de:0114-fqs0002204

STEAM-X: An Exploratory Study Adding Interactive Physical Activity to the STEAM Model

Jina Shin and Jeongyun Heo[✉]

Kookmin University, 77 JeongNeong-Ro, SeongBuk-Gu, Seoul 02707, Korea
jinashinlab@gmail.com, yuniheo@kookmin.ac.kr

Abstract. The philosophy of holistic education, which emphasizes a balance between physical and cognitive development, has been widely considered important for many years. However, Science, Technology, Engineering, Arts, and Mathematics (STEAM) education, which is currently being promoted worldwide, is moving away from the holistic education model, causing an imbalance between subjects due to its heavy emphasis on science and mathematics. This paper proposes a STEAM-X education model that adds physical activity to the STEAM model for the purpose of providing a modern holistic education that includes physical, cognitive, and mental learning and promotes creative and convergent thinking. In this study, we reviewed the existing literature concerning the benefits of physical activity, student preferences for physical activity, and the link between physical activity and STEAM education. Based on this review, we derived four research questions and conducted experimental research. We selected the appropriate tools for STEAM-X education, collected data on their implementation through observation and user interviews, and received positive responses from students and parents about STEAM-X education. The STEAM-X model appears capable of influencing students' body reaction speeds, body coordination, concentration, problem-solving abilities, creativity, sequential thinking, strategic thinking, collaboration skills, and ethical attitudes. Implementing the STEAM-X education program would require creating additional plans for safety, developing content for instruction in conjunction with other subjects, and providing support for teachers, such as operational guides and manuals.

Keywords: STEAM · STEAM-X · Interactive game · Mixed reality

1 Introduction

While education policies have changed as society has changed, the philosophy of education as an experience that cultivates both mind and body has remained the same. Throughout history, prominent philosophers of education, from Plato and Aristotle to Rousseau, have emphasized that intellectual and mental development must be in balance with physical development [1]. Juvenal likewise emphasized the importance of creating harmony between physical strength and mental training, stating, "There is a sound mind in a healthy body" [2].

© Springer Nature Switzerland AG 2020
P. Zaphiris and A. Ioannou (Eds.): HCII 2020, LNCS 12205, pp. 179–193, 2020.
https://doi.org/10.1007/978-3-030-50513-4_14

In the last decade, reforms emphasizing Science, Technology, Engineering, Arts, and Mathematics (STEAM) education have taken place worldwide. STEAM is an educational model which aims to enhance students' interest in and understanding of science and technology and to foster a convergence of thinking skills based on science, technology, and practical problem-solving skills [3]. Its purpose is to integrate elements of each subject area into broader interdisciplinary themes and to pursue a holistic approach to life [4]. In contrast to the traditional education model, in which students independently learn knowledge and concepts from various subject areas, STEAM-based classes focus on project-based inter-disciplinary learning and on fostering problem-solving skills in everyday life. STEAM takes the positive view that students should acquire and use knowledge with the goal of solving a given problem, rather than learning passively, and utilizes a student-centered interactive education model to improve student learning [5].

The move towards promoting and investing in STEAM programs at the national level is necessary to foster science and technology talent. How-ever, the STEAM model allows certain subjects to receive the spotlight, while others remain relatively unlit. This can lead to imbalances between subjects. The STEAM model evolved from the STEM (Science, Technology, Engineering, and Mathematics) model, adding the arts to enhance creativity. The category of "arts" included not only fine arts, but also language arts, physical education, liberal arts, and social studies [6]. Nevertheless, many view the arts as limited to activities such as visual art, design, and music, and there is a need for more active physical and liberal arts education.

Physical activity improves the physical health of children and adolescents, leading to strength development, improved aerobic capacity, and reduced blood pressure and cholesterol levels. It also helps children learn by increasing their cognitive abilities and reducing their stress levels. However, the advent of technologies like computers, smartphones, and television has reduced students' physical activity levels [7]; even in schools, time spent engaging in physical activity is decreasing. This can lead to problems, such as lower overall levels of physical fitness in adolescents and an increase in the obese population.

This study proposes a STEAM-X education model that adds physical activity to the STEAM model to provide a modern holistic education for children and adolescents that enables them to become physically, cognitively, and mentally healthy and facilitates creative and convergent thinking. The purpose of this study is to provide a basis for including physical activity in STEAM and to conduct exploratory research applying STEAM-X to the educational field.

2   Related Work

2.1   Benefits of Physical Activity

Previous theoretical and empirical studies have shown that physical activity has various benefits for children and adolescents and is essential to the formation of a healthy body. Proper physical activity forms the basis for children's growth and has a positive effect on their physical strength [8]. Physical activity in childhood leads to a decrease in body fat in adolescence [9], thereby reducing childhood obesity. Furthermore, physical activity stimulates immune cell growth [8] and reduces the incidence of chronic diseases in adults, including cardiovascular disease, cancer, and diabetes [10].

Studies have also shown that physical activity can improve quality of life through positive emotional changes, altering the negative emotions that occur in daily life [11]. Endorphins released during exercise reduce stress, anxiety, and depression [12]. Physical activity has been shown to have a positive effect on adolescents' sociality, as well as their physical and affective health. The World Health Organization (WHO) reported that sports participation improved self-esteem, self-awareness, and psycho-logical well-being [13], and the Council of Europe argued that sports made an important contribution to the process of personality development [14]. Shields and Bredemeier suggest that sports reflect the dominant climate of society; according to their analysis, sports function both as a cultural symbol and as an intermediary through which young people can learn and experience the core values of their society [15]. Park —who defines sports as competitive recreational activities based on established rules and practices—concludes that learning traditions (such as the rules and customs of sports) allows individuals to develop their abilities as members of society and grow into competent social beings through good-faith competition with others [16].

Physical activity is beneficial for adolescents in a variety of areas of cognition and metacognition [17] and contributes to higher intelligence and improved learning preparation [18]. Sustained physical activity is significantly correlated with cognitive ability, including reaction time, processing speed, executive function, attention, and concentration [19]. Activating brain functions through physical activity affects not only these cognitive functions, but also thinking skills involved in combining, analyzing, and creatively reproducing information [17]. Studies have shown that children's academic achievement improved when they spent more time participating in physical activity and that schools with high academic achievement had higher levels of physical activity than low-achieving schools [20].

2.2 Adopting Physical Activity in Education

Dutch historian Johan Huizinga described humans as "Homo Ludens" (playful creatures) [21]. Human play is spontaneous and regular and involves important elements for happiness, such as relationships and leisure [22]. When the body is voluntarily engaged in physical activity, the brain is more active as well. The experience of pleasure involves a positive emotional reaction and a motivating participatory decision [23]. The pleasure that a person feels during physical activity induces spontaneous participation, which motivates them to continue exercising, exerting tremendous concentration and experiencing a "flow" state of complete immersion and happiness. Furthermore, the effects of physical activity are clear and immediate. Almost as soon as an individual moves their body to perform an action, the task ends, providing immediate results and creating a series of small successes and challenges. This process enables people to feel fulfilled and confident.

As the importance of science and mathematics education has grown, students have tended to achieve more highly in mathematics and science, but their mathematics and science interest has tended to be lower. In particular, in 2015, Korean students' scientific achievements on the Organization for Economic Cooperation and Development (OECD)'s Programme for International Student Assessment ranked fifth among OECD countries, but Korean students' interest in science ranked 26th, below the OECD average. Similarly, Korean students' mathematics scores were the highest among OECD countries as of 2012, but their interest was only 28th—again below the OECD average [24].

On the other hand, students had a higher preference for physical activity than for other subjects. Seo et al. surveyed the subject preferences of 1,694 students in grades 5 and 6 in Korea and Japan and found that their preference for physical education was significantly higher than for other subjects; children who participated in the survey indicated peer group interactions, self-expression, and praise as factors leading to their enjoyment of exercise [25]. As the previous study shows, students enjoy physical education because it allows them to move out of the classroom, engage in a variety of physical activities, and play with friends.

2.3   Integrating Physical Activity with STEAM

Some previous studies have investigated the combination of physical activity and science education. Yoo compared Korean seventh- and ninth-graders' physical education textbooks with their science textbooks to find the connection between the two subjects and suggested the possibility of convergence education [26]. Lee asked students to actually measure the speed and force of objects in physical activities—such as running, tug-of-war, and Korean seesaw—and to analyze the data to reflect new game strategies and tactics [27]. Recently, in the field of computer education, students have been introduced to computer science concepts through "unplugged" activity, which uses physical activity, games, and work-sheets to educate students on computer science without using computers [28].

STEAM and physical activity are also linked in that the skills cultivated through STEAM education can also be developed through physical activity. Critical thinking, creativity, collaboration, and communication—which are called "Four Cs"— are the most important skills of the 21st century for k-12 education defined by National Education Association [29]. STEAM is a suitable training for developing the critical thinking, creativity, collaboration, and communication [30, 31], and physical activity can also help to build these four competencies. Tishman and Perkins contend that, in order to be successful in physical education, students must plan, research, reason, strategize, and use meta-cognition to assess their current level of understanding [32]. Since sports activities often involve teams of many people, participation in sports requires verbal and emotional communication between various team members, coaches, and referees [16]. In addition, when students compete in teams, they develop collaborative skills and experience various cognitive thinking and problem-solving processes in the course of skill and strategy development, exercises, and competitions. Physical activity improves cognitive creativity through sports and play activities and expands artistic creativity through dance education and physical movement activities [33].

While doing physical activity, students may find effective ways to achieve their physical goals through analysis and their own reasoning and verification. For example, students might attempt to shorten their running time, lower their body posture to reduce resistance, change their supporting foot from right to left to use force at the starting point, or take off their shoes and run barefoot. These seemingly simple choices about running movements are based on a variety of scientific principles, and students naturally go through the process of using scientific knowledge to achieve practical goals. This process is similar to the process of critical thinking and problem solving that is cultivated in STEAM education.

3 Exploratory Study on STEAM-X

3.1 Research Questions

In the literature review, we discussed the educational benefits of physical activity, student preferences regarding physical activity, and the relationship between STEAM and physical activity. The purpose of this study is to provide a basis for including physical activity in the STEAM model. Through an exploratory study of STEAM-X, this research seeks to answer the following questions:

1. Do learners have positive perceptions of adding physical activity to STEAM?
2. What effect does adding physical activity to STEAM have on the learner (student)?
3. Do preferences concerning physical activity affect learning about the associated subject?
4. What are the considerations involved in adding physical activity to a STEAM education program?

3.2 Method

We selected the augmented reality sports platform Lü interactive Playground (Lü) as a teaching tool for STEAM-X. Lü is an augmented reality video game that displays content on a large screen. Kinect, which is a motion sensing input device produced by Microsoft, recognizes a player's movement when the player touches the screen using a softball or their body. We used Lü as a tool for the STEAM-X education model for the following reasons:

- Lü involves immediate interaction between the player and the screen, allowing the user to engage in enjoyable physical activity.
- Lü contains approximately 30 types of game content, including both simple content (e.g., requiring a ball to be correctly matched to an object displayed on the screen) and content requiring more complex cognitive skills (e.g., math operations, word quizzes, and picture puzzles) (Fig. 1).
- Since it is possible for multiple individuals to play Lü at the same time, we were able to investigate situations involving multiple users.
- Because Lü uses a softball, rather than a joystick or another separate device, it can be used easily by young children.
- Lü's lighting and sound effects enhance user concentration and interest.

- Lü can be used indoors, so that research can be carried out without being affected by the weather.

Fig. 1. Lü Interactive Playground (Lü) contains approximately 30 types of game content (https://www.play-lu.com/applications)

We used the below Stakeholder Map to identify the stakeholders involved in education and conducted the study using the qualitative survey methods of observation and interviews.

Stakeholder Map. Stakeholders involved in STEAM-X include students, teachers who provide education, parents, and suppliers of education teaching tools (Fig. 2).

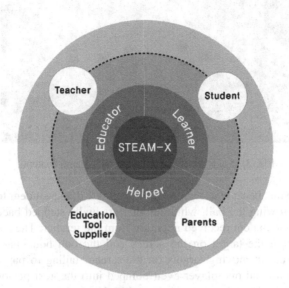

Fig. 2. Stakeholder map of STEAM-X

Observations. Our observations took place in December 2019 at a private agency on Jeju Island, South Korea, which used Lü for its pilot program. In this program, 7 to 8 children experienced 3 to 4 game contents for 15 min each.

Participants were a mix of ages, with the youngest student at age 4 and the highest student at age 13. Children under the age of seven seem to have difficulty using Lü due to their weak throwing power, poor accuracy in matching targets, and poor recognition of and reaction speed to targets appearing and disappearing on the screen. Most of the students who participated in the program actively chose to participate in the program. However, participants in aged 12–13 were a little passive, ashamed about moving their body in front of younger students. Education by similar ages will likely lead to more active student participation.

The teacher often played "DANJA" (a game content which requires the user to follow characters' dances on the screen, but does not require user interaction) for the purpose of relaxation at the beginning of the program. While playing DANJA, some groups appeared to be enjoying themselves and were actively involved, while others remained shy and stood still. The students seemed to move actively when the teacher imitated the action of the character on the screen. The teacher's behavior and energy seem to affect the students a lot.

Fig. 3. Students are playing DANJA game content

As the participants became accustomed to playing Lü, one student touched the wall lightly without throwing the ball, while another gradually stepped back and threw the ball hard. The latter student received attention from the teacher. The students were too focused on catching the target on the screen and the ball bouncing out, When the participants focused on moving targets on the screen, failing to pay attention to the person next to them, and one player even bumped into the next person.

Shorter students typically hit objects that appeared in the lower position, whereas taller and older participants intentionally only hit objects that appeared higher on the screen out of consideration for the younger participants (Fig. 3). When eight students were divided into two teams and played "NEWTON" (a mathematic game), team members talked and worked together to solve problems and one girl stood behind her team to retrieve all the missed balls and deliver them to the next batter. In this way, students showed cooperation, even though the day of the study was the first time they had met.

While the program was in operation, parents and students waiting for their next turn watched the progress of the program from a distance. All parents took pictures and videos of their children on their smartphones, and watched the education program interestingly (Fig. 4).

Fig. 4. Students are playing Target game content using balls

3.3 Data Collection

Interviews. Interviews were conducted with students, parents, and teachers.

Students. We conducted oral interviews with five children between the ages of 8 and 10 years old who had undergone the STEAM-X program. We obtained the consent of both the child participants and their guardians. The questions aimed to identify students' preferences for STEAM-X education (Fig. 5).

User Code		S1	S2	S3	S4	S5
Age		8 years	8 years	9 years	10 years	10 years
Sex		Male	Female	Male	Male	Female
Q1	Interest level (low:1 ~ High: 5)	5	5	5	5	5
Q2	Favorite subject	Assembly blocks	Music	Arts	Physical Education	Physical Education
Q3	What do you think about doing Lü at school?	[S1~S4] I want to do it at school. It seems to be fun. [S5] Doing it everyday would not be good, but sometimes it would be fun.				
Q4	Which game you did is the most memorable?	[S1] Target: It was fun to play, and it might help to lose weight. [S2] Dojo: It was good to work out as a team, and I felt bad because of sweat, but it was fun. [S3] Target: because I did it last. [S4] Newton: Memorize the multiplication table and put it to the body without using your head. [S5] Galactic: A good effect of popping the square when hitting the ball.				
Q5	Did you do enough?	not enough. I want to do more	enough	not enough. I want to do more	not enough. I want to do more	not enough. I want to do more

Fig. 5. Summary of student interviews

Parents. We asked two parents of children who participated in the program about their opinions of the program. Both had positive reactions to their children's engagement in physical activities, and both expected that the program would have cognitive learning effects.

> P1: *"My child has recently become interested in Nintendo, and I like it because he seems to be moving and using his head rather than just sitting at home playing mobile games."*

> P2: *"Children do not play well outdoors because of fine dust, but they can move actively indoors and have good learning effects. It would be nice to have such a facility near the school."*

Teachers. We had an hour-long in-depth interview with one elementary school teacher who is the organizer of an education program that utilizes Lü as "Body Activity Design Tool". He takes in charge of organizing computational thinking and software educational program for the whole school. He also received the Prime Minister's Award for his contributions to the dissemination of software education. This Elementary School in Seoul, Korea, was designated as a "maker hub center" in Seoul. After introducing Lü to this school in December 2019, a two-week pilot program was held for each class. Prior to the implementation of the education program, all teachers learned how to use the relevant tools, received content education through faculty trainings, and utilized Lü for physical education classes, convergent curriculum classes, and non-disciplinary activities one to two times per week.

The teacher introduced Lü for enhancing collaboration and cognitive learning.

"I first saw Lü on Facebook, it seems to be able to use multiple people at the same time, enhancing collaboration and cognitive learning"

Through the education program, he expects students to have learning effects of physical, cognitive, and social such as attitude, concentration, collaboration, creativity, and sequential thinking.

"They can learn order and attitude while waiting for their turn in line. Their concentration becomes stronger by doing the program, and this concentration is likely to affect other classes, as well. I was surprised to see students collaborate on PHŸS [physics puzzles, which require them to move tools so that mice can eat cheese]. In order to solve common problems, they naturally created leaders, shared roles, formulated strategies, and solved problems in creative ways. This process seemed to be able to develop the sequential thinking of software education, and most of all, they seemed to be acquiring these skills without knowing it. The program also develops their speed of response to stimuli as well as their ability to adjust to goals."

The teachers and students responded to the program as follows. Students expressed regret that they wanted to do more but couldn't. Teachers said that the tool motivated students rather than general physical education classes because it scores and has instant interaction. Some teachers who were unfamiliar with the new teaching methods and digital devices felt pressured to conduct the class. In such cases, they worked with their class and the other class at the same time with the help of other teachers.

As an operational improvement, he talked about developing additional equipment for safety and game content for further education.

"Students are so engrossed in the screen that it can be dangerous, as they do not see the person next to them, so it would be nice to display a safety statement before the content is played. It is also likely that a net will be installed so that the ball hitting the wall does not fall back and is not dangerous to the students sitting behind it."

"I would like to add more content suitable for Korean education and more advanced learning, as well as more content that students have done offline so they can easily understand and enjoy it. In math computational content, students did not want to go to a more difficult stage; adding a gamification element so that the amount learned is displayed cumulatively is likely to compete with other classes and motivate them."

"If there is a guide and curriculum on what capabilities each content requires and how many participants can proceed as a team, teachers will likely be able to use it well in conjunction with other classes."

4   Insights and Design Implication

4.1   Insights

Students' perceptions of STEAM-X education were positive, given that all five students interviewed rated their interest at the highest possible level (5) after completing the program. In our interviews, parents were also positive about STEAM-X education.

Although the effect of STEAM-X education on students was not quantitatively measured here, our observations and in-depth teacher interview allow us to hypothesize that STEAM-X education could affect students' physical response rates and coordination, concentration, problem-solving abilities, creativity, sequential thinking, strategic thinking, and ethical attitudes.

In this study, it was difficult to measure the learning effects of whether preferences regarding physical activity affected other subjects linked to it. This is because the program has not yet conducted classes linked to physical activities, and the educational tools used did not have suitable content for other subject areas. Appropriate content in educational tools must be developed to adequately study the influence of physical activity preferences on subject learning.

Two considerations must be taken into account when applying STEAM-X to classes. First, since STEAM-X is an education model that includes physical activities, safety concerns must be addressed by creating safety guides and sharing them with teachers, providing safety training to students, and adding physical safety equipment. Second, support should be provided for teachers who operate classes, including trainings, manuals for educational equipment, and lesson operation guides.

In addition, future studies should consider the following as independent and control variables: (1) conducting programs among groups with similar physical conditions leads to a more active student attitude; and (2) learning effects vary according to teachers' individual competencies.

4.2   Design Implication

Lü—which was selected as an educational tool in this study—includes content related to mathematics and science literacy, but did not have adequate game content to enable the class to proceed.

As a result, it is necessary to develop new content. The researchers have planned content that can be linked to other subjects and that is highly scalable.

Figure 6 displays content designed to solve a set number of problems within a time limit by utilizing the scientific knowledge learned in Korea's third grade science curriculum. This is a quiz that answers the questions such as "What is the object attached to the magnet?", "What is the object that can be burned?", "What can be floated in the water?". Time is numerically displayed in the corners of the screen and is marked with a timeline at the bottom to increase student motivation. Over time, the bomb icon in the bottom corner explodes, adding an enjoyable gameplay element.

Fig. 6. Science quiz

Figure 7 shows content that needs to be addressed using mathematical computational capabilities. If there are three objects on the left side of the scale and the support is horizontal, the ball must be hit three times on the right. If there are three objects on the left side of the support and the left side of the support is tilted, then it is necessary to hit the ball twice. Similarly, if there are three objects on the left side of the support and the support is tilted to the right, you have to hit four times, one greater than three.

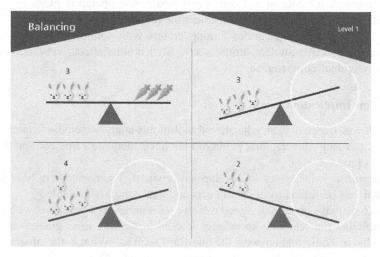

Fig. 7. Balancing game

Before playing this content, the teacher can teach students the scientific concepts of "mass" and "gravity." Students can then use this content to understand and identify the concepts they have learned.

5 Conclusion

This study proposed a STEAM-X education model adding physical activity to STEAM based on the educational advantages of physical activity, the high preference of learners for physical activity, and the correlation between physical activity and STEAM education. An exploratory study revealed students' preferences for STEAM-X, hypotheses about learning effects, and considerations for conducting educational programs. However, we could not confirm the effect on the curriculum linked to physical activity. Content that can be linked with other subjects has therefore been planned for further study. The contents we have planned will be developed in Unity (game engine) and will be uploaded to the equipment with the cooperation of Lü.

As an exploratory study, this research has several limitations. The education programs we examined were run as a pilot program, rather than a regular program, so we could only determine user preferences and hypothetical learning effects. In order to fully measure the educational effects of the STEAM-X model, future research will require a curriculum organized by experts, as well as training periods of sufficient length to identify significant learning effects. Furthermore, the results from this study utilized qualitative research methods to evaluate learners' positive perceptions of the STEAM-X model; future work should examine the qualitative data we obtained using proven measurement tools verified in subsequent studies. Finally, this study was conducted primarily using elementary school students in first through third grade. However, as it is important to study preferences and learning effects at various ages, future studies involving the application of the STEAM-X model to various age groups are necessary.

Acknowledgements. This study has been conducted with support from the "Design Engineering Postgraduate Schools" program, an R&D project initiated by the Ministry of Trade, Industry and Energy of the Republic of Korea. (N0001436).

References

1. Hills, A.: Scholastic and intellectual development and sport. Sports Child. 76–90 (1998)
2. Han, D.: A sound mind in a sound body - Plato's and Aristotle's views. J. Korean Soc. Wellness **9**, 1–11 (2014)
3. About STEAM—STEAM education. https://steam.kofac.re.kr/?page_id=11269. Accessed 23 Feb 2020
4. Lim, Y.: Problems and ways to improve Korean STEAM education based on integrated curriculum. J. Elementary Educ. **25**, 53–80 (2012)
5. Hong, O.: STEAM education in Korea: current policies and future directions. Sci. Technol. Trends Policy Trajectories Initiatives STEM Educ. **8**, 92–102 (2017)

6. Yakman, G.: What is the point of STE@ M?–A brief overview. steam: a framework for teaching across the disciplines. STEAM Educ. **7**, 9 p. (2010)
7. Fogel, V.A., Miltenberger, R.G., Graves, R., Koehler, S.: The effects of exergaming on physical activity among inactive children in a physical education classroom. J. Appl. Behav. Anal. **43**, 591–600 (2010)
8. Sothern, M.S., Loftin, M., Suskind, R.M., Udall, J.N., Blecker, U.: The health benefits of physical activity in children and adolescents: implications for chronic disease prevention. Eur. J. Pediatrics. **158**, 271–274 (1999). https://doi.org/10.1007/s004310051070
9. Moore, L.L., et al.: Does early physical activity predict body fat change throughout childhood? Prev. Med. **37**, 10–17 (2003). https://doi.org/10.1016/S0091-7435(03)00048-3
10. Lee, S.M., Burgeson, C.R., Fulton, J.E., Spain, C.G.: Physical education and physical activity: results from the school health policies and programs study 2006. J. Sch. Health **77**, 435–463 (2007). https://doi.org/10.1111/j.1746-1561.2007.00229.x
11. Paluska, S.A., Schwenk, T.L.: Physical activity and mental health: current concepts. Sports Med. **29**, 167–180 (2000). https://doi.org/10.2165/00007256-200029030-00003
12. Long, B.C.: Stress-management interventions: a 15-month follow-up of aerobic conditioning and stress inoculation training. Cogn. Ther. Res. **9**, 471–478 (1985). https://doi.org/10.1007/BF01173094
13. Micheli, L.J., et al.: Sports and children: consensus statement on organised sports for children. Bull. World Health Organ. **76**, 445–447 (1998)
14. Svoboda, B.: Sport and physical activity as a socialisation environment: scientific review part 1. Council of Europe, Strasbourg, France (1994)
15. Shields, D.L.L., Bredemeier, B.J.L.: Character Development and Physical Activity. Human Kinetics Publishers (1995)
16. Park, J.J.: Can sports build character?: The theoretical, empirical grounds and tasks of character education through sports. J. Curriculum Stud. **29**, 173–202 (2011)
17. Alvarez-Bueno, C., Pesce, C., Cavero-Redondo, I., Sanchez-Lopez, M., Martínez-Hortelano, J.A., Martinez-Vizcaino, V.: The effect of physical activity interventions on children's cognition and metacognition: a systematic review and meta-analysis. J. Am. Acad. Child Adoles. Psychiatry **56**, 729–738 (2017)
18. Getman, G.N.: How to Develop Your Child's Intelligence. Research Publications (1984)
19. Etnier, J.L., Salazar, W., Landers, D.M., Petruzzello, S.J., Han, M., Nowell, P.: The influence of physical fitness and exercise upon cognitive functioning: a meta-analysis. J. Sport Exer. Psychol. **19**, 249–277 (1997)
20. Lindner, K.J.: The physical activity participation–academic performance relationship revisited: perceived and actual performance and the effect of banding (academic tracking). Pediatric Exer. Sci. **14**, 155–169 (2002)
21. Gaver, W.: Designing for homo Ludens. I3 Mag. **12**, 2–6 (2002)
22. Huizinga, J.: Homo Ludens Ils 86. Routledge (2014)
23. Wankel, L.M.: Personal and situational factors affecting exercise involvement: the importance of enjoyment. Res. Q. Exer. Sport **56**, 275–282 (1985)
24. Kwak, Y.: Effects of educational context variables on science achievement and interest in TIMSS 2015. J. Korean Assoc. Sci. Educ. **38**, 113–122 (2018). https://doi.org/10.14697/jkase.2018.38.2.113
25. Seo, Y., Nam, Y., Choi, T., Aoyagi, O., Ikeda, T., Han, N.: A comparative study on the preference of physical education, after school-play and factors of physical pleasure derived from physical activity in Korea and Japan elementary students. Korean J. Growth Dev. **25**, 179–186 (2017)
26. Ryu, S.: Exploration of Middle School Inclusive Education Through Connection of P.E. and Science (2010)

27. Lee, D.: Interdisciplinary Integration in Physical Education Practice. Korean Society for the Study of Physical Education, pp. 37–49 (2018). (We translated Korea title to English)
28. Taub, R., Ben-Ari, M., Armoni, M.: The effect of CS unplugged on middle-school students' views of CS. ACM SIGCSE Bull. **41**, 99–103 (2009)
29. An Educator's Guide to the "Four Cs". http://www.nea.org//tools/52217.htm. Accessed 23 Feb 2020
30. Sen, C., Ay, Z., Kıray, S.: STEM skills in the 21 st century education. Presented at the December, vol. 23 (2018)
31. Taylor, P.C.: Why is a STEAM curriculum perspective crucial to the 21st century? (2016)
32. Tishman, S., Perkins, D.N.: Critical thinking and physical education. J. Phys. Educ. Recreation Dance **66**, 24–30 (1995)
33. Park, H.: A study on the meanings of creativity in the world of sports. J. Korean Soc. Philos. Sport, Dance Martial Arts **21**, 21–42 (2013)

Usability Testing of a Digital Competence Assessment and Certification System

Aleksandra Sobodić[(✉)] ⓘ and Igor Balaban ⓘ

Faculty of Organization and Informatics, University of Zagreb,
42000 Varaždin, Croatia
{aleksandra.sobodic,igor.balaban}@foi.unizg.hr

Abstract. This research study is based on conducted usability evaluation of the CRISS system, which is a cloud-based system for acquisition, evaluation and certification of digital competence in primary and secondary schools, scalable to other educational levels. The usability evaluation included a combination of tasks completion and questionnaires to collect mostly quantitative, but also qualitative data in order to improve the existing system and give some guidelines for future development of systems with similar scope. In total, 14 teachers and 19 students from primary and secondary schools participated in the evaluation. The results revealed that the effectiveness score of the CRISS system was 97% and 94% on behalf of students and teachers, respectively. One of the efficiency measures showed that in average teachers spent 1.7 min, while students spent 1.5 min per task, but it should be bear in mind that they also had differently assigned tasks. Findings showed no significant differences in score ratings of overall task ease, task time and satisfaction with the system performance.

Keywords: Usability testing · Digital competence assessment system · Digital competence certification system

1 Motivation

In recent years, there has been an increasing awareness of the importance of acquiring digital competences (DC) so that an individual does not get excluded from society and the labor market. Many researches have been made on this issue and it has been concluded that the teaching of DC should be started from the earliest age and implemented into the formal educational curriculum [1–3]. Moreover, it has been revealed that DC does not develop equally over the years of education, but that this could be changed by the development of a proper system based on a competency-based learning [4]. There are some initiatives of developing ICT tools for skills development or assessment (such as Ikanos project, Skillage, ACTIC, ECDL, etc. [5, 6]), but literature review has not revealed any attempts of implementing such system into school curricula or its use within classes in primary and secondary schools. Most of the analyzed papers deal with the DC acquisition and evaluation on a theoretical level and within university context.

© Springer Nature Switzerland AG 2020
P. Zaphiris and A. Ioannou (Eds.): HCII 2020, LNCS 12205, pp. 194–206, 2020.
https://doi.org/10.1007/978-3-030-50513-4_15

Therefore, a group of educational institutions and industry partners across six EU countries felt encouraged to start the CRISS project within Horizon 2020 funding program which involved around 52 primary and 93 secondary schools. The main aim was to develop the CRISS system, a cloud-based system for guided acquisition, evaluation and certification of digital competence in primary and secondary schools and to pilot the efficiency of such approach throughout formal curriculum. Upon completion of the project, the system will be released on the market for commercial purposes and usability testing is 'de facto' the standard procedure that should be carried out [7]. After all, the success and longevity of an information system (IS) greatly depend on positive user experience and perception [8].

Unsurprisingly, most of usability testing studies are conducted on health information technology in order to meet users' or patients' needs as to reduce the proneness to failure [9]. Nevertheless, same goals need to be reached for any other technology (web, mobile, tablet) or a product in less critical contexts. The DC assessment and certification CRISS system is unique for its functionalities but share some similarities with other educational systems worth to be studied. Therefore, some examples found in the literature show application of GOMS model on English learning education game which interface is evaluated by elementary school children aged 7–12 years [10], game scenarios for project management education [11], e-books for lectures at university [12], student academic portal [13], and similar. Most common conclusions of research paper reveal that a dynamic change of content (i.e. learning resources) can retain users, a higher degree of system's flexibility can satisfy learning objectives (e.g. design of new content, creation of assessment criteria, etc.), and that interfaces should be easy to use as well as intuitive and user-friendly.

Since usability testing can be costly and time-consuming it was worth considering how many participants is necessary to involve in this activity. The optimal number of users has challenged many researchers and experts to suggest a rule that all could rely on. Two research streams of usability practitioners have stood out, but a final consensus on a sample size was not reached. The first one estimated that 80% of usability issues can be detected by five users [14], while the other criticized it arguing that such a small number can only support relatively straightforward studies with quite closed or specific tasks [15, 16]. Through their usability studies they determined that higher number of users or experts can increase the percentage of usability issues detected. The newer research suggests a rule of at least twelve and a maximum of twenty users [17], but highlights the impact of study complexity and context on choosing the right sample size. This rule was followed in this paper striving to achieve valid usability testing and identification of majority of the system's usability problems. Besides the previous rule, five step procedure [12] of conducting the usability testing is taken into consideration throughout this paper: (1) Determining the purpose of the study; (2) Determining the study methods; (3) Determining the list of tasks and scenarios; (4) Describing the environment and equipment of the study; (5) Determining the participants.

The purpose of this study was to apply the usability test on the CRISS system by including its end-users, teachers and students of primary and secondary schools. Also, a multifaceted research question was proposed: Are there significant differences in opinions between students and teachers regarding the (a) overall task ease, (b) overall task time and (C) overall system's score rating?

Results gathered by conducting and reviewing this study enabled developers to reflect on necessary improvement of current technical and design aspects of the system in order to improve its usability and acceptability by the target group of end-users. The results can also provide directions for developers or usability practitioners interested in developing or evaluating similar systems.

2   Methods

The usability of the CRISS system was assessed through the process of usability testing and usability problems were identified by end-users. Principles of usability testing and structured user tasks would provide a useful insight into system performance, error rate, attractiveness, participants' learnability time and acceptance. The goal was to make the system more usable for both teachers and students, but in the same time to provide a methodology of usability testing that other developers or practitioners could benefit from.

2.1   Research Context

CRISS system is based on the methodological framework that supports key digital competences and pedagogical principles of problem-based and collaborative learning [18]. It represents cloud-based and adaptive technological solution easily scalable to different educational levels, but primarily developed for primary and secondary schools within the pilot project financed by EU's fund program Horizon 2020. The system allows students to have guided acquisition, evaluation and certification of digital competences which will be widely recognized at the European level. It applies a learner-centered approach which actively engages students in a learning process. Technically, system's architecture consists of seven different modules which are in details explained in this paper [19] while some of its main functions will be described in the following text.

Generally, teachers lead their students through various competence assessment scenarios (CAS) which may integrate one or more school subjects or disciplines of the school curriculum. It can also be implemented at any point in the learning process and performed at different time intervals. Depending on teacher's assignment, students perform a different set of activities or tasks which evidence submit through the CRISS system. Teachers assess students' work against a specific set of performance criteria which have different weights of importance. Teachers have also the opportunity to design different CAS, set assessment indicators and select assessment methods and instruments according to their needs and teaching practice. Except for the above, CRISS system also supports advanced techniques such as adaptive intelligent tutoring (e.g. personalized learning), ICT tools set (social network, a visual programming environment, tool for creating multimedia content, mind maps, timelines, etc.), eportfolio, learning analytics, etc.

The system is designed to be used by students without any prior training, but with the assistance of teachers who were provided with the MOOC tutorials and could contact the support service any time. Most of the above functionalities that were considered important for the system quality were tested through the usability testing.

2.2 Participants and Location

Usability testing doesn't require large sample sizes unlike traditional statistical methods, but there are a variety of suggestions from already mentioned practitioners on optimal number of users that can contribute to the validity of the results. For this study, it was decided to follow the rule 16 ± 4 participants [17] with the main objective of identifying as many usability problems as possible. In the following text, the term 'participant' is applied to both teachers and students.

Since CRISS system is developed within the project, three partner institutions (Croatia, Spain and Greece) were asked to ensure at least five teachers who would like to participate in the usability test. It was also recommended that they should seek to achieve equal ratio of primary and secondary school teachers who don't have to be from a same school. On the other hand, it was left to the teachers to select five of their students to take part in the test. For conducting the test, it was necessary for a selected school to have one available classroom with computers and fast Internet connection for three hours on agreed day.

It is necessary to point out the variables that were well controlled during the conducting phase of usability testing:

- All participants used the CRISS system at least for one month.
- All participants evaluated the same system.
- All participants could solve tasks without time restriction or time pressure.
- All participants received the instructions prior to the evaluation with identified evaluation objectives and focus.
- All participants received a certain number of tasks depending on the group they belonged to (ten tasks for teachers and seven tasks for students).

2.3 Design of the Study

All teachers selected by country partners were sent an email containing an introduction to the online tool Loop11, a description of their obligations and rules they had to follow during the usability testing, a number of tasks, a link to a usability test and instructions for guiding their students through usability testing. Further, a remote usability testing with an unmoderated approach was applied, since it provides an opportunity to administer a larger group worldwide and a natural environment where the participants feel comfortable.

The instructions for both groups of participants were written in details to reduce the possibility of errors. In the introductory part of the instructions it was emphasized that both teachers and students are the evaluators of the subject of interest (in this particular case, the CRISS system), and not the test subjects. They also had to give their consent regarding their participation in testing. This was especially important for underage students who had to get the consent signed by the person with parental responsibility.

The testing process consisted of three parts. The first and the last part of testing can be considered as pre-testing and post-testing questionnaires and the second part was task completion. Number of questions and tasks differed per participant group. The first part consisted of socio-demographic questions about the participant (seven questions for teachers and six questions for students). This was followed by ten tasks for teachers and seven tasks for students to solve without time restrictions. Since there were two groups of participants who had different roles in the system, it was necessary to develop a different series of tasks. Developed tasks represented typical activities in the CRISS system. Given user tasks varied in length from one short sentence to a maximum of three. Participants also had the opportunity to skip the task in a case they did not know how to solve it. The third part contained satisfaction questions. Both groups had six questions to answer about their satisfaction and perception of the system they have used for learning or teaching. There were different types of questions from open-ended (e.g. what you liked the best or at least) to close-ended with answer options presented e.g. in a 5-point scale (1 = very dissatisfied, through 3 = neutral to 5 = very satisfied). All three parts were integrated within the mentioned online tool Loop11 which guided each participant through a prototype usability testing.

Teachers could choose whether they want to run their tasks at home or at school while students could only approach the test at school while being supervised by a teacher. Students also had the opportunity to seek for help from a teacher during the usability testing, but only in such cases where it would not affect the test results.

3   Results

Usability testing was conducted in primary and secondary schools in Croatia, Greece and Spain during the June of 2019. Collected data was analyzed by using descriptive and inferential statistics in Microsoft Office Excel. Analysis was made following the recommendations from [20].

3.1   Sociodemographic Characteristics of Participants

The effective sample consisted of 14 teachers (50% male; 50% female) and 19 students (37% male; 63% female) who voluntarily participated in the research. Teachers' age distribution is 25–29 (7%), 30–39 (29%), 40–49 (57%), 50–59 (7%). The ages of students ranged from 11 to 17 years ($M = 14.3$; $SD = 1.8$).

Twelve out of 14 teachers who participated in this research have more than 11 years of teaching experience. Teachers' reported level of computer skill is distributed as following: basic computing and applications (7%), intermediate computing and applications (29%), advanced computing and applications (35%) and proficient computing, applications and programming (29%). Both students and teachers mostly have used desktop computers (45% students; 40% teachers) and laptops (41% students; 48% teachers) to access the CRISS system. In a minority of cases, they have used tablets or smartphones. Table 1 shows a distribution of responses regarding the CRISS usage and participant groups.

Table 1. CRISS usage per participant group.

CRISS usage	Students at home	Students at school	Teachers
(1) Never or almost never	2 (11%)	0 (0%)	0 (0%)
(2) At least once a month, but not every week	11 (58%)	7 (37%)	4 (29%)
(3) At least once a week, but not every day	2 (11%)	5 (26%)	4 (29%)
(4) Almost every day	4 (21%)	7 (37%)	5 (36%)
(5) Every day	0 (0%)	0 (0%)	1 (7%)

3.2 Descriptive Analysis

Descriptive analysis takes into account data collected during usability testing such as number of correctly performed tasks (calculated as task success rate), task completion time, number of page visits, satisfaction and perception ratings.

The effectiveness aspect of CRISS system was measured based on participant's ability to complete a task. Therefore, task success was calculated with respect to '1' indicating completion and '0' indicating abandonment. Of the 140 tasks performed by 14 teachers (ten tasks per teacher), 131 (94%) were completed and nine (6%) were abandoned. On the other hand, 19 students performed 133 tasks (seven tasks per student) of which 129 (97%) were completed successfully and four (3%) were abandoned. In both cases, effectiveness can be taken as 'good' according to [21].

The efficiency aspect was measured by the time it took the participant to complete a task. The mean task time for teachers was between 1.1 and 3.4 min, but the shortest time had also the success rate of 80% which means two abandoned tasks. The second shortest time is 1.2 with success rate of 100% and task success rate above 80% per minute. While solving the tasks, most of teachers visited between 5.3 and 9.8 pages. On the other hand, students had seven tasks for which they mostly spent between 0.9 and 5.8 min per task in average. The fastest student solved each task with over a hundred percent of efficiency, while the slowest one had around 40% of task success per minute. Students visited between 3.7 and 8.7 pages during solving the tasks that is slightly better result in comparison to teachers. In average, a teacher spent 1.7 min per task, while the student spent 1.5 min.

Performance metrics analyzed per each task are presented in Table 2 for teachers and Table 3 for students. The first four tasks had been totally completed by all involved teachers. The most time-consuming task for teachers was to create a group on the social network which is in line with the highest mean number of page visits (11.8). The social network was especially developed for the CRISS system and it had some minor technical issues which affected its less frequent use among teachers that explains the poorer results during testing. The calculated confidence interval showed that there is a 90% chance that true mean time of the last task is between 2.8 and 4.6 min. The task with the shortest time was to find the CRISS Support Service as expected, because it was about pressing a button from the menu. As expected, the task time and task success of teachers depended on the complexity of assigned tasks.

Table 2. Teachers – performance metrics per task.

Tasks	# teachers (ou of 14)[a]	Task success rate	Mean task time (*min*)	90% CI[2]	Task success per min	Mean number of page visits
1 - Login and change the password	14	100%	1.7	[1.0, 2.4]	58.6%	5.0
2 - Find CRISS Support Service	14	100%	0.8	[0.6, 1.0]	125.0%	7.8
3 - Edit the user profile	14	100%	0.9	[0.6, 1.3]	108.8%	7.4
4 - Make a new plan	14	100%	2.1	[1.6, 2.7]	47.4%	4.8
5 - Add content to planning	12	85.7%	2.5	[0.8, 4.2]	34.7%	8.2
6 - Plan the evaluation of a task	13	92.9%	1.8	[1.0, 2.6]	51.9%	7.7
7 - Create portabily	11	78.6%	2.5	[1.6, 3.4]	31%	8.5
8 - Check the Magellan ICT TOOL	13	92.9%	2.0	[1.2, 2.9]	45.6%	6.4
9 - Check the learning analytics	13	92.9%	1.1	[0.8, 1.4]	84.0%	6.0
10 - Create a group on the social network	13	92.9%	3.7	[2.8, 4.6]	25.0%	11.8

Note: a – denotes number of teachers who successfully completed the task; b – 90% confidence interval (CI)

Table 3. Students – performance metrics per task.

Tasks	# Students (out of 19)[a]	Task success rate	Mean task time (*min*)	90% CI[b]	Task success per minute	Mean number of page visits
1 - Login and change the password	18	94.7%	1.2	[0.6, 1.7]	81.3%	3.7
2 - Edit the user profile	19	100.0%	1.4	[0.6, 2.2]	70.3%	7.5
3 - Check the learning analytics	17	89.5%	1.3	[1.0, 1.6]	70.6%	8.2
4 - Create an evidence	18	94.7%	3.4	[2.5, 4.3]	28.0%	6.0
5 - Send the evidence to the evaluation	19	100.0%	1.0	[0.4, 1.6]	101.6%	5.7
6 - Check the social network	19	100.0%	1.5	[1.2, 1.9]	65.7%	7.1
7 - Check the Magellan ICT tool	19	100.0%	1.3	[0.3, 2.3]	77.0%	5.0

Note: a – denotes number of students who successfully completed the task. b – 90% confidence interval (CI)

According to a number of participants who successfully solved each task, checking the learning analytics seemed to be problematic. The evidence of this conclusion is also the mean number of page visits which is equal to 8.2. Although, its mean time of 1.3 min is the same as for the task to check the Magellan ICT tool. Both tasks belong to external modules and it is worth further to explore whether the problem with learning analytics lies in the location of a button or its design. The most time-consuming activity (mean time of 3.4 min) for students was creating an evidence or a story as a solution to the assigned task on behalf of their teacher. All other tasks were solved in less than 1.5 min. The 90% confidence level also has the widest calculated interval (between 2.5 and 4.3 min) for the task of creating an evidence.

In the post-test questionnaire, participants had to evaluate ease of completing the tasks, needed time and overall satisfaction with the CRISS system on a 5-point scale. Figure 1 shows results of task ease according to proposed statement 'I am satisfied with the ease of completing these tasks on the CRISS system' for both teachers and students. Majority students were satisfied (74%) with the ease of completing the assigned tasks while teachers' results were slightly lower (57%). There was also a higher percentage (29%) of teachers who had neutral opinion of task ease.

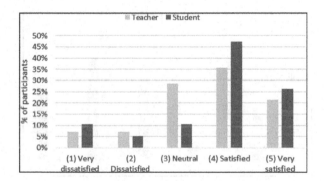

Fig. 1. Teachers and students rating of task ease

Participants' opinion only slightly varied with respect to the statement 'I am satisfied with the amount of time it took me to complete these tasks on the CRISS system' which is clearly shown in bar charts in Fig. 2. It could be said that majority is satisfied with the time taken to solve the tasks (64% of teachers and 63% of students). There is also over 20% of participants with neutral opinion.

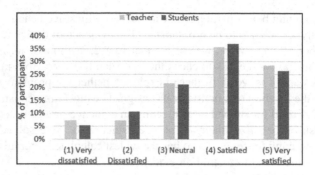

Fig. 2. Teachers and students rating of task time

Figure 3 represents teachers and students overall rating score of the CRISS system. They had to answer to the following question 'On a scale of 1–5, what score would you give to the CRISS system?'. Most of the students (37%) and teachers (43%) rated the system with the score '4 – Very good'.

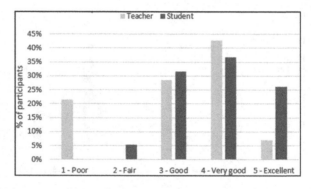

Fig. 3. Teachers and students overall rating score of the system.

In the open-ended questions, students and teachers commended the design of the system, easiness of navigation, interesting content and simple communication in the system with each other. They also agreed that the system was somewhat too slow considering how long they had to wait for its response. Also, in some cases, the system was not regularly updated with students' progress and achievements. Furthermore, students think some of the learning scenarios in the system were too complicated for their level of knowledge and required a lot of time and effort. Teachers added they wanted an open possibility to update the content of the provided scenario according to the needs of their class and teaching practice. They also complained about the complexity of the evaluation process of students' evidences which can become long and tiresome. The provided answers were very helpful in formulating guidelines for improving the system, but they can also serve as recommendations for an optimal design of other educational systems.

3.3   Inferential Analysis

Figure 4 shows average responses for overall task ease, task time and system's score rating. In the same time, it answers to a multifaceted research question. On a 5-point response scale, teachers' perception of tasks ease ($M = 3.6$) is slightly lower than students ($M = 3.7$). On the other hand, they had the same opinion about the amount of time they had to invest to complete the given tasks ($M = 3.7$).

In a narrow sense, teachers and students evaluated their perception of effectiveness (tasks ease) and efficiency (amount of time needed to complete the tasks). On a scale from '1 – Poor' to '5 – Excellent' the CRISS system was rated with an average score of 3.8 by students and 3.1 by teachers.

Two sample t-test was conducted to determine whether there is a significant difference in means between two sets of data. The results are analyzed according to [22] and discussed here:

- There was not a significant difference in the means of task ease rating between students ($M = 3.74$, $SD = 1.21$) and teachers ($M = 3.57$, $SD = 1.12$); $t(31) = 0.39$, $p = 0.70$.
- There was not a significant difference in the means of task time rating between students ($M = 3.68$, $SD = 1.13$) and teachers ($M = 3.71$, $SD = 1.16$); $t(31) = -0.07$, $p = 0.94$.
- There was not a significant difference in the means of overall system's score rating between students ($M = 3.84$, $SD = 0.87$) and teachers ($M = 3.14$, $SD = 1.25$); $t(31) = 1.84$, $p = 0.08$.

Although teachers in two out of three cases gave lower scores than students for the system, the differences between their means were not significantly different ($p > 0.05$).

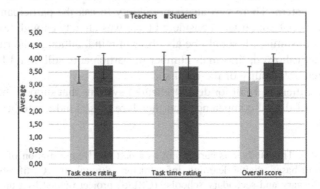

Fig. 4. Satisfaction ratings. Error bars represent the 90% confidence interval.

4   Discussion and Conclusion

This study evaluated the usability of the CRISS system from teachers' and students' perspective. Results indicated the high effectiveness of the CRISS system, 94% on behalf of teachers and 97% on behalf of students. Teachers had a bit more problems during the completion of tasks than students, but their tasks were also different. Although, there could be several factors that favored it, such as less digital literacy on behalf of teachers, non-intuitive interface, complicated usability tasks and many more. On the other hand, students are 'digital natives' who are born using information technology, but it does not have to necessarily influence their ability of handling digital information [4].

Measured task time and number of page visits for both groups revealed minor system flaws that could be easily solved by redesigning or relocating buttons in a more intuitive place. A checklist of items that should be taken into observation while developing such system is based on the observations of open-ended questions. The checklist is structured as follows: system responsiveness, up-to-date system data, interesting content, challenging learning scenarios that could be easily adapted to different teaching practice, easy evaluation process of students' performance, colorful design, intuitive and user-friendly interface. An optimal design of future educational system with similar scope can be achieved by following these recommendations.

Inferential analysis of provided answers regarding overall task ease, task time and satisfaction with system performance showed slightly lower results on behalf of teachers. Although, students were only a bit more critical towards themselves regarding the time they needed to solve the tasks. Findings showed that there were not significant differences in students' and teachers' perception of their interaction with the system. It is also important to emphasize that teachers and students who are selected for the usability testing could be more critical than the rest of the population who participated in the project, because they wanted to express their concerns and problems in relation to the system. Furthermore, participants were limited with predefined tasks, but in this way, the important functionalities of the system, could be tested. Since, this was an unmoderated testing, it would be valuable to conduct the think-aloud-protocol in the future. It would provide insightful information about the system during user's inter-action with the system. There was also a possibility to ask the participant about their opinion after each task, but it was considered there was already enough tasks that were time and effort consuming. It should be also bear in mind, although the rule of at least twelve users was followed, the small number of participants still could have affected the statistical generalizability of the results.

Nevertheless, there is a call for development of systems that support the assessment and certification of digital competence and therefore these kind of studies are of great importance [23].

Acknowledgment. This study was carried out as a part of "Demonstration of a scalable and cost-effective cloud-based digital learning infrastructure through the Certification of digital competences in primary and secondary schools" (CRISS) project funded by European Union's Horizon 2020 research and innovation program under Grant Agreement No 732489.

References

1. Varela, C., Rebollar, C., García, O., Bravo, E., Bilbao, J.: Skills in computational thinking of engineering students of the first school year. Heliyon **5**, e02820 (2019)

2. Tudor, S.L.: The open resources and their influences on the formation of specific competencies for the teaching profession. In: Proceedings of the 10th International Conference on Electronics, Computers and Artificial Intelligence, ECAI 2018, pp. 1–4. IEEE (2018)
3. Siddiq, F., Hatlevik, O.E., Olsen, R.V., Throndsen, I., Scherer, R.: Taking a future perspective by learning from the past - a systematic review of assessment instruments that aim to measure primary and secondary school students' ICT literacy. Educ. Res. Rev. **19**, 58–84 (2016)
4. Lazonder, A.W., Walraven, A., Gijlers, H., Janssen, N.: Longitudinal assessment of digital literacy in children: Findings from a large Dutch single-school study. Comput. Educ. **143**, 103681 (2020)
5. Kluzer, S.: Guidelines on the adoption of DigComp. In: Rissola, G. (ed.) Telecentre Europe, pp. 1–28. Brussels, Belgium (2015)
6. Florián-Gaviria, B., Glahn, C., Fabregat Gesa, R.: A software suite for efficient use of the European qualifications framework in online and blended courses. IEEE Trans. Learn. Technol. **6**, 283–296 (2013)
7. McCreight, S.J., Brinton, C., Kinn, J., Bush, N., Hoyt, T.: Integration of mCare and T2 mood tracker: illustrating mHealth usability testing. J. Technol. Behav. Sci. **4**, 130–138 (2019)
8. Talirongan, F.J.B., Hernandez, A.A.: Issues and challenges on academic information systems: a quantitative study utilizing purdue usability testing questionnaire. In: 2017 IEEE 9th International Conference on Humanoid, Nanotechnology, Information Technology, Communication and Control, Environment and Management (HNICEM), pp. 1–7. IEEE (2017)
9. Maramba, I., Chatterjee, A., Newman, C.: Methods of usability testing in the development of eHealth applications: a scoping review. Int. J. Med. Inform. **126**, 95–104 (2019)
10. Rosyidah, U., Haryanto, H., Kardianawati, A.: Usability evaluation using GOMS model for education game "play and learn English. In: Proceedings - 2019 International Seminor Application Technology Information Communication Industry 4.0 Retrospect and Prospect Challenges, iSemantic 2019, pp. 219–223 (2019)
11. Calderón, A., Ruiz, M., O'Connor, R.V.: Designing game scenarios for software project management education and assessment. IET Softw. **13**, 144–151 (2019)
12. Halim, F.S.S., Widyanti, A.: E-book in Indonesia: reason to use and usability evaluation. In: 2018 International Conference on Information Technology System Innovation, ICITSI 2018 – Proceedings, pp. 154–158 (2018)
13. Rosmasari, et al.: Usability study of student academic portal from a user's perspective. In: Proceedings - 2nd East East Indonesia Conference on Computer and Information Technology, EIConCIT 2018, pp. 108–113 (2018)
14. Nielsen, J., Lewis, J., Turner, C.: Determining usability test sample size. In: International Encyclopedia of Ergonomics and Human Factors, Second Edition - 3 Volume Set. CRC Press (2006)
15. Faulkner, L.: Beyond the five-user assumption: benefits of increased sample sizes in usability testing. Behav. Res. Methods Instrum. Comput. **35**, 379–383 (2003)
16. Hwang, W., Salvendy, G.: Number of people required for usability evaluation: the 10 ± 2 rule. Commun. ACM **53**, 130 (2010)
17. Alroobaea, R., Mayhew, P.J.: How many participants are really enough for usability studies? In: Proceedings of 2014 Science Information Conference SAI 2014, pp. 48–56 (2014)
18. Guárdia, L., Maina, M., Juliá, A.: Digital competence assessment system: supporting teachers with the CRISS platform. In: Central European Conference on Information and Intelligent Systems, Varazdin (2017)

19. Balaban, I., Filipović, D., Peras, M.: CRISS: a cloud based platform for guided acquisition, evaluation and certification of digital competence. In: Multi Conference on Computer Science and Information Systems (MCCSIS), pp. 41–48 (2019)
20. Albert, W., Tullis, T.: Measuring the User Experience: Collecting, Analyzing, and Presenting Usability Metrics. Morgan Kaufmann (2013)
21. Farrahi, R., Rangraz Jeddi, F., Nabovati, E., Sadeqi Jabali, M., Khajouei, R.: The relationship between user interface problems of an admission, discharge and transfer module and usability features: a usability testing method. BMC Med. Inform. Decis. Mak. **19**, 172 (2019)
22. Sauro, J., Lewis, J.R.: Quantifying the User Experience, Second Edition: Practical Statistics for User Research. Morgan Kaufmann Publishers Inc., San Francisco (2016)
23. Siddiq, F., Gochyyev, P., Wilson, M.: Learning in digital networks – ICT literacy: a novel assessment of students' 21st century skills. Comput. Educ. **109**, 11–37 (2017)

Designing 'Embodied' Science Learning Experiences for Young Children

Rhiannon Thomas Jha[1], Sara Price[1(✉)], and Alison Motion[2]

[1] University College London, 23-29 Emerald St, London WC1N 3QS, UK
sara.price@ucl.ac.uk
[2] Learning Through Landscapes, Monarch Way, Winchester SO22 5PW, UK

Abstract. Research in embodied cognition emphasises the importance of *meaningful* 'bodily' experience, or congruent action, in learning and development [1]. This highlights the need for evidence-based design guidelines for sensorimotor interactions that *meaningfully* exploit action-based experiences, that are instrumental in shaping the way we conceptualise the world. These sensorimotor experiences are particularly important for young children as they can provide them with an embodied toolkit of resources (independent of language skills or subject specific vocabulary) that they can draw upon to support science 'think' and 'talk', using their own bodies to develop and express ideas through gesture, that are grounded on sensorimotoric representations from action experiences. Taking an iterative design-based research (DBR) approach [2], this paper reports the design, development and deployment of a programme of outdoor activities for children aged 4–6 years, that drew on embodied cognition theory to foster meaningful action in relation to ideas of air resistance. This research is relevant to researchers, practitioners and designers. It makes a contribution to learning experience design by making explicit the process of applying key components of embodied cognition theory to the design of science learning activities for early years, and how this can effectively inform digital design.

Keywords: Embodied cognition · Early years science · Digital design

1 Introduction

Opportunities for early years science education are expanding due in part to advancements in technology, ongoing research in embodied cognition, increased value being placed on the importance of early intervention by both researchers and educators [3] and increasing awareness of the breadth of educational experiences which need to be nurtured. However, identifying the best tools and pedagogy can often be challenging, and there remains a relative lack of research demonstrating how to translate research in domains like embodied cognition into practice, and how best to assess the effectiveness of this translation.

Science learning from pre-school onwards is typically centred around hands-on interactive activities that utilise visual prompts, objects or apparatus to demonstrate and provide concrete sensorimotor experience of science concepts. Much of this involves

© Springer Nature Switzerland AG 2020
P. Zaphiris and A. Ioannou (Eds.): HCII 2020, LNCS 12205, pp. 207–225, 2020.
https://doi.org/10.1007/978-3-030-50513-4_16

observation and noticing visuo-spatial features related to action experience, with activity design focusing on the objects of science, rather than perhaps the broader embodied activities that might surround these. Alongside this, there is a call to better engage children in outdoor play and learning, where there are increased opportunities for designing for embodied movement and physical activities. Children's movement is a foundation for much of child development, yet is often overlooked [4]. Research in embodied cognition emphasises the importance of 'meaningful' movements and bodily experience in learning and development [e.g. 1, 5–7]. These perceptual and sensori-motor experiences are particularly important for young children as they can provide them with an embodied toolkit of resources (independent of language skills or subject specific vocabulary) that they can draw upon to support science 'think' and 'talk', using their own bodies to develop and express ideas through gesture, that are grounded on sensorimotoric representations from action experiences [e.g. 8–11]. Embodied move-ment and physical activities also contribute to the effective development of physical literacy [e.g. 4] and thus provide both new ways of engaging with science ideas, as well as the more general, but significant, physical literacy skills. Thus, our interactions with the world are significant in our development generally, but also can be drawn on in creating interactions with the world that offer 'lived' experiences relevant to science ideas. "Outdoor play also engages children in physical learning through exploratory experiences which engage them meaningfully, purposefully and with imagination in more extensive and natural environments than can normally be provided indoors [4, p. 113].

However, framing the design of early years science activities from such an embodied perspective is relatively new for educational practitioners and digital design, and calls for more theoretically and empirically grounded embodied design guidelines for sensorimotor interactions that meaningfully exploit action-based experiences, for early years educators and designers. Taking an iterative design-based research (DBR) approach [2] this paper reports the design, development and deployment of a programme of outdoor activities for children aged 4-6 years, that drew on embodied cognition theory to foster meaningful action in relation to the science idea of air resistance. Drawing specifically on the following ideas from embodied cognition the-ory: movement (relating to 'felt'/tacit/kinaesthetic experience); meaning congruency [12], and integrated physical learning tasks [13], we designed activities that provided differently embodied experiences to support engagement with ideas of air resistance, and exploited the outdoors, by drawing on environmental characteristics of space, airflow and outdoor objects (e.g. wearable resistance parachutes) as well as bodily forms of engagement.

2 Theoretical Underpinning

The design of the science learning activities presented here is situated within the context of Embodied Cognition. Theories of Embodied Cognition originate from diverse disciplines bringing various discourses around the role of the body in cognitive development. We situate this work within overarching ideas from enactive cognition where understanding is actively constructed by 'situated living bodies' [14], through dynamic interaction between body (taking into consideration its specific biological and physical affordances), environment and others [10, 15, 16]. Central to this is the idea that meaning and conceptual representation are grounded in *perceptual* and motor experience: "conceptual capacities incorporate and are structured in terms of patterns of bodily activity" [14]. This has important implications for how we design embodied learning activities for young children's science learning. In this work we draw on the following key ideas to inform our design:

2.1 Movement (Felt Experience, Tactile Kinesthetic Movement)

Existentialist and phenomenologists notions of 'lived embodiment' or 'being in the world' claim that we make sense of the world based on the way we perceive it, and each experience, or perception, modifies or shapes our understanding of the world. While our embodied interactions with the world are significant in our development generally, we draw on this idea to create interactions with the world that offer 'lived, felt' experiences relevant to specific science ideas. There are two key related considerations that underpin our designs:

Firstly, a central component of 'lived embodiment' and interaction with the world is movement, which plays a critical role in cognition – it is through our *movement* that we interact with and experience and interpret the world [17]: meaning and thinking being closely linked to movement [18]. Movement capacities have been referred to as the 'ongoing axis of thought and knowing' [19]. Sheets-Johnson (1982) argues that from infancy we 'think in movement' - we learn about the world and our bodies through movement. These early experiences provide a foundation for the development of more complex notions of space and the world. Indeed, as adults we also experience space and the world through attention to movement and kinesthetic qualities when, for example, we walk into a strong wind, or push something heavy across the floor. "Kinesthesia is the gateway to those coordination dynamics that make the world familiar to us and allow us to know what to expect" [18, p. 173]. More than this, embodied interaction with particular objects or features of the world constitute the meaning or understanding we place on these: "As we move in relation to an object or feature in the world, we experience a particular embodied relationship with that feature. This relationship then becomes integral to our understanding of that feature" [4, p. 26].

Secondly, the lived experience – our everyday embodied interactions (movements) with the world - typically occurs at the unconscious level e.g. learning to walk, achieved through repeated trial and error or repeated practice. As adults, once we've mastered 'movement', this process often gets taken for granted ("we may no longer appreciate how thinking in movement informs our lives" Sheets-Johnson, 1982, p. 174) or fades into the unconscious [4], and while important is not necessarily brought to the foreground.

Our design aimed to bring children's awareness of these felt kinesthetic experiences, movements to the foreground in the context of science ideas, to provide links to key components of air resistance. Thus, one aim of our design was to bring to the fore important aspects of the 'typically unconscious lived experience' to develop an activity that brought children's awareness of their 'felt' experience of wind, drag or lift.

2.2   Meaning Congruency

Building on the critical aspect of movement, we also draw on Hald's [12] notion of meaning congruency. Hald also holds the view that "our bodily actions make things happen, which in turn creates meaning" (2016, p. 497), but Hald identifies the important role of motor and *perceptual* experiences more broadly. While recent work in gesture studies framed within embodied cognition suggest the importance of congruent action for fostering learning [e.g. 1], Hald [12] proposes that a broader range of actions – or movements – are also instrumental in eliciting and interpreting changes in our environment, those changes being perceived through different sensory modalities. The notion of congruent action refers to a meaningful action that directly maps to a concept, for example, swinging the forearm with a fixed elbow to learn about a pendulum [1]. Research suggests that congruent actions provide important sensorimotor representations that children can use later through gesture to express and communicate these ideas. However, Hald's notion of 'meaningful' action highlights the role of our multisensory 'embodiment' and multisensory representations in fostering cognition (which links to Barsalou's model of perceptual processing). Recent work examining young children's gestural communication of science ideas, based on interaction with various objects in a water table, indeed shows ways in which children draw on their wider perceptual experiences – including what they observed based on their actions – to generate sensorimotor representations that they used to communicate through gesture about their experience [20]. What is important is the link between action and perception, and how we can design to enable children to make meaningful links between movement and their perceptual and sensorimotor experience.

We draw on these ideas in our design, by providing congruent perceptual, kinaesthetic and physical sensory experiences, using multiple modes of representation of air resistance through the different activities.

2.3   Integrated Physical Learning Tasks

Skulmowski and Rey's [13] review of research on embodied learning noted that the outcome of comparative studies typically showed better learning performance when the embodied learning designs involved 'integrated physical learning tasks', rather than incidental physical learning tasks. Integrated physical learning tasks refer to studies where embodiment aspects were inseparably connected to the learning task [13], for example, running to catch a baseball, as an example of learning to interact with projectile motion in the physical world. This aspect of Skulmowski and Rey's [13] work draws heavily on Wilson and Golonka's paper [21], which positions embodied research as a process of identifying the available resources an organism is actually using and how they are being coordinated into a smart, task-specific framing to solve the task at hand. Wilson and Golonka suggest that four key questions must be addressed in order for the role of embodied cognition to be explored within a research framework. Here we provide a brief overview of how these four questions helped us think through the design of the activities to ensure that they were embedded in physical learning.

1. What is the task to be solved?

    During science themed activities young children engage in exploration, which will help them to effectively interact with a given physical world as well as allowing them to better ingratiate themselves in a given social world. More specifically in each activity children will have a particular task, for example, when running whilst wearing a parachute children need to balance the forces exuded on their bodies to allow them to move forward with control, and to start and finish at predetermined points. When we ask children to hold ribbons and observe the effect of wind on their movement more specifically their task is to maintain grip on the ribbons under changing wind conditions.

2. What are the resources available to solve this task?

    When designing our tasks, we considered the resources we were providing in the context of the role of the body, the brain and the environment as well as through the relationship between these – for example the motion of a body through the environment, and how this might change with different resources.

3. How can these resources be assembled to solve the task?

    When designing our tasks, we considered how the different resources might be drawn upon in a dynamic task solving system, and what each contributes in terms of experiencing and thinking about air resistance.

4. Are these resources actually assembled and used?

    Our research aims to address this question by exploring the extent to which children use the embodied resources provided by each activity to solve each task, and to identify key aspects that could be better supported through digital augmentation.

In summary, the design aimed to provide integrated physical learning tasks, that fostered 'felt' experiences, and provide meaning congruency through children's bodily movement and actions linked to broader multisensory and perceptual experiences. Our research aimed to explore whether and/or how children drew on these resources during each activity.

3 Methodology - Design Based Research

An iterative design-based research (DBR) approach [2] was taken to design, develop and deploy a programme of outdoor activities for children aged 4–6 years, that drew on key ideas from embodied cognition theory to foster meaningful action in relation to science concepts related to air resistance. Design based research aims to improve educational practice through theoretically driven iterative design, development and deployment of educational activities in real world settings, developed through researcher-practitioner collaboration, with a view to informing theory and/or generating design guidelines [2].

The methodology undertaken here reflects key characteristics of DBR [22]. The key focus of this work was to explore ways in which precepts from embodied cognition theory can be explicitly used to inform design of embodied science learning activities, with a view to productively inform digital augmentation design. The activity designs were, therefore, grounded on key precepts from Embodied Cognition theory, outlined above. An initial set of activity designs were developed through a collaborative partnership between embodied learning researchers and a charity that works with educational bodies to enrich, enhance and inspire young children's outdoor learning. These activities were iteratively designed and tested in an embodied learning intervention with children aged 4–6 years. The implementation of the designed activities took place in a primary school's outdoor playground adjacent to their classrooms, as part of the children's normal school day. Children engaged with the activities in pairs, selected by the teacher, and participated in a semi-structured interview afterwards. The activities were led by a researcher-practitioner pair who structured the tasks, provided practical support, engaged children in the tasks and prompted conversation around the activities. The interview aimed to allow children to express any observations, interactions, feelings and ideas which emerged from their interactions. Questions were structured around each of the activities and children were encouraged to describe what they did, what happened, what they could feel, what else they observed and how these sensations and observations differed under different circumstances (e.g. sizes of parachutes, wind levels, states of motion). Interviews were semi-structured to allow the researcher to respond to children's answers, with the aim of encouraging them to build on these responses. All interactions and interviews were video recorded for analysis. Multimodal transcripts were generated for interactions and interviews, capturing children's speech, gestures, gaze, and action. The learning interactions were evaluated in terms of the ways in which children made meaning, or not, from their embodied interaction, to inform a second, and then third iteration of designed activities. A final evaluation was undertaken to generate digital design ideas.

Evaluation of the effectiveness of the activities for communicating aspects of air resistance examined links between the designed perceptual motor experiences and children's communication of these ideas after their experience, undertaken in two ways:

- Through analysis of children's multimodal interactions during the activities - exploring how they systematically used their bodies to explore and make meaning, whilst supported by the designed physical environment.
- Through analysis of children's gesturing in subsequent semi-structured interviews, where the physical environment was pared down and children could no longer directly incorporate the interactive objects into their communication. We chose to focus on gesture as this mode of communication has been established as a source of evidence for embodied cognition as it provides support for the idea that bodily experience assists children's thinking and communication across a number of domains, however gestures were always considered within the multimodal context of children's communication.

4   Design Phase 1

4.1   Air Resistance

As a collaborative team we discussed science themed topics which would particularly benefit from being situated outdoors, from being framed through an embodied lens and which children between 3 and 6 years-of-age would have had minimal formal exposure to, but which they could engage with through action and experience. We chose to design activities around the topic of *air resistance*. Any object in motion through air is subjected to a resistive force to that motion termed *air resistance*. This force is affected by variables including the surface area of the object and its speed of motion. Given their age, we did not have an expectation that children would emerge from the tasks with a concept of *air resistance*, but rather that these activities would provide complementary experiences which drew attention to the relationships/factors which underpin this concept, such as:

- Air is all around us
- When an object moves through air its movement is slowed by the air around it
- The shape and size of the object will influence the extent of this slowing 'force'
- Feeling the effect of this 'force' by moving objects through air, or by observing objects being moved by air.

4.2 Activity Designs

In design phase 1 the experience consisted of three activities which were designed to provide different multisensory experiences with concepts of air resistance, specifically drawing on notions of 'felt' or tacit experiences, movement and other congruent perceptual experiences. The initial activities all made use of parachutes, as we anticipated that this surface level similarity would help children to link ideas across the activities. However, each activity was designed to provide children with different sensorimotor experiences that would enrich their 'embodied toolkit' of resources around the higher order concept of *air resistance* (Table 1).

Table 1. Design Phase 1 - Sensory experiences mapped to potential learning outcomes

Activity	Key sensory experience	Potential learning outcomes
Running with wearable parachutes in two sizes	**Visceral whole body felt** experience of drag	Relationship between size (surface area) and speed Influence of wind speed and direction on speed
Dropping toy parachutes of two sizes	**Observe** parachutes falling at different speeds and their changing shape	Relationship between size (surface area) and speed Shape of parachutes influenced by motion through air
Pulling toy parachutes of two sizes	**Felt** experience of moving parachutes through the air allowing for immediate comparison across sizes **Observe** parachutes changing shape as they moved through air	Relationship between size (surface area) and speed Shape of parachutes influenced by motion through air

Each task consisted of experience with two differently sized parachutes. We choose to present children with only two sizes so that the observable and felt sensations children could engage with would be distinctly different, rather than on a gradation.

Wearable Parachutes
The aim of this activity was to give children a felt sensation of resistance to their motion given the different sizes of parachutes, different levels of wind speed and different states of motion (e.g. stationary vs. in motion). The activity was designed to give children an opportunity to link their felt bodily experience to the observable variables which influenced this felt sensation: these relationships contribute to the higher order concept of *air resistance*. Children wore child-sized resistance parachutes adjusted to have two different surface areas (large/small) (Fig. 1a). They participated in pairs and ran together from a designated start to end point twice, before switching parachute size. Children always ran into the wind, as this allowed them to experience the greatest sensation of resistance and also helped to prevent them from becoming entangled in the parachute. Movement was integral to this activity as children's task was to run between a given start and end point, and the parachutes only inflated whilst in motion – thus only through movement could children have a 'felt' experience of the effect of *air resistance* – a sensation of resistance to their forward momentum, which we predicted would be experienced in part as a pull sensation felt on their shoulders.

Fig. 1. a,b,c: Children interacting with (from left to right): a) wearable parachutes; b) dropping toy parachutes; c) pulling toy parachutes

Dropping Toy Parachutes.
The aim of this activity was to provide children with an opportunity to simultaneously observe the motion of two differently sized parachutes as they travelled through the air (Fig. 1b), allowing children to test and observe the impact that size has on motion/speed, and in turn the impact that motion has on the parachute shape. Children were each provided with two toy parachutes: one large and one small. They initially dropped the parachutes sequentially, and then dropped pairs of parachutes simultaneously to explore and observe how they moved through the air, since the relationship between surface area, shape and air resistance was only available through motion.

Pulling Toy Parachutes
The aim of this activity was to enable children to simultaneously *feel* the resistive force in their hand and arm generated by differently sized parachutes in motion, and in turn to *observe* how these forces and the shape of the parachutes changed as they moved

through air. Using the same toy parachutes as above (Fig. 1c), children were also encouraged to explore ways of moving them through air to experience how the different sized parachutes felt, moved and changed shape.

4.3   Evaluation of Design and Iterative Developments

Through our analysis of the multimodal transcripts generated from the video data of interaction and interviews collected in design phase 1, we assessed how effectively these activities had translated research theory into practice. More specifically we explored how these activities which were designed to enhance awareness of the phenomenon of air resistance through action which was congruently mapped to the underlying science ideas and fully integrated into the task, actually supported meaning making around air resistance for young children. In turn, we explored if and how young children drew on the sensations created through these activities to further support their thinking and communication. This led to us identifying which aspects of the phenomenon were being effectively communicated by the activities and which needed further mediation, leading us to iterate the design and implementation of both the interactive session and the semi-structured interview, as detailed below.

Two key issues emerged in relation to the wearable parachutes: *(i)* a failure to effectively communicate a relationship between parachute size and the speed at which children were able to run; and *(ii)* children were intrigued by their own parachute, which caused them to turn as they ran and this led to the parachute twisting and collapsing.

With the wearable parachute activity in design phase 1, we expected that when children were wearing the larger parachute their maximum running speed would be restricted. However, analysis showed that children's maximum running speed was more strongly linked to their motivation to 'win' than to the size of the parachute they were wearing. Even when they were wearing differently sized parachutes their focus was on racing, rather than 'felt' experience of speed. This was evident from children's performance during the task as well as from their reflections throughout the task and in the semi-structured interviews. Despite the fact that the larger parachute exuded a greater resistive force on children's motion, they were able to compensate for this by increasing the effort they expended. In the semi-structured interview probing children's awareness a relationship between size of parachute and children's running speed, it became apparent that the actual relationship between size of parachute and children's running speed was more complex than initially anticipated. Children tended to suggest that speed was a trait of themselves (e.g. 'I am the fastest') rather than being open to external variables, which in this particular task tended to also hold true. Partly as a result of this, the notion of speed proved to be a problematic way of exploring children's understanding. Their awareness was not drawn to 'differences' in *felt* kinesthetic experiences (either speed or effort) [18], since their focus was on an external goal of winning. To address this issue we changed the context of the task for design phase 2, so that children took it in turns to run, rather than racing against one another. By removing the element of competition, we aimed to foster similar running effort with either parachute, and a better awareness of felt kinesthetic experience. Changing the context of the task in this way also meant that children could observe one another running, and the way the parachutes filled and moved whilst their peer was in motion, addressing the second issue. We expected that if children could observe their peer's parachute then this might discourage them from turning as they ran. During design phase 2 we also mentioned that turning would cause the wearable parachute to collapse. While we aimed to address this issue by changes to the task as described above, we also refocused our questions around the relationship between children's effort and the size of the parachute.

In terms of the toy parachute activities it became clear that children sometimes struggled to clearly observe the relationship between the size of the parachute and the speed at which it fell to the ground (with the smaller parachute travelling faster). This was not surprising, since there was only a short delay between the parachutes being released and reaching the ground (given young children's typical height). In this case the perceptual links between movement and change were not congruent enough to be meaningful [cf, 12]. This led to a researcher demonstrating the releasing of the parachutes simultaneously, as their increased height led to a longer travel time for the parachutes. To address this issue in phase 2 we provided children with a raised platform, which they could stand on to release the parachutes. This meant that they could still control the release, maintaining agency over the process, which we felt was an important factor in allowing children to focus on the sequence of events and the factors contributing to this system [20].

During the semi-structured interviews children struggled to describe their felt experience, perhaps because the experience itself was limited by a lack of wind strength on the day of implementation, but also because the questions themselves did not help children to focus on this sensation. Thus, in design phase 2, it was vital that children had some experience of wind strength (in addition to self-generated air resistance), and increased awareness of the felt experience. To foster this, we encouraged them to engage in active reflection during the interactive experience, e.g. comparing how each run/pull felt, what had changed and what might be different in subsequent trials.

Interestingly, across the activities children's *felt* awareness focused on the notion of 'lift', since they often discussed their potential for flight. This notion may have emerged given that all the tasks related to parachutes, which are strongly associated with motion off the ground and in the sky, and the wearable parachute tended to lift above the level of their shoulders as they ran. This suggests the significant role of felt experience on interpretation [4]. To address this in design phase 2, we introduced an additional task using cardboard sails, with the aim of linking air-resistance and surface area, but which appeared superficially different and did not evoke any imagery of flight or motion through the sky.

Children also frequently referenced colour as a distinctive feature of the objects during and after their interactions. From design phase 2 onwards, all sets of apparatus were matched for colour and other visual features, to ensure that this variable did not interfere with other variables.

5 Design Phase 2

5.1 Activity Designs

Design phase 2 incorporated the adjustments to activities as described above, plus the addition of a task involving cardboard sails. The four activities were presented within an open-ended notion of exploring how different objects behave when moving through air. Thus, children (in pairs) completed four activities in the following order; Pulling toy parachutes, Dropping toy parachutes, Wearable parachutes, Cardboard sails.

Pulling Toy Parachutes
Children were provided with two toy parachutes matched for colour but differing in size, and were encouraged to explore ways of moving them through air when holding the men attached to the parachute cord. The aim of this activity was still to enable children to simultaneously feel the resistive force generated by differently sized parachutes in motion, and in turn to observe how these forces and the shape of the parachutes changed as they were moved through the air. During this phase in particular, children were asked to reflect on the *felt* and *observed* experience produced by the two parachutes. They were also further encouraged to explore ways of moving – this freedom meant that children could run, jump, rotate their arms, rotate their bodies, pull simultaneously, pull sequentially etc., leading to a range of potential sensorimotor experiences.

Dropping Toy Parachutes
Using the same two parachutes, the aim of this activity was still to provide children with an opportunity to *observe* the motion of two differently sized parachutes as they travelled through air, allowing children to explore the impact that size has on motion/speed, and in turn, the impact that motion has on parachute shape. Children initially dropped the parachutes sequentially, and then dropped pairs of parachutes simultaneously to explore and observe how they fell through the air: the relationship between surface area, shape and air resistance was only available through motion. To give children more opportunity for observation in this phase they were provided with a raised platform to stand on. Children were encouraged to reflect on their experiences between each release and to consider how the motion of the parachute differed and the factors which might contribute to this.

Wearable Parachutes
The aim of this activity was still to give children a *felt* sensation of resistance to their motion given different sizes of parachutes, different levels of wind speed and different states of motion (stationary vs. in motion). The activity was designed to give children an opportunity to link their felt bodily experience to the observable variables which influenced this felt sensation: these relationships are captured by the umbrella concept of air resistance. Children wore the same child-sized resistance parachutes adjusted to have two different surface areas (large/small) as in phase 1. They participated in pairs but ran individually from a designated start to end point twice, before switching parachutes. When stationary, children observed their peer running. Once at the end point children waited for their peer to complete the run and then both children walked

back to the designated start point, with assistance from the researcher/practitioner pair. Between each run children were encouraged to reflect on their experience and to consider how the previous or next run might differ. The distance children were required to run was increased from design phase 1 to give children more opportunity to reflect on the felt experience during their run, and to try and reduce the impact of motivation on children's maintained speed. Children always ran into the wind to prevent them from becoming entangled in the parachute.

Cardboard Sails

The aim of this activity was to give children a different *felt* sensation of resistance to their motion given different sizes of 'sails', different levels of wind speed and different states of motion (stationary vs. in motion). Children were provided with two differently sized sheets of cardboard – one large and one small. They were asked to hold these sheets at the edges, with the cardboard in front of their bodies, see Fig. 2. Taking it in turns children were asked to run to a designated end point. They stayed at this end point whilst their peer ran and then both children walked back to the designated start point (start and end points were the same as for the wearable parachutes). Children completed two runs before swapping 'sails'. The activity was designed to give children an opportunity to link their felt bodily experience to the observable variables which influenced this felt sensation – in this case, a more of a push sensation from in front of the body rather than a pull from behind (as with the parachutes). In particular this activity was designed to provide this felt sensation but in a visually and body positionally different context to the wearable parachutes. This activity was also designed to allow children to observe the impact of their motion on the shape of the sails during the activity. Between each run children were encouraged to reflect on their experience and to consider how the previous or next run might differ.

Fig. 2. A child running into the wind with a 'cardboard sail'

5.2   Evaluation of Design and Iterative Developments

Through our analysis of the interaction and interview video data collected in design phase 2 we evaluated the design iterations implemented in terms of how effectively these activities, which were designed to promote congruent science ideas through integrated action, actually communicated these ideas to young children and in turn how young children drew on these experiences to support their thinking and communication. These showed where some modifications were effective, but also highlighted those that suggest further design iterations in both the interactive session and semi-structured interview.

Effective Modifications

During the wearable parachute activity children benefited from running individually. This led to their reflections being more focused on their own experience and their 'felt' effort required to complete a run, rather than on comparative assessments of themselves and their peers. The opportunity for children to observe their peer running meant that they were also able to describe how the parachute's shape and motion changed as it moved, and to draw out some the relationships between variables. This iteration also led to far fewer occasions where children turned during a run to observe their own parachutes, which meant children were able to have more successful experiences of running under the full influence of an inflated parachute.

During the wearable parachute activity and semi-structured interviews children were more able to describe their felt experiences than in design phase 1. The wind strength experienced by children in this phase greatly exceeded that experienced by children in phase 1, which is likely to have enhanced their felt experience and in turn their ability to describe this experience. Furthermore, encouraging children to make observations and reflect during the activities seemed to support their engagement with science processes (observing, describing, predicting). Furthermore, introduction of the card-board sail activity allowed children to express their understanding of the relationship between surface area, and effort by drawing on a new embodied resource.

Giving children a raised platform to stand on as they released the toy parachutes allowed them to reflect on the motion of the parachutes and to report this with more accuracy. This removed the need for an adult to demonstrate releasing the parachutes and allowed children to be embedded within this activity. Focusing interview questions around differences in the effort required to generate motion in the various activities allowed children to express links between size (surface area) and effort. In the case of the toy parachutes children also linked these variables with speed.

Overall, these findings suggest that these activity designs had better meaning congruency, as well as more effectively bringing awareness to kinesthetic felt sensations linked to air resistance.

Iterations in Design

Children continued to talk about their potential for flight. To further address this we re-ordered the activities so that children engaged with the toy parachutes last, with a view to reducing emphasis on the particular 'flight' motion of these parachutes. However, we also broadened our interview questions to further probe this reported phenomenon to better identify whether children were reporting a 'felt' experience.

Few children were aware of any relationship between wind direction or even wind speed and air resistance or their felt experience. To draw attention to this variable in the final design phase we introduced a preliminary task in which children held ribbons and were asked to describe their motion. This aimed to draw children's attention to the dominant wind direction and to changes in wind speed, as these factors would influence the observed ribbon behavior and the strength of grip required by children to maintain hold of the ribbons.

6   Final Evaluation Phase

The final suite of activities consisted of five activities embedded within the context of differently exploring the effects of air on movement. Children completed all five activities in a prescribed order (Ribbons, Cardboard sails, Wearable parachutes, Dropping toy parachutes, Pulling toy parachutes), with the context and structuring of the activities being largely pre-defined, while also allowing room for children to explore and investigate. This final set of activities aimed to enable children to readily identify links between size, force and effort, through both felt and observed experiences, and in the case of the toy parachutes, were also linked to speed (Table 2).

Table 2. Design Phase 3 - Sensory experiences mapped to potential learning outcomes

Activity	Key sensory experience	Potential learning outcomes
Running with wearable parachutes in two sizes	**Visceral whole body felt** experience of air resistance **Observable** change in shape of parachute as another child runs	Relationship between size (surface area) and effort/speed Shape of parachutes influenced by motion through air Influence of wind speed and direction on effort/speed
Dropping toy parachutes of two sizes	**Observe** parachutes falling at different speeds and their changing shape	Relationship between size (surface area) and speed Shape of parachutes influenced by motion through air. Influence of wind speed and direction on parachute motion
Pulling toy parachutes of two sizes	**Felt** experience of moving parachutes through the air allowing for immediate comparison across sizes **Observe** parachutes changing shape as they moved through air	Relationship between size (surface area) and effort/speed Shape of parachutes influenced by motion through air
Running with cardboard 'sails' in two sizes	**Visceral whole body felt** experience of air resistance against the sail **Observe** change in shape of sail as they move	Relationship between size (surface area) and effort/speed Shape of sail influenced by motion through air
Holding ribbons	**Felt** experience of maintaining grip under different wind conditions **Observe** direction and speed of wind	We can observe the effect of air by seeing its influence on static objects or by moving objects through air

6.1   Final Evaluation

Video analysis of interaction and interviews again focused on the effectiveness of the activities for communicating relevant aspects of air resistance. We examined how children systematically used their bodies to explore and make meaning, during the interactive tasks, as well as analysing how children's communication (including gesturing) during the semi-structured interviews incorporated aspects of their felt and wider perceptual experiences.

It was clear from children's interview data that they drew on the embodied nature of the activities to help them express their actions, observations and thoughts through gesture. Children used a range of whole-body gestures and hand gestures to capture the physicality of their experience and noticings, for example, using their whole bodies to re-enact the effort required to run with the different sized 'sails' and using their hands to show how air pushes on the parachutes, and how more air is captured by a larger parachute. These gestures allowed children to re-enact their experiences and in doing so to express the relationships they had become aware of, their developing ideas around these relationships and even support them in thinking through new problems.

The wearable parachute and cardboard 'sail' activities supported children in making connections between the size of the parachutes/sails and the amount of effort required to move these objects through air. Movement, meaningful congruency and integrated physicality was integral to the design of these tasks and to communicating these relationships. One drawback of these tasks was that, as children were embedded in the scenarios, it proved challenging for them to separate their own perceptions of themselves (in particular in terms of their speed) from the immediate experience of the task. This issue was somewhat addressed by the complementary toy parachute tasks which allowed children to consider the same variable of parachute size, but in this case to successfully map its relationship to speed.

Children tended to use the term 'heavy' to capture their observations about and sensations related to force. In this final design phase, we were confident that this was not about them reporting an absolute difference in the weight of the two parachutes when they were static, but was a 'heaviness in motion' - the felt sensation of force. This observation is not incorrect and actually captures a lot about children's sensory experience and their developing concept of force. However, given future iterations we could consider how to foster this developing understanding to help children transition between this way of thinking about 'force' and how this would map to other force scenarios. Below, we also discuss ways this might be addressed through digital design.

Children confidently discussed the pull sensation generated by the wearable parachutes, however the cardboard 'sails' task led to some apparent confusion around push forces – children sometimes appeared confused about whether they were being pushed forwards or backwards by the sail. Further iterations would be required to explore whether this confusion arises from the task itself, whether this confusion is centred around the meaning of the word 'push' or some combination of factors.

Across the activities children had their attention drawn to 'air' as a broad phenomenon – they expressed links between 'air' and the way the objects moved or the way the shape of the objects changed. In some cases children began to build a naïve theory of air resistance where they linked the size of the parachute with the amount of 'push' force it underwent or heaviness they felt due to air. Conveying these developing theories was greatly supported by children's use of their bodies as a mode of communication, based on their perceptuo-motor experiences.

Across all design phases children reported a sensation linked to flight. In the final evaluation phase, we became more confident that this was a genuine felt sensation as children said things like "I knew I was on the ground, but I felt like I almost might fly". This re-emphasised to us the importance of reflecting on the felt experiences that children report, beyond those which have been designed into the activities/tasks.

7   Implications for Digital Design

Drawing on the analysis above, in this section we outline the extent to which children use the physical 'embodied' resources provided by each activity, and begin to identify the different roles that digital technology could play in future designs. In so doing, we demonstrate how an embodied iterative design can most effectively inform digital designs, by isolating the key factors that are unsupported through physical resources alone, or that cannot be easily solved in the physical world.

Children were able to make connections between the felt experience of the effort required to run given different sized parachutes and, in some cases, linked this to ideas of air as a source of resistance. Some children started to express why a larger parachute takes more effort to move, through statements like 'it has more area and the air pushes it'. Children were able to talk about how their own motion (or that of their peers) impacted the shape of the parachutes and sails, and linked this change to ideas of how air might mediate this relationship.

However, the analysis also highlights a number of shortcomings from physical resources, which have implications for digital design. Incorporating technology into the existing physical experiences could specifically help communicate or draw attention to aspects of the science which are not effectively foregrounded. Alternatively, these activities could be presented in a more controlled or simulated environment, which might allow for alternative exploration of science ideas, and could address design implications that cannot be easily overcome in purely physical activities. Here we explore four ideas:

7.1   Wind Speed and Direction

Across the activities we found that very few children were aware that wind speed and direction might affect their experience, even when using ribbons to draw attention to these properties. One reason for this might have been that children were always asked to run into the wind, both to increase their felt experience and to overcome potential safety issues. Technology in the form of sensors could be incorporated into the current physical activities to detect changes in wind speed or direction, and translated into age appropriate cues, for example, a visual cue like a dial ranging from light to strong, colour change or an auditory cue that associates volume or pitch with wind speed. In so doing, it would aim to draw children's attention to important environmental changes which relate to and, therefore, might impact on their felt experience.

7.2   Differentiating Sensations

Children were able to make connections between the size of the parachutes and sails and the amount of effort needed to move through air. In the physical experience this required them to reflect across two sequential experiences and to compare the 're-membered' felt sensations generated. One issue with this approach is that other vari-ables could change in the interim, which would affect the relationship between children's felt experience and the size of the parachute. For example, if the wind speed increased between a child's run with the large parachute and the small parachute then their felt experience could be relatively equivalent. An environment which offers more control over these variables, either through adapting the physical environment or by simulation would help address this, for example, a simulation or mixed reality envi-ronment, which combined the felt sensations children experience in the physical activities with the capacity to set and instantaneously change the variables of interest, such as wind force, parachute size. Using haptic feedback on the shoulders/straps of the parachute may simulate and draw attention to stronger 'pull' sensation in conjunction with more wind. Or mechanisms that enable the automatic opening or closing of the parachute mid-running, would provide clearer and more immediate sensations of change. Or the size of their parachute could be adjusted during a child's run then this is likely to lead to a very compelling felt sensation of the change in air resistance, which would have an impact on their speed and the effort required to run. Allowing for particular variables to be changed instantaneously, might allow children to more readily identify links between felt sensations and given factors.

7.3   Configuration for Variation

If these activities were presented in a controlled or partially simulated environment then this could help to extend the learning opportunities over a wider age range. For example, older children could make predictions about how changes in wind speed, wind direction, parachute size, parachute speed or even air density would affect their speed or the effort required for them to run at a given speed. They could then test these predictions and engage in a process of enquiry learning. This could also help to extend the activities to a lower age range as the number of variables could be reduced to help communicate a simple message.

7.4   Making the Invisible Visible

Air is an invisible entity which we can only observe through its effect on the objects around us. Technology could enable us to make this phenomenon visible, through visualisations, which might help children to better notice the links between the movement of air (or objects movement through air) and the force that this generates. This might help them to think about this force in a different way from the notion of 'heaviness', that they reported in relation to our activities. This might also help them to build on the relationship between size, effort/speed and air to begin to think about how and why the size of a parachute impacts their effort/speed. This might also help children to overcome some of the confusion reported around push forces during the cardboard 'sail' activity, as the direction of net air resistance could be made visible.

8   Conclusion

Through a process of DBR we proposed a series of activities to communicate ideas of air resistance to 4- to 6-year-olds, which were theoretically underpinned by three key concepts: Movement, Meaning Congruency and Integrated Physicality, all of which are grounded in theories of embodied cognition. Air resistance is a phenomenon which arises due to the particular physical world which we live in. As such, physical activity within this world allows us to have direct experience of this phenomenon. We proposed a variety of tasks which drew attention to particular aspects of this experience to foster children's developing understanding of this phenomenon. Meaning congruency across these tasks was easily achieved as children's actions drew their attention to naturally occurring relationships in the physical world (e.g. the relationship between the size of an object and the amount of air resistance it is subjected to). Movement and integrated physicality was essential to all tasks as air resistance is a phenomenon which only arises due to motion of air affecting an object, or motion of an object being affected by air. As such, this topic leant itself to being supported by our three theoretical underpinnings and benefited immensely from being situated outside. One of the challenges of basing ideas about science phenomena on physical interactions with the world is the relatively minimal control one has over extraneous variables, for example wind speed. This can be problematic in educational scenarios as these extraneous variables may have a large impact on children's felt and perceived experiences, and can be a source of misconceptions – particularly if the activities themselves do not draw attention to the role of these extraneous variables. Digital design offers us opportunities to maintain the benefits of children being able to interact with the physical world through action, in meaningful ways, which can support their thinking and communication, whilst also being able to draw attention to/control aspects of the environment, which are important for children's developing meaning making around these contexts.

This research demonstrates how drawing on theory to underpin design and engaging in a process of DBR supports the translation of research in domains such as embodied cognition into practice, allows for reflection on the effectiveness of this translation and in turn can inform digital and physical design.

Acknowledgements. This material is based upon work supported under a collaboration between the National Science Foundation (NSF), the Wellcome Trust, and the Economic and Social Research Council (ESRC) via a grant from the NSF (NSF grant no. 1646940) and a grant from the Wellcome Trust with ESRC (Wellcome Trust grant no. 206205/Z/17/Z). Any opinions, findings and conclusions or recommendations expressed in this material are those of the author(s) and do not necessarily reflect the view of NSF, the Wellcome Trust, or ESRC. We would also like to thank Mizuki Choi and Minna Nygren for their help with data collection, the children who participated in the study, and teachers who made this research possible.

References

1. Lindgren, R., Johnson-Glenberg, M.: Emboldened by embodiment: Six precepts for research on embodied learning and mixed reality. Educ. Res. **42**, 445–452 (2013)
2. Wang, F., Hannafin, M.J.: Design-based research and technology-enhanced learning environments. Educ. Technol. Res. Dev. **53**, 5–23 (2005)
3. Tippett, C.D., Milford, T.: Findings from a pre-kindergarten classroom: making the case for STEM in early childhood education. Int. J. Sci. Math. Educ. **15**(3), 1–20 (2017)
4. Whitehead, M. (ed): Physical Literacy Throughout the Lifecourse. Routledge (2010)
5. Barsalou, L.W.: Grounded cognition. Annu. Rev. Psychol. **59**, 617–645 (2008)
6. Cress, U., Fischer, U., Moeller, K., Sauter, C., Nuerk, H.C.: The use of a digital dance mat for training kindergarten children in a magnitude comparison task. Proceedings of the 9th International Conference of the Learning Sciences, vol. 1, pp. 105–112. (2010)
7. Abrahamson, D., Trninic, D.: Toward an embodied-interaction design framework for mathematical concepts. In: Proceedings of the 10th International Conference on Interaction Design and Children - IDC 2011, pp. 1–10 (2011)
8. Goldin-Meadow, S., Nusbaum, H., Kelly, S.D., Wagner, S.: Explaining math: gesturing lightens the load. Psychol. Sci.: J. Am. Psychol. Soc./APS **12**(6), 516–522 (2001)
9. Alibali, M.W., Nathan, M.J.: Embodiment in mathematics teaching and learning: evidence from learners' and teachers' gestures. J. Learn. Sci. **21**(2), 247–286 (2012)
10. Gallagher, S., Lindgren, R.: Enactive metaphors: learning through full-body engagement. Educ. Psychol. Rev. **27**, 391–404 (2015)
11. Johnson Glenberg, M.: Immersive VR and education: embodied design principles that include gesture and hand controls. Front. Robot. AI **5**, 81 (2018)
12. Hald, L.A., de Nooijer, J., van Gog, T., Bekkering, H.: Optimizing word learning via links to perceptual and motoric experience. Educ. Psychol. Rev. **28**, 495–522 (2016)
13. Skulmowski, A., Rey, D.R.: Embodied learning: introducing a taxonomy based on bodily engagement and task integration. Cogn. Res.: Principles Implications **3**, 6 (2018)
14. Wilson, R.A., Foglia, L.: Embodied cognition. In: Zalta, E.N. (ed.) The Stanford Encyclopedia of Philosophy, Spring 2017 edn. https://plato.stanford.edu/archives/spr2017/entries/embodied-cognition/
15. Varela, F.J., Thompson, E., Rosch, E.: The Embodied Mind: Cognitive Science and Human Experience. MIT Press, Cambridge (1991)
16. Gallagher, S., Bower, M.: Making enactivism even more embodied. AVANT/Trends Interdisc. Stud. **5**(2), 232–247 (2014)
17. Clark, A.: Whatever next? Predictive brains, situated agents, and the future of cognitive science. Behav. Brain Sci. **36**(3), 181–204 (2013)
18. Sheets-Johnson, M.: Thinking in movement. J. Esthetics Art Criticism **39**(4), 399 (1982)
19. Polanyi, M.: The Tacit Dimension. Routledge & Kegan Paul, London (1966)
20. Thomas Jha, R.L., Nygren, M.O., Price, S.: Exploring how children's interactions shape their gestural communication around science ideas. Science Communication (under review)
21. Wilson, A.D., Golonka, S.: Embodied cognition is not what you think it is. Front. Psychol. **4**, 58 (2013)
22. Anderson, T., Shattuck, J.: Design-based research: a decade of progress in education research? Educ. Res. **41**(1), 16–25 (2012)

Learning Analytics, Dashboards and Learners Models

Impact of Constant Work on the Students' Academic Performance

Patricia Compañ-Rosique[✉], Rafael Molina-Carmona[✉], and Rosana Satorre-Cuerda[✉]

Cátedra Santander-UA de Transformación Digital, Universidad de Alicante, San Vicente del Raspeig, Spain
{patricia.company,rmolina,rosana.satorre}@ua.es

Abstract. Current teaching methodologies are based on concepts such as continuous work, constructivism, project-based learning, gamification, etc.; in short, more active methodologies on the part of the student in which they acquire a leading role and are more responsible for their own learning. Teachers always insist students on the importance of working continuously. In a subject of computer programming this is especially important. For this reason, in this subject we provide to students numerous materials in various formats (notes, videos, questionnaires) that we consider to be fundamental in the training of our students. From time to time, teachers consult the access that students make to these materials and they are not as frequent as they should be. This leads us to question whether students who work more continuously with the materials provided do better academically than students who do not. The objective of this work is to analyze if the activities carried out by the students (questionnaires, deliverables, downloads of materials), are related to the performance obtained in the subject. Data have been collected on student activity during the academic year. The data collected are very heterogeneous, in some cases it is a flag that indicates whether the material has been downloaded or not, while in other cases it is the result of more dynamic activities such as a questionnaire. It is necessary to carry out a standardisation process that allows us to work with the data as a whole. There are several analyses that can be carried out. A first study would be to consider the different activities that the student can carry out as input variables and the performance obtained in the subject as output variable and to establish whether there is a dependency relationship. The results of these analyses show that there are not as many relationships as expected but the continuous work is slightly related with the theory exam.

Keywords: Programming teaching · Academic performance · Continuous work

1 Introduction

Society tacitly admits the benefits of effort and continuous work. The teaching world follows this trend and all teachers insist on instilling in their students

© Springer Nature Switzerland AG 2020
P. Zaphiris and A. Ioannou (Eds.): HCII 2020, LNCS 12205, pp. 229–240, 2020.
https://doi.org/10.1007/978-3-030-50513-4_17

the benefits of continuous work to acquire the skills of a subject. It is common that the first class day for a subject, the teacher insists on the need to work continuously in order to acquire the competencies and skills that the subject requires. In the case of subjects that involve a great deal of memory effort, there are students who can rely on their ability and dedicate themselves exclusively to study on the days prior to the exam in order to pass the subject. However, the new teaching methodologies are more and more participative and active on the part of the student and require more continuous work or practice.

In the case of subjects in which it is not a question of memorizing contents, but of acquiring more analytical skills, it seems essential to carry out continuous work from the first day in order to acquire those skills. Several studies have been carried out that deal with the advantages of working on a continuous basis [2,5,6,12]. The continuous effort represents motivation to dedicate time and effort to learn and obtain good results. The benefits are not only for the students. The continuous monitoring allows the teacher to have a feedback of how the subject is working and gives him or her the option to make changes if he or she detects any lack.

In principle, there are many advantages to carrying out activities on a continuous basis by the student, but there are also some disadvantages. To begin with, there are students whose main motivation is the qualification they obtain in the subject. In these cases, for these students to work continuously they must have some kind of reward in the grade. This leads to several possibilities. The first and most traditional option is that the teacher has to spend large amounts of time and effort reviewing, correcting and providing students with feedback on their work. Another possibility, quite in use today, is the use of automatic correction systems that considerably reduce the teacher's workload. This option is very suitable for some subjects, but there are other subjects for which it is more complex to design automatic correction systems. For example, it is very simple to put a math problem and check if the final result is correct, but perhaps what interests the teacher is not the final result, but the process that the student has followed to reach the result. In this case, designing an automatic correction system seems much more complicated. And another problem that inexorably arises when students deliver exercises on a continuous basis is the problem of copying and plagiarism. Several studies have been conducted that show an increase in plagiarism in recent years. New technologies greatly facilitate the increase of this activity. Groups are created where students deposit their work in such a way that any student can download it immediately. It is true that new technologies provide virtually unlimited access to sources of information that allow for deeper learning, but they also provide the means for students who work less to more easily appropriate someone else's work. Some studies have shown that the project-based learning model minimizes the tendency to plagiarize [1]. Copy detection programs can be used to detect copies in source code: jplag, Sherlock, etc. In [4] a study is shown where Open Source tools are analyzed for software plagiarism detection. Student work was used to test them.

In this work we have considered activities that the student has carried out throughout the course that do not represent any benefit for the grade of the subject. The aim is to determine whether there is any kind of relationship between the continuous work that students do and the performance they obtain in an introductory programming subject.

The document is organized as follows. Section 2 presents the context of the research. Section 3 specifies the process followed to carry out the study by explaining the characteristics of the study group and the techniques used. The study carried out to determine the possible relationships between the variables analysed and the results obtained is shown in Sect. 4. Finally, the conclusions obtained, as well as the possible lines of future work, are presented in Sect. 5.

2   Context

This study focuses on the analysis of the potential benefit to students of working on a continuous basis. It tries to analyse whether the continuous work of the students means a higher performance in the subject of study. For this purpose, the information provided by the continuous work done by the students of an introductory programming subject has been used.

The subject of study is taught in the first year of the Degree in Computer Engineering. Since it is a subject with a large volume of students, it is easier to be able to obtain a sufficient amount of data to perform an analysis. There are many papers that deal with the difficulty of this subject [7,10,11]. There are skills that are necessary to acquire computer programming skills. Some of them are the capacity of abstraction, logical-mathematical capacity, and problem-solving ability [9]. On top of this, when a student is faced with a programming exercise, he or she usually does not spend enough time on the problem analysis phase. An expert programmer has acquired skills that allow him or her to understand a problem well and to know which algorithm is suitable to solve it, so he or she does not need to dedicate so much time to the analysis phase and can start programming immediately. In the case of a beginner, especially a student, the phase of analysis of the problem and the approach of the algorithm to solve it, requires much more dedication since he or she has not yet acquired the necessary skills. The problem is that when the student is presented with the problem, he or she immediately starts writing code, without spending the necessary time on the analysis phase.

Various methodologies have been used to facilitate learning: use of role-playing game [13], use of tools to visualize execution [18], learning through programming errors [16], creation of video games in Scratch as an introduction [1], or use of Augmented Reality as a motivating element [8].

Despite all the efforts made by teachers, the fact that for many of the students this is their first contact with this field, learning this subject is very complicated. As if all this were not enough, it is a subject that is taught in the first term of the first year, that is, students have just entered the University so they are disoriented as they are unaware of how the new environment in which they find themselves works. It should also be taken into account that most students come from High School, where they have not studied similar subjects and therefore have some difficulty in dealing with the correct study methodology for learning this subject.

The aim of the study is to determine whether those students who, from the teacher's point of view, work more continuously obtain better results than those who do not seem to take advantage of all the materials and opportunities available to them.

The course uses a content management system[1] that provides students with notes, quizzes, slides and some videos. These materials are organized according to the different topics that make up the course: data types, control sentences (conditionals and loops), modular programming, recursion, arrays, structures and basic notions of computer cost. Notes and slides are available on all topics. With regard to the questionnaires, there are two topics that do not have questionnaires, and there are a couple of videos about control sentences. C language is used under Linux. The main objective of the course is that students are able to propose solutions to the problems they face.

The teachers involved in the subject have used different methodologies to try to improve academic performance [3]. In this study, it is necessary to analyse the completion or not of the questionnaires to see if it means a greater performance in the subject. The score obtained in the questionnaires is not taken into account since what the study tries to analyse is the performance of the activity itself, not its success in doing it. At first, the possibility of using the download information from the notes and slides was considered, but it was concluded that a student could download a file of notes and never look at it. It is for this reason that only the completion of the questionnaires has been considered as it is a task that requires more active participation from the student. It is important to emphasize that the completion of the questionnaires has no influence on the grade of the course so a student could get the maximum grade despite not having done any questionnaire.

The questionnaires are made up of questions to complete some code fragment. For each question there are several options from which the student has to choose one. To motivate them to take the quizzes, they do not have to type anything in, they just have to drag the chosen option into the corresponding slot. This has been done to try to get them to take advantage of any time slot they have, no matter how short it is, for example, when they go by bus to the University. Furthermore, they are insisted that even if they fail to answer the questions, they will not be penalized in any way. To make the questionnaire more instructive, when they fail a question, an explanation is shown as to what the correct option is and why.

Another of the available materials that would be interesting to analyze are the videos, but unlike the questionnaires that can be linked to the student who has worked on them, in the case of the videos, it is only possible to know the

---

[1] https://moodle2019-20.ua.es/moodle/course/view.php?id=727. Access is private with a password, but if you wish you can request access as a guest user.

number of views that each one has had, the identity of the users who have watched them is unknown.

In the course there are three tests, two of practice and one of theory. The practice exams consist of the elaboration of a program. The practice exam 1 consists of developing a program that makes use of modules, it does not include arrays or structures. The practice test 2 consists of developing a program that includes all the contents: control structures, modules, arrays and structures. It is basically a program to handle record arrays with all the relevant modules. The theory exam consists of several programming exercises that assess the knowledge of recursion, vectors, structures, passage of parameters and computational cost. This exam is given on paper and assesses the student's ability to propose a solution to a problem without focusing on the peculiarities of the programming language.

In order to study whether there is any relationship, the performance obtained in each of the examinations carried out will be considered, associating the corresponding materials with each examination.

3   Methodology

The aim of the study is to determine whether there is any kind of relationship between the students' continuous effort and the academic performance obtained by them. To this end, the steps to be followed have been:

1. To identify the study group.
2. To determine the data with which the analysis will be performed.
3. To decide on the statistical technique to be applied taking into account the type of data to be worked with.
4. To perform the analysis.
5. To interpret the results.

The study group is made up of first-year students of the Computer Engineering Degree in an introductory programming subject, 2019–20 academic year. No data have been collected from previous years because the questionnaires have been launched this year. In order to carry out the study, repeaters have not been considered, since, as it is not their first time in the subject, they already have some previous knowledge that would affect the results. In total there are 260 students, 232 men and 28 women. As it can be appreciated, there is a big difference between both numbers. It is usual that there are few women in Engineering, despite the efforts made by universities to promote the study of Engineering among women[2].

---

[2] *Quiero ser ingeniera* (**I want to be an engineer woman**): project coordinated by the *Instituto de la Mujer* (Spanish Women's Institute) which aims to promote the interest of secondary school students, particularly girls, in the study of science, technology, engineering and mathematics, https://eps.ua.es/es/quieroseringeniera/la-sociedad-necesita-tu-talento.html.

The data with which the study will be carried out are the grades obtained in the two practice exams and in the theory exam as variables to assess the academic performance and the completion or not of the available questionnaires as descriptors of the continuous work.

Some of the analyses have been carried out between numerical variables while in other cases categorical and numerical variables have been considered. In order to detect possible relationships between the numerical variables, a linear correlation analysis has been carried out [17]. Various coefficients can be used to quantify the degree of linear relationship between two variables. In the case of working with some categorical variable, the technique ANOVA (ANalysis Of VAriance) has been used [14,15]. In this work, a one-factor ANOVA has been applied, so that only one factor has been analysed for each case. In order to apply this technique, it is necessary for the study group to follow a normal distribution with respect to the factor analysed. Figure 1 shows the distribution of the notes for the completion of any questionnaire, for the completion of questionnaire 4 and for the completion of questionnaire 5. As can be seen, it can be assumed that the distribution of the groups is normal.

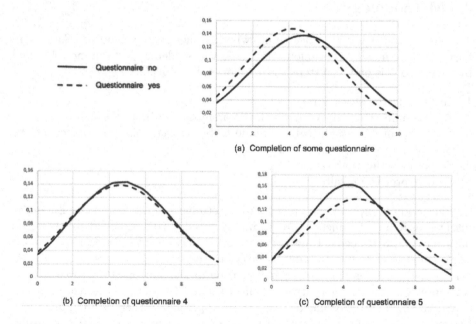

(a) Completion of some questionnaire

(b) Completion of questionnaire 4

(c) Completion of questionnaire 5

Fig. 1. Grade distributions

Figure 2 shows the number of students who have completed each questionnaire. The figure depicts the number of students who have completed the questionnaires at three different time milestones. The first milestone considers the number of students who have done the first four questionnaires before the practice exam 1. The second milestone shows the number of students who have taken the five available questionnaires before the second practice exam. Finally, the number of students who have taken the five questionnaires before taking the theory exam is considered in the third milestone. At the first milestone it can be seen that there is a clear difference between the number of students who have taken the first questionnaire and the rest of the questionnaires. The reason is very simple: the second week of the course a data type control was carried out. The students were very motivated to do the data type questionnaire and also in those dates they are not very busy with other subjects. As the course progresses, students are more saturated with work so they are less motivated to spend time on the questionnaires.

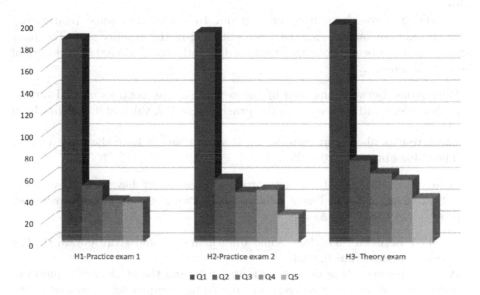

Fig. 2. Questionnaires at the three milestones

The following section shows the studies carried out and the interpretation of the results.

4   Results

This section shows the analyses carried out to assess the students' continuous work. Each subsection corresponds to the performance obtained in each of the three exams taken in the subject.

In each test, only those students who have taken the test considered in the experiment have been included.

4.1   Continuing Work - Practice Exam 1

In this case, the information from the data type, conditionals, loops and modular programming questionnaires has been considered to see the possible relation with the result obtained in the practice test. Since each topic includes the competencies of the previous topics (for example, a loop cannot be programmed if the concepts of data types and variables are not known) a different weight has been assigned to each questionnaire. The weights have been assigned in increasing order, so that the data type questionnaire has weight 1 while the modular programming questionnaire has weight 4. This has been done to reflect the fact that the most advanced questionnaires require more effort to understand the subject.

Several analyses have been carried out to try to find some relationship between different factors and the score obtained in the practice test. The tests carried out have been two correlation studies and two ANOVAs. The results of the correlation are:

- Correlation between the sum of the weights of the controls carried out by each student and their score in the practice test 1. A value of 0.1136 has been obtained.
- Same test as above but considering that all controls have the same weight. The value obtained is 0.1405.

The values obtained from the correlation coefficient have not allowed the detection of any type of linear relationship between the variables considered. The results of the ANOVAs are:

- ANOVA between "has done some questionnaire" and score obtained. The p-value obtained was 0.1163
- ANOVA between "has done questionnaire 4" and the grade, since questionnaire 4 is considered to correspond fully to the competencies assessed in the practice exam 1. A p-value of 0.8456 has been obtained.

One-factor ANOVA assess the importance of one factor by comparing the means of the response variable (grade) at different factor levels. In this case, each factor has two levels (questionnaire done or not). None of the values obtained allowed the rejection of the null hypothesis that all the population averages (averages of the factor levels) are the same, while the alternative hypothesis states that at least one is different.

4.2   Continuing Work - Practice Exam 2

For this second experiment, the five questionnaires available in the subject have been considered, that is, the same ones used in the previous experiment plus the structured data type questionnaire (arrays and structures).

The tests conducted have been analogous to those carried out with the practice test 1 but considering in this case questionnaire 5 which incorporates the contents of structured data types instead of questionnaire 4.

The correlation values obtained were: 0.0147, considering the questionnaires with different weights and 0.0362 in the case that all the questionnaires have the same weight. The experiment that analyzes the ANOVA between "has done some questionnaire" and the grade of the practice test 2 has obtained a p-value of 0.2058. Finally, an ANOVA has been carried out between "has done the questionnaire 5" and the grade, the p-value obtained has been 0.4664.

As with the analyses carried out in practice test 1, no influencing factors could be detected.

4.3 Continuing Work - Theory Exam

The same tests have been carried out as in the previous section. The correlation values obtained were 0.1423 considering the questionnaires with different weights and 0.1753 assigning the same weight to the questionnaires. The experiment that analyzes the ANOVA between "has done some questionnaire" and the grade of the theory has obtained a p-value of 0.0033. Finally, an ANOVA has been carried out between "has done the questionnaire 5" and the grade, the p-value obtained has been 0.5495.

A p-value < 0.05 is usually considered to be statistically significant. The value obtained (0.0033) allows us to reject the null hypothesis that all population means are equal. It can therefore be deduced that both populations do not score the same on the theory test.

Figure 3 shows the average grades obtained by students who have taken a questionnaire and by those who have not taken one. It can be seen that the average of the grades obtained by the students who have taken a questionnaire is slightly higher than that obtained by the students who have not taken any questionnaire.

4.4 Discussion

The aim of these experiments was to detect whether there was a relationship between the work done by the students on a continuous basis and the results obtained in the various tests carried out in the subject. Although no relationship was detected in practice exams 1 and 2, it is true that the fact that a student does not take the questionnaires does not mean that he or she does not work on the subject. The student may do other activities to learn the subject. On the other hand, the acquisition of the skills involved in this subject, requires a lot of time to program and in no case the performance of the questionnaires can replace the program coding by the student.

The tests carried out with the theory exam produce similar results except for test 3. Through the ANOVA it has been detected that the grade averages of the students who have done a control and those of the students who have not done any, are different.

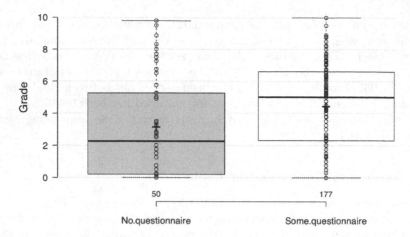

Fig. 3. Grade point average

5   Conclusion

In this work the accomplishment of activities by the students in an introductory course in programming in a continuous way has been analyzed in order to consider whether there is an improvement.

In order to carry out the study, data were collected from a series of questionnaires and different studies were carried out with the grades obtained in the subject three exams. When the variables analysed are numerical, a linear correlation analysis has been carried out, Pearson's coefficient has been used for this purpose. The questionnaires have been assigned an incremental weight since this is a subject in which each topic includes the knowledge of the previous topics. Other tests have also been carried out assigning the same weight to the questionnaires and other studies have been done using categorical variables and the ANOVA technique.

The first study analyses the relationship between the completion of the four questionnaires and the score obtained in the first practice exam. A possible relationship has also been studied with the performance of questionnaire 4 and also with the completion of any quiz. Questionnaire 4 has been considered because it is focused on modular programming, which is precisely the objective of the practice test 1. In the tests carried out by calculating the correlation coefficient, no linear relationship between the variables studied could be detected. Similarly, it was not possible to reject the null hypothesis in the ANOVA tests.

The second study analyses the relationship between the five available questionnaires and the score obtained in the second practice test. A possible relation with questionnaire 5, which is dedicated to structured data types, has also been studied, since the practice exam 2 consists of the handling of an array of structures. The result obtained does not show a relationship between the variables either.

Finally, the third study works with the marks of the theory exam. The same tests have been carried out as with the practice test 2. The tests carried out have obtained similar results to those of previous experiments except in one case. From the experiment that analyzes the ANOVA between "has done some questionnaire" and the grade of the theory exam it can be deduced that both populations do not score the same on the theory test.

In this research, the continuous work has been measured through the analysis of some voluntary questionnaires that do not affect the student's grade. It would be interesting for future analyses to assign a weight to the questionnaires in the final grade. It is expected that the number of students taking them will increase and it is also possible that some more significant relationship will appear with the tests taken in the subject.

References

1. Arwendria, A., Effendi, M., Fauzan, A., Darmansyah, D.: The effectiveness of the problem-based learning- internet information literacy (PBL-IIL) model in minimizing plagiarism among students. In: 1st International Conference on Innovation in Education (ICoIE 2018). Atlantis Press, January 2019. https://doi.org/10.2991/icoie-18.2019.112
2. Busato, V.V., Prins, F.J., Elshout, J.J., Hamaker, C.: Intellectual ability, learning style, personality, achievement motivation and academic success of psychology students in higher education. Pers. Individ. Differ. **29**(6), 1057–1068 (2000). https://doi.org/10.1016/S0191-8869(99)00253-6. http://www.sciencedirect.com/science/article/pii/S0191886999002536
3. Compañ-Rosique, P., Molina-Carmona, R., Satorre-Cuerda, R.: Effects of teaching methodology on the students' academic performance in an introductory course of programming. In: Zaphiris, P., Ioannou, A. (eds.) HCII 2019. LNCS, vol. 11590, pp. 332–345. Springer, Cham (2019). https://doi.org/10.1007/978-3-030-21814-0_25
4. Díaz, J., Banchoff, L., Rodríguez, L.: Herramientas para la detección de plagio de software. un caso de estudio en trabajos de cátedra. In: Workshop de Tecnología Informática Aplicada en Educación (WTIAE), January 2008
5. De Raad, B., Schouwenburg, H.: Personality in learning and education: a review. Eur. J. Pers. **10**(5), 303–336 (1996). https://doi.org/10.1002/(SICI)1099-0984(199612)10:5⟨303::AID-PER262⟩3.0.CO;2-2
6. Dezcallar Sáez, T., Clariana Muntada, M., Gotzens Busquets, C., Badia Martín, M., Cladellas Pro, R.: Conciencia y trabajo continuo como predictores del rendimiento academico en estudiantes españoles. Revista Complutense de Educación **26**(2), 367–384 (2015)
7. Gomes, A., Mendes, A.J.: Learning to program-difficulties and solutions. In: International Conference on Engineering Education-ICEE, vol. 2007 (2007)
8. Gopalan, V., Zulkifli, A.N., Bakar, J.A.A.: A study of students' motivation using the augmented reality science textbook. In: AIP Conference Proceedings, vol. 1761, no. 1, p. 020040 (2016). https://doi.org/10.1063/1.4960880. https://aip.scitation.org/doi/abs/10.1063/1.4960880
9. Insuasti, J.: Problemas de enseñanza y aprendizaje de los fundamentos de programación. Revista Educación y Desarrollo Social **10**(2), 234–246 (2016). https://doi.org/10.18359/reds.1966, https://revistas.unimilitar.edu.co/index.php/reds/article/view/1966

10. Jenkins, T.: On the difficulty of learning to program. In: Proceedings of the 3rd Annual Conference of the LTSN Centre for Information and Computer Sciences, vol. 4, pp. 53–58. Citeseer (2002)
11. Lahtinen, E., Ala-Mutka, K., Järvinen, H.M.: A study of the difficulties of novice programmers. In: ITiCSE 2005 (2005)
12. Lounsbury, J.W., Sundstrom, E., Loveland, J.M., Gibson, L.W.: Intelligence, "big five" personality traits, and work drive as predictors of course grade. Pers. Individ. Differ. **35**(6), 1231–1239 (2003)
13. Sancho Thomas, P., Gómez Martín, P.P., Fuentes Fernández, R., Fernández-Manjón, B.: NUCLEO, aprendizaje colaborativo escenificado mediante un juego de rol. In: Actas de las XIV Jornadas de Enseñanza Universitaria de Informática, Jenui 2008. pp. 453–460. Granada, Julio 2008
14. Smalheiser, N.R.: ANOVA. In: Data Literacy, pp. 149–155. Elsevier (2017). https://doi.org/10.1016/B978-0-12-811306-6.00011-7, https://linkinghub.elsevier.com/retrieve/pii/B9780128113066000117
15. Sthle, L., Wold, S.: Analysis of variance (ANOVA). Chemom. Intell. Lab. Syst. **6**(4), 259–272 (1989). https://doi.org/10.1016/0169-7439(89)80095-4, http://www.sciencedirect.com/science/article/pii/0169743989800954
16. Swigger, K.M., Wallace, L.F.: A discussion of past programming errors and their effect on learning assembly language. J. Syst. Softw. **8**(5), 395–399 (1988). https://doi.org/10.1016/0164-1212(88)90030-1
17. Taylor, R.: Interpretation of the correlation coefficient: a basic review. J. Diagn. Med. Sonography **6**(1), 35–39 (1990). https://doi.org/10.1177/875647939000600106. http://journals.sagepub.com/doi/10.1177/875647939000600106
18. Thomas, L., Ratcliffe, M., Thomasson, B.: Can object (instance) diagrams help first year students understand program behaviour? In: Blackwell, A.F., Marriott, K., Shimojima, A. (eds.) Diagrammatic Representation and Inference, vol. 2980, pp. 368–371. Springer, Heidelberg (2004). https://doi.org/10.1007/978-3-540-25931-2_41

Learning Analytics and MOOCs

Ebru İnan[(✉)] and Martin Ebner[(✉)]

Educational Technology, Graz University of Technology, Graz, Austria
einan@student.tugraz.at, martin.ebner@tugraz.at

Abstract. There are new discoveries in the field of educational technologies in the 21st century, which we can also call the age of technology. Learning Analytics (LA) has given itself an important research field in the area of Technology Enhanced Learning. It offers analysis, benchmarking, review and development techniques for example in online learning platforms such as those who host Massive Open Online Course (MOOC). MOOCs are online courses addressing a large learning community. Among these participants, large data is obtained from the group with age, gender, psychology, community and educational level differences. These data are gold mines for Learning Analytics. This paper examines the methods, benefits and challenges of applying Learning Analytics in MOOCs based on a literature review. The methods that can be applied with the literature review and the application of the methods are explained. Challenges and benefits and the place of learning analytics in MOOCs are explained. The useful methods of Learning Analytics in MOOCs are described in this study. With the literature review, it indicates: Data mining, statistics and mathematics, Text Mining, Semantics-Linguistics Analysis, visualization, Social network analysis and Gamification areas are implementing Learning Analytics in MOOCs allied with benefits and challenges.

Keywords: Educational technology · Learning analytics · MOOCs

1 Introduction

Learning Analytics is a research discipline that is rapidly developing, aims to analyze and optimize learning and learning environments [1]. E-Learning Platforms such as Learning Management Systems (e.g. Moodle) or MOOC-platforms (e.g. edx, Udacity, Coursera etc.) have become frequently preferred tools by educators in high capacity classes. These platforms, which are used with the purpose of supporting learning, incorporating technology into education, introducing information to students, and improving the quality of education, need various analyzes to monitor the availability of the system and the student's performance change. In this way, the concept of learning analytics has emerged along with Technology-Enhanced Learning (TEL) [2].

In our age, the concept of educational technologies is becoming widespread. Teachers and educators need to be aware of the importance of using technologies and tools to increase student's motivation and ensure their participation. New teaching skills in this all-global education transformations should be adopted and implemented [3].

In this study scope, it is aimed to present an overview of existing learning analytics concepts and methods strongly focused in conjunction with Massive Open Online

© Springer Nature Switzerland AG 2020
P. Zaphiris and A. Ioannou (Eds.): HCII 2020, LNCS 12205, pp. 241–254, 2020.
https://doi.org/10.1007/978-3-030-50513-4_18

Courses(MOOCs). At the end of the study, a literature review about the concepts of MOOCs and learning analytics is going to be compiled and the future tools' functionality of learning analytics in MOOCs is going to be presented.

2 Introduction to Learning Analytics and MOOCs

Learning analytics term, initially stated in LAK 2011: 1st International Conference Learning Analytics and Knowledge and used as a base by Society of Learning Analytics (SoLAr) is defined as "the measurement, collection, analysis and reporting of data about learners and their contexts, for purposes of understanding and optimizing learning and the environment in which it occurs" [4].

Learning is a social process that includes interactions with students, teachers, instructors and others. The instructors make an effort in their learning design to maximize these interactions. All these preparations bring many questions as following: "How effective was the lecture? Did it meet the needs of the students? How can it be improved? Is an update required in learning design?" etc. Large data are obtained with approaches towards answering these questions. All these data to be used in developing teaching and learning are statistically evaluated and analyzed with Learning analytics [5].

The first learning analytics conference that took place in Banff City, Canada in 2011, brought together researchers from around the world to explore and develop learning analytics [6]. Since 2011, there are education and learning platforms on the basis of Learning analytics, with unprecedented development. Although it is a young area, there are close relationships between Learning Analytics and Web Analytics, Educational Data Mining (EDM) and Academic Analysis [7] (Fig. 1).

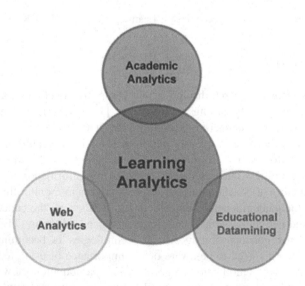

Fig. 1. Learning analytics, educational data mining, web analytics and academic analytics [7].

The concept of distance education, which is method "old concept", has undergone great progress along with today's Internet and technology. By this means of distance education, access information gets easy for users. Learners are positioned as persons who access, produce, shape and analyze information individually. As access to information becomes easier, the change to educate many people at once applied. Thus, the occurrence of the model called Massive Open Online Course or MOOCs was supported.

The term MOOCs has been first appeared in 2008 by Stephen Downes and George Siemens. Subsequently, in 2011, the training videos of Stanford University professors were published on free of charge online learning platforms. Same year, MOOCs exploded around the world; Later, Coursera, Udacity, Udemy, MITx platforms were established. Thus showed great improvement towards [8].

In general, MOOCs support models, which are free learning and independent from time and space. It also examines and follows the success and failure of the students. Moreover, it provides at least free accessibility for all participants.

Massive Open Online Course can be explained with the words of concepts in its name.

1. Massive: Massive means huge and gigantic. A large number of students participated in the MOOCs is symbolized with this letter. Opened training can be held easily with the participation of 100 people or with the participation of 100000 people. In addition to the size of the number of students, with the conception of massive, outside the campus boundaries, the concept of class global class is also defined. At this juncture, learner variations, educational material and transportation network size come into prominence [9].

2. Open: This term symbolizes the openness to each individual with access to the Internet. This is the most distinctive feature of MOOC-based education. Learners are free to join or not to join, interact, analyze in the subjects and getting the education they would like to learn. There are few to no prerequisites necessary to attend courses. There are target groups addressed by courses. These prerequisites are only available in some areas, which require expertise. MOOCs comprise word of open by being mostly free of charge [10].

3. Online: In the MOOCs model, management, data system and education are offered entirely online. There is no physical place. All educations are actualized in the courses which are accessible online and offered on the web [7].

4. Course: With this word, it is stated that the contents of the lectures are structured with pedagogical approaches within the educational plan done by instructional designers.

3 Research Methods

This study aims to describe the methods, benefits and challenges of using and implementing Learning Analytics in evaluating data of MOOCs. In order to support, the effective application of learning analytics in MOOCs, further clarification is required. The trends of Learning Analytics in MOOCs will be examined and will be a guide for future research. This research is supported by the literature review examining keywords such as Learning Analytics and MOOCs.

It includes combinations of search terms deemed appropriate for the potential of the study during the search. The search string used are "Learning Analytics" and "MOOCs" and "Massive Open Online Course" and "Learning Analytics - MOOCs". After specifying these search string, search queries were conducted in selected databases between 2009-2019 dates. A research, investigation and screening series, which started with TUBibliothek Library of University search, was conducted. Afterwards, full-text search of that search strings such as Learning Analytics and MOOCs were done in large databases offering academic publications of Semantic Scholar, Web of Science, Google Scholar, Research Gate, Scopus and Dergipark which is the academic field of research that provides access to information in Turkey. In this way on this study has been intensified with a comprehensive literature review to identify methods, benefits and challenges of Learning Analytics in MOOCs.

3.1 Data Collection Method

The data collection method used within the scope of the article is a thematic literature review. The themes are defined from the revised literature and are based learning analytics on the achievements of MOOCs, which have been built over the last decade and related to education, enabling a better theoretical understanding. The literature reviewed and discussed is comprehensive, the method for successful implementation is based on relevance, taking into account the main purpose of identifying benefits and challenges.

The titles, abstracts, keywords of the articles as a Search String was searched in that literature databases. A temporal filter was applied from 2009 to 2019 since Learning Analytics is a relatively new field that emerged back in recent years. This search data collection resulted in a total number of papers as shown in Table 1.

As a result, as a part of this review, it was referenced a total of 49 articles, which were fully read in the research process and cited in the context of the review of this study.

Table 1. Literature review on databases

Database	Last 10 years publication numbers	Keywords
TUBibliothek	7	Learning analytics
	6	MOOCs
	2	Massive open online course
	2	Learning analytics-MOOCs
Semantic scholar	647.937	Learning analytics
	29.204	MOOCs
	131.640	Massive open online course
	7.146	Learning analytics-MOOCs
Web of science	6.300	Learning analytics
	2.714	MOOCs
	2.447	Massive open online course
	202	Learning analytics-MOOCs
Scopus	10.113	Learning analytics
	3.467	MOOCs
	3.028	Massive open online course
	356	Learning analytics-MOOCs
Google scholar	450.000	Learning analytics
	31.700	MOOCs
	295.000	Massive open online course
	12.900	Learning analytics-MOOCs
DergiPark	4.060	Learning analytics
	45	MOOCs
	43.877	Massive open online course
	4.123	Learning analytics-MOOCs

4   Results of the Literature Review: Learning Analytics and MOOCs

Data Science is a field that allows creating knowledge from data in various shapes that are processed or unprocessed [11]. Learning Analytics is an Educational Data Implementation Science. It is based on the fundamentals of learning analytics, computer science, statistical calculations, data mining, machine learning, and human-computer interaction [12]. MOOCs are a mine to carry out learning analytics because all the behaviors that occur in MOOCs are much higher and higher than the amount of behavior recorded in traditional education [13].

If we explain it in detail, Learning Analytics provides an opportunity to examine student behaviors in MOOCs and to maintain the positive effects of the instructors' behaviors on learners or to clarify their concerns. In this research, methods, benefits and challenges of Learning Analytics and MOOCs are examined as well as their limitations.

Learning Analytics, which contains different disciplines such as Computer Science, Statistics, Psychology and Education, has not only technical and statistical analysis methods but also different analysis methods.

To expand research on MOOCs, Learning Analytics methods described by Khalil et al. have been studied. In MOOCs which is one of the online learning courses, learning analytics is carried out by such methods: data mining technique, statistics and mathematics, Text Mining, Semantics-Linguistics Analysis, visualization, Social network analysis and Gamification [14].

4.1 Data Categories

Data Mining. It is a method in which uses data to explore student's learning ways that have not been found before. It aims to bring on understanding with the available data. Emotions of students and their effects on the performance of the processes they perform in the system can be researched with data mining in MOOCs [15].

Data mining in e-learning is conducted with Classification and Regression Approaches. Future behaviors and attitudes in MOOCs can be designated by analyzing and pointing former data. Collected answers of questions in Classification are always "true" or "false" while they are represented as digits in Regression. The correct classification ensures obtaining correct results from data [16].

Also, Data Mining can be executed on MOOCs due to it is able to be included in e-learning environments. It supports to improve MOOCs environments. In the scope of this method, significant information is procured in MOOCs by using Prediction, Classification, Association Rule in Mining, Cluster and Fuzzy Logic Techniques [17, 18].

Statistical and Mathematical. Statistical and Mathematical methods are used to observe the relationship between participation rates and achievements by analyzing students' educational backgrounds. With this method based on numerical data, it is also possible to inform the instructors on increasing the student motivation, by determining the students with low participation in education [19].

There are data about students' behaviors and actions on MOOCs. Data such as online durations, number of being active, visited pages, percentage of reading and watched materials are stored on the system. The results are obtained with Statistical and Mathematics methods such as Average, Mean and Standard Deviation [20].

Furthermore, this method is used with some data mining techniques while it is applied. A method named Markov Chain, which is a statistical, and mathematics method has been also used on examining students' behaviors [21].

Text mining- Semantics-Linguistics Analysis. Data from user-generated content, discussion sections on forums and blogs are interpreted through Text mining- Semantics-Linguistics Analysis. In the examination of education dropout in MOOC, research and analysis that will take place in the forum and discussion sections can reveal a real result [22].

While this method is implemented, diverse techniques are used. Summarization Technique on summarizing by reducing the length properly, Categorization Technique on classifying technique-documents, Retrievals Technique on obtaining the valuable information inside the text, Extract Technique on picking over information and Cluster Technique on collecting and stacking documents besides analyzing texts are utilized [23].

Visualization. Another applicable method to the MOOCs is the Visualization method. With this method, the visualization of all the data obtained enables the user and researchers to obtain meaningful information and make analyzes through MOOCs the training performed [24].

Visualization is one of the key points about applying e-learning objects for data in education and MOOCs. The power of visualizing data comes from the enhancement of data's processability and enabling explain with occurred arguments [25]. This technique is used for doing proper learning, develop brainstorming and creativity. The followings can be shown as examples for Visualization Technique; Mind map, Concept Map, Cognitive Map, Radial Tree, Semantic Map, Rhizome, Visual Metaphor, Tree Structure, Argument Map and Social Map [26].

Social Network Analysis. Social network analysis now occupies a significant place among the Learning analytics methods. It is a method used by many researchers to understand and optimize the learning environment. Social network analysis provides an in-depth analysis of network structures and participates in training engagement interactions [27].

Social Network Analysis is implemented to interpret and analyze relations among the found data in works as well as interactions in communication tools [28]. It is a technique that is continuously growing and developing new methods and approaches. On implementing this technique, Practices such as Block Modelling and Equivalence, Signed Graphs, Structural Balance and Analysis, and Dynamic Network Analysis are utilized [29].

Gamification. Gamification method increases student motivation, learning platform usage and participation in courses and makes learning entertaining. The practice of gamification in MOOCs enables students and participants to achieve success an immersive experience with high motivation and high participation [30].

There are differences in participation and training completion levels in MOOCs and online learning environments. Students' motivation with simple game features and their commitment to learning processes are increasing. By the help of the secret relationship between computers and games, it is advantageous to use the gamification method in online learning platforms [31]. Learning for learners is available by making transactions in processes. Learners gain ability to manage their time and speed while improving their ability to follow. In this process, learners can experience sense of wonder, mystery, fun, excitement and sadness when they are learning [32]. The most used gamification methods in education are defined as Visual Status, Social Engagement, Freedom of Choice, freedom to fail, Rapid Feedback and Progress [33].

4.2   Current Situations

Considering all these methods, it would not be wrong to state that the application of Learning Analytics on MOOCs has benefits and difficulties. MOOC platforms and similar online learning platforms are data stores. It is a data mine to perform learning analytics in MOOCs with mouse clicks, forums and discussion activities, on-the-fly and post-test performances, entry frequency and active time, time spent on work and assignments, and video interactions. In this way, direct intervention can be provided to the success of the student and the quality of education [34].

Table 2. 6 Areas of Learning Analytics and MOOCs

6 Areas of learning analytics and MOOCs			
	Areas	Description	Techniques
1	Data mining	It is an observation oriented learning analytics technique that contributes to student interaction and teaching models design [35]	•Predictions •Classification •Association rule in mining •Clustering •Fuzzy logic
2	Statistical and mathematical	It is the analysis and interpretation of quantitative data to reach information	•Average •Mean •Standard deviotion •Markov Chain
3	Text mining-semantics-linguistics analysis	It is a method of reaching useful information by discovering and defining meaningful ones from the texts on the system [36]	•Summarization •Categorization •Retrievals •Extract •Cluster
4	Visualization	It is a visual conversion of information by using special engineering techniques in original forms of data [37]	•Mind Map •Concept Map •Cognitive Map •Radial Tree •Semantic Map •Rhizome •Visual Metaphor •Tree Structure •Argument Map •Social Map
5	Social network analysis	Relational bonds and behaviors are measured, defined, analyzed and taken precautions [38]	•Blockmodelling and equivalence analysis •Signed graphs and structural balance analysis •Dynamic network analysis
6	Gamification	It is used to increase the quality and quantity of activity and training outputs by increasing user effectiveness [39]	•Visual Status •Social engagement •Freedom of choice •Freedom to fail •Rapid feedback •Progress

Although MOOCs are among the education trends in the world today, they comprise many challenges within. The determination of the needs of learning and the suitability of education is very complex on the system. In general, in the statistics of MOOCs, it occurs a low rate of fulfilment on education, despite remarkable high rate of the registered participant. The concept of learning analytics supports to solve and analyzes such cases that are mentioned above [40].

According to the study by Khail, Taraghi and Ebner (2016), the benefits of learning analytics in MOOCs are limitless. These are indicated as Prediction, Recommendation, Visualization, Entertainment, Benchmarking, Personalization, Enhance Engagement, Communication Information and Cost Saving [34].

Learning analytics aims to develop students' knowledge and skills with data obtained from online learning platforms and MOOCs. When this method uses, students' learning quality is maximized. Examining, using and analyzing the obtained data provide several benefits for education.

Learning Analytics and MOOCs together enables students to interpret their own results and review their performance, to instructors to affect the learning of students or student groups in MOOCs. Moreover, they also provide an advantage to management about learning outcomes and using personal programs [41].

With the analysis of the data, instructors can determine renewals in the curriculum and students' weaknesses in learning and understanding. Instructors can make educational strategic changes over the curriculum. These renewals provide an advantage for improving curriculum quality and learning potential of students [42]. With the implementation of learning analytics, instructors can easily identify individual errors [43].

In this study, MOOCs and Learning Analytics concepts, methods, benefits and challenges of the implementation of Learning Analytics in MOOCs have been put forth. It is seen that the application of Learning Analytics in online learning platforms and especially MOOC platforms are interdisciplinary studies. There is a need to operate a comprehensive process from all sorts of inputs and outputs on MOOCs, from students and participants to educators. There are many techniques such as Visualization, Statistical and Mathematical etc. and pedagogical methods such as Gamification in order to make learning analysis true. These methods which can be applied in MOOCs are mentioned. As part of the literature review, references to these methods and fields are given in Table 3.

Table 3. 6 areas reference review

Areas	1-Data mining	2-Statistical and mathematical	3-Text mining-semantics-linguistics analysis	4-Visualization	5-Social network analysis	6-Gamification
Literature	1;4;5;7;15;16;17;18; 35;42;44	4;5;7;19;20;21	7;22;23;36;45	1;2;3;4;5;7;24;25; 26;37;42;46	4;5;7;27;28; 29;38;42;47	3;7;30;31; 32;33;39;48

Implementations of these methods gain favors on converting large amounts of data in MOOCs into information and quality. It provides useful information about the needs of students, classroom interactions of teachers, educational activity and curriculum arrangements. In the future, as the usage and the development of technologies advance, new advantages and benefits will arise.

4.3　Typical Examples

In the following paragraphs we would like to list a typical example for each area according to Table 2.

Data Mining: In the study conducted by Mukala et al., Learning behaviours of students have been analyzed by examining the correlation between the students' video course follow-ups and success. Using the data mining technique, it is seen that the student's video surveillance have a direct impact on performance. In addition, it has been observed that behaviour studies can be developed and necessary improvements and measures can be taken for the future with the interesting parts of the course examined and the data of the most skipped or repeated sections [44].

Statistical and Mathematical: In the study carried out by Taraghi et al., Data set analysis was performed by considering the answering time of the students and it has been determined the easiest and most difficult questions in different types. The questions were classified as difficult, medium, easy with the K-means algorithm method. Thus, it was concluded that the question selection algorithm will be developed with the Markov statistical analysis method which will be applied for each question and this will affect the performance of the students [21].

Text Mining-Semantics-Linguistics Analysis: In the study of Tucker and Pursel on MOOCs, they investigated the effects of the texts produced by the students on the student performances and outputs by using the Text mining - Semantics-Linguistics Analysis technique. According to the results of the study, it was found out that the students' feelings had an impact on exam performance and homework. During the research, text data was obtained via MOOCs and the data were arranged on SQL. This technique was applied by using emotional analysis algorithms on the textual data and results were obtained [45].

Visualization: Zhang and Yuan have worked on video recordings in MOOCs to explore the relationship among courses. Within the scope of the study, it was seen that all participants registered at least two courses while there was not any participant in only one course. A visualized network diagram was applied to the relationship between courses and learners. With the performed analysis, it was concluded that it is possible to enroll in lectures at the same time. In this way, an environment will be created to present the other open courses for registered participants [46].

Social Network Analysis: Kellogg, Booth and Oliver have applied the Social Network Analysis technique in their studies in order to present a peer-assisted learning approach in MOOCs. This method has been preferred to measure and visualize interaction patterns within the scope of the study. To implement this statement, they have used the free NodeXL template, which is an add-in to Excel. Thus, they explained the importance and use of peer interaction in training prepared for educators [47].

Gamification: In their study, Vaibhav and Gupta have done Gamified and Non Gamified groups on MOOCs and analyzed the differences. It was seen that the completion rate of courses was more successful in the platforms using gamification technique. The number of students who refused to take the final exam decreased by 14% in gamified platforms. It is explained based on the survey results that students have fun and developments in their education by Gamification application [48].

As it is seen in these studies; learning analytics in MOOCs provides many benefits; On the other hand, it includes ethical, legal, technological and security challenges. On this topic some precautions should be taken on pedagogical transparency, data control and safety.

Generally, the advantages of learning analytics in MOOCs are indicated as follows [42]:

- Determining the target course
- Improvement of the curriculum
- Student learning outcomes, behaviors and processes
- Individualized learning
- Teacher performance improvement
- Post-educational employment.

Although learning analytics in MOOCs provides many benefits over learning, there are some difficulties in the implementation process. The data which is obtained on the platforms is not knowledge. This data should be transformed into information and knowledge by processing, then interpreted correctly. Learning is a complicated process. Learning also contains cultural behaviors. While learning analytics offers technical analysis, it requires trainers to use different culturally and behaviorally educational models in interpretation. To perform and interpret can take time on Learning Analysis. Considering the individuality of learning, these issues can be seen as challenges.

According to Ferguson, some of these challenges [49]:

- The necessity of establishing strong connections with learning science
- Difficulty in understanding and optimizing learning environments and MOOCs.
- Focus on students' point of view
- Not to develop and implement a clear set of ethical rules

There is no doubt that the challenges with envisaged by our age technologies and rapidly evolving platforms will be solved in the future. Learning analysis and MOOCs, with contributions to education and learning, is a scientific field and it is continuously developing.

Learning Analytics and MOOC with all their content are pioneers in education. They will continue to be the focal point on implementing large data analysis in education and online learning platforms.

5 Discussions

That Literature Review provides a comprehensive overview of the Learning Analytics methods, benefits, and challenges of MOOCs. The examination of these features showed positive contributions. However, with the literature review, it has also been revealed from publications that the use of Learning Analytics in education has increased over time.

This study revealed that Learning Analytics is an interdisciplinary field as suggested by Clow [50]. Therefore, learning analytics selects and uses the most appropriate methods and analysis techniques to achieve the goal of making education more efficient at MOOCs. The use of an inclusive method will lead to improved learning experience for students.

6 Conclusions

Learning Analytics is a new area and ever developing concept. In additional to this, MOOCs with the huge data sources have an important role in applying learning analysis. The state-of-the-art methods of learning analytics in MOOC are described in this study. Data mining, statistics and mathematics, Text Mining, Semantics-Linguistics Analysis, visualization, Social network analysis and Gamification areas are implemented Learning Analytics in MOOCs allied with benefits and challenges. In the future, it is expected that the implementation of learning analytics and large data will be effectively used more and more in MOOCs to understand how learning is happening.

References

1. Saqr, M.: A literature review of empirical research on learning analytics in medical education. Int. J. Health Sci. 12(5), 1–6 (2018)
2. Bahçeci, F.: Öğrenme Yönetim Sistemlerinde Kullanılan Öğrenme Analitikleri Araçlarının İncelenmesi. Turk. J. Educ. Stud. 2(1), 41–58 (2015)
3. Chang, V., Gütl, C., Ebner, M.: Trends and opportunities in online learning, MOOCs, and cloud-based tools. In: Voogt, J., Knezek, G., Christensen, R., Lai, K.-W. (eds.) Second Handbook of Information Technology in Primary and Secondary Education. SIHE, pp. 935–953. Springer, Cham (2018). https://doi.org/10.1007/978-3-319-71054-9_64
4. Siemens, G.: Learning analytics the emergence of a discipline. Am. Behav. Sci.t 57(10), 1380–1400 (2013)
5. Elias, T.: Learning analytics: definitions, processes and potential. https://landing.athabascau.ca/file/download/43713. Accessed 23 Apr 2019
6. Dawson, S., Joksimovic, S., Poquet, O., Siemens, G.: Increasing the impact of learning analytics. In: Proceedings of the International Conference on Learning Analytics and Knowledge,https://dl.acm.org/citation.cfm?id=3303784&dl=ACM&coll=DL,last. Accessed 22 Apr 2019
7. Khalil, M.: Learning analytics in massive open online courses. Doctoral thesis, Graz University of Technology, Graz (2018). https://www.semanticscholar.org/paper/E-Learning-Using-Data-Mining-Elaal/16c4625f2e31307dd11223464b551db097c36cc4

8. Baturay, M.H.: An overview of the world of MOOCs. Procedia – Soc. Behav. Sci. **174**, 427–433 (2015)
9. Bozkurt, A.: Kitlesel Açık Çevrimiçi Dersler (Massive open online courses - MOOCs) ve Sayısal Bilgi Çağında Yaşamboyu Öğrenme Fırsatı. Açıköğretim Uygulamaları ve Araştırmaları Dergisi **1**(1), 56–81 (2015)
10. Mali, A.K.: Massive open online courses. EduInspire: Int. E-J. **3**(1) 1–9 (2016)
11. Dhar, V.: Data science and prediction. Commun. ACM **56**(12), 64–73 (2013)
12. Piety, P.J., Behrens, J., Rea, R.: Educational data science and the need for interpretive skills. Am. Educ. Res. Assoc. **27** (2013)
13. O'Reily, U.M., Veeromochoneni, K.: Technology for mining the big data of MOOCs. Res Pract. Assess. **9**, 29–37 (2014)
14. Khalil, M., Ebner, M.: What is learning analytics about? A survey of different methods used in 2013–2015. In: Smart Learning Conference Dubai, pp. 294–304 (2016)
15. Tucker, C., Pursel, B.K., Divinsky, A.: Mining student-generated textual data in MOOCs and quantifying their effects on student performance and learning outcomes. Comput. Educ. J. **5**(4), 84 (2014)
16. Ionita, I.: Data mining techniques for e-learning. J. Appl. Comput. Sci. Math. **10**(22), 26–31 (2016)
17. Abd Elaal, S.A.E.: E-learning using data mining. Chin.-Egypt. Res. J. (2013)
18. Lile, A.: Analyzing e-learning systems using educational data mining techniques. Mediterr. J. Soc. Sci. **2**(3), 403–419 (2011)
19. Al-Shabandar, R., Hussain, A.J., Liatsis, P., Keight, R.: Analyzing learners behavior in MOOCs: an examination of performance and motivation using a data driven approach. IEEE Access **6**, 73669–73685 (2018)
20. Chatti, M.A., Dyckhoff, A.L., Schroeder, U., Thüs, H.: A reference model for learning analytics. Int. J. Technol. Enhanced Learn. (IJTEL) **4**(5), 318–331 (2013)
21. Taraghi, B., Saranti, A., Ebner, M., Schön, M.: Markov chain and classification of difficulty levels enhances the learning path in one digit multiplication. In: Zaphiris, P., Ioannou, A. (eds.) LCT 2014. LNCS, vol. 8523, pp. 322–333. Springer, Cham (2014). https://doi.org/10.1007/978-3-319-07482-5_31
22. Wen, M., Yang, D., Rose, C.P.: Sentiment analysis in MOOC discussion forums: what does it tell us? In: Conference: Educational Data Mining (2014)
23. Dang, S., Ahmad, P.H.: Text mining: techniques and its application. IJETI Int. J. Eng. Technol. Innovations **1**(4), 22–25 (2014)
24. Gama, S., Gonçalves, D.: Visualizing educational datamining patterns. In: Eurographics Conference on Visualization (EuroVis), United Kingdom (2014)
25. Williamson, B.: Digital education governance: data visualization, predictive analytics, and 'real-time' policy instruments. J. Educ. Policy **31**(2), 123–141 (2016)
26. Latha, S., Raj, M.R.C., Sukumaran, R.: Use of visualization techniques for active learning engagement in environmental science engineering courses. Int. Sch. Sci. Res. Innovation **10**(4), 1340–1344 (2016)
27. Filva, D.A., Penalvo, F.J.G., Forment, M.A.: Social network analysis approaches for social learning support. In: Proceedings of the Second International Conference on Technological Ecosystems for Enhancing Multiculturality, Spain, pp. 269–274 (2014)
28. Perovic, D.: Data mining influence on e-learning. In: The Sixth International Conference on e-Learning, Serbia, Belgrade (2015)
29. Butts, C.T.: Social network analysis: a methodological introduction. Asian J. Soc. Psychol. **11**, 13–41 (2008)

30. Khalil, M., Wong, J., de Koning, B.B., Ebner, M., Paas, F.: Gamification in MOOCs: a review of the state of the art. In: IEEE Global Engineering Education Conference, pp. 1635–1644 (2018)
31. Glover, I.: Play as you learn: gamification as a technique for motivating learners, Sheffield Hallam University Research Archive. http://orcid.org/0000-0002-1078-5281,last. Accessed 22 Apr 2019
32. Brull, S., Finlayson, S.: Importance of gamification in increasing learning. J. Continuing Educ. Nurs. **47**(8), 372–375 (2016)
33. Dicheva, D., Dichev, C., Agre, G., Angelova, G.: Gamification in education: a systematic mapping study. Educ. Technol. Soc. **18**(3), 75–88 (2015)
34. Khalil, M., Taraghi, B., Ebner, M.: Engaging learning analytics in MOOCS: the good, the bad, and the ugly. In: International Conference on Education and New Developments (2016)
35. Chang, G., Healey, M., McHugh, J.A.M., Wang, T.L.: Mining the World Wide Web An Information Search Approach. Kluwer Academic Publisher, Boston (2001)
36. Sundari, J.G., Sundae, D.: A study of various text mining techniques. Int. J. Adv. Netw. Appl. (IJANA) **8**(5), 82–85 (2017)
37. Pardos, Z.A., Horodyskyj, L.: Analysis of student behaviour in habitable worlds using continuous representation visualization. J. Learn. Anal. **6**(1), 1–15 (2019)
38. Müller, T.: Social network analysis: a practical method to improve knowledge sharing, hands-on knowledge co-creation and sharing; practical methods and techniques. https://papers.ssrn.com/sol3/papers.cfm?abstract_id=1467609. Accessed 25 Apr 2019
39. Morschheuser, B., Hassan, L., Werder, K., Hamari, J.: How to design gamification? A method for engineering gamified software. Inf. Softw. Technol. **95**, 219–237 (2018)
40. Chea, C.: Benefits and challenges of massive open online courses. ASEAN J. Open Distance Learn. **8**(1), 16–23 (2016)
41. Manderveld, J.: Grand challenges for learning analytics and open & online education. In: Open and Online Education, pp. 70–74 (2015)
42. Avella, J.T., Kebrithchi, M., Nunn, S.G., Knai, T.: Learning analytics methods, benefits, and challenges in higher education: a systematic literature review. Online Learn. **20**(2), 13–29 (2016)
43. Ebner, M., Pronegg, M.: Use of learning analytics applications in mathematics with elementary learners. Int. J. Acad. Res. Educ. **1**(2), 26–39 (2015)
44. Mukala, P., Buijs, J.C.A.M., Van Der Aalst, W.M.P.: Exploring students' learning behaviour. In: Moocs Using Process Mining Techniques, Department of Mathematics and Computer Science, University of Technology, Eindhoven, The Netherlands, pp. 179–196 (2015)
45. Tucker, C., Pursel, B.K.: Mining student-generated textual data in MOOCs and quantifying their effects on student performance and learning outcomes. ASEE Comput. Educ. (CoED) J. **4**(5), 84 (2014)
46. Zhang, T., Yuan, B.: Visualizing MOOC user behaviors: a case study on XuetangX. In: Yin, H., Gao, Y., Li, B., Zhang, D., Yang, M., Li, Y., Klawonn, F., Tallón-Ballesteros, Antonio J. (eds.) IDEAL 2016. LNCS, vol. 9937, pp. 89–98. Springer, Cham (2016). https://doi.org/10.1007/978-3-319-46257-8_10
47. Kellogg, S., Booth, S., Oliver, K.: A social network perspective on peer supported learning in MOOCs for educators. Int. Rev. Res. Open Distrib. Learn. **15**(5), 263–289 (2014)
48. Vaibhav, A., Gupta, P.: Gamification of Moocs for increasing user engagement. In: 2014 IEEE International Conference on MOOC, Innovation and Technology in Education (MITE), pp. 290–295 (2014)
49. Ferguson, R.: Learning analytics: drivers, developments and challenges. Int. J. Technol. Enhanced Learn. **4**(5/6), 304–317 (2012)
50. Clow, D.: An overview of learning analytics. Teach. High. Educ. **18**(6), 683–695 (2013)

On the Design of a Teachers' Dashboard: Requirements and Insights

Pedro Isaias[1](✉) and Adriana Backx Noronha Viana[2]

[1] University of New South Wales (UNSW – Sydney),
Room 2117, Quadrangle Building, Sydney 2052, Australia
pedro.isaias@unsw.edu.au
[2] Business School, University of São Paulo, Av. Prof. Luciano Gualberto,
908 - Butantã, São Paulo, SP 05508-010, Brazil

Abstract. The value that data has in the information society is undeniable. However data per se has limited significance, as it requires structure and it needs to be adequately conveyed to the user. Education is no exception to all the sectors currently harnessing the power of the data that stems from the interaction with their various stakeholders. Learning analytics can assist educators to understand how their students are learning, how successful they are at the accomplishment of certain tasks and to identify if they are at risk of failing. A fundamental part of learning analytics is visualisation, which is responsible for the communication of the data that is collected and becomes central in determining the teacher intervention in the learning process. In this paper the authors will present the results of semi-structured interviews that were conducted with lecturers at UNIV faculties and schools, in order to collect their insights regarding what aspects should be considered when design a teachers dashboard. Main requirements as well as major concerns are compiled and discussed. This is specifically useful to guide the future design of a teacher dashboard at UNIV and other universities.

Keywords: Teacher dashboards · Learning analytics · Dashboard design

1 Introduction

Higher education institutions are increasingly investing in the use of business intelligence applied to education. The pressure to make evidence-based decisions drives the development of sophisticated dashboards where selected data is sorted and visually presented. The present study started with the process of gathering information from university lecturers and researchers about the business requirements to design and build a teacher dashboard. The focus of the questions was to understand the purpose of a dashboard for higher education teachers. Those requirements are the foundation for the project and process definition.

As a strong dyadic relationship, teaching and learning are inseparable. Good teaching only happens where there is authentic learning. At one point in time, this relationship was more clearly defined. The teacher was the only source of information from which the students came to build up their knowledge.

© Springer Nature Switzerland AG 2020
P. Zaphiris and A. Ioannou (Eds.): HCII 2020, LNCS 12205, pp. 255–269, 2020.
https://doi.org/10.1007/978-3-030-50513-4_19

With emerging technologies, learning happens everywhere and anywhere, and teachers are becoming one of the sources of knowledge instead of the main one. Ubiquitous learning changes the perspective of teaching which was merely restricted to classroom interactions. It is necessary to understand what happens beyond the class-room and how the learning process is changing. For teachers to reflect upon their practice, they must look at the way students are responding to the teaching but also they need to have access to data generated by the usage of new learning technologies and the social interactions that take place online. Also, within ubiquitous learning settings, there is usually a higher number of students that the teachers need to support. These challenges create the need for the development of monitoring tools that can be used to track the student's progress and assess the educational process [16]. Teachers can greatly benefit from the information that a visual overview provides about their stu-dents' activities. Through visualization teachers can obtain a picture of what activities are most popular among their students and resort to that information to redesign learning tasks [8]. It is the information that dashboards display that can lead teachers to intervene in the learning process and contact learners that have been identified as potential drop outs [5]. One of the purposes of dashboards is to assist teachers to detect and make sense of behavioral patterns in classes [12]. Moreover, the information that derives from the use of learning analytics can be used for the assessment of the students' competencies. Learning analytics tools can assist assessment to move beyond the conventional use of survey and quizzes' results and provide insight from the data that is collected from richer sources [22].

Khan Academy's proposal is to be a free digital learning platform with its main focus on Mathematics [11]. It is an individualized mastery-based learning tool where learners accumulate points by an algorithm that considers time on practicing exercises, watching video tutorials and skill progressing [17]. Such information is organized on a dashboard to provide teachers with an overview of the class performance as a whole, or focusing on a particular student's profile to have a better understanding of learning behavior and need for early interventions. Khan Academy provides a sophisticated teacher dashboard that can be an inspiration to gather insights into Teacher Dashboard planning.

In this paper authors will present results from semi-structured interviews that were conducted with lecturers at the UNIV (fictitious denomination to protect the entity's anonymity) faculties and schools, in order to collect their insights regarding what aspects should be considered when design a Teachers Dashboard. This is comprised of a qualitative study of 14 academics who were interviewed as representatives of dif-ferent faculties. There were 2 lecturers per school to ensure that some particular operating patterns could be captured and represented. Main requirements as well as major concerns are compiled and presented. This is specifically useful to guide the future design of a Teacher Dashboard at UNIV and in other universities.

2 The Role of Visualization

The field of visual analytics differs from the area of simple data visualisation in the sense that it cannot be reduced to a mere presentation of the information deriving from an analytic process. Instead, it aims to endow those with the power of decision with resources that they can engage with and control in order to obtain a deeper insight into the consequences that the results have in the decisions that they have to make [18]. Learning analytics can be divided into four phases: awareness, reflection, sensemaking and impact. Visualisation is part of the first stage, awareness. This phase is focused on the visualisation of data. The data that is collected through learning analytics can be portrayed in numerous visualisations, namely in activity streams, tabular overviews [27]. The use of activity streams can enrich the learners' awareness and commitment. Also, charts representing progress bars are visualisation tools that can support an objective-oriented strategy [25]. Linear visualisations can be used to represent data from time series [20]. Network visualisations can enhance the students to obtain a deeper insight about how their peers communicate [25].

From the viewpoint of the teachers, visualization tools will help them to have a depiction of the students' progress and based on that information they can reformulate their teaching methods, change the material that is supplied and adjust the learning process to suit the needs of the students. Furthermore, through the visualisation of the students' data, the teachers can produce a more complete and effective feedback on the students' evolution than if they were to use the results of quizzes or tests [20].

From the perspective of the students, they can use the data that is displayed to increase their awareness about their accomplishments and modify their behaviour and learning techniques according to the data [20]. Visualisations aim to drive the students to reflect upon what they have accomplished [25]. Moreover, visualisations are important resources when it comes to allowing the students not only to view their progress, but also to compare it with their colleagues [19].

The fact that data can be visually represented means that is it possible for teachers and students to exchange visualizations, and consequently to be able to discuss and ponder about real data [20]. Social learning can also be measured through learning analytics. Students and teachers' dashboards can include visualisation from social learning analytics to assist the monitoring of the different degrees of social interaction. Visualization such as discourse and content analysis and social networks analytics can be used for this purpose. These visualizations can equally be used to portray the students' progress in the development of collaborative competencies, to assist the timely identification of students that might be disconnected and at-risk and to offer them solutions [24].

3 Teacher Dashboards

Learning dashboards derive from the general idea of visualization based on specific objectives [8]. The visualization of the data that was collected from the students is a crucial step in learning analytics. Namely using dashboards, it is possible to have an understanding about some aspects of the learning process [5]. The use of teacher dashboards is demonstrating the potential that learning analytics have to positively impact education [1]. In an ideal scenario, dashboards should be included in Learning Management Systems. Moodle and Blackboard, for example offer elementary tables where teachers can visualise the students' marks. Also, Brightspace and Schoology have learning analytics features available for teachers [23].

3.1 Challenges

Despite the numerous benefits of teacher dashboards, their use is associated with a series of challenges that can compromise their effectiveness. One of the challenges linked with teacher dashboards is the scarcity of empirical evidence attesting to their real impact on the students' learning [1]. In terms of learning analytics in general, one of the most relevant challenges associated with its use is related to the uncertainty of what aspects are more pertinent and should be measured to ensure the provision of a clear understanding of how learning occurs. There is some question as to the effectiveness of the conventional measurements in obtaining information that actually addresses the core of learning. Traditionally, the aspects that are included in learning analytics measurements are time spent and the number of clicks, accessed material, logins and completed assignments [8]. An important shortcoming that affects learning analytics is the potential that exists for the occurrence of a misinterpretation of the data results, caused by human judgment. It seems that the corrected interpretation of the results can only be done by skilled educators [19]. Furthermore, the low level of interoperability among distinct systems of data constitutes a challenges for analytics that depend on data deriving from assorted and distributed sources [22].

3.2 Design Considerations

There is a lack of research in terms of design guidelines for the development of teacher dashboards. The complete development of tools for learning analytics is the result of the efforts of distinct disciplines, namely human-computer interaction, software engineering and psychology [13]. The design of learning analytics dashboards can be an intricate process when it has to address a great volume of data deriving from various sources with diverse uses [7]. In brief, teacher dashboards need to collect and display student data meaningfully, to have the capacity for complex data aggregation, and they must be user-friendly [16]. The user-friendliness of the visual representation of learning analytics results can enable a better interpretation and analysis of the collected data [4]. Learning analytics' visualisations should address relevance, usability, the satisfaction of the user and general effectiveness [13]. The design of dashboards requires insight about learning analytics and its uses, since dashboards are created according to the peculiar needs and observational aims of the users [7]. It is equally important that this tool can use and portray an extensive range of students' activities and that it includes a recommendation feature to offer options to the teachers [16]. To be effective learning analytics are required to extend its reach further than the collection of data from learning management systems (LMS) and include different types of metrics. Also, the information should be communicated to teachers in a timely manner and in an actionable layout [22].

4 Method

This research is founded on a qualitative approach. Semi-structured interviews were conducted with 14 academics, who participated as representatives of different faculties. There were 2 lecturers per school to ensure that some particular operating patterns could be captured and represented. Lecturers were invited via email by the Head of School and those who volunteered were contacted by the researcher to schedule an interview. The estimated time for the interviews was initially 30 min, but only 1 of the 14 interviews remained within that timeframe. The interviews happened at each lecturer's office. It was during work hours at the most convenient time defined by them. The lecturers were very welcoming and seemed to appreciate the opportunity to share their opinion with the researcher from the central teaching and learning unit.

The interviews were analyzed using constructive grounded theory [3] and thematic analysis [2]. There were semi-structured questions to guide the conversation, but the interviewer also allowed lecturers to introduce any subject that they considered to be relevant. Initially, the interviews were supposed to be for 30 min, but only one stayed within that time frame. The lecturers talked for over one hour about their visions concerning UNIV, their faculties, teaching practice, the students and them-selves. Lecturers were asked about their teaching practice, how they curated and shared the learning resources, how they communicated the learning objectives and the course procedures, and how they received feedback from the students' developmental progress and learning. They were also asked about the information that would be relevant in the dashboard and how it could integrate, correlate and compare some of the data generated by other systems and by the students in the classroom. Based on this information, lecturers commented on how they provided feedback and actions they took to support students' learning and make sure that the learning objectives were achieved. The concept of Feed up, Feedback and Feed Forward was explored to describe the exchange process between a lecturer and the students [10]. Teachers' actions are guided by the first contact with the students via the ECP (electronic course profile on Blackboard) with a clear definition about the learning objectives, learning resources, course procedures and support. This initial stage, Feed-up, ensures that students understand the purpose of the course, assignment, task, or lesson, including how they will be assessed. As students interact with the learning resources, participate in the lecturers and start doing activities, they generate data about their learning process.

Most resources are unidirectional like pdfs, video tutorials and presentation. Some resources have instant feedback, others are peer-evaluated, other need marking from the lecturers of tutors. Some are formative, others are summative. It is from the interaction with the designed resources that students can evaluate their own progress. When they are formative and automatically generated by systems, the lecturers can have an overall and specific snapshot with a clear description of the class performance. It is a representation of how the students are learning. It is a basic feedback that provides students with information about their learning gaps. It is a preparation for the summative assessments. Unless there is a system to create this assignment, the results are consolidated in a separate spreadsheet and then updated to Blackboard. There is not a system for data analysis that could represent for the teachers and the students what are the trends, rankings, successes, needs and recommendations. The same information could help student's self-reflection and the teacher's class and student evaluation. Lecturers were asked about what information they thought would be relevant based on performance data for those reflections and how they would like to visualize it.

The most important question is what the lecturers would do with such information, and if they would be willing to adapt their practice to improve students' learning. If the analysis was made in a way that would be meaningful to the lecturers and learners would they use it to change their learning behavior? Feed-forward guides student learning with recommendations based on performance data. All three, feed up, feedback and feed forward, should be aligned if students are to learn at high levels.

The analyses were performed by grouping the information presented in the interview according to Table 1.

Table 1. Analyses layers: dimensions, aspects and context.

Dimension	Aspect	Context
The concept of a Dashboard	Teaching practice	View of the lecturer's context View of the students: traits and attitudes View of themselves View of their practice
	Feedback	Feed up Feedback from students Feedback to the students Feed Forward
What teacher say they need	Descriptive Data Comparative data Prescriptive data Data sources	
What would they do?	Attitudes towards innovation	

5 Results

Previous findings from a previous survey with university lecturers and researchers, showed that 63% of teachers were not aware if there was a teacher dashboard at their universities even though the majority were respondents from universities that have a teacher dashboard. Either the concept of the dashboard is not clear or the communication and training from Information Technology and Innovative Teaching departments to lecturers needs to be reframed.

Some universities are being cautious about adopting a formal dashboard. Teachers' skills involve having insights about students' progress and adapting their lessons just in time to students' needs and mastery level. However, with increasing cohort sizes and higher standard deviation in students' mastery level and engagement, it is becoming more difficult to assess performance without technology support. 57.1% can identify struggling students with the current level of information they have. The majority has access to LMS information, grades and attendance and this is how they evaluate student performance. Unfortunately, some of that information might only come very late into the course not allowing the lecturer to intervene and adapt lessons to improve students' performance just in time.

Another point of concern is that some teachers have not affirmed that if they would have access to a Teacher Dashboard, that they would use that data to make student learning focused decisions. Some lecturers perceive that having access to extra information might implicate extra workload. Others, on the other hand have declared that they would work manually on spreadsheets to compare cohorts and students within each cohort.

When questioned about using data from the Teacher dashboard to adapt their teaching, the answers were slightly less favorable. Despite having access to the data, there is resistance from teachers to adapt their teaching to meet students' needs and mastery level. Maybe the concept of a Teacher Dashboard was not as understood as presumed from our sample of higher education lecturers familiar with learning analytics. Nevertheless, when asked if they had access to students' mastery level, teachers' response was more positive. It might be related to the fact that mastery level is an indicator easier to assess than the concepts that can be incorporated in a dashboard.

As shown in Table 1, the analyzes were performed considering three dimensions: 1) the concept perceived by the teachers interviewed about Dashboard; 2) what teachers say they need; 3) and what teachers would do. The results, obtained from the analysis of the interviews conducted with the lecturers, are presented considering these dimensions.

5.1 The Concept of a Dashboard

Some of the teachers who have been interviewed were not even familiar with the concept of an analytical dashboard. When the interviews have been conducted, disseminating the concept and explaining the affordances of a dashboard to reflect upon their teaching practice were also a parallel process. There is the idea that a dashboard is about control.

Molenaar, Knoop-van Campen [15] developed a study on how teachers use dashboards, observing the relationship between feedback and teaching practice. The concept of a Dashboard by the interviewees was analyzed considering two aspects: Teaching practice and Feedback.

Teaching Practice

To analyze teaching practices, four concepts were considered: view of the lecturers' context, view of the students (traits and attitudes), view of themselves and view of their practice.

View of the context

Before going into the dashboard concept, it is crucial to explore the context and how the vision of teachers about teaching at UNIV. Head of Schools, Faculties and The central teaching and learning unit (at UNIV) influences their choices and shapes the dynamics. There is a culture of a course existing despite its lecturers. If a lecture is no longer teaching the course, he or she leaves the content and the format behind to be adopted by the successor.

The central teaching and learning unit has an image of bringing proposals ready-made for the lecturers to adopt and implement. That seems to evoke a resistance and undervalue of the information provided.

There is a unique culture in every school and lecturers are proud about their community. When talking about each other, they used the word 'colleague' and referred to each school as almost an autonomous entity. Each School is a relatively independent unit and they have budget and certain autonomy on how to spend that budget. For instance, one specific School had chosen to use an online quiz provider. It costs 15 US dollars per student. There is no formal evidence that this platform improves student learning, but that is the assumption that students are learning more because they are doing more quizzes and their marks are improving in the quizzes. This could mean that they are getting better at doing quizzes. Perhaps the question data bank is not as dynamic and updated to be counteracted by students' online strategies to find out about the answers. Students use Yahoo Answers, Chegg and closed Facebook groups to find out about solutions and publish them online.

Most of teaching methods and administrative tasks have been improved overtime by learning from experience. There is a committee that reflects and discuss how each semester went and propose adjustments.

There is the feeling that there is overregulation at UNIV. Too much regulation can be an obstacle to innovation. Some lecturers feel they do not have the autonomy to implement changes.

It was also questioned the effects of teaching awards as they recognize individuals, not team-effort. The awards also seem to have shifted from teaching excellence to teaching innovation.

In addition, it was acknowledged by one of the lecturers that every time UNIV brings the term innovation it is in fact looking for efficiencies. Moreover, when anything is restructured, UNIV gives nice reasons, but at the end it means that people are going to be losing jobs once the novelty is implemented.

View of the students: traits and attitudes

Lecturers' perceptions of the students inform their teaching practice and the level of relationship and commitment to the students [14]. During the interviews, it was aimed to explore their views by asking about examples, situations in the classroom, evaluation results and participations during the course. Most of the interviewees agree that 1st year and 2nd year students have different learning behavior and attitudes, and therefore teaching strategies should be tailored specifically. One faculty has chosen a computer-based simulation to increase student engagement in one of its 1st year course with over a thousand students. There are the proactive and the cruisers. Some students evaluate the effort and time it will take them to do an assignment versus the potential reward before deciding to do it what a lecturer has described as Super model Syndrome.

If students have a chance to work harder or not, they will always choose the easy path. The blended learning format at first is perceived by the students as extra work. Students feel like they must work more as they have to watch the lectures before coming to class. Sometimes teaching in innovative ways might come across as more efficient, but it can be deceptive as there is no evidence that it improves students' performance.

The fact that students are attending lectures or not attending is an indicator, but it is worth to explore the fact that those who are attending are not necessarily engaged. One lecturer used the expression "absent presence" to describe such phenomenon. One other one talked about mind wondering. The issue about students' well-being and mental health was brought up by some.

View of themselves

Lecturers view themselves as the lectures they give. The nature of the lecture is part of their identity. Lecturers are divided between teaching, research and service. Some of them say that they try to invest the minimum time possible into their teaching practice as they are required to do research and publications to build their academic career.

The fact that lecturers and tutors are easily available online has created a syndrome called Learned Helplessness [9]. Because it is so easy to make contact, some students do not bother to think and look for the information themselves. According lectures, to search and find the right information is another important skill to learn.

It was observed the boundaries between work and personal time seems to have been blurred and students expect to have an immediate answer for their questions.

View of their practice

The support that each lecturer varies from School to School. Some Schools utilize short modules been delivered by experts in a sequence to create a course. In this case, a coordinator is responsible for the communication and follow up. Sometimes there is administrative support to deal with extensions, emails and other tasks, sometimes tutors to engage with the students.

Feedback

Sedrakyan, Malmberg, Verbert, Järvelä, Kirschner [26] presents several publications that discuss the benefits of using panels in education for new feedback opportunities that can improve learning. This article discusses design implications for Learning Analytics Dashboards (LAD) feedback and preliminary responses on how that feedback can be grounded in the learning sciences. Sedrakyan et al. [26] derived a conceptual model that can be used to design information systems as a basis for process-oriented feedback in the context of LADs.

Considering that the learning process is a continuum and organized within the beginning, middle and end aspect, when analyzing the data, and according to the results of the interviews conducted in this research, feedback was analyzed in four contexts: feed up, feedback from students, feedback to the students, feed forward.

Feed up

This is the initial contact of the teaching and learning experience. There is no evidence if students do some research before deciding to enroll in a course. Do they engage student advisors on the decision-making process? Do they ask for information online or informally exchange ideas with other students and lecturers? Do they follow a prescribed pathway? It was declared in one of the interviews that UNIV does not established pre-requisites for courses. It makes recommendations, but there are no formal course requirements for students to enroll.

Is it clear for the students the purpose of the course, the expected level of commitment and the proposed learning outcomes?

Feed-up resources ensure that students understand the purpose of the assignment, task, or lesson, including how they will be assessed.

There are also some tacit rules and some formal ones. Blackboard is compulsory, and every course must be on Blackboard. There is training on how to set up Blackboard, but it is perceived by some teachers as a repository for resources and recorded lectures, the outlet for a weekly announcement, and the station to collect assignments and posting grades.

Some also use blackboard to share learning resources to prepare the students, prior to class, attempting the concept of flipped classroom.

There are many underlying assumptions like it should have a weekly announcement on Blackboard. Some lecturers anticipate and create a page of Frequently Asked Questions either on Blackboard or on Piazza.

Feedback from students

Lecturers have very few outlets to receive feedback from the students. The main source of feedback is an assessment carried out by the institution that happens towards the end of the course. It is too late to implement change in the current course. Based on that, there is an experiment with mid-course evaluation.

Lecturers pay a lot of attention to the results from this assessment which was mentioned in all the interviews as a reference of student feedback. Although there is some criticism about the way it is done and the way it is dealt by their School.

Before the class, one of the lecturers said that she used Wordcloud to gauge the level of understanding from the students. Some lecturers use tech devices to gather information from the students, but do not have time to analyze after to compare knowledge before and after intervention. To use technology to merely substitute what could be done without it seems to be neglecting data potential.

Information from Blackboard is not used for data analysis by all the lecturers who were interviewed. It is not used as a source of information for decision-making by the lecturers.

Feedback to the students

According the results, students mostly receive an indication on their course performance after the first assessment in the middle of the semester. Feedback provides students with information about their successes and needs. The level of feedback that lecturers provide to students is becoming shorter with the increase of formative and summative assessments. Exam over-load has been a recurrent theme in the interviews.

Most lecturers use multiple-choice quizzes to evaluate students' learning. Although there was an instruction from the higher level of command within the university not to use them, most teachers stick with those tests to facilitate the marking process. This is still the most time consuming of their tasks. It is not easy to delegate marking to tutors of subjective and complex task that would assess critical thinking, creativity and problem-solving. For the purpose of fairness amongst diverse classrooms and students, objective answers are easier to mark.

Lecturers have anecdotal data on student attendance and its correlation with attrition that informs their decision

There are patterns that naturally occur that are even labeled. For instance, evasion before the first census day at week six is called "constructive dropout".

Feed forward

Feed-forward guides student learning based on performance data. Based on analysis, comparisons and correlations, teachers can infer about students' learning and reflect upon the course progress. Actions such as making recommendations and even adapting the course design and pedagogical practices might have an impact on students' outcomes.

5.2   What Teachers Say They Need

From the initial survey, when asked to write an open statement about what information would be useful from the dashboard, the results demonstrated that lecturers wanted data to be sorted and compared in a meaningful way to them in the form of graphs, statistics and indicators to enable forecasting and prediction of student outcomes.

In a way, virtual environments have so many possibilities for information that they often end up hampering their use. According to the interviews, there is a need to simplify the process, facilitating the deeper use of available resources. Thus, according to the interviewees, they could be organized considering the following categories: Descriptive Data, Comparative data, Prescriptive data.

Descriptive Data

This first category corresponds to descriptive data on the progress of students and the class in general; it would present interactions between students and lecturers (for example, system messages). The use of this category would allow the lecturers to have an overview of the course's progress, identifying possible students with difficulties or even delayed activities, in a more objective and quick way. In this category students' grades and evaluations in the activities proposed during the course would also be included.

Comparative Data

The second category would consist of information considering comparisons between students and classes. For example, comparing current students with performance in previous courses. This would make it possible to identify students with certain difficulties more easily. It would also be possible to analyze the interaction of students (in messages or forums) in relation to other students or in relation to the development of the course. In general, this category brings information that allows comparisons to be made and then reorganizes improvements in the teaching-learning process. Correlation analysis tools or cluster analysis could be used in relation to the available data for more information on possible comparisons.

Prescriptive Data

Considering the history of information in the course (for example, other editions of the course could be considered), using data analysis tools (for example, regression analysis), to understand possible scenarios in the students' performance. In general, many of these analyzes are developed, but at the end of the course, seeking to relate performance with a set of activities carried out and students' profile. However, using historical data, trying to do this analysis previously, can help to rethink and change routes in the course development.

5.3   What Would They Do?

Most of them think carefully about the time investment to design a course. One of the lecturers said that it is expected that designing a course would last for at least 3 years. Other said that changes could only be made once a year after deliberation with other lecturers involved in the course. Change is a slow and not a desirable process.

There is the feeling that big classrooms need big data for the lecturers to get information on how the course is going. When the lecture is recorded, there is no evidence if the students are really participating or not. They were questioned if they felt like they were teaching in a blind way, without any information being provided to them. There are tools that allow to interact with a video while watching it (for example, stops to answer questions). Only Business School lecturers reported that they would be using this aspect.

Based on the concept of meta-learning, a particular School from one of the studied Faculties has started to use quizzes to encourage the students to reflect upon their learning strategies. It is essential that all students are provided with opportunities to develop an understanding of their own knowledge and learning processes [6]. This metacognitive understanding of learning, or 'meta-learning', is the process of developing an awareness of one's own knowledge, motives and learning; literally 'learning about learning'.

On the other hand, one lecturer talked about not being interested in data from Blackboard at all. He believed acknowledging it and using it to chase the students would not change their behaviour.

This shows the need for, in addition to having a dashboard with several possibilities, it is important to consider a cycle of teacher engagement. For this, one should consider starting with an awareness, training and monitoring process. This last step would aim to verify how much the process has contributed to improve the teaching-learning process.

There are very few examples of innovation from the group of lecturers interviewed and the level and openness to innovation also varies according to the School. There is one School that has funding for innovation and supports its lecturers to take risks. There is even a computer simulation activity to develop team-based skills for students in their first semester at University.

Most of the examples of innovative teaching practice like computer-based simulations, team-based selection using computer programs, online student feedback surveys came from the same School. At first, they follow the SMAR model proposed by Puentedura [21] where traditional activities are mere substituted by online versions.

When asked if they would want a system that would flag students who are not participating, not coming to the lectures, not handing in the activities, most of the interviewees asked for the system to launch reminders to the students, instead of this being one extra attribute for the lecturer. If the student has the same indifferent absent behavior for all the courses that he/she is taking, one email from UNIV saying that it was noticed that he was accessing instead of 4 emails from lecturers saying the same thing. According interviewed, the students are complaining that they are having too much surveys, too many emails.

6 Conclusions

With mass education, the size of cohorts has changed dramatically and the teaching spaces, and teaching methods had to be adapted to accommodate the large and diverse number of students. Educational technologies are not a choice anymore, the question has shifted to how they are going to be implemented to improve and enhance the students' learning experience. Teachers still need to interact with students before introducing new concepts and estimating the level of previous understanding, similarly to how it was done before when the lecturers asked a question and the students responded by raising their hands. It was a rough indicator of comprehension that a lecturer would use as a learning opportunity. Technology enables not only to have a precise indicator of the answers but also to store them for further comparison, and to use them either at a granular or at an aggregated level. Digital traces are abundant and not difficult to capture. The challenge is to define what information needs to be gathered and for what purpose to further define the sources, the dimensions, the hierarchies, the navigation, the presentation, the users' groups and the reports.

With the advances in technology and online learning, student generate significant digital traces. Despite the abundance of rich digital data, Higher Education Institutions are still in the development process of a formal Teacher Dashboard.

As a foundational research, it has provided interesting insights on teachers' perceptions and dispositions towards a Teacher Dashboard. Despite the importance of the topic, it is rare to find a project where teachers are directly involved in the development process with a focus on its applicability. If educators can see the value of learning data as a reflection of their practice, they can draw upon evidence-based information keep learning instead of perceiving it as monitoring tool for intervention.

From the research carried out, it was observed that:

- Teachers have little knowledge about the use or tools available on Dashboards
- Dashboards are often understood as tools of control and not aggregation for the teaching-learning process
- Teachers' need to better understand the use of these possibilities in the context of digital educational technologies.

Thus, two points stand out: the need for simpler and easier-to-use Dashboards as well as a training process for the development of this tool composed of the following cycle: awareness, training and monitoring.

For awareness, examples of use should be presented and how this facilitated the development of activities and improvements in the teaching-learning process in other courses. Thus, successful cases could be presented. Another possibility in this context would be for the lecturer to accompany another lecturer already experienced in using the teacher dashboard and understand how much this tool can help.

In the context of training, the main point is to equip the teacher with the tools of the teacher dashboard that will be used or even bring some benefit. If it only presented existing tools, the training wouldn't solve much. It should present its routine use and how it can collaborate to bring improvements in the teaching-learning process, being these aspects clearly more important.

Finally, to prevent the awareness of the lessons learned in training from being overlooked, a third phase must be considered: monitoring. This third phase considers providing lecturers with support in the use of the teacher dashboard and how that use can be improved.

In the literature it is possible to identify several works showing how the use of teacher dashboards can help in improving the teaching-learning process. However, the main point is teacher engagement and culture exchange. As identified in the interviews, many teachers were not trained to operate in a digital context, which makes greater integration with these tools difficult. Thus, the proposed cycle (awareness, training and monitoring) can help in the development of the culture for the use of the dashboard.

Acknowledgements. The first author would like to acknowledge the work of Solange M. Lima, as a research assistant, in a Teacher Dashboards' grant, led by the first author, which originated findings that have been used as the basis for this paper.

References

1. Aleven, V., Xhakaj, F., Holstein, K., McLaren, B.M.: Developing a teacher dashboard for use with intelligent tutoring systems. In: Proceedings of the 4th International Workshop on Teaching Analytics, IWTA at the 11th European Conference on Technology Enhanced Learning, Lyon, France (2016)
2. Braun, V., Clarke, V.: Using thematic analysis in psychology. Qual. Res. Psychol. **3**(2), 77–101 (2006)
3. Charmaz, K.: Constructivist grounded theory. J. Posit. Psychol. **12**(3), 299–300 (2017). https://doi.org/10.1080/17439760.2016.1262612
4. Chatti, M.A., Dyckhoff, A.L., Schroeder, U., Thüs, H.: A reference model for learning analytics. Int. J. Technol. Enhanc. Learn. **4**(5–6), 318–331 (2012)
5. Clow, D.: The learning analytics cycle: closing the loop effectively. In: Proceedings of the 2nd International Conference on Learning Analytics and Knowledge – LAK 2012, pp. 134–137. ACM, Vancouver (2012). https://doi.org/10.1145/2330601.2330636
6. Colthorpe, K., Sharifirad, T., Ainscough, L., Anderson, S., Zimbardi, K.: Prompting undergraduate students' metacognition of learning: implementing 'meta-learning'assessment tasks in the biomedical sciences. Assess. Eval. High. Educ. **43**(2), 272–285 (2018)
7. Dabbebi, I., Iksal, S., Gilliot, J.-M., May, M., Garlatti, S.: Towards adaptive dashboards for learning analytic: an approach for conceptual design and implementation. In: Proceedings of 9th International Conference on Computer Supported Education (CSEDU), Porto, Portugal, pp. 120–131 (2017)
8. Duval, E.: Attention please! Learning analytics for visualization and recommendation. In: Proceedings of LAK11: 1st International Conference on Learning Analytics and Knowledge, pp. 9–17. ACM (2011)
9. Firmin, M.W., Hwang, C.-e., Copella, M., Clark, S.: Learned helplessness: the effect of failure on test-taking. Education **124**(4), 688 (2004)
10. Hattie, J., Timperley, H.: The power of feedback. Rev. Educ. Res. **77**(1), 81–112 (2007)
11. Khan, S.: The One World Schoolhouse: Education Reimagined. Twelve, New York (2012)
12. Kitto, K., et al.: The connected learning analytics toolkit. In: Proceedings of the Sixth International Conference on Learning Analytics & Knowledge, pp. 548–549. ACM, Edinburgh (2016)

13. Martinez-Maldonado, R., Pardo, A., Mirriahi, N., Yacef, K., Kay, J., Clayphan, A.: LATUX: an iterative workflow for designing, validating and deploying learning analytics visualisations. J. Learn. Anal. 2(3), 9–39 (2016)
14. Melesse, S., Jirata, E.: Teachers' perception and practice of constructivist teaching approach: the case of secondary schools of Kamashi Zone. Sci. Technol. Arts Res. J. 4(4), 194–199 (2015)
15. Molenaar, I., Knoop-van Campen, C.A.: How teachers make dashboard information actionable. IEEE Trans. Learn. Technol. 12(3), 347–355 (2018)
16. Mottus, A., Kinshuk, H.R., Graf, S., Chen, N.-S.: Use of dashboards and visualization techniques to support teacher decision making. In: Kinshuk, H.R. (ed.) Ubiquitous Learning Environments and Technologies. Lecture Notes in Educational Technolog, pp. 181–199. Springer, Heidelberg (2015). https://doi.org/10.1007/978-3-662-44659-1_10
17. Muñoz-Merino, P.J., Valiente, J.A.R., Kloos, C.D.: Inferring higher level learning information from low level data for the Khan Academy platform. In: Proceedings of the Third International Conference on Learning Analytics and Knowledge, pp. 112–116 (2013)
18. Ochoa, X.: Visualizing uncertainty in the prediction of academic risk. In: Proceedings of the Workshop on Visual Aspects of Learning Analytics held at the International Conference on Learning Analytics and Knowledge (LAK 2015), Poughkeepsie, USA, pp. 4–10 (2015)
19. Papamitsiou, Z., Economides, A.: Learning analytics and educational data mining in practice: a systematic literature review of empirical evidence. Educ. Technol. Soc. 17(4), 49–64 (2014)
20. Pesare, E., Roselli, T., Rossano, V., Di Bitonto, P.: Digitally enhanced assessment in virtual learning environments. J. Vis. Lang. Comput. 31(Part B), 252–259 (2015)
21. Puentedura, R.: The SAMR Model and Digital Learning (2015)
22. Rayón, A., Guenaga, M., Núñez, A.: Integrating and visualizing learner and social data to elicit higher-order indicators in SCALA dashboard. In: Proceedings of the 14th International Conference on Knowledge Technologies and Data-Driven Business. ACM, Graz (2014)
23. Reimers, G., Neovesky, A., der Wissenschaften, A.: Student focused dashboards. In: Proceedings of the 7th International Conference on Computer Supported Education, Lisbon, Portugal (2015)
24. Rose, C.P., et al.: Analytics of social processes in learning contexts: a multi-level perspective. In: Looi, C.K., Polman, J., Cress, U., Reimann, P. (eds.) Transforming Learning, Empowering Learners: Proceedings of the International Conference of the Learning Sciences, vol. 1, pp. 24–31. International Society of Sciences, Singapore (2016)
25. Santos, J.L., Verbert, K., Govaerts, S., Duval, E.: Addressing learner issues with StepUp!: an evaluation. In: Proceedings of the Third International Conference on Learning Analytics and Knowledge, Leuven, Belgium (2013)
26. Sedrakyan, G., Malmberg, J., Verbert, K., Järvelä, S., Kirschner, P.A.: Linking learning behavior analytics and learning science concepts: designing a learning analytics dashboard for feedback to support learning regulation. Comput. Hum. Behav. 107, 105512 (2018)
27. Verbert, K., Duval, E., Klerkx, J., Govaerts, S., Santos, J.L.: Learning analytics dashboard applications. Am. Behav. Sci. 57(10), 1500–1509 (2013)

Mudpoint: Evaluating Instructor Perception on a Continuous and Non-specific Feedback System

Jamshidbek Mirzakhalov[✉], Anoop Babu, and Marvin Andujar

University of South Florida, Tampa, FL 33620, USA
{mirzakhalov,anoopbabu}@mail.usf.edu, andujar1@usf.edu

Abstract. In this paper, we introduce a platform called Mudpoint. It is an educational system that: a) allows students to provide real-time, continuous and anonymous feedback on their comprehension levels using a mobile application and b) enables instructors to visualize an aggregated form of student comprehension feedback on a web dashboard in real-time. A number of studies show that real-time feedback on instructor methodologies has several benefits including improvement in teaching [1] and better communication between instructors and students [2]. Also, student response systems (SRS) in classroom teaching have been explored in several studies previously [3–5], including the effects of instantaneous and anonymous feedback. Therefore in this study, we explore the instructor's perception of receiving student feedback that, in addition to being instantaneous and anonymous, is also continuous and non-specific. Through interviews with instructors, we found that the system resulted in significantly more feedback on student confidence in the material, improved the pace of the class, and encouraged more responsible learning behaviour for students. This work shows that, from the instructor's perception, continuous and non-specific feedback systems can improve the classroom experience for both instructors and students.

Keywords: Classroom · Web application · Mobile application · Feedback · Education · Instructor perception

1 Introduction

Performance-based feedback in classrooms can help instructors evaluate their teaching materials and methodologies, which in turn facilitates better learning experiences for students [6].

Traditionally, instructors use non-verbal cues such as facial expressions or postures as a means to obtain feedback on student comprehension levels. This allows them to assess the efficiency of their teaching methods and content while making continuous efforts to ensure all students have their concerns addressed. However, due to the subtlety and high internal variations of these non-verbal cues, this information can be compromised. Coupled with other external factors

© Springer Nature Switzerland AG 2020
P. Zaphiris and A. Ioannou (Eds.): HCII 2020, LNCS 12205, pp. 270–278, 2020.
https://doi.org/10.1007/978-3-030-50513-4_20

such as class size and peer pressure, this may affect the students' ability to engage with the class and ask questions.

Obtaining rapid and formative feedback enables instructors to evaluate their methodologies and content much more effectively, leading to better performance in classrooms. Tools such as Student Response Systems (SRS) have been developed to facilitate this process in an efficient and scalable manner. SRS are "instructional technologies that allow instructors to rapidly collect and analyse student responses to questions posed during class" [7]. Over the years, they have been shown to improve students' attitudes towards classes [8], increase attentiveness [9], and enhance student-instructor communication [10,11] even when student responses are kept anonymous [12]. However, there are multiple challenges associated with the use of SRS in classrooms. Firstly, SRS require special electronic hardware to collect feedback and responses from students which brings a financial burden either for the university or the student. Additionally, the finite amount of features and the lack of sophisticated graphical interfaces for clickers limit the ability to receive descriptive feedback.

In recent years, the ubiquity and accessibility of smartphone devices sparked an interest in education communities to use them as an alternative for SRS. It has also been shown that mobile-phone-based response systems can retain the pedagogical advantages of SRS, while overcoming some challenges associated with them [13]. Most of them are designed to use internet connection to transit real-time feedback from devices to a central instructor interface, usually in the form of a web dashboard. Studies above also implement features where student responses are anonymous which provide the students with a safe space to ask questions. Our work builds upon these two main features by incorporating continuous student feedback, which allows students to provide their level of understanding at any point during the class. A web dashboard designed for the instructor reflects the feedback in real-time. Another substantial difference is the type of formative feedback students are allowed to provide in the system. Students can provide self-evaluation using three commonly understood emojis (*Sad, Neutral* and *Happy*). Through face-to-face interviews with instructors who used the system, we found that the non-specific nature of the feedback allows students to relay their understanding of the material more efficiently and seamlessly.

2   Related Work

Several studies employing smartphone-based SRS have made use of commercially available applications. In a study conducted among first-year, sports science students [4], researchers used a freely available mobile application, Socratis. Among many features, Socratis enables instructors to ask "on-the-fly" questions which students can respond to from their mobile devices or PCs. Authors used the software to allow instructors to receive real-time responses to discussion questions and quizzes. As a caution against the abuse of the system, these responses were not anonymous. Through the survey designed to evaluate the system, almost all students indicated that the system increased their interaction during the class and highlighted gaps in their knowledge. In another study [5], authors used a commercially available polling website, PollEverywhere. Similar to Socratis, PollEverywhere allows for real-time collection of responses to prompted questions. Although the setup and findings resembled the previous study, authors of this work noted that one of the challenges with the system was the fact that students did not follow instructions properly and faced issues with the software later on. Similar to Mudpoint, these systems are also smartphone-based and collect feedback in real-time; however, their main differences lie in the timing and type of feedback received.

An example of continuous SRS comes from a 2009 study in New Zealand, where researchers used a system called TXT-2-LRN (text-to-learn) in a classroom of almost 1200 students for five lectures. One feature of the system called *open channel* "allows students to send their questions and comments via SMS without interrupting the class. The instructor is able to read the messages on the laptop screen (using a special software) and decides whether and when to comment on the message received. Replies to questions that were not addressed during class could then be supplied by the instructor afterwards via SMS or a traditional discussion forum" [14]. TXT-2-LRN creates a continuous feedback system that allows students to provide comments and ask questions any time during the class as opposed to being discretely tied to instructor prompts and quizzes. Results from the study show that over 90% of student participants perceived the ability to send the instructor SMSs during the class to be useful. In addition, the instructor involved in the trial reported a very positive experience with the system noting the perceived increase in the quality and quantity of feedback. Similar to TXT-2-LRN, our system can receive feedback continuously at any point during class without interrupting the flow of the instructor, however the main difference is the type of feedback received. In TXT-2-LRN, students can send questions or comments, while our system limits the responses to discrete states of *Confused, Neutral* and *Confident.*

3   User Interaction

3.1   Student View - Mobile Application

To begin the process of interaction in Mudpoint, students are prompted to download a mobile application available through Android and iOS app stores. After the download is complete, each student is prompted to enter a class code which is provided by the instructor once at the beginning of the class (Fig. 1). Students can use this code to join the class session which will be valid until the end of the semester. On the active session page, there are three buttons representing students' comprehension status through commonly understood emoji signs: *Sad, Neutral* and *Happy* corresponding to *Confused, Neutral* and *Confident* respectively. Students have the ability to toggle between those options at any point during the class period, and it is reflected on the instructor's dashboard in real-time.

Fig. 1. Mudpoint Mobile Application. Main Page allowing students join a session using a instructor-provided code (on the left). Active Session Page allows students send feedback to the instructor (on the right).

Having only three options for the comprehension status makes the process of providing feedback more simple and intuitive, which is essential in order for the application to distract as little as possible from the course material. While their status is tracked in real-time, the identity of the student is kept anonymous, allowing for more voluntary and honest feedback.

3.2 Instructor View - Web Application

Meanwhile, instructors create an account via a web application where they can manage multiple classes and sessions. When the instructor initiates a new session for their class, a new "join code" is generated which the students can use to access the course. After the code is generated, the instructor will be shown a dashboard with the total number of students that are currently in the session, numeric breakdown of comprehension levels, as well as a chart representing an aggregated version of this data. The dashboard gets updated in real-time based on changes in student confidence in the course material. Through this interface, the instructor can assess the comprehension level of the class with minimal effort. Once the lecture is over, the instructor can end the session and the graph depicting the student comprehension levels is saved for future analysis (Fig. 2).

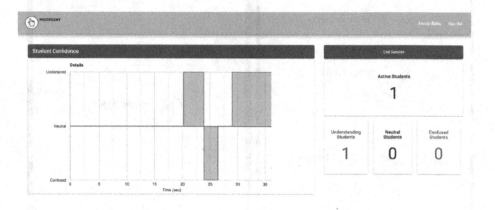

Fig. 2. Instructor Dashboard. Chart representing aggregated student feedback is shown on the left. Numerical analysis of student feedback is shown on the right.

4   System Design

The Mudpoint smartphone application is developed for Android and iOS devices and is freely available in Google Play Store and Apple Store respectively. The app is relatively small in size at around 8 megabytes, and can run in more than 95% of all available smartphones. It is built using an open-source, cross-platform mobile application development framework, React Native.

The web dashboard, which is primarily used by the instructors, is publicly available on https://www.mudpoint.com. This website is built with the SPA (Single-Page Application) Framework Angular 8 so that the instructor's interactions with the website is quicker and thus more preferable to use.

Our database and backend servers are implemented using Google's BaaS (Backend-as-a-Service) framework, Firebase. It allows for reliable, low-cost, and secure communication between devices and servers, and can be easily scaled as the users grow. With the current setup, our calculations show that the cost of the servers would not exceed more than $10 to support 10,000 users simultaneously (Fig. 3).

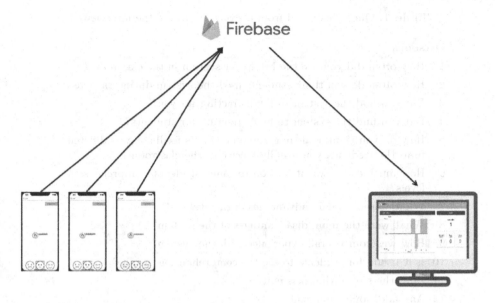

Fig. 3. System Design Overview. The mobile application sends their status to Firebase, which is then sent to the web dashboard.

5   Methodology

This education tool was employed in five (3 upper-level elective and 2 introductory) computer science classrooms at a large public university through four different instructors. After the system was used in their classrooms as described above, one-on-one interviews were conducted with each of the instructors in reference to their experience. More specifically, the questions referred to the overall integration of the system into their classrooms. A full list of questions asked during the interview are shown in Table 1.

6   Results

Based on the responses obtained during the interviews, it is believed that the effects of the system were positive as it seemed to generate significantly more feedback, increase the pace of the class, and encourage a more responsible learning behaviour.

6.1   Usability

Throughout the course of each of their one hour and 15 min class periods, each instructor checked the comprehension graph on average five times, primarily between every major discussed concept. Some of the instructors thought that the students utilized the system minimally and increased their use of the system when the instructor prompted them to update it, while another instructor

Table 1. Questions asked from instructors during the interviews

Questions	
1	How often did you use the Mudpoint system in the classroom?
2	How often do you think students used the system during the class?
3	Did you find the system to be distracting for you?
4	Did you find the system to be distracting for students?
5	How do you think real-time and anonymous feedback was different from the feedback you usually receive in the classroom?
6	How much easier was it for you to gauge students' comprehension levels?
7	What were the main advantages of the system?
8	What were the main disadvantages of the system?
9	How was your overall experience with the system?
10	Is it useful for students to see the comprehension graph ?
11	Does the size of the class matter?
12	Any additional comments?

believed that the students updated their comprehension status regularly. From these responses, the teachers and students all seemed to use the system more during the transitory stage of changing topics. When asked whether it would be beneficial to show the student the comprehension graph, one instructor agreed saying that it would encourage students to note that they were confused if others were confused too, while the other instructors either thought that it would alienate students who were confused and discourage them from noting it, or that it would make the student question the professor more.

Even though both the students and the instructors used the system during more discrete points, the continuous nature of the comprehension graph may still be beneficial since it both can be used for reflection, and does not force the instructor to follow a particular structure. Additionally, the differing of opinions of the whether to show the students the comprehension graph shows that Mudpoint can support many different teaching styles that instructor may want to follow depending on the class.

6.2 Distraction

Although it seemed that distraction would be a major concern in the adoption of the system, the instructors all unanimously perceived the distraction to be minimal. One instructor noted that most students only seemed to be particularly motivated to update their status when they started to become confused much more than when they understood the course material. Additionally, all instructors agreed that the system was relatively seamless, with the exception of requiring a dedicated monitor since it could be challenging in certain classroom settings, especially if they are already using slides or other teaching tools.

6.3 Primary Difference from Existing Teaching Experience

With the inclusion of Mudpoint in each classroom, all of the instructors received significantly more feedback from the student than without Mudpoint. They did not have to rely on their own perception of what the class understood, which made it more helpful with larger class sizes. In another instructor's perspective, this change gave students a responsibility to facilitate their learning because, with the system, there are less barriers to communicate with the instructor. Another instructor noted that the system allowed them to improve the pace of the class, likely due to being able to quickly make adjustments to their own teaching style. Based on the responses from the instructors, the biggest factor that changed for the instructor of the class with the inclusion of Mudpoint was that they had another metric the instructor can use in order to understand the comprehension the students have of the course material.

6.4 Overall Experience

When asked about the primary advantage of this interaction, the consistent response was receiving the real-time and anonymous feedback. While the anonymous part of the feedback encouraged students to update their comprehension status in the first place, the instantaneous responses helped instructors to adapt their techniques more efficiently. Additionally, another instructor said "...the system really was incredibly easy to adopt in the class, both for me and students. It also increased the pace of my class by letting me understand the comprehension level of students with minimal effort". This instructor also believes that the easy and effective adoption of the system is possibly due to the non-specific nature of the feedback.

When asked about the limitations of the system, two instructors mentioned how requiring a dedicated monitor can be challenging in certain classroom settings, while another instructor addressed difficulty in determining how current student responses are on the dashboard since the system does not automatically revert back to *Neutral* state after a certain period of time. This may be problematic in cases where students forget to update the comprehension level after their questions have already been answered by the instructor. A mechanism for changing the state of the student should be further explored.

7 Summary

Overall, Mudpoint is a platform for collecting and visualizing real-time and anonymous student feedback in a continuous manner. Students are able to relay their level of understanding using one of three easily recognized emojis (*Sad, Neutral, Happy*) at any point during the lecture using their mobile devices. This data gets aggregated and visualized on a web dashboard designed for instructors. We launched the system in five computer science classes at a large public university, and conducted one-on-one interviews with four instructors involved in the study. All of the instructors reported a pleasant experience with the system, and felt that its integration into the classroom was seamless. They also agree that Mudpoint received significantly more feedback and positively affected the learning behaviour in students. Limitations of the system included the initial setup overhead for instructors and inability to determine if student feedback is up-to-date. Future work will focus on overcoming these limitations as well as focusing on Mudpoint's effect on student engagement and performance.

References

1. Poulos, A., Mahony, M.J.: Effectiveness of feedback: the students' perspective. Assess. Eval. High. Educ. **33**(2), 143–154 (2008)
2. Calders, T., Pechenizkiy, M.: Introduction to the special section on educational data mining. ACM SIGKDD Explor. Newsl. **13**(2), 3–6 (2012)
3. Lu, J., et al.: User centred mobile aided learning system: student response system (SRS). In: 2010 10th IEEE International Conference on Computer and Information Technology, pp. 2970–2975. IEEE (2010)
4. Dervan, P.: Increasing in-class student engagement using Socrative (an online Student Response System). AISHE-J: Irel. J. Teach. Learn. High. Educ. **6**(3) (2014)
5. Wong, A.: Student perception on a student response system formed by combining mobile phone and a polling website. Int. J. Educ. Dev. Using ICT **12**(1) (2016)
6. Scheeler, M.C., Ruhl, K.L., McAfee, J.K.: Providing performance feedback to teachers: a review. Teach. Educ. Spec. Educ. **27**(4), 396–407 (2004)
7. Bruff, D.: Teaching with Classroom Response Systems: Creating Active Learning Environments. Wiley, Hoboken (2009)
8. Barnett, J.: Implementation of personal response units in very large lecture classes: student perceptions. Australas. J. Educ. Technol. **22**(4) (2006)
9. Kaleta, R., Joosten, T.: Student response systems. Res. Bull. **10**(1), 1–12 (2007)
10. Lantz, M.E.: The use of 'clickers' in the classroom: teaching innovation or merely an amusing novelty? Comput. Hum. Behav. **26**(4), 556–561 (2010)
11. Caldwell, J.E.: Clickers in the large classroom: current research and best-practice tips. CBE—Life Sci. Educ. **6**(1), 9–20 (2007)
12. Hoekstra, A.: Vibrant student voices: exploring effects of the use of clickers in large college courses. Learn. Media Technol. **33**(4), 329–341 (2008)
13. Dunn, P.K., et al.: Mobile-phone-based classroom response systems: students' perceptions of engagement and learning in a large undergraduate course. Int. J. Math. Educ. Sci. Technol. **44**(8), 1160–1174 (2013)
14. Scornavacca, E., Huff, S., Marshall, S.: Mobile phones in the classroom: if you can't beat them, join them. Commun. ACM **52**(4), 142–146 (2009)

Characterization of Learners from Their Learning Activities on a Smart Learning Platform

Alberto Real-Fernández, Rafael Molina-Carmona$^{(\boxtimes)}$, and Faraón Llorens Largo

Smart Learning Research Group, University of Alicante,
San Vicente del Raspeig, Spain
albertorealfdez@gmail.com, {rmolina,faraon.llorens}@ua.es

Abstract. An smart learning system is a computer system that allows to personalize and adapt the learning process to the learner's needs. To do so, it is necessary to characterize the student so that we can know how he or she learns. The aim of this research is to propose this characterization through a vector of characteristics that are measurable, significant, discriminating and independent, so that the information can be processed by a computer program. The characteristic vector is obtained by observing the student's behavior in the learning system, that is, we know the student through the results of the learning activities that he or she performs in the smart learning system. We propose a mathematical formulation that allows calculating the student's characteristic vector from his activity in the system. Finally, in order to evaluate the robustness of the proposed formulation we have carried out a set of simulations and we have verified that the system behaves as expected.

Keywords: Learner model · Characteristic vector · Smart learning · Learning style

1 Introduction

It is widely assumed that each person has different skills and learns in a different way, so that some individual features, such as learning level, types of intelligence or learning style, can be an important factor in academic performance. So, when designing a smart learning system, it is important to consider these factors to provide an actual personalized and adaptive learning experience.

A formal way of considering the learning factors is constructing a learner model, which is a compact definition of the features that characterize the individual as a learner. A useful learner model to be considered in a computational system must include meaningful, measurable, discriminating and independent variables describing the individuals.

Supported by *Unidad Científica de Innovación Empresarial* "Ars Innovatio" and Smart Learning Research Group, University of Alicante (Spain).

P. Zaphiris and A. Ioannou (Eds.): HCII 2020, LNCS 12205, pp. 279–291, 2020.
https://doi.org/10.1007/978-3-030-50513-4_21

A first step is characterizing the learning activities to be performed by the learner. Learning activities, can be characterized by a set of features that form their activity model. The features of an activity can be very varied in nature and include aspects such as difficulty (the cost in time and effort any learner has to pay to successfully finish the activity), the levels of reasoning skills of the Bloom's Taxonomy required to complete de activity, as well as the learning styles that are fostered when practicing the activity.

In our proposal, features apply first and foremost to activities. The learner model is then created as a consequence of their actions in the smart learning system and the results in the activities they carry out. In short, the smart learning system establishes a cycle of updating the learner model as they complete the proposed learning activities.

The objective of this paper is defining the learner model and the way it is updated from the activities they perform. All in all, the learner model is extracted from the activity model, and it is built progressively as the student interacts with the smart learning system. Furthermore, a second objective is evaluating the validity of the formulation we present. A simulation with artificial data is a first step to prove the validity.

The document is structured in the following way: in Sect. 2 we present the background of the research, including a brief review about learning styles, cognitive levels knowledge types, activity difficulty and the concept of characteristic vector. Next, in Sect. 3, the characteristic vectors, both for activities and learners, are presented. Section 4 is devoted to present the formulation for calculating the learner vector from the performed activities. We also validate the formulation in Sect. 5 using a simulation. Finally, in Sect. 6, we present the main conclusions.

2   Background

The main objective of this paper is to define a learner model in the form of a computable feature vector. In order to do so, a review of previous research is required, dealing with the main variables that will be part of the vector (learning styles, cognitive levels and knowledge types, and difficulty), as well as with the concept of characteristic vector.

2.1   Learning Styles

The fact that each person has different skills and learns differently seems to be confirmed by different authors [7,27]. Among all the factors that affect the academic performance of a student, some authors consider that the individual characteristics of the person (intelligence, learning style, motivation, character ...) are the most important factor [2,13–15]. Thus, the intellectual capacity and motivation of the individual account for up to 50% of her or his performance, compared with the factors considered to be external [14]. When designing a learning process, therefore, it is important to be aware that within the same group there will be students with different learning styles, distinct types of intelligence and diverse motivations [12, 26].

The so-called learning styles refer to a set of theories and methods defined in the literature that propose the classification of students according to the way they learn. Although there are many theories and they are very diverse, the scientific basis of these theories has been widely criticized in the sense that they often consider styles as separate compartments. In spite of these criticisms and without valuing them, it is interesting to review some of the most renowned theories in order to try to understand the learning processes that students develop and to try to characterize them.

Some of the most renowned theories that aim to classify the learning style of students have the form of inventories [23]. This is the case of the Kolb Learning Style Inventory [17], with four identified styles: diverging, assimilating, converging and accommodating. An extension of this theory is the new Kolb Learning Style Inventory 4.0 [16], which is one of the theories considered in the definition of our model. It defines nine styles: initiating, experiencing, creating, reflecting, analyzing, thinking, deciding, acting and balancing. Kolb's inventory collects the information about the learning styles through self-report questionnaires that evaluate the attitudes of the students about learning and studying.

2.2   Cognitive Levels and Knowledge Types

The learning of a subject not only depends on the student's way of learning, but also on the subject to be learned and the form of the activities in which it is presented, such as the reasoning abilities and the cognitive level necessary for its successful completion.

A widespread way of categorizing the levels of reasoning skills required during learning is Bloom's Taxonomy [5]. By extension, it can be considered that these levels can also be used to categorize learning activities according to the reasoning skill they foster [22]. There are six levels in the taxonomy, each requiring a higher abstraction level from the students. According to Bloom, teachers should attempt to move students up the taxonomy as they progress in their knowledge, so that students become thinkers as opposed to simple information gatherers.

In 2001 Anderson and Krathwohl proposed a revision [3] that emphasizes the dynamism of the original proposal proposing two dimensions: the cognitive process dimension and the knowledge dimension. They use verbs for the cognitive process dimensions to label the actions associated and nouns for the knowledge dimension to describe what knowledge students are expected to acquire or construct. These authors identify six categories for the cognitive process dimension (remember, understand, apply, analyze, evaluate and create) and four categories for the knowledge dimension (factual, conceptual, procedural and metacognitive).

The authors propose a double-entry table with the categories corresponding to each dimension. The activities can be placed in each cell according to the cognitive process and the knowledge to which they refer, described through a verb and an object.

2.3 Activity Difficulty

A learning activity is a task that allows students to develop their learning. The task-centered principle is one of the key aspects of the instructional theory [24], which states that instruction is better developed if a progression of increasingly complex relevant tasks is used.

In order to model the instruction based on activities with progressive complexity it is essential to first define the concept of activity difficulty. The concept of difficulty is not easy to define, although intuitively we all understand that a task is difficult when performing it becomes laborious, requiring a significant effort and in which skills with a certain complexity must be put into practice [18]. Attempts have been made to measure difficulty from different points of view, such as the analysis of the results of activities carried out by students [20], the estimation of difficulty by means of a linear regression analysis of user data [8] or the automatic generation of exercises with a certain established difficulty [19,25]. Whatever the case, one common factor to all these definitions can be established: difficulty can be considered as a cost so that students must pay this cost in time and effort to successfully complete an activity, thus the effort is considered to be indirectly related to progress [9–11].

2.4 Characteristic Vectors

In a learning system, a learner model is a resource that stores all the learners features, such as their preferences or their behavior along the learning process [6]. It is the same for the activity model, which stores all the features of an activity such as their learning style or their difficulty level. Both models will be processed by the smart learning system and interpreted by an algorithm that perform the corresponding selection of the most appropriate activity at any time [21]. Therefore, these models must be prepared to be correctly read and computed, that is why they are stored as a collection of features in the form of a vector. Each of these features is a measurable variable used to characterize a concrete aspect of an individual or phenomenon. So a feature vector will end up being a set of explanatory variables of a phenomenon being observed [4].

As feature vectors are used to characterize the individuals and make decisions by the corresponding algorithm depending on their values, each of those features must be meaningful, discriminating, independent and, as we mentioned before, measurable, so that they will have an interpretable value for the algorithms, which can be quantitative, such as integer or real; or qualitative, also named categorical, that contains a value inside a pre-defined range [1].

A feature is meaningful if it makes sense to a human observer, that is, if the mathematical representation it assumes is interpretable by a person and if it corresponds to what it actually represents. In this case, the features presented are based on models proposed by researchers to explain the complex learning process. Although a mathematical representation is necessary, the basis on which this representation is developed is solid from the point of view of educational research.

Those features must also be discriminating to be correctly differentiated into categories and so to classify the learner.

And also independent, which means their values does not depend on other variables, eliminating redundant information and simplifying the task from a computational point of view.

3 Vectors Definition

As we have already mentioned, the characteristic vector of the learner is obtained from the characteristic vectors of the activities that the learner performs. Therefore, the first step is to correctly characterize the activities.

The first variable in the activity characteristic vector to be considered is the learning style. Among the different possible theories referring to categorize learning styles, we will use the Kolb Learning Style Inventory 4.0 [16], due to this theory is the most suitable one to define an activity and so the learners through the activities they do. Then there are two more features: the cognitive level and knowledge type, which both can be measured for learner and activity, respectively taken from the cognitive dimension and knowledge dimension of Bloom's Taxonomy revision [3]. Finally, difficulty is another essential variable one to be taken into account for each activity.

In the case of the learner model, it will contain all previous variables, excepting activity difficulty, and one of its own, the time log. This variable will contain the history of the learner's actions in the system. Concretely, referring to the activities they have done, when and how, in order to obtain as more information about the learner as possible.

In the following sections, we will analyze each variable and the interpretable value to assign to them.

3.1 Activities' Vector Definition

Firstly, the variables describing the activities' feature vector are actually a data structure formed by the variables in Table 1 and set by the corresponding teacher when an activity is created.

3.2 Learners' Vector Definition

Then, the learner is also characterized with a feature vector, containing the same variables than the activities and some specific of the learner, having in total four variables (Table 2). The variables must represent the same categorical values as for the activities, but each of them has a percentage value associated. So that, instead of being just a concrete sub-type, there will be different values for each one, representing the level of completion the learner has for each learning style sub-type. This will be represented using a dictionary in which the keys are the style sub-type and the value is a floating point value representing the corresponding percentage.

Table 1. Variables of the activity vector.

Variable	Type	Possible values	Description
Difficulty	integer	[0 100]	Numerical value (measurable), normalized between 0 and 100
Learning style	enum	Initiating, Experiencing, Creating, Reflecting, Analyzing, Thinking, Deciding, Acting, Balancing	Categorical value, according to the Kolb Learning Style Inventory 4.0 [16]
Cognitive level	enum	Remember, Understand, Apply, Analyze, Evaluate, Create	Categorical value, according to the cognitive process dimensions of Bloom's Taxonomy [3]
Knowledge type	enum	Factual, Conceptual, Procedural, Metacognitive	Categorical value, according to the knowledge types of Bloom's Taxonomy [3]

Table 2. Variables of the learner vector.

Variable	Type	Record fields	Description
Learning style	record	initiating: floating experiencing: floating creating: floating reflecting: floating analyzing: floating thinking: floating deciding: floating acting: floating balancing: floating	Percentage value for each possible learning style, because no learner has a pure learning style
Cognitive level	record	remember: floating understand: floating apply: floating analyze: floating evaluate: floating create: floating	Percentage value for each possible cognitive level, because no learner is only prepared for a given cognitive level activity
Knowledge type	record	factual: floating conceptual: floating procedural: floating meta-cognitive: floating	Percentage value for each possible knowledge type, because no learner is only prepared for a given knowledge type activity
Time log	array of records	[Starting date: date Finishing date: date Starting time: time Finishing time: time Activity Id: integer Time Spent: floating Score: floating]	Array or records containing the history of the learner's actions in the system related to the activities

4   Vector Calculation

When a learner completes an activity, a resulting value is computed, in a way that can completely vary according to the type of the activity, but to be able of measuring how the learner has achieved the activity, we need a numerical value. Then, the learner's feature vector is updated depending on the activity's vector that has just been done and the result obtained. It is, as we said before, a cycle of updating the feature vectors of the learners as they complete the proposed learning activities. In that way, a learner will be characterized by the activities they have done.

In this process, the learner's feature vector, will be updated variable by variable in a different way, since each variable needs to be computed according to different factors. But there will be a common factor that affects all the variables: the time. While the learner goes forward in the learning process, their skills develop and their experience increase and so their features will also change. Therefore a recently done activity is more relevant than another one done time ago.

This is specially important in the case of those variables whose values represent a percentage of completion, such as Learning Style, Cognitive Level and Knowledge Type. These variables are represented by the percentage that each of their own sub-types is developed, so each time a new activity of that concrete sub-type is completed, the corresponding existent value is updated using the resulting evaluation of the new activity, hereafter called E. To have the time aspect into account, we firstly introduce a time-dependent variable understood as the instant an activity has been completed, following a chronological order, called t, so the activity made in the instant t is previous to one made in the instant $t + 1$. Also we use a reduction factor λ with a value between 0 and 1, which represents how the weight of the older activities is being decreased.

The computation of the new value for each corresponding sub-type is named as v_x, where v corresponds to the value of the sub-type and x to the sub-type affected. This value depends on the instant t the current activity has been made, representing $v_x(t)$ as the value for the sub-type x obtained in an instant t, and on all the previous values computed for each activity belonging to the same sub-type. It is performed in a recursive way, given $e(a_i)^{(t)}$ as the value obtained for an activity a_i made in the instant t. In the case of the first instant $(t = 1)$, the new value v_x is the same than the recently obtained, so:

$$v_x^{(1)} = e(a_i)^{(1)} \tag{1}$$

Then, any v_x computed in the instant t is obtained as follows:

$$v_x^{(t)} = \frac{v_x^{(t-1)} \cdot (t - 1) \cdot \lambda + e(a_i)^{(t)}}{(t - 1) \cdot \lambda + 1} \tag{2}$$

Therefore, when the learner completes an activity, in the learner's feature vector all Learning Style, Cognitive Level and Knowledge Type variables will use this formula to update their values, considering only the sub-types corresponding to the activity's feature vector. But in order to avoid that only one sub-type of any of those variables is updated and keep the rest of them updated too, we use the same formula for the rest of them, but with a value $e(a_i)^{(t)} = 0$, with whom the value of the corresponding sub-type will be decreasing. So that besides reducing the weights of all the previous activities done of a concrete sub-type, the value of the other sub-types will be also affected, aiming to keep the time factor into account for them.

Let us consider an example. Given an activity a1 vector $A = \{ difficulty = 5.6, Learning\ Style = $ "Creating", $Cognitive\ Level = $ "Remember", $Knowledge\ Type = $ "Conceptual"$\}$, that has been completed with a score $e(a_1) = 76$, the following variables of the learner vector L will be modified in the following way:

- Learning Style. The value corresponding to Creating sub-type will be updated using Eqs. 1 and 2, including the current activity and all the previous ones that have Creating as value of Learning Style variable in their feature vector. For the rest of the sub-types the same equations will be used, but with the value $e(a_1) = 0$ instead of $e(a_1) = 76$.
- Cognitive Level. In this case, the Remember sub-type will modify its value in the given $e(a_1) = 76$ and the rest of the sub-types with $e(a_1) = 0$.
- Knowledge Type. As in the previous cases, this variable will update its Conceptual sub-type value using the current value of $e(a_1) = 76$ and the rest of the sub-types with $e(a_1) = 0$.

Now it is the turn for the variable that is exclusive of the learner's vector: Time Log. It is updated any time the learner makes an activity. It is important to consider that a learner can complete an activity in different periods of time, that means they can start in one day, stop and exit the system, and complete it another day. That's why it is important to store starting and finishing dates and times. So Starting Date and Starting Time will be set in the moment the learner starts an activity for the first time, and the Finishing Date and Finishing Time when they complete the activity. For computing Time Spent, it will be increasing only while the learner is doing the activity, and set when they finish it. Finally, given an activity a_i, Activity Id is i and Score is $e(a_i)$.

5   Experiments

In order to validate the algorithm for calculating the student's characteristic vector, a simulation has been carried out in which, synthetically, activity characteristic vectors are created and the system is tested. The simulation has the following parameters:

- $n_a = $ Total number of activities operated by the system
- $n_s = $ Number of activities performed by every student
- $\lambda = $ Reduction factor

In this simulation, activity vectors are created so that it is randomly chosen which learning style it reinforces, which cognitive level it has and which type of knowledge it deals with. Then, the performance of a random activity by the student is simulated, with a random score between e_{min} and e_{max}. Finally, the student's vector is recalculated according to Eqs. 1 and 2, and the process is repeated until n_s activities are achieved.

It should be noted that the activities are not eliminated from the activity bag when they are performed. It has been considered that in the simulation it is not necessary since the score that the student reaches is random and is not conditioned by the knowledge of the student. In a real system the activities performed must be eliminated from the bag of eligible activities, since once performed they must not be assigned again.

There some interesting results. Firstly, when the activities performed grow, the value of the student's vector for each variable tends to converge to the mean of the score obtained $(e_{min} + e_{max})/2$. We must bear in mind that the vector reflects the student's behavior and the nature of the simulation produces this effect. In a real system, the vector will end up converging to the average of the scores obtained for each type of activity. Graphs in Figs. 1 and 2 reflect this behavior. In Fig. 1 the score has been considered to be a random value between 80 and 100, so the values converge to 90, while in Fig. 2 the value is between 0 and 100 and the values converge to 50. Moreover, the convergence is faster in the first case because the initial variability is lower.

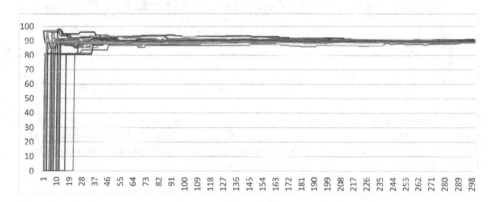

Fig. 1. Convergence value of the simulation of the learner's vector calculation. Parameters: $n_a = 1000$, $n_s = 300$, $\lambda = 0.9$, $e_{min} = 80$, $e_{max} = 100$. Each line represents the changes in the value of each variable (vertical axis), in each iteration (horizontal axis). The value of every variable converges to 90.

The λ reduction factor also modulates the convergence speed of the system. The larger it is, the faster it converges. This occurs in the simulation because a higher value means that more recent activities have a much greater weight than earlier ones and therefore changes are faster. According to this, it would seem

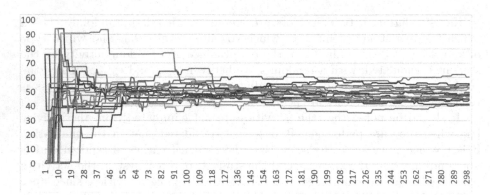

Fig. 2. Convergence value of the simulation of the learner's vector calculation. Parameters: $n_a = 1000$, $n_s = 300$, $\lambda = 0.9$, $e_{min} = 0$, $e_{max} = 100$. Each line represents the changes in the value of each variable (vertical axis), in each iteration (horizontal axis). The value of every variable converges to 50, and the convergence speed is lower, due to the higher initial variability. Most variables stabilize at iteration 60, approximately.

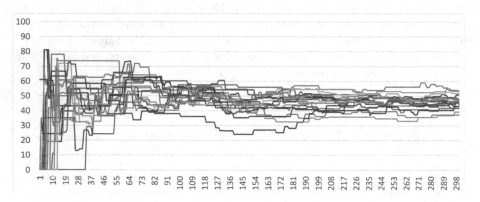

Fig. 3. Convergence speed of the simulation of the learner's vector calculation. Parameters: $n_a = 1000$, $n_s = 300$, $\lambda = 0.5$, $e_{min} = 0$, $e_{max} = 100$. Each line represents the changes in the value of each variable (vertical axis), in each iteration (horizontal axis). Most variables stabilize at iteration 100, approximately

convenient to incorporate a high value, however in a real case this parameter must be studied in detail since the implications are not only of convergence but also of remembering the older activities. Figures 2, 3 and 4 compare the behavior of the system for three λ values.

This simulation allows the mathematical validation of the equations to calculate the learner vector. However, the usefulness must be validated in a real environment with learners performing actual activities.

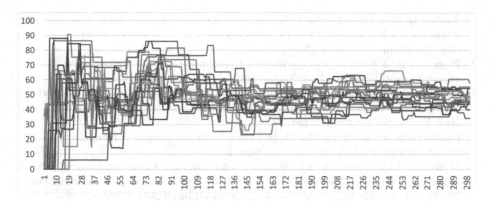

Fig. 4. Convergence speed of the simulation of the learner's vector calculation. Parameters: $n_a = 1000$, $n_s = 300$, $\lambda = 0.2$, $c_{min} = 0$, $c_{max} = 100$. Each line represents the changes in the value of each variable (vertical axis), in each iteration (horizontal axis). Most variables stabilize at iteration 160, approximately.

6   Conclusions

For a smart learning system to be able to personalize learning, it is necessary to characterize the learner so that a computer program can process that information. We propose the characterization through a vector of characteristics that are measurable, meaningful, discriminating and independent.

The characteristic vector is obtained by observing the learner's behavior in the learning system. That is, if we label the features of the learning activities that the learner must perform, we can use these features to know the learner better. In this article we have proposed a series of features for the activities and a way to calculate the learner's characteristic vector from his or her activity in the system. The result is a mathematical way to obtain the vector that can be easily computed.

In addition, we have carried out a set of simulations to evaluate the robustness of the proposed formulation, and we have verified that, after a series of iterations, the system converges to the expected values. We have also introduced a reduction parameter that allows us to modulate the speed of convergence, although it has other implications for learning that we should explore.

In the future, we propose to incorporate these methods in a learning system to validate the calculation of the vectors with real users.

References

1. Aggarwal, C.C.: Machine Learning for Text. Springer, Cham (2018). https://doi.org/10.1007/978-3-319-73531-3
2. Ahn, S., Ames, A.J., Myers, N.D.: A review of meta-analyses in education: methodological strengths and weaknesses. Rev. Educ. Res. **82**(4), 436–476 (2012). https://doi.org/10.3102/0034654312458162

3. Anderson, L.W., Krathwohl, D.R. (eds.): A taxonomy for Learning, Teaching, and Assessing: A Revision of Bloom's Taxonomy of Educational Objectives, complete edn. Longman, New York (2001)
4. Bishop, C.M.: Pattern Recognition and Machine Learning. Information Science and Statistics. Springer, New York (2006)
5. Bloom, B.S., Krathwohl, D.R., Masia, B.S.: Taxonomy of Educational Objectives. The Classification of Educational Goals: Cognitive Domain Handbook 1. Longman, New York (1956). OCLC: 929425977
6. Carberry, S., et al.: User Models in Dialog Systems. Springer, Heidelberg (2011). Softcover reprint of the original, 1st edn. 1989
7. Castejon, J.L., Perez, A.M., Gilar, R.: Confirmatory factor analysis of project spectrum activities. A second-order g factor or multiple intelligences? Intelligence **38**(5), 481–496 (2010). https://doi.org/10.1016/j.intell.2010.07.002
8. Cheng, I., Shen, R., Basu, A.: An algorithm for automatic difficulty level estimation of multimedia mathematical test items. In: 2008 Eighth IEEE International Conference on Advanced Learning Technologies. ICALT 2008, pp. 175–179, July 2008. https://doi.org/10.1109/ICALT.2008.105
9. Gallego-Durán, F., Molina-Carmona, R., Llorens-Largo, F.: Estimating the difficulty of a learning activity from the training cost for a machine learning algorithm. In: Proceedings of the Sixth International Conference on Technological Ecosystems for Enhancing Multiculturality - TEEM 2018, pp. 654–659. ACM Press, Salamanca (2018). https://doi.org/10.1145/3284179.3284289
10. Gallego-Durán, F.J.: Estimating difficulty of learning activities in design stages: a novel application of Neuroevolution. Ph.D. thesis, University of Alicante (2015)
11. Gallego-Durán, F.J., Molina-Carmona, R., Llorens-Largo, F.: An approach to measuring the difficulty of learning activities. In: Zaphiris, P., Ioannou, A. (eds.) LCT 2016. LNCS, vol. 9753, pp. 417–428. Springer, Cham (2016). https://doi.org/10.1007/978-3-319-39483-1_38
12. Gardner, H.: Intelligence Reframed: Multiple Intelligences for the 21st Century. Basic Books, New York (2000). OCLC: 247819868
13. Hattie, J.: Visible Learning: A Synthesis of Over 800 Meta-Analyses Relating to Achievement, 1st edn. Routledge, London (2008)
14. Hattie, J.: Visible Learning for Teachers: Maximizing Impact on Learning. Routledge, Abingdon (2013)
15. Hattie, J., Anderman, E.M. (eds.): International Guide to Student Achievement, 1st edn. Routledge, New York (2012)
16. Kolb, D., Kolb, A.: The Kolb Learning Style Inventory 4.0: Guide to Theory, Psychometrics, Research & Applications (2013)
17. Kolb, D.A.: Facilitator's Guide to Learning. Hay Group Transforming Learning, Philadelphia (2000)
18. Nicholls, J.G., Miller, A.T.: The differentiation of the concepts of difficulty and ability. Child Dev. **54**(4), 951 (1983). https://doi.org/10.2307/1129899
19. Radošević, D., Orehovački, T., Stapić, Z.: Automatic on-line generation of student's exercises in teaching programming. Central European Conference on Information and Intelligent Systems, CECIIS (2010)
20. Ravi, G.A., Sosnovsky, S.: Exercise difficulty calibration based on student log mining. In: Mdritscher, F., Luengo, V., Lai-Chong Law, E., Hoppe, U. (eds.) Proceedings of DAILE 2013: Workshop on Data Analysis and Interpretation for Learning Environments, Villard-de-Lans, France, January 2013

21. Real-Fernández, A., Llorens-Largo, F., Molina-Carmona, R.: Smart learning model based on competences and activities. In: Sein-Echaluce, M.L., Fidalgo-Blanco, A., García-Peñalvo, F.J., Tomei, L. (eds.) Innovative Trends in Flipped Teaching and Adaptive Learning. Advances in Educational Technologies and Instructional Design, pp. 228–251. IGI Global (2019). https://doi.org/10.4018/978-1-5225-8142-0

22. Real-Fernández, A., Molina-Carmona, R., Llorens-Largo, F.: Instructional strategies for a smart learning system. In: Proceedings of the Seventh International Conference on Technological Ecosystems for Enhancing Multiculturality - TEEM 2019. ACM Press, León (2019)

23. Real-Fernández, A., Molina-Carmona, R., Pertegal-Felices, M.L., Llorens-Largo, F.: Definition of a feature vector to characterise learners in adaptive learning systems. In: Visvizi, A., Lytras, M.D. (eds.) RIIFORUM 2019. SPC, pp. 75–89. Springer, Cham (2019). https://doi.org/10.1007/978-3-030-30809-4_8

24. Reigeluth, C.M.: Instructional Theory and Technology for the New Paradigm of Education. Revista de Educación a Distancia (32) (2012)

25. Sadigh, D., Seshia, S.A., Gupta, M.: Automating exercise generation: a step towards meeting the MOOC challenge for embedded systems. In: Proceedings of the Workshop on Embedded Systems Education (WESE), October 2012

26. Sternberg, R.J.: Beyond IQ Paperback: A Triarchic Theory of Human Intelligence. Cambridge University Press, Cambridge (2009)

27. Sternberg, R.J., Castejón, J.L., Prieto, M.D., Hautamäki, J., Grigorenko, E.L.: Confirmatory factor analysis of the Sternberg triarchic abilities test in three international samples: an empirical test of the triarchic theory of intelligence. Eur. J. Psychol. Assess. **17**(1), 1–16 (2001). https://doi.org/10.1027//1015-5759.17.1.1

AI-Driven Assessment of Students: Current Uses and Research Trends

José Carlos Sánchez-Prieto[1,4(✉)] , Adriana Gamazo[1,4] ,
Juan Cruz-Benito[2] , Roberto Therón[1,3,5] ,
and Francisco J. García-Peñalvo[1,3,4]

[1] GRIAL Research Group, University of Salamanca, Salamanca, Spain
{josecarlos.sp,adrianagamazo,theron,fgarcia}@usal.es
[2] IBM Quantum, IBM Research, IBM T.J. Watson Research Center,
Yorktown Heights, NY 10598, USA
Juan.cruz@ibm.com
[3] Computer Science Department, University of Salamanca, Salamanca, Spain
[4] Research Institute for Educational Sciences (IUCE),
University of Salamanca, Salamanca, Spain
[5] VisUSAL Research Group, University of Salamanca, Salamanca, Spain

Abstract. During the last decade, the use of AIs is being incorporated into the educational field whether to support the analysis of human behavior in teaching-learning contexts, as didactic resource combined with other technologies or as a tool for the assessment of the students.

This proposal presents a Systematic Literature Review and mapping study on the use of AIs for the assessment of students that aims to provide a general overview of the state of the art and identify the current areas of research by answering 6 research questions related with the evolution of the field, and the geographic and thematic distribution of the studies.

As a result of the selection process this study identified 20 papers focused on the research topic in the repositories SCOPUS and Web of Science from an initial amount of 129.

The analysis of the papers allowed the identification of three main thematic categories: assessment of student behaviors, assessment of student sentiments and assessment of student achievement as well as several gaps in the literature and future research lines addressed in the discussion.

Keywords: Artificial intelligence · Education · Assessment · Algorithmic evaluation

1 Introduction and Background

The word artificial intelligence is every day in everyone's mouth. It is one of the most over-hyped research areas in media, and society is permeable to such publicity. It is true that artificial intelligence and its advancement are revolutionizing many aspects of our daily lives [1–4] and can improve the efficiency of different processes, but are those advancements adequately communicated?

© Springer Nature Switzerland AG 2020
P. Zaphiris and A. Ioannou (Eds.): HCII 2020, LNCS 12205, pp. 292–302, 2020.
https://doi.org/10.1007/978-3-030-50513-4_22

For years, artificial intelligence has been interacting with users in digital environments in more or less obvious ways [5]. In many cases, users are not aware that their activity is continuously evaluated or intervened by software agents with a minimum of intelligence. However, this non-obvious interaction affects these users and conditions the resources, actions, or states that users reach in the digital environments they use [5, 6]. Today, one of the natural trends in different areas is to introduce intelligent software agents to improve specific areas of computer systems. This has introduced an intense discussion [7–9] about the effects of these agents, giving rise to reflections about the privacy of the users, the ethics in such systems, or the need to create common working frameworks that respect the users and their human characteristics. Too often, disrespectful behavior towards users has been observed, sometimes creating a negative image of the algorithms and how they are used in conjunction with people [7, 10].

These issues are relevant in general, but even more so when they affect such fundamental social and human issues like behavior, freedom, education, or social good. In the case of this article, we will focus on how artificial intelligence is involved in a specific case related to education and the social sciences, such as educational evaluation.

For years, progress has been made in applying computer solutions to the education process, with more or less success [11–14]. These computational approaches are increasingly common in STEM (Science, Technology, Engineering, and Mathematics) areas, while in other areas, they present some difficulties that limit the emergence of such solutions. In the STEM areas, it is possible to assess the results of many operations or learning outcomes using calculation or mathematical processes. Therein lies the growth of computational approaches related to education in such areas and the appearance of algorithmic evaluations or algorithm-based educational approaches [15]. Something as simple for a computer as checking the result of a set of operations, calculations, or processes regulated by mathematics can facilitate the work of teachers and educators when correcting exercises, exams, or assignments within a regulated context. This benefit is even more evident in contexts with many students or people involved in similar processes (like in MOOCs). As a related context, it is possible to cite several works in the field of research in Learning Analytics or Educational Data Mining[16–18] that deal with this type of questions or the use of tools such as Jupyter notebooks [19] in STEM areas to support the educational process and evaluation (through Jupyter-related packages such as *nbgrader* [20, 21]).

However, to the extent of our knowledge, due to the novelty of the field, there is still a lack of secondary studies that provide a systematic overview of the state of the art that allows the clear identification of lines of research.

This paper deals with these issues and related aspects aiming to fill a research gap through a systematic literature review (SLR) and mapping study [22] focused on how artificial intelligence or similar algorithmic methods have been used for the educational assessment of students.

To do so, the article is composed of the following sections: Sect. 2 describes the methodology employed to perform the SLR, including the research questions, the search string, the repositories and the selection process; Sect. 3 exposes the results of the SLR answering the research questions, and, finally, Sect. 4 provides a discussion on the most relevant findings.

2   Methodology

As we have seen, this study combines two different techniques for literature review, namely a systematic literature review and a mapping study. These two techniques have in common the structured and planned examination of large amounts of information in a replicable way [23]. However, while the main objective of mapping studies is to provide a general overview focused on characteristics external to the content of publications such as the geographical distribution or the evolution of the number of studies over time, SLRs aim to answer more in-depth questions related to the areas of study, the variables used or the methodology among others[22, 24].

In consequence, this investigation employs a combination of this two techniques aiming to answer the following six research questions.

1. What has been the evolution of the number of documents covering the use of AIs in student assessment?
2. Who are the most relevant authors in the field?
3. What is the most common source for the dissemination of results in the field?
4. Where do the studies take place?
5. Which is the population of the study?
6. Which are the most frequent uses of AIs in student assessment?

Following the proposal by Kitchenham and Charters [22], the following inclusion criteria were designed to guide the selection process and ensure the adequacy of the papers selected:

1. The research papers are related to the use of IAs for student assessment.
2. The research papers include empirical research.
3. Research papers have been published after being subjected to a peer review process.
4. Research papers are written in English.

If a study did not meet all the inclusion criteria it was excluded from the research during the selection process.

In order to identify the papers in the databases we employed the following search string considering both the research questions and the possible alternative spellings and synonyms: (AI OR "artificial intelligence") AND ("students assessment" OR "students evaluation" OR "assessment of the students" OR "evaluation of the students").

This search string was introduced in the two databases: SCOPUS and Web of Science (WOS). This two databases were selected considering that both of them allow the use of logical expressions, searches in specific fields or full-length searches and are relevant to the field. Additionally the use of this two databases is considered enough to perform valid SLR and mapping studies [25–27]. The introduction of the search string on the two databases provided an initial number of 120 studies (109 from SCOPUs and 20 from WOS) on December of 2019.

These initial results were recorded on a spreadsheet and, after the removal of the duplicates, were subjected to the inclusion criteria screening the titles abstracts and keywords of the papers. When such elements did not include enough information the researchers also screened the full text of the publications (Fig. 1).

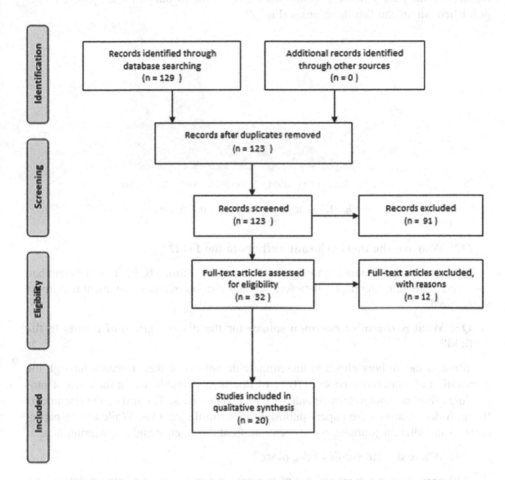

Fig. 1. Selection process. Reported in line with the PRISMA statement [28]

3 Results

The application of the inclusion and exclusion criteria yielded a total of 20 papers on the topic of the use of AI for student assessment. This section presents the analysis of the characteristics of the selected documents in order to answer the research questions posed in the method section, both for the mapping and the SLR.

Q1: What has been the evolution of the number of documents covering the use of AIs in student assessment?

Regarding the evolution of the research field, we can see in figure X that, while there is not a clear upward trend, there does seem to be an evolution towards more research in the past years, especially since 2017, with 14 out of the 20 papers (70%) published within the last three years (Fig. 2).

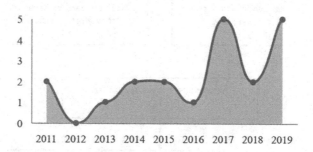

Fig. 2. Year of publication of the studies

Q2: Who are the most relevant authors in the field?

There were 66 different authors in the 20 selected documents, but none of them had authored more than one paper, therefore no author stood out as a prominent researcher in the field.

Q3: What is the most common source for the dissemination of results in the field?

Most of the authors chose to disseminate the results of their research through the elaboration of conference papers (70%, 14 documents), published in the form of proceedings from computer science and AI-based conferences. The rest of the documents (60%, 6 documents) were papers published in scientific journals. While all the papers come from different journals, all of them are from the science and engineering field.

Q4: Where do the studies take place?

Although there is a large variety of countries where the selected studies take place, there are two countries that stand out: the United States of America, with 5 papers [29–33], China with 3 papers [34–36], and Pakistan with 2 papers [37, 38].

Figure 2 shows the dispersion of studies conducted in the European region, which are located in Greece [39], Macedonia [40], Norway [41], Poland[42], Serbia [43] and the United Kingdom [44].

Other countries represented in the selection are Mexico [45] in North America, Turkey [46] in Asia, Mauritius [47] in Africa, and Fiji [48] in the Pacific region[1].

---

[1] The last two countries are not represented in the map in Fig. 3 due to their small size.

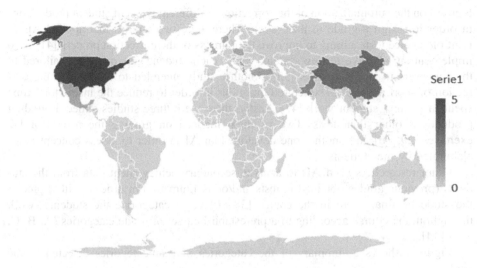

Fig. 3. Countries where the studies took place

Q5: Which is the population of the study?

Out of all 20 papers, 14 were focused on Higher Education students and 1 focused on Secondary Education Students [39]. The other 5 were not aimed at a particular group of students, since they were theoretical in nature [32, 40, 41, 44, 47].

Q6: Which are the most frequent uses of AIs in student assessment?

Aiming to characterize the main aim of the papers analyzed for this study, three thematic categories emerged: assessment of student behaviors, assessment of student sentiments and assessment of student achievement.

There were four papers focused on the study of student behaviors with different aims. Two studies analyzed the social interactions performed by students within the framework of an online course in order to predict their final outcome or achievement in the course [32, 48]. The other two used information on the behavior of students during the performance of a given task in order to personalize their user experience. In one of them, the aim was to provide the student with useful assistance during the task [45] and the other aimed to tailor an enemy bot during a gaming experience [43].

Six studies were focused on student feelings or sentiments, aiming to assess and determine the emotional state of the students when performing a given task or participating in a given course. The aim of four of them was to analyze the students' opinions on the teaching and learning processes and models developed in the course [31, 33, 34, 37, 42], and the other one intended to use the data on student emotions to predict their chances of finishing a MOOC and subsequently provide personalized messages to encourage the students who are less likely to finish the course based on their emotions [36].

There was another block of papers (10) whose main focus was the assessment of student achievement through AI-based methods. More than half of these papers were focused on the automatization of the correction of different types of student productions in order to assign a grade to their work. There were two studies that applied AIs to multiple-choice tests aiming to improve the fairness of the correction process [41] or to implement an adaptive testing system, where each student gets questions tailored to their answers to previous ones [35]. Another study intended to automatize the correction of short answers to structured questions in order to reduce the instructors' time spent in grading student work [47]. Lastly, there were three studies aimed at grading productions other than tests. Two of them focused on grading the results of lab exercises [29, 46] and another one developed an AI in order to assess concept maps elaborated by the students.

Other researchers used AIs to analyze secondary achievement data from the students (previous grades obtained in tests and/or assignments) in order to either predict the students' final score in the course [38–40] or to categorize the students' work throughout the course according to a pre-established set of grade categories (A, B, C, etc.) [44].

Figure 4 shows a summary of the categories and subcategories detected in the study.

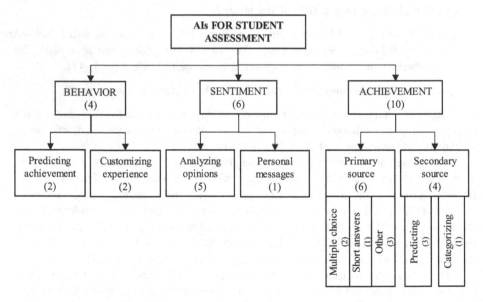

Fig. 4. Summary of AI uses in student assessment

4   Discussion and Conclusions

This literature review has served to address some issues regarding the status of research on the use of AIs for student assessment.

Firstly, the answer to the first research question points out that the research in this field is still at a very early stage of development given that all the selected works have been published in the last decade and more than half of them in the last five years.

This short period of development may have resulted in a wide dispersion both in the number of publications per author and in the geographical distribution, although USA and China concentrate most of the research.

In the same vein, it is striking that all publications have been made in conferences and journals in the field of computer engineering existing a lack of studies focused on the use of AIs for the assessment of the students from a pedagogical perspective. This is a usual phenomenon in the early stages of integration of any technological innovation in the educational field [49] and constitutes a very interesting line of research for future studies.

Additionally, all of the studies except one are focused on the higher education level, therefore extending the research to other formal education levels may constitute another line for the future development of investigations.

In the answer to research question 6, three major thematic areas have been identified, focusing on the study of student behavior, feelings and achievement. Future studies should extend this lines including the use of IAs in more ambitious didactic designs, paying attention to the assessment of different competences or the detection of educational needs.

Finally, this study presents some limitations. In the first place, although SCOPUS and WoS are the more relevant databases of scientific publications they may not include some works of interest published in less relevant journals or conference proceedings, therefore future studies could consider the use additional databases such as Google Scholar in order to diminish the effect of the publication bias.

Secondly, this review has only considered the direct results obtained in the two databases as a first approach to the field, future studies may find of interest to include additional records identified through other sources to increase the number of publications analyzed.

Acknowledgement. This work has been partially funded by the Spanish Government Ministry of Economy and Competitiveness through the DEFINES project (Ref. TIN2016-80172-R).

References

1. Makridakis, S.: The forthcoming Artificial Intelligence (AI) revolution: its impact on society and firms. Futures **90**, 46–60 (2017)
2. Roll, I., Wylie, R.: Evolution and revolution in artificial intelligence in education. Int. J. Artif. Intell. Educ. **26**, 582–599 (2016). https://doi.org/10.1007/s40593-016-0110-3
3. Gunning, D.: Explainable artificial intelligence (XAI). Defense Advanced Research Projects Agency (DARPA). http://www.darpa.mil/program/explainable-artificial-intelligence. Accessed 24 Feb 2020

4. Abdul, A., Vermeulen, J., Wang, D., Lim, B.Y., Kankanhalli, M.: Trends and trajectories for explainable, accountable and intelligible systems: an HCI research agenda. In: Proceedings of the 2018 CHI Conference on Human Factors in Computing Systems, pp. 1–18. ACM, April 2018
5. Amershi, S., Cakmak, M., Knox, W.B., Kulesza, T.: Power to the people: the role of humans in interactive machine learning. Ai Mag. **35**, 105–120 (2014)
6. Cruz-Benito, J.: On data-driven systems analyzing, supporting and enhancing users' interaction and experience. Doctoral dissertation, Universidad de Salamanca (2018)
7. O'neil, C.: Weapons of Math Destruction: How Big Data Increases Inequality and Threatens Democracy. Broadway Books, New York (2014)
8. Etzioni, A., Etzioni, O.: Incorporating ethics into artificial intelligence. J. Ethics **21**, 403–418 (2017). https://doi.org/10.1007/s10892-017-9252-2
9. Russell, S., et al.: Letter to the editor: Research priorities for robust and beneficial artificial intelligence: an open letter. AI Mag. **36**, 3–4 (2015)
10. Peirano, M.: El enemigo conoce el sistema: Manipulación de ideas, personas e influencias después de la economía de la atención. Debate (2019)
11. Miller, T.: Explanation in artificial intelligence: insights from the social sciences. Artif. Intell. **267**, 1–38 (2019)
12. Aoun, J.E.: Robot-Proof: Higher Education in the Age of Artificial Intelligence. MIT Press, Cambridge (2017)
13. Henrie, C.R., Halverson, L.R., Graham, C.R.: Measuring student engagement in technology-mediated learning: a review. Comput. Educ. **90**, 36–53 (2015)
14. Jonassen, D., Davidson, M., Collins, M., Campbell, J., Haag, B.B.: Constructivism and computer-mediated communication in distance education. Am. J. Distance Educ. **9**, 7–26 (1995)
15. Perrotta, C., Williamson, B.: The social life of learning analytics: cluster analysis and the 'performance' of algorithmic education. Learn. Media Technol. **43**, 3–16 (2018)
16. Papamitsiou, Z., Economides, A.A.: Learning analytics and educational data mining in practice: a systematic literature review of empirical evidence. J. Educ. Technol. Soc. **17**, 49–64 (2014)
17. Roll, I., Winne, P.H.: Understanding, evaluating, and supporting self-regulated learning using learning analytics. J. Learn. Anal. **2**, 7–12 (2015)
18. Rienties, B., Cross, S., Zdrahal, Z.: Implementing a learning analytics intervention and evaluation framework: what works? In: Kei Daniel, B. (ed.) Big Data and Learning Analytics in Higher Education, pp. 147–166. Springer, Cham (2017). https://doi.org/10.1007/978-3-319-06520-5_10
19. Kluyver, T., et al.: Jupyter notebooks-a publishing format for reproducible computational workflows. In: Loizides, F., Schmidt, B. (eds.) Positioning and Power in Academic Publishing: Players, Agents and Agendas, pp. 87–90. IOS Press, Canada (2016)
20. Hamrick, J.B.: Creating and grading IPython/Jupyter notebook assignments with NbGrader. In: Alphonce, C., Tims, J. (eds.) Proceedings of the 47th ACM Technical Symposium on Computing Science Education, p. 242. ACM Press, New York (2016)
21. Blank, D. S., Bourgin, D., Brown, A., Bussonnier, M., Frederic, J., Granger, B.,... Page, L. nbgrader: A tool for creating and grading assignments in the Jupyter Notebook. The Journal of Open Source Education2, 32–34 (2019)
22. Kitchenham, B., Charters, S.: Guidelines for performing Systematic Literature Reviews in Software Engineering. Version 2.3 (EBSE-2007–01) (2007). https://www.elsevier.com/__data/promis_misc/525444systematicreviewsguide.pdf. Accessed 24 Feb 2020

23. Cruz-Benito, J., García-Peñalvo, F.J., Therón, R.: Analyzing the software architectures supporting HCI/HMI processes through a systematic review of the literature. Telematics and Inform. **38**, 118–132 (2019)
24. Kitchenham, B.A., Budgen, D., Brereton, P.O.: Using mapping studies as the basis for further research – a participant-observer case study. Inf. Softw. Technol. **53**, 638–651 (2011)
25. Kitchenham, B.: What's up with software metrics? – a preliminary mapping study. J. Syst. Softw. **83**, 37–51 (2010)
26. Neiva, F.W., David, J.M.N., Braga, R., Campos, F.: Towards pragmatic interoperability to support collaboration: a systematic review and mapping of the literature. Inf. Softw. Technol. **72**, 137–150 (2016)
27. García Sánchez, F., Therón, R., Gómez-Isla, J.: Alfabetización visual en nuevos medios: revisión y mapeo sistemático de la literatura. Educ. Knowl. Soc. **20**, 1–35 (2019)
28. Moher, D., Liberati, A., Tetzlaff, J., Altman, D.G.: Preferred reporting items for systematic reviews and meta-analyses: the PRISMA statement. PLoS Med **6**, 1–6 (2009)
29. Floryan, M., Dragon, T., Basit, N., Dragon, S., Woolf, B.: Who needs help? Automating student assessment within exploratory learning environments. In: Conati, C., Heffernan, N., Mitrovic, A., Verdejo, M.F. (eds.) AIED 2015. LNCS (LNAI), vol. 9112, pp. 125–134. Springer, Cham (2015). https://doi.org/10.1007/978-3-319-19773-9_13
30. Gurupur, V.P., Pankaj Jain, G., Rudraraju, R.: Evaluating student learning using concept maps and Markov chains. Expert Syst. Appl. **42**, 3306–3314 (2015)
31. Newman, H., Joyner, D.: Sentiment analysis of student evaluations of teaching. In: Penstein Rosé, C., Martínez-Maldonado, R., Hoppe, H.U., Luckin, R., Mavrikis, M., Porayska-Pomsta, K., McLaren, B., du Boulay, B. (eds.) AIED 2018. LNCS (LNAI), vol. 10948, pp. 246–250. Springer, Cham (2018). https://doi.org/10.1007/978-3-319-93846-2_45
32. Ma, J., Kang, J.-H., Shaw, E., Kim, J.: Workflow-based assessment of student online activities with topic and dialogue role classification. In: Biswas, G., Bull, S., Kay, J., Mitrovic, A. (eds.) AIED 2011. LNCS (LNAI), vol. 6738, pp. 187–195. Springer, Heidelberg (2011). https://doi.org/10.1007/978-3-642-21869-9_26
33. Tzacheva, A., Ranganathan, J., Jadi, R.: Multi-label emotion mining from student comments. In: Proceedings of the 2019 4th International Conference on Information and Education Innovations, pp. 120–124. ACM, New York (2019)
34. Lin, Q., Zhu, Y., Zhang, S., Shi, P., Guo, Q., Niu, Z.: Lexical based automated teaching evaluation via students' short reviews. Comput. Appl. Eng. Educ. **27**, 194–205 (2019)
35. Wang, M., Wang, C., Lee, C., Lin, S., Hung, P.: Type-2 fuzzy set construction and application for adaptive student assessment system. In: Proceedings of the 2014 IEEE International Conference on Fuzzy Systems (FUZZ-IEEE), pp. 888–894. IEEE (2014)
36. Wang, L., Hu, G., Zhou, T.: Semantic analysis of learners' emotional tendencies on online MOOC education. Sustainability **10**, 1–19 (2018)
37. Akhtar, J.: An interactive multi-agent reasoning model for sentiment analysis: a case for computational semiotics. Artif. Intell. Rev., 1–18 (2019). https://link.springer.com/article/10.1007/s10462-019-09785-6#citeas
38. Mahboob, T., Irfan, S., Karamat, A.: A machine learning approach for student assessment in E-learning using Quinlan's C4.5, Naive Bayes and Random Forest algorithms. In: Proceedings of the 19th International Multi-Topic Conference (INMIC), pp. 1–8. IEEE (2017)
39. Livieris, I.E., Drakopoulou, K., Kotsilieris, T., Tampakas, V., Pintelas, P.: DSS-PSP - a decision support software for evaluating students' performance. In: Boracchi, G., Iliadis, L., Jayne, C., Likas, A. (eds.) EANN 2017. CCIS, vol. 744, pp. 63–74. Springer, Cham (2017). https://doi.org/10.1007/978-3-319-65172-9_6

40. Simjanoska, M., Gusev, M., Bogdanova, A.M.: Intelligent modelling for predicting students' final grades. In: Proceedings of the 37th International Convention on Information and Communication Technology, Electronics and Microelectronics (MIPRO), pp. 1216–1221. IEEE (2014)

41. Hameed, I.: A fuzzy system to automatically evaluate and improve fairness of multiple-choice questions (MCQs) based exams. In: Proceedings of the 8th International Conference on Computer Supported Education - Volume 1: CSEDU, pp. 476–481. SciTePress (2016)

42. Dudek, D.: Survey analyser: effective processing of academic questionnaire data. In: Borzemski, L., Świątek, J., Wilimowska, Z. (eds.) ISAT 2018. AISC, vol. 852, pp. 245–257. Springer, Cham (2019). https://doi.org/10.1007/978-3-319-99981-4_23

43. Kuk, K., Milentijević, I.Z., Ranđelović, D., Popović, B.M., Čisar, P.: The design of the personal enemy - MIMLebot as an intelligent agent in a game-based learning environment. Acta Polytechnica Hungarica 14, 121–139 (2017)

44. Boongoen, T., Shen, Q., Price, C.: Fuzzy qualitative link analysis for academic performance evaluation. Int. J. Uncertainty Fuzziness and Knowl.-Based Syst. 19, 559–585 (2011)

45. Zatarain-Cabada, R., Barrón-Estrada, M.L., Ríos-Félix, J.M.: Affective learning system for algorithmic logic applying gamification. In: Pichardo-Lagunas, O., Miranda-Jiménez, S. (eds.) MICAI 2016. LNCS (LNAI), vol. 10062, pp. 536–547. Springer, Cham (2017). https://doi.org/10.1007/978-3-319-62428-0_44

46. Caliskan, E., Tatar, U., Bahsi, H., Ottis, R., Vaarandi, R.: Capability detection and evaluation metrics for cyber security lab exercises. In: Bryant, A.R., Mills, R.F., Lopez, J. (eds.) Proceedings of the 2017 International Conference on Cyber Warfare and Security, pp. 407–414. Academic Conferences and Publishing International Ltd., UK (2017)

47. Luchoomun, T., Chumroo, M., Ramnarain-Seetohul, V.: A knowledge based system for automated assessment of short structured questions. In: Proceedings of the 2019 IEEE Global Engineering Education Conference (EDUCON), pp. 1349–1352. IEEE (2019)

48. Singh, S., Lal, S.P.: Educational courseware evaluation using Machine Learning techniques. In: Proceedings of the 2013 IEEE Conference on e-Learning, e-Management and e-Services, pp. 73–78. IEEE (2013)

49. Petrova, K., Li, C.: Focus and setting in mobile learning research: a review of the literature. Commun. IBIMA 10, 219–226 (2009)

Generating Dashboards Using Fine-Grained Components: A Case Study for a PhD Programme

Andrea Vázquez-Ingelmo[1](✉) , Francisco J. García-Peñalvo[1] ,
and Roberto Therón[1,2]

[1] GRIAL Research Group, Computer Sciences Department, Research Institute
for Educational Sciences, University of Salamanca, Salamanca, Spain
{andreavazquez, fgarcia, theron}@usal.es
[2] VisUSAL Research Group, University of Salamanca, Salamanca, Spain

Abstract. Developing dashboards is a complex domain, especially when several stakeholders are involved; while some users could demand certain indicators, other users could demand specific visualizations or design features. Creating individual dashboards for each potential need would consume several resources and time, being an unfeasible approach. Also, user requirements must be thoroughly analyzed to understand their goals regarding the data to be explored, and other characteristics that could affect their user experience. All these necessities ask for a paradigm to foster reusability not only at development level but also at knowledge level. Some methodologies, like the Software Product Line paradigm, leverage domain knowledge and apply it to create a series of assets that can be composed, parameterized, or combined to obtain fully functional systems. This work presents an application of the SPL paradigm to the domain of information dashboards, with the goal of reducing their development time and increasing their effectiveness and user experience. Different dashboard configurations have been suggested to test the proposed approach in the context of the Education in the Knowledge Society PhD programme of the University of Salamanca.

Keywords: Domain engineering · SPL · Information dashboards · Information systems · Educational dashboards

1 Introduction

Data visualization is gaining relevance as a method to understand and generate knowledge [1] from datasets. However, the exponential growth in data generation due to the widespread of data-driven technologies [2] asks for new methodologies to support informed decision-making even if relying on complex and large datasets.

Visual analytics [3, 4] is a popular methodology to foster the comprehension of large quantities of data. This field focuses on analytical reasoning and how interactive tools and visual interfaces can support it.

Visualizing data and generating knowledge from them through information visualizations or information dashboards [5–7] require proper representations, that is,

© Springer Nature Switzerland AG 2020
P. Zaphiris and A. Ioannou (Eds.): HCII 2020, LNCS 12205, pp. 303–314, 2020.
https://doi.org/10.1007/978-3-030-50513-4_23

appropriate encodings and visual metaphors to convey the information contained (and mainly hidden) within large datasets.

However, although practitioners can follow general guidelines to design information visualizations [8], the process of building these tools is costly, because it is important not only to take into account but also to deeply understand the context in which these tools will be employed.

The audience and the context of application are essential to build an effective dashboard. One of the challenges in this field is the adaptation of visualizations and dashboards based on their context [9]. But the adaptation of these tools is complex; it requires several resources to design and implement an adapted version of the same tool.

That is why some approaches that leverage reusability are extremely useful in these domains [10]. Especially, approaches like the Software Product Line (SPL) [11, 12] paradigm and the Model-Driven Development (MDD) [13] foster the reusability of components and knowledge by abstracting common features of a concrete domain.

A dashboard meta-model has been previously developed [14–16] to account for not only for technical features of these tools but also to account for their users. Involving the end-users' characteristics and goals regarding information is crucial to obtain a dashboard adapted to the context and audience.

This work focuses on the application of the developed dashboard meta-model to generate information dashboards in the context of a PhD programme. The goal of this application is to test the suitability of a generative pipeline to tailor information dashboards in a real-world scenario.

A requirement elicitation process has been carried to identify the information requirements and goals of each involved user profile to achieve the mentioned goal. With this information, it has been possible to map the goals into concrete dashboard features.

The rest of this paper is organized as follows. The next section contextualizes the PhD Programme on Education in the Knowledge Society. Section 3 explains the different materials and methods employed to carry out this work. Section 4 presents the results of the requirement elicitation process, as well as the results regarding the generation of customized dashboards based on the previously identified requirements. Finally, Sect. 5 discusses the obtained results, concluding with Sect. 6, in which the conclusions derived from this work are described.

2   PhD Programme on Education in the Knowledge Society

The PhD Program on Education in the Knowledge Society emerges from the Research Institute for Educational Sciences (IUCE – http://iuce.usal.es) at the University of Salamanca (Spain), following the Spanish Royal Decree 99/2011. The primary motivation behind this PhD Program is to feature the teaching-learning forms as main impetus of the Knowledge Society, so as to examine and create new information about the learning as a key component of the Knowledge Society, including both the Social Sciences considers and the new mechanical advances yet inside a synergic and harmonious methodology [17, 18].

The focus of this program is completely interdisciplinary, mainly upheld by the Recognized Research Groups at the University of Salamanca: GRIAL (http://grial.usal.es) [19], GITE (http://gite213.usal.es), OCA (http://campus.usal.es/~oca/), VISUALMED (http://visualmed.usal.es), Robotics and Society Group (http://gro.usal.es) y E-LECTRA (http://electra.usal.es).

The PhD Program gives a context where knowledge generation and its visibility and dissemination are primary objectives. In order to reach them, the scientific knowledge management of the Programme is supported by a technological ecosystem that fusion methodology and technology to provide tools for both PhD candidates and researchers. The fundamental parts of the ecosystem are the PhD portal (http://knowledgesociety.usal.es) and a set of social instruments, such as SlideShare to share presentations (http://www.slideshare.net/knowedgesociety) or a YouTube channel to share seminars and meetings (http://youtube.com/knowledgesocietyphd).

3 Materials and Methods

3.1 Dashboard Meta-model

Meta models are the starting point of the Model-Driven Development paradigm [13]. These artifacts allow the high-level definition of entities and relationships, without focusing on the technical details of the domain.

In this case, a dashboard meta-model has been developed to capture the abstract characteristics that define dashboards. As can be seen in Fig. 1, the user is also part of the meta-model because they are the drivers of the design process and the final consumers of the information displayed through these tools, so their characteristics must be accounted for to deliver a properly designed dashboard.

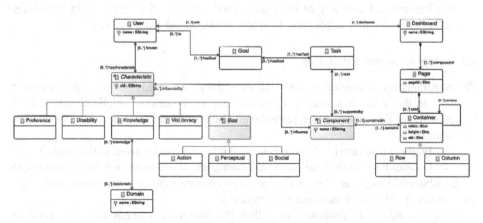

Fig. 1. Overview of the dashboard meta-model. The component definition has been omitted for legibility reasons, but it can be consulted at [20].

The entire meta-model design process is out of the scope of this paper, but it can be consulted in [15, 16].

3.2   Feature Model

The goal of software product lines (SPLs) is to derive final products from different core assets and software components [11, 12], and to allow the adaptation of products to match specific requirements without consuming significant time and resources.

This paradigm has two main phases: the domain engineering phase and the application engineering phase. The mentioned core assets are developed during the first phase by identifying commonalities and variability points within the products' domain. This phase supports the implementation of base components that hold the common logic of the domain as well as the variability points.

Variability points are sections of the logic that can be modified, parameterized, or configured to change the functionality of the products during the second phase (application engineering phase). In SPLs, products' functionalities are seen as features. Stakeholders can select different features for their products to be injected in the base logic, thus obtaining personalized systems that fit their specific requirements. These personalized products are built by reusing and assembling the core assets developed during the domain engineering phase, which reduces the time-to-market of tailored software systems as well as their development efforts.

The features of software product lines can be specified by different means. One of the most popular methods to identify and arrange SPL features are feature models [21]. Feature models are useful for documentation purposes, but also essential artifacts for guiding the development process of the product line. These models provide a skeleton for designing the core assets and for materializing the variability points at code level.

In this specific domain (i.e., the dashboards domain), the feature model captures the dashboards' visualizations' low-level characteristics, corresponding with visual encodings, visual marks, etc. [8]. Figure 2 shows an excerpt from the feature model employed to design the core assets for the dashboards product line.

The hierarchical structure of the feature model enables the definition of high-level characteristics and their refinement to reach finer-grained features [22].

3.3   Requirements Elicitation

The requirements elicitation phase is an essential phase in any software development process. In this case, it is crucial to understand the context of application (the PhD Programme on Education in the Knowledge Society) to generate adapted information dashboards.

Firstly, there is a variety of profiles to take into account involved in the programme: from PhD candidates to their advisors and managers. These users will be the drivers of the dashboards' design and generation processes because the outcome must match their information needs and functional requirements.

A questionnaire is proposed to gather the information needs of each involved profile. However, to ensure the proper design of this questionnaire, an initial interview was conducted. The goal of this interview was to collect information regarding the business processes of the PhD programme, as well as the available data and their structure.

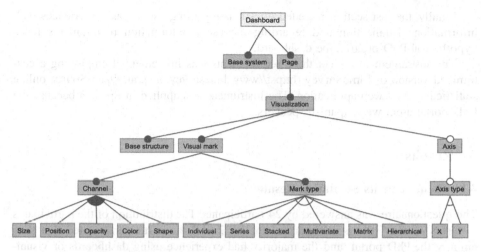

Fig. 2. Simplified feature model of a dashboards product line.

A few questions were asked to a member of the PhD programme's quality committee to understand which data could be displayed in a potential information dashboard. The PhD portal gathers information about the milestones achieved by the members of the PhD programme. For example, data about publications, research visits, conferences, reports, awards, seminars, patents, etc., are collected in a semi-structured way.

On the other hand, the PhD programme on Education in the Knowledge Society has a series of minimum requirements to be able to defend the thesis or to obtain some recognitions like an international PhD mention. These requirements are covered in [23].

In addition, other aspects of the PhD candidates are stored, such as their academic year, associated research lines, PhD advisors, scholarships, contracts, PhD modality (full- or part-time), etc.

Finally, the users of the portal can have different roles: students (including current PhD candidates or post-doctoral students), PhD advisors, and managers.

This interview supported not only the development of the questionnaire, but also the comprehension of the variables available to be displayed in potential PhD information dashboards.

3.4   Instrumentation

Once the interview was carried out, an instrument to collect information regarding the users' information requirements was designed. First, some demographic variables are collected to contextualize the sample: age, gender, and birthplace.

The next section focuses on the collection of the user situation within the PhD programme: role, research lines, PhD modality, and academic year (in the case of PhD students) and the number of PhD thesis being directed (in the case of PhD advisors). Questions regarding the usage of the PhD portal were also included in this section to understand how users employ this platform.

Finally, the last section included questions regarding users' past experiences with information visualization and regarding the users' information requirements for a hypothetical PhD programme dashboard.

The instrument to collect these requirements was implemented employing a customized version of LimeSurvey (https://www.limesurvey.org), an Open Source online statistical survey web application. The instrument was applied in Spanish because the PhD portal users were Spanish speakers.

4   Results

4.1   Requirements Elicitation Results

The questionnaire was answered by 24 participants. The distribution of the participants in terms of their role is summarized in Fig. 2. All the participants stated that they employ the PhD portal, and the majority had experience using dashboards or visualization tools (70.83%).

Regarding how the PhD students save their milestones, an interesting pattern of answers were found. The information regarding their milestones is scattered among different research profiles (Mendeley, Scopus, WoS, Google Scholar, etc.) and/or the PhD programme portal, in personal Microsoft Word files created by themselves and even some students state that they don't save their milestones at all. These aspects are summarized in Fig. 3.

Finally, the collected requirements for a hypothetical personal dashboard within the PhD programme portal suggest that users have different information goals. On the one hand, PhD advisors were very interested in obtaining information regarding the publications (count, typology, and the number of citations), conference attendance/participation, and research profiles of their PhD students (Fig. 4).

In relation to managers or academic committee members, in addition to the information related to the progress of all the PhD students and their deadlines, some pointed out as an information requirement the number of PhD students associated to each research group, as well as metrics regarding the interactions between their PhD advisors. Another participant asked for information about publications by research line and the number of publications during specific periods of time.

As will be discussed, the most diverse requirements were found within the PhD students' answers. The majority share the necessity of displaying information related to their PhD progress and their achieved milestones (publications, conferences, seminars, etc.), but other requirements were also mentioned:

- Remaining required activities.
- Recommended activities vs. required activities.
- Comparison with other PhD students.
- Distribution of activities/milestones (publications, seminars, etc.) by type.
- Percentage of progress based on the requirements of the PhD programme.
- Status of each research milestone uploaded to the portal.
- Deadlines and enrollment dates.

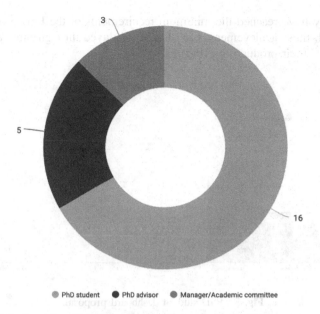

Fig. 3. Distribution of participants regarding their role in the PhD programme (n = 24).

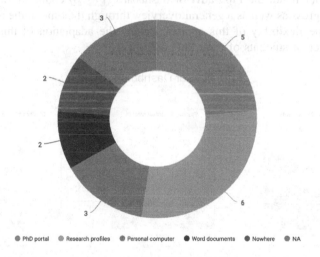

Fig. 4. Distribution of the methods employed by PhD students to save their progress/milestones obtained within the PhD programme (n = 16; some participants pointed out more than one method to save their milestones).

4.2 Dashboard Generation Results

Based on some of the requirements identified through the questionnaire, three dashboard prototypes for each major PhD role have been generated by using the software product line paradigm. These proposals can be seen in Figs. 5, 6, and 7.

For example, based on the collected requirements, a student dashboard might be composed of views that show their achievements classified by type and reference marks to show if they have reached the minimum requirements of the PhD programme. On the other hand, these achievements can also be displayed through time, allowing students to inspect their productivity (Fig. 5).

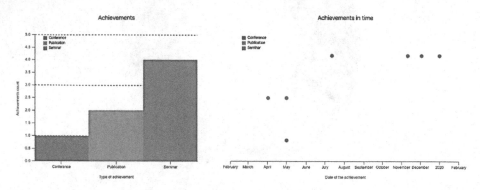

Fig. 5. PhD student dashboard proposal.

On the other hand, the PhD advisor dashboard (Fig. 6) could show each student individual progress as well as a general overview through the time of the advisors' PhD candidates. The flexibility of this approach allow the adaptation of this view to the specific number of students of each PhD advisor.

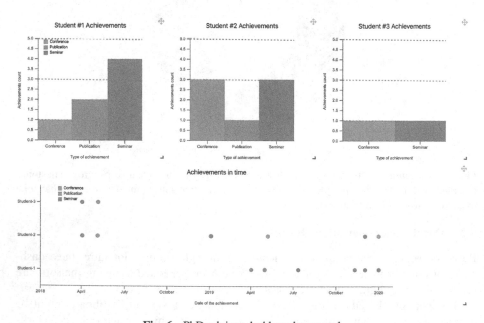

Fig. 6. PhD advisor dashboard proposal.

Finally, the PhD manager dashboard (Fig. 7) could hold information regarding the workload (in terms of directed thesis) of each PhD advisor and research group involved in the programme. Also, following the collected requirements, this dashboard can also have a view displaying the achieved publications through time by research line.

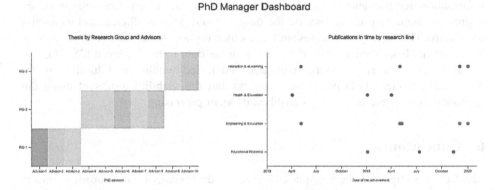

Fig. 7. PhD manager dashboard proposal.

5   Discussion

The questionnaire yielded very interesting results and confirmed that dashboards must take into account different user roles and user requirements. There is not a "universal" dashboard that fits for any user; that is why dashboards should be tailored depending on their context.

Three main roles have been identified within the PhD programme through an interview with a member of the quality committee: PhD students, PhD advisors, and the programme managers. The questionnaire asked different questions depending on the role of the participant. While students asked for information about their progress or publications, PhD advisors wanted to gain insights regarding their own students' process. On the other hand, managers mostly asked to gain overall insights regarding all the students enrolled in the programme.

The greatest diversity of requirements was found among PhD students; although these users share the same role, significant differences were encountered regarding their information goals. In this work, a single dashboard proposal was presented for PhD students, but different dashboards could be developed for this role; for example, one user asked for comparisons with other students' progress.

While this could be a beneficial feature for this user, it could be counterproductive for other users (for example, showing their progress compared with other pre-doctoral users could have a negative impact on some students' motivation [24]).

The three dashboards were generated using a DSL based on the feature tree and meta-model presented in Sect. 3. This approach not only improved the development time of the dashboards, as the tools were automatically generated through code templates (the core assets of the SPL, in this case) but also improved the requirements management of the users.

A requirement file using the DSL could be maintained for each user, supporting fine-grained management of requirements and controlling changes in a straightforward manner.

The main effort, however, is still in the requirements' elicitation process. If users' information requirements are taken for granted or are given low relevance, the approach would be useless, because the output would be an inefficient and ineffective dashboard. That is why current research is focused on how to automatize or infer users' requirements from their characteristics or from the data to be displayed [25, 26].

This approach is yet to be integrated and tested within the Education in the Knowledge Society PhD programme context, but the viability results of using this approach to generate information dashboards seem promising.

6   Conclusions

The SPL paradigm has been applied to generate dashboards in an educative context; specifically, in a PhD programme context.

The diversity of information goals and requirements ask for flexible design and development process to build these tools in order to accelerate the delivery time and leverage the information displayed.

The application of the SPL paradigm requires initial efforts to identify the domain's abstract features and to develop the different core assets, but relying on these artifacts have subsequently reduced the required time to develop tailored dashboards.

The presented dashboard generative process has been driven by the PhD programme involved actors and their information goals, which were gathered through an online questionnaire.

Future research lines will involve the improvement of the dashboard product line to automatize the generation process, as well as in-depth user testing to validate the utility of this approach to integrate tailored dashboards in learning contexts.

Acknowledgments. This research work has been supported by the Spanish *Ministry of Education and Vocational Training* under an FPU fellowship (FPU17/03276). This work has been partially funded by the Spanish Government Ministry of Economy and Competitiveness throughout the DEFINES project (Ref. TIN2016-80172-R).

References

1. Zeleny, M.: Management support systems: Towards integrated knowledge management. Hum. Syst. Manag. **7**, 59–70 (1987)
2. Patil, D., Mason, H.: Data Driven. O'Reilly Media Inc., Sebastopol (2015)
3. Keim, D., Andrienko, G., Fekete, J.-D., Görg, C., Kohlhammer, J., Melançon, G.: Visual analytics: definition, process, and challenges. In: Kerren, A., Stasko, J.T., Fekete, J.-D., North, C. (eds.) Information Visualization. LNCS, vol. 4950, pp. 154–175. Springer, Heidelberg (2008). https://doi.org/10.1007/978-3-540-70956-5_7

4. Keim, D., Kohlhammer, J., Ellis, G., Mansmann, F.: Mastering the Information Age Solving Problems with Visual Analytics. Eurographics Association, Goslar (2010)
5. Tufte, E., Graves-Morris, P.: The Visual Display of Quantitative Information. Graphics Press, Cheshire (1983, 2014)
6. Ware, C.: Information Visualization: Perception for Design. Elsevier, Amsterdam (2012)
7. Few, S.: Information Dashboard Design. O'Reilly Media Inc., Sebastopol (2006)
8. Munzner, T.: Visualization Analysis and Design. AK Peters/CRC Press, Boca Raton (2014)
9. Sarikaya, A., Correll, M., Bartram, L., Tory, M., Fisher, D.: What do we talk about when we talk about dashboards? IEEE Trans. Vis. Comput. Graph. **25**, 682–692 (2018)
10. Vázquez-Ingelmo, A., García-Peñalvo, F.J., Therón, R.: Information dashboards and tailoring capabilities - a systematic literature review. IEEE Access **7**, 109673–109688 (2019)
11. Clements, P., Northrop, L.: Software Product Lines. Addison-Wesley, Boston (2002)
12. Gomaa, H.: Designing Software Product Lines with UML: From Use Cases to Pattern-Based Software Architectures. Addison Wesley Longman Publishing Co., Inc., Boston (2004)
13. Kleppe, A.G., Warmer, J., Bast, W.: MDA Explained. The Model Driven Architecture: Practice and Promise. Addison-Wesley Longman Publishing Co., Inc., Boston (2003)
14. Vázquez-Ingelmo, A., García-Holgado, A., García-Peñalvo, F.J., Therón, R.: Dashboard meta-model for knowledge management in technological ecosystem: a case study in healthcare. In: UCAmI 2019. MDPI (2019)
15. Vázquez-Ingelmo, A., García-Peñalvo, F.J., Therón, R.: Capturing high-level requirements of information dashboards' components through meta-modeling. In: 7th International Conference on Technological Ecosystems for Enhancing Multiculturality (TEEM 2019), León, Spain (2019)
16. Vázquez-Ingelmo, A., García-Peñalvo, F.J., Therón, R., Conde González, M.Á.: Extending a dashboard meta-model to account for users' characteristics and goals for enhancing personalization. In: Learning Analytics Summer Institute (LASI) Spain 2019, Vigo, Spain (2019)
17. García-Holgado, A., García-Peñalvo, F.J., Rodríguez Conde, M.J.: Definition of a technological ecosystem for scientific knowledge management in a PhD programme. In: Proceedings of the Third International Conference on Technological Ecosystems for Enhancing Multiculturality (TEEM 2015), Porto, Portugal, 7–9 October 2015, pp. 695–700. ACM, New York (2015)
18. García-Peñalvo, F.J.: Engineering contributions to a knowledge society multicultural perspective. IEEE Revista Iberoamericana de Tecnologías del Aprendizaje (IEEE RITA) **10**, 17–18 (2015)
19. García-Peñalvo, F.J., Rodríguez-Conde, M.J., Therón, R., García-Holgado, A., Martínez-Abad, F., Benito-Santos, A.: Grupo GRIAL. IE Comunicaciones. Revista Iberoamericana de Informática Educativa, 33–48 (2019)
20. Vázquez-Ingelmo, A., García-Holgado, A., García-Peñalvo, F.J., Therón, R.: Ecore version of the metamodel for information dashboards (2019). https://doi.org/10.5281/zenodo.3561320
21. Kang, K.C., Cohen, S.G., Hess, J.A., Novak, W.E., Peterson, A.S.: Feature-oriented domain analysis (FODA) feasibility study. Carnegie-Mellon University, Software Engineering Institute (1990)
22. Vázquez-Ingelmo, A., García-Peñalvo, F.J., Therón, R.: Addressing fine-grained variability in user-centered software product lines: a case study on dashboards. In: Rocha, Á., Adeli, H., Reis, L.P., Costanzo, S. (eds.) WorldCIST'19 2019. AISC, vol. 930, pp. 855–864. Springer, Cham (2019). https://doi.org/10.1007/978-3-030-16181-1_80
23. Programa de Doctorado Formación en la Sociedad del Conocimiento. https://www.slideshare.net/knowedgesociety/kickoff-phd-programme-20192020

24. Teasley, S.D.: Student facing dashboards: One size fits all? Technol. Knowl. Learn. **22**, 377–384 (2017). https://doi.org/10.1007/s10758-017-9314-3
25. Hu, K., Bakker, M.A., Li, S., Kraska, T., Hidalgo, C.: VizML: a machine learning approach to visualization recommendation. In: Proceedings of the 2019 CHI Conference on Human Factors in Computing Systems, p. 128. ACM (2019)
26. Dibia, V., Demiralp, Ç.: Data2Vis: automatic generation of data visualizations using sequence to sequence recurrent neural networks. IEEE Comput. Graph. Appl. **39**, 33–46 (2019)

Language Learning and Teaching

Learning Analytics and Spelling Acquisition in German – The Path to Individualization in Learning

Markus Ebner[2]([⊠]) [iD], Konstanze Edtstadler[1], and Martin Ebner[2] [iD]

[1] Institute of Early Childhood and Primary Teacher Education,
University College of Teacher Education Styria,
Hasnerplatz 12, 8010 Graz, Austria
Konstanze.Edtstadler@phst.at
[2] Department Educational Technology, Graz University of Technology,
Münzgrabenstraße 36/I, 8020 Graz, Austria
markus.ebner@tugraz.at

Abstract. This paper shows how Learning Analytic Methods are combined with German orthography in the IDeRBlog-project (www.iderblog.eu). After a short introduction to the core of the platform – the intelligent dictionary – we focus on the presentation and evaluation of a new training format. The aim of this format is, that pupils can train misspelled words individually in a motivating and didactic meaningful setting. As a usability test was run with twenty one third graders, we are able to present the results of this evaluation.

Keywords: Learning Analytics · German orthography · Qualitative analysis of misspellings · Technology enhanced learning · Educational media · K-12 education

1 Introduction

During the last years IDeRBlog was used in many schools in German speaking countries as well as schools who offer German language courses in foreign countries, therefore we were able to gain a better insight in the acquisition of German orthography [4–7]. Due to the success of the project a follow up project called IDeRBlog ii was started with the following goals:

1. further implementation in schools in order that more students can benefit from the platform;
2. further individualization of the training material to foster the orthographic competence;
3. extension of the number of words, which give a specific feedback for correcting the mistakes (see following chapters).

The purpose of this paper is to show, how the individualization is achieved and how the extension of the words is accomplished.

© Springer Nature Switzerland AG 2020
P. Zaphiris and A. Ioannou (Eds.): HCII 2020, LNCS 12205, pp. 317–325, 2020.
https://doi.org/10.1007/978-3-030-50513-4_24

1.1   The IDeRBlog-Platform

German orthography is known to be quite difficult to master, especially for primary-and secondary-school pupils. Therefore, we try to make writing and spelling activities as attractive and useful as possible. Our system is an attempt to bridge Learning Analytics (LA) research and daily writing activities for pupils aged from eight years on by offering a web-based platform with various functions, some of them we will present later in this paper. The core system is designed to support the acquisition of German orthography during the text-writing process - that is focused on writing blog entries - as well as with individualized material when focusing exclusively on problematic orthographic areas.

For assisting children during the text writing process, the developed web-based platform for German-speaking users offers an "intelligent dictionary" [5]. This is the attempt to combine spelling and LA. The intelligent dictionary works on different levels:

a) During the text-writing process the intelligent dictionary provides specific feedback that encourages pupils to think about the spelling and to correct it when an orthographic mistake occurred. In contrast to a conventional auto correction system, which only provides information that the word is (probable) wrong and may suggest the correct word or a list of possibly words, our systems helps to gain deeper insights in the system of German orthography and its acquisition.

b) After and besides the text-writing process the intelligent dictionary supports teachers and students to train problematic orthographic areas specifically. To do so, teachers and pupils are provided with a qualitative analysis based on the occurred orthographic mistakes identified by the intelligent dictionary. Consequently, teachers and students can focus on specific explanations and selected (predefined) online and offline exercises, which are provided by the system.

c) For an even more specific training of the German orthography the new approach is to develop new training formats, which are even more specific. In contrast to predefined exercises, the new training formats should be generated automatically based on the occurred mistakes. For example, an exercise is developed that trains exactly the occurred misspelled words in combination with a meaningful didactic approach.

2   Individualization

2.1   Extension of the Intelligent Dictionary

In order to improve the platform, we need to extend the intelligent dictionary. Selecting the words for this extension is quite hard. Therefore, we decided on the following strategies for the word selection:

The first strategy is, that the texts written between October 2016 and October 2019 are analyzed in order to select the most frequently used words either spelled correctly or incorrectly. Consequently, they are implemented in the intelligent dictionary by deriving all their word forms and the mistakes corresponding to the categories.

The other strategy is that teachers could suggest words that should be implemented in the intelligent dictionary. For this purpose, an interface was designed that should encourage teachers to participate in order to gain a more individualized intelligent dictionary (see Fig. 1). If teachers discover important words while correcting/reading blog entries that have not yet been categorized, they can suggest them for inclusion easily. They just need to click on the encountered word that is used by a pupil in a blog entry and tick the box: "I think that this word is important and suggest it for inclusion in the intelligent dictionary." Furthermore, they can – but need not to – fill in the form by mentioning the intended word for a misspelled word and suggest the category of the mistake.

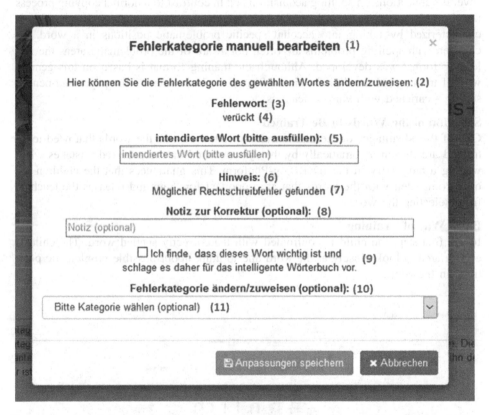

Fig. 1. Interface for suggesting words to be included in the intelligent dictionary. Translation: (1) Editing the Category of Mistakes; (2) Here you can edit the category of a selected word, (3) Misspelled word:, (4) crazy; (5) Intended word (please fill in); (6) Feedback; (7) Possible mistake encountered; (8) Note for correcting (optional); (9) I think that this word is important and suggest it for inclusion in the in the intelligent dictionary.; (10) Editing the category (optional); (11) Please choose a category (optional)

2.2 A New Training Format

When training the German orthography, it is necessary to consider two approaches: One is to focus on problematic orthographic areas based on the qualitative analysis of mistakes. This was the focus of the first IDeRBlog-project (see chapter The IDeRBlog-Platform). The other one is to train the specific words that are spelled incorrectly. This is a more individualized way that will be implemented in the second IDeRBlog-project.

Example of a New Training Format: Incorrectly Spelled Words

In order to train incorrectly spelled words, a specific didactic approach is necessary. For example, it is not enough to just read the words or write them several times. Rather the words should be trained by applying the strategy of conscious copying as described in several publications on spelling acquisition [1]: In contrast to a normal copying process that is probably based on a letter by letter approach a conscious copying process is characterized by taking into account specific problematic positions in a word. As children with spelling problems are often not aware of the problematic areas the following format was developed. Although the training format is based on this general way of training [1] the digital training format is - in contrast to the paper-and-pencil-setting - enriched with various features.

Selection of the Words to Be Trained

One of the advantages of the digital training format is, that the words that need to be trained are chosen automatically by the system based on the occurred mistakes when writing a blog entry in the IDeRBlog-Platform. This guarantees that the children are only confronted with the words that are important for them and releases the teachers from selecting the words.

Basic Way of Training

In the first step, the child is confronted with the correctly spelled word. The child is encouraged to look closely at the word and to think about possible problematic positions in the word.

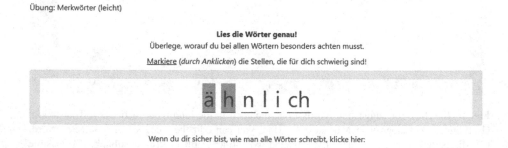

Fig. 2. Screenshot of the first step for the word ähnlich 'similar' [2]

As can be seen in the screenshot (see Fig. 2) the child is led trough the by the orders. On top the orders say: "Read these words closely! Think about problematic orthographic positions. Highlight the positions that seem difficult to you!"

After highlighting the possible positions, the order says:" In case you are sure how to spell these words, click here!"

In the second step (see Fig. 3), the child should write the word by heart without seeing the correctly spelled word. This prevents a letter-by-letter-copying approach. The child is encouraged to remember how the possibly problematic position of the word are spelled correctly. As soon as the child thinks, that she/he is ready for writing she/he can press the button "hide word" in order to get to step three.

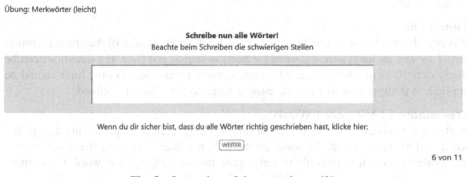

Fig. 3. Screenshot of the second step [?]

In the third step, the child gets a feedback on the spelling attempt in contrast to the correct spelling. In case, the spelling attempt is correct, the spelled word and the target word appear in green. In case the spelling attempt is not correct, the incorrectly spelled word appears in red and the target word in green (see Fig. 4). Consequently, the child is encouraged to look again closely at the correctly presented word.

Fig. 4. Screenshot of the third step in case the word is spelled incorrectly (Color figure online)

Possible Ways of Modification

In order to create more attractive exercises that also fit better the needs of different children, we offer several ways to modify the format. The settings can be changed by the teacher for each pupil individually. The possibilities for changing the settings are:

Number of presented words: Up to five words can be presented at the same time in the first step. We suggest the following settings: Easy level: one word; medium level: three words; most difficult level: five words;

Marking of Problematic Positions

In order to lead the children to a conscious approach, they can mark specific positions of the word by clicking on them in the first step. Consequently, they appear highlighted in red. In case, children do not want or need not to highlight anything, this function can be deactivated.

Time Limit

It is possible to choose a time limit as well as for the presentation of the correct word in step 1 as well as for typing the word by heart in step 2. For both, the time limit can be freely defined in number of seconds. Zero seconds means that no time limit should be applied. It is suggested that for the easiest level no time limit is defined.

Presentation of Misspelled Words

In step 3 the children get a feedback on their spelling attempt by presenting the spelled word and the target word. As some teachers do not like to confront the children with misspelled words, it is possible to only show the correctly spelled word. Concerning the presentation of the spelled and the intended word, it is also possible to define a time limit. Our suggestion is to not give a time limit.

3   Evaluation of the Training Format

According to [9] the interaction with a game by the user requires a constant cycle of hypothesis formulations, testing and reworking during the play. This requires instant feedback while the game is running. E.g. to easy games are not engaging the learning for a long time. The game must adjust itself to the skillset of the player.

To ensure a good quality of the game we conducted a field test to detect possible problems or bad game design before the official release, which we will describe in the following section.

Further, using the Training Formats on PC or iPads comes also with some points to keep in mind as a teacher [10]:

- check if the existing infrastructure is able to support you in a meaningful way,
- make sure that the login procedure is understood by everyone,
- let them play with the app so that they can get familiar with it,
- take your time to assist the children
- children are open minded – assist them in their creativity
- provide them with immediate feedback when they have done the exercises
- competition is not the priority; collaboration should be the goal.

During our field test, we were able to further train the teachers to become better at using digital exercises as support in teaching.

3.1 Method

In a first step the training format was designed in an interdisciplinary team consisting of professionals of the area of language education (Konstanze Edtstadler and Elisabeth Herunter from University College of Teacher Education Styria, Graz, Austria) and media informatics (Markus Ebner, Marko Burazer and Markus Friedl from Graz University of Technology, Graz, Austria). This interdisciplinary work is crucial in order to offer training formats that are not only database-based and online, but also didactically valuable formats following the research on the acquisition of German orthography [2, 3]. In a second step, the training format was programmed in a pre-version. Before this pre-version can get online, it is necessary to conduct a usability test.

This usability test was conducted in June 2019 with twentyone 3rd graders (eleven girls and ten boys) of the school that is part of the Teacher Training College Styria. The children were supervised by their class teacher and the group of researchers assisted the children during the whole usability test (90 min).

As more training formats than the described one were tested on this day, this format was run on four computers in two different difficulty levels. The easy level was prepared with one word without time limitation for reading and writing and the possibility to highlight problematic positions. The harder level was prepared with two words at the same time, 20 s time for reading and 40 s time for writing. Of course, the time limit could be exceeded [2].

The children received for each training format a questionnaire with four statements in German [2]:

1. I knew what the task was. (Ich wusste, was die Aufgabenstellung war.)
2. I could solve the task myself. (Ich konnte die Aufgabe selber lösen.)
3. It was fun to practice. (Es hat mir Spaß gemacht zu üben.)
4. I also want to do the exercise at home. (Ich möchte die Übung auch zuhause machen.)

For these statements one of five smileys needs to be chosen, ranging from 1 (very happy) to 5 (very sad). Therefore, the lower the average level the better the feedback.

4 Results

All twentyone pupils gave feedback, although the number of questionnaires is varying because sometimes two children filled out one questionnaire together or decided on the same feedback on two different feedback sheets [2, 8] (Table 1).

Table 1. Results of the feedback on the two different difficulty levels [8]

Statement	Easy level	Hard level
I knew what the task was	1.41	1.74
I could solve the task myself	1.41	1.53
It was fun to practice	1.35	1.89
I also want to do the exercise at home	1.71	2.47

4.1   Interpretation

It is clear that the easier and the harder level differ from each other. In fact, the harder level seems to be more exhausting and more error-prone. This is also derivable from the log-data. Concerning the easy mode out of 17 sessions 7 were conducted without any mistake whereas in the hard mode out of 24 sessions no one was error-free.

4.2   Further Findings

This training formats offers a number of possibilities for analyzing the way children encounter spelling problems. As children can highlight problematic positions of the word to spelled, we can analyze the most problematic positions of a word from the learner's perspective. For example, in the word "ähnlich" (which means similar) the <h> was marked in five sessions, the <ch>in three sessions and the <ä> in two sessions.

Looking at the spelling attempts after presenting the word for memorizing we can see the following mistakes in the easy mode: *ahndlieh, ahnlicheres, anhlich (2x), anlich* and the following mistaktes in the harder mode *nothing (7), ählich, ähnlichere, Än, änhlich, Änlhich, Änli, änlich (4), Blege* (cf. Burazer Masterarbeit). In contrast to easy mode children do not only make more mistakes in total but also show a greater variety of spelling mistakes. The "nothing" answers point in the direction that either the working memory was overwhelmed or that the time for typing was running out.

5   Outlook

Currently we are working to develop additional training formats and to extend the intelligent dictionary by analyzing the texts written so far. To speak frankly, our system will not be able to cover all the words pupils use when writing blog-entries, but we are able to show that the combination of Learning-Analytic-Methods and German orthography is possible and fruitful. Furthermore, we offer a lot of trainings for teachers – in class and online – in order to disseminate the project.

Further, we are working on the extension of the intelligent dictionary by analyzing the texts written so far. Concerning the possibility to suggest words for the intelligent dictionary the results so far are quite disappointing as teachers do not make use of this possibility, although the feature has been promoted via newsletters and webinars. Since the activation of the feature in October 2016 only 83 suggestions have been made.

Acknowledgements. The IDeRBlog-project and the IDeRBlog-ii project are funded by the European Commission in the framework of Erasmus+ (IDeRBlog: VG-SPS-SL-14-001616-3, 2014-2017; IDeRBlog-ii: VG-IN-SL-18-36-047317, 2018-2021).

Project-team of IDeRBlog-ii: Germany: LPM Saarland (M. Gros = coordinator, N. Steinhauer); Gebundene Ganztagsschule Dellengarten (S. Pfeifer, J. Gregori); Austria: PH Steiermark (K. Edtstadler, E. Herunter); TU Graz (M. Ebner, M. Ebner); Belgium: Gemeindeschule Raeren (A. Huppertz, V. Kistemann).

References

1. Sommer-Stumpenhorst, N.: Lese-und Rechtschreibschwierigkeiten: vorbeugen und überwinden. In: Cornelsen Scriptor (1991)
2. Burazer, M., Ebner, M., Ebner, M.: Implementation of interactive learning objects for German language acquisition in primary school based on learning analytics measurements. In Proceedings of EdMedia: World Conference on Educational Media and Technology, Amsterdam (2020, in print)
3. Friedl, M., Ebner, M., Ebner, M.: Mobile learning applications for android und iOS for German language acquisition based on learning analytics measurements. Int. J. Learn. Anal. Artif. Intell. Educ. (2020, in print)
4. Ebner, M., Edtstadler, K., Ebner, M.: Learning analytics and spelling acquisition in german – proof of concept. In: Zaphiris, P., Ioannou, A. (eds.) LCT 2017. LNCS, vol. 10296, pp. 257–268. Springer, Cham (2017). https://doi.org/10.1007/978-3-319-58515-4_20
5. Edtstadler, K., Ebner, M., Ebner, M.: Improved German spelling acquisition through learning analytics. eLearn. Pap. **45**, 17–28 (2015)
6. Edtstadler, K., et al.: Analysis of Misspellings in German Orthography in Grade 3 to 6. Postersitzung präsentiert bei European Dyslexia Autumn Seminar, München, Deutschland (2018)
7. Ebner, M., Edtstadler, K., Ebner, M.: Tutoring writing spelling skills within a web-based platform for children. Univ. Access Inf. Soc. **17**, 305–323 (2017). https://doi.org/10.1007/s10209-017-0564-6
8. Burazer, M.: Implementation of interactive learning objects for German language acquisition in primary school based on learning analytics measurements. Master thesis at Graz University of Technology, Graz, Austria (2019)
9. Van Eck, R.: Digital game-based learning: It's not just the digital natives who are restless. EDUC. Rev. **41**(2), 16 (2006)
10. Ebner, M., Schönhart, J., Schön, S.: Experiences With iPads in Primary School. Profesorado, revista de currículum y formación del profesorado **18**(3), 161–173 (2014)

Building Student Interactions Outside the Classroom: Utilizing a Web-Based Application in a University Flipped Learning Course for EFL Learners

Yasushige Ishikawa[1]([✉]) [iD], Yasushi Tsubota[2] [iD],
Takatoyo Umemoto[1] [iD], Masayuki Murakami[3] [iD],
Mutsumi Kondo[1] [iD], Ayako Suto[4] [iD], and Koichi Nishiyama[5] [iD]

[1] Kyoto University of Foreign Studies, Kyoto, Japan
{y_ishikawa, t_umemoto, mu_kondo}@kufs.ac.jp
[2] Kyoto Institute of Technology, Kyoto, Japan
tsubota-yasushi@kit.ac.jp
[3] Osaka University, Toyonaka, Japan
masayuki@murakami-lab.org
[4] Uchida Yoko Co., Ltd., Tokyo, Japan
a.suto@uchida.co.jp
[5] Infinitec Co., Ltd., Tokyo, Japan
nishiyama-koichi@infinitec.co.jp

Abstract. This research project developed a web-based application to facilitate out-of-class collaborative learning; the aim was to transform a student culture that facilitated very little independent study outside the classroom and classroom learning that treated students mainly as passive participants. Additionally, an innovative flipped learning course utilizing this web-based application was implemented in order to integrate online and in-class collaborative learning. We hypothesized that students' online collaborative learning could be activated and sustained throughout the semester. Based on pre- and post-questionnaire results, it was apparent that the students actively participated in discussions outside class (Active Learning (AL): $p < .10$, AL externalization: $p < .05$). Furthermore, Spearman's rank correlation analysis for the frequency of category appearances and the indicators for social and cognitive presences, which was guided by the Community of Inquiry framework with regard to out-of-class student interactions and the pre- and post-questionnaire gains revealed that the cognitive presence was strongly correlated with the pre- and post-questionnaire gains ($p < .001$). These results indicate that the web-based application developed in this study supported out-of-class student collaboration.

Keywords: Out-of-class student interactions · A web-based application · Flipped learning

© Springer Nature Switzerland AG 2020
P. Zaphiris and A. Ioannou (Eds.): HCII 2020, LNCS 12205, pp. 326–338, 2020.
https://doi.org/10.1007/978-3-030-50513-4_25

1 Introduction

1.1 Defining Flipped Learning

Blended learning (BL) is "the integration of face-to-face and online learning activities" (p. 8) [1]; it aims to enhance "engagement through the innovative adoption of purposeful online activities" (p. 9) [1].

Teachers interested in BL may seek ways to utilize rapidly expanding easily accessible online learning resources. Technology usage aimed at connecting learning environments inside and outside the classroom has recently received a boost thanks to two educational resource-related developments: 1) the availability of free online access to university courses via software such as iTunes U and websites such as Coursera (https://www.coursera.org/) and 2) the sophisticated communication capabilities offered by mobile devices such as smartphones and tablet computers.

The flipped learning (FL) approach is a promising response to these developments, especially in combination with the BL teaching methodology [2, 3], which has reversed conventional classroom learning patterns. Hamdan, McKnight, McKnight, and Arfstrom [4] defined the differences between FL practices and distance learning and BL courses as follows: if the use of computers and online content does not alter conventional direct instruction patterns in teacher-centered classrooms, the learning method in question is not FL. In FL courses, students are provided with out-of-class online learning materials that are usually presented in class by the teacher. Students are instructed to utilize class time to seek teachers' advice and to help each other as they complete tasks that are usually undertaken as out-of-class assignments [5].

Yarbro, Arfstrom, McKnight, and McKnight [6] define FL as "a pedagogical approach in which direct instruction moves from the group learning space to the individual learning space, and the resulting group space is transformed into a dynamic, interactive learning environment where the educator guides students as they apply concepts and engage creatively in the subject matter" (p. 5). FL allows teachers to respond to individual differences in students' comprehension of course content, thus facilitating active collaborative learning during class time. At the same time, students receive opportunities to find and utilize learning methods and materials that suit their own learning styles [5]; furthermore, they are encouraged to engage in project-based learning activities such as small-group discussions and problem-solving activities. Thus, FL has the highest chances of success in small-sized classes that facilitate manageable peer interaction and allow teachers to take on coaching roles.

In this paper, BL is defined as an integration between in-class and out-of-class online collaborative learning tasks that aims to achieve the desired learning outcomes. FL is defined as a BL-type interaction where students in small groups engage in out-of-class collaborative learning tasks by using a web-based application, which was developed to assist in-class collaborative learning activities.

1.2   Flipped Learning Within an EFL Environment

Recent encouraging studies have indicated that the application of the Jones Model of Learning [7] to FL approaches in language teaching should be further investigated through classroom-based action research methodologies. The Jones Model of Learning can serve as a guideline for constructing experimental FL collaborative-learning modules in English as a foreign language (EFL) classes provided that it is reasonable to assume that the learners' creation of new knowledge with regard to language through collaborative peer interaction will lead them to make connections with previous knowledge; this could be beneficial because, ideally, interaction with peers can accommodate different learning styles more effectively than a one-size-fits-all approach [7].

Stuntz [2] reported that students participating in an FL Computer-Assisted Language Learning EFL course required considerable instruction and practice while using communication and study media, such as Gmail and Google Docs, to complete out-of-class assignments. Students who improved their application usage skills effectively used class time to discuss out-of-class learning tasks with both peers and instructors. Thus, such collaborations can result in higher-quality task performance. Learning Management System platforms can help students accomplish out-of-class online collaborative activities [8]. Sharing FL course learning-task products with the class and members of a broader community via YouTube can increase students' satisfaction, which, in turn, enhances their learning motivation [9]. Engaging EFL students in FL video conferences with students from other countries can help to achieve interactive communication with the international community [10]. FL courses offer many authentic language-use opportunities of this nature, which could decrease students' in-class language use anxiety [11]. Hughes [12], who compared a flipped and a traditional model in an Advanced Presentation and Discussion course at a university in South Korea, reported that students taught under the traditional model achieved better objective assessment outcomes compared to those who were taught under the flipped model, thus suggesting that teachers should consider an effective instructional design to achieve desired learning outcomes when creating a course.

1.3   Collaborative Learning

Collaborative learning has been defined as a communication situation where expected interactions between people create learning mechanisms; thus, it needs to be ensured that such expected interactions do take place [13]. Dillenbourg [13] discussed studies that focused on small-scale groups—for example, two to five people working together for about an hour, which is similar to the group size and work activities within typical foreign language classrooms. Often, problem-solving activities that depend on collaboration in order to develop certain skills necessary for reaching solutions are used for examining collaborative learning effects. Dillenbourg [13] identified two main challenges in the planning of collaborative learning activities: 1) increasing the chances of collaboration occurring and 2) enhancing and sustaining learning quality and effectiveness through task design i.e., role assignment and role responsibility decisions, task participation requirements, and distinguishing individual members' works—work achieved toward their own interests, toward the interests of other team members, and toward the interest of the team as a whole. Teachers working within collaborative learning environments are often referred to as facilitators; they carefully monitor interactions, make any necessary adjustments to the task, and also offer advice—even mid-process—to aid students.

Within the past few decades, with increasing classroom technology use, collaborative learning-based activities are being increasingly supplemented by, or conducted using, web-based environments; such environments facilitate interaction and provide more opportunities for active and participatory learning [14, 15]. Social networking sites, co-authorship sites, and folksonomies are three popular examples of web-based social media. Social networking spaces, including Facebook and YouTube, offer learners multiple chances to interact with members from their own learning communities and individuals outside their communities by sharing ideas and receiving rapid feedback. These media allow users to easily connect and build rapports with their fellow learners. Co-authorship media, such as Wikis, provide learners with an open space to utilize collaborative writing and editing as well as a base for communities to practice knowledge building. Folksonomies are systems that classify and describe online content by using tags or keywords. Learners are able to tag resources that are relevant to their group through social tagging, thus creating useful resources that meet the group's specific needs and providing opportunities for sharing resources and ideas [15].

Waters [16] provided an example of online discussion board usage in a North American university's graduate online courses; it was used for facilitating interactions between peers and between students and teachers as well. The study found that instructors' responsiveness on online discussion boards was not related to students' satisfaction levels. At the same time, it was observed that, as instructors began to post more questions, students became more responsive in terms of numbers of posts, the amount they contributed, and time spent responding to instructors' posts. This, however, resulted in lesser peer interaction, as students prioritized interactions with instructors. This study suggests that instructors using web-based media for collaborative learning may not have to support online interactions with large numbers of posts for such effective interaction to occur, especially if peer interaction is desired.

Collaborative learning, in this paper, is defined as a type of interaction between people that is expected to achieve the primary purpose of the learning: the achievement of the desired learning product.

2 Purpose of the Study

The purpose of this study is to transform a student culture in which very little independent study was being done out of class and classroom learning mainly involved students as passive participants. According to a survey of 48,233 Japanese university students, approximately one out of four of them believe that everything necessary to learn should be taught in class and that they should not have to learn independently out of class. The survey found that on average only 4.6 h per day were spent on study; 2.9 h were used for in-class activities; and 1.7 h were for out-of-class activities [17].

Therefore, a web-based application for an outside-of-class collaborative study was developed. Additionally, an innovative FL course utilizing the web-based application was implemented which integrated the online and in-class collaborative study.

3 Research Question

This study sought to answer the following research question about the potential use of an FL-based approach in BL within EFL courses to transform an educational culture where learning is primarily expected to occur through teacher-directed face-to-face instruction [17]: Would the use of the specially-developed web-based application in this study encourage students to build and sustain semester-long interactions in an out-of-class active collaborative learning activity?

4 The Web-Based Application

The web-based application functions as a learning environment within students' and teachers' smartphones. All the functions (See Fig. 1) were delivered using a server via the Internet. Various data, including student participation logs, texts, comprehension tests for the texts, and students' performance data, were stored in MySQL.

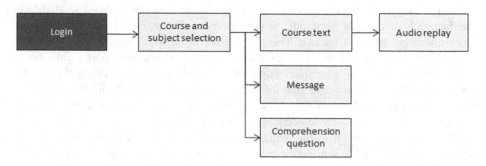

Fig. 1. A diagram illustrating the functional components of the application

Students and teachers wishing to use the application were required to create their own accounts. A list of such students and teachers was then registered on the application. Teachers used the administration functions to divide students into small groups and assign texts to them before each unit. The students studied the texts through collaborative learning tasks. The teachers administered reading comprehension tests on these texts to the students. The application allowed students and teachers to attach files and materials to the messages they posted to the message board.

5 Transforming a Conventional Classroom Lesson into a Flipped Learning Class: The EFL Flipped Learning Course Design

A conventional EFL in-class methodology typically involves three activity phases: input, intake, and output. Students are exposed to a comprehensive English text input so that they will be able to learn about a language feature that is new to them. If they understand the new feature of the given language they are learning and if it becomes a part of their language knowledge, intake has occurred [18]. After engaging in learning tasks that are designed to facilitate intake occurrence, students conduct output activities to practice using the new language feature. At the end of class time, the teacher usually assigns homework as an individual out-of-class learning task to reinforce the in-class learning. The teacher's grading of the homework assignment confirms whether the intended teaching aims have been achieved.

Under FL, as part of the input component, students work together on out-of-class learning tasks in an interactive online learning environment. In class, after reflecting on their out-of-class activities, students perform collaborative small-group work on intake and output learning tasks, which the teacher facilitates within the collaborative learning environment. Before class time ends, the students reflect on what they have accomplished. Figure 2 shows a conceptual diagram illustrating an FL lesson.

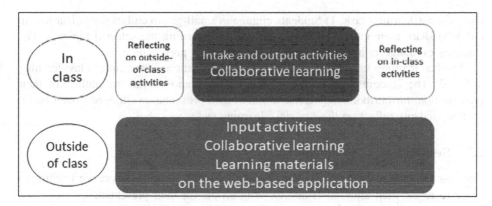

Fig. 2. A conceptual diagram of a flipped learning lesson

The EFL course was mandatory for first-year students at a university in Japan. It consisted of three units with each having four sessions (one session per week). The students were divided into groups of 4–5 people during the first week of the semester and were registered in the web-based application (See Sect. 4). The weekly outline of course topics was as follows:

1. Week 1: Registration and instructions about the web-based application; pre-questionnaire
2. Week 2–Week 5: Unit 1

3. Week 6: Midterm evaluations, reflections, and feedback
4. Week 7–Week 10: Unit 2
5. Week 11–Week 14: Unit 3
6. Week 15: Evaluations, reflections, feedback, and post-questionnaire

The following outline shows the learning tasks' flow during the four sessions of one unit. The students used their first language, Japanese when they engaged in small-group collaborative learning tasks.

5.1 Session 1

Out-of-class learning task: Students engage in small-group collaborative learning tasks in order to understand a course text and to answer a reading comprehension test; these activities are designed to ensure that they have understood the text.

In-class learning task: 1) Students reflect on what they have done in the out-of-class learning tasks. 2) The students collaborate in small groups and write a summary of the text in order to completely understand the text; furthermore, they use a mind map to brainstorm on a topic from the text. 3) The students decide their own topic, which should be relevant to the text they have read, for a presentation during Session 4. The students reflect on the in-class learning tasks.

5.2 Session 2

Out-of-class learning task: 1) Students engage in small-group collaborative learning in order to share their individual research findings regarding the selected topic. 2) The students exchange opinions about an outline for their presentation.

In-class learning task: 1) Students reflect on their actions in the out-of-class learning tasks. 2) The students collaborate in small groups and decide the outline of their presentation; furthermore, they create drafts of their presentation slides on Power Point. 3) The students reflect on their in-class learning tasks.

5.3 Session 3

Out-of-class learning task: 1) Students engage in small-group collaborative learning in order to revise their slideshows and to write scripts for their presentation.

In-class learning task: 1) Students reflect on what they have done in the out-of-class learning tasks. 2) The students collaborate in small groups and finalize the slideshows; furthermore, they revise the scripts for their presentation. 3) The students reflect on the in-class learning tasks.

5.4 Session 4

Out-of-class learning task: 1) Students pair up in order to practice their presentations, upload video clips, and evaluate their presentation deliveries among their peers.

In-class learning task: 1) Students reflect on what they have done in the out-of-class learning tasks. 2) The students use the slideshows to present their research findings within their groups. They hold discussions on the presentations. 3) The teacher supports the students by providing comments and advice. 4) Students reflect on the in-class activities.

6   The Study

6.1   Participants

Twenty-four first-year students (20 females and 4 males) at a university in Japan, members of one section of a general English-skill building course in which students were assigned to sections in alphabetical order of their surnames, voluntarily participated in this study.

6.2   Methods

We defined the out-of-class learning environment in this study as a Community of Inquiry (CoI) [19]. Since no extensive teacher intervention was provided in this study, our analysis considered only the social and cognitive presences. Guided by the CoI framework, all student interactions on the message board in the web-based application were coded into categories and the indicators for these two presences. In order to improve the coding trustworthiness of the student interactions, investigator triangulation [20] was employed. We finalized the categorization of all student interactions as follows:

1. The student interactions were coded using NVivo qualitative data analysis software.
2. Two external researchers were invited.
3. Both the researchers categorized the student interactions.
4. The two researchers discussed and revised the categorization until a consensus was achieved.
5. We finalized the categorization of the student interactions.

Moreover, in order to monitor student active participation in out-of-class discussion, a pre- and post-questionnaire measuring the quality of students' active learning (AL) and that of the AL externalization [21] were administered at the beginning (April, 2017) and end (July, 2017) of the course (Please see Tables 1 and 2). The AL externalization means externalization of cognitive process in activities such as writing, discussion, and presentation [22].

A 6-point Likert Scale (from 1–strongly disagree, to 6–strongly agree) was used to measure the responses in a way that would adequately allow for the expression of a range of participants' beliefs about students' AL and AL externalization.

7 Results and Discussion

The pre- and post-questionnaire, which measured the quality of students' AL and that of the AL externalization, were administered at the beginning (April, 2017) and end (July, 2017) of the course (See Tables 1 and 2 below).

Table 1. Descriptive statistics for the pre- and post-questionnaire

	Item	Pre		Post	
		Mean	SD	Mean	SD
1*	I clearly stated my opinion in the discussion	4.08	1.06	4.50	0.78
2	I noticed that the opinions of other group members are different from my own opinions	4.54	1.10	4.75	0.79
3	I deeply understood the course contents through the discussion	4.33	1.20	5.21	0.66
4*	I stated my opinion, showing evidence that supported it	4.13	1.19	4.63	0.88
5*	I considered ways in which I was able to convey my opinion to other group members	3.71	1.12	4.58	0.78
6	I was stimulated by the opinions of other group members that are different from my own opinion	4.67	1.13	4.79	0.83
7	I noticed that my way of thinking was wrong through the discussion	4.17	1.13	4.38	1.01
8	I increased my knowledge about the course contents through the discussion	4.67	1.20	5.08	0.72
9	The discussion helped me understand the ways in which I had been thinking before the discussion	4.25	1.11	4.67	0.70
10	I noticed new ways of looking at things differently through the discussion	4.63	1.13	4.71	0.86
11	I noticed that my opinion was one-sided through the discussion	3.96	1.08	3.92	0.83
12	I understood the course contents from various points of view through the discussion	4.46	1.18	5.08	0.83

$N = 24$
*AL externalization

Table 2. Results of the t-test ($N = 24$)

	Pre		Post		t	d
	Mean	SD	Mean	SD		
AL	4.30	0.90	4.69	0.47	−2.03†	0.54
AL externalization	3.97	0.94	4.57	0.66	−2.79*	0.74

†$p < .10$, *$p < .05$

As Table 2 illustrates, the students actively participated in discussions outside class (AL: $p < .10$, AL externalization: $p < .05$).

Table 3 shows the frequency of category appearances; furthermore, it depicts the indicators for the two above-mentioned presences in the out-of-class student interactions during Sessions 1–4 of the three units (See Sect. 5).

Table 3. Frequency of category appearances and the indicators for the social and cognitive presences

Presence	Category	Session 1	Session 2	Session 3	Session 4	Total
Social presence	Affective expression	50	62	37	59	208
	Open communication	80	66	53	56	255
	Group cohesion	58	50	50	34	192
	Total	188	178	140	149	655
Cognitive presence	Triggering event	9	3	4	13	29
	Exploration	101	129	73	49	352
	Integration	6	4	5	6	21
	Resolution	3	1	0	4	8
	Total	119	137	82	72	410

Table 4 shows the Spearman's rank correlation analysis between the frequencies of appearances in the categories of the indicators for the two above-mentioned presences in students' out-of-class interactions and the gains of the pre- and post-questionnaire.

Table 4. The result of Spearman's rank correlation analysis

		Gain of AL	Gain of AL externalization
Social presence	Total	.24	.19
	Affective expression	.21	.14
	Open communication	.25	.19
	Group cohesion	.27	.23
Cognitive presence	Total	.63***	.58**
	Triggering event	.41*	.29
	Exploration	.64***	.59**
	Integration	.56**	.42*
	Resolution	.25	.14

$*p < .05, **p < .01, ***p < .001$

This result revealed that the cognitive presence was strongly correlated with the gains of the pre- and post-questionnaire $(p < .01, p < .001)$.

8 Summary of the Findings

The research question of the study—that is, whether the use of this specially-developed web-based application would encourage students to build and sustain semester-long interactions in out-of-class active collaborative learning—was answered positively as follows:

- The results of the pre- and post-questionnaire, which measured the quality of students' AL and that of AL externalization, revealed that the students actively participated in out-of-class discussions.
- Spearman's rank correlation analysis indicated that the cognitive presence was strongly correlated with the gains of the pre- and post-questionnaire. This result reveals that the cognitive presence is closely related to externalization of cognitive process [22] in students' out-of-class discussions.

9 Conclusion

Research results showed that use of the web-based application, which was specially-developed for this study, may encourage students to build and sustain interactions during collaborative learning tasks, especially out-of-class learning tasks, by helping them develop collaborative communication skills and enabling them to support each other's learning; furthermore, the findings of this study may potentially transform a student culture where very little independent study is carried out outside the class, and classroom learning treats students mainly as passive participants. Thus, this specially-developed web-based application may support out-of-class student collaboration.

Further research is being planned to quantitatively measure whether the EFL FL approach helps improve active student participation in in-class activities; such improvements could lead to improvements in EFL written and oral communication skills and, consequently, better academic performance on standardized proficiency tests.

Acknowledgement. While conducting the research project described in this paper, we were deeply saddened to hear that our co-researcher, Craig Smith, died suddenly on January 3, 2019. He was a Professor of the Department of Global Affairs, the Director of the Community Engagement Center at Kyoto University of Foreign Studies (Japan), and the Advisor of the United Nations Association for Development and Peace (UNADAP). As a member of the Kyoto University Academic Writing Research Group, he received the 2011 Japan Association of College English Teachers Award for Excellence in Teaching. We offer our sincere condolences to his family.

This study was supported by the Grant-in-Aid for Scientific Research (#18K00763) provided by the Japan Society for the Promotion of Science. The data presented, the statements made, and the views expressed are solely the responsibility of the authors.

References

1. Vaughan, N.D., Cleveland-Innes, M., Garrison, D.R.: Teaching in Blended Learning Environments: Creating and Sustaining Communities of Inquiry. Athabasca University Press, Athabasca (2013)
2. Stuntz, D.F.: Flipped classrooms and CALL sustainability: a rationale for the development of flipped classrooms for sustainable CALL. In: WorldCALL 2013: Global Perspectives on Computer-Assisted Language Learning, Glasgow, 10–13 July 2013, pp. 323–326. Papers, University of Ulster, Coleraine (2013)
3. Bishop, J.L., Verleger, M.L.: The flipped classroom: a survey of the research. In: 120th ASEE Annual Conference & Exposition, Conference Proceedings, pp. 1–18. ASEE, Washington DC (2013)
4. Hamdan, N., McKnight, P., McKnight, K., Arfstrom, K.M.: A review of flipped learning, the flipped learning network (2013)
5. Lage, M., Platt, G.L., Treglia, M.: Inverting the classroom: a gateway to creating an inclusive environment. J. Econ. Educ. **31**(1), 30–43 (2000)
6. Yarbro, J., Arfstrom, K.M., McKnight, K., McKnight, P.: Extension of a review of flipped learning, the flipped learning network (2014)
7. Jones, N.A.: From the sage on the stage to the guide on the side: the challenge for educators today. ABAC J. **26**(1), 1–18 (2006)
8. Sung, K.: A case study on a flipped classroom in an EFL content course. Multimedia-Assist. Lang. Learn. **18**(2), 159–187 (2015)
9. Leis, A., Cooke, S., Tohei, A.: The effects of flipped classrooms on English composition writing in an EFL environment. Int. J. Comput. –Assist. Lang. Learn. **5**(4), 37–51 (2015)
10. Kuhn, K., Hoffstaedter, P.: Flipping intercultural communication practice: opportunities and challenges for the foreign language classroom. In: Colpaert, J., Aerts, A., Oberhofer, M., Gutiérez-Colón Plana, M. (eds.) Proceedings of Seventeenth International CALL Conference Task Design and CALL, pp. 338–345. Universiteit Antwerpen, Antwerp (2015)
11. Egbert, J., Herman, D., Chang, A.: To flip or not to flip? That's not the question. exploring flipped instruction in technology supported language learning environment. Int. J. Comput. Assist. Lang. Learn. **4**(2), 1–10 (2014)
12. Hughes, C.: The effects of flipping an English for academic purposes course. Int. J. Mob. Blended Learn. **11**(1), 26–41 (2019)
13. Dillenbourg, P.: What do you mean by collaborative learning? In: Dillenbourg P (ed.) Collaborative Learning: Cognitive and Computational Approaches, Emerald, Bingley, pp. 1–19 (1999)
14. McLoughlin, C., Lee, M.J.: Social software and participatory learning: pedagogical choices with technology affordances in the Web 2.0 era. In: Atkinson, R.J., McBeath, C., Soong, S. K.A., Cheers, C. (eds.) Proceedings Ascilite Singapore 2007, pp. 664–675. Centre for Educational Development Nanyang Technological University, Singapore (2007)
15. Wheeler, S., Yeomans, P., Wheeler, D.: The good, the bad and the wiki: evaluating student-generated content for collaborative learning. Br. J. Educ. Technol. **39**(6), 987–995 (2008)
16. Waters, J.: The impact of instructor intervention style on student activity in asynchronous online learning discussion boards. In: Bastiaens, T, Marks, G. (eds.) Proceedings of World Conference on E-Learning in Corporate, Government, Healthcare, and Higher Education 2012, pp. 831–840. Association for the Advancement of Computing in Education, Chesapeake (2012)

17. Center for Research on University Management and Policy, The University of Tokyo: Zenkoku daigakusei chosa [National survey of university students]. Center for Research on University Management and Policy, The University of Tokyo, Tokyo (2007)
18. Ishikawa, Y., Kondo, M., Smith, C.: Design and implementation issues of interoperable educational application: an ICT application for primary school English education in Japan. In: Lazarinis, F., Green, S., Pearson, E. (eds.) Developing and Utilizing E-Learning Applications, pp. 100–124. Information Science Reference, Hershey (2010)
19. Garrison, D.R.: E-learning in the 21st Century: A Framework for Research and Practice, 3rd edn. Taylor & Francis Group, New York (2017)
20. Denzin, N.K.: The Research Act, 3rd edn. McGraw-Hill, New York (1989)
21. Mizokami, S., et al.: Bifactor model niyoru active learning (externalization) shakudo no kaihatsu [developing the active learning (externalization) scale by bifactor model]. Kyoto Univ. Stud. High. Educ. 22, 151–162 (2016)
22. Matsushita, K. (ed.): Deep Active Learning: Toward Greater Depth in University Education. Springer, Singapore (2018). https://doi.org/10.1007/978-981-10-5660-4

The Impact of Corpus Linguistics on Language Teaching in Russia's Educational Context: Systematic Literature Review

Marina Kogan[1]([✉]), Victor Zakharov[2], Nina Popova[1],
and Nadezhda Almazova[1]

[1] Higher School of Language Teaching and Translation,
Peter the Great St. Petersburg Polytechnic University, St. Petersburg, Russia
m_kogan@inbox.ru, ninavaspo@mail.ru,
almazovanadial@ya.ru
[2] Department of Mathematical Linguistics, Saint Petersburg State University,
St. Petersburg, Russia
v.zakharov@spbu.ru

Abstract. Corpus linguistics (CL) is one of the most dynamic and rapidly developing areas of modern linguistics. It affects all areas of linguistics, including methodology of teaching foreign languages, translation and other linguistic disciplines. The reviews of publications on this subject include only the works published in English and do not reflect the contribution of Russian researchers. This article fills this gap by presenting an overview of the disparate publications of Russian authors by examining the dynamics in the growth of the publication number, the geographic distribution, publication outlets, citations, focusing on the studies on the application of CL methods in education in Russia since 2011 till the first half of 2019. Methods of finding relevant publications and processing the resulting body of the data in order to obtain answers to the research questions are described. The discussion indicates that most of the work contains guidelines on the CL use in teaching various aspects of the Russian and foreign languages with the involvement of large general-purpose corpora that are freely available on-line. Only a small number of studies present the results of pedagogical experiments. It is noted that the selected indicators make it possible to assess the degree of CL approach influence on education. Drawing on the analysis, we propose the ways of expanding the implementation of CL methods in language teaching by increasing their use in different disciplines of the pre-service teacher training program and in-service training of contemporary foreign language teachers.

Keywords: Corpus linguistics · Systematic literature overview · Language teaching · Russia's educational context

1 Introduction

Corpus linguistics is a new direction in linguistics, existing for a little over than half a century and involved in the creation and use of corpora for solving various linguistic and non-linguistic problems.

© Springer Nature Switzerland AG 2020
P. Zaphiris and A. Ioannou (Eds.): HCII 2020, LNCS 12205, pp. 339–355, 2020.
https://doi.org/10.1007/978-3-030-50513-4_26

Is it right, though, to call it direction? This, probably, seemed right at the beginning, when Henry Kučera and Nelson Francis, in the Brown University (USA), created the first corpus, which is called Brown University Standard Corpus of Present-Day American English. Nowadays, corpus linguistics is something more than that. Today, corpora have become an integral part of linguistics, one of its cornerstones, such as vocabulary and grammar. After the appearance of the corpora, the whole linguistic science became different, and we can say that the whole linguistics became corpus linguistics, because it is used in various fields of linguistics either as a method or as a data source.

The number of corpora in the world is constantly growing, and currently there are thousands of corpora [1]. Modern corpora are multilingual (both independent and parallel) and multifunctional. Examples include portal Wortschatz at the University of Leipzig (393 corpora representing 252 languages), the Sketch Engine corpus system (588 corpora, 94 languages) [2], the Aranea corpora at Comenius University in Bratislava consisting of 66 corpora, 31 languages, and a number of others.

A special role is played by national corpora. Such projects are supported at the national level, and leading corpus linguists of the country take part in their creation. Countless studies are carried out on corpora basis, the corpora serve as a source of information on language functioning. Due to the corpora we can quickly and effectively check the features of the use of an unfamiliar word or grammatical form by competent authors. Thus, the national corpus is useful to everyone who, by virtue of the profession, out of necessity or out of simple curiosity, is looking for an answer to questions about the structure and functioning of the language, that is, in fact, to the majority of educated speakers of the language and to all those who study it as a foreign language. The national corpus of the Russian language, available online since April 2004, enjoys well-deserved authority among specialists [3].

Corpus linguistics has had a direct impact on teaching foreign languages since the advent of large online corpora. In 1991, Professor Tim Jones from the University of Birmingham introduced the concept of Data Driven Learning (DDL) and was an ardent supporter of the use of corpora by students to test their hypotheses about word compatibility, grammatical constructions, usage contexts, etc., explaining that "research is too important to be left to the researchers". Boulton and Cobb's meta-analysis of studies (from 1989 to 2014) on the use of corpora in foreign languages teaching [4] and Pérez-Paredes' systematic analysis of the literature on the uses and spread of the corpora and data-driven learning in CALL research [5] help to understand better what has been done in the DDL for the recent decades. Neither of the review works contains papers published in non-English languages. The Boulton and Cobb's meta-analysis concludes that the DDL is effective and efficient in different learning environments with different categories of learners in pursuing different language goals. However, the research articles by Russian authors on the influence of CL on foreign language teaching were not considered by the above authors of the reviews. For example, in an annotated list of references to all 205 studies which Boulton and Cobb selected for their meta-analysis[1] there is not a single paper either by Russian authors or devoted to

---

[1] The full list is available in Supporting Information Folder at the Publisher's website https://onlinelibrary.wiley.com/doi/pdf/10.1111/lang.12224.

teaching the Russian language using corpora. They are missing among the 32 articles selected by Pérez-Paredes for his analysis either.

We decided to fill this gap and analyze the impact of corpus linguistics on the education system in Russia.

1.1 Criteria for Assessing the Impact of Corpus Linguistics on Education in Russia

The authors of this work agreed that the following indicators can be chosen as criteria for the influence of CL on the sphere of education in the Russian Federation:

1. The total number of publications on this topic written by researchers/with the participation of researchers from Russia registered in recognized databases and their growth dynamics over a certain period of time.
2. The number and geographic distribution of Russian universities conducting research in this area.
3. Publication outlets (the number of publications of various types that publish materials presenting research interest to us).
4. Citations. Despite several shortcomings of this indicator described in literature (e.g., not distinguishing between positive and negative citations) they are helpful in identifying papers that, for one reason or another, are popular [6].
5. The goals of applying corpus linguistics approaches in the educational process, which the authors pursued.

These criteria were formulated as research questions (RQ), to which the authors decided to find the answers in the course of the undertaken study.

2 Research Questions

RQ1: What is the number of corpus linguistics research related to the sphere of education in Russia (CLR-RE)? What is their distribution by a year of publishing?

RQ2: How is CLR-RE research geographically distributed?

RQ3: What are preferable publication outlets for this research: journal or conference proceedings? In which journals and conference proceedings is CLR-RE research currently being published?

RQ4: What CLR-RE studies in Russia are most cited?

RQ5: What goals of applying CL approaches do researchers in Russia's educational settings pursue?

3   Methods

In this section we describe the approaches we took to answer the research questions. We describe the methods we used to gather literature (data collection) and the analytic methods we used to examine the literature on corpora we gathered (data classification and analysis).

3.1   Data Collection

As the issue of author affiliation with Russian universities was of fundamental importance to us, we began a search for publications on international databases (Scopus, Web of Science) that allow us to choose the country/university of the author of the publication and the Russian platform Russian Science Citation Index (RSCI).

To search for articles in international databases, standard queries were used: different combinations of *corpus/corpora/corpus linguistics and data-driven learning, DDL, and concordance/concordancer/concordancing with language learning/ teaching, higher education* indicating the authorship of the Russian Federation (in the Scopus database) and all identified Russian universities in the Web of Science database. As the result of the search several dozen of items were found. After getting familiarized with the article titles and abstracts, we discovered that the problem of using corpus approaches in teaching is reflected in 16 papers by the authors from Russia, with 7 of them being journal articles, while the rest of them were conference proceedings published in 2014–2018. All this means that the number of publications by Russian authors on the subject registered in international bibliographic databases is scarce.

The main source of publications on this topic was the scientific electronic library eLIBRARY.RU, the leading electronic library of scientific periodicals in Russian in the world, which includes the Russian Science Citation Index (hereinafter RSCI). The number of registered users is 1.7 million. The RSCI is a national information and analytical system that accumulates more than 11 million publications of Russian authors, as well as information on citing these publications from more than 6,000 Russian journals. The project started in 2005 [7]. The system is based on a bibliographic abstract database, which indexes articles in Russian scientific journals. In recent years, other types of scientific publications have also begun to be included in the RSCI: conference proceedings, monographs, study guides, patents, PhD and doctoral dissertations. The database contains information on the output data, authors of publications, places of their work, keywords and subject areas, as well as abstracts and cited references. The integration of the RSCI with the scientific electronic library (e-library) allows users, in most cases, to get familiarized with the full text of the desired publication. The chronological coverage of the system is from 2005 to the present day; for many sources the archives cover longer time period. More than one and a half million publications of Russian scientists are annually added to the RSCI. The RSCI is a non-profit project and is in the public domain, which allows all Russian scientists to use this powerful analytical tool without any restrictions.

Advanced Search offers an opportunity to search for information by type of publication, keywords, abstracts, title, author, subject, journal. We searched for publications containing combinations of expressions/phrases typical for a given topic in Russian (query category *What to look for*), with the following search filters (category *Where to search*): in the title, in the abstract, in the keywords, in the full text of the publication. The search was carried out for the following types of publications: articles in journals, books, conference proceedings, dissertations (category *Type of publication*). We also used the option, very important for inflectional languages like Russian, – taking into account morphology (category *Parameters*). Search settings in all sessions were kept the same for all queries. The variable was the *What to search* field, into which different combinations of keywords were entered. There were no restrictions on publication dates.

In response to the query, the search engine returned the search results in the form of a table containing the title of the article, the names of the authors, the name of the journal/conference materials in which the paper was published, the year of publication and the number of references to this publication. A hyperlink leads to a page with a description of the publication.

The search results obtained in the form of a table were saved and analyzed. At the first stage of the analysis, the works whose title and/or abstract did not contain information on the CL use in the educational process were excluded from the lists obtained.

On the other hand, to search for relevant works, lists of publications citing highly cited works in our original "trawl" were analyzed. We attributed as highly cited the works that were referenced more than 10 times. These works are given in Table 1. Figure 1 illustrates how the citation hyperlink was used for forward citations search.

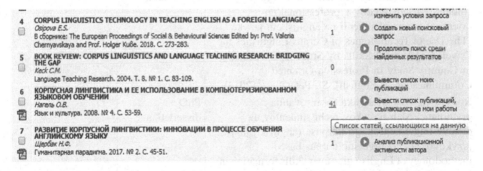

Fig. 1. An example of how original tables generated by eLIBRARY search engine were used in a forward referencing process (Hyperlink 41 leads to a list of papers referring to the particular one.)

Table 1. Highly cited works used as sources to replenish the database of relevant publications

Publication	Type	Number of citations in RISC (2019)
Sysoyev, P.V.: Linguistic Corpus in Teaching Foreign Languages Jazyk i kul'tura [Language and culture], 1(9), 99–111 (2010)	Article	132
Zakharov, V.P, Boganova, S.Yu.: Korpusnaja lingvistika [Corpus Linguistics]: a textbook for humanities students. Irkutsk (2011)	Textbook (1-st edition)	101
Sysoyev, P.V.: Linguistic corpus, corpus linguistics, and methods of teaching foreign languages Inostrannye Jazyki v Shkole [Foreign languages at school], 5, 12–21 (2010)	Article	78
Sysoyev, P.V., Kokoreva, A.A.: Teaching professional terms to EFL students using parallel corpus. Jazyk i kul'tura [Language and culture], 21 (1), 114–124 (2013)	Article	71
Nagel', O.V.: Corpus linguistics and its use in computer assisted language teaching. Jazyk i kul'tura [Language and culture], 4, 53–59 (2008)	Article	41
Zagorovskaya, O.V., Litvinova, T.A., Litvinova O.A.: Electronic corpus of student essays in Russian and its potentials to modern human studies. Mir nauki, kul'tury, obrazovanija [world of science, culture and education], (3), 387–389 (2012)	Article	32
Zakharov, V.P, Boganova, S.Yu.: Korpusnaja lingvistika [Corpus Linguistics]: a textbook for Linguistics students. St-Petersburg (2013)	Textbook (2-nd edition)	31
Gorina O.G. Ispol'zovanie tehnologij korpusnoj lingvistiki dlja razvitija leksicheskih navykov studentov-regionovedov v professional'no-orientirovannom obshhenii na anglijskom jazyke [The Use of Technologies of Corpus Linguistics for Developing Lexical Skills by Students Specializing in Country Study in Profession-Oriented Communication in English]. St. Petersburg (2014)	PhD dissertation	25
Rjazanova, E.A. Metodika formirovanija grammaticheskih navykov rechi studentov na osnove lingvisticheskogo korpusa (anglijskij jazyk, jazykovoj vuz) [Linguistic corpus based methodology of English grammar skills formation in Linguistics students] Tambov (2012)	PhD dissertation	17
Chernyakova, T.A. The use of linguistic corpus in teaching a foreign language Jazyk i kul'tura [Language and culture], 16(4), 127–132 (2011)	Article	15

Another source of information on the search for relevant articles was the materials of the international conference Magic INNO, which is held every 2 years by MGIMO University[2]. At each of the past conferences, one of the Plenary speakers was a specialist in the field of corpus linguistics. For example, at the first conference held in 2013, there was Geoffrey Leech, Prof. from Lancaster University[3]. Search for relevant publications was carried out on PDF versions of conference materials. All articles containing the word *korpus* were scanned.

In addition, the accounts of the individual promising authors containing lists of their publications were studied in the eLIBRARY.RU. We also considered the eLIBRARY.RU' accounts of all the authors whose works were found in the international databases in order to obtain a more complete picture of their research being conducted in Russia on the subject of our interest.

Duplicates were excluded from the lists obtained. The remaining works were supplemented with abstracts available on the publication page in the electronic library and information on the availability of the full text. If the full text was available, it was downloaded for later analysis. If there was no full text, and the abstract was short and uninformative, the work was excluded from the database. This situation is typical for conference proceedings before 2010–2011. Therefore, it was decided to conduct further analysis on publications issued in 2011 – the first half of 2019. An exception was made for the materials of the conference "National Corpus of the Russian Language and Problems of Humanitarian Education", held in 2007, the materials of which are available on the RNC website[4]. An explanation to this decision will be given in the Discussion section.

Thus, the body of the publications for further analysis and the search for answers to the research questions were the materials presented in Table 2.

Table 2. Data Collection Methods, Results, and Dates

Method	Identified number	Date
Search: Scopus, Web of Science	17 (16 articles and conference papers, 1 book chapter)	2014–July-2019
Search: RISC data base (mixed search methods including Forward Referencing search queries)	116 (106 articles and conference papers, 6 PhD diss., 2 book chapters, 2 textbooks)	2011–July-2019
Search: MGIMO The magic of Innovation conference proceedings	11	2013–July-2019
RNC web site	8	2007–2009

---

[2] The materials of the past conferences are freely available on the university website https://inno-conf.mgimo.ru/materials.

[3] Videorecording of Geoffrey Leech Plenary talk at Magic INNO 2013: https://www.youtube.com/watch?v=CdpOSAIzIfc&feature=youtu.be.

[4] https://studiorum-ruscorpora.ru/education/articles/.

4 Results and Discussion

4.1 The Number of Publications and Their Distribution by Year of Publication

The final number of published papers that constituted the corpus of this study was 152. 77 works were published in conference proceedings, 64 – in journals, (7 of which – in journals registered in the Scopus database), 2 textbooks, 6 PhD dissertations, 3 book chapters. Concerning the years of publications (2011 – the first half of the year 2019), the materials were distributed as shown below in Fig. 2.

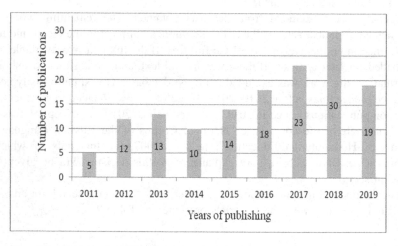

Fig. 2. The distribution of publications by Russian authors/researchers on CLR-RE by publication year across the period studied (2011 – the first 6 months of 2019)

4.2 Geographic Distribution and Publication Outlets (RQ2 and RQ3)

The collected articles were classified and analyzed using qualitative and quantitative methods. To determine the geographical location of the universities where the CLR-HE studies are conducted, a list of universities where the authors of the articles work is compiled. As a rule, the name of the university allows us to immediately determine its location. However, in some cases, we used the Google search engine to find out the location of the university. To determine the type of material publication from our corpus (article, conference materials, chapters of a collective monograph, dissertation), we calculated how many times each type appeared in the corpus. The list of journals in which the articles were published was further analyzed in order to find out which publications were preferred by the researchers of this subject.

The only journal that regularly publishes the articles on the use of corpus linguistics in teaching foreign languages is Tambov University Review, Series: Humanities (11 works from our corpus were published in it). Filologicheskie nauki. Voprosy teorii i praktiki [J. of Philological Sciences. Issues of Theory and Practice] is in the 2nd place.

This journal is also published in Tambov (Publishing House Gramota Publishers), Jazyk i Kul'tura [Language and Culture] (4 publications each), 4 more journals (Industrija perevoda [Translation Industry], Aktual'nye voprosy obrazovanija [Topical Educational Issues], Uchenye zapiski Krymskogo federal'nogo universiteta imeni V.I. Vernadskogo [Scientific Notes of the Crimean Federal University named after V.I. Vernadsky], European Social Science Journal = European Journal of Social Sciences, published in Moscow (publisher: Autonomous Non-Profit Organization International Research Institute)) published 2 articles each. In each of the remaining 37 journals over the period under consideration, one article from our database was published. No special issues of journals focusing on the topic have been discovered.

Conferences in which the research results from our corpus were presented are characterized by a variety of subjects, with the predominance of interdisciplinary conferences devoted to innovative methods of teaching foreign languages and translation, intercultural communication, translation discourse, problems of modern education in general, etc. Only one conference brings together specialists in the area of corpus linguistics. This is the International Conference of Corpus Linguistics, which is held every 2 years at the Department of Mathematical Linguistics of St. Petersburg State University. However, papers related to the use of corpus linguistics approaches in teaching are an exception at this conference, because the main subjects of the conference are the studies on corpora creation, their markup and corpus data analysis rather than the use of CL approaches in teaching.

Authors of the publications work in 59 universities of different regions of Russia. Most of the research is expectedly carried out in large Russian scientific and educational centers, Moscow and St. Petersburg, however, CL in the sphere of education studies are also conducted in regional universities. Table 3 shows the universities that published more than 4 works from those collected in our database.

Table 3. Universities conducting research on the use of CL in the educational process

University	Number of publications
Peter the Great Saint Petersburg Polytechnic University	14
G.R. Derzhavin Tambov State University	12
National Research Institute "Higher School of Economics"	8
The Crimean Federal University named after V.I. Vernadsky	7
Saint-Petersburg State university	7
Buryat State University	6
Lomonosov's Moscow State university	5
Tyumen State University	5
National Research Tomsk Polytechnic University	4

In some cases, publication activity is associated with preparation for the defense of a candidate dissertation. Not all authors of PhD theses (6 in our database) continue research in this area. It is all the more important that some of them continue active research and publication on this topic after receiving the Ph.D. title (candidate of sciences) [8, 9]. In this regard, we note that at least 10 works in our corpus were written by students independently or in collaboration with their scientific advisers, which was reflected in the meta-data for publications. Three of them are registered in the international Scopus database [10–12]. Perhaps there are more of them: "suspected" are those authors who do not have an account in the electronic library eLIBRARY.RU. As registration in the e-library is a mandatory requirement in Russia for university teachers in recent years, it can be assumed that the authors affiliated with a specific university, but not registered in eLIBRARY.RU, are students. However, this issue requires further investigation.

4.3 Most Cited Papers (RQ4)

Finding the answer to RQ4: *Which CLR-RE studies in Russia are cited the most?* led to the following results. At the time of this writing, 93 articles were not cited, 38 articles were cited 1 to 4 times, with the majority of them being cited once (20). 14 articles were cited from 5 to 11 times, with the most highly cited publications from the corpus being presented in Table 1. Of these, in the period under consideration (2011 - July 2019) 7 publications (2 editions of the textbook on CL), 2 Ph.D. dissertations and 3 articles published in peer-reviewed journals. The lack of references to many articles selected for analysis in a systematic review of the literature was noted by researchers even in such an intensively developing field as empirical MOOC studies. For example, Veletsianos and Shepherdson found that out of 183 works in their corpus, 87 (47.5%) had not been cited at all [6, p. 210]. The lack of references to most of the works in our corpus may indicate a lack of interest in the use of CL in teaching among the professors of Russian universities and/or a lack of distinction of a particular author in a professional environment, or a lack of interest in other people's experience, including the CL use in teaching among the professors of Russian universities.

On the other hand over half of the works in our corpus are the conference proceedings referenced, as a rule, less than articles in journals or monographs. Until recently, in Russia there were restrictions on the number of references allowed in conference materials, while in some cases they were completely excluded. Another aspect of the citation problem is low informativeness of headings, abstracts and keywords in the works of the Russian authors on humanitarian subjects. This conclusion was made on the basis of a specially conducted study, in which, using a corpus analysis of the texts of the articles by Russian authors, it was shown that many authors of humanitarian articles were not able to clearly formulate the novelty of their research and present information in the texts of scientific articles so that it could be easily extracted and processed [13, 14].

4.4 Goals of Applying Corpus Linguistics Approach in Language Teaching (RQ 5)

In search of an answer to RQ 5 on the research objectives pursued by the authors, we wanted to find out which corpora they used, who were the members of the experimental group, and what aspects of the study, language or translation, the research was aimed at.

The authors of the publications investigated the use of CL approaches for teaching English (77% of all publications), German (6%), and Russian (17%). The following corpora were considered:

When teaching **English** the researchers used BNC (35%), COCA (20%), LOB (Lancaster-Oslo-Bergen Corpus) (10%). Also mentioned were English Grammar Corpus, Cambridge Learner Corpus, DANTE, BAWE, RNC, Russian annotated Learner Corpus (REALEC[5]), TED talks, Web corpus, NOW corpus, ERUK (hose-made) corpus for training students focusing on regional studies and some other house-made corpora for ESP classes.

For teaching **German**, DeReCo, DWDS, COSMAS corpora are recommended, as well as DGD (Datenbank für gesprochenes Deutsch), with the possibility of accessing colloquial archives: das "Forschungs und Lehrkorpus gesprochenes Deutsch" (FOLK); das Korpus "Deutsche Mundarten" (Zwirner-Korpus), das Korpus "Deutsche Umgangssprachen" (Pfeffer-Korpus). Kod.ING (Korpus der Ingenieurwissenschaften) (house-made corpus based on the texts of Ph.D. dissertations defended at Leibniz University Hannover [12]), Leipzig Corpora, corpora of the German Language Institute LIMAS-Korpus, NEGRA, and RNC were also used.

When learning the **Russian** language the RNC and a sound corpus "One speech day" compiled at SPbSU [15] were used.

When teaching **translation** COCA, RNC, Russian Learner Translator Corpus (RusLTC)[6], an electronic specialized corpus of English-language texts on military-technical topics, created by the author of the study were useful.

From the above information we can draw a preliminary conclusion that non-specialized general language corpora freely available on-line are more commonly used than specialized ones.

The main aspects proposed to be studied using the approaches of corpus linguistics are the following: vocabulary (18.3%), grammar, vocabulary-grammar (lexicogrammar) (15.6%), translation (20%). Some works are devoted to teaching written discourse, phonetics, upgrading foreign language textbooks, working out test papers and exam materials. A number of articles are aimed at familiarizing readers with corpus resources, showing their possible applications (25.6%). For example, corpora may be helpful in organizing students' research work, involving them in project activities, and developing their cognitive skills.

Most authors consider the possibilities of using CL in tertiary education (in an ESP course for students of different areas of study (17.6%), for linguists (45.8%), and in postgraduate foreign language courses (3.2%)), which corresponds to global trends, because most studies on the use of CL approaches in teaching have been carried out in a university setting. However, the authors of 4 works (two – on teaching German, two – on teaching Russian) discuss the possibility of applying CL approaches in secondary school. Interest in introducing data-driven learning in secondary school (for younger learners/pre-tertiary learners) for studying foreign and native languages is manifested in different countries of the world, as evidenced by the recently published collective

---

[5] Homepage of REALEC: http://web-corpora.net/RLC.

[6] Homepage of RusLTC: http://rus-ltc.org/search.

monograph. Its authors consider the use of DDL at school to be very promising, noting that current young learners are well aware of computers and are happy to use them to learn new learning resources, such as linguistic corpora [16].

The authors of only 14 articles described their experiment in detail, with a description of the students' characteristics in the experimental group. In all cases, positive results were achieved, and a positive attitude of students to new ways of learning a foreign language was shown.

It is surprising that the authors of Ph.D. theses, whose articles constitute approximately 15% of the works in our corpus, do not describe the stages and the results of the experiment in the articles, confining themselves only to the general conclusions. For example, they conclude that the results of the experiment "showed that the mastery of future translators' work with a linguistic corpus algorithm provides an adequate expression of the meanings embedded in the idiomatic speech units, expands their translation horizons, promotes the development of linguistic thinking, contributes to building the skills of learners' independent work with information and communication resources" [17]. In the dissertations as such, the experiment is described in sufficient detail, while in the articles there is no description of the pedagogical experiment and the processing of its results.

Most authors focus on discussing the didactic advantages of using CL in teaching certain aspects of foreign language or translation, developing a number of competencies provided by educational standards (information & communication competence (ICT), computer literacy, information culture, research competence), acquaint readers with available corpus resources, and offer a number of relevant questions from their own pedagogical practice, the answers to which helped to find the corpora, analyze possible algorithms/scenarios of teaching with the help of corpora, gives examples of the corpora use in the students' project activities, corpus-based research projects, recommendations for organizing independent work of students with corpora, leading to an increase in their autonomy and motivation, development of cognitive and meta-cognitive skills and strategies (for instance, contextualization, resourcing, translation, inferencing, self-monitoring, self-management, directed attention, selective attention). It is obvious that the criteria for evaluating CL approaches in the development of many of these competencies or skills have yet to be developed. Pérez-Paredes believes that the criterion for the successful development of cognitive skills is the use of concordance programs by students, but none of the 32 articles of 2011–2015 considered in his systematic analysis investigated this subject [5, p. 16].

As in most works there is no description of the experiment, the question of the degree of students' corpora awareness and the ways of using them in the study of foreign languages remains unclear. In some works where the authors described the experiment, it is noted that before the experiment students did not know about the corpora and did not use them before the start of the experimental training. This is noted in the works describing experimental training for both linguists [18] and non-linguists [12, 19]. A special study conducted by a student of IvSU among her fellow students of the Faculty of Romano-Germanic Philology showed that out of 52 respondents, 75% knew about the existence of corpora thanks to the disciplines of Analytical Reading and IT. However, only 43% were actively using corpora [20].

Knowing the situation in the higher education system in Russia, we can assume that most students majoring in linguistics and philology get familiarized with the corpora and approaches of corpus linguistics in the process of studying at university. However, the question remains whether or not familiarity with corpus technologies means their use by young specialists in their own teaching practice, and it requires a separate serious study, as indicated by Boulton and Tyne [21]. The few available studies on this problem in the world give somewhat mixed results. On the one hand, Charles' s more than a half post graduated students from different disciplines used their Do-It-Yourself corpora on a regular basis a year after the completing the experimental writing course [22]. Lenko-Szymanska showed that one specially designed course for students – future teachers of foreign languages is not enough to build sustainable technical, corpus-linguistic, and pedagogical skills [23]. She believes that students should be exposed to corpora in their language and linguistics classes and be familiarized with DDL methods and techniques in general teacher training courses, which will enhance DDL methodology acquisition and contribute to its sustainability [23].

We proposed our own solution to the problem of updating and supplementing various disciplines of the foreign language teachers majoring in computer assisted language teaching program at Peter the Great St. Petersburg Polytechnic University with tasks for accessing corpora and analyzing corpus data in an article [24].

The low "corpus literacy" [25, p. 148] of teachers prevents their widespread use in the educational process. This applies to the teaching of the Russian language and the use of RNC. One of the reasons seems to be insufficient integration of two areas – corpus linguistics and methods of teaching foreign languages. Linguistic corpora are created mainly by linguists who are not teachers of a foreign language, and teachers themselves are characterized by low corpora awareness, a lack of understanding innovative methods of language teaching, which dictates the need to master new competencies, skills in handling complex computer programs. The increasing sophistication of corpus linguistics tools functionality due to the complex set of programming, linguistic and mathematical means makes these intellectual programs much superior to conventional concordancers [26]. The former provide a wide range of multiple linguistic functions such as lexical-semantic fields formation, detection and visualization of the collocations, text key word list production, and a set of relevant study examples selection. There is an obvious controversy between CL researchers' interests and ordinary language learners' and teachers' needs in terms of complexity and functionality of special software. The former are eager to master state-of-the-art software for intellectual processing of corpus data, providing a wide range of multiple linguistic functions such as lexical-semantic fields formation, detection and visualization of the collocations, text key word list production, and a set of relevant study examples selection. Although conventional concordancers are essentially information storage, searching and retrieval systems with elaborated query and sorting functions these are complex enough for ordinary users who need more training than foreseen by the syllabus to achieve the level of confident users and take advantage of them in their independent teaching and research.

The main directions of the RNC use in teaching will be discussed in the following section.

4.5   RNC Use in Learning and Teaching

The RNC is the largest, national scale reference corpus in the Russian language. Available on-line, free of charge, it is a linguistic resource, which can be used without registration. Its present day size is 288727494 million word tokens taken from spoken genres, fiction, and written media (including academic and non-academic texts) in Russian from the mid-18th century to the present. The Russian National Corpus currently uses four types of annotation: metatextual, morphological, accentual and semantic; the introduction of syntactic annotation is planned for the near future. The system of annotation is constantly being improved, which allows for quite complex syntactic and morphological queries.

The RNC has a number of subcorpora of different types including a set of bidirectional parallel text subcorpora. In the latter subcorpora, Russian is complemented by its translation into a different language, and vice versa. The units of the original and the translated texts (usually, a unit is a sentence) are matched through an alignment procedure. At the time of publishing, 19 bidirectional parallel text corpora are available including English/Russian, German/Russian and French/Russian parallel corpora.

All the work on the RNC use is of great methodological value, as they contain a detailed description of the tasks developed for addressing the corpora, for example, for studying diminutives typical for the Russian language [27]. The work of Olkhovskaya and Paramonova [28] contains a description of 8 different types of tasks in the RNC corpus with lexical ambiguity, neologisms in Russian and their graphic variability, the time of the word emergence in Russian using the diachronic corpus, the study of functional styles, work with literary images of different writers, intertextuality assignments, etc. The authors also note the fact that Russian teachers are familiar with the corpus as a linguistic resource, but practically do not use it as a tool for teaching. At the same time, characterizing the ongoing educational work on the pedagogical potential of the corpora, the authors call it "hyperactive", but refer to the well-known works of their colleagues published more than 10 years ago. Many works were published in the proceedings of the only specialized international conference "National Corpus of the Russian Language and Humanitarian Education Issues", organized in 2007 by the Higher School of Economics (HSE) in Moscow [29].

In our opinion, the problem of familiarizing practicing teachers of foreign languages and the Russian language with the basics of corpus linguistics can be solved within the framework of continuing education courses taking into account their needs, which is the cornerstone of the effectiveness of such courses [for details see 30]. Another important condition for the effectiveness of such in-service training courses is the use of modern resources and training formats. First of all, such technologies as blended learning and flipped classroom were included in the curriculum with the available MOOC courses on corpus linguistics. We mean the Corpus Linguistics: Method, Analysis and Interpretation (Massive Open Online Course) course on the FutureLearn platform, created by teachers and offered by Lancaster University, under the direction of T. McEnery[7] and Introduction to Corpus Linguistics on the Open Education

---

[7] Corpus Linguistics: Method, Analysis and Interpretation MOOC course URL: https://www. futurelearn.com/courses/corpus-linguistics.

platform developed at the Higher School of Economics National Research University under the direction of A. Levinson[8].

5 Conclusions

- The selected criteria for the research were the number of publications, their dynamics, the number of citations, types of publications, the geographical distribution of universities conducting research in the field of CL and the target settings of the research authors as a whole. All these factors made it possible to get an idea of the CL methods influence in the higher education system in Russia in 2011–2019. The available data allow us to conclude that CL methods are used by teachers at many universities, and most students majoring in linguistics are familiar with the corpora.
- The question of whether young teachers who studied CL at the university use this knowledge in their teaching practice requires further study.
- The use of CL approaches in teaching a foreign language, mother tongue, and translation in Russia, as well as in other countries, is one of the innovative methods in linguodidactics, but it does not belong to the main methods of teaching these disciplines. Researchers focus on building students' linguistic competence with the help of corpora, and the available publications contain a large number of recommendations and examples of the corpora use for the development of linguistic competence. Less than 10% of the works contain descriptions of the experimental training results.
- One of the existing problems is low awareness of the foreign language teachers of CL use in teaching students, majoring in different areas. It is evident, though, that the CL has a certain potential for building competencies to be formed among graduates in accordance with the requirements of the Federal educational standards. One of the possible solutions is specially developed continuing education programs using available modern resources, like MOOC on CL, and innovative training formats.
- It is possible that a special scientific journal on the CL use achievements in pedagogical practice and holding special scientific conferences will contribute to the wider dissemination of this promising teaching method and its sustainable usage in modern pedagogical practice.

Acknowledgements. The authors would like to acknowledge Inga Kuznetsova, English language instructor for ITMO University (St. Petersburg), Master student at Higher School of Language Teaching and Translation (SPbSPU), for her help in preparing this paper.

---

[8] Introduction to Corpus Linguistics MOOC course URL: https://openedu.ru/course/hse/CORPUS/.

References

1. Kopotev, M.V.: Introduction to Corpus Linguistics. Animedia Company, Praha (2014). (in Russian)
2. Kilgarriff, A., et al.: The sketch engine: ten years on. Lexicography **1**(1), 7–36 (2014). https://doi.org/10.1007/s40607-014-0009-9
3. Plugnjan, V.A.: Why do we need the National Corpus of the Russian Language? Informal introduction. In: The National Corpus of the Russian Language: 2003–2005, pp. 6–20. Indrik, Moscow (2005). (in Russian)
4. Boulton, A., Cobb, T.: Corpus use in language learning: a meta-analysis. Lang. Learn. **67**(2), 348–393 (2017). https://doi.org/10.1111/lang.12224
5. Pérez-Paredes, P.: A systematic review of the uses and spread of corpora and data-driven learning in CALL research during 2011–2015. Comput. Assist. Lang. Learn. (2019). https://doi.org/10.1080/09588221.2019.1667832. Published online: 26 Sept 2019
6. Veletsianos, G., Shepherdson, P.A.: Systematic analysis and synthesis of the empirical MOOC literature published in 2013–2015. IRRODL **17**(2), 198–221 (2016). https://doi.org/10.19173/irrodl.v17i2.2448
7. Zimina, T.: Citation index in Russian: Dr. Eugene Garfield approved Russian Science Citation Index. Nauka i Zhizn [Science & Life] 19 September 2006. http://www.nkj.ru/news/6301/. (in Russian)
8. Osipova, E.S.: Corpus linguistics technology in teaching English as a foreign language. In: Chernyavskaya, V., Kuße, H. (eds.) The European Proceedings of Social & Behavioural Sciences EpSBS, vol. 51, pp. 273–283. Future Academy, London (2018). https://doi.org/10.15405/epsbs.2018.12.02.30
9. Gorina, O.G.: Corpus research tools in L2 teaching. Vestnik Tomskogo gosudarstvennogo universiteta [Tomsk State Univ. Bull.] **435**, 187–194 (2018). https://doi.org/10.17223/15617793/435/24. (in Russian)
10. Fenogenova, A., Kuzmenko, E.: Automatic generation of lexical exercises. In: Chernyak, E., Ilvovsky, D., Skorinkin, D., Vybornova, A. (eds.) CEUR Workshop Proceedings, vol. 1886, pp. 20–27 (2016). http://ceur-ws.org/Vol-1886/
11. Kuzminykh, I., Khoroshilova, S.P.: Investigating the impact of corpus-based classroom activities in english phonetics classes on students' academic progress. Novosibirsk State Pedagogical Univ. Bull. **7**(4), 40–51 (2017). https://doi.org/10.15293/2226-3365.1704.03
12. Kogan, M., Yaroshevich, A., Ni, O.: Corpus-based teaching of German compound nouns and lexical bundles for improving academic writing skills. Lidil, **58** (2018). http://journals.openedition.org/lidil/5438. https://doi.org/10.4000/lidil.5438
13. Belyaeva, L.N., Chernyavskaya, V.E.: Scientific and technical texts in the framework of information 4.0: content analysis and text synthesis. St. Petersburg State Polytech. Univ. J. Hum. Soc. Sci. **10**(2), 53–63 (2019). https://doi.org/10.18721/JHSS.10205
14. Beliaeva, L., Chernyavskaya, V.: Technical writer in the framework of modern natural language processing tasks. J. Sib. Fed. Univ. Humanit. Soc. Sci. **12**(1), 20–31 (2019). https://doi.org/10.17516/1997-1370-0377
15. Bogdanova-Beglarian, N., Martynenko, G., Sherstinova, T.: The one day of speech corpus: phonetic and syntactic studies of everyday spoken russian. In: Ronzhin, A., Potapova, R., Fakotakis, N. (eds.) SPECOM 2015. LNCS (LNAI), vol. 9319, pp. 429–437. Springer, Cham (2015). https://doi.org/10.1007/978-3-319-23132-7_53

16. Boulton, A.: Foreword. Data-driven learning for younger learners: obstacles and optimism. In: Crosthwaite, P. (ed.) Data-Driven Learning for the Next Generation: Corpora and DDL for Pre-tertiary Learners, pp. 2–9. Routledge, London (2020). https://doi.org/10.4324/9780429425899

17. Tarnaeva, L.P., Osipova, E.S.: Corpus linguistics resources use in training translators in the sphere of professional communication. Voprosy Teorii i Praktiki **63**(9), 205–209 (2016). (in Russian)

18. Oveshkova, A.N.: Work with english corpora as a means of promoting learner autonomy. Obrazovanie i Nauka [Educ. Sci.] **20**(8), 66–87 (2018). https://doi.org/10.17853/1994-5639-2018-8-66-87

19. Almazova, N., Kogan, M.: Computer assisted individual approach to acquiring foreign vocabulary of students major. In: Zaphiris, P., Ioannou, A. (eds.) LCT 2014. LNCS, vol. 8524, pp. 248–257. Springer, Cham (2014). https://doi.org/10.1007/978-3-319-07485-6_25

20. Shamova, N.A.: Corpus technologies in the academic process from students' perspective. In: All-Russia Student Convent "Innovation" Proceedings, pp. 472–476. Ivanovo State University Press, Ivanovo (2016). (in Russian)

21. Boulton, A., Tyne, H.: Corpus-based study of language and teacher education. In: Biglow, M., Ennser-Kananen, J. (eds.) The Routledge Handbook of Educational Linguistics, pp. 301–312. Routledge, New York (2015). https://doi.org/10.4324/9781315797748

22. Charles, M.: Getting the corpus habit: EAP students' long-term use of personal corpora. Engl. Specif. Purp. **35**(1), 30–40 (2014). https://doi.org/10.1016/j.esp.2013.11.004

23. Leńko-Szymańska, A.: Training teachers in data-driven learning: tackling the challenge. Lang. Learn. Technol. **21**(3), 217–241 (2017). https://doi.org/10125/44628

24. Dmitrijev, A.V., Kogan, M.S.: The potential of corpus linguistics in training foreign language teachers majoring in computer assisted language teaching. St. Petersburg State Polytech. Univ. J. Hum. Soc. Sci. **10**(4), 69–85 (2019). https://doi.org/10.18721/JHSS.10407. (in Russian)

25. Dikareva, S.S., Chernobrivetc, S.G.: Corpus technologies in Russian syntax studying. In: Orekhova, V.V., Titarenko, E.Ja. (eds): Dialogue of Cultures. Theory and Practice of Teaching Languages and Literature. VI International Scientific Conference Proceedings, pp. 146–149. Arial Publishing House, Simferopol (2018). (in Russian)

26. Zakharov, V.P.: Corpus linguistics tools functionality. In: Nikolaev, I.S. (ed.) Strukturnaja i prikladnaja lingvistika Mezhvuzovskij sbornik [Structural and Applied Linguistics], pp. 81–95. Saint Petersburg State University Press, St. Petersburg (2019). (in Russian)

27. Rezanova, Z.I., Shilyaev, K.S.: Russian National Corpus in teaching the use of Russian diminutives. Mezhdunarodnyj Zhurnal Prikladnyh i Fundamental'nyh Issledovanij [Int. J. Appl. Basic Res.] **5–4**, 634–639 (2015). (in Russian)

28. Paramonova, M., Olkhovskaya, A.: Corpus in teaching Russian language and literature. Rhema **1**, 93–123 (2019). https://doi.org/10.31862/2500-2953-2019-1-93-123

29. Dobrushina, N.R. (ed.): Nacional'nyj korpus russkogo jazyka i problemy gumanitarnogo obrazovanija [The National Corpus of the Russian Language and Issues of Humanitarian Education]. SU-HSE Press, Moscow (2007)

30. Kabanova, N., Kogan, M.: Needs analysis as a cornerstone in formation of ict competence in language teachers through specially tailored in-service training course. In: Zaphiris, P., Ioannou, A. (eds.) LCT 2017. LNCS, vol. 10295, pp. 110–123. Springer, Cham (2017). https://doi.org/10.1007/978-3-319-58509-3_11

Framework of Manga Application
for Teaching Japanese Language

Masahide Kuwano[1]([⊠]), Ryosuke Yamanishi[1], Yoko Nishihara[1],
and Naoko Takei[2]

[1] Ritsumeikan University, Kusatsu, Shiga 525-8577, Japan
is0305pk@ed.ritsumei.ac.jp, ryama@media.ritsumei.ac.jp,
nisihara@fc.ritsumei.ac.jp
[2] Simon Fraser University, Burnaby, BC V5A 1S6, Canada
ntakei@sfu.ca

Abstract. This paper proposes a framework to use Manga (i.e., Japanese comics) as the teaching materials for the Japanese language education and develops a prototype that enables teachers to easily retrieve the intended grammar, words, and contexts from Manga. Japanese pop-culture has been widely known and is becoming popular all over the world, e.g., Manga and Anime. Manga-related culture is currently no longer just Japanese domestic but universal culture. Through enjoying the Manga-related culture, people may have the opportunity to learn Japanese traditional and present cultures. Japanese teaching materials are prepared in various languages. It is thus easy to understand basic grammar. However, it is still difficult to learn how to use the Japanese language in real life in Japan. Some of the expressions and nuances of the phrases are deeply related to the Japanese culture which is unconsciously obtained through the lives in the native environment; those are hard to know even if it is explained in the text. We believe that Manga can be useful materials for such education. So, this paper proposed a framework to help teachers to retrieve the intended educational topics (i.e., words and phrases). The user easily obtains the frames where the intended words and phrases are included by using the system. While the teachers made the problem for the Japanese language, the usability of the proposed framework was confirmed.

Keywords: Application of Manga · Language education · Retrieval of teaching materials

1 Introduction

Japanese pop-culture has been widely known and is becoming popular all over the world, e.g., Manga and Anime. Manga and Anime, that is Manga-related culture, are highly appreciated not just as entertainment contents but also the unique arts. So many people watch Anime on media-streaming services. During May through August in 2019, British Museum, which is a well-known museum in

© Springer Nature Switzerland AG 2020
P. Zaphiris and A. Ioannou (Eds.): HCII 2020, LNCS 12205, pp. 356–367, 2020.
https://doi.org/10.1007/978-3-030-50513-4_27

the world, held a special exhibition for Manga. Manga-related culture is currently no longer just Japanese domestic but universal culture. Through enjoying the Manga-related culture, people may have the opportunity to learn Japanese traditional and present cultures. Besides, it can be a trigger to study the Japanese language. Based on the survey for Japanese language education in foreign countries conducted by The Japan Foundation [4], the third most common purpose for learning the Japanese language was "I like manga, anime, pop culture, etc."

Almost 3.7 million people outside of Japan learn the Japanese language. The number of learners has increased continuously in these years. Japanese teaching materials are prepared in various languages. It is thus easy to understand basic grammar and some words themselves. However, it is still difficult to learn how to use the Japanese language in real life in Japan. The skill to talk in natural Japanese is dramatically hard to get for the learners outside of Japan because they can not experience Japanese-native lives in real, especially daily conversations. To resolve this experience-depend problem, language teachers have tried so various ways to teach the nuance and context for the words. Even though the learners know the Japanese culture, it is still hard to figure out the word usage in real if they do not experience the culture. For example, Vancouver in Canada is a city greatly influenced by Asian culture, where the fourth author is teaching Japanese. The learners there tend to have a higher level of understanding of Asian culture than other regions. However, a sentence "After dinner, the family shared an apple to eat." evokes their emotion that is differed from the native Japanese sensitivity. This sentence can be assumed as the sentence showing a happy family though North Americans may feel the opposite understanding like "the family is so poor that they need to share an apple." In Japan, native Japanese naturally imagine a relatively big kind of apple "Fuji" when they see "apple." However, the common "apple" in North America is usually an apple small enough to fit in a hand.

In teaching materials that focus on only the introduction of sentences and words, it should be limited to teach the difference in nuance and appropriate usage of words corresponding to the context. The differences in expressions and nuances are deeply rooted in Japanese culture and should be learned through real life. Even if it is explained in textbooks, those are most difficult to understand and master for especially language learners outside of Japan. We believe that Manga can be useful materials for teaching such complicated things that are not shown in the textbook directly because Manga mainly consists of speech dialogues and images showing the corresponding contexts. However, retrieving the pages and scenes showing the intended topics to teach takes a lot of time for the language teacher; he/she has to manually read all of the content in Manga and Anime. We consider that automating this task should help the teachers to make more attractive and useful lectures in real. As learning languages with living contextual examples, the language learning should be changed from "learning to target the understanding of grammatical syntax and words" to "learning to educate context understandings and affective sensitively for language."

In this paper, we propose a prototype to support to retrieve Japanese teaching materials from Manga. In the proposed system, we use the Manga 109 [8,10] dataset, which stores 109 comic books drawn by professionals and is prepared for media processing research of Manga. We conducted an evaluation experiment for the retrieved comic frames as the teaching materials.

2   Related Work

The comic is no longer just an entertainment content but an interesting target for multimedia research. Comic Computing is the concept for the research related to Comic-related entertainment [15]. So many types of research related to comics have been proposed: analysis [1,14], processing [3,11], generation [2,7], and application [13,16].

As the application of comics, many studies using Japanese Manga and Anime to support Japanese language learning; e.g., the comic is used as teaching material for Japanese language learning in European countries [6]. Our previous study proposed a support system using comics scenes for learning Japanese role words [9]. The understandings of the role words, which are the especially hard part of the Japanese language, was improved by using the proposed system. Anime is the most typical entertainment related to comics. We have also proposed a framework to use Anime as additional educational materials for listening skills [13]. It has been confirmed that the framework introduced practical and effective learning for language and cultures.

This paper is the extended approach of the previous studies and is designed as the support system, not for only role words but also various words and phrases. The proposed system enables us to easily use comics as the teaching sub-materials corresponding to the textbook for language learning.

3   Proposed Framework

We propose a framework to support teaching the Japanese language as using Manga for teaching materials. As the resource of Manga, we used Manga 109 dataset with annotations that are stored in XML files in this paper.

3.1   The Procedures in the Proposed Framework

The proposed framework works as the following steps.

Step 1 The proposed system obtains three types of annotations for each spread of two pages from one XML file in the Manga 109 dataset. The obtained annotations are the coordinate data of each frame, the text of a speech for each speech bubble, and the coordinate data for each speech bubble.

Step 2 The proposed system detects which frame each speech is included concerning to the coordinate data for each frame and speech. And then, the coordinate data of the speech for each spread of two pages are prepared. Here, each speech is morphologically analyzed and is shown as the sequence of the part-of-speech.

Step 3 The proposed system accepts the query from the user, i.e., the teacher for the Japanese language. The query should be words, phrases, and contexts corresponding to the target of the lesson. As same as Step 2 for speech in Manga, the input query is morphologically analyzed and is shown as the sequence of words with the part-of-speech.

Step 4 The proposed system searches which area on the page of Manga include the sequence of words with the part-of-speech of the input query. According to the result of the search, the system outputs all frames with the speech including input query.

Manga109 has an XML file for annotations corresponding to one title of the comic. Each comic includes every page with the images for each spread two pages and some kinds of annotation. The proposed system uses three types of annotation: the coordinate data for each frame, the text for each speech in the speech bubbles, and the coordinate data for each speech. In Step 1, the coordinate values for each frame, text, and speech bubbles are provided as a rectangular area which is shown as x-min, y-min, x-max, and y-max. Then, the coordinate data of each angle can be calculated by using x-min and y-min for the upper left, x-min and y-max for the lower right, x-max and y-max for the lower right and x-max and y-min for the upper right, respectively. As the detail of Step 2, Fig. 1 shows the example of detecting frames including the speech. Figure 1 (a) shows an example that is detected as the frame including the speech; the frame surrounded by a blue frame includes the coordinate data of the speech surrounded by a red frame in its area. On the other hand, Fig. 1(b) shows an example that the speech surrounded by a red frame is not included in the frames surrounded both blue and green frames; both of the frames do not include all of four coordinate data of the speech.

As the morphological analysis in Steps 2 and 3, the proposed system uses MeCab [5] for morphological analysis and NEologd [12] for the dictionary. To output the frames including the query as the retrieval results, the proposed system crops the coordinate of each frame including the input query from the image of the spread two pages.

3.2   The Merit of Proposed Framework

Using the proposed framework, the user easily obtains the frames of Manga that include the intended words and phrases in the speech. We believe that the user saves significant time on tasks to retrieve the Manga scenes for teaching materials.

In Fig. 2, (a) and (b) each shows a conceptual comparison between the architecture of the proposed system and conventional tasks, respectively. Without using the system to retrieve comics, the teacher has to read every page of the comics and find the speech including the intended words and phrases by his/herself. So it takes a great number of times as in Fig. 2 (a): the number of pages times number of comics. On the other hand, in Fig. 2 (b), the retrieving is automatically conducted by the system. The user has to only input the query and the retrieval results are provided in a second.

(a) The proposed system detects that the speech in the red rectangle is included in a frame of the blue rectangle.

(b) The proposed system detects that the speech in the red rectangle is included in none of the frames.

Fig. 1. Examples of how the proposed system detects speech included in the frame. (a) shows the speech detected as the speech included in the frame. (b) shows that none of the frames does not include the speech. (Color figure online)

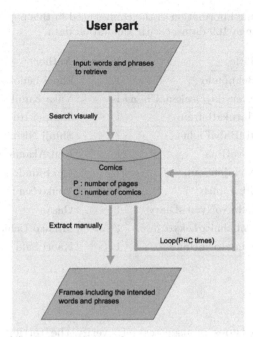

(a) The task for teachers to retrieve appropriate comic scenes. The teachers have to read so many pages of comics by themselves.

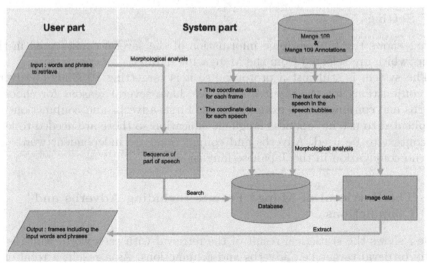

(b) The system architecture and the user interaction. The teachers have to only input the query and the retrieved scenes for the query would be output.

Fig. 2. Comparison of traditional tasks and the proposed system architecture.

Table 1. Bibliographic information of the comics used in this paper. All of the comics are stored in the Manga 109 dataset with annotation data.

ID	Title	Volume	Author
1	Belmondo	1	Shoei Ishioka
2	EverydayOsakanaChan	1	Yuka Kuniki
3	HarukaRefrain	1	Shinpei Ito
4	JijiBabaFight	1	Shinji Nishikawa
5	LoveHina	1	Ken Akamatsu
6	NichijouSoup	1	Uni Shindou
7	OL_Lunch	1	Youko Sanri
8	UchiNoNyan'sDiary	1	Gasan
9	UnbalanceTokyo	1	Minako Uchida
10	YamatoNoHane	1	Kaori Saki

4   User Test

We conducted two types of user tests to verify the retrieval results and the effectiveness of the retrieved frames as teaching materials. We have the discussion for the retrieval results for the future direction.

4.1   Settings

Table 1 shows the bibliographic information of the several comics used in this paper, which are selected from the Manga 109 dataset.

The system is still just a prototype so it is targeting 10 kinds of adverbs and conjunctions for the input queries. We have several reasons for choosing adverbs and conjunction as example input. First, adverbs and conjunctions are complicated to use in Japanese language education so those are needed to learn the context to be used. Adverbs and conjunctions are independent words and have no conjugation in the Japanese language.

4.2   The Retrieval of Manga Frames Including Adverbs and Conjunctions

Table 2 shows the statistical result of the retrieval with each word, which is set as the retrieval target i.e., adverbs and conjunctions. As a result, a total of 66 frames were detected as the frames including each from a total of 10 comics.

In the results, 17 frames out of 66 frames showed the conversation between more than two characters. The examples of the retrieved frames are shown in Fig. 3. Though it is not so much than we expected, the system automatically

Table 2. The stastical results of the retrieval. The values in the table indicate the number of frames detected by the proposed system for each comic title. Note, (a): adverb, (c): conjunction.

	ますます (a)	いまにも (a)	おそらく (a)	すでに (a)	せっかく (a)	それとも (c)	だけど (c)	つまり (c)	ところが (c)	ところで (c)
Belmondo	0	0	0	0	0	0	1	5	1	1
EverydayOsakanaChan	2	0	0	3	3	0	1	0	1	4
HarukaRefrain	0	0	0	2	0	0	0	2	0	0
JijiBabaFight	1	0	1	2	1	0	0	0	0	1
LoveHina	0	0	0	0	1	0	0	0	0	0
NichijouSoup	0	0	0	0	2	0	0	0	0	2
OL_Lunch	0	0	0	1	1	0	0	1	0	1
UchiNoNyan'sDiary	0	0	2	0	3	1	0	0	4	0
UnbalanceTokyo	0	0	0	0	1	2	1	4	1	3
YamatoNoHane	0	0	0	0	0	0	1	2	0	0

Table 3. Evaluation of the retrieved frames for some words. The values in the table are shown in %. Note, (a): adverb, (c): conjunction.

	あまり (a)	でも (a)	まだ (a)	もう (a)	ちょっと (a)	よく (a)	ところで (c)
Good	33.3	58.6	16.7	29.4	61.5	16.7	100
Bad	66.7	41.4	83.3	70.6	38.5	83.3	0

found the frames showing the conversation using the intended words. The conversations were like the daily conversation of native speakers. The usage of the intended words and phrases corresponded to the speaker's profile and emotion in the conversational context. And the context was shown in the mix of texts and images. So we consider that the retrieved results can be used as the teaching materials for Japanese language learning especially for daily conversation.

The number of the retrieved frames including the query word in the conversation was less than we expected. We believe that these results were caused by the characteristics of the Manga conversation. In Manga, each frame usually shows only one character speech because of lack of space and for identification of the speaker: that is a kind of drawing technique. So the direction to improve the proposed system should be detecting multiple frames showing a conversation with a reasonable breaking. Also, the system retrieved multiple frames including only text without any images. It seems that these results did not show the advantage of Manga, which is the mixed media of text and image. Another future direction will be detecting only frames in which the character expressly has a conversation. Then the character ID annotated to each frame should be useful to detect whether the frame includes characters.

Let us focus on an adverb "いまにも" in Table 2. The system could not find any frames including the word from the dataset. This was the fact that the intended word did not exist in the comics used in this retrieval. However, we could know the results in a moment as the retrieval result though it takes much longer time to know that by human manual retrieval. It suggested that the proposed system reduced the time for retrieval.

© Yuka Kuniki

(a) Frame including " (more and more)"

© Minako Uchida

(b) Frame including " (however)"

© Shinpei Ito

(c) Frame including " (that is)"

© Shinji Nishikawa

(d) Frame including " (great deal)"

Fig. 3. Examples of frames including the intended query retrieved from comics with the conversation between more than two characters.

4.3 The Evaluation of the Retrieved Frames

We prepared three participants as the test users. They were university students whose filed is computer science. And, they had no experience of language instruction before. The goal for the participants was to retrieve some frames for the sub-materials of elementary Japanese teaching, which is shown in the textbook

Fig. 4. Example of frames including "by the way (ところで)" retrieved from "Nichijou Soup." Those were evaluated as appropriate sub-materials.

Fig. 5. Example of frames including "あまり" retrieved from "EverydayOsakanaChan." The usage of the word can be not distinguished.

"Genki." The participants were asked to use the proposed system for retrieving frames to be used as the sub-materials from the three comics listed in Table 1.

The participants chose the adverbs and conjunctions that should be necessary for learning Japanese from the textbook. The participants retrieved the chosen words by using the proposed system. And the retrieved results were subjectively evaluated by a teacher of Japanese language, who is the fourth author of this paper. The stastical results of the evaluation is shown in Table 3. From the table, it was confirmed that the participants retrieved the frames appropriate teaching materials for some of the words without any experience of teaching the language. However, some of the retrieved frames were evaluated as inappropriate for teaching materials because of some reasons.

Let us focus on some typical cases. The retrieved results for "ところで," which is a conjunction, were good as the teaching materials. Figure 4 shows the examples of the retrieved frames. The retrieved frame showed the conversational context with only one frame. However, the evaluation for conjunction "あまり," which examples are shown in Fig. 5 was not good. The word has several types of usages and is used in different contexts; in Fig. 5, the left side concerened "degree" but the right side concerned "too much." However, the current prototype did not focus on the difference. It will be the future improvement of our system.

5   Conclusions

In this paper we proposed a framework to use Manga frames as the sub-materials for Japanese language learning. The prototype of the retrieval system was developed.

It was confirmed that the proposed system detected the frames including the intended query in the speech. Some of the retrieved results showed conversation that should be effective to show real use cases of the query word with the context shown in texts and image. We found the future directions to improve the proposed system based on the discussions for the results. The conversation may not be in one frame but be continued over multiple frames. To show the context in which the intended word is used, the multiple frames shoudl be provided as the retrieved results. Also, the retrieval should be controlled for usage and meaning of the word. The context itself should be categorized in the language education too.

This paper is positioned as a basic study for using comics as teaching materials to promote understanding rooted in the background and culture of the Japanese language. We will improve the accuracy and usability of the system in the future based on the findings in this paper.

References

1. Chu, W.T., Cheng, W.C.: Manga-specific features and latent style model for Manga style analysis. In: 2016 IEEE International Conference on Acoustics, Speech and Signal Processing (ICASSP), pp. 1332–1336 (2016)
2. Fukuda, K., Fujino, S., Mori, N., Matsumoto, K.: Semi-automatic picture book generation based on story model and agent-based simulation. In: Leu, G., Singh, H.K., Elsayed, S. (eds.) Intelligent and Evolutionary Systems. PALO, vol. 8, pp. 117–132. Springer, Cham (2017). https://doi.org/10.1007/978-3-319-49049-6_9
3. Ito, K., Matsui, Y., Yamasaki, T., Aizawa, K.: Separation of Manga line drawings and screentones. In: Eurographics (Short Papers), pp. 73–76 (2015)
4. Japan Foundation: Survey report on Japanese-language education abroad (2012)
5. Kudo, T., Yamamoto, K., Matsumoto, Y.: Applying conditional random fields to Japanese morphological analysis. In: 2004 Conference on Empirical Methods in Natural Language Processing, pp. 230–237 (2004)
6. Lammers, W.P.: Japanese the Manga Way: An Illustrated Guide to Grammar and Structure. Stone Bridge Press Inc., Berkeley (2004)
7. Martens, C., Cardona-Rivera, R.E.: Generating abstract comics. In: Nack, F., Gordon, A.S. (eds.) ICIDS 2016. LNCS, vol. 10045, pp. 168–175. Springer, Cham (2016). https://doi.org/10.1007/978-3-319-48279-8_15
8. Matsui, Y., et al.: Sketch-based Manga retrieval using Manga109 dataset. Multimed. Tools Appl. **76**(20), 21811–21838 (2016). https://doi.org/10.1007/s11042-016-4020-z
9. Nishihara, Y., Matsuoka, K., Yamanishi, R.: Effects comparison between English and Chinese speakers in learning Japanese role words with comic scenes. In: International Symposium on Affective Science and Engineering, pp. 1–6 (2018)

10. Ogawa, T., Otsubo, A., Narita, R., Matsui, Y., Yamasaki, T., Aizawa, K.: Object detection for comics using Manga109 annotations. CoRR. arXiv preprint arXiv:1803.08670 (2018)
11. Qu, Y., Wong, T.T., Heng, P.A.: Manga colorization. ACM Trans. Graph. (TOG) **25**(3), 1214–1220 (2006)
12. Sato, T.: Neologism dictionary based on the language resources on the web for MeCab (2015). https://github.com/neologd/mecab-ipadic-neologd
13. Shan, J., Nishihara, Y., Yamanishi, R., Fukumoto, J.: Analysis of dialogues difficulty in anime comparing with JLPT listening tests. Procedia Comput. Sci. **112**, 1345–1352 (2017)
14. Sun, W., Burie, J.C., Ogier, J.M., Kise, K.: Specific comic character detection using local feature matching. In: 2013 12th International Conference on Document Analysis and Recognition, pp. 275–279. IEEE (2013)
15. Yamanishi, R., Matsushita, M.: Comic computing: a conceptual framework for decomposition and utilization of comic contents. In: The Proceeding of the Sixth Asian Conference on Information Systems 2017, p. TH2-2 (2017)
16. Yamanishi, R., Tanaka, H., Nishihara, Y., Fukumoto, J.: Speech-balloon shapes estimation for emotional text communication. Inf. Eng. Express **3**(2), 1–10 (2017)

Individualized Differentiated Spelling with Blogs - Implementing and Individualizing (IDeRBlog ii)

An Example of a Learning Analytics Platform for the Text-Based Acquisition of Spelling Skills of Students in German

Nina Leidinger[1](✉), Michael Gros[1](✉), Martin Ebner[2],
Markus Ebner[2], Konstanze Edtstadler[3], Elisabeth Herunter[3],
Jessica Heide[4], Sabine Peifer[4], Anneliese Huppertz[5],
and Vera Kistemann[5]

[1] Landesinstitut für Pädagogik und Medien, Saarbrücken, Germany
{nleidinger,mgros}@lpm.uni-sb.de
https://iderblog.lpm.uni-sb.de
[2] Graz University of Technology, Graz, Austria
[3] PH Steiermark, Graz, Austria
[4] Grund- und Ganztagsgrundschule Saarbrücken, Dellengarten,
Saarbrücken, Germany
[5] Gemeindeschule Raeren, Raeren, Belgium

Abstract. The paper depicts the Erasmus+ project "Individual DifferEntiated correct writing with Blogs - Individualizing and Implementing (IDeRBlog ii)". IDeRBlog ii is a follow-up project evolving the result of IDeRBlog, a blogging platform for pupils aged eight and above. The project is an international cooperation between 3 countries in Europe. This paper presents an overview of possibilities in context of individualization of the exercises. Further, it covers the benefits of using the platform, e.g. learning about media competences, how to communicate online and the possibility to get individualized exercises for supported during their writing process by the feedback of the intelligent dictionary.

Keywords: Learning analytics · Blog · Writing · Spelling · Orthography · Communication

1 Consortium

The partners perform various tasks within the project. The distribution of tasks and milestones formulated in the application are discussed and evaluated in regular virtual and face-to-face meetings. A precise allocation of the individual work packages has already been made in the application. The PH Steiermark is mainly responsible for the extension of the intelligent dictionary and didactic advice in the creation of spelling

© Springer Nature Switzerland AG 2020
P. Zaphiris and A. Ioannou (Eds.): HCII 2020, LNCS 12205, pp. 368–379, 2020.
https://doi.org/10.1007/978-3-030-50513-4_28

exercises. Graz University of Technology is technically implementing the individual work packages. The two practice schools test new functionalities and give feedback on usability. Based on their feedback, adjustments to the system are made as required.

The LPM as coordinating institution is integrated in all work packages and creates didactic materials for teaching such as lesson preparations for the individual spelling categories. Like all other partners, the LPM is also responsible for the dissemination of the project.

2 Writing Lessons at School - Analogue Writing Versus Digital Writing in a Blog

In school, a wide variety of texts are written in the classroom. In German lessons in the area of writing, process descriptions, narrations and stories are written. In factual lessons, texts are written on the respective subject matter. Students also write texts in religion, visual arts and music.

All these texts are often written in analogous form in the booklet and then ideally read and improved by the teacher. This requires the students to correct what they have written until the text is finished, which in turn requires the complete rewriting of the text again and again, which slows down the completion of the text. In addition, the complete rewriting of the text is not motivating.

Since the analogue text is only available in the booklet, it is not or rarely read by others. The author of the text - in this case the pupils - has no audience. Unless the teachers give other pupils the opportunity to read or present the resulting texts (exhibition, posters ...). This means that an essential aspect of writing texts is lost in analogue text production. Texts are usually written for others to pass on information to the reader. This has a negative effect on the pupils' motivation to write. It is often very low due to the missing readership of the text and decreases more and more in the course of school attendance. Wanting to write often turns into having to write.

In the digital form of writing on a blogging platform the procedure is similar. Students write their text. The teacher gives feedback. On the one hand, this can be in terms of content. On the other hand, spelling can also be discussed in the feedback. The students improve their text.

Here, a first advantage of writing with digital media becomes clear. Pupils do not always have to rewrite the text after the teacher has corrected it, but can continue writing and improve the text once it has been written.

After completion of all improvements in the context of the writing conference between teachers and pupils, the text is published and is then available for reading to an audience (fellow pupils within the class community, within the school community or all users of the Internet). The resulting text thus gains an audience. Hence, the pupils' motivation to write increases because the text can be read by others.

3 Relevance of Spelling

Spelling is of great importance in all areas of life. The legibility of texts is increased and facilitated by standardized spelling. Misunderstandings are avoided if words are orthographically correct. Especially in the school system, but also in professional life in Germany, the importance of spelling is very high. In primary schools there is a separate grade for spelling and in secondary schools the results are rated one grade lower if the spelling is not sufficient. In professional life, too, great importance is attached to correct spelling in many professional fields. This goes as far as that applicants handing in application documents with poor spelling are not considered when selecting potential new employees.

4 IDeRBlog ii Tool for Free Writing and Spelling Improvement

The blogging platform IDeRBlog ii picks up on this by enabling a phase of automated spell checking after the creation of the text throughout the process of text creation described above.

The procedure remains basically the same as described above. However, after the text creation phase, students are given feedback on the text they have written and the spelling errors it contains by clicking on "Check now".

The feedback is differentiated between that of the "intelligent" dictionary and that of the intelligent dictionary.

In the "normal dictionary" a potential error is displayed. Students can use the normal methods of finding the correct spelling of the word. They look words up in dictionaries. They ask questions or they search the Internet for the correct spelling. After having improvement their text, students can click on "check again" to see if the word is now spelled correctly (Fig. 1).

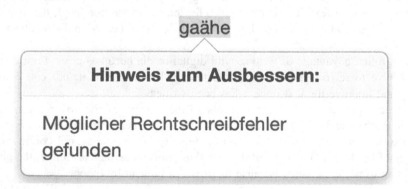

Fig. 1. Note of the general dictionary in IDeRBlog ii (Screenshot https://iderblog.eu 22.01. 2020)

The feedback from the intelligent dictionary relates to the mistake made by the students and gives specific feedback on the error to improve the word. After reading the feedback, students should be able to correct the mistake immediately using the feedback. This requires knowledge of spelling strategies (Fig. 2).

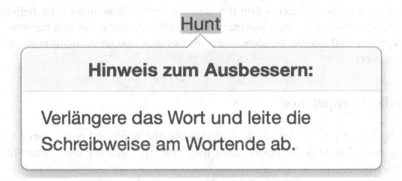

Fig. 2. Note of the intelligent dictionary in IDeRBlog ii (Screenshot https://iderblog.eu 22.01. 2020)

In this phase of spell checking the self-written text, students receive feedback on their spelling mistakes. This makes it easier for them to improve their spelling skills. At the same time, they apply the spelling strategies they have learned and internalize them by applying them during the improvement process. The described improvement process suggests an increase in spelling competence.

Ideally, the students improve their texts until they are presented correctly and then hand them over to the teacher.

This correction process, which is carried out by the students, makes the teachers' work easier, as they receive texts from the students that are ideally free of errors.

However, context-based spell checking is not available even in the dictionaries used in IDeRBlog ii. Therefore, it is possible that teachers will find a few more mistakes in the text and report them back to the students. This feedback will also give students an insight into the finite nature of the digital improvement of texts due to the technical structure of spell checkers, which will only allow a context-based improvement of misspellings to a limited extent by 2020.

Apart from that, teachers mainly focus on content corrections of the text and give students feedback on the content of their texts. By using the platform IDeRBlog ii, a digital writing conference between teachers and students is possible. Due to the fact that they can communicate with each other asynchronously.

The aim of the writing conference is to produce a well written text, which will be published in the final step. Only the students can publish the text they have written after the teachers have given their approval.

5 Digital Texts Versus Analogue Texts

The texts created and published by the pupils can be read by members of the class, school-wide or by all users of the Internet, depending on settings made by the teacher. Thus, the texts and their authors gain a potential readership. In addition, classmates can comment on texts being read within the class or school community after registration. Hence, the text loses its static character and becomes dynamic through the interaction between reader and author. Readers and authors enter into an asynchronous dialogue with each other.

6 Media Competence

By writing with digital devices as described above, the pupils not only acquire German language skills but also the media skills they urgently need for their future life in a digital society.

In addition to basic skills such as orientation on the computer keyboard and the basics of writing with digital devices for example punctuation, the basic handling of the input device is also trained. Switching on and off as well as the correct operation of the browser will be learned. These skills are more likely encompassed in the area of "operation and use".

But also, competencies in the area of "acting safely and thinking about media" are addressed by using the platform. Dealing with each other in digital communication is not only theoretically trained, but also applied in acting on the platform. The effect of texts can also be discussed in class, as can the way we deal with each other on the Internet. Likewise, competences in the safe use of the Internet are trained while using the website. The competent use of passwords can also be addressed while working with the platform in class. At the same time, students directly apply the acquired knowledge.

In this way, the platform pursues a subject-integrated approach in which digital knowledge and skills are imparted in German. The acquisition of skills goes far beyond the basic skills of the operator and user. A particularly large number of skills are developed in the area of "communication and safe handling when using the Internet".

7 Easy Usability

Despite all the complexity of the platform, attention is paid in all areas to increase the usability of the platform. Navigation within the platform is kept as simple as possible so that students have little difficulty in using the platform. Usability tests were carried out in the first phase of the development of the platform with students who gave important hints for the improvement of the platform. Whenever new functionalities are programmed into the platform, they are tested by the practice schools and their feedback flows back into a continuous improvement process.

8   Learning Analytics and IDeRBlog ii

The learning analytics approach, first systematized by Mohamed Chatti and colleagues in 2012 [1], plays a major role in the IDeRBlog ii platform.

Chatti and colleagues [1] describe learning analytics (LA), or educational data mining (EDM), as a process of collecting and evaluating data in digital environments and provision of materials to the learner based on the evaluation. IDeRBlog ii has implemented this approach of LA or EDM.

All of the words of the intelligent dictionary are assigned to 22 spelling categories. The systematics of the different spelling phenomena were developed by the project team, as well as the intelligent dictionary that picks up the spelling phenomena. All misspelled words of a student in the intelligent dictionary are evaluated and assigned to the corresponding error categories. After a certain number of misspellings (50) and written words (500) a qualified statement can be made about the spelling problems of the student. This evaluation is made available to each student (Fig. 3).

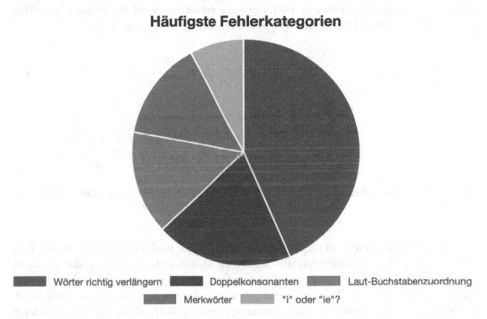

Häufigste Fehlerkategorien

| Wörter richtig verlängern | Doppelkonsonanten | Laut-Buchstabenzuordnung |
| Merkwörter | "i" oder "ie"? |

Fig. 3. Evaluation display of the error focus for students of general dictionary in IDeRBlog ii (Screenshot https://iderblog.eu 22.01.2020)

Students will be provided with "online exercises" or "worksheets" for the individual error focus of the students, which may vary from student to student. These can be worked on in exercise phases and thus improve their spelling competence in their individual error focus.

To refresh knowledge, one online course is available for each error category, which is to be worked on by the students. The individual courses are all structured in the same way. They offer a mixture of knowledge transfer and application of the knowledge acquired within the course. In all courses, care is taken to alternate analogue and digital practice phases.

On the first page, the spelling phenomenon is explained. The knowledge acquired on page 1 is to be applied on the second page by the students working on a corresponding online exercise which focuses on the respective spelling phenomenon. On the third page there is a phase of knowledge transfer paired with an offline exercise in which the students apply their acquired knowledge. On page 4 the students are provided with another online exercise to work on. Finally, the students can download and print out a worksheet, which can also be worked on at home.

Thus, IDeRBlog ii makes an important contribution to individualized spelling learning.

The evaluation provided to the students can also be viewed by the teachers. In addition, the teacher's view shows the spelling mistakes of the individual students, sorted by spelling category, so that the teacher can see a detailed performance level of the students. This allows an individualized support of the students in other teaching scenarios as well. Teachers can also view the performance of the entire class. This gives them important information for planning their lessons (Fig. 4).

Auslautverhärtung   Walt (105), Hunt (92), Flugzeuk (12) ⊜   286

mak (10), kald (10), Pfert (9), gap (7), mid (6), dord (6), Abent (6), gud
(5), laud (2), wilt (2), starg (2), Tak (2), nichd (2), Deutschlant (1), Helt
(1), Urlaup (1), Zeid (1), Strant (1), Gud (1), liept (1), weid (1)

Fig. 4. Example of a directory of misspelled words by students (Screenshot https://iderblog.eu 22.1.2020)

The evaluation adapts to the learning progress of the students and is not static. This means that it changes automatically according to the texts written by the students. Hence, the student evaluation loses its static character and is always up-to-date through the use of the platform. This is a great advantage for teachers and makes their work easier, because they do not have to evaluate the spelling skills of the individual students anymore, but can always access the current evaluation with one click.

9   Exercises in IDeRBlog ii

The exercises and worksheets used in IDeRBlog ii are mostly the result of online research. Researched exercises (online or print) were assigned to the corresponding spelling categories and sorted by level of difficulty. In the IDeRBlog project, the PH Vienna has created and published exercises in areas where few or no exercises were found. The same happened with worksheets created by the LPM in the first phase of the project.

All exercises have been reviewed and checked by the partner consortium. Special attention was paid to the correctness of all exercises and worksheets. Other criteria included common file formats in the print exercises and age-appropriate explanations in the online exercises.

All exercises referenced in IDeRBlog ii can be accessed by students in the student area "Practice" as well as by teachers in the adult area without registration at IDeRBlog ii.

10   The Teachers and Parents Site on the Platform

In principle, the platform is divided into the "Children's World" (http://iderblog.cu) and the "Teachers and Parents Site" (https://iderblog.eu/fuer-erwachsene/aktuelles/). The structure of the children's page and its possibilities for pupils were discussed above. On the teachers and parents site, teachers in particular, but also other users or interested parties can get an overview of the platform.

Besides the provision of the above mentioned online (https://iderblog.eu/fuer-erwachsene/uebungsdatenbank-online/?no_cache=1) and print exercises (https://iderblog.eu/fuer-erwachsene/uebungsdatenbank-print/?no_cache=1) sorted by spelling mistake categories, users can get an insight into the structure of the platform. A total of 15 videos describing how to use the platform are available for teachers (https://iderblog.cu/fucr-erwachsene/uebungsdatenbank-print/?no_cache=1). In addition, teachers have access to a manual describing how to use the platform. A user manual for pupils can also be downloaded and made available to pupils when they use the platform (https://iderblog.cu/fuer-erwachsene/materialien/handbuecher/). Another supporting material is the digital self-learning course, which also explains the basic use of the platform (https://iderblog.lpm.uni-sb.de/moodle/course/view.php?id=4).

Teachers are also provided with an overview of the idea and the main features of the platform as well as the basic requirements that students should meet before they start working on the platform.

In the materials section, teachers will find information about possible scenarios for using IDeRBlog ii. It is explained how and in which teaching scenario IDeRBlog ii can be used. The goals to be achieved in the field of media education when using IDeRBlog ii are also presented in the adult area.

Especially interesting in this context are the writing occasions (https://iderblog.eu/fuer-erwachsene/schreibanlaesse/). The 100 writing events contain ideas about what pupils can write on the platform if they have no idea what text to write (Fig. 5).

The writing events are arranged according to topics and contain not only suggestions for what the pupils can write about but also tips on what the pupils should think about during the writing process.

The writing events are published digitally, but can also be downloaded collectively and used as flashcards. This gives the pupils the opportunity to choose topics for writing in other lesson sequences and to use them in an analogue writing process (Fig. 6).

Schreibanlässe nach Thema

SA - Erlebnisse	SA - Farben	SA - Gegenstand
SA - Geographie	SA - Geschichte	SA - Jahreszeiten
SA - Kleidung	SA - Lebensmittel	SA - Literatur
SA - Personen	SA - Privates	SA - Schule
SA - Spannung	SA - Sport	SA - Sprichwort
SA - Textgattung	SA - Tiere	SA - TV
SA - Werbung		

Fig. 5. Writing occasions sorted by topic (Screenshot https://iderblog.eu 22.01.2020)

SA 001) Wenn Pause ist ...

Verfasse einen Blogbeitrag zu einer interessanten Pause. Berichte uns, was du erlebt hast.

Tipps:

- Wann?
- Was?
- Mit wem?
- Wo?

Kategorie: SA - einfach, SA - Schule

SA 002) Sport

Du betreibst eine Sportart in einem Verein; dann berichte uns von deinem letzten Wettkampf / Spiel.

Tipps:

- Sportart
- Art des Wettkampfes
- Ort
- Ergebnis

Kategorie: SA - Sport, SA - einfach

Fig. 6. Example: Writing occasions (Screenshot https://iderblog.eu 22.01.2020)

Teachers can subscribe to the IDeRBlog ii newsletter, which informs about news and is published monthly. Teachers can also get an overview of the next training dates in the area of further education.

11 News in IDeRBlog ii

The IDeRBlog ii platform will be funded as part of the European Erasmus+ project from 2018 to 2021. The follow-up project is divided into different work packages. In the following, the changes of the platform that will alter the use of the platform will be addressed.

In order to expand the user groups, a second design of the platform will be created, so that older pupils can also use the platform with an appropriate design according to their age.

The process of writing on the platform will be didacticized so that pupils can enter the headline in an extra field. This way every text has a headline, which is also better displayed on the platform.

Texts can be provided with keywords so that they are easier to find. This additional function makes it easier to find texts as well as to work with the pupils in media education. Keywords or tags can be discussed in class. By using this function pupils become aware of the necessity of keywording content to make it easier to find it.

The teacher's comments after the text has been submitted by the pupil are highlighted. This allows students to find teachers' improvements or comments more quickly and incorporate them into their text.

Copyright free images can be incorporated into texts, so that the appearance of the texts and the blog changes. By implementing images, the aesthetics of the individual blog posts is increased. Additionally, other teaching scenarios become possible. For example, it is possible to describe images and thematize their appearance or content in blog posts. The possibility of adding images to the blog allows media-pedagogical content to be discussed with the pupils when using the platform. Copyright aspects in the use of images on the Internet are taken into account in the lessons (Fig. 7).

It should be possible to use created Blogs in other digital scenarios. For this purpose, an export function of blogs or individual contributions will be programmed. The exports can then be processed digitally. An export as a word processing file is planned in order to be able to further process blogs. This makes it possible to create a student magazine from blogs. The possibility of a PDF export is also planned. Or teachers can export blogs or blog posts in EPUB format so that they can be read in other contexts.

In IDeRBlog ii the intelligent dictionary will be extended. While about 500 words have been included in the dictionary so far, the vocabulary will be extended to 1200 words. The selection of words is based on an analysis of the blog posts written by students. In addition, the words to be recorded are compared with the total vocabulary and the number of words in the existing spelling categories to ensure a valid spelling analysis of the students.

Bild wählen ...

Fig. 7. Screenshot https://learningapps.org 25.01.2020

In IDeRBlog ii, own exercises are programmed to enable students to work on the spelling phenomenon they encounter individually e.g. to work with exactly the words they misspelled. The exercises are additionally displayed within the evaluation and can be worked on by students during the exercise phases. By programming and providing own exercises it is also possible to provide students and teachers with an evaluation of the exercise results.

In addition to purely technical changes, IDeRBlog ii also creates other pedagogical materials that are made available to teachers for their lessons. For each spelling category, lesson preparations are made available that can be integrated into the spelling lessons of the respective class. Each teaching unit is designed for 10 lessons and can be used or adapted by teachers. The teaching units correspond to the latest didactic requirements. During the preparation of the lessons, great importance is attached to teaching students in analogous teaching scenarios. However, phases are also included which enable digitally supported learning. This must always be seen in relation to the equipment available at the school.

In order to illustrate the use of the platform, another 15 videos will be produced which explain and discuss the use of the new functionalities. These videos will be integrated into the platform at appropriate places, but are also available in the teachers' area.

12   Scientific Aspects in the Digital Storage of Data in IDeRBlog ii

By storing the data in the IDeRBlog ii platform, many different scientific statements can be made in the field of research for writing and spelling in German. The amount of data and submitted texts is much higher than in normal studies. This also allows for more valid evaluations, because the validity of the data increases due to the large amount of data. At the end of 2019, 12000 texts were available for evaluation.

The total number of data can be analyzed in many different ways, some of which are described below. The selection of analyses should be seen as an example and does not claim to be complete.

With the totality of all written texts, statements can be made about the length of texts depending on the age group. The assumption is that older students write longer texts than younger students. By evaluating the written texts, however, more precise statements can be made on the basis of the available data.

The texts as a whole can be used to analyze the active vocabulary of students. Since the texts are not always influenced by the teacher's instructions, an exact evaluation of the vocabulary in its entirety is possible. Regional differences can also be worked out when evaluating the data.

A regional analysis of the spelling performance of students using IDeRBlog ii is also possible. Thus, it may be possible to make statements on the different spelling performance of students depending on the regional dialect used. It is also possible to make statements on the spelling performance of students in different federal states.

If IDeRBlog ii is used continuously, the change in spelling competence of students can be assessed in long-term studies. Likewise, the change in text length when using IDeRBlog ii can be determined. And these are just some possible scenarios.

13   Summary

To sum up, the blogging platform IDeRBlog ii encompasses three out of four aspect of German language learning. Pupils can write, read and comment on texts. They are supported during their writing process by the feedback of the intelligent dictionary, in order to improve their spelling abilities. In addition, students enhance their media competency while working with IDeRBlog ii, ranging from the proper handling of their passwords to acquiring adequate online communication skills. What is more, is that from a research point of view the platform offers through the implementation of learning analytics not only an analysis and evaluation of each students or every single classes orthographic abilities, but a whole new level of data concerning orthography research. Hopefully, allowing researchers to gain new insights into the acquisition of spelling abilities.

Acknowledgements.   The IDeRBlog-project and the IDeRBlog-ii project are funded by the European Commission in the framework of Erasmus+ (IDeRBlog: VG-SPS-SL-14-001616-3, 2014-2017; IDeRBlog-ii: VG-IN-SL-18-36-047317, 2018-2021).

Reference

1. Chatti, M.A., Dyckhoff, A.L., Schroeder, U., Thüs, H.: A reference model for learning analytics. Int. J. Technol. Enhanced Learn. (IJTEL) 4(5/6), 318–331 (2012)

Applied Webservices Platform Supported Through Modified Edit Distance Algorithm: Automated Phonetic Transcription Grading Tool (APTgt)

Cheryl D. Seals[✉], Sicheng Li, Marisha Speights Atkins,
Dallin Bailey, Jueting Liu, Yang Cao, and Robertson Bassy

Auburn University, Auburn, AL 36949, USA
{sealscd,szl0072,mls0096,djb0053,jzl0122,yangcao,
rzb0053}@auburn.edu

Abstract. The abstract should summarize the contents of the paper in short terms, i.e. 150–250 words. This research proposes a platform to improve the user experience of Communications Disorders (CMDS) faculty and their students. Traditionally CMDS faculty have the task of training new scholars in the field on communication disorders in the craft of phonetic transcription utilizing the using the International Phonetic Alphabet (IPA). This can be a phoneme by phoneme transcription of words that have to be analyzed in a phoneme by phoneme process. In the department of Computer Science (CS), we had to opportunity to engage in this participatory design exercise with CMDS to analyze and automate this process. This project utilizes a variant of the Edit Distance algorithm for preprocessing the distance between the phonetic transcriptions of the professor's provided key and student's response. We call this platform, the Automated Phonetic Transcription grading tool, APTgt. The platform dramatically speeds up the grading process (i.e. instant feedback) as compared to traditional manual grading. The case discussed is a complex multivariate problem in the field of Communications Disorders of using the International Phonetic Alphabet (IPA) as a transcription language to support students learning the IPA language. Our focus was to develop an engaging, easy to use platform that can support interactive online learning and reduce complexity of evaluation and feedback for transcript tasks.

Keywords: User Interface Design · Web development · E-Learning · Edit distance tools for linguistic education · User experience

1 Introduction

Today everyone is excited about new technologies, especially the Internet, and adapting to a new era in human history. It is sensible that there is a growing need for educational tools in communications disorders and this online web application provides flexible access for the learners and immediate reinforcement of the subject matter. Technology has become a prime necessity in the classroom, as it plays an important role in helping young people achieve promising careers. The use of technology allows

P. Zaphiris and A. Ioannou (Eds.): HCII 2020, LNCS 12205, pp. 380–398, 2020.
https://doi.org/10.1007/978-3-030-50513-4_29

educators to display more information in creative forms. It augments students' learning capability through interaction. In a world where the power of technology will fit in the palm of our hands, it is no longer admissible to train students only through traditional learning approaches. The trending usage of the Internet drives a shift in the way people learn and will have a profound impact on the evolution of computer usage. This in return gives birth to the need for new learning technologies.

Subsequent paragraphs, however, are indented. In the field of User Interface Design, we focus on users as the center of the design process. We design and develop interactive systems to support users improving their work practice, and also as a training mechanism to reinforce the software engineering student's design and development skills. We utilize applied service-learning projects to provide more intrinsic motivation and interesting opportunities for student learning. We began to investigate this case study, i.e. creating an online phonetics educational training tool, the Automated Phonetic Transcription grading tool (APTgt), as design and development challenge with opportunities to provide a rich learning experience. This specific case supports Communications Disorders (CMDS) faculty to provide more efficient instruction and reinforcement in linguistic transcription. The implemented system prototype calculates the difference between the phonetic transcripts of the student's answer and the professor's answer. The student reviews a phonemic string as an audio recording providing and transcripts the speech using a dedicated phonetic keyboard developed for this application (i.e., a variant of the IP International Phonetic Alphabet keyboard). The APTgt planform is designed to upload exams online for educators and learners can take exams online and reduces the possibility of errors during transcription evaluation. This application will perform a string-wise comparison of phonemes created by phonetics professionals and novice transcribers, which is not a trivial process. For phonetic string representation, it is even harder than traditional string comparisons, since this type of comparison has to utilize diacritics, diphthongs, and double consonants as a single unit instead of several characters. This effort combines a suite of front-end and back-end web development techniques (i.e. advanced development skills possessed by full-stack developers). APTgt will save the teachers from manually grading the exams by hand since the exams involve phonetic transformation. It is not an easy work to do manually. APTgt is a standalone online educational content management system (CMS) that provides specialized services not currently supported by other CMSs. The goal of this project is to help instructors in creating and managing their online courses and their corresponding resources in a convenient way. And more importantly, it will help the teachers to handle exams automatically, and the system will present meaningful statistical results of individual and class exam results. Also, it helps students have ready access to real-time practice and reinforcement of their transcription skills through the use of this web application.

APTgt improves the user experience for CMDS faculty and their students by utilizing this application to automatically assess language transcriptions and immediately provide feedback to the student to improve their learning outcomes and transcription efficacy. This advanced technology application supports student learning through reinforcement and educator's creativity through this time-saving application. The trending usage of the Internet drives a shift in the way people learn and will have a profound impact on the evolution of computer usage. This in return gives birth to the need for new learning technologies [1–3]. Students are excited about new technologies, especially the Internet, and most of our student population are digital natives [3–6] who are accustomed to powerful technology right in the palm of their hands. It is no longer admissible to train students with only traditional learning approaches. Over the past few years, there has been a growing emphasis on the course content, but not much focus has been placed on this specific task-oriented system. Our focus was to develop an engaging, easy to use platform that reduces the effort for instructors and supports interactive learning for linguistics education. The APTgt webservice platform with the edit distance component diagram as seen in Fig. 1.

2 Background

2.1 User Interface Design and User Experience

The Business to Business to Customer (B2B2C) model is a new e-commerce sales method, which originates from B2B and B2C models and supports merchants to directly act as sellers to shorten the sales chain. For User Experience, according to James's definition, it refers to the parts of the product or service that the user can experience, including the man-machine interface and divides UX into five elements namely presentation, framework, structure, scope and strategy layers [19]. They began with the user as the center of our design process and denote user experience design as a user-centered process [20].

This study [20] investigates online shopping behavior and they concluded that user experience had a significant impact on online shopping in terms of usability, functionality, content, and performance. The necessary elements in developing E-commerce website are to determine positioning and target audience. The designer needs to analyze the target users (i.e. one of the keys to a user-centered process) and realize the users' shopping flow. Their steps in website interface design included the following: (1) Interface flow design, (2) Interface function design, and (3) The visual design [19, 20].

In a study of a mHealth application [21], the authors investigated the User Interface (UI) design and effectiveness and effect on the user's performance. This paper discusses the role of the UI design in a mobile application. Based on the Effective Use Theory, the experiment used four different UIs treatments. The result indicates that UI design has a significant impact on task completion time [21]. The experiment is based on Effective Use Theory, which is proposed by Burton-Jones and Grange has two main concepts: effective use and performance, the effective use improves performance. This theory indicates three dimensions of effective use - 1) transparent interaction, 2) representational fidelity, 3) informed action; and two dimensions of performance - a) effectiveness and b) efficiency.

This paper [21] focuses on touch-based techniques and target direction as the independent variables of the experiment. Two touch-based techniques were studied (i.e. tap and slide), and two target direction in the experiment were vertical and horizontal. The combination of these two variables suggests four UIs conditions to test. Tap-Vertical (UI#1), Tap-Horizontal (UI#2), Slide-Vertical (UI#3), Slide-Horizontal (UI#4). The author tested the efficiency of four UIs by measuring the task completion time and error rate. The experimental data indicated that tap-based UIs have better performance than slide-based UIs in task completion time and based on the Effective Use Theory, the results indicate that tapping is more effective than sliding. So, the tap-based UI have higher efficiency than slide-based UI. However, in this paper, the author could not examine the potential differences in the effectiveness part, because none of the participants made an error during the experiment.

2.2   E-Learning

E-Learning is one of the most significant new instructional approaches available; it drives progress in both the teaching and learning process in a wide range of schools around the world today. E-Learning is delivered and supported using a variety of electronic media. These technologies allow us to deliver individualized and comprehensive learning content that facilitates learning, anytime and anywhere. It does not replace the traditional classroom approach, but creates an augmented learning environment. This approach rather promotes combined usage of teaching techniques in order to maximize the student's participation in the learning process. Accessing the learning materials allows students to go beyond the limits on time and place imposed by the traditional classroom [16].

E-Learning [7, 8] is one of the most significant new instructional approaches available; it drives progress in both the teaching and learning process in a wide range of schools around the world today. E-Learning is delivered and supported using a variety of electronic media. These technologies allow us to deliver individualized and comprehensive learning content that facilitates learning, anytime, and anywhere. It does not replace the traditional classroom approach but creates an augmented learning environment. This approach rather promotes combined usage of teaching techniques to maximize the student's participation in the learning process. Accessing the learning materials allows students to go beyond the limits on time and place imposed by the traditional classroom [16].

Case-based learning (CBL) is an effective educational method for enhancing students' learning and reasoning skills and is an alternative method to the traditional classroom approach. Sek-Ying Chair [9] and coauthors utilized a sequential mixed-methods study using both quantitative and qualitative research to conduct an exploration of CBL experience for nursing students in Hong Kong. The researchers compared traditional and Web-based approaches and concluded that although their qualitative data support that CBL enhanced self-learning ability and critical thinking skills of participants, they found no difference between two methods in self-learning ability and clinical reasoning ability. The participants reported that CBL helped them apply learned knowledge to clinical situations and they appreciated the flexibility of a web-based approach. The authors concluded that a rigorous structural design, real-time synchronized e-discussions, and cultural sensitivity to students' learning behavior are all crucial components of a successful Web-based CBL approach in the context of their nursing education [9, 16].

The development of The Automated Phonetic Transcription Grading Tool (APTgt), served as a mechanism for providing case-based learning in the communication disorders courses. Theoretical instruction is applied through case-studies in the advanced speech disorders courses. The case studies serve as a means of cultivating the ability for students to think critically to formulate clinical diagnostic decisions. One skill that students in these courses learn is the ability to code spoken words (phonetic transcription) using the International Phonetic Alphabet (IPA) system. Phonetic transcription involves capturing the sounds of speech in written form to create a transcript that represents how words were produced by an individual speaker [14]. This written phonetic transcript is important for continued assessment and clinical diagnostics. Mastery of this skill for students requires regular practice and performance feedback. One factor that impedes the provision of applied practice opportunities is the widely agreed upon problem of grading phonetic transcription assignments by hand [13, 16].

2.3   Phonetic Transcription

The predominantly used technology for phonetics instruction is paper and pencil. Student transcribe by hand words spoken by the instructor and the instructor in turn grades the assignments by hand. The approach has two key intrinsic limitations 1) adult speech without the presence of a speech disorder is not reflective of the populations training clinicians will encounter and 2) the instructor can become burdened with grading large volumes of assignments reducing consistency in grading and timely feedback. Current learning management systems such as Canvas and Blackboard do not currently support the use of a dedicated IPA keyboard for transcription of the unique symbol set. A Canvas Q & A board user asked in October 2018, how IPA can be used on Canvas pages. Recommendations were made to use third-party sites such londonschool.com, IPA typeit.com, Microsoft Word to copy and paste the symbols. However, this approach also requires students to access these web browsers during an exam which is inefficient and prone to decreased test taking integrity [18]. Addressing this problem presented a unique pedagogical opportunity for enhancing student learning with the use of an online learning platform that uses an embedded IPA keyboard and supports automated the grading in order to provide students with timely feedback that supported deep learning of applied clinical concepts [11]. Additionally, the design of such an application created an applied learning opportunity for students in a user interface design course by engaging students in a case-based learning approach to solve a real client presented need that allowed for instruction in the iterative process of web application design.

3   Methods

3.1   Advanced Learning Technology

Operationalizing and automating the phonetic transcription grading process in the APTgt learning system was implemented through the use of edit distance calculation by phonetic rules and word-length normalization. Edit distance is an accepted method for string-to-string comparisons when comparing differences between characters in words. The work of Bae et al. [10] proposed the well-known algorithm for string-to-string comparison in the context of the Korean language. This Edit Distance method applied a consonant normalization factor for syllable-structured word similarity. Their method was designed to improve the performance of the syllable-based and letter-based metrics for word similarity. They concluded that the performance of edit distance was improved with their strategy via the phonetic pronunciation rules and word-length normalization. They reported that the phoneme-based metric provided a better result compared to the approaches of letter-based, syllable-based and hybrid distance methods. Modifications to the traditional [12, 17] edit distance calculation were applied to the APTgt algorithm to account for the complexities of spoken language and the phonetic representation.

3.2   UID Learning Model

The User Interface Design course, taken by software engineering upper-level undergraduate and graduate course, incorporates a component of the class that supports service learning. Addressing this problem within this course introduced the opportunity to provide a rich learning experience for the User Interface Design student that was practical and engaging. The course teams began this effort by gathering requirements from the subject matter experts in the field of communication disorders. Then based on these requirements, user scenarios were crafted for the Student User, Teacher User and Admin User of the system. The scenarios were captured utilizing UML (Unified Modeling Language) that is utilized to capture a pictorial view of the system and cataloging roles, actors, actions and classes within a system. Once the system scenario is captured, software requirements created, software language identified and environment identified the software development team will begin iteratively developing software to instantiate this software system. We also will need to pilot test the software, and at the end of the first cycle of development, the team will need to test the software and have users to validate that the system works as anticipated. At the end of the first cycle of development the development team, design team, and the content experts reach an agreement that the planned scenario meets the specified requirements for the user [11, 16].

3.3   Experimental Study

To evaluate our project, we will have approximately 60 young adults will be selected for the usability component of the experiments. Two faculty will participate in testing APTgt project. All participants are expected to be at least novice computer users with experience using Internet. We will assess their user experience with the application and the impact of this framework. The participants will complete pre and post assessments and will utilize a combination of both quantitative closed-ended and qualitative open-ended questions will be included in the instruments and we will follow a user-centered lifecycle throughout the design process. Based on this feedback, we will iteratively update the development process until our design partners are satisfied with our application outcomes.

4   System Requirements

Based on the specification given by communications disorders design partners (Drs. Bailey and Speights Atkins), the following requirements were gathered for the development of an algorithm for scoring the accuracy of phonetic transcriptions done by students within our learning management system [16]:

1. Use the instructor-provided transcription (string1) as the model.
2. Strings consist of vowels, consonants, and diacritics. Diacritics always appear in combination with a vowel or a consonant, appearing as a one-character unit. Automatically include the diacritic as null if it is unspecified.
3. Find the optimal alignment of strings that minimizes the number of transformations (substitutions, deletions, and insertions) required to transform the model (string1) into the student's transcription (string2). In general, characters that are identical in both strings align with each other, except when that violates these conditions:
   3.1. Not allowed to change the order of characters in either string.
   3.2. Vowels may only align with vowels, and consonants may only align with consonants.
   3.3. Prioritize aligning vowels with each other if the number or order of consonants and vowels in the strings differs.
4. Perfect correspondence between the strings indicates a score of 0. Each transformation of a consonant (see list of consonants) or a vowel (see list of vowels) counts as a penalty of 1. If the diacritic changes, score .5. If the consonant or vowel and the diacritic changes score 1.5.

4.1   Exam Management Webservices Platform Design

The APTgt is an interactive learning environment supporting CMDS faculty in providing online pedagogical support and transcription reinforcement for their students. As displayed in Fig. 1, the APTgt will take requests from users (i.e. the initial users are faculty) that are building examinations in the system through the insertion of questions and corresponding audios in the system. The system will save these created questions in the backend (i.e. system database) to be preserved for future usage. The system will send affirmative responses back to end-users (i.e. faculty) to validate the proper creation of practice or exam questions. The algorithm discussed in this paper is in the component of the "edit distance algorithm". This algorithm is the core of the application. Assignments and exam questions are evaluated by calculating the edit distance of two strings (one is obtained from the expert answer; the other is collected from the student's response using a specifically designed keyboard, as shown later). The system has three main groups of users: Admin (to monitor users), Teacher (to create exams and monitor students), and most common user − Student (to benefit from practice exams and automatic phonetic transcription evaluation), as seen in Figs. 2, 3 and 4 [16].

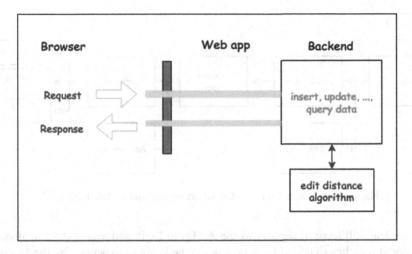

Fig. 1. The APTgt webservice, including the modified edit distance algorithm as core [16].

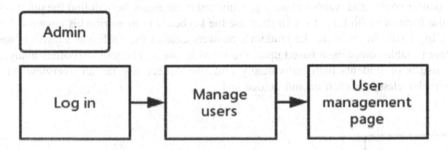

Fig. 2. The Admin user in the APTgt system and its functions [14].

The admin will be able to approve the credential of new user registration, or removal of a user from the system.

The Faculty (teacher) can upload and manage lesson files, manage users in their designated courses, and manage exams as well as practice tests. The lesson files are in the video format and the questions added to the exams and practice tests are of audio format. The teacher will have a user account for himself using which he will login to the APTgt.

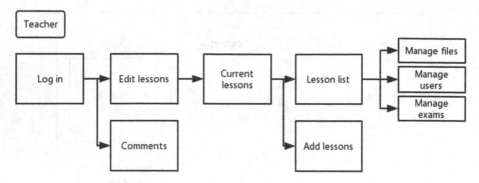

Fig. 3. The Teacher role in the APTgt system and its functions [14].

A student will have to register to the APTgt to login and access the functionality. The student then has to added for a course that he is about to access, by the faculty of that course. After this procedure, the student will be able access the course material, exams or practice tests related to the course. When a student reviews a video for a particular course and wants to take a practice test or an exam, he will find the questions in the form of audio files. He will then use the keyboard to transcribe his answers. The grading tool will compare the student's answers against the professor's answers and offers reliable comparison based upon the saved answers. The tool also offers analysis of results of students both individually and also collectively (as an overview for a particular class) for each exam/practice test.

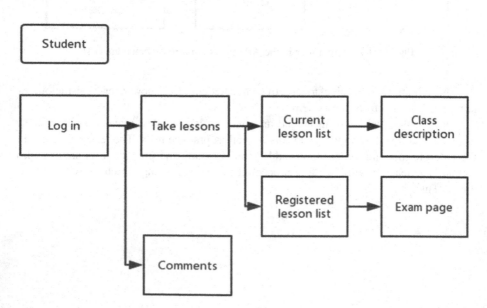

Fig. 4. The Student role in the APTgt system and its functions [14].

The APTgt v2.0 has been developed to incorporate all these functionalities. The APTgt is a web application which enables teachers to create an account, manage lessons, and exams as well as manage students and approve their registration to a particular class. The grading tools enables the teachers to provide course material through an online medium, which facilitates them to make the material available to students at all times. It also enables the teachers to provide tests and exams to students which they can take according to their convenience.

The APTgt enables students to register to the application, login using these credentials. The students can access the course materials, attempt the practice tests (for which they can access the result immediately) and also the exams (for which they can only access the result after the due date). The students can also see a comparison of their answer to that of the teacher's through a character-wise comparison.

The application allows the students to transcribe the speech of audio samples (exam or practice questions) and their ability to type characters and click on the International Phonetic Alphabet (IPA) keyboard, as seen in Fig. 5, to insert phonetic symbols, based on their understanding of these audios. The main scenario of the application includes playing audio files of words and students type its phonetic symbol to get a score based on their typed input against professors uploaded answers. For multi-level learners (basic, advanced), the APTgt tool provides various keyboards with different phonetic symbols, which includes most languages' phonetic symbol all over the world. It is a web-based application built in a Responsive Web Design framework promoting a User-Centered Design, which allows the students to use the application on desktop, smartphones and other hand-held devices [16].

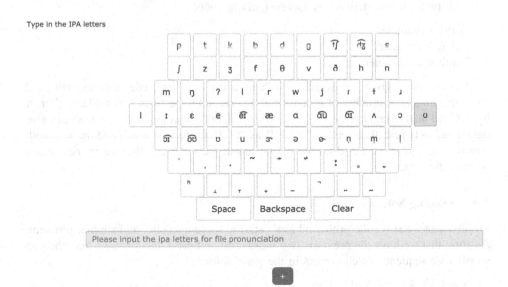

Fig. 5. A specifically designed keyboard that allows teacher and student to type in the IPA symbols.

Automatic grading aims at improving the level of feedback given to students and optimizing the professor time. Several researches have reported the development of software tools to support this process. The grading tool should support grading mechanism with precision, accuracy, consistency and security along with making a temporal comparative analysis. The lack of a grading model for assignments is identified as an important gap in the existing tools. Thus, a characterization of evaluation metrics to grade has to be provided as first step to get a model.

The APTgt is an application that facilitates e-learning and mobile learning for students as well as convenience, grading and student management for faculty. This project is aimed to help professors in educational department to manage their lectures and practices and exams. Current canvas system could not meet the specific requirements of our clients. So, we designed and implemented a special system according to their requirements [16].

4.2   The Problem [16]

Assume you have to listen to an audio of a word (sound). You have to write down the phonetic representation of that word you heard of using a specialized phonetic coding system (IPA). Then someone else has to tell the difference between your answer and the real phonetic representation of that word (sound).

If it is about the difference between two words, then that is the classic edit distance. By definition, edit distance is a way of quantifying how dissimilar two strings (e.g., words) are to one another by counting the minimum spelling correction of operations required to transform one string into the other. One of the simplest sets of operations one can perform was defined by Levenshtein in 1966:

- Insert a character
- Delete a character
- Replace a character

For example, given the words A = "cat" and B = "cars", edit distance will be 2 since the minimum number of transformations needed to perform is to replace "t" in A by "r" and then delete the "s" from B. After that, both words will be car. One can also delete "s" in B first, then replace "r" in B as "t". That procedure will end up with both words as cat. And we can do other operations as well. All the distance in these cases will be the same, 2.

4.3   Existing Solution [16]

So how can we solve the problem? Let's start to solve a smaller and simpler problem. Assume that we have the previous two words (cat and cars), this time we treat the two words as a sequence of characters in the general form:

A = [A0, A1, ... Am]
B = [B0, B1, ..., Bn]

Notice that initially, the lengths of A and B (m and n respectively) can be different.

We know that in the end, m and n will be the same since we want to transform one word into another. And on the other hand, one character at a given position must be the same. Now, imagine if we are dealing only with the first character of A and B, what choices do we have? We have 3 operations to perform, that means we have three choices:

1. We can insert a character into A to match the character in B[0], which has a cost of 1. After this operation, we still need to take care of the first character of A. However, we will go to the next character in B, since we already know A[0] is the same as B[0] now. The left job is to compute the edit distance for A[0...m] and B [1...n]. The final result will be the cost of insertion (1 in this example) plus the edit distance of A[0...m] and B[1...n].
2. We can delete a character in A to match B[0]. The cost is also 1. After this step, we have processed the first character in A, but we still have all the initial characters in B. Thus, we need to compute the edit distance of A[1...m] and B[0...n]. Again, the final result will be this value + 1 (the cost of deleting [0]).
3. The last choice we have is to replace the first character in A by the first character in B. The cost of this operation will be 1 if the two characters are different and 0 if they are the same. At this point, we only need to calculate the edit distance A[1...m] and B[1...n]. The final result will be 1 + the remaining edit distance of processing [1... m] and B[1...n] [16].

Let's summarize what we have so far:

$$ed(A, B) = min \begin{cases} ed(A[1...n], \ B[1...m]) + replace \ (a) \\ ed(A[1...n], \ B[0...m]) + delete \ (b) \\ ed(A[0...n], \ B[1...m]) + insert \ (c) \end{cases} \qquad (1)$$

The first (a) is the case when we replace A[0] as B[0]. (b) is corresponding to the deletion of A[0] and (c) is when we insert a character into A.

The base cases are:

editDistance(A, "") = length(A)
editDistance("", B) = length(B)

The recursive implementation of the above solution is in Algorithm 1 [12, 17].

Algorithm 1: Recursive version of edit distance
m: length of string A
n: length of string B
    a.   If the last character of the two strings is the same, do nothing. Ignore the last characters and get the distance for remaining substrings. So we recur for lengths of m -1 and n -1
    b.   Else, we consider all operations on string A. We have three options here and we obtain the minimum distance of them:
    c.   Insert: Recur for m and n - 1
    d.   Delete: Recur for m - 1 and n
    e.   Replace, Recur for m - 1 and n - 1

However, the time complexity of the above implementation is O(3n), where n is the maximum length of the two words. The problem here is could we do better than that? Of course, we can. However, the above implementation is letter-based implementation, which is not suitable for phonetic representations of words because a single phonetic representation may be represented by one, two, or even three letters. Then we run the edit distance algorithm to comparatively process two lists of strings. Hence comes the proposed solution.

4.4   Proposed Solution: String Processing [16]

As mentioned above, the character-based solution is not suitable in our case, since one has to take the diacritics, diphthongs, and double consonants as a single unit instead of several characters. Therefore, the recipe is to group these thought groups together, counting as one single unit. The original version of this implementation was provided by our client, which was developed in Visual Basic (VB). It generated the correct results for the phonetic transcription but was a very complicated and long process with poor user-experience. The previous process was a tedious task of gathering hand-written data from students, and then our teachers manually entered all the students' answers into a Microsoft Excel sheet and exported the results out to the VB system to obtain the edit distances and grades for each student's assignment.

We also endeavored to improve the evaluation process and after thoughtful consideration, the system treats all the diacritics, diphthongs, and double consonants logically by dividing the initial input from the student into an array of characters, then combine the corresponding units into one position. As a result, instead of calculating the edit distances of two string representations of the words, we compute the edit distance of thought-group position-based edit distance. For instance, if we have the phonetic representation fɪŋɡə-neɪl, the result from the preprocessing will be [f, ɪ, ŋ, ɡ, ə, n, eɪ, l]. In this way, eɪ will be in one single unit, as it should be. The time complexity for the preprocessing is $O(n)$. The preprocessing is done by applying the preprocessing algorithm and, on the other hand, achieved by restricting the users to use only the keyboard provided by our implementation, for the reason that we only allow users to type legitimate input string. Otherwise, it is very complicated to do the tokenization step, since there are millions of possibilities of input strings.

> Algorithm 2: String preprocessing [16]
> m: length of input string
> result = empty list
>
> The algorithm goes for 0...m:
>
> 1.   If this character is belonging to a diacritic, a double vowel or consonant, based on the information in Table 1: find the whole group of characters, and add them as a group into the result list
> 2.   Else (not in any of diacritics, double vowels, or double consonants): add this single character to the result list

4.5   Dynamic Implementation of Edit Distance [16]

Once we obtain the list of strings from the preprocessing step, we can run the dynamic programming version edit distance, as the time complexity of recursive edit distance is O(3n). This algorithm is shown in Algorithm 3.

> Algorithm 3: Dynamic programming implementation of edit distance
> M[][] is the matrix to store the edit distance
> For the list of strings S1 = [S1,0, S1,1, ... S1,m]
> For the list of strings S2 = [S2,0, S2,1, ... S2,n]
> M[i][j] = case 0: M[i-1][j-1] + 0 if S1[i-1] == S2[j-1]
>   case 1: M[i-1][j-1] + replaceCost if replace
>   case 2: M[i-1][j] + deleteCost if delete
>   case 3: M[i][j-1] + insertCost if insert
> return M[S1.length][S2.length] as the final edit distance

Costs are calculated based on the requirements, shown in the requirements section.

5   Results and Analysis

Let's look at one specific example here to illustrate the algorithms. Say the student's answer for a word is $pre\widehat{dʒ}$, while the key is $bɪ\widehat{dʒ}$. The first step is to get the list of strings for both of them. Thus, [p, r, ɛ, $\widehat{dʒ}$] and [b, ɪ, ɪ, $\widehat{dʒ}$] for the above two words, respectively. Then the dynamic programming version of edit distance is run to get the difference (distance) for them. The matrix representation of the execution process is shown in Table 1. As we can tell from the matrix, the final distance is listed in the last cell. So, the distance is 3.0. For comparison, we list the test cases for the algorithm with and without the preprocessing procedure. As we can tell clearly from Tables 2 and 3, the preprocessing procedure will affect the words that have diacritics, double vowels, and/or double consonants. Without appropriate preprocessing, the edit distance will be inaccurate for most of the cases involving the above-mentioned scenarios.

Table 1. The matrix representation of the distance of $pre\widehat{dʒ}$ and $bɪ\widehat{dʒ}$. The bolded values make up the final transformation path [16].

	.	b	ɹ	ɪ	$\widehat{dʒ}$
.	**0.0**	1.0	2.0	3.0	4.0
p	1.0	**1.0**	2.0	3.0	4.0
r	2.0	2.0	**2.0**	3.0	4.0
ɛ	3.0	3.0	3.0	**3.0**	4.0
$\widehat{dʒ}$	4.0	4.0	4.0	4.0	**3.0**

Table 2. Test cases for edit distance results without preprocessing procedure. For the path, we use 's' to denote replace, 'i' to indicate insert, '|' to mean same consonant, and '*' to denote the same vowel [16].

Case #	key	Answer	Path	Distance
case1	dʌk	dæt	|ss	2.0
case7	keɪd͡ʒ	keɪd͡ʒ	|***|*|	0.0
case8	geɪt	geɪt	|***|	0.0
case9	kɪŋ	kɪŋ	|*|	0.0
case10	fɪs	geɪt	%is*s	4.0
case11	fænd	fænt	|*|s	1.0
case12	d͡ʒaɪ	d͡ʒɔr	|*|ss	2.0
case13	t͡ʃiz	t͡ʃiz	|*|*|	0.0
case14	wat͡ʃ	wat͡ʃ	|*|*|	0.0
case15	klaʊn	klaʊn	||***|	0.0
case16	glʌv	gləv	||s|	1.0
case19	bɹɪd͡ʒ	prɛd͡ʒ	sss|*|	3.0
case21	bæskɪtbɔl	bæskɛtba	|*||s||ds	3.0
case22	pɛɹəʃut	peɪrəʃut	|iiss*|*|	4.0

Table 3. Test cases for edit distance results with preprocessing procedure. For the path, we use 's' to denote replace, 'i' to indicate insert, '|' to mean same consonant, and '*' to denote the same vowel [16].

Case #	key	Answer	Path	Distance
case1	dʌk	dæt	|ss	2.0
case7	keɪd͡ʒ	keɪd͡ʒ	|**	0.0
case8	geɪt	geɪt	|*|	0.0
case9	kɪŋ	kɪŋ	|*|	0.0
case10	fɪs	geɪt	sss	3.0
case11	fænd	fænt	|*|s	1.0
case12	d͡ʒaɪ	d͡ʒɔr	*ss	2.0
case13	t͡ʃiz	t͡ʃiz	**|	0.0
case14	wat͡ʃ	wat͡ʃ	|**	0.0
case15	klaʊn	klaʊn	||*|	0.0
case16	glʌv	gləv	||s|	1.0
case19	bɹɪd͡ʒ	prɛd͡ʒ	sss*	3.0
case21	bæskɪtbɔl	bæskɛtba	|*||s||ds	3.0
case22	pɛɹəʃut	peɪrəʃut	|ss*|*|	2.0

5.1 Student Perspective on APTgt

In our initial study, more than 90% of students (N = 67) reported that their confidence increased by greater than 30% and that they appreciated the ease of use of the keyboard, more opportunities to practice transcription was helpful. The students also indicated that more access to real clinical speech samples was helpful and they gained valuable experience from automated transcription feedback [14].

5.2 Faculty Perspective

Using the APTgt tool has allowed me to engage students in phonetic training in a novel way. The interactive learning management system allows me to build practice assignments that are relevant to course lecture material providing a means for active, hands-on learning. Traditionally, instruction is often limited to healthy adult speech that does not represent the technical challenges of transcribing speech that is less intelligible because of the presence of a speech disorder. The ability to upload a variety of speech samples and the use of the keyboard allows for a richer learning experience.

The automated grading allows me to provide many opportunities for practice and to focus on helping students to apply the learning rather than having my time consumed by grading. It also gives me more confidence in knowing that the grading is consistent since it is quite tedious to grade each symbol by hand. Students also greatly benefit from the conversations they have when they can compare their work with others to understand how everyone is learning and that some areas may be more challenging than others. I have experienced students increasing confidence in the task as they have the opportunity to practice and discuss their results with the professor and peers in a timely manner. The benefits for me have been tremendous.

5.3 Learning Outcomes for Engineering Course

We deliver instruction for our Computer Science & Software Engineering (CSSE) students to understand the theory of user interface design and development, and engage in applied software development projects as practical exercise and fully elaborated case study. They experience an iteration of this process during User Interface Design courses and can extend this experience as a member of our UID research team. The typical learning episode begins with requirements elicitation, design, development, testing, and a project presentation of findings from preliminary user evaluations pertaining to the analysis of user satisfaction and system effectiveness. We have found that this gives students a great understanding of the user interface design process. Research experiences give students a brief introduction to the entire process of research (i.e., problem, method, analysis, presentation of solution) and students have the opportunity to review scholarly articles or conference style papers that will inform their future writing practice. With respect to research, it also gives them a great experience in teamwork as they have to collaborate with a team of 4–8 individuals based on the size of the project and also give them more practice in programming skills that are indispensable for CSSE students. The additional practice supports the writing of technical reports, a skill needed for transition to the industry. We have found that many upper-level engineering students do not have as much writing content to provide (i.e., as compared to freshman English and English composition classes). Writing opportunities provided by research experiences yield work products that provide students with opportunities to refine their writing skills and to produce scholarship, which they can reference when preparing for job interviews. Writing practice is particularly important for students pursuing the completion of a thesis or dissertation [11, 16].

6   Conclusions and Contributions

6.1   Conclusions

This research proposes a platform to improve the user experience of Communications Disorders (CMDS) faculty and their students. Traditionally CMDS faculty have the task of training new scholars in the field of communication disorders in the craft of phonetic transcription utilizing the using the International Phonetic Alphabet (IPA). The research question that we addressed was, "How do we provide more timely and consistent feedback for students on their linguistics transcriptions with feedback on their transcription goodness and accuracy?". The research team focused on developing an engaging, easy to use platform that reduces the effort for CMDS faculty and support interactive online learning for their students with immediate feedback on their transcriptions practice. In this research, we have proposed and developed the APTgt system to support CMDS faculty as a content management system that provides specialized support for phonetics training and reinforcement. This effort provides a great opportunity for software engineers to refine their professional requirements, algorithm design and development, and system implementation practice. The core algorithm utilized supports immediate feedback and evaluation of transcription accuracy and is a variant of the Levenshtein algorithm and is used to calculate the distance between two phonetic representations of a word. During this project, we have improved the user experience for two university CMDS professors by reducing tedious and possibly error-prone hand-grading approaches to transcription evaluation. This approach has been piloted in multiple courses for two years. This tool has also improved student learning based on information from evaluations of APTgt, we have discovered that it has improved their students' efficacy and learning of transcription. We hope that this tool becomes a standard for all CMDS and linguistics professionals that utilize transcription in their teaching and practice.

6.2   Contributions

APTgt provides a novel approach to language transcription and assessment. APTgt improves the user experience for CMDS faculty and their students by utilizing this application to automatically assess language transcriptions and immediately provide feedback to the student to improve their learning outcomes and transcription efficacy. APTgt enhances the pedagogical practice of phonetics instruction with great potential to improve their teaching experience and efficiency. Another unique contribution is a new IPA education-centric keyboard set supporting multiple-levels of course difficulty (i.e., beginner, intermediate, advanced) to improve the student experience by scaffolding novice users with simpler keyboard and fully functional keyboards to advanced users. We automate the process of teachers adding audios to enhance exam questions, and support reviewing of these audios as exam questions for the students, and students enter their responses through these new keyboards. This transcription process is also enhanced and not like the standard multiple-choice learning management system as we support partially correct responses to increase their transcription efficacy.

References

1. Cheng, I., Basu, A., Goebel, R.: Interactive multimedia for adaptive online education. IEEE Multimed. Mag. **16**, 16–24 (2009)
2. Seals, C., Zhang, Q., Cook, T.: An M-learning application to enhance children's learning experience. Int. J. Recent Innov. Trends Comput. Commun. (IJRITCC) **4**(10), 214–222 (2017). ISSN 2321-8169
3. Tripp, L.O., Seals, C.D., Bassy, R.: Spectrum educational tool: animated scenarios for teacher preparation. J. Online Learn. Res. Pract. **7**(2), 15–36 (2019)
4. Margaryan, A., Littlejohn, A., Vojt, G.: Are digital natives a myth or reality? University students' use of digital technologies. Comput. Educ. **56**(2), 429–440 (2011). https://doi.org/10.1016/j.compedu.2010.09.004
5. Nagler, W., Ebner, M.: Is your university ready for the Ne(x)t-Generation? In: Proceedings of 21st World Conference on Educational Multimedia, Hypermedia and Telecommunications (EDMEDIA), Honolulu, Hawaii, USA, 22–26 June 2009, pp. 4344–4351 (2009)
6. Nemo, J.: The $107 Billion Industry That Nobody's Talking About Inc.com (2016). https://www.inc.com/john-nemo/the-107-billion-industry-that-nobodys-talkingabout.html
7. Anshari, M., Alas, Y., Guan, L.S.: Developing online learning resources: big data, social networks, and cloud computing to support pervasive knowledge. Educ. Inf. Technol. **21**(6), 1663–1677 (2015). https://doi.org/10.1007/s10639-015-9407-3
8. Kazmer, M.M., Haythornwaite, C.: Multiple perspectives on online learning. ACM SIGGroup Bull. **25**(1), 7–11 (2004)
9. Chan, A.W.K., Chair, S.Y., Sit, J.W.H., Wong, E.M.L., Lee, D.T.F., Fung, O.W.M.: Case based web learning versus face-to-face learning: a mixed-method study on university nursing students. J. Nurs. Res. **24**(1), 31–40 (2016). https://doi.org/10.1097/jnr.0000000000000104
10. Bae, B., Kang, S.S., Hwang, B.Y.: Edit distance calculation by phonetic rules and word-length normalization. In: Proceedings of the European Computing Conference (ECC 2012), Prague, Czech Republic, pp. 315–319 (2012)
11. Speights Atkins, M., Seals, C., Bailey, D.J.: At the intersection of applied sciences: integrated learning models in computer science and software engineering and communication disorders. Sci. Educ. Civic Engagem. Int. J. **11**(1), 37–43 (2019)
12. Levenshtein, V.I.: Binary codes capable of correcting deletions, insertions, and reversals. Sov. Phys. Dokl. **10**(8), 707–710 (1966)
13. Heselwood, B.: Teaching and assessing phonetic transcription: a roundtable discussion. Centre for Languages Linguistics & Area Studies (2007). https://www.llas.ac.uk/resources/gpg/2871. Accessed 16 2015
14. Speights-Atkins, M., Seals, C.D., Bailey, D.: The automated phonetic transcription grading tool: where computer science meets clinical problem solving in communication disorders. In: SENCER Summer Institute August 2018, National Center for Science & Civic Engagement (Highly Acknowledged in Education Scholarship) (2018)
15. Knight, R.A.: Sounds for study: speech and language therapy students' use and perception of exercise podcasts for phonetics. Int. J. Teach. Learn. High. Educ. **22**(3), 269–276 (2010)

16. Li, S., et al.: Software engineering to develop online phonetics educational training: interdisciplinary research with communications sciences and disorders. In: American Society of Engineering Education (ASEE-SE 2020), Auburn AL, p. 11 (2020)
17. Wagner, R.A., Fischer, M.J.: The string-to-string correction problem. J. ACM **21**(1), 168–173 (1974). https://doi.org/10.1145/321796.321811
18. Walsh, W.: How Can I use PA on Canvas Pages? Canvas Community Discussion Board (2018). https://community.canvaslms.com/thread/28472-how-can-i-use-ipa-on-canvas-pages
19. Garrett, J.J.: Elements of User Experience, pp. 52–56. Mechanical Industry Press, Beijing (2011)
20. Cai, L., He, X., Dai, Y., Zhu, K.: Research on B2B2C E-commerce website design based on user experience. J. Phys: Conf. Ser. **1087**(6), 1–5 (2018)
21. Choi, W., Tulu, B.: Effective use of user interface and user experience in an mHealth application. In: Proceedings of the Hawaii International Conference on System Sciences (2017)

Digital Competences for Language Teachers: Do Employers Seek the Skills Needed from Language Teachers Today?

Tord Talmo[1]([⊠]), Maria Victoria Soule[2] [iD], Mikhail Fominykh[1] [iD],
Antonio Giordano[3], Maria Perifanou[4] [iD], Vilma Sukacke[5],
Anna Novozhilova[6] [iD], Roberta D'Ambrosio[7], and Alev Elçi[8] [iD]

[1] Norwegian University of Science and Technology, Trondheim, Norway
{tord.m.talmo,mikhail.fominykh}@ntnu.no
[2] Cyprus University of Technology, Limassol, Cyprus
mariavictoria.soule@cut.ac.cy
[3] Pixel, Florence, Italy
antonio@pixel-online.net
[4] University of Macedonia, Thessaloniki, Greece
mariaperif@gmail.com
[5] Kaunas University of Technology, Kaunas, Lithuania
vilma.sukacke@ktu.lt
[6] Tallinn University, Tallinn, Estonia
anovozilova@gmail.com
[7] University of Bari, Bari, Italy
robertadambrosio85@gmail.com
[8] Aksaray University, Aksaray, Turkey
dr.alevelci@gmail.com

Abstract. Language proficiency is essential for 21st Century skills, and for the ability to obtain and utilize new competencies in the future. Digitalization is greatly affecting the language learning settings, and more digital skills are needed amongst teachers. Thus, it is interesting to see what kind of demands the new working life puts on the future language teachers in all areas of the sector. To better understand the role of national policies on digital competence and their impact on language teacher's recruitment, this study investigates existing strategies for digital competence for language teachers in 11 countries, and their representation in job announcements. The study uses qualitative content analysis as well as quantitative analysis represented by descriptive statistics. The former includes document analysis of strategies on different levels and gives an overview of existing trends and new tendencies considering digital skills for language teachers. The latter comprises a search and classification of 854 job announcements throughout Europe according to three levels of digital competences to see which skills are being asked for when hiring language teachers. The results indicate that there are discrepancies between strategies being implemented at overarching levels and the institutional practices. We also demonstrate discrepancies between the needs described for the 21st Century and the defined skills in the job announcements. Among other results, the study highlights the need for more targeted job announcements to attract teachers with the desired digital skills.

© Springer Nature Switzerland AG 2020
P. Zaphiris and A. Ioannou (Eds.): HCII 2020, LNCS 12205, pp. 399–412, 2020.
https://doi.org/10.1007/978-3-030-50513-4_30

1 Introduction

It is widely acknowledged that language proficiency is key for a common under-standing between the EU citizens and for the practice of shared cultural values. However, recent studies demonstrate that we still have a long way to go until Infor-mation and Communication Technologies (ICT) get truly integrated into the work of the European foreign language teachers. According to surveys, the availability of ICT facilities in the foreign language classrooms of European schools is low: "In almost all countries, students have experienced small decreases in the availability of desktop computers and tablets for use in their reading, math and science lessons, as well as less desktop computers available in school" [1]. But even a greater barrier to spreading the best practices in Computer-Assisted Language Learning (CALL) is the level of teachers' digital literacy, which is a challenge for Higher Education: "[...] between 45% (ISCED 1) to 52% (ISCED 2 and 3) of European teachers can be defined as being less digitally active, confident and supported" [2]. In order to improve the uptake of ICT tools in foreign language teaching, the educators' digital skills need to be regularly upgraded. Moreover, there needs to be a clear distinction between the ICT skills that teachers use in regular classrooms and those that are required for teaching languages online, as online tutoring becomes increasingly popular. This new educational reality requires novel pedagogies, open learning environments, open educational resources, and open adult training environments.

Digital skills are vital 21st-century skills and are much appreciated in the educa-tional sector. Worldwide demand for higher education is expected to grow exponen-tially from 100 million students currently to 250+ million by 2025 [3]. This raises the question of how Higher Education Institutions (HEIs) and other institutions providing education will be able to sustain and improve the quality of the learning experience in the face of continuing growth and diversity in the student population. According to Scott, it is largely acknowledged that the pedagogical approaches need to be trans-formed in order to support the acquisition of these skills, but there has been little focus on how to teach these 21st-century skills; including elements like critical thinking, communicative skills, innovation, problem solving and collaboration [4].

In her report to UNESCO, Scott emphasizes the role of Educational Technology (EdTech) in this transformation: "Promoting learner autonomy and creativity is part of the solution. Technologies can be used to support efforts to transform pedagogy, but it is essential to recognize that 21st century learning experiences must incorporate more than just technology" [4]. Scott emphasizes the need for technologies as a part of both the new pedagogy in general, but also as a variation to more conservative learning methods to redevelop these into enquiry and problem-based approaches. New inno-vative technologies can enhance the teacher's ability to use strategic questioning, capitalize on learners' interest in mobile technologies, utilize social media, design relevant and real-world learning activities in order to teach metacognitive skills and build the right relationships for learning. Accordingly, technologies include learners more actively in learning, they emphasize learner centered models and EdTech pro-motes learning without borders like time, place and age.

In this context, the objective of the study presented in this paper was to analyze the needs of the education market and evaluate if digital skills and methodological approaches are required from language teachers. This study presents findings from the Erasmus+ project Digital Competences for Language Teachers. We analyzed job announcements for language teachers in several countries to understand whether digital skills are mentioned as requirements and if yes, how they are formulated. We discuss the results in the context of relevant European and national strategies and policies. In the conclusions, we highlight the discrepancies between the strategies and their practical implementation.

2 Literature Review

In all countries, there are governing policies for the education system. In addition, most of the countries researched in this study are partially obliged to follow international policies, or at least relate to these, more specifically, policies and strategies from the European Commission. We identified and investigated policies in different European countries in order to find guidelines that could be recognized in the study. As a base for the national and institutional strategies, EU's policies were included.

In order to have a better reasoning and background for the job market study, we focused on strategies at three different levels: 1) Macro; international and national policies, 2) meso; strategic work being done at the institution and 3) micro; the performative level between educator and student [5]. This was done to obtain more knowledge about what is demanded politically to be a language teacher in Europe today. A question is, of course, if there are any correlations between the demands at a political level and the actual skills being asked for in the announcements from the institutions. This functions as a backdrop for the discussion and conclusions in this article.

In the following, important findings in EU policies as well as two of the involved countries will be presented. The main reason for focusing on two countries is to be able to analyze the findings more thoroughly, and also because the policies are quite similar in all countries analyzed. In this study Norway and Cyprus are used as examples due to the fact that the number of announcements is app. the same (40 and 33), the results show some difference (30% vs. 15.2% mentioning's) (see Table 1), the countries represents north and south in Europe and the governmental strategies are implemented in different ways. Considering the research questions for this study, the article will not emphasize findings at the performative level.

The results will be presented briefly and will be used later for a broader discussion combined with the results of the market study.

2.1   Policies Concerning Digital Skills Europe

The study aims at identifying whether job announcements looking for language teachers mention digital skills, and if there is a relationship between strategic demands and the actual announcements at institutional level considering digital skills for language teachers. In order to do this, it is vital to acknowledge that the digital technologies do not exist in a vacuum, there are different actors and policies that affect the realization and development of these skills. Educational specialists concerned about education and digitalization often refer to the three different levels of the educational system that affect the quality of digitalization, called macro, meso and micro level [5]. It is therefore obvious that one needs to consider all levels in order to understand which digital competencies language teachers need to inherit or develop in order to improve their skills. It is also interesting to analyze how the three levels influence each other, for example, through job announcements. In the following, we will analyze how the policies and strategies at the first two levels affect the job announcement being published. The analysis will be exemplified with updated strategies from Norway and Cyprus.

As literature shows (see introduction), EdTech is essential to everyone in order to cope with the demands of the contemporary societies and their working life. This should also have an important impact on the educational institutions worldwide and across Europe. Therefore, The European Union has decided to take important actions in this direction.

More concretely, the European Framework for Digitally Competent Educational Organizations is one of the key elements in the Europe 2020 strategy, which thus acknowledges and emphasizes the need for a digital boost in the following years:

Digital technologies are enablers of a step change in learning and teaching practices; however, they do not guarantee it. To consolidate progress and to ensure scale and sustainability, education institutions need to review their organisational strategies, in order to enhance their capacity for innovation and to exploit the full potential of digital technologies and content [6].

This is further underlined seeing that digitalization on all areas is one of the ten priorities that the European Commission has emphasized in the period 2015–2019. The importance is stated already in the first paragraph: "The internet and digital technologies are transforming our world. Barriers online can deny people the full benefits that digital developments can offer" [7]. Through this work, the EU shows the importance of reevaluating and increasing the knowledge of digital skills in all sectors.

This includes, of course, the educational sector, and the Commission is developing initiatives towards a European Education Area. They have already worked on several initiatives that impact the digitalization of the educational system in Europe. One example is how they have developed a new way to distribute digitally-signed qualifications through the Europass platform. This will further enhance the work with strengthening the digital competence of both employers and employees in the future, but it also raises new challenges, like diversity on learning processes, ways of validating the qualifications and ability to provide the certificates in a safe electronic format [8].

Technology is nothing without methodology, though. It can be suggested that "Pedagogy and technology are intertwined in a dance: the technology sets the beat and creates the music, while the pedagogy defines the move" [9]. This is recognized at all levels. Strategies and visions for the future are therefore essential in order to succeed: "Each nation must examine new ideas put forward by its citizens and increase the collective impact of resulting innovation by tackling these challenges through regional partnerships and coalitions that accommodate local needs and contexts." [7]. Thus, institutions and learning providers also need to implement technology that transforms and changes the pedagogical model that we find being dominant today. Digital tools are a fundamental instrument in this change, but it is just as important who, why and how the tools and skills should be developed and implemented. Each country and each institution have their own ways of dealing with the digital era to prepare students and other learners for the 21st Century skills.

2.2 National Policies: Norway and Cyprus

The Norwegian government issued in 2017 a new strategy for digitalization of Higher Education in Norway [10]. Even though a survey from 2014 shows that there have been several initiatives that have improved the digital conditions in the sector, especially considering digital exams and digital assessments methods [11], it is obvious that in Norway the digitalization strategy has been connected to single persons initiatives and anchored solemnly in the management. It is also interesting that new teachers have not been provided sufficient training in developing their digital skills [10]. As it is shown in the latest report from the Norwegian Agency for International Cooperation and Quality Enhancement in Higher Education (DIKU) [12], promoting the use of digital skills in workplace is one of the priorities that has been successfully introduced in Norway's tertiary education and this is a positive step towards its digitalization. In fact, 7 out of 10 respondents have confirmed this interesting finding [12]. This underlines that the governmental policy should include a high focus on digitalization in the institutions.

The first paragraph in the strategy for digitalization of Higher Education in Norway [10] lists aims that concern research and education. The main aims of this strategy include both "Høy kvalitet i utdanning og forskning" ("High quality in research and education") and "God tilgang til utdanning" ("Good access to education") [10]. Those are directly connected to digitalization and to specific initiatives which promote not only the idea of accessible blended and online learning to everyone, but also other differentiated learning methods which support the use of ICT in the classroom. This is further elaborated in paragraphs 3.21 Målbilde for studenten (Future visions for the student) and 3.2.2 Målbilde for læreren (Future visions for the teacher) [10].

The future visions for the student are focused on digital opportunities and tools in order to develop digital skills and engage in active learning. It is also emphasized that the student should have "access to a modern, personalized learning environment that facilitates individual learning experiences, efficiency, collaboration and flexibility in the studies" [10] (English translation is made by the authors). Accordingly, the future visions for the teacher are also focused on applications, digital tools and services to support both the learning process, but also the professional development of the teacher. This is necessary to fulfill the aim that *"The teachers have good digital and pedagogical competence"* [10].

In the following sections of the report on Norway's strategy for digitalization of Higher Education, several means connected to the development of teachers' basic competences are presented, supposed to lead to the achievement of its future promising goals. Teachers should be better equipped to cope with new methods of teaching and to adapt to new demands for digital skills. The aims include the demand that all students should be exposed to methods of teaching where digital opportunities are explored and the demand for basic pedagogical competence and experience in teaching when hiring in all professional positions (in order to provide incentives for developing teaching skills). It also suggests a recognition system for educational competence and pedagogical development at all higher education institutions as well as strengthening of the teachers' digital competence in order to implement restructuring and development of learning processes based on the new opportunities provided through digitalization. The aim presented in 5.4.5 shows a high ambition from the government in Norway towards the digitalization of Education. Here it is stated that "Solutions for study administration, digital Learning Management Systems and processes are organized for personal learning environments and mobile and dynamic studies, and are adapted to more flexible arrangements for going through the studies" [10] (English translation is made by the authors).

This corresponds well with the policies and statements provided by the European Commission, showing that there is a common understanding for, and awareness of the importance of ICT skills at the macro-level, and also an aim to use technology in order to personalize learning.

It is nevertheless important to recognize in the Norwegian strategy that the responsibility for implementation and ensuring that the policies are conducted is often shared between the governmental instructions/strategies and the institutions themselves. Even though the government designs strategies and puts power behind the words, it is the institutions that need to implement the new demands in their plans for the future, allocate resources and create incentives for actual development in the scientific staff, as it is seen for example at the point 5.2.5, where there is presented a demand for a recognition system for pedagogical development in all institutions [10].

Of high interest for this study is the point 5.2.4, where the government demands "pedagogical base competence and experience in teaching when hiring in all professional positions, and successively higher demands concerning teaching competence for employment in positions at higher levels" for scientific staff at higher education institutions in order to get the position [10]. Having done training, taught at lower levels or taken external courses, makes scientific staff more capable of adjusting to new demands concerning ICT. This is something that should be reflected also in the job announcements, which are written and published at the institutional level.

In Cyprus, the policies are implemented in a different way, but still show some of the same tendencies. Europe's Digital Progress Report (EDPR) tracks the progress made by Member States in terms of their digitalization. As for Cyprus, the EDPR showed that the country ranks 22nd out of the 28 EU Member States [13]. Overall, Cyprus progresses slowly. Nevertheless, it showed significant progress in connectivity compared to previous years. However, despite the fact that Internet users engage in a wide variety of online activities, low level of digital skills risk acting as a brake to the further development of its digital economy and society. In Human Capital, Cyprus's performance is below the EU average. According to the Education and Training Monitor Report in 2016 only 43% of the Cypriot population possessed at least basic levels of digital skills [14]. Nowadays, digital skills and competences are needed for nearly all jobs where digital technology complements existing tasks, and shortages can be an important barrier to the country's economic development. As a result, awareness actions were planned in 2017, such as role model visits to schools and universities, by important ICT industry figures to explain the importance of ICT professionals in the future. Another action that illustrates this process was the introduction of the European Computer Driving License (ECDL) Certification in 2017 for secondary students in public and private schools. It is worth mentioning that this was the first time that public schools were provided vocational ICT certification. This is considered to be a break-through for the Cypriot education system.

In terms of teachers' continuing professional development (CPD) in the area of digital education, the EURODYCE Digital Education at School in Europe Report from 2019 highlights that Cyprus has adopted the European self-assessment tool (TET-SAT) to help teachers evaluate their level of digital competence and define their development needs [15]. Moreover, according to this report, the Cypriot authorities support teachers' professional development by combining three different approaches: CPD activities, teacher networks and the aforementioned self-assessment tool. CPD activities are offered by training agencies and educational centers. An example of the latter can be found in the continuous teacher training programs offered by the Cyprus University of Technology, particularly in the fields of EdTech, teacher professional development, and CALL.

As mentioned earlier, the same tendencies can be seen in all countries researched for this study. The aims are relatively high, and the need for heightened digital skills in all levels of the educational system is recognized. There are still few examples on how to do it, and exactly what is needed. Thus, it is often left to the institutions themselves to define and implement their strategies.

3   Study Objectives and Methodology

3.1   Objectives

The objective of the study presented in this paper is to analyze and evaluate the needs of the education market based on the request for digital skills in job announcements directed towards language teachers. The analysis of the job announcements for language teachers revealed that very few job descriptions mentioned digital skills as requirements or even desired. Therefore, it was interesting to analyze the share of job announcements for language teachers that require digital skills. This is even more interesting because of the strong focus on digital skills in the policies and strategies analyzed. Thus, the study aims to answer the following research questions:

1. To what degree do job announcements looking for language teachers mention digital skills?
2. Is there a relationship between strategic demands and the actual announcements at an institutional level considering digital skills for language teachers?

We adopted the methodology of a market study, a process of determining the viability of new services and products through research conducted directly with potential customers. Market study allows to discover the target market and get opinions and other feedback from both education providers about the needs required by the market and consumers about their familiarity with the defined skills and competences.

3.2 Data Collection

The present paper draws on a qualitative and quantitative analysis of qualitative data, namely, job advertisements. Therefore, the sampling unit is a job advertisement offering employment for language teachers. The sampling strategy employed in collecting the data were non-probability convenience sampling as the team of nine researchers in seven different countries applied certain criteria for data collection. The final sample consists of 854 such job advertisements from 11 countries.

When it comes to the design of the present study, it was conducted in three stages. In the first stage, the researchers collected relevant job advertisements. In the second stage, a qualitative and quantitative analysis was performed and the results were compared. In the third stage, the report was written up.

According to Bryman [16], to ensure high quality of research, such quality criteria as reliability, replication, and validity should be applied. In terms of reliability and replicability, the present study ensures them by describing and explaining the measures and methods used in a transparent manner. Bryman notes that probably the most important quality criteria are validity, which can be classified into measurement, internal, external, and ecological validity [16]. It should be noted that because of the design of the present study, only external validity is relevant. In this case, it means that the results presented in this paper can be generalized to other contexts as well.

Furthermore, according to Yin [17], triangulation is one of the criteria to ensure robust and high-quality research. The present study draws on data and investigator triangulation. More precisely, data are collected in a variety of contexts. Moreover, they are collected and analyzed by a number of researchers.

The data collection was done country by country because the majority of online platforms list job announcements by country. The search in each country was done by a different researcher (or a group of researchers). In each country, one or multiple online job platforms were selected to provide a higher number of relevant results.

We used the country-specific keywords to match the name of the job "language teacher" or "English teacher" or "Norwegian teacher" or similar equivalents. The keywords were used both in English and in local languages. Multiple searches were performed either on different dates, on different job portals or with different keywords to be able to collect 100 relevant job announcements (or as many as possible if 100 could not have been reached). The data were collected between February and August 2019. A job announcement was considered relevant if it offers a job for a language teacher in any organization or any other profession that focuses primarily on language learning or teaching, including researchers, managers, policymakers, and administrators. For example, an administrator's position in a language school is relevant, while an administrator's position in a regular school that also teaches languages is irrelevant. For each search, the following information was collected:

- Date
- Name of the job portal
- Keyword(s) used
- The total number of results returned by the search on the given portal and keyword.

3.3   Analysis of the Relevant Job Announcements

Each relevant job announcement was opened and read to find if the description mentioned digital competences or skills. Most job announcements contain a list of required qualifications or skills or sometimes have such requirements mentioned in the description of the work tasks or elsewhere. Any mention of the digital competences and skills was noted.

For each relevant job announcement, we noted if it contained any mentions of the digital competences or skills. For those job announcements that mentioned digital competences or skills, the following information was collected:

- in which search the job announcement was found
- the exact formulation of the digital competences or skills (later translated to English)
- job title
- name of the hiring organization
- type of the hiring organization (university, school, company, etc.)
- link to the announcement.

In addition, all data were analyzed, and information that could be biased or irrelevant was rejected from the dataset. As an example, the analysis showed that some job announcements in some countries were published at different platforms, or on different dates. Such announcements were considered duplicates, thus were included only once. Very similar job announcements by the same organization with only small differences (e.g., different languages, but the rest of the announcement texts are the same) were also considered duplicates. The same applies when the same job description was announced at different dates. Job announcements that were unclear about the main tasks of the prospective employees were not included either.

4   Results

In this study, we identified a total of 854 job announcements in 11 countries. For the analysis, we selected 128 announcements – only those that mention ICT skills. The breakdown by country is presented below (Table 1).

Table 1. Total number of mentions of digital skills in all countries analyzed

Country	#of search results	# mentions	% mentions
Estonia	42	15	35.7%
Norway	40	12	30.0%
Lithuania	109	28	25.7%
Turkey	88	22	25.0%
Italy	40	9	22.5%
France	30	5	16.7%
Spain	30	5	16.7%
Cyprus	33	5	15.2%
Russia	132	13	9.8%
Germany	106	9	8.5%
Greece	204	5	2.5%
Total/average	854	128	15.0%

As we can see, there are very few announcements that mention digital skills at all. It is important to keep in mind that the total number of search results in different countries might have been affected by several factors (such as season, choice of keywords, and choice of job platforms). However, the total rate of job announcements that mention any digital skills required for language teachers (15%) is an important indicator for our research.

We found 128 announcements mentioning digital skills. It is necessary to implement a distinction between the typologies of the required digital skills in order to identify and analyze the needs of the market. One example can be the excessive requirement of proficiency in PC usage or expertise in MS Office, which could have been an essential digital skill 10 years ago. The vast and varied pedagogical opportunities offered by modern ICT (blended learning, distance learning, game-based learning, etc.) require updated digital skills rather than simply "typing speed" or "general PC literacy". Normally it should be considered that teaching languages does not necessarily require sophisticated digital skills. One can get by even today without using all the innovative and modern digital tools. However, seeing the strategies implemented in different countries as well as remembering the need for languages in order to obtain the 21st Century skills, it is reasonable to believe that digitalization should be vital also in the future language classrooms at HEI.

The 128 job announcements identified can be listed and classified on the basis of how digital skills by language teachers are described and required: Generic digital skills, old fashioned digital skills or specific digital skills.

In the category *Generic digital skills*, we classified job announcements that simply stated the fact that some digital skills are required, without specifying which exact skills, for example:

- good ICT competences
- good IT skills
- confident user of modern technologies and business software
- skilled user of PC, webcam and internet
- familiarity with new technologies

The *Old-fashioned digital skills* category includes job announcements that require an ability to operate a computer and use basic office software, for example:

- knowledge of MS Office
- demonstrated experience using a personal computer, Office software such as MS Office
- typing speed and general PC literacy
- strong skills in Power Point
- MS Office proficiency
- proficient PC user
- expert in MS Office

The third category *Specific digital skills* include skills that describe abilities to use specific tools, platforms or methods, for example:

- knowledge of blended programs and new technologies in the training sector (preferential requirement)
- experience working with online educational platforms/research in the online educational
- platforms' domain
- new interactive teaching methods
- desirable expertise in online teaching

The categorization in old-fashioned, generic and specific skills is defined by the researchers in this study. The figure below shows how often the skills of these categories appeared in job announcements for language teachers in 11 countries (Fig. 1).

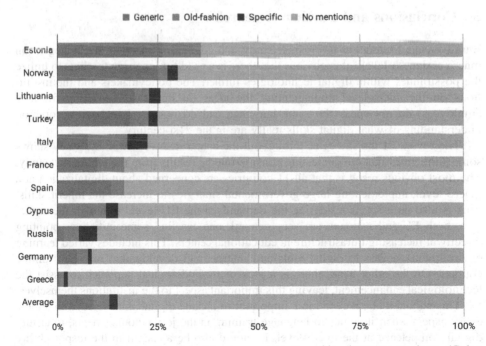

Fig. 1. Types of skills mentioned in job announcements seeking language teachers. (Color figure online)

The overview figure above can be used to compare the proportion of the announcements that mention digital skills (green, yellow and red on Fig. 1) and those that do not mention them (grey on Fig. 1).

Figure 1 can be supplemented by comparing the job announcements that mention digital skills of different categories, excluding announcements that do not mention digital skills. It can help to understand the needs and the requirements of the market. The percentage in which those required digital skills are recurring in the job announcements can help defining a more organic state of the art:

- Generic digital skills: 59%
- Old fashioned digital skills: 27%
- Specific and updated digital skills: 14%

As mentioned, most job announcements analyzed did not include any reference to digital skills. These are also included in the results of the survey (see Fig. 1).

The results are quite clear. Only 15% of the announcements analyzed mentions digital skills at all. When digital skills are mentioned, most of the job announcements for language teachers require generic digital skills (59%), i.e. being confident about ICT in general. Specific digital skills appear in 14% of the announcements that mention any digital skills. However, from the total of 854 announcements there are only 18 that asks for specific digital skills (2%), and when specific digital skills are required, they are not mandatory, but rather "preferential" and/or "desirable" are quite recurrent in the announcements.

5   Conclusions and Further Research

Based on the findings in the market study and comparing them to the strategies on macro and meso-levels, it is obvious that there is a need for language teachers to utilize the possibilities within digital technologies further. The policymakers and the institutions on the micro-level implementing the ideas (in this case, searching for new employees) do not speak the same language and do not seem to have a common understanding of what digital skills really are in the 21st century.

The review of the strategies throughout the countries involved in the study shows some similarities that are interesting considering the results from the job market study. The most obvious result is that all 11 countries are concerned about digitalization at a macro level, implementing large governmental strategies to increase the inherit skills. This is also necessary considering the demands at the EU-level. Although the strategies, both EU and national, are very general, one can find some initiatives pointing directly at increasing infrastructure in educational centers. This includes varied learning environments, access to digital tools and internet and development of (open) online courses. On the other hand, there is a lack of methodological approach to assist the technological enhancement, leaving this important aspect to the institutions themselves.

This should make it even more important to include digital skills needed in almost every aspect when it comes to language training in the job announcements, to ensure digital competence at the micro-level. It should also be apparent in the responsibility for implementing digital skills at all levels.

Another interesting finding in the strategies is that at a meso level the responsibility for implementing the actions are very differentiated. The responsibility is separated on different providers, including private and public sector, Non-Governmental Organizations and even industry. This means that there are several different ways and methods for implementing the strategies, allowing for considerable autonomy at a single institution and the micro level, i.e. the individual teacher.

Even though there are several actions implemented at the macro level, for example, national actions in all involved countries, it appears that few of these actions are directed towards methodological use of digital tools and/or skills defined at the macro level to ensure a common understanding of digitalization. Thus, this is left to the institutions themselves, or even the individual teacher. This can be part of the reason why we seldom find these skills defined in the job announcement.

Still, the majority of job announcements do not mention the need for digital skills at all. One could, of course, discuss the necessity for what we have defined as old-fashioned skills, but at least these announcements relate to the strategies at some level.

It is also worth mentioning that the number of announcements analyzed is not significant per country, even if the total number of 854 is enough to show a tendency. There are also some countries where more announcements have been analyzed than others, which can also provide some bias in the results. We have also included both private and governmental institutions in the research, without dividing these in the final results presented in this paper. It could be interesting to look further into this difference, and to analyze qualitatively the process for developing and writing job announcements for teachers of languages and other subjects.

Acknowledgement. The work presented in this publication has been partially funded by the European Union's Erasmus Plus programme, grant agreement 2018-1-NO01-KA203-038837. This publication reflects the views only of the authors, and the European Commission cannot be held responsible for any use which may be made of the information contained therein.

References

1. Vincent-Lancrin, S., Urgel, J., Kar, S., Jacotin, G.: Measuring Innovation in Education 2019. OECD Publishing, Paris (2019)
2. Deloitte, Mori, I.: 2nd Survey of Schools: ICT in Education. Objective 1: Benchmark progress in ICT in schools. European Commission (2019). https://ec.europa.eu/digital-single-market/en/news/2nd-survey-schools-ict-education
3. European Commission: High level group on the modernisation of higher education: report to the European Commission on new modes of learning and teaching in higher education. Luxembourg (2014)
4. Scott, C.L.: The Futures of Learning 3: what kind of pedagogies for the 21st century? UNESCO (2015). https://unesdoc.unesco.org/ark:/48223/pf0000243126
5. Fossland, T.: Digitale læringsformer i høyere utdanning. Universitetsforlaget, Oslo (2015)
6. EU Science Hub: European Framework for Digitally Competent Educational Organisations (2019). https://ec.europa.eu/jrc/en/digcomporg

7. European Commission: Priorities, Digital Single Market (2019). https://ec.europa.eu/commission/priorities/digital-single-market_en
8. European Commission: Digital Education Action Plan - Action 3 Digitally-Signed Qualifications (2019). https://ec.europa.eu/education/education-in-the-eu/european-education-area/digital-education-action-plan-action-3-digitally-signed-qualifications_en
9. Anderson, T., Dron, J.: Three generations of distance education pedagogy. Int. Rev. Res. Open Distrib. Learn. **12**(3), 80–97 (2011). https://doi.org/10.19173/irrodl.v12i3.890
10. Kunnskapsdepartementet: Digitaliseringsstrategi for universitets- og høyskolesektoren 2017–2021 (2017). https://www.regjeringen.no/contentassets/779c0783ffee461b88451b9ab71d5f51/no/pdfs/digitaliseringsstrategi-for-universitets–og-hoysk.pdf
11. Norgesuniversitetet: Digital tilstand 2014 *Norgesuniversitetets skriftserie* (2015). https://diku.no/rapporter/digital-tilstand-2014
12. DIKU: Digital tilstand 2018: Perspektiver på digitalisering for læring i høyere utdanning *Rapportserie* (2019). https://diku.no/rapporter/digital-tilstand-2018-perspektiver-paa-digitalisering-for-laering-i-hoeyere-utdanning
13. European Commission: Europe's Digital Progress Report (EDPR) Country Profile Cyprus. Publications Office of the European Union, Luxembourg (2017). http://ec.europa.eu/newsroom/document.cfm?doc_id=44294
14. European Commission: Education and Training Monitor Report. Publications Office of the European Union, Luxembourg (2018). https://ec.europa.eu/education/sites/education/files/document-library-docs/et-monitor-report-2018-cyprus_en.pdf
15. European Commission, EACEA, & Eurydice: Digital Education at School in Europe. Eurydice Report. Publications Office of the European Union, Luxembourg (2019). https://eacea.ec.europa.eu/national-policies/eurydice/content/digital-education-school-europe_en
16. Bryman, A.: Social Research Methods. Oxford University Press, Oxford (2012)
17. Yin, R.K.: Case Study Research: Design and Methods. SAGE Publications, Thousand Oaks (2003)

Study on Learning Effects and Platform Design Strategies of English Short Videos from the Perspective of Flow Experience

Chang Zong and Zhang Zhang[✉]

East China University of Science and Technology,
Shanghai 200237, People's Republic of China
2830545180@qq.com, zhangzhang@ecust.edu.cn

Abstract. Short video + education is currently on the rise, but video English learning platforms still have the following difficulties. First, whether this learning method is effective and whether it can improve the enthusiasm and efficiency of the learners. Second, such platforms do not have much direct feedback on learning, which is not conducive to the next learning.

This article starts with the flow theory. Flow theory represents the best user experience in the learning process. This article will address the following questions: (1) Compared with traditional English learning, will video English learning platforms produce a powerful flow experience? (2) What are the factors that affect the video stream of the video English learning platform? (3) How to apply the elements that stimulate learner flow to the design of video English platform? Research process: (1) The experimental method is used to compare and analyze the flow experience of learners in traditional English learning platform and video English learning platform, as well as their memory status. (2) Investigate the students who have experienced the video English learning platform to understand their feedback. (3) Based on these factors, the concept of video English learning platform is proposed. Conclusion: Compared with traditional learning methods, learning English through video does bring a better learning experience to learners. This article aims to provide some reference for the construction of video English learning platform and build a sustainable development direction.

Keywords: Flow experience · Short video education · English learning · User experience · Contrast experiment

1 Research Status of Video English Learning App

There are two types of video English learning platforms. The first type is mainly 15 s short videos, such as second bear English, second learn English, fresh sense of language, etc. The operating mechanism of these video platforms is similar to that of vibrato. Quickly play English in the form of short videos, which is convenient for learners to learn in a fragmented manner. However, whether the learning time of 15 s can meet the real needs of learners and facilitate learners to enter the heart stream experience remains to be verified. Moreover, these platforms are still in the new stage,

P. Zaphiris and A. Ioannou (Eds.): HCII 2020, LNCS 12205, pp. 413–422, 2020.
https://doi.org/10.1007/978-3-030-50513-4_31

and the content is that foreigners share their daily activities on the platform. Life can really bring new experience to users, but it does not form a closed-loop system. Another kind of platform starts from watching videos, such as Tangyuan English and seagull watching the world. Their videos cover a wide range of content, including American dramas, films, news information, etc., and sell some courses to bring revenue to the platform. This kind of video is usually long, lasting for 3–5 min, with key vocabulary, sentence by sentence listening, follow-up scoring, and speed adjustment functions. A relatively complete learning system has been formed. From the perspective of current market and research, the trend of learning English is indeed changing from picture based to video-based; however, from the perspective of research field, there are few related papers retrieved, insufficient research on the effectiveness of video English learning platform, and less on how to design a video English learning platform with better user experience. To sum up, this paper will first study the learning effect, choose a relatively mature long video platform such as a little English as an example to study the effectiveness of video English learning. Then we need to investigate the user's experience in learning video English, and find out the lack of a platform. Finally, the optimization research is performed from several perspectives such as aesthetics, ease of use, and usability.

2   Overview of Flow Experience

The concept of flow experience was first proposed by the famous psychologist Csikszentmihalyi. The specific definition is that when an individual is engaged in a job or activity that he likes, he or she will ignore the passage of time, forget the things in the real world, enjoy the current work and present a state of happiness in it. This theory was initially applied in the field of psychology, and now it is introduced into the field of Internet, and applied to games, online shopping, online learning, online communication and many other emotional scenes. Mihari and Australian scholar Jackson summed up the factors that affect the production of heart flow, and got nine characteristics that produce the experience of heart flow, and divided these nine characteristics into three stages. The former reason is the condition that needs to trigger the heart flow, the experience, which will last for a period of time; the result is to trigger the experience of heart flow to give users a good feeling. [1] As shown in Table 1.

Table 1. Flow chart

Stage	Antecedents	Experience	Result
Feature	1. Have clear tasks 2. Timely and accurate feedback 3. People have a sense of control in their activities	1. Match your own skills with the difficulty of the task 2. Fully integrated behavioral awareness 3. Enjoy it	1. High concentration and loss of consciousness. 2. The sense of time of the supervisor will change during the event 3. Participation from the heart

3 Correlation Between Flow Theory and English Learning

3.1 Flow Theory Enhances Learning Effects

The application of flow theory to network learning is a research topic that scholars have been paying attention to, and some scholars have shown that flow experience can have a positive effect on learning. For example, in a virtual network environment, generating a flow experience can reduce people's loneliness and stimulate people's motivation for learning next time, that is, they can stimulate the intrinsic motivation of learners and make learners more active in learning. Therefore, promoting learners into a state of flow during video English learning can improve learning efficiency [2].

3.2 Flow Experience Enhances User Learning Stickiness

In the age of Internet, products emerge in endlessly. To improve the user experience of Internet products is the goal of Internet companies, and flow experience is the highest goal of user experience. User experience involves multiple dimensions of the platform, such as usability, ease of use, emotional consistency, aesthetics, etc. In the process of using the product, once the flow experience occurs, it will produce continuous behavior and improve user stickiness. Novak, for example, built a theoretical model of the adhesiveness of educational games based on the theory of heart flow. Therefore, it is necessary to optimize the user's heart flow experience to enhance the stickiness between the video English learning platform and users.

4 Research Hypothesis

The purpose of this research is to explore an English learning process with a better user experience, which can harvest knowledge while harvesting happiness, and can effectively improve the efficiency of English learning. Therefore, first assume that this English learning style can have a certain positive impact on students. Taking randomly selected graduate students in various colleges of Huali University as test samples, we can use two teaching methods and three low-to-high learning tests to test whether video English learning in a context can bring a more amazing learning experience effect. Research hypothesis:

From the perspective of the conditions that stimulate the flow, it is speculated that the traditional text learning method and video English learning method, the latter can stimulate the flow experience and improve the user's enthusiasm for English learning.

The study of flow theory shows that skills and challenges must be matched, so it is inferred that the learning status of medium difficulty is more likely to stimulate the flow experience of the tester among the three difficulty levels from low to high.

The flow theory shows that the generation of flow experience can stimulate the learner's brain and can promote students to learn more quickly and lastingly. Therefore, the flow experience is positively correlated with the effect of English learning.

5 Experimental Research Process: Flow Experience in Two Kinds of Teaching

5.1 Test Phase

A total of 40 graduate students from various colleges were convened and told about the experimental process. After preliminary judgment, 8 of the invalid questionnaires and 12 of the subjects who misinterpreted the experimental tasks were deleted, and 20 of them were finally tested, which were divided into two groups: one group was tested by traditional learning; the other group was tested by short video English learning.

5.2 Experimental Materials

First, the flow state scale. Second, this test should ensure that the English words, time and other external factors are the same in traditional learning and video English learning. This paper chooses a little English platform. The videos on this platform are divided into six difficulties. Considering the overall English level of graduate students, three videos from grade four to grade six are randomly selected as test samples, and the key words in the videos are selected for learning. In addition, add these words to the app, which are also divided into three levels for learning. After learning, we use the word test table to test the influence of two English learning methods on the memory of these English words.

5.3 Experiment Design Process

The short video learning method is to randomly select three videos of different difficulty levels to learn, and you can learn key vocabulary, listen to sentences in detail, and follow-up. For each difficulty word learning, fill in a flow experience questionnaire immediately, three groups in total. The traditional way of teaching is to learn the words by using the app, which has the meaning and pronunciation of the words. Learners can learn words by speaking and writing. Similarly, a flow experience test is conducted once for each study, with a total of three groups. After the two groups of people have completed their studies, they will conduct a comprehensive test on the learned words to check the learning effect.

5.4 Experimental Results

After three difficult vocabulary tests, the results of the flow experience presented by the traditional teaching testers and video English learners are as follows.

This paper uses a two-factor repeated measurement analysis of variance method to determine the impact of different learning methods on the tester's flow experience with changes in vocabulary of different difficulties. Through SPSS analysis, the main effect of different learning styles on the heart flow experience is obvious. $F (1, 9) = 5.168$, $P = 0.049$. The main effect of different difficulty English words on the flow experience of the examinees is not particularly obvious. $F (2, 18) = 2.868$, $P = 0.083$. And the mean value of heart flow experience in short video learning process is 0.460 higher than that in traditional learning process, showing significant difference.

This process still uses the two-factor repeated measurement analysis of variance method to determine the impact of different learning methods and vocabulary changes of different difficulties on the number of vocabulary memory of the tester. After SPSS analysis, it is found that the traditional learning method and video learning have little effect on testers' memory vocabulary, and the main effect is not obvious. $F (1, 9) = 6.612$, $p = 0.030$. However, English words of different difficulty have a greater impact on testers' memorizing words. $F (2, 18) = 19.914$, $p = 0.002$. Although the short video learning method ($M = 4.2$, $SE = 0.311$) is better than the traditional learning method ($M = 3.4$, $SE = 0.311$), but in these two Among the factors, the impact of vocabulary difficulty is greater. Under the influence of two factors, the descriptive statistics of English learning are as follows (Table 2):

Table 2. Descriptive statistics of English learning in two factors

Different learning styles	English vocabulary difficulty	Average value	Standard error	95% confidence interval	
				Lower limit	Cap
Video English learning	Low difficulty	4.000	.258	3.416	4.584
	Medium difficulty	4.900	.277	4.274	5.526
	High difficulty	3.700	.300	3.021	4.379
Traditional APP English learning	Low difficulty	3.900	.233	3.372	4.428
	Medium difficulty	3.800	.416	2.858	4.742
	High difficulty	2.500	.224	1.994	3.006

Based on the experimental method, this chapter tests the students with the same English level, and verifies that the way of video English learning does bring high flow experience to the tester. Further research finds that the memory performance of the tester on vocabulary is indeed affected by the teaching method. The results show that the memory of words is related to the difficulty of words. It can be seen that in the learning process of low-level vocabulary, the experimental results of traditional teaching methods and video English learning methods are not much different; while in the middle and high difficulty vocabulary learning, video English learning effect is better. The overall result is consistent with the hypothetical process at that time.

After the end of this experiment, the testers of video learning were surveyed again to understand their views on video English learning platforms, and analyze which elements of video English learning platforms will have a flow experience for testers? The experimental data is as follows. Then use these elements to optimize the video English learning platform. First, the people surveyed met the requirements of the research subjects. Secondly, from the fourth question, the reason why users learn on the video English learning platform is that they can exercise listening, increase English learning activity, and feel more happy. As shown in Fig. 1, it also further proves the above assumption.

From the perspective of the factors that users pay attention to in the learning process, we can optimize the design of the platform from the factors that affect their flow experience. The research results are shown in Table 3:

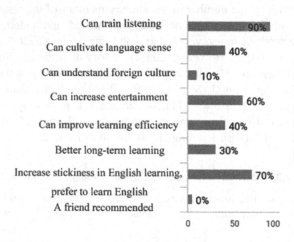

Fig. 1. Reasons to study on a video English learning platform

From the data point of view, the needs of learners are English subtitles needed during playback = Chinese subtitles required during learning = video difficulty > video course continuity > video subject matter > platform ease of operation > video duration > video speed.

Table 3. Attention of each element of the platform

Focus on the elements	Not concerned	General concern	More concerned	Very concerned	The average score
Video theme	0	20%	70%	0	3.9
Video rate	20%	30%	40%	10%	3.4
Video duration	10%	40%	40%	10%	3.5
Video course coherence	0	10%	60%	30%	4.2
Ease of platform operation	0	40%	40%	20%	3.8
English subtitles required during playback	0	0%	70%	30%	4.3
Chinese subtitles required during playback	0	10%	50%	40%	4.3
Video difficulty	0	20%	30%	50%	4.3

According to the user's investigation on the problems existing on the current platform, as shown in Fig. 2:

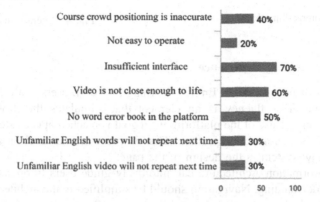

Fig. 2. Platform problem

From the above results, it can be seen that users believe that the interface of the current platform is insufficiently coherent, there are no wrong title books on the platform, and the targeted audience is not detailed enough, resulting in the platform being untargeted and affecting the user's flow experience. Combining the above problems, from the above several elements, the platform's operation and content are given targeted improvement measures, including the setting of interface content and the elements of video content.

6 Principles and Strategies for Designing Flow Experience in Video English Learning Platform

6.1 Clear Learning Goals

The flow theory mentions that a clear task is required to produce a flow experience, but in the process of English learning, learners have different conditions, so in the current era of big data, the future direction is to use research processes and big data analysis The user's gender, age, and motivation, in order to derive a suitable user data model, and then arrange different tasks for learners, and recommend different learning solutions. For example, in the pre use design test stage, we can judge the learners' own situation through an audio or word test. Learners may not have a very deep understanding of their own English learning situation, and they are likely to start from the lowest difficulty. It can be seen that a little English APP has set a small icon in the upper left corner of the page. You can select different levels of modes when you click in it. However, the sense of fresh language has added an interesting icon in this interface, from simple to overly difficult. The growing beak symbolizes the enrichment of knowledge, which is more humane and interesting (Figs. 3 and 4).

Fig. 3. Interaction effect (1)

Fig. 4. Interaction effect (2)

6.2   Fluent Learning Experience

In the process of using a video English learning platform, users can clearly perceive how to operate. This fluency is an element that stimulates the flow experience. Therefore, during the use of the platform, what goal is reached at each step and what is the next goal is extremely important. That is presented as a clear and scientific architecture flow system in the design of the page.

A clear information architecture can intuitively guide users to operate and reduce the cost of understanding. Navigation should be simplified in the architecture; in order to obtain better learning results, the architecture and flow system of the mobile-side learning app must conform to scientific learning methods. In the content of the study textbooks, most of them use the straight line arrangement method of Gagne, and the content to be learned is arranged from simple to complex. The transformation into visual language can take the form of increasing. [3] As shown in Fig. 5, the tasks under a video are broken down into words, sentences, and read. However, the task visualization here can be optimized to appear in a step-like form; or as the user uses it in depth, commonly used task icons can appear in color changes or appear in more obvious ways. No effect is shown here.

Fig. 5. Interaction effect (3)

In addition, the interface design can be presented in a visual form (setting dynamic controls). The learner's learning process does not require too much information, and too much interference information will not be conducive to the generation of a flow experience. Therefore, the interface design should control the amount of information, important information should be taken out from the secondary information, and the target information should be highlighted through the contrast of color and size in order to attract the learner's attention in the shortest time [4].

6.3   Timely and Effective Feedback

During the survey, testers stated that feedback was an important factor in stimulating the flow experience. Feedback is an indication of the action that has been performed and is reflected in the learning process as a response to the act of giving. [5] For learning testers, it is possible to build a better experience feedback system based on the needs of the learners. Learners should provide timely feedback during the learning process. Feedback includes positive feedback and negative feedback. Positive feedback includes incentives. Negative feedback can provide feedback from multiple dimensions such as hearing, vision, and smell. [6] In video English learning platforms, visual and auditory feedback methods are usually used. For example, in the process of learning a word of English, when the vocabulary learning is wrong, the correct page appears and stays for a period of time. And the tips of the example sentences, let it try to figure out the meaning in the example sentences. From the test results, this is a more preferred and more effective way of learning for testers.

6.4   Situational Construction in Video English Learning

Contextual learning can motivate users to a certain extent. This is why survey users have shown that video-based English learning is more pleasant than other methods of learning. During the contextual learning process, the learner's content is related to past experience, it is easier to stimulate self-confidence and passion for learning, and help to understand knowledge. [7] For example, freshly squeezed language sense. The learning videos inside are produced by UGC (user Generated Content) or PGC (professional Generated Content). Similar B stations, Xiaohongshu, Douyin and other platforms also have special learning blogs. Master, similar to these platforms is that learners can follow the UP master, comment on videos, and interact in the comment area. One of the great advantages of this form of video is the scenes in daily life, through which the scenes can increase the immersion of the learner. See Fig. 6 and Fig. 7.

Fig. 6. Interaction effect (4)   **Fig. 7.** Interaction effect (5)

7 Conclusion and Outlook

In the 5G era, short video presentations have exploded. The emergence of short videos has empowered knowledge-based applications. The content of video presentations is mostly 2 to 5 min of film and television, animation segments, fragmented and entertaining. However, it has not been verified whether this learning method is truly effective and can generate user stickiness. And there is no systematic theoretical method to support the construction of video English learning platform. Based on comparative experiments, this paper verifies that compared with traditional text learning methods, short video English learning can stimulate people's flow experience and improve the memory level to a certain extent. Based on the factors that stimulate the user's flow experience, some suggestions are helpful to the video English learning platform, which is conducive to improving the user experience and helping learners to obtain better learning results. Further research will follow, which of the factors that influence the user's flow experience is more valuable. Based on this, the English learning platform is further optimized.

References

1. Weibin, D., Shihui, L., Yijuan, S., Yulei, Q.: Innovative design of entertainment products based on flow theory. Packag. Eng. **39**(06), 187–191 (2018)
2. Qiao, H.: Research on Mobile MOOC Platform Experience Design Based on Heart Flow Theory. Jiangnan University (2018)
3. Qiankun, H., Renke, H.: Research on interactive design of mobile learning application based on heart flow theory. Packag. Eng. **39**(04), 188–192 (2018)
4. Xiaodong, X., Huang, S., Wu, J.: Instructional game design integrating flow theory and big data technology. J. Jiaxing Univ. **31**(06), 130–135 (2019)
5. Lan, X., Jiang, X.: Research on mobile health application design from the perspective of flow experience. Design **32**(17), 140–142 (2019)
6. Zhao, W.: Research on Interactive Design of Music Short Video App Under Heart Flow Experience. Jiangnan University (2019)
7. Peilin, C., Xiaochen, Y., Jing, L.: Research on mobile reading application design based on pat model. Design **32**(09), 100–103 (2019)

Technology in Education: Policies and Practice

A Comparative Study of the Application of Lesson Study in Different University Learning Environments

Efraim Centeno[1] , Marian Alaez[2] , David Fonseca[3(✉)] ,
Fidel Fernández-Bernal[1] , Sonja Wogrin[1] , Susana Romero[2] ,
Ane Ferrán[2] , Maria Alsina[3] , and Silvia Necchi[3]

[1] Comillas Pontifical University, 28015 Madrid, Spain
{efraim.centeno,sonja.wogrin}@comillas.edu,
fi-delf@icai.comillas.edu
[2] University of Deusto, 48007 Bilbao, Spain
{marian.alaez,sromeroyesa,aferran}@deusto.es
[3] Ramon Llull University, La Salle, 08022 Barcelona, Spain
{fonsi,maria.alsina,silvia.necchi}@salle.url.edu

Abstract. This paper presents the application of Lesson Study technique to seven subjects in different faculties in three Spanish universities. Lesson study is a methodology for the improvement of any teaching activity based on the detailed observation of lessons and analysis, carried out mainly by team of teachers. This technique has been extensively used for schools and high schools in particular in Japan and UK, but its use at University is not that common. In order to make a comparison of the application of the technique, a set of surveys were designed including two surveys for teachers (before and after the session) and one for students (only after the session). This paper makes an overall description of the experience and presents some of the results of the students' survey. The survey includes questions about usefulness, motivation, and attention of the session and an overall assessment of the lesson study technique. It also contents qualitative questions using a Bipolar Laddering Assessment (BLA). The comparison of the results of the different subjects provides interesting insight about the strong and weak points of the use of the methodology in the different areas and allows for a faster improvement of the sessions in the framework on Lesson Study.

Keywords: Lesson Study · University learning environments · Active methodologies · Mixed method · Collegiality

1 Introduction

The beginning of 21th century has been characterized by a change in all the levels of our society, including education and specifically, higher education. Not only the pace of this change is fast, but it's also continuously increasing. Some of the changes are especially significant in the context of education: the ubiquitous immediate availability of information through internet, the automation of a number of intellectual task (i.e.

© Springer Nature Switzerland AG 2020
P. Zaphiris and A. Ioannou (Eds.): HCII 2020, LNCS 12205, pp. 425–441, 2020.
https://doi.org/10.1007/978-3-030-50513-4_32

data or image analysis) that had never previously performed (not even conceived that it was possible) by machines, the easy availability of technologies such as data, sound and video, recording and real-time transmission [1, 2]. Additionally, in this context, the educational profiles required by industry and society are also undergoing a substantial and fast change. A lucid description of the challenges that education is facing can be found in [3].

Faced to the previously described situation, many educational institutions are becoming more and more conscious of the need of adaptation. Innovative educational experiences are developed here and there, both in an informal way and as part or strategic actions fostered by governments, schools or universities.

Many new ideas are proposed worldwide trying to adapt higher education to this fast-changing environment. Nevertheless, the implementation of any new idea risks to be inadequate in the particular situation that is used, to not adjust to the continuous adaptation that is nowadays constantly required, or to be unsuccessful for not being able to adequately include those who at the end of the day have to put in practice any change: teachers.

Taking into account the need for a quick and effective adaptation of any innovative educational action, the work presented herein, explores a methodology that effectively addresses the previously mentioned risk that may act as barriers to an effective adaptation of higher education to the present situation.

2 Lesson Study Methodology and Its Advantages

Lesson study is a methodology for the improvement of any teaching activity based on the detailed observation of lessons and analysis carried out mainly by the team of teachers. There is plenty of literature that explains in detail the use of lesson study [4–9], only a brief idea of the technique will be presented herein. The main features of lesson study methodology are:

- Lesson study it is a methodology based on the cooperation of teachers that teach the same subject as a teamwork.
- It's based in the detailed observation of the lessons by teammates in order to improve lessons (or any classroom activity) in order to make them more effective as learning tools. The work focuses on particular lessons, and not in the whole subject. Any kind of innovative classroom technique may be assessed using this methodology.
- Teachers that take the role of observers collect the information about the lesson. They try to detect when and how effective learning has taken place, and when it has been not properly worked. Additionally, the information may be collected using questionnaires and interviews with students.
- Because of the observation, improvements are proposed and implemented in the next repetition of the lesson.
- The work is based on a continuous cycle: selecting a lesson, setting lesson objectives, planning the session, rehearsing it, assessing the results and introducing

changes, the lesson itself, a new assessment of results and dissemination of obtained results.

- The results of lesson study intend to go beyond the improvement of specific session but to create a collaborative culture among teachers that help to promote motivation and a proactive attitude towards teaching. In this way, the methodology will naturally extend to other lessons, other subjects and other teams of teachers.

As a consequence of lesson study characteristics, we consider it is especially useful in the previously mentioned changing environment. Firstly, as it mainly relies on teacher's experience, it may quickly detect the need for adaptation to particular situation or students' characteristics. Secondly, as the process promotes to work continuously in the same way, a fast rhythm of change may be followed. Finally, as it fosters innovation and teacher's creativity, it is likely to produce a high level of motivation for teachers, even when changes and the need of reaction overlap and presents high intensity.

In the present work, lesson study has been introduced and used in three different universities during two years, in seven different subjects form different studies and backgrounds in order to test its effectiveness to adapt to different teaching environments.

3   Recrea Project Description

Recrea project gets its name from a play on words in Spanish than can be partially translated into English. It conveys both the idea of recreation in a ludic sense and in the sense of create again, including the aspects of innovation and motivation. It was designed and developed during academic years 2018–2019 and 2019–2020 with the objective of promoting a positive and collaborative teaching and learning culture among the three universities: Comillas Pontifical University (Madrid), University of Deusto (Bilbao) and Ramón Llul University (Barcelona). These three institutions constitute a strategic alliance known as Aristos Campus Mundus.

From a practical point of view, the objective was to design and implement lesson study in several subjects of these universities in order to check how it adapted to different matters and learning environments and also to check how it could help, not only to promote innovation and cooperation inside each of them, but also among the three institution.

3.1   Project Steps

A description of the main steps of the project follows:

- Preparation of documentation by the project leader. It included some guidelines for implementing lesson study for each subject, mainly following [10, 11], and some questionnaires: two for teachers (to be answered before and after the lesson study session), and one for students (to be answered only after the session). This questionnaire will be described in more detail later.

- Team enrolment. The project was proposed through the innovation units of the universities and several teaching teams volunteered to be part of the experience.
- Kick-off meeting. Representatives of all the teams participated in a whole day session. This session included a general introduction to lesson study and the presentation of the decisions about the subjects in which the lesson study methodology would be applied, as well as the objectives that would be tackled. (See next steps).
- Session selection. The teams of teachers selected the sessions they were going to work on (which could go from one hour of classroom to four). The reasons for selecting them were that it might be considered specially challenging or because it had presented previous difficulties when teaching, or just because it was particularly motivating for the team concerned.
- Session preparation including the setup of a session schedule with all the activities and the required materials (work documents, slides and so on).
- Session rehearsal, with observers. It could be done with a reduced group of students.
- Discussion and assessment of the rehearsal, drawing conclusions about the improvements that could be introduced in the session.
- Lesson in the definitive version with the students, again with observers.
- Lesson assessment and new conclusion drawing.
- Final meeting with representatives of all the teams participating comparing the results of all the subjects.
- Dissemination of results (papers and presentations to non-participating teachers).

4 Hands-on Experiences

This section describes the different subjects that have been included in the lesson study experience. They are included in a variety of graduate and post-graduate studies, in three different universities located in Madrid, Barcelona and Bilbao. The main conclusions drawn for each one are presented. A comparison among the entire subject is presented in the next section.

4.1 Electromagnetic Fields (Course #1)

Electromagnetic Fields is a mandatory subject in the second year of the Bachelor's Degree in Engineering for Industrial Technology at the ICAI School of Engineering at the Comillas Pontifical University in Madrid. It includes sixty hours of lectures (6 ECTS) and no laboratory classes. It provides a comprehensive introduction to electromagnetics, covering basic phenomena in the areas of electric fields, magnetic fields and electromagnetic induction. Some innovative activities had already been included in the previous years that are detailed in [12]. The subject is oriented towards a conceptual understanding rather than a numerical approach. This makes the subject difficult for students as they have to develop "understand why" skills rather than "how to do" ones.

The lesson study was developed for the two first sessions of the chapter about "electromagnetic induction" where this phenomenon, how the variation of a magnetic field produces an electric current, is presented. Each lesson lasted one hour and there was one observer for each session. Additionally, both sessions were recorded in video and observed by three more teachers (with different levels of engagement). A particular student was chosen to be observed in more detail.

The main innovation that was introduced in these sessions is that they were oriented to examples. A very brief theoretical introduction was made, and then a large number (around fifteen) of different situations were analyzed, first by the teacher and then by the students both individually and in pairs. The examples were designed to highlight not the quantitative analysis of this physical phenomenon but its behavior, asking the students to determine for each situation what was the direction of the inducted current, if it appeared and why. Some examples were proposed for personal work after the first and the second session.

As a results of the lesson study process, new slides were created with emphasis in the quality of figures, and a list of examples that anticipates the situation that are analyzed in deep in the subsequent sessions. In addition, some strategies to deal with the differences in the pace of students' understanding were proposed, as giving the faster students in the classroom the work that is later proposed for personal work for all of them. Some examples were discarded for next years, as they were too complicated for a basic introduction.

4.2   Operations Research (Course #2)

Operations Research is a mandatory subject in the fourth year of the Bachelor's Degree in Engineering for Industrial Technology at the ICAI School of Engineering at the Comillas Pontifical University in Madrid. It includes sixty hours of lectures (6 ECTS).

It provides a comprehensive introduction to optimization, modelling, simulation and other important techniques in Operations Research. Some innovative activities had already been included in the previous years. The subject is oriented towards a both a conceptual understanding and practical applications using several different software tools. The difficulty for students is that they have to take complex theoretical content and translate it so that it makes sense in the software, and apply it to industry problems.

The lesson study was developed to two sessions within the topic of simulation, and in particular, to apply the (previously learned) theoretical concepts of simulation and implement them in a software called ARENA. The two sessions were intended as a laboratory, in which students come with their laptops and the practice is implemented jointly. Each lesson lasts one hour. Last year, when we did this lesson study in class there was one observer for each session. Last year we observed that while students were able to follow the first simple practical case, they were not able to follow the second one in the time available. In summary, we observed that the simple case took excessively much time because not everybody paid attention, and if you missed a step, then you could not proceed. Hence, it took very long to get everybody to the same point. Therefore, there was too little time left for the second, more complicated case that was the second session. Once the instructor started going a bit faster, students got lost (or many of them did) and disconnected from the class.

As a remedy, the main innovation that was introduced this year was to convert these practical case studies into tutorials that the students have to do at home. In particular, the instructors designed two tutorial videos of the practice cases, and a self-evaluation questionnaire for the students. The advantage of the tutorial videos (in contrast to the in-class tutorial) is that each student can go at his/her individual pace, stop/pause or repeat the video whenever he/she seems fit. By doing so, we tailor the content to the need of each student. The mandatory self-evaluation questionnaire allows students to check whether or not they have understood the context.

As results of the lesson study process, new slides, tutorial videos and online- self-assessment questionnaires have been developed.

4.3   Introduction to Economics (Course #3)

The experience in the Faculty of Law has focused on the first-year subject Introduction to Economics. It is of a basic training nature and involves 6 ECTS, which means a total workload for the student of 150 h (50 h in class). In three large blocks, the student's total time is distributed among activities of analysis and reflection (70 h), reading and study of documents (50 h) and presentations given by the teacher (30 h). The lecturers encourage students to consider the impact of Economics on society and on people's lives, rather than just the technical aspects. For this reason, it has been considered appropriate to respond to the call of the United Nations to work on the Objectives of Sustainable Development (SDGs). Furthermore, the employers of law students convey in the quality meetings of the degrees that the students should deepen their competence in Teamwork. This is why the lecturers have designed the transversally of this generic competence on the specific one of economic problems.

The approach has been focused on the specific competence SC3 - Interpreting the great current economic problems - and on the generic competence GC - Teamwork. We have designed our proposal as a transversal one on the mentioned SC3.

During the 2018/2019 academic year, the four teachers who teach the subject in six different groups proceeded to the collegiate design of the Lesson Study. Firstly, a Didactic Unit on GC was elaborated, starting with a call to the students' experience and their reflection on the importance and keys of Teamwork; then a joint presentation was elaborated for the conceptualization of this GC and it was decided that the practice and assessment would be transversal to the SC3. In particular, the SDG No. 8 Decent Work and Economic Growth was chosen and, amongst it, the problem of Unemployment. The teachers prepared a document containing instructions on the work to be carried out by students as a team, as well as their assessment, which included, among other things, a rubric with the descriptors of the grade for each indicator assessed.

The experience was carried out in the first semester of the 2019/20 academic year. The students devoted 20 h to it, 7 of which took place inside the classroom and 13 outside. In the classroom, 2 h were devoted to the GC Teamwork Teaching Unit, 1 h to the explanation of instructions on work, 2 h of group meetings with tutoring by the teacher and 2 h of presentations of the work done. Afterwards, each group received feedback in the teacher's office.

Three different agents evaluated the experience. Firstly, the students, who evaluated the overall experience by means of a questionnaire; secondly, the lecturer responsible for the group who also filled in a questionnaire; and thirdly, the other three lecturers in the subject. This peer evaluation took place through direct observation in the classroom during the two hours of the presentation of the papers. The observation between teachers of the different groups was scheduled over two weeks in order to keep a time after each observation to share the strengths and opportunities for improvement observed, so that this feedback could be taken into account in subsequent observation sessions.

4.4 Programming III (Course #4)

Programming III is a compulsory second year course in the Computer Engineering Degree at the University of Deusto (DU). It has a student workload of 6 ECTS (150 h of work in and out of the classroom). It's structured on the basis of teacher presentations, exercises and computer practices. In addition to the specific competences of the area, it develops the generic competence of Planning and is what we have focused on. In accordance to the guidelines of the university, the planning competence is stated as: Methodically organizing one's work, resources and time, depending on available possibilities and priorities. This competence is key in the performance of any profession, and especially in Engineering, as it must be applied to each new project. However, the current engineering students not only do not see the importance of this competence but also find it difficult both to plan in the long term and subsequently to monitor what has been planned.

The new class was organized around two sessions and an intermediate work. In the first one, the competence was contextualized and students were given a small exercise to reflect on its importance, as well as the conceptualization that had to be considered. This first session was more participative than what had been done up to then. A new ingredient was then introduced, the experimentation by the students by planning a whole week of their "daily life", which they had to share with the teacher. Finally, in a second session, the experience was evaluated - both from the point of view of motivation and satisfaction with the experience, and from the point of view of the results of the planning exercise. The students should put those aspects seen during the development of the Planning competence into practice during the development of the final project of the subject. The difference with previous years is that they had already done a first trial of planning and they were able to draw their own conclusions about the importance and difficulties of it.

In both sessions, there were three lecturers who were observers, collecting data on the teacher, the class in general and any particular student. The experience was developed in a parallel way in two carefully formed groups: one in which the new process was introduced and another one considered as "control". The latter was taught as in previous years, but was also involved in the final results.

4.5 Processes and Techniques of Social Intervention (Course #5)

The experience in the Faculty of Social and Human Sciences is part of the course "Processes and techniques of social intervention" in the third year, second semester of the Degree in Social Work offered at the San Sebastian campus. It is a compulsory training course, with 6 European Credits, taught in two different groups by two lecturers. It is included in the curriculum of the Social Work Degree in Module I, namely

Social Work: Concepts, Methods, Theory and Application. This course contributes to the profile of the graduates in the development and acquisition of skills, abilities, competences and attitudes for the use of specific methods and techniques of professional intervention at individual, family and group level. In this course, students will propose and build alternative interventions to solve psychosocial problems and situations of an individual, family and group nature. In order to do so, students are trained to reflect on their attitudes and to build and strengthen their own style of intervention that enables them to give adequate answers and solutions to the problems they face, always in a responsible way. One of the competences assigned to this subject is, precisely, that the student develops active listening and empathy skills.

In this project, the teaching team that offers this course has focused on improving the methodology of Role Playing. This is one of the active techniques or psychodramas that allows students to face professional situations that worry them or cause them fear or insecurity. This way, through the adoption of roles and the dramatization of these situations, they are progressively more capable of identifying and analyzing their shortcomings, reducing their concerns and learning from a proactive and group position.

The teaching team has experienced certain disadvantages in the development of this technique that make it difficult to achieve the above-mentioned competence: the students' "stage fright", which blocks the naturalness of the presentation; the scarce capacity for self-observation, which makes it difficult to later analysis the situation being staged; and the need to perceive the classroom as a "safe context" in order to be able to study the relevant personal aspects in depth. These matters have led to the preparation of this Lesson Study. Thus, bearing in mind the limitations detected, a change of technique has been proposed in order to be able to go deeper into the analysis and evaluation of active listening skills and empathic attitudes, in the context of helping relationship processes: stop using Role Playing and experiment with video recording.

During the 2018/19 academic year, in the second semester, the initiative has been carried out, based on a case analysis. The students devoted 10 h to this activity, 6 of which took place in the classroom and 4 outside. The classroom hours were spent viewing the videos and giving feedback on the experience.

Three different agents carried out the evaluation of the experience. Firstly, the students, who evaluated the overall experience through two questionnaires; secondly, the teacher responsible for the group who also completed a questionnaire and, thirdly, the other teacher of the subject. This peer evaluation carried out by the teaching staff took place through direct observation in the classroom. This observation was scheduled over two weeks in order to provide a space after each observation to share the strengths and opportunities for improvement observed. This way, this feedback could be taken into account in the following observation sessions.

4.6   Project Manager (Course #6)

The subject of Project Management is mandatory in the different curricula of Engineering degrees at La Salle Campus Barcelona (Ramon Llull University-URL). It's a fourth-year subject with students enrolled of seven different degrees: Computer Engineering, Multimedia Engineering, Telematics Engineering, Audiovisual Systems

Engineering, Telecommunications Systems Engineering, Electronics Engineering and ICT Organization Engineering.

The subject is 3 ECTS credits with lecture model of 30 teaching hours plus the workload students perform out of class. Within this subject student works basic concepts in project management and understands the entire life cycle of a project. To achieve this objective, concepts are learned in a very practical way. The challenge for students is a real assignment so they must apply all the tools explained directly to the project.

The methodology used is the learning by doing strategy. Teachers supply all the necessary material in the virtual learning platform. The course is structured in the different presence-based sessions. It contains all the resources and, together with small explanations and group consultations, students develop the project in charge.

Presentation sessions were planned in order to share experience between different groups. In these sessions, each teamwork presented its project proposal and progress to the rest, and contributions to the presented work from the rest of groups were expected. However, the result of these sessions was not satisfactory: the attitude of the rest of the groups was passive in these sessions, and the contributions were scarce and of poor quality.

The lesson study application was developed in one of these presentation sessions. The dynamics were changed looking for an active attitude of students. To this end, the following dynamics were proposed: a) The team was divided into 2 subgroups: one that presented and another that listened to the other teams and gave feedback; b) The first subgroup was responsible for explaining the project to the other subgroups of other teams. It stayed at his exhibition table and the other subgroups of other teams were listening to the presentation; c) The second subgroup listened to the different presentations and gave feedback to each of them; d) In the last part of the session the team returned to gather and integrate all the contributions received on their project and shared them for all team members; e) Finally, each team presented its conclusions.

The main objective was to ensure that students understood the work of the other groups while maintaining an active attitude, and that they could improve their work with the rest of the classmates' contributions, apart from developing a critical attitude. On the other hand, students reinforce the concepts by having to analyze the work of other classmates. This dynamic seems to favor participation and contributions since these should be done in a small group and not in front of the whole class.

4.7 Transversal Project of Architecture (Physics, Descriptive Geometry, History, Mathematics and Computer Tools) (Course #7)

This experience was carried out in the context of a transversal activity in first year of Architecture Studies and Technical Architecture and Building Engineering of La Salle, Ramon Llull University. This work is a continuation of an outgoing initiative since 2016–17 Academic Year. In the case study, a series of transversal visits have been established, under the name of Aula Barcelona, in which the objective is to interrelate contents of the first-year subjects of the degree from visits to buildings or emblematic areas of Barcelona metropolitan area. These visits, not only seek to improve synergies between subjects and teachers, but increase interest and improve learning methods based on the study of real cases informally.

The subject has been endowed with 6 ECTS credits, with a minimum impact of 10% on the grade for all first-year subjects. In addition to the scheduled visit (4–5 h in one morning), 2 h per week of workshop class have been scheduled, where students must carry out a joint practice about the visit in teamwork, relating contents of various subjects, under the support of the teachers of the same. These activities, seek to reinforce the motivation of the first-year students, and despite the fact that, at the beginning of the studies, the basic and more instrumental subjects abound, they can glimpse the dimension that their profession will reach, so that early abandonment in First year decrease [13].

For the project proposed, the design of the activity has focused on defining an intervention proposal in a specific area that can be visited for the student's knowledge. In this way, while the professors of the Architectural Analysis subject have defined a statement for a proposal for the occupation of a plot, the History subject has reflected on the historical occupation of the space in the working area. On the other hand, Construction subject made students reflect on the typology of materials and needs of the environment at the level of uniformity, and finally Computer Tools trained students for digitally presenting his proposal considering volumes, materials, lighting, etc., generating a photo-realistic model that can be accessed through interactive systems.

A rubric has been created for the evaluation, with various indicators associated with the subjects that include the competences/skills that have been sought to be enhanced. The final grade of the activity is the average of each indicator, impacting with the same grade the percentages assigned for each subject, ranging from a minimum of 10% (subjects such as History or Computer Tools), to a maximum of 15% (Architectural Analysis or Construction).

5   Comparative Analysis

As part of the methodology of the Lesson Study, two surveys were carried out among the teachers of each subject, in order to get information about perception and motivation about this way of working. The objective was to compare the answers before and after the classroom session, and as an internal control variable for the project. Additionally, a single survey was made to ask questions to the students. This article will focus only on the latter. The survey included a set of closed questions, and additionally a Socratic- interview known as Bipolar Laddering Assessment, that has shown its validity when applied to the assessment of innovative education [14–17], both individually and combined with quantitative methods [18–23]. The designed survey was tabulated using the 6-level Likert type (from 1: strongly disagree, to 6: strongly agree), divided into four main domains/variables:

- Usefulness of the method:
    - U1: The session has been more useful to my learning than a regular session,
    - U2: The session provided was more useful for working on values than the regular session.

- Motivation:
  - M1: The teacher has been more motivated to teach this session than a regular one,
  - M2: As a student, I have been more motivated to participate in the class than in a regular one,
  - M3: My classmates have been more motivated to participate in the class compared to a regular one.
- Attention:
  - A1: My level of attention has been higher than in a regular class,
  - A2: My classmates' level of attention has been higher than in a regular class.
- Lesson Study final assessment:
  - F1: The presence of observers in the class has been an inconvenience for the normal development of the class,
  - F2: The class was more enjoyable than usual,
  - F3: My overall class assessment is very positive.

In Table 1, we can observe the results by Course (from #1 to #7 according the description in Sect. 4 of the paper), related to the indicators of the two first variables studied: Utility (U1 & U2), and Motivation (M1, M2 & M3). The results are tabulated in six Likert scale, and we also have incorporated the Standard Deviation (SD). The sample is linked with all courses.

Table 1. Results by Course of Utility and Motivation variables.

Course (Sample)	U1	SD	U2	SD	M1	SD	M2	SD	M3	SD
Course #1 (20)	4.8	0.7	4.3	1.0	4.9	1.3	4.2	1.2	4.3	0.8
Course #2 (29)	4.0	1.7	3.5	1.6	3.9	1.1	3.9	1.5	3.5	1.4
Course #3 (216)	4.4	1.0	4.5	1.1	4.3	1.1	4.5	1.2	4.2	1.2
Course #4 (11)	3.4	1.3	3.5	1.3	4.5	1.2	**2.9**	1.3	**2.8**	1.3
Course #5 (19)	**5.1**	0.8	4.9	0.9	4.8	1.0	**5.0**	1.0	4.8	0.8
Course #6 (10)	4.4	1.5	4.5	1.5	3.6	0.9	4.4	1.8	4.2	1.6
Course #7 (10)	3.9	1.9	3.9	1.7	4.1	1.9	4.6	1.9	4.4	1.5
Global Average	**4.3**	*1.3*	**4.2**	*1.3*	**4.3**	*1.2*	**4.2**	*1.4*	**4.1**	*1.2*

As it can be seen, the average value of all the studied variables ranges from 4.1 to 4.3 over a maximum of 6, with only two instances with a value equal or larger than 5, what corresponds to an excellent answer (both for Course #5). In this sense, this course students, value it from a personal point of view as very useful (5.1/6) and report a motivation much higher than for a traditional session (5.0/6). On the opposite side, we only found two values lower than 3 (pass threshold for the experience), that, similarly as before, correspond to the same course, #4. In this course, the values for perceived usefulness and motivation are the lowest, being only over the average value the perceived teacher motivation (M1:4.5). The teacher's perception about this course is that, as it was a very practical course in all the sessions, and not only on those that were improved, the students could not find a big difference with respect to regular sessions.

In Table 2, we can observe the results by Course related to the indicators of Attention (A1 & A2), and Lesson Study assessment (F1, F2 & F3). The results are tabulated also in six Likert scale, and we can also observe the SD.

Table 2. Results by Course of Student's attention and Lesson Study final assessment. F1 uses an inverted scale, where the results near to 1 are better than 4 or 5.

Course (Sample)	A1	SD	A2	SD	F1	SD	F2	SD	F3	SD
Course #1 (20)	4.6	0.9	4.7	1.0	**1.3**	0.8	4.8	1.0	**5.0**	0.7
Course #2 (29)	3.9	1.4	3.7	1.2	2.5	1.5	3.8	1.6	4.1	1.5
Course #3 (216)	4.5	1.1	4.3	1.1	2.3	1.5	4.8	1.2	4.6	0.8
Course #4 (11)	3.0	1.4	3.0	1.4	3.0	1.5	3.3	1.5	3.5	1.6
Course #5 (19)	4.9	1.1	4.8	1.2	**1.9**	1.4	**5.0**	1.2	**5.1**	0.7
Course #6 (10)	4.7	1.8	4.5	1.7	2.3	1.6	4.4	1.7	4.2	1.8
Course #7 (10)	4.3	1.5	4.2	1.3	2.3	1.6	4.7	1.2	4.5	1.2
Global Average	**4.3**	**1.3**	**4.2**	**1.3**	**2.2**	**1.4**	**4.4**	**1.3**	**4.4**	**1.2**

As a confirmation of the low results obtained for the Usefulness and Motivation variables, course #4 shows the lowest values for students' attention and overall assessment of Lesson Study. These results suggest the need for a substantial improvement for the session proposal in that course, as the changes introduced have not obtained the desired significantly higher results in comparison to the conventional session. Also, in Table 1, and as an opposite value, the course that obtains the highest value for satisfaction is Course #5 with all the indicators with average values around 5/6.

Figure 1 shows a comparison between Satisfaction (F2) and overall assessment (F3) and the average value for Utility, Motivation and Attention variables (UMA). As can be seen, the courses that require paying a higher attention for a second edition of the session and introducing changes for a better fitting are the above-mentioned course #4, and partially courses #2, #6 and #7.

As already mentioned above, in order to obtain answers more detailed that quantitative results, a qualitative survey was carried out using BLA method. This method allows us to identify strong and weak points of the application of Lesson Study from the point of view of university students, giving valuable clues about issues with room for improvement. Tables 3 and 4 show positive and negative common aspects (mentioned by more than one student) for each course:

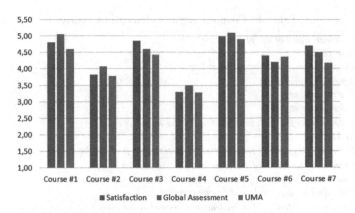

Fig. 1. Course Comparative of indicators.

Table 3. Common positive elements by course

Course #1	*Participation* *Clear explanations* *Attention of the students*
Course #2	*Clear documentation* *Rhythm of the session* *Entertaining session*
Course #3	*Entertaining session with high student participation* *Clear rules previously explained* *Better learning process with previous research of the topic*
Course #4	*The observation tasks are useful* *More clear contents and detailed explanation* *Better interaction and collaboration of the students*
Course #5	*A visual learning process more real to understand the future tasks* *The system helps to do an auto critic work* *Visualizing videos at class, helps to understand errors and problems*
Course #6	*Very dynamic class with more participation and collaboration of the students* *Work in reduced groups* *It is necessary to pay more attention for having more reflections about the contents*
Course #7	*In situ visit to understand practical topics* *Documentation of the teachers Implication to complete the explanations*

In order to complete this procedure, the next step was to ask about improvement proposal associated to each item identified individually, either positive or negative. Following the BLA procedure in Table 5, you can see the common suggested improvements (those that are repeated, positive or negative) that are more mentioned. These improvements are part of the implementing process of the Lesson Study for the second session edition that will be carried out during 2019–2020 academic year.

Table 4. Common negative elements by course

Course #1	*Not clear slides of the presentation* *Slow rhythm* *The presence of the camera recording*
Course #2	*Informatics problems* *Too much data* *Video Image quality*
Course #3	*Reduced time for each presentation (Pecha-Kucha is too fast)* *Nervous* *It is necessary to have more corrected materials to prepare the exam*
Course #4	*Change the schedule of the class (outside the scholar time)* *Duration* *More time used to explain the same contents*
Course #5	*Asynchronous feedback of students not present in the class (difficult)* *Bad quality of the videos, specially the audio* *It is necessary more time*
Course #6	*It is necessary documentation to understand better the contents of the class* *More time to explain* *Doubts about the equal system to assess between pairs*
Course #7	*Duration of the class* *Duration of some contents and explanations* *Very complex explanations not according the level of the class*

Table 5. Common solutions and improvements proposed

Course #1	*Improve the rhythm of the class* *Avoid the visual presence of the camera* *Increment the number of practical sessions* *Do some exercise in pairs*
Course #2	*Improve the quality of the video* *Increment the duration of the class* *Eliminate the project after the practical session* *More teachers as a supporter of the students with the program*
Course #3	*Do more works and classes with the same system* *More time to present and time to view all the presentations* *The participation of the students must be equal in time* *Do a previous rubric for the assessment*
Course #4	*Do inside of the approved schedule and with some breaks* *Use the flip-classroom to improve the participation of the student* *Students must analyze the final data*
Course #5	*Explain better the exercise previously to do it* *Allow to make breaks in the recording* *Apply these types of approaches in the first courses of the degree* *Focus on three topics for a better understanding and learning process*
Course #6	*Share the results with the teachers after the class* *More Teachers and observer's rotation in the class* *Reduce the contents of the class* *view real examples of topics application*
Course #7	*Reduce the duration of the class and of the explanations in general* *focus on the main aims and activities to do after the class* *Reduce the size of the groups* *More documentation about the visit*

6 Conclusions

After the application of Lesson Study methodology in seven different courses corresponding to different subjects, faculties and universities, we can observe a number of common behaviours that allows the identification of strengths and weaknesses of the methodology, that can be very useful for its subsequent improved replication. On the one hand, there is a generally positive attitude towards the method, as it provides an opportunity for students and teachers to work in a more collaborative way. Students perceive any variation from the master class as positive. On the other hand, taking into account that we are facing a first experience, there are some points that clearly require improvement, being more significant the session length, the support material used in the session (both quantity and quality), and the attitude and presence of the observers. We suggest as key aspects to improve in its re-edition an inclusive design of the classroom, making the presence of observers and cameras more discreet, improvement of the contents and a sound connexion between the session typology and learning objectives.

The data presented herein correspond to the first iteration defined by Lesson Study, carried out during 2018–2019 academic year. From the analysis of the data presented in this paper in a synthetic way, a second iteration will be done, taking into account the strong and weak points detected and also the improvements suggested by students.

Acknowledgment. The research that has given rise to these results has been carried out through funds from the Secretariat of Universities and Research of the Department of Business and Knowledge of the Generalitat de Catalunya, Spain.

References

1. Fonseca, D., Conde, M.Á., García-Peñalvo, F.J.: Improving the information society skills: is knowledge accessible for all? Univers. Access Inf. Soc. **17**, 229–245 (2018). https://doi.org/10.1007/s10209-017-0548-6
2. Fonseca, D., García-Peñalvo, F.J.: Interactive and collaborative technological ecosystems for improving academic motivation and engagement (2019). https://doi.org/10.1007/s10209-019-00669-8
3. Myers, J., Adams-Budde, M.: Creative schools: the grassroots revolution that's transforming education. Int. Rev. Educ. **62**, 375–378 (2016). https://doi.org/10.1007/s11159-016-9539-8
4. Cerbin, W., Kopp, B.: Lesson study as a model for building pedagogical knowledge and improving teaching. Int. J. Teach. Learn. High. Educ. **18**, 250–257 (2006)
5. Lewis, C., Perry, R., Murata, A.: How should research contribute to instructional improvement? The case of lesson study. Educ. Res. **35**, 3–14 (2006). https://doi.org/10.3102/0013189X035003003
6. Lewis, C.C., Perry, R.R., Hurd, J.: Improving mathematics instruction through lesson study: a theoretical model and North American case. J. Math. Teach. Educ. **12**, 285–304 (2009). https://doi.org/10.1007/s10857-009-9102-7
7. Fernández, M.L.: Investigating how and what prospective teachers learn through microteaching lesson study. Teach. Teach. Educ. **26**, 351–362 (2010). https://doi.org/10.1016/j.tate.2009.09.012

8. Yoshida, M.: Mathematics lesson study in the United States: current status and ideas for conducting high quality and effective lesson study. Int. J. Lesson Learn. Stud. **1**, 140–152 (2012). https://doi.org/10.1108/20468251211224181

9. Nami, F., Marandi, S.S., Sotoudehnama, E.: CALL teacher professional growth through lesson study practice: an investigation into EFL teachers' perceptions. Comput. Assist. Lang. Learn. **29**, 658–682 (2016). https://doi.org/10.1080/09588221.2015.1016439

10. Brown Easton, L.: An introduction to lesson study, Washington (2009)

11. Larssen, D.L.S.: An introduction to lesson study. In: Lesson Study in Initial Teacher Education: Principles and Practices (2019). https://doi.org/10.1108/978-1-78756-797-9201 91002

12. Centeno-Hernáez, E.: A hands-on experience of the use of active learning and some innovative teaching techniques in a basic engineering subject Una experiencia práctica del uso de aprendizaje activo y técnicas docentes innovadoras en una asignatura básica de ingeniería. Teach. Learn. Innov. J. Rev. Innovación en la Enseñanza y el Aprendiz. **2**, 14–19 (2018)

13. Fonseca, D., et al.: Evaluación mixta de actividades transversales en el grado de Arquitectura basadas en la metodología de la "Lesson Study." In: Proceedings of CINAIC 2019. Congreso Internacional sobre Aprendizaje, Innovación y Cooperación, pp. 331–336. Universidad Politécnica de Madrid, Madrid (2019). https://doi.org/10.26754/CINAIC.2019.00073

14. Pifarré, M., Tomico, O.: Bipolar laddering (BLA): a participatory subjective exploration method on user experience. In: Proceedings of the 2007 Conference on Designing for User eXperiences (DUX 2007), pp. 2–13. Association for Computing Machinery, New York (2007). https://doi.org/10.1145/1389908.1389911

15. Vicent, L., Villagrasa, S., Fonseca, D., Redondo, E.: Virtual learning scenarios for qualitative assessment in higher education 3D arts. J. Univers. Comput. Sci. **21**, 1086–1105 (2015). https://doi.org/10.3217/jucs-021-08-1086

16. Llorca, J., Zapata, H., Redondo, E., Alba, J., Fonseca, D.: Bipolar laddering assessments applied to urban acoustics education. In: Rocha, Á., Adeli, H., Reis, L.P., Costanzo, S. (eds.) WorldCIST 2018. AISC, vol. 747, pp. 287–297. Springer, Cham (2018). https://doi.org/10.1007/978-3-319-77700-9_29

17. Fonseca, D., Navarro, I., de Renteria, I., Moreira, F., Ferrer, Á., de Reina, O.: Assessment of wearable virtual reality technology for visiting world heritage buildings: an educational approach. J. Educ. Comput. Res. **56**, 940–973 (2018). https://doi.org/10.1177/0735633117 733995

18. Fonseca, D., Redondo, E., Villagrasa, S.: Mixed-methods research: a new approach to evaluating the motivation and satisfaction of university students using advanced visual technologies. Univers. Access Inf. Soc. **14**, 311–332 (2015). https://doi.org/10.1007/s10209-014-0361-4

19. Fonseca, D., Martí, N., Redondo, E., Navarro, I., Sánchez, A.: Relationship between student profile, tool use, participation, and academic performance with the use of augmented reality technology for visualized architecture models. Comput. Hum. Behav. **31**, 434–445 (2014). https://doi.org/10.1016/j.chb.2013.03.006
20. Fonseca, D., Valls, F., Redondo, E., Villagrasa, S.: Informal interactions in 3D education: Citizenship participation and assessment of virtual urban proposals. Comput. Hum. Behav. **55**, 504–518 (2016). https://doi.org/10.1016/j.chb.2015.05.032
21. Fonseca, D., Redondo, E., Valls, F., Villagrasa, S.: Technological adaptation of the student to the educational density of the course a case study: 3D architectural visualization. Comput. Human Behav. **72**, 599–611 (2017). https://doi.org/10.1016/j.chb.2016.05.048
22. Sanchez-Sepulveda, M., Fonseca, D., Franquesa, J., Redondo, E.: Virtual interactive innovations applied for digital urban transformations. Mixed approach. Futur. Gener. Comput. Syst. **91**, 371–381 (2019). https://doi.org/10.1016/j.future.2018.08.016
23. Sanchez-Sepulveda, M.V., Torres-Kompen, R., Fonseca, D., Franquesa-Sanchez, J.: Methodologies of learning served by virtual reality: a case study in urban interventions. Appl. Sci. **9** (2019). https://doi.org/10.3390/app9235161

Exchanging Challenge Based Learning Experiences in the Context of RoboSTEAM Erasmus+ Project

Miguel Á. Conde[1](✉) ⓘ, Francisco Jesús Rodríguez-Sedano[2] ⓘ,
Camino Fernández-Llamas[1] ⓘ, Manuel Jesus[3], María-João Ramos[4],
Susana Celis-Tena[5], José Gonçalves[6] ⓘ, Ilkka Jormanainen[7] ⓘ,
and Francisco J. García-Peñalvo[8] ⓘ

[1] Department of Mechanics, Computer Science and Aerospace Engineering,
Robotics Group, University of León, Campus de Vegazana S/N, 24071 León, Spain
{mcong, cferll}@unileon.es
[2] Department of Electric, Systems and Automatics Engineering, Robotics
Group, Universidad de León, Campus de Vegazana S/N, 24071 León, Spain
francisco.sedano@unileon.es
[3] Departamento de Tecnologias, Colégio Internato dos Carvalhos,
Rua do Moeiro s/n, 4415-284 Carvalhos, Portugal
manuel.jesus@cic.pts
[4] Department of Languages, Agrupamento de Escolas Emídio Garcia,
Rua Eng. Adelino Amaro da Costa, 5300-146 Bragança, Portugal
f33laepq@gmail.com
[5] IES Eras de Renueva, Comandante Cortizo S/N, 24008 León, Spain
susanact@ieserasderenueva.org
[6] Department of Electrical Engineering, Instituto Politécnico Bragança,
Campus de Santa Apolonia, 5301-253 Bragança, Portugal
goncalves@ipb.pt
[7] School of Computing/Joensuu Campus, University of Eastern Finland,
Länsikatu 15, Joensuu 80101, Finland
ilkka.jormanainen@uef.fi
[8] GRIAL Research Group, Computer Science Department,
Research Institute for Educational Sciences, University of Salamanca,
37008 Salamanca, Spain
fgarcia@usal.es

Abstract. In the context of the digital society, educational systems should prepare the students to succeed in a really volatile environment. In order to do so they require to acquire some specific competences that use to be related to STEAM Education. However, integrating STEAM is hard and requires of new methodologies and tools. RoboSTEAM is an Erasmus+ project that aims to facilitate this by using Challenge Based Learning and applying Physical Devices and Robotics. In order to know if what RoboSTEAM proposes work properly it must be tested in different contexts with different educational systems. The results of these tests should be compared, which requires of a common knowledge background. In order to achieve it RoboSTEAM proposes students and teachers exchanges between similar and different sociocultural

P. Zaphiris and A. Ioannou (Eds.): HCII 2020, LNCS 12205, pp. 442–455, 2020.
https://doi.org/10.1007/978-3-030-50513-4_33

environments, so they can learn how other people work in the project challenges and if what they do can be addressed by them in a similar way. The present work describes these exchanges, how they were planned and carried out and the main results obtained. From the exchanges carried out until now it is possible to say that they facilitate sharing knowledge that later can lead to better results in the project challenges and that they are enriching experiences both for students and for teachers.

Keywords: STEAM · Exchange · Competence · Challenge Based Learning · Robotics · Physical Devices

1 Introduction

Educational systems should adapt themselves to their ecosystem. Nowadays we are involved in what is known as digital society. A changing context that requires of flexible and well-prepared professionals, that know the tools and methodologies to succeed in so heterogeneous landscape. In order to do this the students need to develop what are known as 21st century competences such as: computational thinking, problem solving, teamwork, critical thinking. These competences are linked to what is known as STEAM Education [1].

STEAM (Science, Technology, Engineering. Arts & Mathematics) Education is critical to improve countries innovation capacity and students employability [2, 3]. Given this fact it must be integrated in current educational systems. However, this is not an easy task, because STEAM Education is not only a set of subjects, they should be integrated along educational institutions curricula by applying new methodological approaches [4, 5]. A sample of these approaches can be active methodologies such as Problem based Learning (PBL) [6], Project based Learning (PrBL) [7] or in the last years Challenge Based Learning (CBL) [8].

RoboSTEAM project is a proposal granted by Erasmus+ Strategic Partnership call in 2018. It aims to experiment with STEAM integration projects that help learners to develop 21st century skills by using a Challenge Based Learning methodology and applying Robotics and Mechatronics. In order to do so the project proposes the exchange in the European Context of experiences related to this topic [9, 10].

The project is coordinated by the University of León and beyond this institutions it includes in the partnership another 4 universities (Instituto Politécnico de Bragança - IPB, Karlsruher Institut Fuer Technologie - KIT, University of Eastern Findland - UEF and University of Salamanca - USAL) and 4 schools (Colégio Internato dos Carvalhos - CIC, Agrupamento de Escolas Emídio Garcia - AEEG, IES Eras de Renueva - IER and the Secondary School of the University of Eastern Finland UEF-SS). As associate partners are also involved an additional school (Karl Benz School) and a company (Arduino). This means that institutions of five different countries and different socioeconomic contexts will collaborate in the project.

RoboSTEAM project is described as a set of activities, outcomes, multiplier events and learning teaching and training actions, following the schema defined by the Erasmus+ call. The activities are related to project progress including tasks such as management, quality assurance, dissemination and two pilot phases employed to test the results of the project. The outcomes of the project define a set of challenges and tools to address them, and a digital environment to facilitate accessing to all those materials and managing the experiences and knowledge exchanges. The multiplier events are devoted to disseminate the project results and the project has scheduled one of them in each of the partners countries. Last but not least, RoboSTEAM teaching and training actions that facilitates knowledge exchange. The project includes one staff training exchange for teachers and four students exchanges.

This paper is focused on the latter of the exchanges, that is the students exchange. Why are they necessary? As we commented above, during the project students from the partnership schools will be addressing challenges, following a CBL approach and applying Robotics and Mechatronics kits. To do so they will define their own challenges and described the kits to address them. As part of the pilot phase 2 the schools will exchange challenges between them and will address such challenges with their own kits. These exchanges can be between similar or different sociocultural contexts, so for the project is interesting carrying out students exchanges in order to compare how they work and share good practices and knowledge when addressing the challenges. This work describes the students' exchanges and their results.

The rest of the paper is structured as follows. Section 2 describes the students exchanges planned in the proposal and the way in which they are evaluated. Section 3 details two exchanges already carried out. Section 4 presents and discusses the results of such exchanges and finally in Sect. 5 some conclusions are posed.

2 The Students' Exchanges

As commented above, students' exchanges are carried out during the project piloting in order to facilitate sharing knowledge and good practices about specific challenges or kits. The first pilot phase requires that students develop their own challenges with their kits, but for the second phase challenges are exchanged between schools. It is desirable to have knowledge about how students from a different socioeconomic context can deal with them, so during the first pilot phase students travel to other institutions in order to know how students from a different country work in the project. In this section the challenge schedule and the assessment methodology are described.

2.1 Description

The exchanges included in RoboSTEAM have a duration of 5 days each, including travelling time. They involve students and teachers from the partnership schools although the people travelling from each institution is not the same in all the exchanges.

The exchanges proposed are (we use the same actions ids employed in the proposal for the exchanges):

- C2. First exchange between Portuguese and Spanish school students. It aims that students from two similar sociocultural contexts can see how the others work. It is a short-term exchange of groups of pupils. It involves 5 students from AEEG and 5 from CIC and 2 teachers per institution. The hosting institution is IER and the exchange was developed in October 2019. During this action Portuguese students participated in challenges of the Spanish institution, so they saw how the latter address the challenges and the type of PD&R solutions they used.

- C3. Second exchange between Spanish and Portuguese school students. It is similar to C2 but in this case 5 Spanish students and 2 teachers from IER travelled to Bragança. The hosting institution was AEEG and the exchange was carried out in November 2019. In this case the Spanish students participated in Portuguese challenges.
- C4. Exchange between Finnish and Spanish students. In this case 5 Finnish students and 2 teachers travelled to Spain in order to know how students from a different sociocultural contexts addressed the challenges. The hosting institution was IER and the action was developed in February 2020.
- C5. Exchange between Finnish and Portuguese students. Similar to C4 but in this case Finnish students travelled to Portugal and the hosting institution was AEEG. It was carried out in February 2020.
- C6. Exchange between Spanish, Portuguese and Finnish students. This exchange involves 5 students from IER, 5 from CIC and 5 from IER. The hosting institution is UEF and the exchange will be developed in March 2020. During this action Spanish and Portuguese students will participate in challenges of the Finish institution.

A schema of the exchanges can be seen in Fig. 1. It is necessary to point out that C4 and C5 were carried out in the same week with different students and teachers and that C6 has not yet developed when writing this work.

2.2   Working and Assessment Methodology

To better understand how the exchanges were carried it is necessary first briefly describe CBL.

CBL is a flexible methodology that encourages students to leverage the technology they use in their daily lives to solve real-world problems [11]. CBL is a collaborative methodology. It is going to involve the students' groups, but also other peers, teachers, experts, parents, etc. in order to solve a real problem. A CBL approach requires to propone to the students a big idea, this idea will be discussed in order to find some main questions. The students analyze the questions and define a challenge. The challenge is addressed by the students in a collaborative way and involving people from their educational contexts and from the outside [8].

The main problem we found out regarding the methodology is the time each institution can devote to a challenge. Some of them can employ the whole term while others only a concrete number of hours and always orienting the challenges to fulfil their learning pathways. Given this context it was necessary to look for a challenge description that fits with all the involved partners requirements, so the challenge granularity was explored. In [12] we described how this issue is addressed during the project, that basically consist of the definition of challenges, mini-challenges and nano-challenges. This was based in Nichols, Caters and Torres work [13], that understands the challenge as the higher granularity level element, composed by mini-challenges with a lower level of granularity, up to the nano-challenge that is the lowest one. Thus, nano-challenges have a higher level of detail and requires less hours to be addressed.

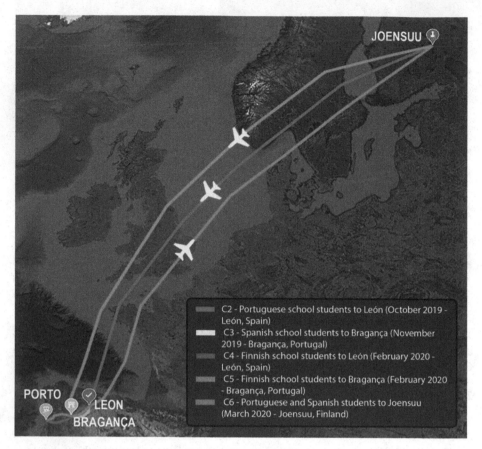

Fig. 1. Schema of the different exchanges carried out in RoboSTEAM project.

As the exchanges last only 5 days and they include also travel time, the decision was that the students that travel address a nano-challenge proposed by the hosting institution with the hosting institution kits. In addition, in order to share knowledge and to foster the interaction between the students, the teams includes members from both the hosting and the visiting institution.

For the evaluation of the exchanges we have applied a mixed methodology [14] taking into account quantitative and qualitative information.

As quantitative indicators we have:

- The grade for the outcome. After addressing a nano-challenges each team should present their results which will be graded by the teachers.
- In addition, we have used a co-measure rubric. "Co-Measure is a rubric focused on evaluating student collaborative problem solving when participating in STEAM activities, tasks, or units of study" [15]. We use this rubric during the pilots to measure the collaboration of students when addressing the challenges. However, in this case they are working together just a few days, so instead of rating each of the group members they have rated themselves as kind of peer review assessment.

- Time devoted to the challenges. That is how many hours the students have employed to address the challenges. Although we have measure it, this indicator is not so interesting in the exchanges, because it depends not only in the difficulty of the challenge but in the number of working days and working hours that the students employ, which is constrained by the duration and agenda of the exchange.
- Number of persons involved in the challenge. Both team members and external people that participate solving the work.

As qualitative indicators we have:

- Students perception about the exchanges. Gathered through the open questions of an anonymous questionnaire. The students describe their opinion about the exchange and the collaboration with students from other countries to solve the challenges.
- Teachers perception about the exchanges. The teachers were asked in semi-structured interviews about their perception regarding challenges. This information is analyzed to know the positive issues and the drawbacks of the activities and how they can be improved in the future.

In next sections two exchanges and the results about teachers perception are presented.

3   C2 and C3 Exchanges

In this section we described some details of the exchanges specially the persons involved and the challenge addressed.

3.1   C2. First Exchange Between Portuguese and Spanish School Students

This challenge took place from the 21th to the 25th of October of 2019. On it the educational institutions that participate were CIC with 2 teachers and 6 students, AEEG with 2 teachers and 5 students and IER, as the hosting institution, with 13 students and 2 teachers (although the initial proposal includes fewer visiting students the CIC involved more with their own funds).

The visit included working activities and also social and cultural activities to foster students' interaction. We focused our research in the former. In this case the students deal with a mini-challenge divide in several nano-challenges. Teams of four students were defined by the teachers. The teams mixed students from the different schools. It should be noted that although CIC and IER students had a technological background AEEG students come from the arts field which enriches students work.

The mini-challenge selected for the exchange consisted of improving school festival and it was especially focused on guiding students to the auditorium. Table 1. Summarizes the challenge. It was split in several nano-challenges with the same difficulty level as the described in Table 2. In order to address the nano-challenges students should use a kit, in this case Arduino: ELEGOO UNO Project Basic Starter Kit with Tutorial and UNO R3 Board Compatible with Arduino IDE for Beginner [16]. The results of these challenges are shown in Fig. 2.

Table 1. Mini - challenge description for C2

Title	Illuminated sign

Description

The school festival will be held in the auditorium. Students' relatives and friends will be welcome to the event. We want to signal how to get to the auditorium from the main entrance. To do this you will have to design the light signaling

Design a program to get 8 different color LEDs to turn on and turn off in a simple sequence. Insert them in a board to get the route correctly marked

It is required to use a simulator program before making the model

Goal/S

General Objectives
- Know the basics of computational thinking and acquire the skills to use it when solving simple problems
- Understand and practice basic programming concepts acquiring the ability to create simple programs using them
- Address diversity in the classroom: use methodologies and resources that have been specifically selected for STEAM teaching with students with different cultural, academic and competence levels
- Identify and use relevant everyday real-life contexts and scientist reasoning to promote the essential values of our society
- Foster inclusive education and intercultural learning through the use of STEAM contexts

Specific Objectives
- Know how a LED diode works
- Calculate the current limiting resistors you should place in a circuit with LED diodes
- Send different values to an Arduino digital pin
- Work with loops to send different values with different delays

Evaluation

An active methodology, based on learning making, will be used. Special emphasis is placed on the social and connected nature of learning when designing the activities, by encouraging communication among participants

Teachers will act as facilitators, monitoring the activities and providing the necessary support for a fruitful experience. Teachers will be also in charge of proposing the challenges students will rise to and provide them with web sources where to obtain the necessary information to carry out these challenges

In addition, every participant will be able to help and collaborate with other participants to solve difficulties and challenges that could arise

Every participating group of students will generate a solution to solve the challenge

The realization of the activity plan will contribute to the development and improvement of digital competence, particularly in the Digital contents generation and Solving problems areas

Fig. 2. Results of C2 exchange.

Table 2. C2 nano-challenge sample

Title	Make an LED turn on and off

What is an LED?

What type of component is an LED?
How is it connected? What resistor is required?

Description

• Research into the necessary components for the circuit to work
  correctly
• Calculate the resistor needed to prevent LED from blowing
• Create a program to turn on an LED
• Simulate the circuit using, for example, Tinkercad and send
  different values to an Arduino digital pin
• Connect the components to the breadboard
• Power on the Arduino board by connecting it to a computer using
  an USB cable
• Check that the real circuit works

Goal/s

Know how to connect an LED to turn it on and off

Kits to use

Simulator program, Arduino Uno or similar Arduino board, a
breadboard (preferably with a positive and negative rail), an LED,
a resistor, jumper wires, USB cable, a computer, IDE Arduino

Evaluation

The students should connect correctly all the components and
calculate the value for the resistor

3.2   C3. Second Exchange Between Portuguese and Spanish School Students

This exchange was carried out during from the 18th to the 22nd of November 2019. The institutions involved were IER and AEEG as the hosting institution. 8 students per institution take part in the experience (IER funded 3 more visiting students than the described on the proposal). The challenge was carried out by Art students (Portuguese) and the Spanish ones with an educational background related to technologies. There were four groups of four students in each. All groups were made up of Portuguese and Spanish students; all of them with mixed abilities concerning STEAM related competences. Therefore, the groups were heterogeneous.

As in previous exchange there was a cultural agenda and a working plan. Regarding the latter we have again a mini-challenge (Table 3) and some nano-challenges (Table 4).

In this case students programmed mBots [17] to follow straight lines with some turnings by the use of infrared sensors. The students created a fire detector which emits a sound whenever detects heat. Afterwards, students programmed ultrasonic sensors to create alternative ways so that mBots could avoid obstacles. All students achieved a good level at this skill. Results are shown in Fig. 3.

4   Results and Discussion

Regarding the results, the presentation of all the indicators gathered have not sense specially when not all the exchanges have finished, so we show the qualitative analysis of teachers' perspectives about each of the challenges and the time that students devoted to complete the nano-challenges.

Regarding C2, we should point out that students have devoted 7,5 h per day to work, which means 35 h during the exchange. They were distributed between: challenges work, visits to different ICT companies and cultural acts. In this first exchange students have worked a total of 15 h. That is around a 42% of the time.

In this exchange have participated 6 teachers, 4 from Portugal and 2 of the hosting institutions. We have asked them about the experience and the positive and negatives issues that they found. Their answers have been explored qualitatively. In order to do this, we grouped teachers' answers following a proximity criterion to the positive of the exchanges, the drawbacks found and other relevant issues. The results are combined and shown in a matrix (Table 5) as suggested by authors such as [18].

From the table it is possible to see that most of the upsides are referred to collaboration, interaction and knowledge exchange, which was very profitable both for visiting and hosting teachers and students. The main drawbacks were related to the fact that this was the first RoboSTEAM exchange, which requires to adapt some of the initially planned strategies, only half of the teachers described drawbacks. In addition, the teachers pointed out that cultural activities were very positive to break the ice between students and visits to know some of the hosting country ICT companies.

Fig. 3. Results of Exchange C3.

Table 3. Mini – challenge description for C3

Title	Use mobile robots to detect and avoid the cause(s) of wildfires and reduce the impact of global warming on this issue

Description

Can mobile robots prevent fire(s)? (acts of arson, lack of cleanliness, global warming – drought and severe heat- etc.)

Human activities such as lighting campfires, discarding lit cigarettes, acts of arson, bushfires etc. are mainly responsible for starting a fire. However, hotter weather makes forests drier and more prone to burn Rising temperatures, a key indicator of climate change, evaporate more moisture from the ground, drying out the soil and making vegetation more flammable. Think about how to employ mobile robots to reduce the impact of global warming on environment and avoid other causes of wildfires

Goal/s

• Study mobile robots
• Develop computational thinking
• Study possible ways to apply mobile robots to improve environment
• Develop soft skills
• Implement collaborative solution/strategy that involves students, parents, teachers and experts in this field
• Design and explore the scenarios where mobile robots can be applied
• Develop creativity

Evaluation

• Time employed to solve the challenge (stds will fill in a grid)
• Degree of success producing a solution (stds will fill in a self and hetero evaluation report)
• Number of people involved in the challenge (information sheet including age, role/status and Education level)
• Perception about STEAM (stds will be asked to talk about their experience throughout the whole process of this challenge – they can make a video, around two minutes)
• Assessment of STEM skills and CT skills before and after the challenge (online questionnaires)

Table 4. C3. Nano – challenge sample

Title	Follow lines with a mobile robot to patrol the forest
Specific Issue to deal with	
Use or built a robot that was able to follow a line	
Description	
Human activities in the countryside namely forests have a great impact on the environment A possible solution to address this issue can be the use of mobile robots We want to find out how to use a robot to follow a line in order to patrol the forest	
Goal/s	
• Study navigation issues in mobile robots • Study possible ways to make a mobile robot follow a line • Explore scenarios where mobile robots can be applied • Implement collaborative solution/strategy that involves students, parents, teachers and experts in this field • Develop soft skills • Develop CT skills and Enhance creativity	
Kits to use	
mBot, a STEAM educational robot for beginners	
Evaluation	
Checking if the mobile robots are following properly the line and number of possible errors. Assessing students' collaboration and the acquisition of knowledge about mobile robots	

C3 followed the same schema defined in C2. Students worked 7,5 h per day (for a total of 35 h during the exchange), from them 16,5 were applied to address the challenges, which means a 47% of the total working time. As in C2 rest of the time was divided in visits and cultural activities. In this case 5 teachers were involved, 3 from the hosting institution and 2 from IER. Table 6 shows their opinions by the topics also explored in C2.

In this case the upsides were similar to C2, teachers pointed out issues such as collaboration and knowledge exchange. They are especially happy with the fact that their students, with a background of arts, could complete challenges that are more related to use of robots and programming, thanks to the collaboration with the visiting students. Regarding drawbacks in this case the problem is that the school has not previous experience with Erasmus+ projects so the exchange required new dynamics that are not always easy to implement. In addition, during the exchange students from the hosting institution had exams so their participation in solving the nano-challenges was not easy. Some teachers point out that the experience carried out C2 helped them to develop this exchange.

Table 5. Matrix with teachers' opinions about C2 upsides, drawbacks and other issues.

	Positive issues	Drawbacks	Other
T1	Very good collaboration and interaction. Really enriching experience	Improve resources and planning	Visits were very interesting
T2	Quality of results and Collaboration	Clarify the process	Visits
T3	The was very enriching and profitable	–	Cultural activities
T4	Knowledge Exchange and the quality of products	–	–
T5	Getting to know the methodology and educational context of a foreign school. Materials and human resources	Language barriers in some cases	–
T6	Know a different educational system and the performance of my students there	–	–

Table 6. Matrix with teachers' opinions about C3 upsides, drawbacks and other issues.

	Positive issues	Drawbacks	Other
T1	Very interesting challenges and very good collaboration	–	Excellent facilities for the challenges and good visits
T2	Knowledge Exchange, lessons learned	It is necessary to motivate students to work together	Previous work done to complete the challenges
T3	The chance to share knowledge and educational ideas was enriching	Different dynamic	–
T4	Students and teachers can learn from the exchange experience and broaden their mindset	Logistic constraints	–
T5	The intercultural exchange among students and teachers	Few students for artwork	–

5 Conclusions

The present work has described a key element in RoboSTEAM project, the students and teachers exchange. These activities facilitate sharing knowledge with peers from other countries or even from different socioeconomical contexts. This means with people that have different educational systems, customs, languages, etc. Why is this so relevant for RoboSTEAM? Because one the main aims of the project is the application of CBL in STEAM Education by using Robotics and Mechatronics, but it is not enough to test this in one country, we should check how it works and how to adapt it in different environments. That is why two different pilot phases are carried out, with the idea of checking it what is used in a context is also applicable in a different one. In order to do so it is necessary to build a common knowledge base to address challenges and the exchanges make this possible.

RoboSTEAM exchanges plan has included institutions with similar and different sociocultural context and with similar and different educational background, so a wide choice of possibilities is being considered.

From the exchanges that have already taken place the perception both of students and teachers were really positive and has help addressing the challenges from a different perspective. This can be seen as a success but it is necessary to evaluate it once all the exchanges and pilots phases have finished.

In order to conclude the work it is important to say that exchanges are really helpful to know how other students live and work, so it is a desirable activity even beyond the Erasmus+ initiatives.

Acknowledgement.   This paper is supported by ROBOSTEAM Erasmus+ KA201 Project with reference 2018-1-ES01-KA201-050939.

References

1. Ramírez-Montoya, M.S. (ed.): Handbook of Research on Driving STEM Learning With Educational Technologies. IGI Global, Hershey (2017)
2. García-Peñalvo, F.J.: A brief introduction to TACCLE 3 – coding European project. In: García-Peñalvo, F.J., Mendes, J.A. (eds.) 2016 International Symposium on Computers in Education (SIIE 2016). IEEE, USA (2016)
3. TACCLE 3: Coding Erasmus+ Project website https://goo.gl/f4QZUA. Accessed 23 Feb 2020
4. García-Peñalvo, F.J.: Computational thinking and programming education principles. In: García-Peñalvo, F.J. (ed.) TEEM 2018 Proceedings of the Sixth International Conference on Technological Ecosystems for Enhancing Multiculturality, Salamanca, Spain, 24–26 October 2018, pp. 14–17. ACM, New York (2018)
5. García-Peñalvo, F.J., Mendes, J.A.: Exploring the computational thinking effects in pre-university education. Comput. Hum. Behav. **80**, 407–411 (2018)
6. Barrows, H.S., Tamblyn, R.M.: Problem-Based Learning: An Approach to Medical Education. Springer, Heidelberg (1980)
7. Kilpatrick, W.H.: The Project Method. Teachers College. Columbia University, New York, USA (1918)
8. Apple-Inc: Challenge Based Learning - Take action and make a difference, US (2009). http://ali.apple.com/cbl/global/files/CBL_Paper.pdf
9. RoboSTEAM Consortium: RoboSTEAM Project Management Handbook (2019). https://doi.org/10.5281/zenodo.3338671
10. European-Comission: RoboSTEAM Project Description (2019). https://ec.europa.eu/programmes/erasmus-plus/projects/eplus-project-details/#project/2018-1-ES01-KA201-050939
11. Johnson, L., Adams, S.: Challenge Based Learning: The Report from the Implementation Project. The New Media Consortium, Austin (2011)
12. Conde, M.Á., et al.: RoboSTEAM - definition of a challenge based learning approach for integrating STEAM and develop computational thinking. In: Seventh International Conference on Technological Ecosystems for Enhancing Multiculturality (TEEM 2019). ACM, León, Spain (2018)

13. Nichols, M., Cator, K., Torres, M.: Challenge Based Learning Guide. Digital Promise, Redwood City (2016)
14. Green, J.L., Camilli, G., Elmore, P.B.: Handbook of Complementary Methods in Education Research. American Educational Research Association by Lawrence Erlbaum Associates Inc, Mahwah (2006)
15. Herro, D., Quigley, C., Andrews, J., Delacruz, G.: Co-Measure: developing an assessment for student collaboration in STEAM activities. Int. J. STEM Educ. **4**, 26 (2017)
16. Elegoo UNO Project Super Starter Kit with Tutorial for Arduino. https://www.elegoo.com/product/elegoo-uno-project-super-starter-kit/. Accessed 21 Feb 2020
17. mBot - Entry-level educational robot kit. https://www.makeblock.com/mbot. Accessed 21 Feb 2020
18. Miles, M.B., Huberman, A.M.: Qualitative Data Analysis: An Expanded Sourcebook. Sage Publications, Thousand Oaks (1994)

Development of a Flipped Classroom Approach to Teaching Lung Pathology: The Evaluation of a Formative On-Line Quiz Primer to Encourage Active Learning

Mark Dixon[1](✉) and Katherine Syred[2](✉)

[1] School of Engineering, Computing and Mathematics, University of Plymouth, Drake Circus, Plymouth PL4 8AA, UK
mark.dixon@plymouth.ac.uk
[2] Pathology Department, Derriford Hospital, Plymouth PL6 8DH, UK

Abstract. Within the UK there are concerns around the implications of reduced staffing levels within medicine for meeting clinical demand and teaching commitments. There are also concerns regarding limited pathology content in undergraduate medical courses, reductions in postgraduate pathology enrolments, and the proportion of current staff approaching retirement age. As a result, there is interest in approaches, such as the flipped classroom, to reduce medical teaching resource requirements and improve effectiveness. This paper describes the rationale, development, and evaluation of a formative online quiz primer for tutorial sessions delivered to third year undergraduate medical students to improve student engagement, understanding and staff satisfaction. A student perception questionnaire was administered to attendees of two teaching sessions, with thirty one students responding. Student behaviour during the teaching session was influenced (rather than their immediate pre-exam behaviour). Students reported using a range of devices to access the quiz, good usability, general improvements in understanding and engagement during the teaching sessions, which was also supported by participant observation. This required a significant investment of preparation time, which would be sustainable if the quiz questions could be used for several years and shared across multiple sites. Further work is needed to compare student perceptions with actual measured understanding and to look at the process of creating additional resources.

Keywords: Pathology education · Flipped classroom · Interface design · User requirements

1 Introduction

1.1 Pathology Education: UK Staff Shortage

A workforce census by the Royal College of Pathologists has indicated that only around 3% (3 out of 103) of UK histopathology departments have enough staff to meet clinical demand [1]. This is echoed across other medical and wider healthcare

© Springer Nature Switzerland AG 2020
P. Zaphiris and A. Ioannou (Eds.): HCII 2020, LNCS 12205, pp. 456–465, 2020.
https://doi.org/10.1007/978-3-030-50513-4_34

disciplines. These staffing difficulties have been identified as an issue for pathology teaching, with a lack of specific pathology content in undergraduate medical courses leading to a reduction in postgraduate pathology training enrolments [2]. Also, reduced staffing leaves fewer resources to deliver pathology teaching. The situation seems unlikely to improve as a significant number of current staff are approaching retirement age (55 years or over) and workloads are likely to increase (due to increased cancer diagnosis demand and cases becoming more complex). Staff shortages are not a recent phenomenon [3] and it is not surprising that work has been done to consider moving away from resource heavy teaching [4].

Medical schools vary in how teaching is organised, with some having a small number of people employed with a large teaching workload and others engaging a large number of staff (primarily working clinically for the UK National Health Service) to deliver a small number of teaching hours per year. Transient users may find IT learning systems difficult to access and use effectively within the limited hours available.

1.2 Flipped Classroom Within Medical Education

The flipped classroom (FC) approach seeks to move information dissemination activities (often focusing on fundamental concepts) out of teaching sessions, to be replaced with more cognitive activities that use active learning to focus more in-depth on applying knowledge and problem solving (often involving case-studies). This moves lecture material outside teaching sessions and bring activities often regarded as 'homework' into the class. Material moved to before teaching sessions is often online and may include more passive learning activities (such as video collections, and digital slideshows) and more active learning events (such as discussions between students and between teachers and students).

In 1993, Alison King advocated focusing on the construction of meaning (a constructivist view of learning), rather than the transmission of information (a transmittal model of teaching-learning process) [5]. At the core of this was that students should be active (rather than passive) in their learning activities, which is key to the FC approach.

The effectiveness of the FC approach may be evaluated by the measurement of both student satisfaction and student understanding [6]. Chen et al. has conducted a review of the effectiveness of the FC approach in medical education [7]. This showed positive student perceptions of FC, but less evidence of improvements to actual knowledge and skill levels.

Variations in student perceptions have been reported: some students naturally gain quick benefits from FC, while others experience difficulty. At times tutors and students view differ [8]. Common concerns raised by students include: having to teach themselves, a lack of appropriate guidance, and an increased student workload [9]. This may be related to differences in learning styles, previous educational experiences and levels of maturity. There have been some concerns regarding the digital divide and the amount of time younger people are spending working with screens (including computers, phones, tablets, and television).

Bijol et al. used a formative online quiz for teaching renal pathology [10]. Although this reported an improvement in summative exam results, the usage data showed that use of the quiz was highest the day before the final summative exam (by a factor of 10) suggesting that the quiz was used as preparation for the exam rather than improving the learning process across the course delivery.

1.3   Evaluation of an Online Quiz Primer

This paper describes the rationale, development, and evaluation of an online quiz primer for tutorial sessions delivered to third year undergraduate medical students. The intention was to improve student engagement and staff satisfaction during the teaching sessions by providing:

- some form of primer task for students to undertake in the week before the session, and
- altering the delivery for the session itself (reducing the amount of formally delivered factual material and focusing more on interactive discussions of a small number of case studies - talking in pairs about a real case, related to diagnosis and treatment - so very similar in structure to the quiz, but the cases in the sessions were more detailed and concrete than the quiz cases)

The online quiz primer was chosen as it is more interactive (including an element of formative feedback) and problem based. It was therefore more aligned with active learning (the underlying intention of the FC) than the use of video recordings of lectures (which is inherently passive). The intention was also to align the quiz directly to the session rather than the summative assessment (although both the quiz and session were aligned to the assessment to make them relevant for the students and encourage engagement).

There was a focus on transient users undertaking a small number of hours teaching per year. This raises issues of limited preparation time and difficulty becoming familiar with large learning systems (such as Moodle). These staff require a simple system and a simple user interface for content creation. As staff time is limited, the intention was to embed aspects of staff knowledge into software that could be used by students prior to teaching sessions as a primer, accessible outside the teaching session.

2   Method

Students were prompted to use the formative online quiz over the week prior to the session - they could do it as many times as they liked from any location. No other form of preparatory activity was required. The teaching session was an hour long, conducted in a classroom environment with projection facilities. The perception questionnaire was administered at the end of the teaching session (consisting of both quantitative and qualitative elements).

Within the medical school each year's cohort are divided into three groups and the session is delivered once per group - three times over the year (in October, January, and April). Hence, at the time of writing two out of the three sessions have been conducted.

2.1 Software

A set of 31 multiple choice questions were developed for the quiz, to align with the format and level of the Applied Medical Knowledge (AMK) test used within the medical school for summative assessment (where students are required to select one correct answer from five options). The AMK test is intended to present clinical scenarios requiring the application of medical knowledge at the level of a newly qualified doctor. It is applied across all years with consistent difficulty, where student performance is expected to improve as they progress from year to year. This is unusual compared to the rest of the Higher Education sector, where different assessments are created for each year of study, progressively becoming more challenging.

The intention was to explicitly link the teaching to the assessment with the hope of improving student engagement (based on the principles of constructive alignment). A single clinician led the question development, eliciting opinions from colleagues to cover a mixture of anatomy, epidemiology, and diagnostic content (similar to the AMK). The quiz software was developed using ASP.Net C# and an SQL Server database.

A link was sent to students approximately one week prior to the session, the session was delivered with a focus on student active learning (presenting detailed case-studies, with multiple questions, where students were asked to discuss their ideas within pairs or threes). The perception survey was returned from students who wished to participate at the end of the session.

The quiz begins with an initial screen that gives an overview. A total of ten questions are asked (randomly selected from the 31 questions in the question bank). After each question is posed, the student selects a response and automatic feedback is given (indicating whether their choice was correct or not, and if not what the correct answer was). Figure 1 shows a screenshot of the lung pathology quiz, where a student has selected the correct answer. Once all ten questions have been answered a summary page is shown indicating how many correct answers (out of ten) were given by the user, and encouraging them to undertake the quiz again.

2.2 Student Perception Questionnaire

A student perception questionnaire consisting of nine questions (shown in Table 1) was given to all attendees of the first and second (of three) teaching sessions (held at the end of September 2019 and mid-January 2020). Questions 3, 4, and 5 used a Likert scale with five categories. Questions 2, 6, 7, and 8 asked for a yes/no response with a free-text follow-up question. Questions 1 and 9 were free text.

The questionnaire was intended to elicit information regarding the correct functioning of the quiz, changes in student understanding, engagement and the impact of its use.

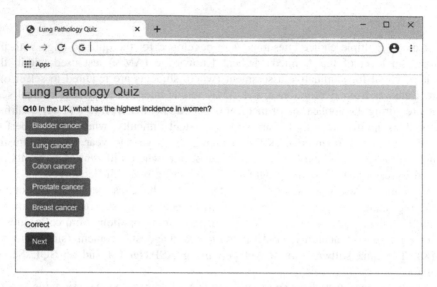

Fig. 1. Screenshot of Lung Pathology Quiz, where the user has just selected a response and the computer has automatically given feedback (in this case the answer selected was correct).

Table 1. Questionnaire questions. * Small Cell Carcinoma, Squamous Cell Carcinoma, Mesothelioma, Adenocarcinoma, Lung Cancer

Question	Text
1	What device (phone/computer) did you use to view the quiz website?
2	Did the quiz website work properly on your device?
3	How easy to use (user-friendly) was the quiz website?
4	Before using the quiz, how would you describe your understanding of *
5	After using the quiz, how would you describe your understanding of *
6	Did you look anything up (online or in books) as a result of using the quiz?
7	Did using the quiz help your understanding?
8	Did using the quiz help prepare you for the tutorial?
9	Any other comments or suggestions

2.3 Participant Observation

A short semi-structured debrief interview was conducted with the pathologist who ran the teaching session regarding their perceptions of the process, student engagement and understanding.

3   Results

3.1   Student Perception Questionnaire

Ninety six students are enrolled across the three sessions, so each session should have approximately 32 attendees. Twelve students completed the questionnaire during the first session (about one third of the attendees for that session) and nineteen students completed the questionnaire during the second session (about two thirds of the attendees for that session). This gave a total of thirty one responses.

The first question identified the range of devices used by students to access the quiz (shown in Table 2). Mobile phones were the most popular device (used by thirteen out of thirty one students). One student responded with 'PowerPoint presentation' to this question, which is difficult to interpret. The total comes to thirty two as one student indicated that they used both a phone and a iPad.

Table 2.   Q1: range of devices used to access the quiz.

	Count
Phone	13
Computer	7
iPad	7
Laptop	3
PowerPoint presentation	1
Total	32

The next two questions (Q2, and Q3) considered the performance of the quiz system. The intention here was to detect any operational issues that may have a negative effect on student engagement and/or understanding and therefore act as confounding factors.

Table 3 shows the response count for the quiz functioning correctly. Almost all (29) students indicated that the system functioned correctly. Free-text comments associated with this response included 'all absolutely fine, no issues' and 'it worked completely fine and the instructions were clear'. Two students indicted that the quiz functioned partly, with associated comments mentioning two minor issues. One student suggested using a larger font and another indicated that the same question was posed twice, which would happen if the quiz was run several times, but should not happen within the same group of ten questions. Unfortunately, there was no indication which of these was the case.

Table 4 shows the ratings given by students for the usability of the quiz, which were generally very positive (with twenty nine students rating the system good or very good).

The next two questions (Q4 and Q5) considered student understanding before and after using the quiz. A Likert scale was used where student understanding was categorised as very poor, poor, ok, good, very good and coded from 1 to 5 respectively. Table 5 shows the mean student perception scores and the difference pre and post quiz

Table 3. Q2: indication of correct functioning of the quiz.

	Count
Worked properly	29
Partly worked	2
Did not work properly	0
Total	31

Table 4. Q3: usability of the quiz.

	Count
Very good	18
Good	11
Ok	2
Poor	0
Very poor	0
Total	31

(a positive number indicates an improvement, while a negative number would indicate a reduction in understanding). All of the differences were positive, showing a slight improvement of approximately one category in understanding being reported across all topics, with a small variation between topics. There was no indication of any negative effects in understanding (i.e. students being confused by the quiz).

Table 5. Mean student perception scores, using categories from 1 (very poor) to 5 (very good) of self-understanding pre and post quiz.

	Before (Q4)	After (Q5)	Difference
Small Cell Carcinoma	1.94	2.81	0.87
Squamous Cell Carcinoma	1.90	2.81	0.90
Mesothelioma	2.03	3.10	1.06
Adenocarcinoma	1.71	2.77	1.06
Lung Cancer	2.19	2.94	0.74
Overall Average	1.95	2.88	0.93

The next three questions (Q6, Q7, and Q8) considered the impact of using the quiz (shown in Table 6). The total for these questions is thirty as one student did not respond to questions 6 to 9. Twenty (out of thirty) students indicated that the quiz prompted them to look up material (either online or on paper copies). Twenty one students indicated that their understanding had improved as a result of using the quiz. Eighteen students indicated that the quiz prepared them for the subsequent teaching session. These were not the same students for each question.

Table 6. Numbers of students looking up material and indicating that the quiz helped them understand and prepare for the tutorial.

	Yes	Partly	No	Total
Q6: Looked up material	20	0	10	30
Q7: Quiz helped understanding	21	2	7	30
Q8: Quiz helped prepare for tutorial	18	1	11	30

The final question (Q9) asked for any other comments or suggestions. Emergent themes were identified from the free-text responses given by eleven students (shown in Table 7). Twenty students left this blank or wrote 'n/a'. The most recurrent themes were an indication that the quiz was useful (three responses) and a request for more detailed explanations of correct and incorrect answers (three responses).

Table 7. Emergent themes identified from free-text responses to Q9 asking for comments and suggestions.

	Count
Useful/helpful concept	3
Request for quiz explanations	3
Request for additional questions/scenarios	2
Request for additional notes/background material	2
Thank you	2
Request for basic physiology questions	1
Too many abbreviations	1
I should have spent more time on the quiz	1

3.2 Participant Observation

The tutor referred to the quiz during the teaching session. They indicated that it 'helped me see the relevance of the content in terms of treatment and diagnosis'. In previous years the material was a little detached from treatment and diagnosis. This year it was more case based. The tutor checked the question content with colleagues as part of the development process, which 'made questions more up-to-date' than in previous years.

They indicated that 'there were certainly a proportion of the students who were asking more questions and were more engaged'. In previous years, 'I was talking for much of the hour with very little student engagement' - the students were very reluctant to both ask and answer questions. They indicated that 'this year, I felt much more engaged as I wasn't talking as much. It was refreshing that some of them had actually looked up relatively new terms [such as EBUS and SABRE] and understood them. It felt better in terms of it being more peer-to-peer rather than me being the sage'. The tutor said that 'it changed the dynamic - I wasn't having to explain every little test, it raised the bar of the group for that session a lot and made it more interactive'.

4   Conclusions

4.1   Student Understanding and Engagement

There was a dual aim of improving both student engagement in sessions and their understanding. The results suggest that the approach taken was successful in both respects. Part of the benefit was that students could see the link between the learning activities they were undertaking (the online quiz and the teaching session) and their summative exam. However, the link between the quiz and the exam was not too direct. It influenced their behaviour during the teaching session rather than their immediate pre-exam behaviour. There may be a benefit in providing on-line quiz material for a targeted time to directly support teaching sessions and thereby enhance student engagement with the generic learning process rather than over longer periods (where it is likely to be used for last-minute examination preparation). This is similar to the findings of Bikol et al. [10].

Given the positive feedback regarding the functioning and usability of the quiz it is unlikely that this would have had a limiting influence on the student engagement and learning. The data excludes students who did not attend the session and students who declined to respond to the questionnaire. In both cases, it seems likely that a potentially high number of these students did not attempt the quiz, so their views are not represented. On this basis, the engagement rate seems to be about 50%.

4.2   Preparation Time and Sustainability

It is remarkable, how much of an impact a relatively small change in delivery can make to the student experience. However, this required a significant investment of time (estimated as a solid day and a half's work in creating the quiz questions). This investment would be sustainable assuming it could be re-used over several years and across multiple hospital sites with a smaller amount of effort for additions and modifications. This could have an added benefit of providing consistency in delivery and content across multiple sites.

4.3   Further Work

Another session is scheduled to take place in April 2020, which will be included in further work. The question set will be expanded for next year's sessions.

There is also an intention to include questions regarding images (specifically diagrams and macroscopic digital images of specimens) and free-text explanations as part of the feedback (indicating why a response was correct or incorrect - as suggested by some of the student feedback).

Having established that the quiz has been well received by students, there are two additional activities that are planned. Firstly, to measure any actual improvement in student understanding (as opposed to that perceived by students, and to compare the two). Secondly, to look at the process of creating new questions (resource requirements in terms of time and the development of a question editing system with a simple user interface that seeks to minimise the time taken to generate and modify questions, by transient users).

There is also the intention to investigate the development of a mobile app for the students to use. This was delayed for the current study as the web-based delivery targeted multiple technology platforms (such as phone, computer, and tablet) without requiring the development of separate systems.

References

1. Meeting pathology demand: histopathology workforce census. Royal College of Pathologists (2018)
2. Al Nemer, A.: Undergraduate medical students' perception of pathology. Ann. Diagn. Pathol. **44**, 151422 (2020)
3. Mattick, K., Marshall, R., Bligh, J.: Tissue pathology in undergraduate medical education: atrophy or evolution? J. Pathol. **203**, 871–876 (2004)
4. Syred, K., et al.: Pathological pots: a valuable physical and virtual resource. J. Anat. **224**, 21–22 (2014)
5. King, A.: From sage on the stage to guide on the side. Coll. Teach. **41**(1), 30–35 (1993)
6. Betihavas, V., Bridgman, H., Kornhaber, R., Cross, M.: The evidence for 'flipping out': a systematic review of the flipped classroom in nursing education. Nurse Educ. Today **38**, 15–21 (2016)
7. Chen, F., Lui, A., Martinelli, S.: A systematic review of the effectiveness of flipped classrooms in medical education. Med. Educ. **51**(6), 585–597 (2017)
8. Awidi, I., Paynter, M.: The impact of a flipped classroom approach on student learning experience. Comput. Educ. **128**, 269–283 (2019)
9. Rotellar, C., Cain, G.: Research, perspectives, and recommendations on implementing the flipped classroom. Am. J. Pharm. Educ. **80**(2), 34 (2016)
10. Bijol, V., Byrne-Dugan, C., Hoenig, M.: Medical student web-based formative assessment tool for renal pathology. Med. Educ. Online **20**(1), 26765 (2015)

Facilitating Access to the Role Models
of Women in STEM: W-STEM Mobile App

Alicia García-Holgado[(✉)] ⓘ, Sonia Verdugo-Castro ⓘ,
Mª Cruz Sánchez-Gómez ⓘ, and Francisco J. García-Peñalvo ⓘ

GRIAL Research Group, University of Salamanca, Salamanca, Spain
{aliciagh, soniavercas, mcsago, fgarcia}@usal.es

Abstract. W-STEM is a research project funded by the European Union through the Erasmus+ program in order to develop concrete actions to modernise the government, management and operation of higher education institutions in Latin America to improve women's access to STEM programs. Among the main objectives of the project, there is the development of a mobile app to be used in attraction campaigns conducted by the Latin American higher education institutions involved in the project. Specifically, the app aims to facilitate access to the role models of women in areas related to science, technology, engineering and mathematics. The main content inside the app will be a set of video interviews with women from different ages, cultural backgrounds, profiles, sharing their experiences about their careers, occupation and future plans. This work aims to describe the prototype of the mobile app and the exploratory study conducted with a group of students from secondary education to know their perceptions and opinions about the proposed app and the video interviews.

Keywords: Gender gap · Women visibility · STEM · Mobile app · Acceptance · User perception · Secondary school · Students

1 Introduction

Women are one of the least represented groups in science, technology, engineering and mathematics (STEM) areas. The underrepresentation of women in these areas, for reasons unrelated to their talent or preferences, represents significant economic losses for modern societies [1]. In general, the greater participation of women is related to economic growth, the promotion of human development, the strengthening of the competitiveness of the region and the increment of productivity [2]. According to the European Commission's strategy [3], increasing women's participation in the technology sector will boost the economy and enable their full participation in society. In particular, according to the report "Women in the Digital Age", the incorporation of more women into digital jobs would benefit Europe's Gross Domestic Product (GDP) by up to 16 billion euros per year [4].

Improving the recruitment, retention and training of the next generation of STEM professionals remains an area of political priority and concern [5]. There are initiatives across the world promoted by governments, companies, associations, working on reducing the gender gap in STEM [6]. For example, international associations such as

© Springer Nature Switzerland AG 2020
P. Zaphiris and A. Ioannou (Eds.): HCII 2020, LNCS 12205, pp. 466–476, 2020.
https://doi.org/10.1007/978-3-030-50513-4_35

ACM or IEEE have projects to improve the representation of women in the scientific and technological field, ACM-W (https://women.acm.org) and IEEE Women in Engineering (https://goo.gl/p9xgyH).

The European Advisory Committee on Equal Opportunities for Women and Men [7] identifies the promotion of non-stereotypical education, training and career choices as one of the actions to tackle gender segregation labour-market. Among the suggested recommendations, they propose to ensure that educational curricula at all levels eliminate gender stereotypes, as well as the need to perform extensive reviews of current educational material with a view to gender equality. Also, the OECD emphasises in "reviewing and where necessary, adapting school and early childhood education curricula, teaching and school practices to eliminate gender discrimination and stereotyping" [8]. Equity in the development of STEM competencies must look beyond the educational offer or the promotion of professions focused on science and technology, taking into account the need to empower young women before choosing a university career [9].

Several studies analyse gender bias and stereotypes in educational resources [10]. Kerkhoven et al. [11] analysed online science education resources provided through the Scientix and OERcommons websites; they found the ratio of women depicted with a science profession was 25%. Parkin and Mackenzie [12] presents a tool to measure the gender bias in textbooks; the tool is tested in science textbooks used in the secondary education in the UK concluding that they have a strong bias towards males. López Navajas [13] analyses the presence of women in the textbooks used in the Spanish secondary education; she found that only 12.7% of all the characters mentioned in the textbooks are women, and these only appear in the textbooks on 7.6% of the cases.

According to Smith [5] encouraging young girls to imagine employment in STEM areas is an important step towards improving their representation. However, women in STEM are made invisible by society not only in educational material but also in the media [14]. In the case of Latin America, the low representation of women in scientific and technological areas does not allow for the production of reference models for their incursion into these areas [9].

The revision and modification of the school textbooks in the different countries, suppose a huge investment of the publishers and also from families and schools who have to replace the existing textbooks. Although this process must be implemented to eliminate gender discrimination and stereotyping, it requires time and investment. Moreover, the school textbooks and the educational system depends on the national governments, so each country manages different times to achieve this type of objectives as a measure to avoid the gender gap in STEM. For this reason, other measures have to be implemented to reduce gender bias and stereotyping at schools and encourage young girls to select STEM careers.

The W-STEM project funded by the European Union through the Erasmus+ program arises in order to develop concrete actions to modernise the government, management and operation of higher education institutions in Latin America to improve women's access to STEM programs [15, 16]. Among their goals is the promotion of STEM studies vocation and choice in girls and young women in secondary schools. The ten Latin American higher education institutions involved in the project will define a gender equality action plan focused on three processes: attraction, access and guidance/retention. The actions associated with secondary schools are related to the attraction processes. The ten Latin American higher education institutions (Table 1) will define and implement attraction campaigns with the support of two software tools. First, the profiling tool based on [17] to identify prospective students, successful graduates and current students, with key aptitudes correlated to STEM disciplines/ professions. On the other hand, a mobile app to share women in STEM stories as a way to facilitate reference models to young girls.

Table 1. W-STEM project details.

Heading level	Example
Title	Building the future of Latin America: engaging women into STEM
Acronym	W-STEM
Funding entity	European Union
Call	ERASMUS+ Capacity-building in Higher Education Call for proposals EAC/A05/2017
Reference	598923-EPP-1-2018-1-EN-EPPKA2-CBHE-JP
Coordinator	P1. University of Salamanca - USAL (Spain)
Partners	P2. Universidad del Norte - UNINORTE (Colombia)
	P3. Oulu University - OULU (Finland)
	P4. Politecnico di Torino - POLITO (Italy)
	P5. Technological University Dublin - TUD (Ireland)
	P6. Nothern Regional College - NRC (United Kingdom)
	P7. Tecnológico de Monterrey - ITESM (Mexico)
	P8. University of Guadalajara - UG (Mexico)
	P9. Federico Santa María Technical University - UTSM (Chile)
	P10. Pontifical Catholic University of Valparaíso - PUCV (Chile)
	P11. Technological University of Bolívar - UTB (Colombia)
	P12. Costa Rica Institute of Technology - ITCR (Costa Rica)
	P13. University of Costa Rica - UCR (Costa Rica)
	P14. Private Technical University of Loja - UTPL (Ecuador)
	P15. Technical University of the North - UTN (Ecuador)
Budget	862.268 €
Dates	3 years. 01/15/2019–01/14/2022
Web	https://wstemproject.eu

This work describes the prototype of the mobile app and the exploratory study conducted with a group of students from secondary education to know their perceptions and opinions about the prototype and the contents that will be shared through the app in the attraction campaigns.

The work is set out as follow. The second section describes other mobile apps to give visibility to women in STEM. The third section describes the prototype of the W-STEM mobile app. The fourth and fifth sections describe the students' perception and opinions of the prototype. The last section concludes the work with its more significant contributions.

2 Related Mobile Apps

A search in Apple Store and Play Store was conducted to analyse other mobile apps focused on women in STEM. There are four apps available for iOS and Android related to women in STEM:

- "Women in STEM and Medicine": a free mobile app available for iOS and Android with 100 women who contribute to STEM and medicine in the United States forward. The app is available only in English.
- "Women Who Changed the World": a non-free mobile app available for iOS and Android that introduces several historical women - artists, scientist, civil rights activists, etc. - through illustrations. The app is available in different languages, including Spanish and English.
- "Femmes de Science": free mobile app available for iOS and Android with information about the women professors at the École polytechnique fédérale de Lausanne (Switzerland). Each woman professor share information about her scientific field through a short film.
- "Girls can do I.T.": free mobile app available for iOS to learn more about career opportunities in computer science and information technology. Among the information provided, there are 50 profiles of women in tech.

Although mobile apps are continually appearing, no similar applications to the one proposed in the W-STEM project were found when this search was conducted (01/2020).

3 Prototype of the W-STEM App

The purpose of the W-STEM mobile app is to give visibility to women in STEM careers, not only women of a very high level in STEM, but also young women with different profiles – last year students, PhD students, young researchers, developers, etc. The app will be used as a tool in schools and high schools all over Latin America to show young women in STEM, since the books and materials used in the classroom only show examples of men. It is intended to give young people ideas about what it means or why to study STEM careers.

The app handles two types of content: articles and profiles of women in STEM. The articles are used to share news, events or information related to women in science, technology, engineering or mathematics. They consist of a title and a body with text, links and at least one pictures (Fig. 1). Although articles are not the main objective of the W-STEM mobile app, it provides updated information that can be used to engage young girls.

Fig. 1. Screenshots in Spanish of the prototype: article list, article example and favourites.

Regarding the profiles of women in STEM (Fig. 2), each profile is composed of a 2–3 min interview and a set of metadata: the country, the field of work/study, a brief description and a set of links to social profiles. The team from the Tecnologico de Monterrey (Mexico) has defined a protocol to collect, edit and translate the interviews. Each institution involved in the project have to collect 25 women's profiles, so a total of 375 videos will be available through the mobile app. Moreover, video interviews to world-renowned scientists are conducted in the L'Oreal UNESCO awards ceremonies during the three years of the project with the support of the Columbus Association and UNESCO.

The application is organized into four main screens. The start screen shows featured articles and women's profiles (Fig. 2). A menu in the top of the screen allows access to the other screens of the app: a list of articles, a list of women's profiles and the contents marked as favourites.

The W-STEM mobile app should be available for Android (to be used in devices with different prices) and iOS. The development of native mobile apps supposes a double effort and increases the maintenance cost. For this reason, the prototype was developed using Flutter [18], a Google software development kit (SDK) that allows native development for iOS and Android, based on a unique code.

The main problem of the prototype is the storage and streaming video. Although videos long 2–3 min, they are recorded in high quality with an average of 100–200 MB after the editing process. Videos can be available through a cloud storage service such as Amazon S3 or Firebase Storage, but this solution involves a store and

Fig. 2. Screenshots in Spanish of the prototype: start screen and women profile example.

streaming cost according to the files size and the number of users of the app. To reduce maintenance cost and allow the free availability of the final version of the app in the Play Store and Apple Store, the video storage and streaming is based on YouTube.

4   Exploratory Study

4.1   Participants

The exploratory study was conducted in the IES Venancio Blanco, a public high school in Salamanca (Spain). In particular, the questionnaire was shared among all students in the first and second year of Spanish Baccalaureate, the post-16 stage of education in Spain. The population was composed of a total of eight groups of students from two baccalaureate branches - science and technology, and humanities and social science.

4.2   Instrument

The questionnaire was developed ad-hoc to collect qualitative data about the perception and opinions of the students. The instrument was divided into three sections: context, contents of the app, and usability and usefulness of the app. The first section is a set of questions to contextualise the answers. This section has the following demographic questions:

1. Age (Age ranges).
2. Country.
3. The country where you were born.
4. The country where your parent or guardian was born.
5. The country where your mother or guardian was born.
6. Gender (male, female, not mentioned above, no answer).

Later, a set of questions to find out what the student uses his mobile phone for:

7. Do you have a smartphone? (Yes/No)
8. Select how many apps on your mobile have been downloaded (those that did not come in the mobile when you bought it)
9. Have you ever paid for a mobile app? (Yes/No)
10. If yes, what type of mobile app? (Games, social networks, photography, education, music, sport, etc.)

The last part of the contextualization section has a set of questions to analyse the need for information related to support their decisions after finishing high school:

11. Are you looking for information on the Internet about what you would like to study after high school? (Yes/No)
12. If yes, why on the Internet? What kind of information are you looking for?
13. If not, what are your reasons for not seeking information?
14. Do you know women who work in science, technology, engineering or mathematics? What is your opinion of them?

The next section is focused on getting feedback about the video interviews that will be available through the app. A demo video was recorded and edited. The person interviewed is a 25-year-old woman, a computer engineer who is studying for a doctorate at a Spanish university. The video is followed by two questions:

15. What do you like the most about the video?
16. What do you like least or not like about the video?

Finally, regarding the usability and usefulness of the app, a video showing the prototype and set of screenshots in Spanish are provided at the beginning of this section (Fig. 1, Fig. 2 and other two screenshots):

17. When you watch the start screen, can you identify at a glance what the most relevant content offered was? Can you describe it?
18. Can you see on the screens, how to navigate through the different screens? Is it easily distinguishable?
19. After a first look, is it clear to you what the purpose of the app is? What contents and functions does it offer? Can you list them?
20. Do you think the contents and tools that will be offered in this app are useful for you? Why?
21. What is your opinion about the design of the app? Design means the colours, how the profiles are shown, the menu, how you navigate from one content to another, etc.

22. What caught your attention the most about the usefulness of the app from a positive point of view?
23. What caught your attention the most about the usefulness of the app from a negative point of view?
24. What should we add in the app for you to use?
25. What should we remove from the app for you to use?

The definition of the instrument was conducted in three phases. First, the people involved in the definition of the app defined a draft of questions. Second, two experts in qualitative analysis review the questionnaire and provided feedback. The updated version of the instrument was shared with two teachers from secondary education who completed it to ensure that it was understood properly by the students.

4.3   Data Collection

The prototype is not available to be tested in mobile phones without supervision. Moreover, due to the legal issues to organize a focus group with students, the authors decided to use a qualitative approach based on a questionnaire. Besides, the questionnaire has made it possible to cover a larger population.

The instrument was implemented using a customized version of LimeSurvey, an Open Source online statistical survey web application. The instrument was applied in Spanish.

Regarding the data collection, the questionnaire was shared with the support of a teacher from the high school. He shared the link to the questionnaire with their students during his class sessions. The link was available one month. During that period, two reminders were shared by the teacher to request more answers.

4.4   Sample

The questionnaire was answered for 26 students, 9 are male (34.61%), 16 are female (61.54%), and 1 prefer not to answer (3.85%). Regarding the age, 3 students are 13–15 years, 22 are 16–18 years, and 1 is 19–21 years. There are two students who born outside Spain (Morocco and Venezuela) and other three students with a migrant background (one of the parents is foreign).

Regarding the use of mobile apps, only three students have paid-for apps in the categories of games, photography and education. All of them has some apps installed in their phones, although only four students have more than 31 apps.

5   Results

5.1   Contextualization

The main objective of the mobile app is to facilitate reference models in STEM to young girls, although it could be useful to provide information about different careers. In this sense, most of the participants (80.77%) look for information on the Internet about what study after high school. Mainly, they seek information to decide which career study, to know the job opportunities that a specific career may offer and to get more details about universities, prices requirements. Noteworthy the following answer:

"I look for experiences of people who have been in my situation to know what they did and to guide me a little. Honestly, it hasn't helped me at all" (woman, 16-18 years)

Regarding the information that they have about women who work in STEM, 38.46% does not know women in those areas. Those who do know women in STEM relate them with the following terms: smart, confident, commitment, perseverance, hardworking, self-reliant and professionals. In the words of some of the participants:

"I think they are there by their own efforts and merits, therefore they deserve it like anyone else" (woman, 16–18 years)

"no opinions, they're just doing their job like a normal person" (man, 16–18 years)

"It seems to me that as long as you like what you do, you are welcome, with motivation everything is done well, whether you are a woman or a man." (woman, 16–18 years)

"I think it does a great job" (man, 16–18 years)

5.2   Contents of the App

The mobile app will have video interviews of women in STEM with different characteristics and profiles. Although it is not possibly getting an evaluation of all the videos that will be available through the app, the example used shows the main elements of those videos.

In particular, 73.98% of the participants answer the questions related to the video interview. The positive comments are related to the way the interviewee express herself and her answer to the questions. The most frequently repeated terms are honesty and clearness. Other positive comments of the participants:

"That a woman studies things which people have usually classified as "men's studies" and that she is so empowered" (man, 16–18 years)

"That she has specialized in what she really liked as a child and had a vocation to start in something that everyone says is bad or gives a lot of vice." (woman, 16–18 years)

"That she's come to study something she's wanted since childhood" (woman, 16–18 years)

Regarding the question about things that least like about the video, only 5 students answered these questions (19.23%). The main comments are related to technical issues:

"The background, the stereo noise and that at the beginning of each question after the pause the camera moves." (man, 16–18 years)

"The place where the interview is given and not asked the questions on the video. Transitions make some of the interest in the video go away." (man, 16–18 years)

5.3   The Interface

Regarding the usability and usefulness of the app, only 6 students provided some information (26.92%). All users identify the purpose of the app, the contents available and the way to navigate through the different screens. There are 4 students that consider that the contents offered in the app are useful for them:

"They are useful for anyone, it just depends on that person's interest" (man, 16–18 years)

"If they can help your way of life" (woman, 16–18 years)

"I really don't think so, because it seems to me that it's more aimed at women who want to go into science careers and not like me who really knows what career I want and what branch it's from" (woman, 16–18 years)

All comments about the design are positive: original, well organized, good, right colours, minimal.

6 Conclusions

Governments and international organisms highlight the need for eliminating gender discrimination and stereotyping from the educational systems. The W-STEM project has among their goals the promotion of STEM studies vocation and choice in girls and young women in secondary schools. To achieve this objective, a mobile app will be developed to share women in STEM stories as a way to facilitate reference models to young girls.

The review conducted in the leading app stores shows that there are no other apps with the same objective, in which real women from different ages, cultural backgrounds and, in general, different profiles, share their own life and working experience in STEM.

On the other hand, the study conducted in a high school in Spain has provided useful information to improve the development of the contents available in the W-STEM mobile app. No criticism has been received of the questions asked; in fact, the comments highlight the content of the interview itself as something to be valued. The comments on elements to be improved have focused on the technical aspects, which allow to improve the protocol for recording and editing the interviews that each partner has to carry out.

However, the comments related to the usability and usefulness of the app are not enough. It is necessary to conduct other study with real users and a functional version of the mobile app to get more information about these aspects.

Acknowledgments. This research was partially supported by the Spanish Ministry of Science, Innovation and Universities under a FPU fellowship (FPU017/01252).

This work has been possible with the support of the Erasmus+ Programme of the European Union in its Key Action 2 "Capacity-building in Higher Education". Project W-STEM "Building the future of Latin America: engaging women into STEM" (Reference number 598923-EPP-1-2018-1-ES-EPPKA2-CBHE-JP). The content of this publication does not reflect the official opinion of the European Union. Responsibility for the information and views expressed in the publication lies entirely with the authors.

References

1. Gomez Soler, S.C., Abadía Alvarado, L.K., Bernal Nisperuza, G.L.: Women in STEM: does college boost their performance? High. Educ. 1–18 (2019). https://doi.org/10.1007/s10734-019-00441-0
2. UN Women: Facts and Figures: Economic Empowerment (2018)
3. European Commission: Women in Digital (2019)
4. Quirós, C.T., Morales, E.G., Pastor, R.R., Carmona, A.F., Ibáñez, M.S., Herrera, U.M.: Women in the Digital Age. Publications Office of the European Union, Brussels (2018)
5. Smith, E.: Women into science and engineering? Gendered participation in higher education STEM subjects. Br. Educ. Res. J. 37, 993–1014 (2011)
6. González, C.S., et al.: Gender and engineering: developing actions to encourage women in tech. In: 2018 IEEE Global Engineering Education Conference (EDUCON), 17–20 April 2018, Santa Cruz de Tenerife, Canary Islands, Spain, pp. 2082–2087. IEEE, USA (2018)
7. Advisory Committee on Equal Opportunities for Women and Men: Opinion on how to overcome occupational segregation. European Commission (2015)
8. OECD: 2013 OECD Recommendation of the Council on Gender Equality in Education, Employment and Entrepreneurship. OECD Publishing, Paris, France (2017)
9. Arredondo Trapero, F.G., Vázquez Parra, J.C., Velázquez Sánchez, L.M.: STEM y Brecha de Género en Latinoamérica. Revista de El Colegio de San Luis 9, 137–158 (2019)
10. Makarova, E., Aeschlimann, B., Herzog, W.: The gender gap in STEM fields: the impact of the gender stereotype of math and science on secondary students' career aspirations. Front. Educ. 4, 60 (2019)
11. Kerkhoven, A.H., Russo, P., Land-Zandstra, A.M., Saxena, A., Rodenburg, F.J.: Gender stereotypes in science education resources: a visual content analysis. PLoS One 11, e0165037 (2016)
12. Parkin, C., Mackenzie, S.: Is there gender bias in key stage 3 science textbooks?: Content analysis using the gender bias 14 (GB14) measurement tool. Adv. J. Prof. Pract. 1, 23–40 (2017)
13. López Navajas, A.: Las mujeres que nos faltan. Análisis de la ausencia de las mujeres en los manuales escolares. Universitat de València, Valencia, Spain (2015)
14. González, D., Mateu, A., Pons, E., Domínguez, M.: Women scientists as decor: the image of scientists in Spanish press pictures. Sci. Commun. 39, 535–547 (2017)
15. García-Holgado, A., Camacho Díaz, A., García-Peñalvo, F.J.: Engaging women into STEM in Latin America: W-STEM project. In: Conde-González, M.Á., Rodríguez Sedano, F.J., Fernández Llamas, C., García-Peñalvo, F.J. (eds.) Proceedings of the 7th International Conference on Technological Ecosystems for Enhancing Multiculturality (TEEM 2019), León, Spain, 16–18 October 2019, pp. 232–239. ACM, New York (2019)
16. García-Peñalvo, F.J.: Women and STEM disciplines in Latin America: The W-STEM European Project. J. Inf. Technol. Res. 12, v–viii (2019)
17. Ballatore, M.G., et al.: Increasing gender diversity in STEM: A tool for raising awareness of the engineering profession. In: Conde-González, M.Á., Rodríguez Sedano, F.J., Fernández Llamas, C., García-Peñalvo, F.J. (eds.) Proceedings of the 7th International Conference on Technological Ecosystems for Enhancing Multiculturality (TEEM 2019), León, Spain, 16–18 October 2019, pp. 216–222. ACM, New York (2019)
18. https://flutter.dev/

The Current State of m-Learning in Higher Education: A Survey Study of Mobile Technology Usage in the Classroom

Tiantian Jin[(⊠)] [iD], Kinta D. Montilus [iD], Alison Moore [iD],
and Quincy Conley [iD]

Pearson, Boston, MA, USA
jin.tiantian121@gmail.com, kmontilus@gmail.com,
alisonlindseymoore@gmail.com, quincyconley@gmail.com

Abstract. Existing research acknowledges the proliferation of mobile devices in society, but very few studies have sought to understand the demographics of the students who actually utilize mobile technology for their learning needs. Despite the pervasiveness and attention given to m-learning, there is still a lot of unknowns about how to integrate mobile technology into learning practices. Therefore, this paper describes an exploratory survey study that examined U.S. college and university students' responses to collect data about current mobile technology use. Novel to this study, gaining a clearer picture of mobile technology from students, educators and researchers can better apply m-learning to target desired learning behaviors and outcomes. Results suggest students have access to many mobile devices, however, they tend to be very selective in what device they choose to use for their learning. The findings indicate that their use of mobile technology is highly dependent upon the characteristics of the learning activity they are engaging in, and the subject matter. Students also reported mobile devices having a positive impact on their learning for quick, just-in-time learning activities.

Keywords: Higher education · m-Learning · Mobile technology · Survey study

1 Introduction

The use of mobile technology for educational purposes is referred to as mobile learning, or m-learning [1–3]. Mobile technology consists of devices such as smartphones, tablets, and even laptops [4]. More recent form factors for m-learning consist of wearable technology such as smartwatches and eyewear. Even before the arrival of smartphones in 2007, educators and researchers have worked diligently to investigate best practices for incorporating earlier iterations of mobile technology into their instructional practices with the hopes of enhancing the learning experience for students. With the premise of access to information "anytime, anywhere" [5, 6], the study of mobile devices as a learning tool has shown to increase students' perceptions of engagement, enjoyment, and collaboration [2, 7, 8].

© Springer Nature Switzerland AG 2020
P. Zaphiris and A. Ioannou (Eds.): HCII 2020, LNCS 12205, pp. 477–498, 2020.
https://doi.org/10.1007/978-3-030-50513-4_36

Research efforts also suggest that using mobile devices for learning generally has positive effects on learning gains [9, 10], however, there are still only a few studies that actually focus on measuring learning outcomes [11]. At the same time, the implementation of mobile devices for learning purposes may be prevented from going more mainstream due to common technological challenges associated with learning activities and improper consideration of learning content [12–15]. Due to the smaller screen size, more restrictive input abilities, processing and battery power, research in this area suggests not all learning tasks are appropriate for mobile devices [16–19].

Existing research acknowledges the proliferation of mobile devices in society, but very few studies have sought to understand the demographics of the students who actually utilize mobile technology for their learning needs. Despite the pervasiveness and attention given to m-learning, there is still a lot of unknowns about how to integrate mobile technology into instructional practices. Therefore, this chapter describes an exploratory survey study that examined U.S. college and university students' current mobile technology use for learning. By gaining a clearer picture of mobile technology usage from the students' perspective, educators and researchers are more likely to achieve desired learning behaviors and outcomes with m-learning.

2 Scholarly Justification

2.1 Current State of Mobile Technology in Higher Education

Over the years, mobile technology has revolutionized the way people interact and engage in the world around them, including in academia. With the creation of mobile technology such as laptops, smartphones, tablets, and smartwatches, demand for constant and immediate access to information and communication has increased. Currently, approximately more than 5 billion people use mobile devices, and over half of these connections can be attributed to smartphones [20]. In a 2018 survey of over 64,000 undergraduate students from 130 international institutions including the United States, it was found that less than 1% of students reported having no access to mobile devices [21].

In other related research, students report that they are indeed using mobile technology to engage in a variety of academic activities. Previous research has reported students' reliance on mobile devices to communicate and collaborate, view grades and assignments, participate in "live" classroom activities, and research information [22]. There is evidence that mobile devices are allowing students to uniquely manage and engage in their learning experience by equipping them with access, just-in-time information, and connectedness [23]. Yet, higher education institutions and faculty members are still hesitant to embrace mobile learning due to the uncertainty of best practices in implementing in the learning environment without causing disruptions [24]. What might be a source of trepidation, there is a lack of empirical evidence of best practices for integrating mobile technology in educational settings to enhance teaching and learning experiences [25].

2.2 The Potential of m-Learning

Educators and researchers continue to consider m-learning, in large part, due to its practical ability to provide instant, on-demand access to a personalized world filled with tools and resources for students [16]. Mobile devices are also typically smaller and cheaper than larger technology, such as desktops, making them more affordable, accessible, portable, and useful for students [26, 27]. Another reason educators and researchers consider mobile technology as a learning tool is due to its ability to provide new learning possibilities beyond conventional learning environments. In theory, students can participate in learning activities in remote geographies who do not typically have access to computers. Likewise, mobile technology has been at the forefront of a new wave of educational innovations designed to meet the learning needs of students with learning exceptions (physical or cognitive) [28, 29]. Furthermore, the form factor of mobile devices naturally creates the ability to create more authentic and collaborative learning experiences that other computing technology cannot, integrating learning science thought to provide deeper learning opportunities [30].

The learning potential of mobile technology has advanced with the evolution of the internet. Web 2.0 is often referred to as the second phase of the evolution of the internet. The technology and services of Web 2.0 encourage flexible web designs, richer user interfaces, collaborative content, new apps, social networks, and continued collective intelligence [31]. m-Learning embodies 2.0 as it involves the use of wireless-enabled mobile devices within and between pedagogically designed learning environments [32]. Learners can utilize mobile to improve critical reflective skills, facilitate group communication, develop an online e-portfolio, curate a world-wide network, and learn how to leverage technology and maximize their learning experiences [33]. Embedding mobile devices in the classroom can help instructors facilitate group collaboration and empower both instructors and students to apply technology in a variety of learning environments and activities seamlessly [34].

Insight to the actual learners who are using mobile devices to engage in mobile learning also remains unclear. The assumption is often made that the most frequent group to use mobile devices are younger learners, who are considered to be tech-savvy or *digital natives*. Prensky [35] described digital natives as young people born after 1980 who possess unique knowledge and skills regarding technology because they are growing up in the digital age. A childhood during this age of technology, however, does not automatically bestow technological expertise. Margaryan, Anoush, and Littlejohn [36] found that younger students are far from being technologically-fluid digital natives, but instead, they tend to use mobile devices more actively than older students. More interestingly, younger and older students were both described to be unaware of how to use new technologies to support their learning effectively. Higher education students today are a diverse mix of younger and older learners, who may be employed, are potentially parents or caretakers, and are much more mobile than previous generations [37]. They possess a unique set of needs with solutions that are both inside and outside the classroom. Students have strong expectations of constant access to learning platforms, instructional materials, and resources to learn anywhere and anytime [38]. Considering the portability, mobile technology uniquely offers many opportunities to engage with learning, but their use does not always guarantee that effective learning has or will take place [39]. Notwithstanding the gap in the research of just how to integrate m-learning to enhance learning outcomes, the potential for mobile learning is evident. More research is required to understand learners' mobile device usage and perceptions who are engaging in mobile learning, and thus to identify how to best support their needs to achieve desired learning outcomes.

2.3 Measuring the Impact of m-Learning

To assess the impact of mobile technology to date, past research interests heavily relied on understanding m-learning using instruments such as the Unified Theory of Acceptance and Use of Technology (UTAUT) and the Technology Acceptance Model (TAM) questionnaires. Both instruments have shown to be useful to understand why a user may first decide to use a particular technology and for what purposes. Specifically, the UTAUT is designed to identify the intention to accept or use a given technology based on performance expectancy, effort expectancy, social influence, and facilitating conditions [40]. The Technology Acceptance Model (TAM) is a model that also describes the behavioral factors that influence technology use such as perceived usefulness, ease of use, intention, and actual usage of the technology [41, 42]. Both instruments have been used to identify the reasons for the adoption of mobile devices by students for learning purposes, the potential of the devices, how much time they use mobile devices, and what challenges they face when using mobile devices.

2.4 Overview of the Present Study

As such, the purpose of this survey study was to better understand mobile devices usage trends in higher education by answering the following questions:

Q1: What devices do students own?
Q2: How do students use mobile devices to learn?
Q3: What learning activities do students use mobile devices for learning?
Q4: How much time do students spend using mobile technology for learning?
Q5: How has mobile technology impacted students learning?
Q6: What challenges do students encounter while using mobile devices for learning?

3   Method

3.1   Design and Analysis

This research was an exploratory survey study with the goal of investigating postsecondary students' mobile device usage for learning. A survey design was suitable since the purpose was to collect primary data to ascertain students' behaviors and attitudes of m-learning [43]. One electronic survey form was developed and distributed to collect both quantitative and qualitative data. A visual display of the results was created for quantitative results; at the same time, the qualitative data was parsed into themes.

Only fully completed surveys were included in the final analysis. A total of 475 individuals began the survey, out of which 250 either did not meet eligibility requirements for the study or did not complete the form in entirety. After these incomplete survey attempts were removed from the data records, the survey submissions of 225 eligible participants created the final data set.

3.2 Participants

Participants for this study (N = 225) were recruited from 2-year and 4-year post-secondary schools (e.g., colleges, universities, and vocational schools) across the United States. To be eligible for the study, participants were required to have experience using a mobile device (i.e., smartphone, tablet, or smartwatch) within a learning context. Ages ranged from 18 to 60 (Median = 25), representing 15 different majors, most prominently business (25%), health sciences (20%), and natural sciences (14%) majors, as shown in Table 1. At the time of completing the survey, most students reported that they were going to school full-time taking 4–5 courses (49%) on average. Other demographic information is presented in Fig. 1 and Table 1.

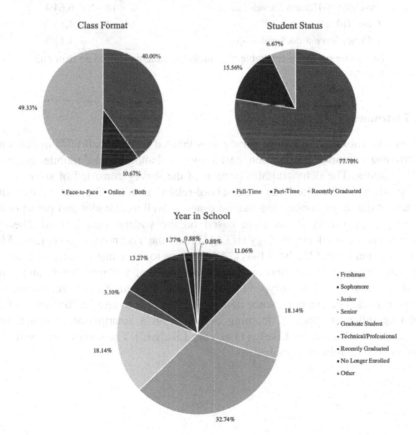

Fig. 1. Participant demographics including their typical class format, student status, and year in school.

Table 1. Breakdown of students' majors participating in the present study.

Majors	Count	%
Accounting/Business/Economics/Finance/Hospitality	58	21.40%
Anthropology/Sociology/Social Work	9	3.32%
Art/Architecture/Music/Performance	6	2.21%
Biology/Chemistry/Earth Sciences/Physics	32	11.81%
Communications	7	2.58%
Computer Science/Information Science	18	6.64%
Criminal Justice/Government/Law	10	3.69%
Education	16	5.90%
Engineering	21	7.75%
English/Composition/Literature	4	1.48%
History/Languages/Philosophy/Religious Studies	10	3.69%
International studies	4	1.48%
Mathematics/Statistics	2	0.74%
Medicine/Pharmacology/Nursing/Wellness	50	18.45%
Psychology/Human Development	18	6.64%
Other (please specify):	3	1.11%
I do not have a declared major	3	1.11%

Note: The results in this table also includes students with more than one major.

3.3   Instrument

As shown in Table 2, the online survey was created in the Qualtrics© online survey platform and captured information pertaining to demographics, mobile usage, and mobile attitudes. The demographics portion of the survey consisted of six items capturing participant characteristics and school-related details. The rest of the survey consisted of questions concerning mobile usage as well as attitudes and perceptions of m-learning. The survey items were based on the widely used Unified Theory of Acceptance and Use of Technology (UTAUT) and the Technology Acceptance Model (TAM) questionnaires [21, 40, 44–47]. Adaptations to these instruments were made to incorporate recent literature and measure finer points of students' habits and perceptions of m-learning [48]. Item-types for the survey consisted of Likert scales and open-ended responses. For example, some items asked students to rate the likelihood of them completing different types of learning activities on a smartphone, a tablet, and a smartwatch from Not At All Likely (1) to Very Likely (5). The survey took participants approximately 15 min to complete.

Table 2. Summary of survey questions.

	Item
Demographics	1. Age 2. Year in school 3. Field of study 4. Student status 5. Course load 6. Class format
Mobile usage	7. Have you used mobile devices for learning-related purposes? 8. What mobile devices do you own? 9. How often do you carry your mobile devices with you? 10. What is the likelihood of you using a mobile device to complete learning activities? 11. How often do you use mobile devices to learn? 12. What type of mobile devices do you use for learning? 13. What type of learning apps do you use on your mobile device? 14. What apps do you use most frequently for learning on your mobile devices? 15. How much time do you typically spend engaging with learning on your mobile devices? 16. What are the challenges you have encountered while using mobile devices for learning? 17. I'm easily distracted if I use a mobile device for learning 18. I'm easily distracted if I use a computer/laptop for learning 19. I'm easily distracted if I use paper and pencil for learning
Attitude towards mobile learning	20. How has the development of mobile technology impacted your learning?
Instructors' role in m-learning (students' perception)	21. How often do you expect your course assignments and materials to be accessible on your mobile devices? 22. How often do your instructors assign you an assignment that requires the use of mobile devices? 23. How often have you received formal training (e.g., tutorial, guide, expert training) to assist you in using mobile devices in your courses or to enhance your learning? 24. Based on your learning preferences, how important is it that your instructors incorporate mobile learning experiences in your course(s)?

(*continued*)

Table 2. (*continued*)

	Item
Mobile technology policy and procedures	25. Does owning mobile devices change how often you would use a computer lab on campus? 26. Does owning mobile devices change how often you would use a library? 27. Does your institution have a mobile strategy? A mobile strategy is a plan on ways to incorporate and leverage the use of mobile devices to ensure success for the school and all people who use the mobile experiences 28. Are you aware of any policies that prohibit the use of mobile devices in your course(s)?
Future of mobile technology	29. Have you used mobile devices to engage with augmented reality or virtual reality? 30. How do you see your use of mobile devices for learning change in the next two years? 31. Is there anything else you would like to mention in regards to mobile learning and the future of education?

3.4 Procedure

Participants for this study were recruited from a research pool managed by an educational software company of post-secondary students from schools located across the U.S. Through various ways of contact (i.e., public ads, social media, and in-class announcements), students voluntarily opt into the pool by providing their permission to be contacted to participate in educational research efforts. Having previously elected to join the research pool, participants received invitations via email to participate in a survey study. The recruitment email stated the purpose of the study was to learn how students used mobile devices in learning experiences, and that eligible individuals must possess experience using a mobile device within a learning context. Interested volunteers accessed the survey link within the email and proceeded to complete the survey in a new tab. After accessing the survey, participants first viewed a brief landing page that summarized the purpose of the study, outlined the monetary incentive, stated that no known risks were associated with the survey, along with contact information for the research team. Students provided their informed consent to participate voluntarily by clicking "continue" at the bottom of this screen. The online survey form recorded responses for three days, after which the link closed. Upon successful completion, a "thank you" message displayed to participants as confirmation. An incentive of $7 (USD) was paid to participants who submitted fully completed surveys.

4   Results

4.1   Ownership by Mobile Device Type

For brevity, only the most informative results and findings were selected for inclusion in this paper. Of the 225 participants who reported having used mobile devices for learning purposes, 99.56% owned a smartphone, 57.78% owned a tablet, and just 29.33% owned a smartwatch. As shown in Table 3, the overall ownership trend was consistent across majors, however, there were noticeably more owners of mobile devices by those who took online and blended courses.

Table 3. Participants' ownership of mobile devices breakdown by major and class formats.

	Smartphone	Tablet	Smartwatch
Majors			
Accounting/Business/Economics/Finance/Hospitality	100.00%	66.67%	24.56%
Anthropology/Sociology/Social Work	100.00%	60.00%	20.00%
Art/Architecture/Music/Performance	100.00%	66.67%	0.00%
Biology/Chemistry/Earth Sciences/Physics	96.88%	37.50%	28.13%
Communications	100.00%	57.14%	42.86%
Computer Science/Information Science	100.00%	55.56%	16.67%
Criminal Justice/Government/Law	100.00%	70.00%	20.00%
Education	100.00%	68.75%	31.25%
Engineering	100.00%	52.38%	33.33%
English/Composition/Literature	100.00%	25.00%	50.00%
History/Languages/Philosophy/Religious Studies	100.00%	37.50%	12.50%
International Studies	100.00%	25.00%	0.00%
Mathematics/Statistics	100.00%	50.00%	50.00%
Medicine/Pharmacology/Nursing/Wellness	100.00%	66.67%	44.44%
Psychology/Human Development	94.12%	41.18%	23.53%
Other	100.00%	42.86%	33.33%
I do not have a declared major	100.00%	100.00%	0.00%
Class Formats			
Online	100.00%	70.83%	37.50%
Face-to-face	98.89%	43.33%	30.00%
Both	100.00%	66.67%	27.03%

Note: The results in this table also includes students with more than one major.

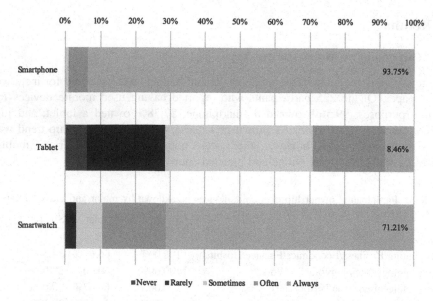

Fig. 2. The rate of students regularly carrying three mobile devices with them.

Additionally, as shown in Fig. 2, 93.75% of participants always carry their smartphones with them, about 71.21% always wear their smartwatches, and 8.46% of participants always carry their tablets. As far as conducting learning activities on a mobile device, smartphone owners did so 96% of the time, tablet owners 79.23% of the time, despite not constantly carrying tablets with them; and smartwatch owners only 9.10% of the time.

4.2   Mobile Device Usage for Learning

As shown in Fig. 3, while most of the participants majoring in most disciplines all reported using smartphones for learning, students majoring in English/Composition/Literature reported the lowest usage rate of 75.00%. For mobile learning with tablets, the usage rates vary widely by major with a range from 0% to 66.67%. The top five majors include Criminal Justice/Government/Law, Medicine/Pharmacology/Nursing/Wellness, Education, Accounting/Business/Economics/Finance/Hospitality, and Anthropology/Sociology/Social Work. Students who use smartwatches for learning were concentrated in five major categories with usage rate from 3.31% to 10%: Medicine/Pharmacology/Nursing/Wellness, Criminal Justice/Government/Law, Education, Engineering, and Biology/Chemistry/Earth Sciences/Physics.

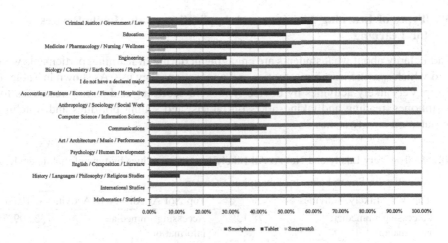

Fig. 3. The usage rate of mobile learning of students majoring in different areas.

Further comparison was conducted to discover whether the usage for learning on devices differs across class format. Across the three class formats, high usage for learning on smartphones was consistent, as shown in Fig. 4. Students who typically enroll only in face-to-face courses tend to use tablets for learning less than students who take only online courses or a combination of the two. Moreover, students who typically take online courses were 10 times more likely to use smartwatches than students in face-to-face or both formats of courses.

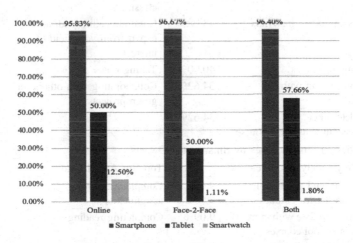

Fig. 4. The usage rate of mobile learning of students who typically take different formats of classes.

4.3   Types of Learning Activities and Applications with Mobile Devices for Learning

To add clarity about what students are engaging in during m-learning, participants were asked which specific learning activities and applications they use. As shown in Table 4, the top Very likely activities by device type were accessing and storing resources for smartphones, reading and taking notes on tablets, and setting priorities and watching due dates on smartwatches.

Table 4. Top Very Likely and Not At All Likely learning activities by type of mobile devices.

	Activities on Smartphones by Smartphone Owners			
	Top Very Likely Activities		Top Not At All Likely Activities (>10%)	
1	Accessing immediate information	78.13%	Accessing immediate information	20.09%
2	Increasing the number of available resources/sources	74.11%	Increasing the number of available resources/sources	14.29%
3	Saving/storing information	70.54%	Saving/storing information	11.61%
4	Looking up grades	55.80%		
5	Receiving feedback or help	53.57%		
	Activities on Tablets by Tablet Owners			
	Top Very Likely Activities		Top Not At All Likely Activities	
1	Completing reading	47.69%	Listen to your audio version of your textbook	16.92%
2	Taking notes	43.08%	Communicating with a classmate	15.38%
3	Accessing course materials	43.08%	Communicating with an expert from your field of interest	15.38%
4	Looking up grades	40.00%	Taking notes	13.08%
5	Communicating with professors	34.62%	Collaborating with others for group projects	13.08%
5	Complete other tasks/assignments for a course	34.62%		
	Activities on Smartwatches by Smartwatch Owners			
	Top Very Likely Activities		Top Not At All Likely Activities	
1	Monitoring and prioritizing task/to-do list for courses	9.09%	Completing writing assignments	74.24%
2	Staying up to date with current events in school/courses	9.09%	Completing reading	72.73%
3	Accessing immediate information	4.55%	Taking notes	72.73%
4	Communicating with a classmate	4.55%	Accessing course materials	72.73%
5	Increasing the number of available resources/sources	3.03%	Complete other tasks/assignments for a course	71.21%

Participants were also asked about which applications they use for mobile learning. To narrow down the list for smartphones and tablets, only the top five m-learning applications with over 50% of responses were reported, as shown in Table 5. Only the top three m-learning applications for smartwatches were reported. Internet apps were listed most often via smartphones and tablets, and productivity tools such as email apps was list first for smartwatches. Flashcards was accessed the second most often across all three mobile device types. In the follow-up, open-ended questions that asked participants to name three applications that they use most frequently, flashcards including Quizlet, Pearson Prep, Study Blue, and Smart Flashcards, and productivity apps such as Google Doc, Translate, and Mail were listed as the most commonly listed. The pattern of learning activities and applications with mobile devices appeared to be consistent in participants taking different class formats and majoring in disparate areas.

Table 5. Top mobile applications that students use.

	Smartphone	Tablet	Smartwatch
1	Internet browser (e.g., Safari, Chrome) (84.33%)	Internet browser (e.g., Safari, Chrome) (78.64%)	Tools (e.g., calculator, email apps, dictionary) (50.00%)
2	Flashcards (e.g., Pearson Prep, Brainscape, Quizlet) (76.96%)	Flashcards (e.g., Pearson Prep, Brainscape, Quizlet) (68.93%)	Flashcards (e.g., Pearson Prep, Brainscape, Quizlet) (33.33%)
3	Tools (e.g., calculator, email apps, dictionary) (72.81%)	Note taking (e.g., OneNote, Evernote) (65.05%)	Task organization (e.g., Smart Study Plan, Reminder) (33.33%)
4	Documentation (e.g., iWork, MS Office, Google Drive) (57.14%)	Tools (e.g., calculator, email apps, dictionary) (62.14%)	
5	Note taking (e.g., OneNote, Evernote) (52.53%)	eReading (e.g., Kindle, Pearson eText, iBook) (59.22%)	

4.4 Time Spent Using Mobile Technology for Learning

As shown in Table 6, participants were also asked about how much time they perceive they engage with learning on their mobile devices. Overall, 30% of students spend 1–2 h a day using mobile devices for learning purposes; another 33% spend 60 min a week; only around 13% of them spend more than three hours a day. If breaking the data down by class format, differences can be observed. About 42% of students typically taking online courses spend 60 min a week, which is about 10% higher than students typically taking face-to-face and both class formats. In the group of students who reported that they spend more than three hours a day on mobile learning, the number of students typically taking both class formats nearly doubled the number of students typically taking online courses. Inspecting the data across majors, it can be found that 50% or more of our participants use mobile devices for learning daily in majors such as art, international studies, and medicine. Interestingly, 33.33% of students who majored in art, 25% international studies, and 23.53% computer science were the top three disciplines reporting they spend three hours or more per day on mobile learning.

Table 6. Time spent on mobile learning by class format and by major.

	10 min a week	20 min a week	30 min a week	60 min a week	1-2 h a day	3 h + a day
Overall	2.28%	9.13%	12.33%	32.88%	30.14%	13.24%
Class Format						
Online	4.17%	4.17%	12.50%	41.67%	29.17%	8.33%
Face-to-face	2.35%	11.76%	11.76%	32.94%	29.41%	11.76%
Both	1.82%	8.18%	12.73%	30.91%	30.91%	15.45%
Major						
Accounting/Business/Economics/ Finance/Hospitality	1.79%	3.57%	12.50%	33.93%	33.93%	14.29%
Anthropology/Sociology/Social Work	0.00%	40.00%	0.00%	40.00%	20.00%	0.00%
Art/Architecture/Music/Performance	0.00%	0.00%	0.00%	33.33%	33.33%	33.33%
Biology/Chemistry/Earth Sciences/Physics	3.33%	6.67%	3.33%	40.00%	36.67%	10.00%
Communications	0.00%	0.00%	28.57%	28.57%	28.57%	14.29%
Computer Science/Information Science	5.88%	23.53%	11.76%	11.76%	23.53%	23.53%
Criminal Justice/Government/Law	0.00%	10.00%	10.00%	70.00%	10.00%	0.00%
Education	7.14%	14.29%	7.14%	57.14%	7.14%	7.14%
Engineering	9.52%	4.76%	14.29%	38.10%	28.57%	4.76%
English/Composition/Literature	0.00%	0.00%	25.00%	50.00%	25.00%	0.00%
History/Languages/Philosophy/Religious Studies	0.00%	12.50%	12.50%	62.50%	12.50%	0.00%
International studies	0.00%	0.00%	0.00%	50.00%	25.00%	25.00%
Mathematics/Statistics	0.00%	0.00%	50.00%	50.00%	0.00%	0.00%
Medicine/Pharmacology/Nursing/Wellness	2.22%	8.89%	15.56%	22.22%	35.56%	15.56%
Psychology/Human Development	6.25%	6.25%	6.25%	43.75%	25.00%	12.50%
Other (please specify):	0.00%	14.29%	19.05%	33.33%	19.05%	14.29%
I do not have a declared major	0.00%	0.00%	33.33%	0.00%	66.67%	0.00%

Note: The results in this table also includes students with more than one major.

4.5 Impact of Mobile Technology on Students Learning

According to the results from the impact of learning on mobile devices question, mobile learning has played an important role in their learning experience. As shown in Fig. 5, 76.26% of participants reported that mobile technology had a positive impact on their learning and only less than 4% reported negative impact. Moreover, none of the students who typically take online classes think mobile technology impacted their learning negatively. There were about two times of students typically taking face-to-face classes reported negative impacts than students typically taking both formats of classes, as shown in Fig. 6.

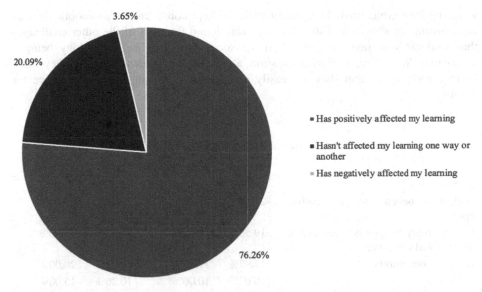

Fig. 5. Impact of the development of mobile technology on students' learning.

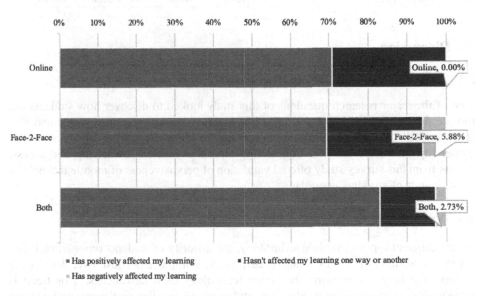

Fig. 6. Impact of the development of mobile technology on students' learning by class format.

4.6 Challenges of Using Mobile Devices for Learning

Participants were also asked what challenges they met while using mobile devices for learning. The biggest challenge reported by students was the small screens, followed by bad user experience/design of mobile applications, compatibility of applications, and internet connectivity. Price of devices and availability of device brands and versions were the least concerned. The pattern basically kept consistent across mobile devices for learning, as shown in Table 7. It was also found that half of the other challenges that students specified was related to the social aspect of the technology being a distraction. Moreover, in another question, almost 50% of students reported they agree or extremely agree that they are easily distracted when using a mobile device for learning.

Table 7. Challenges of using mobile devices for learning.

	Overall	Smartphone	Tablet	Smartwatch
Small screens	24.01%	24.10%	23.51%	20.00%
Bad user experience/design of mobile apps	21.14%	21.48%	20.20%	20.00%
Compatibility of apps between mobile devices and computer	19.55%	19.18%	21.52%	15.00%
Internet connections	17.97%	17.87%	17.22%	20.00%
Price	10.02%	10.00%	10.26%	15.00%
Various availabilities	5.56%	5.57%	5.96%	10.00%
Other (please specify):	1.75%	1.80%	1.32%	0.00%

5 Discussion

5.1 Q1: What Devices Do Students Own?

One of the major research questions of this study looked to discover how students use mobile devices for learning, if at all. Prior to understanding students' usage and attitudes regarding mobile learning, it is necessary to know the current situation of their ownership of mobile devices. Considering almost unanimous ownership and access, results from this survey study offered validation of pervasiveness of mobile technology in the hands of students everyday.

5.2 Q2: How Do Students Use Mobile Devices to Learn?

Of the different types of mobile technology, the majority of students reported that they complete learning activities using smartphones, compared to just over half using tablets, and only a few using the newer technology of smartwatches. This trend is supported by the fact that modern smartphones are smaller and more portable yet packed with comparable processing power as tablets. Smartwatches on the other hand are the epitome of portability, however, the small screen size makes it challenging to complete any learning activities on them. Of those students from majors who reported owning and using smartwatches for learning, most of them come from disciplines that require them to use their hands (i.e., doctor conducting surgery, chemists in a research lab, or an engineer crafting or manipulating materials), or are not expected to use their phones openly (i.e., lawyer in a courtroom or a teacher in a classroom). The majors currently using smartwatch technology might just be early adopters, because smartwatch use is expected to grow in other disciplines as and software developers and educators continue to acquaint themselves with better ways to provide learning experiences on the relatively new smartwatch technology. Examining the m-learning across majors, interestingly, students in more writing-centric majors reported using mobile devices the least. This trend could be attributed to the form factor. One of the main constraints of mobile technology is the smaller, compact screen sizes make tasks such as writing papers, and switching between numerous sources complicated and time-consuming.

5.3   Q3: What Learning Activities Do Students Use Mobile Devices for Learning?

Additionally, based on the question about what type of learning activities students per device, the applications the list of top applications they access for learning appear to be more lower-level learning activities such as quick, short bursts of time. Learning activities that require more challenging and complicated activities such as writing papers, designing projects, and the like are better reserved for more stationary computing. On the contrary, smartwatches serve more immediate, brief, finite tasks. Regarding reading and writing tasks, smartphones may serve more quickly accessible tasks, whereas tablets are used for more prolonged reading and writing tasks.

5.4   Q4: How Much Time Do Students Spend Using Mobile Technology for Learning?

In alignment with the question about how much time students spend using mobile technology for learning, what was found is that, indeed, mobile technology, including newer form factors smartwatches, are frequently used amongst students. Almost at a rate of complete saturation, higher than projections [49, 50], almost all students are in contact with a computing device even more so than standard computers like desktops and laptops. Furthermore, the results from the time spent using mobile devices for learning rival those of other means of learning such as desktops and laptops. As much as a third of students reported spending an hour using mobile technology for learning. That is approaching the behavior for standard study habits which suggest average college students spend about 1–3 h studying per day [51–53]. Additionally, the major students reported that m-learning has had a positive impact on their learning. Only a small percentage reported an adverse reaction to m-learning. It could be the case that with a more strategic approach to designing mobile learning activities, even fewer students will have a negative response to m-learning. Nevertheless, any educational technology product would be elated with such low adverse numbers. These findings together give credence to the notion that students are comfortable engaging in learning activities using mobile devices. Moreover, this finding is encouraging that more should continue to be done to design and develop learning activities for mobile devices.

5.5   Q5: How Has Mobile Technology Impacted Students Learning?

Given the rates of both mobile device ownership and engagement in learning activities on mobile devices, educators can assume that, required or not, students are comfortable with performing learning activities on their mobile devices. And this finding is not isolated to students studying in certain disciplines. Does this mean that all instruction should be designed for delivery via mobile devices? The present study suggests otherwise. Students who reported taking online courses also more often indicated that they perform learning activities with their mobile devices. Perhaps students who are more comfortable with technology in general lean towards both online courses and newer technological ideas, such as m-learning. However, the *cause in effect* could not be determined from this study. Instructors may also play a role in this finding as well. For example, instructors who teach online or blended (e.g., incorporate both online and face-to-face elements) courses may be more comfortable using technology in their instructional practices and, subsequently, m-learning appears more frequently within those courses.

5.6   Q6: What Challenges Do Students Encounter While Using Mobile Devices for Learning?

Based on the challenges students reported, m-learning is limited by the small viewing area. To compound this issue, educational software despite being accessible via mobile technology would benefit from better design considerations for mobile devices. Technology heuristics such as responsive design might need better design considerations so the user experience is more user-friendly [54, 55]. Moreover, distraction was largely recognized in students' m-learning experience. The self-management element was suggested to be helpful to address the distraction issue. Therefore, learning designers might also need to consider embedding this element in the design of m-learning applications [56].

5.7   Limitations

A limitation of this study is the small sample size with respect to the number of students nationwide. Without a larger sample size, it is difficult to generalize these results beyond the superficial. However, the findings of this study can serve as a provisional indication of how mobile technology is currently used in higher education in the United States. Another possible limitation is the potential propensity of respondents and the instructors who taught the respondents might have had towards technology. Participants in this study were recruited from a pool created by an educational courseware company. It could be the case that they are more comfortable with educational technology and hold a more positive attitude towards educational technology as a result of their respective instructors exposing them to educational courseware.

6 Conclusion

Given how mobile devices seem *sine qua non* to students in the United States and across the globe, educators would be remiss not to consider ways to integrate the technology into their teaching practices. Suggested by the results from this survey study students have access to many mobile devices, however, they tend to be very selective in what device they choose to use for their learning. The findings indicate that their use of mobile technology is highly dependent upon the characteristics of the learning activity they are engaging in, the subject matter, and can be motivated by many things including their interest to have immediate access to information or course materials. Regardless of the class formats, face-to-face, online, or both, today's student appears to recognize the positive impact mobile devices have on their learning. As such, the results from this study should be encouraging that more research is needed to help explore the ways educators can help support learners as they engage in mobile learning experiences.

Past research for m-learning offers many definitions and frameworks, which can make it hard for practitioners and learners to determine which one to consider. Each day mobile technology continues to evolve and advance, sparking changes in how we view and experience learning. Already the next phase of mobile, Mobile 3.0, is anticipated to include artificial intelligence and machine learning that will result in a virtual classroom that can be viewed on mobile devices [57]. Soon learners will be able to engage in mobile learning experiences that include location-based learning, augmented reality, wearable learning, learning implants, and ambient intelligence [58]. Therefore, creating successful mobile learning experiences will require careful planning, appropriate pedagogy, and sufficient technological support [33]. Sharples et al. [59] emphasize that we cannot determine how technology will be used until we explore its use in real settings with real people. Future research should continue to explore mobile learning from the instructors perspectives, paying close attention to the existing challenges. Additionally, there is a dire need for an evidence-based framework for designing m-learning experiences in higher education for face-to-face or virtual environments. The best way to develop a concrete definition and framework for mobile learning is to continue to explore the characteristics of those who are currently using mobile devices to help identify the areas where they need the most support.

References

1. Crompton, H., Burke, D.: The use of mobile learning in higher education: a systematic review. Comput. Educ. **123**, 53–64 (2018). https://doi.org/10.1016/j.compedu.2018.04.007
2. Martin, F., Ertzberger, J.: Here and now mobile learning: an experimental study on the use of mobile technology. Comput. Educ. **68**, 76–85 (2013). https://doi.org/10.1016/j.compedu.2013.04.021
3. Davison, C.B., Lazaros, E.J.: Adopting mobile technology in the higher education classroom. JOTS **41**, 30–39 (2015)

4. Kobus, M.B.W., Rietveld, P., van Ommeren, J.N.: Ownership versus on-campus use of mobile IT devices by university students. Comput. Educ. **68**, 29–41 (2013). https://doi.org/10.1016/j.compedu.2013.04.003

5. Pimmer, C., Mateescu, M., Gröhbiel, U.: Mobile and ubiquitous learning in higher education settings. A systematic review of empirical studies. Comput. Hum. Behav. **63**, 490–501 (2016). https://doi.org/10.1016/j.chb.2016.05.057

6. Sung, E., Mayer, R.E.: Students' beliefs about mobile devices vs. desktop computers in South Korea and the United States. Comput. Educ. **59**, 1328–1338 (2012). https://doi.org/10.1016/j.compedu.2012.05.005

7. Bosman, J.P., Strydom, S.: Mobile technologies for learning: exploring critical mobile learning literacies as enabler of graduateness in a South African research-led university. Br. J. Educ. Technol. **47**, 510–519 (2016). https://doi.org/10.1111/bjet.12441

8. Giannakas, F., Kambourakis, G., Papasalouros, A., Gritzalis, S.: A critical review of 13 years of mobile game-based learning. Educ. Technol. Res. Dev. **66**, 341–384 (2018). https://doi.org/10.1007/s11423-017-9552-z

9. Sevillano-García, M.A.L., Vázquez-Cano, E.: The impact of digital mobile devices in higher education. J. Educ. Technol. Soc. **18**, 106–118 (2015)

10. Wu, W.-H., Wu, Y.-C.J., Chen, C.-Y., Kao, H.-Y., Lin, C.-H., Huang, S.-H.: Review of trends from mobile learning studies: a meta-analysis. Comput. Educ. **59**, 817–827 (2012). https://doi.org/10.1016/j.compedu.2012.03.016

11. Mayer, R.E.: Where is the learning in mobile technologies for learning? Contemp. Educ. Psychol. 101824 (2019)

12. Cochrane, T.D.: Critical success factors for transforming pedagogy with mobile Web 2.0. Br. J. Educ. Technol. **45**, 65–82 (2014). https://doi.org/10.1111/j.1467-8535.2012.01384.x

13. Levene, J., Seabury, H.: Evaluation of mobile learning: Current research and implications for instructional designers. TechTrends **59**, 46–52 (2015). https://doi.org/10.1007/s11528-015-0904-4

14. Martin, F., Pastore, R., Snider, J.: Developing mobile based instruction. TechTrends **56**, 46–51 (2012). https://doi.org/10.1007/s11528-012-0598-9

15. Wang, M., Shen, R.: Message design for mobile learning: learning theories, human cognition and design principles. Br. J. Educ. Technol. **43**, 561–575 (2012). https://doi.org/10.1111/j.1467-8535.2011.01214.x

16. McQuiggan, S., McQuiggan, J., Sabourin, J., Kosturko, L.: Mobile Learning: A Handbook for Developers, Educators, and Learners. Wiley, Hoboken (2015)

17. Nielsen, J., Budiu, R.: Mobile Usability. New Riders, Berkeley (2013)

18. Reychav, I., McHaney, R.: The relationship between gender and mobile technology use in collaborative learning settings: an empirical investigation. Comput. Educ. **113**, 61–74 (2017). https://doi.org/10.1016/j.compedu.2017.05.005

19. Tseng, H.W., Tang, Y., Morris, B.: Evaluation of iTunes university courses through instructional design strategies and m-learning framework. J. Educ. Technol. Soc. **19**, 199–210 (2016)

20. Taylor, K., Silver, L.: Smartphone Ownership is Growing Rapidly Around the World, But Not Always Equally. Pew Research Center, Washington (2019)

21. Galanek, J., Gierdowski, D., Brooks, D.C.: ECAR study of undergraduate students and information technology, 2018 (2018)

22. Foti, M.K., Mendez, J.: Mobile learning: how students use mobile devices to support learning. J. Lit. Technol. **15**, 58–78 (2014)

23. Shih, Y.E., Mills, D.: Setting the new standard with mobile computing in online learning. IRRODL **8**, 1–16 (2007)

24. Khaddage, F., Müller, W., Flintoff, K.: Advancing mobile learning in formal and informal settings via mobile app technology: where to from here, and how? J. Educ. Technol. Soc. **19**, 16–26 (2016)
25. Chergui, O., Begdouri, A., Groux-Leclet, D.: A classification of educational mobile use for learners and teachers. Int. J. Learn. Technol. **7**, 324–330 (2017). https://doi.org/10.18178/ijiet.2017.7.5.889
26. Schachter, R.: Mobile devices in the classroom. Dist. Admin. **45**, 31–34 (2009)
27. Zaranis, N., Kalogiannakis, M., Papadakis, S.: Using mobile devices for teaching realistic mathematics in kindergarten education. Creat. Educ. **4**, 1–10 (2013)
28. Qahmash, A.I.M.: The potentials of using mobile technology in teaching individuals with learning disabilities: a review of special education technology literature. TechTrends **62**, 647–653 (2018). https://doi.org/10.1007/s11528-018-0298-1
29. Fernández-López, Á., Rodríguez-Fórtiz, M.J., Rodríguez-Almendros, M.L., Martínez-Segura, M.J.: Mobile learning technology based on iOS devices to support students with special education needs. Comput. Educ. **61**, 77–90 (2013). https://doi.org/10.1016/j.compedu.2012.09.014
30. Conley, Q.: Exploring the impact of varying levels of augmented reality to teach probability and sampling with a mobile device. Arizona State University (2013)
31. Murugesan, S.: Understanding Web 20. IT Prof. **9**, 34–41 (2007). https://doi.org/10.1109/MITP.2007.78
32. Cochrane, T., Bateman, R.: Smartphones give you wings: Pedagogical affordances of mobile Web **20**(26), 1–14 (2010). https://doi.org/10.14742/ajet.1098
33. Cochrane, T.: Mobile Web 2.0: the new frontier. Hello! where are you in the landscape of educational technology? In: Proceedings ascilite Melbourne 2008 (2008)
34. Liu, T.-C., Wang, H.-Y., Liang, J.K., Chan, T.-W., Ko, H.W., Yang, J.-C.: Wireless and mobile technologies to enhance teaching and learning. J. Comput. Assist. Learn. **19**, 371–382 (2003)
35. Prensky, M.: Digital natives, digital immigrants part 2: do they really think differently? On the Horizon. **9**, 1–6 (2001). https://doi.org/10.1108/10748120110424843
36. Margaryan, A., Littlejohn, A., Vojt, G.: Are digital natives a myth or reality? University students' use of digital technologies. Comput. Educ. **56**, 429–440 (2011). https://doi.org/10.1016/j.compedu.2010.09.004
37. Hilton, E.: Today's students: Inspiration for higher education. https://higherlearningadvocates.org/2019/11/14/todays-students/
38. Alexander, B., et al.: Educause Horizon Report 2019 Higher Education Edition (2019)
39. Chen, B., Denoyelles, A.: Exploring students' mobile learning practices in higher education. Educause Rev. **7**, 1054–1064 (2013)
40. Venkatesh, V., Morris, M.G., Davis, G.B., Davis, F.D.: User acceptance of information technology: toward a unified view. MIS Q. **27**, 425–478 (2003). https://doi.org/10.2307/30036540
41. Davis, F.D.: A technology acceptance model for empirically testing new end-user information systems: theory and results (1985). https://dspace.mit.edu/bitstream/handle/1721.1/15192/14927137-MIT.pdf
42. Huang, J.-H., Lin, Y.-R., Chuang, S.-T.: Elucidating user behavior of mobile learning. The Electronic Library (2007)
43. Creswell, J.W.: Educational Research: Planning, Conducting, and Evaluating Quantitative and Qualitative Research. Pearson, Boston (2012)
44. Brooks, D.C., Pomerantz, J.: ECAR study of undergraduate students and information technology, 2017 (2017)

45. Seilhamer, R., Chen, B., Bauer, S., Salter, A., Bennett, L.: Changing mobile learning practices: a multiyear study 2012–2016. Educause Rev. (2018)
46. Davis, F.D.: Perceived usefulness, perceived ease of use, and user acceptance of information technology. MIS Q. **13**, 319–340 (1989). https://doi.org/10.2307/249008
47. Venkatesh, V., Davis, F.D.: A theoretical extension of the technology acceptance model: four longitudinal field studies. Manag. Sci. **46**, 186–204 (2000). https://doi.org/10.1287/mnsc.46.2.186.11926
48. Computer Lab Management: Student Smartphone Survey - Winter 2011. https://computerrooms.ucdavis.edu/pubs/survey/student-w11-2.html
49. Holst, A.: Number of smartphone users in the United States from 2010 to 2023 (2019). https://www.statista.com/statistics/201182/forecast-of-smartphone-users-in-the-us/
50. Dover, S.: Study: Number of smartphone users tops 1 billion (2012). http://www.cbsnews.com/8301-205_162-57534583/study-number-of-smartphone-users-tops-1-billion/
51. Müller, S., Koch, I., Settmacher, U., Dahmen, U.: How the introduction of OSCEs has affected the time students spend studying: results of a nationwide study. BMC Med. Educ. **19**, 146 (2019). https://doi.org/10.1186/s12909-019-1570-6
52. Kudryavtsev, M.D., Kramida, I.E., Iermakov, S.S.: Influence of studying in higher educational establishment on students' harmful computer habits. Phys. Educ. Student **20**, 17–23 (2016). https://doi.org/10.15561/20755279.2016.0503
53. Blasiman, R.N., Dunlosky, J., Rawson, K.A.: The what, how much, and when of study strategies: comparing intended versus actual study behaviour. Memory **25**, 784–792 (2017). https://doi.org/10.1080/09658211.2016.1221974
54. Ricker, B.A., Roth, R.E.: Mobile maps and responsive design. GIS&T Body Knowl. **CV–40** (2018). https://doi.org/10.22224/gistbok/2018.2.5
55. Bhuttoo, V., Soman, K., Sungkur, R.K.: Responsive design and content adaptation for e-learning on mobile devices. In: 2017 1st International Conference on Next Generation Computing Applications (NextComp), pp. 163–168 (2017). https://doi.org/10.1109/NEXTCOMP.2017.8016193
56. Montilus, K.D., Jin, T.: Embedding self-management into mobile learning experiences. ELDj **7**, 12–15 (2020)
57. Wang, S., Heffernan, N.: Mobile 2.0 and mobile language learning. In: Handbook of Research on Web 2.0 and Second Language Learning, pp. 472–490. IGI Global (2009). https://doi.org/10.4018/978-1-60566-190-2.ch025
58. Oller, R.: The future of mobile learning. ECAR Research Bulletin, Educause Center for Applied Research (2012)
59. Sharples, M., Arnedillo-Sánchez, I., Milrad, M,, Vavoula, G.: Mobile learning. Technol.-Enhanced Learn. 233–249 (2009) http://dx.doi.org/10.1007/978-1-4020-9827-7_14

Creating the Profile of Participants in Mobility Activities in the Context of Erasmus+: Motivations, Perceptions, and Linguistic Needs

Panagiotis Kosmas[1]([⊠]) [ID], Antigoni Parmaxi[1], Maria Perifanou[2],
Anastasios A. Economides[2], and Panayiotis Zaphiris[1]

[1] Cyprus Interaction Lab, Cyprus University of Technology,
3075 Limassol, Cyprus
panayiotis.kosmas@cut.ac.cy
[2] University of Macedonia, Thessaloniki, Greece

Abstract. With millions of participants, Erasmus+ is a unique opportunity to study, train, gain work experience or volunteer abroad. However, the lack of language competences is still one of the main barriers to participation in European education, training, and youth programs. This work aims to identify, analyze and present the language needs of the participants involved in mobility activities supported under Erasmus+ Key Action 1. Data were collected by means of an online questionnaire to identify all the necessary information regarding the language needs of the Erasmus+ KA1 Mobility participants as well as their motivations to participate in the mobility. Also, in order to collect additional information in creating a profile and identifying the linguistic needs of all the Erasmus+ participants, a series of semi-structured interviews with Erasmus+ key stakeholders and with Erasmus+ National Agency Officers was conducted. Findings from the online questionnaire and interviews revealed important considerations regarding the language needs of the participants, their motivations and expectations, as well as their challenges/difficulties during the mobility. The contribution of this manuscript is to provide a piece of new knowledge regarding the Erasmus+ KA1 participants profiles emphasizing the need for new strategies to facilitate further mobility in the context of Erasmus + and enhance the idea of multilingualism across Europe.

Keywords: Erasmus · Language learning · Mobility · Students · Higher education

1 Introduction

Over the past few decades, international student mobility has significantly increased [1], as there are many opportunities, specifically in the context of Erasmus+ activities. There is a considerable amount of research regarding the impact of mobility on participants' language and intercultural skills, but there is limited research on the profiles of Erasmus+ KA1 mobility participants.

Previous literature regarding students' mobility and Study Abroad (SA) has revealed that students participate in mobility activities, mainly for personal development [2, 3].

P. Zaphiris and A. Ioannou (Eds.): HCII 2020, LNCS 12205, pp. 499–511, 2020.
https://doi.org/10.1007/978-3-030-50513-4_37

The study of Mitchell [4] showed that the initial motivation of Erasmus students is to discover a country and learn about its culture. Other researchers have argued that participants in those mobilities intend to develop their language proficiency [3, 5–7] and to acquire skills in a foreign language. Other reasons for students to participate in mobility actions are to enhance their professional and career profile so as to find a job [8], to increase their self-confidence, to widen their horizons, to acquire academic or profession-specific skills, to experience adventure, or to have a good time [9]. However, along with their motivations, students face several difficulties in participating in a mobility program [10]. Some of the barriers, according to the literature, include language difficulties and lack of foreign language skills [11], lack of awareness about studying abroad opportunities, family and social commitments in the home country, and uncertainty about the positive impact of participating in mobility [12].

Having all the above challenges in mind, this study aims to map Erasmus+ participants' needs, expectations, difficulties, and challenges in order to create a piece of new knowledge for Erasmus+ KA1 participants profiles. Various other stakeholders can use the findings and conclusions from this research (e.g., all Erasmus+ KA1 Mobility Participants, Partners' Institutions, Universities, Schools, Businesses, National Authorities, National Erasmus+ Offices, Erasmus+ program, European Language Council, and other EU officials) who are interested in gaining knowledge about the profiles of Erasmus+ KA1 mobility participants.

In particular, the findings of this study could positively impact the people who would like to participate in a mobility by informing them about possible language and cultural requirements and needs. Our data could also be helpful for Higher Education Institutions, National Erasmus+ Offices and Erasmus+ program officials, as the conclusions will enhance their knowledge regarding the profiles of Erasmus+ KA1 mobility participants and help them to design better Erasmus+ policies and strategies to support all the participants.

In the sections below, first, an overview of the literature on mobility and study abroad is provided with a focus on language skills and competences. Subsequently, the method of the study is detailed, followed by the main findings. We conclude with some important insights regarding the Erasmus+ participants' profiles.

2 Literature Review

With 4 million participants by 2020, Erasmus+ is a unique opportunity to study, train, gain work experience, or volunteer abroad. However, according to the European report [13], the lack of language competences is still one of the main barriers to participation in European education, training and youth programs. Having in mind the need to cultivate Erasmus+ mobility participants' language skills, the European Union has decided to offer linguistic support through the Online Linguistic Support [14] to all Erasmus+ participants for studying, carrying out a traineeship or volunteering abroad in the framework of long-term mobility activities supported under Erasmus+ Key Action 1. This action is the only online linguistic support opportunity that Erasmus + participants have had so far. Existing literature on Erasmus+ mobility emphasizes the need for more organized actions as, to date, limited information has been provided on the needs of mobile students, in particular, their linguistic and cultural needs. Indeed, while there is great interest in participating in Erasmus+ mobility activities and generally in studying abroad [15], there is lack of a comprehensive tool to enhance and facilitate the mobility of participants in terms of linguistic [11] and cultural needs and challenges [12].

With regard to the Erasmus+ participants' incentives, responses from several surveys in different studies have shown two main motivation factors for participating in mobility activities: first is the willingness for acquiring living abroad experience and intercultural skills; second, participants see this mobility experience as an opportunity to increase their competitiveness in the labor market [16–18]. Moreover, the Erasmus Student Network (ESN), which is the biggest and most known organization for Erasmus+ mobility, often shares online surveys to gather related information from Erasmus+ participants. For example, in the study "ESN Survey 2005" [19] where Erasmus+ participants were asked to mention the skills acquired during the mobility, participants mentioned skills such as the acquisition of cultural knowledge and skills, personal development, social development, academic enrichment and last the discovering - exploiting of new opportunities in their area of interest. Along the same lines, previous studies explored the expectations, perceptions, and experiences of students involved in Erasmus programs to better understand the students' cultural and intercultural needs [2], pointing out the most important motivating factors in participating in mobility abroad.

Previous works focusing on Erasmus students have reported on the benefits and gains experienced by students. Aslan and Jacobs' work [5] showed that language learning and living in a country with a different culture are the main reasons for participating in Erasmus mobility. With regard to language skills, studies in the area, of outgoing and incoming Erasmus students, reported a statistically significant increase of communication skills in the language of the host country [18], while other studies have shown the development of listening skills, reading comprehension skills, writing skills, as well as grammatical accuracy [20]. Similar findings with a focus on the linguistic and cultural needs of the participants can be found in previous studies [e.g., 3, 21, 22]. Based on the literature, there are several ways in which language educators can help students prepare for mobility in terms of guidance and understanding of both what and how they may learn while they are abroad [23].

3 Data Collection Methods

The study adopted a mixed research method [24], which is suggested as a successful method to enhance case studies or empirical research. Data were collected through a questionnaire distributed online and by means of semi-structured interviews with EU KA1 Mobility key stakeholders.

3.1 Questionnaire

An online questionnaire was created to collect all the necessary information that would help the researchers explore and identify the language and cultural needs of the EU

KA1 Mobility participants as well as their preferred pedagogical methods and learning preferences. This technique is a common method that is being used by many other researchers in the area of Erasmus+ mobility for collecting information about participants' expectations, experiences, difficulties, challenges, and gains [2, 3].

The overall aim of the questionnaire was to address the language and cultural needs of the Erasmus+ mobility participants and to identify their motivations, expectations, challenges and language needs. For that reason, the questionnaire was divided into five parts and included questions pertaining to the overall experience of the participants during the mobility:

1. Profile
2. Needs, expectations, and benefits
3. Language and cultural needs
4. Learning delivery mode and learning preferences
5. Demographic information

Specifically, the questionnaire started with a brief introduction and overview of the purpose of the study and continued with the consent form. Part A consisted of general questions regarding the participants' profile. This part aimed to identify in which activity of KA1 mobility they participated and for how long, the country of work and the country of the mobility of those participants. Part B focused on participants' needs, expectations and benefits of the mobility. The aim of the part was to identify what participants expected from their mobility and what they finally gained. It also aimed at establishing an understanding of the rationale the mobility. Part C included questions regarding the language and cultural needs of the participants. This part aspired to determine the participants' linguistic priorities and challenges. Part D focused on the modes of learning, preferences and participants' expectations in an online language environment. Last, Part E gathered demographic information of the participants (i.e., country of origin, age, current status, and gender).

3.2   Interviews

The purpose of conducting interviews was to collect additional information for identifying the linguistic and cultural needs of all the Erasmus+ participants who would like to study, train, gain work experience, or volunteer abroad. To that end, a series of semi-structured interviews with key stakeholders (representatives of organizations who enhance and facilitate the EU KA1 Mobility activities in HE, VET, Schools, leaders of specific networks among others) was conducted. This method of data collection is very common in qualitative research and is appropriate for the exploration of the perceptions, opinions, and attitudes of respondents and enables probing for more information and clarification of answers [25–27].

For the purposes of this study, we created a protocol with some predetermined questions and topics that were deemed important, but with a flexible order that can be modified based upon the interviewer's perception of what seems most appropriate. Specifically, this interview protocol included several questions and topics to be asked or discussed during the interviews (see Table 1 for a list of selected questions asked in the interview sessions).

Each interview lasted approximately 20–30 min. In total, nine semi-structured interviews were conducted; three interviews with KA1 National Agency officers and six interview sessions with KA1 University officers.

Table 1. List selected questions asked in the interview sessions

Question	
1	As National Agency Officer/Erasmus University officer, what linguistic difficulties have you noticed for students/staff participating in Erasmus+ KA1 mobilities? (both incoming and outgoing)?
2	As far as you know, what kind of linguistic and/or cultural support is needed for KA1 mobility participants in your country of residence? (both incoming and outgoing)?
3	How does your office address these difficulties?
4	From your point of view, what are the most important gains/benefits for KA1 mobility participants (both students/staff/other)?
5	In terms of language, what extra activities would your organization like to offer to Erasmus+ KA1 mobility participants?
6	What challenges do you encounter during your work as a National Officer/Erasmus University Officer?

4 Findings

This section presents the findings from the analysis of the online questionnaire and the findings derived from the interviews with Erasmus+ KA1 key stakeholders. As mentioned earlier, the aim of the questionnaire and interviews was to address the language and cultural needs of the Erasmus+ KA1 mobility participants, to identify their expectations, challenges and needs, and to collect useful information from Erasmus+ participants who participated in a mobility for study, train or gain work experience.

4.1 Results of the Online Questionnaire

In this part, we present the main results that emerged from the analysis of the online questionnaire, focusing on data regarding the participants' profile, language, and cultural needs during their mobility, as well as their motivations. Responses to the online questionnaire were received from 168 people, 71% out of whom were women while 27.4% were men. The rest preferred not to state their gender. We received responses from 32 countries, namely Austria, Belgium, Bulgaria, Croatia, Cyprus, Czech Republic, Denmark, Estonia, Finland, France, Germany, Greece, Hungary, Ireland, Italy, Latvia, Lithuania, Luxemburg, Malta, the Netherlands, Poland, Portugal, Romania, Slovakia, Slovenia, Spain, Sweden, United Kingdom, Albania, Serbia, USA, North Macedonia. As shown in Fig. 1, most participants were Cypriots (29%), followed by Greek (27.4%), Romanian (8.9%) and Italian (8%).

44.4% of the participants in the survey were Higher Education students whose mobility took place as a part of their studies. 16.9% were Higher Education staff, 10.5% were school education staff (teachers), and 8.1% were youth workers who used their mobility especially for training purposes (see Fig. 2). Most participants were Higher education students. This was only to be expected as those participants have many opportunities for mobility under the Erasmus+ activities and that is why many researchers have focused on the investigation of university students' mobility activities [2, 3, 18].

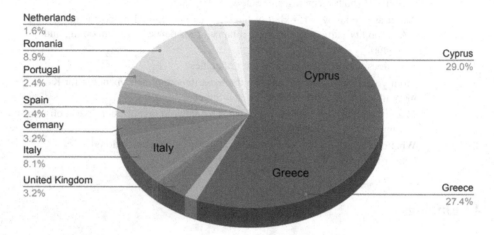

Fig. 1. Participants' country of origin

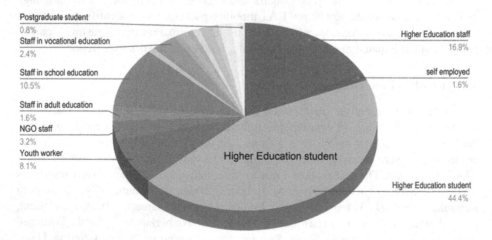

Fig. 2. Current status of participants

Participants were involved in many different activities under the umbrella of Erasmus+ KA1 mobility. As the majority of participants were Higher Education students and staff, the main activities in which the respondents participated in belong in the Erasmus+ for Higher Education students (44.4%) and Erasmus+ for staff working in Higher Education (18.9%). The rest of the participants were involved in other Erasmus+ activities such as VET, Youth Workers, Youth Entrepreneurs, and Staff mobility for training.

Focusing on the participants' expectations and reasons for participation in the mobility, most respondents (82) chose to get involved in those activities in order to gain academic, work or study experience in another EU country. Seventy-five of them participated in an Erasmus+ mobility to learn a new culture, while 71 of them to discover a new place. Other reasons for participating in a mobility include: to improve their academic or professional qualifications, to improve or gain language skills for basic communication, or to improve or gain language skills for specific purposes, etc. Figure 3 presents the three most popular answers selected by the respondents on the questionnaire.

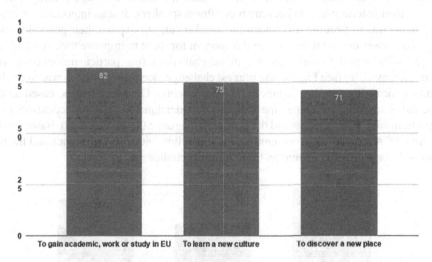

Fig. 3. Reasons for participation in an Erasmus+ mobility

Additionally, according to the participants, the language skills Erasmus participants needed during the mobility varies. As indicated in Fig. 4, most respondents (21%) believed that Erasmus participants need to have a C2 level of language. Based on CEFR of Council of Europe, the C2 level is the capacity to deal with material that is academic or cognitively demanding and to use language to good effect at a level of performance.

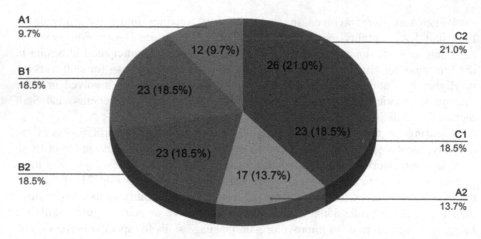

Fig. 4. Participants' perceptions about the needed language level (CEFR) for mobility

Moreover, participants claimed that the most important language priority was to improve their listening and to become more fluent speakers. Just as important for many participants was to become more accurate speakers and to expand their general vocabulary. To a lesser degree it was deemed important for them to improve their reading and writing. With regard to the main linguistic challenges that participants encountered during their mobility (see Fig. 5), the biggest challenge, according to them, was to be able to communicate in everyday instances (60 respondents). Other challenges, based on the participants' responses, included the difficulty to understand the regional accents/dialects (56 participants) and to understand the academic language (48 participants). Based on the participants' responses, the communication with fellow students/colleagues and the use of jargon/slang were considered as less important challenges.

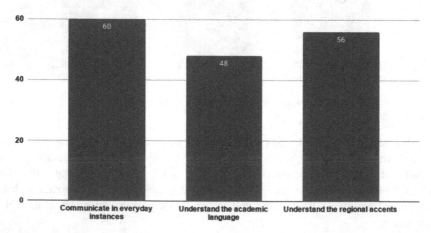

Fig. 5. Linguistic challenges during the Erasmus+ mobility

Another point to consider is the mode of learning in an online language learning environment during the mobility, in order to identify the learning preferences of

Erasmus+ participants. Regarding the participants' learning preferences in an online environment, most of the respondents preferred to have the information be presented to them in visual (using images, and spatial understanding) (23.2%) and interactive ways and to learn in groups or with other people (23.2%). A smaller percentage of respondents (17.1%) preferred the verbal-linguistic way, while 16.4% of the participants preferred the social way of learning (see Fig. 6).

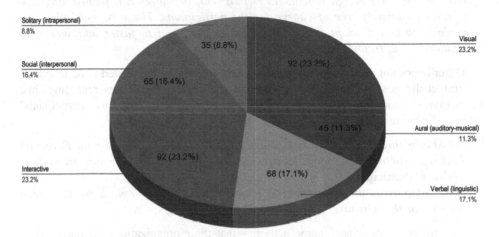

Fig. 6. Learning preferences in an online language learning platform

4.2 Interview Results

To gather additional data, nine semi-structured interviews were conducted; three interviews with Erasmus+ KA1 National Agency officers and six interview sessions with Erasmus+ KA1 University officers. All the interviews were recorded and transcribed. The interview analysis focused on the following themes:

- Linguistic and cultural needs of Erasmus participants
- Motivations - expectations of the mobility

According to the responses obtained, the linguistic needs of both outgoing and incoming participants were an important factor for an effective and successful mobility. A selection of interesting comments is presented below:

– *"For the outgoing mobility, one important difficulty is the language of instruction, which is an enormous barrier for mobility and our collaboration with other universities"* (Participant 1).
– *"Students are afraid of a foreign language - they face many difficulties because of the language. This is one of the factors that people don't want to participate in Erasmus mobility"* (Participant 2).
– *"A major difficulty can be considered the lack of knowledge by the users of the specific jargon of the Erasmus+ program and in general of the academic setting"* (Participant 5).

Additionally, the key stakeholders pointed out some extra activities which the universities or organizations offer to address these language needs. Some indicative quotes from the interviews are:

- *"There is help for students who participate in non-English lessons (translation of the material in English, assignments instead of exams, etc.)"* (Participant 3).
- *"For incoming and outgoing students, the International Mobility Office, in cooperation with the Foreign Languages Department, organizes E.U funded language courses completely free of charge for the participants. These courses allow the students to better adapt to foreign countries that lead to faster and successful academic integration"* (Participant 7).

Other important factors that emerged from the interviews are related to participants' cultural challenges. As interviewees claimed, there are some issues regarding this. Interviewees made the following comments with regard to Erasmus+ participants' cultural difficulties:

- *"Most incoming students are experiencing a cultural shock. However, the European Students Network (ESN, https://uom.esngreece.gr/) offers valuable support to these students"* (Participant 3).
- *"One difficulty is the adjustment in a new place. Some people leave their own country for the first time"* (Participant 8).

The interviewees shared some activities that their organizations do during their participants' mobility to address the cultural needs of participants. Below we present some examples:

- *"We try to engage all incoming Erasmus participants in different social and cultural events. Our goal is to encourage students to do this kind of thing and not the office. We created an organization regarding where students can have the initiative to help other Erasmus students/participants"* (Participant 2).
- *"Usually, we organize twice a semester cultural excursions/visits exclusively for Erasmus participants to introduce them in our culture"* (Participant 4).

Finally, interviewees argued that a mobility offers a lot to the participants enabling them to develop significant academic, social, and personal skills. To sum up, based on the interview data, interviewees discussed the beneficial role of a mobility in many sectors and pointed out the following strengths/benefits:

- Developing collaborations, friendships, and networking
    - *"They develop collaborations with other people in other countries. Some of these friendships last for many years. They become aware of different academic environments and mentality, different cultures and ways of life"* (Participant 9).
- Intercultural communication
    - *"People will learn to communicate and collaborate with other people with a different mindset, language, and culture. They learn to respect other cultures. The people's management I believe, is very important, specifically in the workplace. Only with the mobility, you can acquire all these skills"* (Participant 1).

- Cultural benefits/understanding
  - "[…] *learn new worlds, people and cultures*" (Participant 9).
  - "*The participants acquire valuable experience and important skills, such as to work apart from your comfort zone, to collaborate with people with different rhythm and mindset, to organize/manage your time. These skills are very important for their future life*" (Participant 6).
- Professional opportunities
  - "*They see what other opportunities exist abroad for education and work - we have many cases of students who chose (after the mobility period) to continue their studies abroad or to work there*" (Participant 5).
- Developing academic competencies
  - "*The experience they will gain by spending a period abroad, knowing a new culture and being involved in it, meeting lots of new people, creating networks of contacts which might be useful in the future, start building their own future, enhance their CV*" (Participant 1).

5 Discussion

Combining the results of questionnaires and interviews, the study found that the participants in the Erasmus+ KA1 mobility need linguistic support. It seems that this is the main priority of the participants, as most of them have difficulties communicating in everyday instances in the language of the host country. This necessity was supported by the participants' responses in the questionnaire, as many of them claimed that the biggest linguistic challenge during their mobility was the communication with local people in everyday occasions. Also, this difficulty arose from the interviews with Erasmus+ KA1 stakeholders, who claimed that the linguistic needs for both outgoing and incoming participants were an important factor for an effective and successful mobility.

Focusing on participants' expectations and needs of the mobility, the majority of participants chose to get involved in those activities in order to gain academic, work or study experience in another EU country. Other reasons included to learn a new culture, to discover a new place, to improve professional qualifications or to gain language skills. This finding is in line with the work of Gallarza, Fayos, Currás, Servera, and Arteaga [8] who assert that language learning and living in a different culture are the main reasons for participating in an Erasmus mobility. Language learning is one of the main reasons for participating in an Erasmus mobility [8]; This draws attention to the participants' need to interact successfully with professors and instructors at the host university as well as with other students in their host country. Similarly, a previous study by Asoodar, Atai, and Baten [2] found that mobility participants considered the following factors as important: becoming more independent, gaining another perspective on the way things are at home, and interacting with people from different origins. Other studies in the area of study abroad demonstrated that Erasmus students are mainly motivated by experiential instead of academic goals (e.g., 28).

Furthermore, according to the participants' language needs, the biggest challenge was to communicate in everyday instances, the difficulty to understand the regional dialects in the host country and to understand the academic language. For those reasons, prior knowledge of the target language is crucial. These results are in line with previous empirical studies, which have argued that the level of language proficiency in the host country plays an important role in the outcomes of the experience [22]. Previous studies have revealed that Erasmus students have some difficulties in terms of communication in the host country and for that reason, the lack of foreign language becomes a barrier for mobility [3, 20]. In the same lines, in the study of Klimova [21] students reported not having many language difficulties in terms of listening comprehension, but in terms of speaking in the foreign language and expressing their ideas.

The analysis of the questionnaire and interviews brought to light the necessity for the creation of a new approach to address participants' language and cultural needs during their mobility. This could be achieved via training, seminars, or language courses. The results of this work could be used by various stakeholders who are interested in gaining knowledge about the profiles of Erasmus+ KA1 mobility participants. It could also further enhance mobility in the context of Erasmus+ by informing future participants about the language and cultural challenges and helping them to take appropriate actions before they embark on their mobility. Finally, it is also important to mention that this study aims to emphasize the necessity of promoting new ideas that will facilitate multilingualism within Europe.

Acknowledgments.   This work has been partially funded by the European Union's Erasmus Plus programme, grant agreement: 2018-1-EL01-KA203-047967 (Project: OPENLang Network). This publication reflects the views only of the authors, and the European Commission cannot be held responsible for any use which may be made of the information contained there.

References

1. Van Mol, C., Ekamper, P.: Destination cities of European exchange students. Geografisk Tidsskrift-Danish J. Geograph. **116**(1), 85–91 (2016)
2. Asoodar, M., Atai, M.R., Baten, L.: Successful Erasmus experience: analysing perceptions before, during and after Erasmus. J. Res. Int. Educ. **16**(1), 80–97 (2017)
3. Van Maele, J., Vassilicos, B., Borghetti, C.: Mobile students' appraisals of keys to a successful stay abroad experience: hints from the IEREST project. Lang. Intercult. Commun. **16**(3), 384–401 (2016)
4. Mitchell, K.: Student mobility and European identity: Erasmus study as a civic experience? J. Contemp. Eur. Res. **8**(4), 490–518 (2012)
5. Aslan, B., Jacobs, D.B.: Erasmus student mobility: Some good practices according to views of Ankara University exchange students. J. Educ. Future (5), 57–72 (2014)
6. Borghetti, C., Beaven, A.: Lingua francas and learning mobility: Reflections on students' attitudes and beliefs towards language learning and use. Int. J. Appl. Linguist. **27**(1), 221–241 (2017)
7. Llanes, À., Tragant, E., Serrano, R.: The role of individual differences in a study abroad experience: the case of Erasmus students. Int. J. Multiling. **9**(3), 318–342 (2012)
8. Gallarza, M.G., Fayos-Gardó, T., Arteaga-Moreno, F., Servera-Francés, D., Floristán-Imizcoz, E.: Different levels of loyalty towards the higher education service: evidence from a small university in Spain. Int. J. Manage. Educ. **14**(1), 36–48 (2019)

9. King, R., Findlay, A., Ahrens, J.: International student mobility literature review. Report to HEFCE, and co-funded by the British Council, UK National Agency for Erasmus, Utrecht University Repository (2010)

10. Dessoff, A.: Who's not going abroad? Int. Educ. 15(2), 20 (2006)

11. Mas-Alcolea, S.: 'I Thought I Was Prepared.' ERASMUS students' voices on their transition from L2 learners to L2 users. In: Second Language Study Abroad, pp. 223–255. Palgrave Macmillan, Cham (2018)

12. Beerkens, M., Souto-Otero, M., de Wit, H., Huisman, J.: Similar students and different countries? An analysis of the barriers and drivers for Erasmus participation in seven countries. J. Stud. Int. Educ. 20(2), 184–204 (2016)

13. European Union: Annual Report 2013 on the European Union's Development and external assistance policies and their implementation in 2012. Luxembourg: Publications Office of the European Union. https://ec.europa.eu/europeaid/sites/devco/files/annual-report-2013-eu-dev elopment-external-assistance-policies-implementation-in-2012_en.pdf

14. OLS Homepage. https://erasmusplusols.eu/en/. Accessed 21 Dec 2018

15. Varela, O.E.: Learning outcomes of study-abroad programs: a meta-analysis. Acad. Manage. Learn. Educ. 16(4), 531–561 (2017)

16. Carlson, J.S., Burn, B.B., Yachimowicz, D., Useem, J.: Study Abroad: The Experience of American Undergraduates, no. 37. Greenwood Publishing Group (1990)

17. Findlay, A.M., et al.: Motivations and Experiences of UK Students Studying Abroad, no. 8. BIS Research Paper, London (2010)

18. Souto Otero, M., McCoshan, A.: Survey of the Socio-economic Background of ERASMUS Students. Final Report. European Commission, DG Education and Culture. Brüssel (2006). http://ec.europa.eu/education/erasmus/doc/publ/survey06.Pdf

19. Krzaklewska, E., Krupnik, S.: Research report. The experience of studying abroad for exchange students in Europe. Erasmus Student Network in cooperation with Petrus Communications: Brussels (2006)

20. Isabelli-García, C., Bown, J., Plews, J.L., Dewey, D.P.: Language learning and study abroad. Lang. Teach. 51(4), 439–484 (2018)

21. Klimova, B.F.: EAP needs of Czech ERASMUS students. Proc.-Soc. Behav. Sci. 171, 294–298 (2015)

22. Schwieter, J.W., Ferreira, A., Miller, P.C.: Study abroad learners' metalinguistic and sociocultural reflections on short-and long-term international experiences. Intercult. Educ. 29(2), 236–257 (2018)

23. Kinginger, C.: Enhancing language learning in study abroad. Ann. Rev. Appl. Linguist. 31, 58–73 (2011)

24. Creswell, J.W., Plano Clark, V.L., Gutmann, M.L., Hanson, W.E.: Advanced mixed methods research designs. In: Handbook of Mixed Methods in Social and Behavioral Research, vol. 209, p. 240 (2003)

25. Harrell, M.C., Bradley, M.A.: Data collection methods. Semi-structured interviews and focus groups. Rand National Defense Research Institute, Santa Monica – CA (2009)

26. Ayres, L.: Semi-structured interview. In: The SAGE Encyclopedia of Qualitative Research Methods, pp. 811–813 (2008)

27. Kosmas, P.: Online sharing of knowledge among in-service teachers for professional development purposes. In: Proceedings of the 2017 9th International Conference on Education Technology and Computers, pp. 162–166 (2017)

28. Teichler, U.: Temporary study abroad: the life of ERASMUS students. Eur. J. Educ. 39(4), 395–408 (2004)

Designing a Virtual Exchange Intervention for the Development of Global Competence: An Exploratory Study

Anna Nicolaou(⊠)

Cyprus University of Technology, 31 Archbishop Kyprianos, PO Box 50329, 3036 Lemesos, Cyprus
anna.nicolaou@cut.ac.cy

Abstract. This study demonstrates the process of designing a virtual exchange intervention aiming at developing English for Specific Purposes (ESP) learners' global competence. The study adopted a three-phase Design-Based Research (DBR) approach which included the exploration phase, the implementation phase, and the reflection phase. In this paper, the exploration phase of the study is presented, which was conducted in order to gain insight on various aspects pertaining to virtual exchange embedded in ESP learning. The study was formulative in nature as it aimed to examine the feasibility of the intervention and determine the best intervention design. It also aimed at examining students' attitudes towards telecollaborative learning, their perceptions regarding the anticipated benefits and challenges of virtual exchange, as well as their suggestions concerning the implementation of the intervention. The study combined a mixed methods approach with secondary data collection through a review of similar studies, quantitative data collection by means of an opinion questionnaire, and qualitative data collection through focus groups with university students. The findings of the research provided a thorough understanding of the design of virtual exchange and formed the basis of a more conclusive subsequent study.

Keywords: Virtual exchange · Global competence · DBR · Exploratory study

1 Introduction

In response to the changing landscape and the complexity of our world today, there is an increasing need for educational reforms at all levels. In this context, various educational institutions and professional associations are beginning to acknowledge the need to add a global dimension to their education [1] and to enhance interculturality in young people [2]. Foreign language educators are constantly responding to the changing trajectories, by embracing new pedagogies and by taking advantage of the vast technological developments and seamless digital connectivity. The abundance of new technologies which characterizes our world today has created new teaching and learning opportunities that can be employed to support underpinning pedagogies and accomplish diverse learning goals, including the development of intercultural awareness and global competence. Among the recent technologically-mediated pedagogical approaches that have been practised aiming at building students' intercultural

© Springer Nature Switzerland AG 2020
P. Zaphiris and A. Ioannou (Eds.): HCII 2020, LNCS 12205, pp. 512–529, 2020.
https://doi.org/10.1007/978-3-030-50513-4_38

communicative competence is virtual exchange. Also known as telecollaboration, virtual exchange is a well-known pedagogical approach which involves engaging classes in online intercultural interaction and collaboration projects with geographically dispersed partners [3].

Virtual exchange has generally been positively received by teachers and students [4] and many studies have reported on various benefits of this pedagogical approach. These include the development of students' target language [5] the enhancement of intercultural awareness [6, 7] as well as the development of intercultural communicative competence as defined in Byram's model [8] in 1997 [9–11]. Virtual exchanges have also been reported to successfully accomplish other pedagogical goals, such as increasing student motivation [12] and learner autonomy [13] developing students' computer literacy [14] and enhancing multiliteracy skills [15]. However, in a world that is characterized by increased global communication, mobility, and digital connectivity, there is a need to reconsider the role of virtual exchange in education and explore its potential to develop informed, responsible and engaged citizens. McCloskey [16] argues that "foreign language ability, global awareness, and intercultural communication skills are increasingly recognised as essential dimensions of productive participation in the emerging economic, civic, political and social arenas of the 21st century". With this in mind, virtual exchange can provide a fertile ground for crossing global boundaries and meeting the demands of 21st century learners as empowered citizens of a democratic society who can advocate innovative solutions in response to many global and local problems, through their transnational partnerships.

The present study was an attempt to build the learners' global profile through virtual exchange projects that adopt a critical design. The goal was to create a telecollaborative habitat, rich in affordances for the development of global competences and active citizenship with a view to promoting a democratic culture in internationalised university language education. Considering that learning is most effective if it is relevant to students' needs, this study was situated at the nexus of global competence and content-based learning. The study adopted a three-phase Design-Based Research (DBR) approach which included the exploration phase, the implementation phase, and the reflection phase. DBR has been defined by Wang and Hannafin [17] as "a systematic but flexible methodology aimed to improve educational practices through iterative analysis, design, development, and implementation, based on collaboration among researchers and practitioners in real-world settings, leading to contextually sensitive design principles and theories". In this paper, the exploration phase of the study is presented, which was conducted in order to gain insight on various aspects pertaining to virtual exchange embedded in ESP learning. The findings of the research provided a thorough understanding of the design of virtual exchange and formed the basis of a more conclusive subsequent study.

2 Methodology

Exploratory research is conducted when problems are in a preliminary state, to generate formal hypotheses. Exploratory studies often rely on secondary research, such as reviewing available literature or adopting qualitative approaches such as focus groups in order to form the basis of the final study. As Singh [18] explains, exploratory research "can even help in determining research design, sampling, methodology and data collection method". The present study was formulative in nature as it aimed to examine the feasibility of the intervention and determine the best intervention design. It also aimed at examining students' attitudes towards telecollaborative learning, their perceptions regarding the anticipated benefits and challenges of virtual exchange, as well as their suggestions concerning the implementation of the intervention.

The exploration phase comprised of an investigatory study which included a secondary research with extensive review of similar studies taken in order to learn from their results, and a primary research which involved quantitative data collection by means of an opinion questionnaire, and qualitative data collection through focus groups with a purposive sample in order to lay the groundwork that subsequently led to the actual study. The exploration phase also served as a useful terrain to test data collection instruments and consider situational factors that could facilitate or hamper the planned interventions. Administering the pre-intervention questionnaire and rehearsing the focus groups helped gather preliminary information and establish an understanding of the context and target respondents' attitudes and opinions with regard to the study's scope. The approach followed in the exploration phase is in line with design-based research methodology which begins with a detailed analysis of the problem, context, participants and existing solutions. DBR often includes a pilot study so as to establish an understanding of contextual aspects and requirements. Subsequently, designers analyze the findings using multiple methodologies and based on systematic analysis, reflection, and theoretical guidance, they generate design localized principles [19]. Apart from the secondary research and primary research, exploration also included the quest for a virtual exchange partner to collaborate as a practitioner and a researcher in the planned interventions.

2.1   Secondary Research

Secondary research involved reviewing previous virtual exchange initiatives which aimed at expanding telecollaboration beyond the intercultural competence scope, adding a global outlook to this pedagogical approach. Furthermore, previous studies that adopted a lingua franca configuration or focused on content-based learning were explored. In addition, the review of previous studies aimed at investigating theoretical paradigms and design principles with an emphasis on the constituent parts of the virtual exchange ecosystem and how these, and interaction amongst them, can support or hamper opportunities for competence learning. Specifically, in the exploration phase, the elements of technological and linguistic mediation, task design and themes were examined.

2.2   Primary Research

The exploration phase included the collection of quantitative and qualitative data in order to develop a well-grounded picture of various aspects pertaining to telecollaboration embedded in content-based learning. Issues explored include expected affordances, limitations, feasibility and implementation, as well as anticipated challenges.

Quantitative data were gathered by means of questionnaires which were administered to a purposive sample of students that fit the characteristics of the sample of the planned subsequent interventions. In the exploration phase, the pre-intervention questionnaire was used for piloting purposes, as well as for gaining insights with regard to the target audience's intercultural experiences, motivation for language learning, and perceived affordances of virtual exchange embedded in language learning at university level.

Qualitative data collection was conducted by means of focus groups with a purposive sample of university learners. Focus groups are a form of group interview that capitalizes on communication and interaction between research participants in order to produce data. This method is considered useful for generating data by exploring people's knowledge and experience and can be utilized for examining what people think, how they think and why they think that way [20]. In the exploration phase, the focus groups revolved around the use of technology in language learning, opportunities of learning languages in culturally diverse settings, student collaboration, the mono-cultural character of the university, perceived benefits and pitfalls of telecollaboration, perceived gains, anticipated challenges, feasibility and implementation of virtual exchanges, possible modes and configurations, duration of exchange, possible partner countries, groupings, learner matching, tasks, and expected outcomes.

3   Findings

This part presents the findings of the exploratory phase of the DBR research. These findings led to the evolution of the preliminary principles which guided the design of the intervention that was implemented in the next phase of the research.

3.1   Review of Previous Studies

The exploration research was initiated with an extensive review of similar studies undertaken in the context of virtual exchange. Virtual exchange is not a completely new pedagogical approach [21] and numerous telecollaboration projects have been established to date in various educational contexts, involving different types of partners, web tools, and pedagogical practices [22]. Many virtual exchanges currently reported in the literature describe tandem projects whereby the learners communicate with their partners who are based in a different country in order to practice their language [13]. Under this model, learners adopt the roles of peer tutors who provide corrective feedback on their partners' language use. A different model of virtual exchange is the telecollaboration model whereby the focus extends from communicative competence to intercultural competence [23]. Intercultural telecollaborative projects are very often bicultural involving communication in the two partners' target languages. Lingua franca initiatives are sporadic in the virtual exchange arena despite the acknowledged benefits of using a shared language in intercultural partnerships. Kohn [24] sketches the lingua franca pedagogy adopted in the *Telecollaboration for Intercultural Language Acquisition* project (TILA) whereby "focus is on intercultural communicative exchanges between peers who are in the same language boat". According to Hoffstaedter and Kohn [25] who report on the TILA project, the lingua franca constellation can be highly motivating as it offers authentic communication on an equal footing. Learners seem to feel more confident and less worried to make mistakes as the focus is on getting the message across rather than on producing accurate utterances. Grazzi and Maranzana [26] similarly report on an intercultural telecollaboration project that was configured based on the ELF approach arguing that "this project has shown that the use of English as a lingua franca (ELF) by non-native speakers (NNS) of English within a networked-based context is not a hindrance to communication and mutual understanding. On the contrary, it proves to be an appropriate affordance that L2-users develop through social cooperative practices in order to carry out pragmatic communicative goals". With this in mind, a lingua franca approach was considered as an appropriate configuration in an emerging model of virtual exchange which aspires to add a global perspective to telecollaborative learning. As Graddol cited in O'Dowd [3] argues, today's graduates are more likely to use English as a lingua franca with non-native speakers in their prospective professional careers. Therefore, using a shared language in virtual interactions and in collaborative productions of common artefacts seems to be a suitable approach for affording opportunities to university learners for more realistic intercultural encounters.

Despite the recognized benefits of the aforementioned lingua franca initiatives, what seems to be missing from various virtual exchange projects is criticality, a notion that has been emphasized in Byram's [8] concept of Critical Cultural Awareness (CCA), as part of his broader model of Intercultural Communicative Competence. CCA implies a personal and social transformation through intercultural dialogue. This transformation emanates from critical exploration, analysis and evaluation of self and other [27]. Criticality is at the heart of intercultural citizenship education. However, very few virtual exchange projects have embraced the notion of criticality in their objectives. One remarkable example is *Soliya's Connect Program*, a dialogic model for telecollaboration [28] designed to address the tensions between Western and Arab and Muslim societies [21]. What differentiates the Soliya Connect Program from more traditional models of telecollaboration is the fact that participants are gradually taken out of their comfort zones and are encouraged to synchronously engage in discourse on conflicting topics In fact, divisive topics are deliberately addressed and conflict is not considered to be a barrier to dialogue; instead, potential conflicting views are seen as an opportunity for transformation [28]. This echoes Barnett's [29] 'transformatory critique' or a' refashioning of traditions'. The Soliya Connect Program offers a valid pedagogical approach by engaging participants in intercultural dialogue which is not limited to safe topics. Instead, it dares to encourage participants to delve into conversations that may spark conflict. This affords a significant opportunity for participants to "engage with multiple subjectivities and perspectives in a safe environment where they are free to dig deeper to acquire intercultural understanding" [28].

In addition, very few virtual exchange initiatives have been framed in the concepts of global interconnectivity [30] and critical social engagement. Global competence and active citizenship have been explicitly reported as project goals in limited virtual exchange projects to date. One such project is the Malvinas/Falklands online intercultural citizenship action research project implemented in an EFL classroom in Argentina [31]. Through comparative tasks and collaborative artefact creation that revolved around the Malvinas/Falklands war fought between Argentina and the UK in

1982, learners developed a critical perspective on different texts, reaching the highest level of criticality as defined by Barnett [29] which is the transformatory critique in action especially because the participants' activities were not confined within the partnership; instead they were expanded to the participants' local communities through the creation and sharing of artefacts in the learners' local contexts [31]. Such projects place human rights education at the heart of the exchange and empower learners to act as responsible citizens towards addressing global or local conflict and justice. These initiatives take intercultural discourse beyond the 4Fs - Food, Festival, Folklore, and Fashion [32] which many times results in a reduced perspective of cultural difference. Projects like the Soliya Connect Program and the Malvinas/Falklands online intercultural citizenship initiative are designed with a social perspective, capitalizing on international groups' dynamics towards addressing the critical current issues our world is faced with today. These initiatives require the development and deployment of various global competences, such as valuing cultural diversity, respect, responsibility, empathy, and knowledge of self, among others, which will enable the partners to achieve their common social goals.

Virtual exchange projects embedded in a content-based language context are also scarce in the literature. Most telecollaborative projects are implemented in general language courses or teacher education programs. For the purposes of this study, a review of studies reporting on projects undertaken in the context of English for Specific Purposes (ESP) or Language for Specific Purposes (LSP) modules was conducted. Among the studies that have been reviewed is one that concerns a project implemented in an intercultural tandem between language teachers as part of their teacher training or practicum [33]. A different project by Rolinska, Guariento and Al-Masri [34] reports on a telecollaboration between the University of Glasgow and the Islamic University of Gaza. In this dual project, postgraduate students of Science Engineering and Technology in Glasgow (SET) were mentored by SET graduates with strong language skills in Gaza (EAST 1), while at the same time, postgraduate Biomedical students in Glasgow were partnered with Biomed graduates in Gaza (EAST 2). These two projects relied on a lingua franca, subject-specific, peer review telecollaboration model aiming at responding to the students' need to perform effectively in global communication and increase their employability prospects. The EAST projects demonstrated how technology-enabled interventions to subject-specific language courses may positively affect the learning experience enabling participants to start working towards global competence [34].

A different content-based virtual exchange project is a multiliteracies model for telecollaboration which was designed to address the specific needs of students of Business and Economics [35]. The project was grounded in the theories of Foreign Language Learning (FLE) and Global Virtual Teams (GVT) and was carried out between students at the University of Paderborn in Germany and Masaryk University in Brno in the Czech Republic. The exchange was embedded in ESP courses for Business and Economics at each university in a blended learning framework which included elements from both telecollaboration and GVT models, providing students with valuable situated practice for workplace settings that they are likely to come across in their future careers. A final example of content-based telecollaboration is the X-Culture Project [36]. The X-Culture project was an attempt to enhance learning in

International Business courses by affording business students the opportunity to experience the challenges and learn best practices of international collaboration by working with their international counterparts. Communication and coordination among the X-Culture participants has been conducted using free online collaboration tools, such as email, Skype, Google+ , Facebook, Dropbox, and Doodle. These tools were selected as they are the ones that are commonly used by employees of multi-national companies. The particular project has involved over 4,000 students to date and the results reported so far indicate enhanced learning between pre- and post-project cultural intelligence.

3.2   Technological Mediation

The secondary research included an exploration of the available technologies that can be used to mediate virtual exchange aiming to develop learners' global competence while enhancing their understanding of discipline-specific content. Considering the vast affordances and potential that new technologies offer in learning today, various Web 2.0 applications were examined for the purposes of this study in order to select the most appropriate ones that would serve as the mediating online environment where inter-action and communication among students would occur. Tools were examined and analyzed in terms of modes and potential for synchronous, asynchronous communication, support of autonomy, interactivity, and multimodality. Technologies exploration was performed having in mind the mediating effect of online tools [15] and their potential to foster sustained communication and interaction between students [37].

For the purposes of this study, Google+ was investigated for its pedagogical value, and its potential to serve as a mediating online milieu for virtual exchange. Google+ is a relatively new social networking service that was launched by Google Inc. in 2011. Despite the fact that Google+ was discontinued in 2019 for business use and consumers, during its short life cycle it provided an alternative to other popular social networking sites, such as Facebook. Google+ is similar to Facebook but with some additional features that can afford a rich and diverse intercultural experience for users. Google+ is free and can be joined with a Google Account. Features include the ability to post photos and status updates to the stream or interest-based communities, group different types of relationships into Circles. It also features multi-person instant messaging, text and video chat called Hangouts, events, location tagging, and the ability to edit and upload photos to private cloud-based albums [38]. Google+ Communities allow users to create ongoing conversations about particular topics and can function as a locus for discussion and exchange of views rather than as a way to teach the language. Posts on the Communities can be responded to or commented on.

Google+ user's profile includes basic social networking services like a profile photo, an About section, background photo, cover photo, previous work and school history, interests, places lived, an updates space, contact information, places visited, and other profiles the user has or pages the user contributes to. Google+ Hangouts are free video conferencing calls with up to 10 people, done through the Google+ website or mobile app. Many apps can be used inside the hangout, allowing users to share documents, a scratchpad, or their screens with other users, as well as many built-in apps such as YouTube, Google Docs, and the new Capture [39]. Google+ has a +1 Button which allows people to recommend sites and parts of sites, similar in use to Facebook's Like button. Finally, Google Drive is a file storage and synchronization service created by Google. It allows users to store files in the cloud, share files, and edit documents, spreadsheets, and presentations with collaborators. Google Drive encompasses Google Docs, Sheets, and Slides, an office suite that permits collaborative editing of documents, spreadsheets, presentations, drawings, forms, and more [40].

3.3 Findings from Questionnaires

A questionnaire was administered to 53 ESP students enrolled at the Cyprus University of Technology (CUT). A total of 53 completed questionnaires were returned. All participants were of Cypriot origin and thirty-three students were male while 20 were female. All participants were first-year students at the CUT, with 28 majoring in Agriculture, Biotechnology and Food Science and 24 majoring in Mechanical Engineering and Materials Science. Participation was voluntary and anonymity was ensured.

One of the aims of the pre-intervention questionnaire was to collect data pertaining to the learners' perceptions about technological mediation in language learning at tertiary level. Since virtual exchanges are inherently technologically supported, there was a need to map the learners' online profile with emphasis on their experience with various Web 2.0 tools and the extent to which they felt comfortable with the integration of technology in language learning. The participants in the exploration phase, as well as in the subsequent interventions in the implementation phase, comprise the 'digital natives' population [41]; therefore, they are expected to be technologically-savvy. However, the varied technological implications of the planned virtual exchange mandated a deeper exploration of the learners' technological profile in order to facilitate the selection of appropriate tools for the exchange as well as to determine the level of training that might be needed to enable students to carry out the project tasks. A multiple-response analysis was computed to identify the social networks learners were mostly engaged in. The analysis indicated that the most widely used social media sites were Facebook, followed by Skype, YouTube, Oovoo, and Google+ . This analysis was taken into consideration during the selection of available social networks to facilitate synchronous and asynchronous interaction between the virtual exchange partners.

A different type of analysis measured the participants' attitudes towards the integration of technology in their language learning modules at university. On a Likert scale 1–4 whereby 1 meant 'Not at all' and 4 meant 'Very much', students indicated that their previous experience with technology-enhanced language learning was adequate (3.43), and that their attitudes towards the use of technology in language learning were considerably above average. The exploration phase aimed at gaining insight in the participants' views about virtual exchange as a pedagogical practice embedded in university language learning. This information was deemed important as it would give an indication of the students' attitudes towards telecollaboration with emphasis on the expected gains of this approach and was expected to facilitate the smooth integration of virtual exchange in the module under scrutiny. The analysis indicated that the most anticipated benefit of telecollaboration would be the development of students' linguistic skills, followed by the opportunity to get closer to other cultures. A similar analysis was performed to explore the participants' expected challenges of telecollaboration. This information was considered to be important for the design of the project as it provided insights into the learners' concerns, inhibitions, or insecurities. The analysis indicated that the participants' most anticipated challenge pertained to individual insecurities or lack of confidence in interacting with people who are not members of their immediate environment. Other anticipated challenges included concerns about an increase in their workload and lack of openness to interact with people of diverse cultural backgrounds.

With regard to cultural awareness, students were asked to respond to 20 Likert-type questions from 1–4 whereby 1 meant 'Strongly Disagree' and 4 meant 'Strongly Agree'. The questions were devised by the researchers of the study, drawing from literature on intercultural competence and global citizenship. This set of questions aimed at exploring students' level of cultural awareness and was relevant to their views and perceptions of other cultures, their curiosity and willingness to interact with people from different cultural backgrounds, as well as their reactions and attitudes in cases of discrimination based on cultural differences. Some of these questions were the following: *I think that all cultures have something to offer the world; When I notice cultural differences, my culture seems to have the best approach; I think that my culture is the only right one; I speak up if I witness another person being humiliated or discriminated against; Most of my friends are from my own ethnic background; I'm interested in the ideas and beliefs of people from different ethnicities; It's really hard for me to feel close to a person of another ethnicity.* A Cronbach's Alpha reliability test was carried out in SPSS in order to measure the internal consistency ("reliability") of the set of 20 questions. The analysis indicated a high level of internal consistency for the scale with the specific sample (0.796). Table 1 demonstrates the Cronbach's Alpha analysis computed in the exploration phase:

Table 1. Cultural Awareness Cronbach's Alpha analysis

Reliability statistics		
Cronbach's Alpha	Cronbach's Alpha based on standardized items	N of Items
0.796	0.799	20

After conducting the reliability test, the participants' level of cultural awareness based on the 20 items was measured. The analysis indicated a medium level of cultural awareness with a mean score at 2.94. This information was considered important in the design of the intervention as it depicted the participants' intercultural profile. Table 2 demonstrates the learners' level of cultural awareness based on the set of 20 items:

Table 2. Participants' level of Cultural Awareness

Cultural awareness		
N	M	SD
53	2.94	0.321

Overall, the quantitative data analysis yielded useful information regarding the targeted learners' attitudes towards technology-enhanced language learning and pointed to a number of technological tools that could be utilized in the planned exchanges. In addition, the attitudes of the learners towards telecollaboration were explored, placing emphasis on the anticipated benefits and challenges. The students' indication of inhibition towards interacting with people of diverse cultural backgrounds, coupled with their medium level of cultural awareness based on the analysis of their responses in the respective 20 items, was taken into consideration in the design of the interventions. Finally, the piloting of the questionnaire led to minor modifications in the wording of a few questions and typographical corrections.

3.4 Findings from Focus Groups

The findings from quantitative data analysis were corroborated in the qualitative analysis which was performed by means of focus groups with a small sample of learners fitting the description of the target group in the planned interventions. The sample comprised of 12 ESP learners at the Cyprus University of Technology. Two rounds of focus group took place which lasted approximately 45 min each. Six Agriculture, Biotechnology and Food Science ESP students participated in the first round (4 female and 2 male students), and 6 Mechanical Engineering and Materials Science ESP students participated in the second round (1 female and 5 male students). The focus groups aimed to build a synergistic partnership comprised of the teachers and learners in order to negotiate the planned study in terms of design and implementation. The focus groups aspired to bring the learners' previous experiences into the research process and utilize them to inform the study. This phase was also an effort to rehearse guided questions with subjects similar to the target group. Questions asked were open-ended, specifically related to the main issues of the survey. Topics discussed included the use of technology in language learning, opportunities of learning languages in culturally diverse settings, student collaboration, the monocultural character of the Cypriot university, as well as anticipated benefits and challenges of telecollaboration. In addition, the focus groups aimed at collecting data regarding the feasibility and implementation of the virtual exchange, with emphasis on configurations and situational factors, such as possible modes, duration, partner grouping, and preferred activities. Data from focus groups were analyzed qualitatively in NVivo. The findings from both rounds of focus groups provided great insights on where students stand on the issue of technology and intercultural learning and formed the basis of the subsequent study. Emergent themes included the extensive use of technology both for educational and recreational purposes and the view that technology-enhanced language learning can be beneficial. At the same time, the participants' limited opportunities for cross-cultural encounters both in their personal and educational lives were highlighted. Participant 6 says: *"I think that studying at CUT deprives us of the opportunity to learn more new cultures in foreign countries. We would meet new people, we would talk with each other, we would collaborate with other people, we would learn the language better, and our job prospects would increase."*

During the focus groups, positive attitudes towards telecollaborative learning were expressed by the participants referring to the anticipated gains of this pedagogical approach. The benefits reported pertain to the opportunity to meet people from different cultures and learn new things, the encouragement of reserved or low-achieving learners to participate, the challenge of stereotypes and the fight against racism, as well as the potential that telecollaboration may entail in fostering global perspectives: *I believe it is essential because in our times of technology and globalization being able to communicate with many people and exchange ideas with as many people and groups is possible is very useful. This way you will absorb as much information as possible and you will draw the best conclusions. Being one-sided and staying in your own place... it's not even your own place, there is no 'my', we share everything whatsoever. We are a big village.* (Participant 2).

Despite the acknowledged benefits of telecollaboration, some learners exhibited reluctance and feelings of inhibition towards participating in telecollaborative learning. Some of the reasons behind their negative attitudes included the increase of workload, and the lack of technological resources: *With all this workload that we have, all the studying, we would see it as a chore, as a burden because it would keep us behind in our other courses* (Participant 12). Other participants expressed feelings of skepticism and doubtfulness with regard to the usefulness of this activity in language and intercultural learning, compared to face-to-face communication which was considered to afford more potential in achieving these goals: *It won't be of any help in any of these aspects. It will just be a good experience. You can't learn the language by talking to somebody three times or by doing a task together; you won't increase your ICT knowledge either; you won't get to know the other culture because you will speak 3-4 times about the task; it will just be a new experience* (Participant 9).

With regard to the feasibility and implementation of the telecollaboration project, the focus groups yielded useful data that were considered in the design of the first iterative cycle. This approach is in line with design-based research whereby 'subjects' are acknowledged as part of the design process [42], contributing with their insights and constructive comments. To ensure feasibility of the project, the participants suggested that the telecollaboration should be carefully embedded in the course curriculum. Participant 1 comments: *"Basically this should be part of a program and you should be able to cope in this program because you won't have an alternative time to communicate with the other person".*

In addition, the students recommended a lingua franca approach which would place all participants "in the same language boat" [24]. A participant explains that "*...it would be much easier to communicate with someone who doesn't speak English well than with somebody who speaks English well because you will be on the same level. Easy stuff will be easy stuff for both",* (Participant 12). In addition, participants exhibited preference for project work rather than isolated tasks, and they would like to be engaged in domain-specific projects which are relevant to their field of study: *"If we* *had a project, it would be more helpful in terms of motivation. Not just a task in English which is irrelevant to what you are majoring in"*, (Participant 9).

As for the mediating tools, the students recommended the usage of multiple technologies in order to benefit from the affordances of each type and achieve the project goals. A participant explains that *"...there should be a combination of technologies, you will connect to Skype to talk, and you will also log on Moodle and see certain things about the tasks. I believe you need more than two-three modes so as to collaborate with someone*, (Participant 9). This view is reinforced by another participant who believes that *"...you will definitely want to talk on Skype, but also use email to send a document, show your work to the other person and exchange views*, (Participant 8).

As far as the duration of the project is concerned, most participants recommended a three-month period for collaboration with the possibility of sustaining the exchange on a personal basis: *"It could last for three or four months in order to do the assignments, but then you could have the option to continue communicating as friends; that would be even better"*, (Participant 2). Finally, discussing the possibility for individual or group work, the participants were in favor of working in groups so as to feel more confident and comfortable: *"...it would be better if you had groups, so as to be able to have conversations together. You might feel scared. Being in a group will make you feel more comfortable"*, (Participant 10).

3.5   Virtual Exchange Partnership

The virtual exchange partnership was established via the UNICollaboration platform. UNICollaboration is an online platform designed to support telecollaboration at university level. The platform resulted from the INTENT (Integrating Telecollaborative Networks in University Foreign Language Education) project [43] and it has been developed in order guide university educators towards setting up, implementing and evaluating telecollaboration exchanges. Educators can find the resources and training materials necessary to learn about and to set up telecollaborative exchanges. The platform includes a partner-finding tool, a task databank, an e-portfolio for evaluating telecollaborative projects, a databank of sample projects, a project-planning tool, as well as text- and video-based training materials. A class was added on the UNICollaboration platform, in search of a partner class. After the initial contact was made by email and several online meetings that followed, a telecollaboration exchange was set up between a university in Cyprus and a university in Spain. Official invitations were sent by each partner university and an agreement was signed between the two teachers/researchers.

The two teachers/researchers conducted numerous online meetings on Skype prior to the initiation of the intervention in order to tune in to each other, discuss the research plan, and negotiate the various elements of the virtual exchange ecosystem. The two partner teachers exhibited openness to alternate pedagogical beliefs, a willingness to adapt to other approaches, compromise in task design, and find common ground [44]. The two practitioners agreed on their defined role as facilitators who would prepare their students for the exchange, debrief them following contact with their partners, and embed the themes of interaction into their courses ensuring that tasks were well-integrated into the course objectives of both modules [44]. In addition, the two teachers established an agreement on objectives of the intervention, the selection and structuring of task sequence, the technological mediation, the project's timeline, and assessment. Since both teachers were bound by a course syllabus which included other content-based assignments and comprehensive examinations, they agreed to assign a percentage of the total work to active participation in the virtual exchange project and completion of tasks. Furthermore, the two teachers positioned themselves as researchers in the project who would rigorously observe competence learning via multiple methods. The teachers recognized the importance of overcoming any asymmetries in their institutional contexts in terms of technological affordances, abundance of resources, learners' intercultural profiles and biographies, and the value placed in language learning at each context. Both teachers acknowledged their personal contribution in the success or failure of the intervention; therefore, they committed to continuously monitoring the project in order to achieve the intended learning outcomes. Together they carefully planned the intervention, exhibiting flexibility, adaptability, and willingness to modify the original plans along the way.

4 Discussion

In general, the analysis of both quantitative and qualitative data, as well as the review of previous studies facilitated the identification of the main issues that should be considered in the design of the first intervention. The multiple data collected at this phase helped establish an understanding of the target participants' opinions and attitudes associated with the study's central themes and questions. The exploration phase contributed to the familiarization with the settings and the constituent elements of the virtual exchange ecosystem, forming a well-grounded picture of the situation under investigation. The exploration phase resulted in the proposed first intervention which was identified as a pilot inter-disciplinary lingua franca virtual exchange project between ESP learners at a university in Cyprus and a university in Spain. The targeted modules were benchmarked at B1-B2 CEFR level and the targeted participants were ESP learners majoring in undergraduate degrees at the respective universities. The interventions were designed to last for one academic semester (13–15 weeks). Communication modes included synchronous and asynchronous communication in a blended learning environment and a friendly, non-threatening atmosphere.

4.1 Preliminary Design Guidelines

The exploration phase, informed by secondary research and mixed-methods data collection, led to the evolution of preliminary principles which guided the design and implementation of the first intervention aimed at developing learners' global competence through an internationalised ESP curriculum.

The first preliminary design principle concerned the adoption of a monolingual configuration whereby participants would communicate, interact and collaborate using a shared target language, English as a Lingua Franca (ELF). This would enable learners to engage in the exchange with confidence, adopting the role of collaborator rather than the role of tutor. The lingua franca approach would render all participants equal in the exchange, and each one would contribute to the discussion constructively without worrying about making mistakes. This was mentioned in the focus groups whereby students highlighted the importance of using a common language for facilitating communication. Therefore, in the planned virtual exchange, language would be viewed as a mediating vehicle that would facilitate the exchange of views, foster meaningful interaction and support the creative collaboration on shared tasks. This design principle was also informed by the extensive review of literature in ELF and global citizenship. The adoption of a lingua franca rather than a bilingual/bicultural configuration is in accord with a 'global' paradigm in learning, shifting away from the 'intercultural' paradigm, offering a more realistic opportunity for interaction, which resembles the kind of encounters learners will engage in their future life and career. As Lenkaitis and Loranc-Paszylk [45] argue, the use of a common language between and among interlocutors has the ability to create shared territories and it provides a suitable space to discuss topics that reflect their distinct ideologies. This can be crucial in the enhancement of global citizenship.

The second preliminary principle pertained to the participants in the exchange, namely the learners and the teachers who create together synergistic partnerships in order to inform the exchange and contribute towards the success of the intervention. The students are considered as significant stakeholders who contribute to the design, implementation and evaluation of the exchange in an effort to leverage the intervention and allow the affordances to emerge. Similarly, the teachers/researchers are cautious observers, rigorously recording instances of competence learning, and exhibiting flexibility in modifying the design if the need arises. This principle was guided by the methodological approach that was adopted in this study. Design-based research considers students as significant stakeholders who contribute to the design, implementation and evaluation of interventions. This form of participatory design is also in line with a global citizenship approach which advocates democratic participation, experiential engagement, and critical reflection upon learning [46].

The third design principle concerned the technological mediation of the exchange. The choice and deployment of technological tools should be examined thoroughly as it might affect the success or failure of the project. The different tools must be evaluated based on their unique features to support the project goals and their appropriateness in relation to the designed tasks and expected outcomes. In a global competence oriented virtual exchange, the tools and technologies selected must facilitate the development and deployment of clusters of competences, such as openness to cultural otherness or skills of listening and observing, via the use of tools that allow synchronous communication in order to establish social presence and a sense of connection with the partners. Similarly, the development of cooperation skills which is central in global competence learning should be facilitated through technologies that afford opportunities for collaborative work and co-creation of meaning and common products. Therefore, as students mentioned in the focus groups, a combination of technologies should be selected consisting of at least two or three modes, each serving a different purpose and facilitating different objectives. The analysis of the exploratory questionnaire as well as the focus groups highlighted the students' extensive use of technology and the variety of tools and applications they are engaged with. This suggests that a multimodal environment whereby students engage with multiple technologies for interaction and collaboration would be positively received. Therefore, the planned intervention would be mediated by a technology-rich environment, affording an array of opportunities for cross-cultural communication and meaningful cooperation. A careful examination of Google+ and its features led to the selection of Google+ Communities, Hangouts and Drive as the locus of interaction, communication and collaborative task completion among the telecollaboration partners. Google + Communities were determined as a free stage for students to voice their views with confidence and creativity. The possibility to respond to or comment on posts was expected to initiate authentic, social interaction and meaningful discussions. Activities on Google+ Communities support peer interaction through informal exchanges and students can be encouraged to share their opinions without worrying about their writing styles, tones of voices, or language errors since lenient ground rules can be established in order to cultivate a freedom-of-speech atmosphere [47]. Google Hangouts were used for synchronous exchanges either via chat, audio, or video interactions. To ensure participation of all learners in the tasks and to accommodate all participants' preferences or technological limitations, students were allowed to choose between synchronous oral communication sessions or asynchronous written communication. Google Docs were used as cloud-based alternatives for word processing, utilizing their feature of simultaneous work on the same document by many users which makes it a powerful tool for collaborative writing. In addition, Moodle, the institutional learning management system used at the Cypriot university, and Aula Virtual, the institutional learning management system used at the Spanish university, were included in the technologies used within the interventions in order to manage the project locally. Moodle and Aula Virtual are password-protected, open source platforms that allow for data storage, file sharing and asynchronous and synchronous interaction. Other Web 2.0 tools and applications included Google Forms for completing the pre- and post-intervention questionnaires, Kahoot! and blubbr for playing intercultural games, Moviemaker, iMovie, animoto and other multimedia software for creating the digital stories, YouTube for creating and uploading videos, as well as PowerPoint and Prezi for developing and delivering oral presentations [48].

The fourth design principle concerns the design of tasks. Informed by weak approaches to telecollaborative task design, the planned intervention aimed at bridging the gulf between mere exchange of cultures and real global learning within an international collaboration. Therefore, task design should be established with a social perspective, aiming at facilitating the emergence of affordances for global competence learning. Tasks should be designed with a view to promoting meaningful interaction and collaboration towards achieving common goals which go beyond the sharing of and exchanging cultural information. In addition, as it was emphasised in the focus groups discussions, the tasks should be embedded in the respective courses' curricula and be informed by them in order to place the learners' academic and professional needs at the centre of the exchange. Students clearly highlighted the importance of communicating around tasks that reflect their majors; therefore, this was taken into account in the design of the proposed intervention.

The final principle is related to the choice of themes that underpin the exchange. In an emerging model that aspires to develop global competence, the topics should not be limited to the 4Fs - Food, Festival, Folklore, and Fashion. Instead, themes should revolve around critical 21st century issues, highlighting the interconnectedness of our world today and the dynamics of international partnerships in the global arena. This principle was informed by a critical review of previous virtual exchange projects which engaged learners in superficial discourse. In addition, this principle was guided by the analysis of the focus groups which pointed to the inclusion of themes that are grounded in related domain-specific areas in order to enable learners to relate with the topics. In the present study, the themes were selected with a global view, reflecting the realities of the 21st century. The selected themes underlined the construct of culture in a transnational perspective, highlighting the interconnectedness and interdependence of the world and the need for learners to consider international dynamics in order to effectively live, work and prosper in the global arena. In addition, a content-based ESP perspective informed the selection of themes in order to accommodate the learners' academic and future professional needs.

5 Conclusion

The exploratory study, undertaken as part of a three-phase design-based research, provided significant insights pertaining to the design and implementation of a virtual exchange project aiming at building ESP learners' global competences through internationalized discipline-specific language learning. Using exploratory research to guide the design of the subsequent studies helped identify the main issues that should be addressed and established an understanding of the most important contextual elements of the virtual exchange habitat before attempting to implement the interventions. The thorough exploration of the context through secondary and primary research resulted in a set of useful preliminary guidelines while rendering the learners significant contributors in the design process.

Acknowledgments. Portions of this manuscript are drawn from my unpublished doctoral thesis: Nicolaou, Anna (2020). The Affordances of Virtual Exchange for Developing Global Competence and Active Citizenship in Content-Based Language Learning. Unpublished doctoral thesis, Trinity College Dublin, the University of Dublin.

References

1. Cushner, K., Brennan, S.: Intercultural Student Teaching: A Bridge to Global Competence. Rowman & Littlefield Education, Blue Ridge Summit, PA (2007)
2. Jackson, J.: Cultivating cosmopolitan, intercultural citizenship through critical reflection and international, experiential learning. Lang. Intercult. Commun. **11**(2), 80–96 (2011)
3. O'Dowd, R.: A transnational model of virtual exchange for global citizenship education. Lang. Teach. J. **1**, 1–14 (2019)
4. Helm, F.: The practices and challenges of telecollaboration in higher education in Europe. Lang. Learn. Technol. **19**(2), 197–217 (2015)

5. Dooly, M.: Telecollaborative Language Learning. Peter Lang, Bern (2008)
6. Furstenberg, G., Levet, S., English, K., Maillet, K.: Giving a virtual voice to the silent language of culture: the cultura project. Lang. Learn. Technol. **5**(1), 55–102 (2001)
7. Kramsch, C., Thorne, S.: Foreign Language Learning as Global Communicative Practice, pp. 83–100. Globalization and language teaching (2002)
8. Byram, M.: Teaching and Assessing Intercultural Communicative Competence. Multilingual Matters, Clevedon (1997)
9. O'Dowd, R.: Telecollaboration and the Development of Intercultural Communicative Competence. Langenscheidt, Berlin (2006)
10. O'Dowd, R., Ritter, M.: Understanding and working with 'failed communication' in telecollaborative exchanges. CALICO J. **23**(3), 623–642 (2013)
11. Belz, J.A.: Linguistic perspectives on the development of intercultural competence in telecollaboration. Lang. Learn. Technol. **10**(1), 42–66 (2003)
12. Ware, P.: "Missed" communication in online communication: tensions in a German-American telecollaboration. Lang. Learn. Technol. **9**(2), 64–89 (2005)
13. O'Rourke, B.: Models of telecollaboration (1): eTandem. Lang. Intercult. Commun. Educ. **15**, 41 (2007)
14. Hauck, M.: Critical success factors in a TRIDEM exchange. ReCALL **19**(2), 202–223 (2007)
15. Fuchs, C., Hauck, M., Müller-Hartmann, A.: Promoting learner autonomy through multiliteracy skills development in cross-institutional exchanges. Lang. Learn. Technol. **16**(3), 82–102 (2012)
16. McCloskey, E.M.: Global teachers: a model for building teachers' intercultural competence online. Sci. J. Med. Educ. **38**(XIX), 41–49 (2012)
17. Wang, F., Hannafin, M.J.: Design-based research and technology-enhanced learning environments. Educ. Technol. Res. Dev. **53**(4), 5–23 (2005)
18. Singh, K.: Quantitative Social Research Methods. Sage (2007)
19. Cobb, P., Confrey, J., DiSessa, A., Lehrer, R., Schauble, L.: Design experiments in educational research. Educ. Res. **32**(1), 9–13 (2003)
20. Kitzinger, J.: Introducing focus groups. Br. Med. J. **311**(7000), 299–302 (1995). [Electronic version]
21. Helm, F.: The long and winding road... J. Virtual Exch. **I**, 41–63 (2018). Research-publishing.net
22. O'Dowd, R.: The competences of the telecollaborative teacher. Lang. Learn. J. **43**(2), 194–207 (2015)
23. O'Dowd, R.: From telecollaboration to virtual exchange: state-of-the-art and the role of UNI Collaboration in moving forward. J. Virtual Exch. **1**, 1–23 (2018)
24. Kohn, K.: From ELF communication to lingua franca pedagogy. English as a Lingua Franca: Perspectives and Prospects: Contributions in Honour of Barbara Seidlhofer Boston. De Gruyter Mouton, Berlin (2016)
25. Hoffstaedter, P., Kohn, K.: Telecollaboration for intercultural foreign language conversations in secondary school contexts: task design and pedagogic implementation. TILA Research Results on Telecollaboration (2015)
26. Grazzi, E., Maranzana, S.: ELF and intercultural telecollaboration: a case study. Intercult. Commun., New Perspectives from ELF (2016)
27. Houghton, S.A.: Intercultural dialogue in practice: managing value judgment through foreign language education. Multilingual matters (2012)
28. Helm, F.: A dialogic model for telecollaboration. Bellaterra J. Teach. Learn. Lang. Lit. **6**(2), 28–48 (2013)

29. Barnett, R.: Higher Education: A Critical Business. McGraw-Hill Education, New York City (1997)
30. Rizvi, F.: Towards cosmopolitan learning. Discourse: Stud. Cult. Polit. Educ. **30**(3), 253–268 (2009)
31. Porto, M.: Affordances, complexities, and challenges of intercultural citizenship for foreign language teachers. Foreign Lang. Ann. **52**(1), 141–164 (2019)
32. Meyer, C.F., Rhoades, E.K.: Multiculturalism: beyond food, festival, folklore, and fashion. Kappa Delta Pi Rec. **42**(2), 82–87 (2006)
33. Krajka, J., Marczak, M., Tatar, S., Yildiz, S.: Building ESP teacher awareness through intercultural tandems–post-practicum experience. Engl. Specif. Purp. World **14**(38), 1–18 (2013)
34. Guariento, B., Al-Masri, N., Rolinska, A.: Investigating EAST: A Scotland-Gaza English for Academic Study Telecollaboration between SET Students. Investigating EAST: A Scotland-Gaza English for Academic Study Telecollaboration between SET Students (2016)
35. Lindner, R.: Developing communicative competence in global virtual teams: a multiliteracies approach to telecollaboration for students of business and economics. CASALC Rev. **1**, 144–156 (2016)
36. Taras, V., et al.: Changing the face of international business education: the X-culture project. AIB Insights **12**(4), 11–17 (2012)
37. Hampel, R., Hauck, M.: Computer-mediated language learning: making meaning in multimodal virtual learning spaces. JALT CALL J. **2**(2), 3–18 (2006)
38. Gundotra, V.: Introducing the Google+ project: real-life sharing, rethought for the web. Google Official Blog (2011)
39. Diaz, S.: As Google+ opens to everyone, hangouts get boost to challenge more than Facebook. Googling Google (blog of ZDNet) (2011). Accessed 26 Jan 2016
40. Pichai, S.: Introducing Google Drive… Yes, Really. Google Official Blog (2012)
41. Prensky, M.: Digital natives, digital immigrants. Horizon **9**(5), 1–5 (2001)
42. Barab, S., Squire, K.: Design-based research: putting a stake in the ground. J. Learn. Sci. **13**(1), 1–14 (2004)
43. O'Dowd, R.: The INTENT project: integrating telecollaborative networks into foreign language higher education. EuroCALL Rev. **21**(1), 54–59 (2013)
44. O'Dowd, R., Ware, P.: Critical issues in telecollaborative task design. Comput. Assisted Lang. Learn. **22**(2), 173–188 (2009)
45. Lenkaitis, C.A., Loranc-Paszylk, B: Facilitating global citizenship development in lingua franca virtual exchanges. Lang. Teach. Res. (2019). https://doi.org/10.1177/13621688198773711
46. Annette, J.: Service learning in an international context. Front.: Interdisc. J. Study Abroad **8**(1), 83–93 (2002)
47. Chen, W.C., Shih, Y.C.D., Liu, G.Z.: Task design and its induced learning effects in a cross-institutional blog-mediated telecollaboration. Comput. Assist. Lang. Learn. **28**(4), 285–305 (2015)
48. Nicolaou, A., Sevilla-Pavón, A.: Exploring telecollaboration through the lens of university students: a Spanish-Cypriot telecollaborative exchange. In: Jager, S., Kurek, M., O'Rourke, B. (eds.) New Directions in Telecollaborative Research and Practice: Selected Papers from the Second International Conference on Telecollaboration in Higher Education, pp. 113–120. Research-publishing. Net (2016). https://doi.org/10.14705/rpnet.2016.telecollab2016.497

Global Impact of Local Educational Innovation

María Luisa Sein-Echaluce[1](✉) [ID], Ángel Fidalgo-Blanco[2] [ID],
Francisco J. García-Peñalvo[3](✉) [ID], and Ana María Balbín[4] [ID]

[1] Department of Applied Mathematics, University of Zaragoza, Saragossa, Spain
mlsein@unizar.es
[2] LITI Laboratory, Technical University of Madrid, Madrid, Spain
angel.fidalgo@upm.es
[3] GRIAL Research Group, University of Salamanca, Salamanca, Spain
fgarcia@usal.es
[4] Management School, Pontifical Catholic University of Peru, Lima, Peru
abalbin@pucp.edu.pe

Abstract. The innovation is carried out according to the demands or needs of an industrial, social or economic sector and is aimed at the widest possible target audience. In teaching educational innovation, the demand for innovation is very local, it is generated in each subject and for the students of it. This causes that educational innovation cannot be easily transferred between subjects. But, to meet the demands of an educational sector, the target audience for which innovation is designed must be global. The objective of this work is to study whether teaching educational innovation can be considered globally (for a global target audience and for a need in the education sector), so that it can be applied and transferred between subjects from different contexts. The information provided, during 8 training courses, by 130 university professors belonging to 12 different universities has been analyzed. It has been shown that for a given need for improvement (passive habit in students), the profile of the target audience, the demand of the learning sector and the indicators to measure educational innovation can be raised in a common way for an entire educational sector; in this case, higher education. The conclusion is that educational innovation can be designed globally, applied locally and transferred to other contexts.

Keywords: Educational innovation · Active learning · Innovation indicators · MAIN method

1 Introduction

For decades, the innovation, in the industrial sector innovation has been widely recognized as a key factor in improving the competitiveness of companies [1]. Due to the importance of the innovation in the industrial sector, standardized systems for innovation management have been developed and they have positive influence in these facts [2]. In addition to the procedures and standards established in the innovation management standards, still it is recognized the need to use knowledge management tools and continuous improvement of innovation, because are also some of the aspects that

© Springer Nature Switzerland AG 2020
P. Zaphiris and A. Ioannou (Eds.): HCII 2020, LNCS 12205, pp. 530–546, 2020.
https://doi.org/10.1007/978-3-030-50513-4_39

promote such systems. The Organization for Economic Co-operation and Development (OECD) mentions, through the Oslo manual [3], important barriers that can slow down or speed up the innovation: financing, demand from the own innovation sector, the availability of qualified personnel and administrative obstacles.

As described above, it can be affirmed that in the industrial sector its competitive value is recognized. Indicators that promote the innovation have been identified as well as the standard and certifiable procedures for its management.

Educational innovation is the innovation that is applied in the education sector. Depending on the type of the context of application of such innovation, three types are recognized [4]: 1-innovation is carried out in international projects, which have a similar management to the industrial sector (mainly because it is carried out in collaboration with the industry), 2-the institutional innovation, as per for example, the MOOC, which usually pursue common objectives by the different universities and 3-the educational innovation that is applied in the classroom, which is often called teaching innovation [5].

Educational teaching innovation is one in which teachers innovate in their own subjects [6], trying to improve learning outcomes. But in this context there are no standards for innovation management and the barriers that can curb innovation, defined by the OCDE, they are very accentuated:

- Financing is usually very little or nothing.
- The target audience is the students of a certain subject and, therefore, the demand for innovation is local and very low.
- Innovative teachers need training in pedagogical tools and approaches [7]. Therefore, universities usually offer this type of training. However, since it is not mandatory for teachers to carry out, their training is very heterogeneous.
- The main administrative obstacle is that educational teaching innovation is not a key or determining factor for teachers to obtain accreditation or professional progress.

The barriers that exist for the realization of educational teaching innovation have important consequences, both for the advancement of the innovation itself, and for the impact it produces in the education sector. The main consequences are:

- Difficult transferring educational teaching innovation. When developing educational innovation in a very local scope, with conditions associated with each teacher and without standardized procedures, it is very difficult to transfer innovation between subjects, even if they belong to the same area of knowledge.
- Repetition of innovative experiences both synchronously (in the same period of time) and asynchronously (in different periods of time). Teaching staff usually carry out educational innovation individually, as there is no adequate transfer of innovation, the same processes are often repeated. This produces a huge effort investment by teachers and does not optimize the low economic resources that are invested to carry out innovation.
- Low impact and consequence on the sector. The main consequence of the existence of the mentioned barriers is that educational teaching innovation progresses slowly and does not produce a transformative effect of the educational model.

Following is a set of proposals that could reduce the consequences of the characteristic constraints of teaching educational innovation:

- Consider the demand for innovation globally, not only thinking about the students of the subject where the innovation is carried out. To make this possible, it must be demonstrated that the profile of the target audience that demands the innovation, is global. This would mean that the target audience ceases to be local scope and, therefore, their teaching staff could collaborate with each other to apply that innovation (since the beneficiary would not only be their own students, but also those of other subjects). In that case, the collaboration would have an impact on the improvement of the training process [8].
- Consider that the improvements achieved in a given subject, through the application of innovation, are global improvements. That is, they affect all subjects of any educational level. This would result in a greater transformative effect, since it could move more rapidly in the innovation itself [9]. For this to be possible, it must be demonstrated that the current situation presents the same problems in different educational fields.
- Consider that any innovation can be transferable and applicable at any educational level. The transfer of innovation is important as it affects the transformation of education itself [10]. This is possible if teaching educational innovation can be measured through global indicators.

In this work an application model is used based on the previous approaches. The model is called MAIN (Method for Applying Innovation in educatioN) and is based on a sequence of phases that include processes so that innovation can be considered globally (for the entire education sector) even if applied locally (in a certain subject) [11].

The mentioned model has been applied, for this work, in the university context for educational innovations whose main objective is to get students to participate actively in learning. The objectives of the work, for the defined educational purpose, are based on proving:

- Objective 1: That the profile of the target audience that demands innovation is global. For this, the characteristics of the students, to whom innovation is directed, must be similar.
- Objective 2: The demand of the sector that has the same need for educational teaching innovation. This must be proved, either that there is a common vision of the need for innovation, or that there is a current problem that would be improved with innovation.
- Objective 3: That there are common measurable indicators that measure the impact of educational teaching innovation in a global way.

The following sections show the theoretical model, the context of conducting the research to submit the results of said research and the conclusions obtained.

2 Theoretical Model

The MAIN method is composed of four phases that allow the design and application of an educational innovation project regardless of the innovation method to be applied, the technology to be used and the area of knowledge where educational innovation you want to apply [12].

Each of the four phases has a full-time sequence and some main objectives. Figure 1 shows the relationship of the phases.

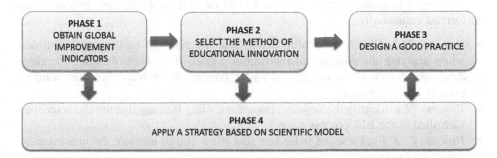

Fig. 1. Name and relationship between the phases of the MAIN method

The main objectives of each phase are:

Phase 1. Obtain global improvement indicators. The professors know the improvements they want to get. These improvements should be measured by indicators that can be common and transferable among the education sector.

Phase 2. Select the method of educational innovation. There are multiple innovation methods that can serve to achieve the same learning achievement [12]. Likewise, there are different technologies that can be used to support each method [13]. In this phase the keys are indicated to choose the method and technology that is most suitable, both to the achievement that is wanted to achieve and to the level of knowledge of the teaching staff (technological, on educational innovation, etc.).

Phase 3. Design a good practice. A good practice of educational innovation must involve a set of indicators based on effectiveness, efficiency, sustainability and transferability [14]. This phase shows how to: get the indicators associated with good practice, plan the activities to be carried out and value the effort required by each activity.

Phase 4. Apply a strategy based on the scientific model. The main objective of this phase is to create and apply educational innovation in such a way that it can be measured and divulge it scientifically.

On the other hand, the MAIN method is totally oriented to the end users of the process; that is, the students and teachers who will use concrete innovation and identify the problems of said end users (phase 1). Based on the problem detected, innovative models are devised and used to solve the problems, providing improvements (phase 2).

Likewise, a prototype is planned and developed to be used with end users (phase 3). A test and validation of the result is carried out (phase 4). In this sense, the MAIN method can be considered a method based on the principles of "Design Thinking" [15].

In turn, the MAIN method must achieve results quickly, since an educational innovation project applied to a subject is developed and applied during its teaching period. Very often, at the beginning of the project the improvements to be achieved have been identified, but not the most appropriate technologies, processes and methods to be used, therefore, they must be incorporated during the completion of the project. In this sense, the MAIN method can be considered to be an "Agile Method" [16].

This work focuses on phase 1 of the MAIN method, in which three processes are performed sequentially:

- *Process P1.1.* Obtain the profile of the students that will be the target audience when applying the educational innovation project. It is about obtaining the characteristics presented by the students who present the problem that they want to correct with the project.
- *Process P1.2.* Identify the negative impact regarding learning that the characteristics identified in the P11 process have.
- *Process P1.3.* Find a set of indicators that allow you to measure the improvement you want to obtain.

Processes P1.1, P1.2 and P1.3 correspond to the objectives 1, 2 and 3 of this work. Therefore, the use of phase 1 of the MAIN model is a methodological support to develop this research work. But before starting these processes, it is essential to identify the improvement you want to obtain when applying innovation during the development of a subject. Usually, this improvement has an impact on: an increase in academic results (such as grades obtained), deeper learning, the acquisition of certain skills or an increase in student and teacher satisfaction.

However, the identification of the problem that prevents these improvements or others, can be formulated with different levels of abstraction. Phase 1 of the MAIN method identifies three levels of abstraction, as shown in Fig. 2.

Level 1 is called "sheet problem" and has a low level of generalization. We usually identify a specific problem that occurs in a specific subject. For example, in the subject "Maintenance and safety of vehicles" and in the topic "car engines", a "problematic sheet" would be "to improve the learning of the operation of a combustion engine." The formulation of the problem with this level of generalization is intrinsic to the subject and it is not usually possible to transfer even to similar subjects.

Level 2 is called " branch problem". It is a more generic level than the previous one and it is about identifying global problems that are known to influence improvement, for example, demotivation. The demotivation of students can be caused by various reasons: he does not like the subject, does not have sufficient prior knowledge or it is the teacher himself who demotivates them. The formulation of the problem at this level is global, but if the origin is not identified, it cannot be transferred to other subjects, since this may be different.

Level 3 is called "root problem" It is the most generic problem since it is usually caused by the own educational model from the institution. These are problems that are always present, regardless of the quality of the teaching staff or the nature of the

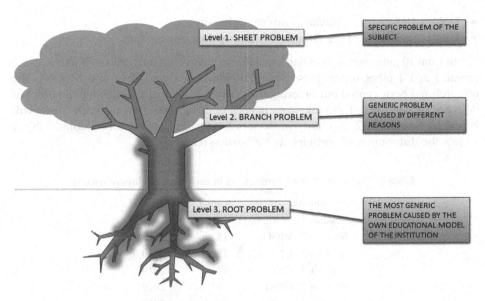

Fig. 2. Different levels of problems

subject. The problem formulated at this level of abstraction can be transferred to any subject that follows an educational model with similar characteristics.

When the level of abstraction to be solved is higher, more global will be the measurable indicators of improvement and, therefore, the result of the innovation will be more transferable. Thus, if phase 1 of the MAIN method is applied to a root problem, global improvement indicators can be achieved from an individual experience, which is the main objective of the work, since it would reduce the current barriers to application and transfer of educational innovation.

3   Research Context

This research has been carried out during teacher training courses have taught by the authors during the years 2018, 2019 and 2020 in different universities, and that have been demanded by them within their training plans. In all of them, the main improvement to be obtained was to increase the active participation of students, since the problem with which they worked was the passive habit of students, level 3 (root). The courses, from which the data for this work have been obtained, have been taught at the following universities:

- UNIZAR 1 and UNIZAR 2. University of Zaragoza (public university).
- UVIGO- University of Vigo (public university).
- USJ. University San Jorge (private university).
- USAL- University of Salamanca (public university).
- MMCo- Conference MoodleMoot Colombia 2019. Universities in Colombia, Ecuador, Chile and Mexico (private and public universities).

- UNA - University of Navarra (private university).
- UPV - University of the Basque Country (public university).

In total 10 universities have participated. Seven Spanish universities (5 public and 2 private) and 4 other universities, from Colombia, Ecuador, Chile and Mexico. The research has been carried out ordering the courses sequentially, following the order of delivery of them, in order to take data in each of them. From now on, each course will be called Session. 132 university professors have participated in all sessions. Table 1 shows the distribution of participants by Session (course).

Table 1. Total number of participants in each session chronologically

Session-course	Participants	Year
Session 1. UNIZAR 1	14	2018
Session 2. VIGO	15	2018
Session 3. UNIZAR 2	15	2019
Session 4. USJ	14	2019
Session 5. USAL	13	2019
Session 6. MMco	19	2019
Session 7. UNA	21	2019
Session 8. UPV	21	2020

In these sessions, phase 1 of the MAIN method was applied (Phase 1. Obtain global improvement indicators) and the tool used to obtain the data was the forum, where the participants responded to an open demand. Three forums were used with the following requests to the participants:

- Forum 1. Provide the characteristics of students who present a passive habit.
- Forum 2. Contribute the consequences in the learning process of a passive student.
- Forum 3. Include measurable indicators to verify the impact of the educational innovation to be carried out to solve the root problem (students' passive habit).

The responses of each forum are used to analyze each of the objectives of this work: the forum1 to analyze the objective 1 (Profile of the target audience that demands innovation is global), the forum 2 to analyze the objective 2 (Demand of the sector which has the same need for educational innovation) and forum 3 to analyze objective 3 (Common measurable indicators that measure the impact of educational innovation on a global basis). In seven sessions, the forums were included in the Moodle e-learning platform, used to manage the contents, and in one session the BlackBoard was used.

In next section, the results of the study and the conclusions obtained from it are shown.

4   Results

The results obtained in each forum and session are presented below. For each session, the response types, the number of total responses and the unique responses are analyzed. Overall, for all sessions, the unique responses and the progression of the analysis performed in each session are analyzed. The following subsections will include the analyzes performed for each of the three objectives of the work.

4.1   Objective 1: Forum 1. Provide Global Characteristics of Passive Students

The teachers were asked, as a result of their own experience, to indicate aspects of the students that would allow them to intuit that the students are passive.

Table 2 shows for each session (S1 to S8) the number of people who participated in each forum (row 2), the total number of messages provided in the forum (row 3), the number of unique (different) messages in each session (row 4) and the number of global single messages in the investigation, that is, unique messages (different from each other) that have not appeared in the previous sessions (row 5). In the last column the totals of each row are expressed.

Table 2. Participants and messages in forum 1 for each session

Forum 1	S1	S2	S3	S4	S5	S6	S7	S8	Totals
Participants (PT)	12	15	15	13	15	20	27	19	136
Total Messages (MT)	25	44	39	46	34	30	57	52	327
Single Messages per Session (MU)	18	16	16	22	21	15	13	16	137
Global Single Messages (MUT)	18	5	4	3	2	0	0	0	32

In Table 2, 136 professors from at least 8 different universities have given 327 responses (MT), of which 32 have been different. This means that 136 participating teachers (PT) have contributed 32 different characteristics (MUT) that define passive students. Figure 3 shows the evolution of the participants and the messages through the different sessions.

The evolution expressed in Fig. 3 shows that different characteristics are defined in the first sessions, 84% of the different characteristics are defined in the first three sessions (of 8 sessions). In addition, as of the fifth session, different characteristics are no longer provided, although there are a greater number of participants and responses in these last two sessions.

It is observed that if a greater number of participants (PT), more total responses (MT) are obtained, which is logical. However, the evolution of the different responses (MUT) is independent of the number of participants, since it is observed that it tends to zero.

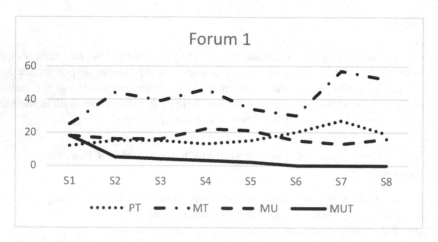

Fig. 3. Evolution of participants and types of messages by sessions in the forum 1

On the other hand, there is a certain stability between the number of different responses per session (MU), being also independent of the number of participants in the session.

The open responses were categorized and the following 5 categories were established:

- AT. Attitude
- PA. Proposed activities
- LK. Learning/Knowledge
- CR. Attitude in the classroom
- TA. Action tutorial

Total responses and total unique responses are grouped by categories, as shown in Table 3. Column 1 represents the category of the classification, column 2 the number of total responses that have been given between all sessions and column three the number of total unique responses.

Table 3. Number of total and unique responses for each category

Category	Total answers	Global unique responses
AT	106	7
PA	60	6
LK	10	5
CR	145	12
TA	6	2

In the analysis, a permanence factor has been established, which measure the presence of a certain different characteristic in all sessions. There are different characteristics that have only been indicated in one or two sessions, so these characteristics can not be considered global. On the other hand, there is a set of characteristics that have occurred in at least 7 of the 8 sessions; that is, they have a minimum permanence of 87.5%. These characteristics can be considered global.

Analyzing the unique answers, organized by categories, which have been obtained in at least 7 of the 8 sessions, Table 4 is obtained. The first column represents the category of the question, the second column is the characteristic expressed by the teaching staff and the third column is the percentage of sessions where the same response was obtained (100% indicates that this response has been given in all sessions and 87.5% has been given in 7 of the 8 sessions).

Table 4. Number of unique responses in at least 7 of the 8 sessions

Category	Characteristic	%
AT	Easily mislead in class (look at the mobile, lost look, etc.)	100
	He has no interest in the subject	100
PA	Does not participate in proposed individual and group activities	100
CR	Does not participate in proposed activities in class	100
	Does not answer the questions	100
	Does not ask questions	87.5
	Does not take notes	87.5

Of the five categories (AT, PA, LK, CR and TA) established, the most different and global responses accumulate are the AT, PA and CR categories (AT. Attitude, PA. Proposed activities and CR. Attitude in the classroom).

4.2   Objective 2: Forum 2. Contribute Consequences in the Learning Process of a Passive Student

In this forum, teachers were asked to indicate, from their experience, the impact that the student's passive habit has in the context of learning the subject under investigation.

Table 5 shows, for each session (S1 to S8), the number of people who participated in each forum (row 2), the total number of messages contributed in the forum (row 3), the number of unique messages (row 4) and the number of global single messages in the investigation (row 5). The last column includes the totals of each row. And Fig. 4 shows the evolution of these participants and types of messages.

As Table 5 shows, 135 participants (PT) have provided 299 responses (MT), of which 26 are globally different (MUT). In the first two sessions, 77% of the different responses have been obtained and as of the fifth session no new one has been contributed, although more people have participated in these sessions.

Thus, as shown in Fig. 4, there is a convergence in teachers' opinions about the impact of passive activity on learning. In the same figure it can be seen that the answers provided are related to the number of participants in each session. However, the number of different responses per session and overall does not keep that relationship. The differences per session are similar.

Table 5. Participants and messages in forum 2 for each session

Forum 2	S1	S2	S3	S4	S5	S6	S7	S8	Totals
Participants (PT)	12	15	15	14	13	19	26	21	135
Total Messages (MT)	19	32	28	37	31	44	56	52	299
Single Messages per Session (MU)	11	16	10	14	15	20	11	16	113
Global Single Messages (MUT)	11	9	2	3	1	0	0	0	26

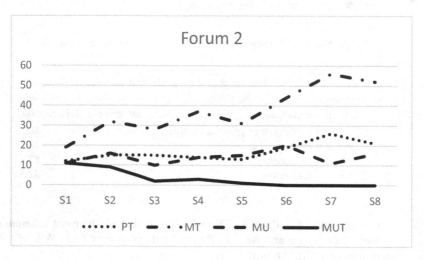

Fig. 4. Evolution of message types by sessions in forum 2

Total open responses and total unique responses are grouped by the aforementioned categories (AT. Attitude, PA. Proposed activities, LK. Learning/Knowledge, CR. Attitude in the classroom, TA. Tutorial action), as shown in the Table 6.

Table 6. Number of total and unique responses for each category

Category	Total answers	Global unique responses
AT	57	6
PA	12	2
LK	123	10
CR	102	6
TA	5	2

Table 7 shows the analysis of unique responses obtained in at least 7 of the 8 sessions. For each category the characteristic included in the messages by the teaching staff is included and the percentage of sessions where that characteristic has appeared (100% if the characteristic appears in all sessions and 87.5% if it has appeared in 7 of the 8 sessions).

Table 7. Unique responses appeared in at least 7 of the 8 sessions

Category	Characteristic	%
AT	Lack of interest in the subject	87.5
	Lack of motivation	87.5
LK	There is no Deep Learning and there is great volatility of content	87.5
	It is necessary to increase the effort and reinforcement for your learning	87.5
CR	It infects assets	87.5
	Desmotiva al profesorado	87.5

In this forum 2, the different global responses have been more numerous in the AT categories. Attitude, LK. Learning/Knowledge and CR. Attitude in the classroom, and correspond to a permanence factor greater than or equal to 87.5% in the sessions.

4.3 Objective 3. Forum 3. Include Measurable Indicators to Verify the Impact of the Educational Innovation to Be Carried Out to Solve the Root Problem (Students' Passive Habit)

The objective of this analysis is to obtain measurable indicators that allow measuring the impact of any innovation in reducing the passive habit of students. The teachers were asked, as a result of their experience, to indicate which indicators could help them to measure the improvement in their own subjects.

Table 8 shows for each session (S1 to S8) the number of people who participated in each forum (row 2), the total number of messages contributed in the forum (row 3), the number of different messages in the session (row 4) and the number of global single messages in the investigation (row 5). In the last column the totals of each row are expressed. Figure 5 shows the graphical evolution of the total quantities in Table 8.

Table 8. Participants in forum 3 for each session

Forum 3	S1	S2	S3	S4	S5	S6	S7	S8	Totals
Participants (PT)	12	14	15	14	14	19	22	20	130
Total Messages (MT)	17	60	36	46	55	75	68	67	424
Single Messages per Session (MU)	10	25	19	21	20	25	16	15	151
Global Single Messages (MUT)	10	19	3	2	0	0	0	0	34

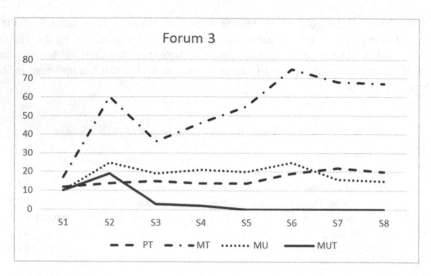

Fig. 5. Evolution of message types by sessions in the forum 3

Table 8 shows that 130 participants (PT) have generated 424 responses (MT) of which 34 have been different (MUT). In the first two sessions, 85% of the different responses have been provided and as of the fourth session, they have not contributed any.

The graph in Fig. 5 shows that the total different responses are not related to the number of participants and that it tends to zero as the sessions progress. The number of different responses per session (MU) has stability in the sessions and does not depend on the number of participants.

The open answers, as in the previous section, correspond to the same 5 categories (AT. Attitude, PA. Proposed activities, LK. Learning/Knowledge, CR. Attitude in the classroom, TA. Tutorial action). Total responses and global single responses are grouped by categories, as shown in Table 9.

Table 9. Number of total and unique responses for each category

Category	Total answers	Global unique responses
AT	91	7
PA	80	5
LK	121	16
CR	137	5
TA	17	1

Analyzing the number of unique responses that have been obtained in at least 7 of the 8 sessions, Table 10 is obtained, with the category of the response, the characteristic expressed by the teaching staff and the percentage of sessions where the same response has been obtained (100% indicate that this response has been given in all sessions and 87.5% has been given in 7 of the 8 sessions).

Table 10. Number of unique responses in at least 7 of the 8 sessions

Category	Characteristic	%
PA	Students create knowledge and share it	87.5
	Greater participation in activities that do not influence the grade	87.5
LK	Teachers change roles (coordination, advice and facilitator)	87.5
	The teacher evaluation survey improves	87.5
CR	Greater class attendance without being mandatory	87.5
	Greater participation in class activities (questions, forums, answers)	100

Similarly, the responses have been grouped into the same previous categories, being more numerous (both in number of responses and in different responses) in the PA categories. Proposed activities, LK. Learning/Knowledge and CR. Attitude in the classroom).

5 Conclusions

The work has been based on the problematic root "passive students", which is very common and frequent in the university system. All the teachers from whom the data from this study have been obtained participated in the training courses to try to alleviate this problem.

The main objective of this research work is to demonstrate that, although there is an innovation by and for a given subject, it can be designed in a global way to serve any other subject of the same educational sector, for example, for the sector "college". For this, three objectives were raised:

- Demonstrate that the characteristics of passive students are similar regardless of the university where they study. This would mean that educational innovation can be considered for all passive students, not just that of a certain subject.
- Demonstrate that teachers share a common vision of the impact that student passivity has on their learning. This would mean that there is a real and common need in the educational sector.
- Demonstrate that there is a set of measurable and global indicators to measure the improvement of learning by alleviating the problem of passive student habits. This would mean that the innovation that has managed to improve a root problem can be transferred between subjects that wish to improve that same root problem.

With regard to obtaining characteristics of passive students, the results and interpretation of the messages in forum 1, it follows that there is a set of common characteristics that define passive students and these characteristics are shared by the teaching staff, since that the global number of different characteristics arises in the first sessions of the study (83% in the first three sessions), then they are repeated. Therefore, it can be affirmed that there is a common vision of these characteristics.

A coincidence has been detected, in at least 7 of the 8 sessions, in the characteristics that define the passive students (of the categories AT. Attitude, PA. Proposed activities, and CR. Attitude in the classroom). Thus, it can be affirmed that there is a consensus among the participating teachers regarding the characteristics that define the passive students, and are the following:

- Easily mislead in class (look at the phone, have lost eyes, etc.)
- Has no interest in the subject
- Does not participate in proposed individual and group activities
- Does not participate in activities proposed in class
- Does not answer questions
- Does not ask questions
- Does not take notes

Regarding the second objective, analyze characteristics that allow us to measure the impact of the passive habit of students in their learning, Thus, it can be seen that teachers share a common vision regarding the impact of student passivity and that in the first two sessions the total global unique characteristics have already been obtained.

The analysis of the answers gives the same classification as in the previous section. Total and different responses have been more numerous in AT, LK and CR (AT. Attitude, LK. Learning/Knowledge and CR. Attitude in the classroom). If we take a permanence factor greater than or equal to 87.5%, the impact on learning is:

- Lack of interest in the subject
- Lack of motivation
- There is no Deep Learning and there is great volatility of content
- It is necessary to increase the effort and reinforcement for your learning
- Students with passive habit transmit their passivity to other students
- Students with passive habits demotivate teachers

Finally, with respect to the third objective, to establish the measurable indicators that allow verifying the impact of educational innovation in the improvement of active habit, it is demonstrated, as in the previous objectives, that there is a global and common vision of the indicators measurable improvement.

After the analysis of permanence above 87.5%, it is observed that the most global common and measurable indicators in forum 3 correspond to the PA categories. Proposed activities, LK. Learning/Knowledge and CR. Attitude in the classroom and are the following:

- Students create knowledge and share it
- Greater participation in activities that do not influence the grade
- Teachers change their rol (coordination, advice and facilitator)
- Improves the teachers survey
- Increased class attendance without being mandatory
- Greater participation in class activities (questions, forums, answers, etc.)

All the graphs results, for the three forums, show that there is a common vision in the different objectives since the identification of these characteristics does not depend on either the university or the number of participants, but on the sequence of the session. Most of the characteristics are defined in the first sessions and according the advance with new contributions reduced to zero. That convergence to zero of the number of global single messages in each of the forums would be accelerated if the order criteria of the sessions had been different, and not the temporality in the delivery of the respective sessions. As an example, if in forum 3 (Table 8) the session 2 had been placed first, 25 of the 34 unique global responses had already been obtained and 0 would have been reached before reaching the fifth session, as with the current order. This is only to illustrate that the order of the sessions only affects in that sense but that the conclusion is the same in each one of the forums, there is a convergence of teachers when interpreting the problem, its impact and the measurable indicators.

It is concluded, therefore, that although each teacher has thought about their own subject, in different universities and even countries, they all agree on the identification of the characteristics of passive students, the consequences it has on their learning and the measurable indicators. Which shows that although educational innovation is locally done, in the subject context, can be raised globally.

In addition, these characteristics and global indicators, obtained in this work from that consensus, will be very useful for any teacher who wants to propose an educational innovation project to palliate the effect of passive students since they will know how to recognize it, anticipate its impact on their learning and apply the indicators to measure the expected improvement. This will allow to design the educational innovation in a global way, apply it locally and transfer it to other contexts.

The work has been done on the root problem "passive habit" of students. As future work, similar studies are planned for other root problems such as lack of prior knowledge and personalized teaching.

Acknowledgments. This work has been partially funded by the Spanish Government Ministry of Economy and Competitiveness throughout the DEFINES project (Ref. TIN2016-80172-R) and the Educational Innovation Service of the Technical University of Madrid (project Ref IE1920.0601). The authors would like to thank the research groups EtnoEdu (https://socioconstructivismo.unizar.es/), GRIAL (http://grial.usal.es) and LITI (http://www.liti.es) for their support.

References

1. Roberts, R.: Managing innovation: the pursuit of competitive advantage and the design of innovation intense environments. Res. Policy **27**(2), 159–175 (1998)
2. Mir, M., Casadesús, M., Petnji, L.H.: The impact of standardized innovation management systems on innovation capability and business performance: an empirical study. J. Eng. Technol. Manage. - JET-M **41**, 26–44 (2016)
3. OECD: Oslo Manual 2018, 4th edn. OECD, Paris (2018)
4. Fidalgo-Blanco, Á.: Últimas tendencias en innovación docente ¿cómo aplicarlas en el aula? IX Jornada Universitaria de Innovación y Calidad. Universidad de Deusto, November-2019. https://zenodo.org/record/3554296#.XfzxP1VKiUk

5. Fidalgo-Blanco, Á., Sein-Echaluce, M.L., García-Peñalvo, F.: Tendencias de Innovación Educativa. Algo más que un desfile de moda. In: Conferencia Internacional en Tendencias de Innovación Educativa. CITIE II, (2018)
6. Fidalgo-Blanco, Á., Sein-Echaluce, M.L., García-Peñalvo, F.: ¿Pueden las tendencias de innovación educativa predecir los cambios que transformarán el modelo educativo? 08 May 2019. https://zenodo.org/record/2672967#.XRU4UugzaUl
7. Cruz-Rojas, G.A., Molina-Blandón, M.A., Valdiri-Vinasco, V.: Vigilancia tecnológica para la innovación educativa en el uso de bases de datos y plataformas de gestión de aprendizaje en la universidad del Valle, Colombia, REVISTA DE INVESTIGACIÓN, DESARROLLO E INNOVACIÓN, vol. 9, no. 2, February 2019
8. Bell, T., Urhahne, D., Schanze, S., Ploetzner, R.: Collaborative inquiry learning: models, tools, and challenges. Int. J. Sci. Educ. **32**(3), 349–377 (2010)
9. Sein-Echaluce, M., Fidalgo-Blanco, Á., García-Peñalvo, F.J.: Diseño de un proyecto de innovación educativa docente a partir de indicadores transferibles entre distintos contextos, 1st edn. Servicio de Publicaciones Universidad de Zaragoza, Zaragoza (2019)
10. Varpio, L., et al.: Is transferring an educational innovation actually a process of transformation? Adv. Health Sci. Educ. **17**(3), 357–367 (2012)
11. Fidalgo-Blanco, Á., Sein-Echaluce, M.L.: Método MAIN para planificar, aplicar y divulgar la innovación educativa. Educ. Knowl. Soc. (EKS) **19**(2), 83–101 (2018)
12. Vera, C., Félez, J., Cobos, J.A., Sánchez-Naranjo, M.J., Pinto, G.: Experiences in education innovation: developing tools in support of active learning. Eur. J. Eng. Educ. **31**(2), 227–236 (2006)
13. Sánchez-Canales, M., García-Aranda, C., Morillo-Balsera, M.C., Miguel S-de-la-Muela, A., Fernández-GutiérrezdelAlamo, L.: Clasificación de los diferentes modelos de Aula invertida y su aplicación en la Universidad Politécnica de Madrid. In: Aprendizaje, Innovación y Cooperación como impulsores del cambio metodológico. actas CINAIC 2019, pp. 607–611 (2019)
14. Fidalgo-Blanco, Á., Sein-Echaluce Lacleta, M.: ¿Qué hay que hacer para que una innovación educativa se consolide? In: Fores Miravalles, A., Subias Valeccillo, E. (eds.) Pedagogías emergentes : 14 preguntas para el debate, 1st edn. p. 203. Ediciones Octaedro, Barcelona (2018)
15. Fidalgo-Blanco, Á.: Qué es el Design Thinking y su relación con la innovación educativa. Blog Innovación Educativa, MADRID, p. 1 (2019)
16. Fidalgo-Blanco, Á.: Qué son las metodologías ágiles y su aplicación a la innovación educativa. Blog Innovación Educativa, MADRID, p. 1 (2020)

"RemoteMentor" Evaluation of Interactions Between Teenage Girls, Remote Tutors, and Coding Activities in School Lessons

Bernadette Spieler[1]([✉]), Jana Mikats[2], Sophi Valentin[2], Libora Oates-Indruchová[2], and Wolfgang Slany[3]

[1] Institute of Mathematics and Applied Informatics,
University of Hildesheim, Hildesheim, Germany
bernadette.spieler@uni-hildesheim.de
[2] Department of Sociology, University of Graz, Graz, Austria
{jana.mikats,libora.oates-indruchova}@uni-graz.at,
sophi.valentin@outlook.com
[3] Institue of Software Technology, University of Graz, Graz, Austria
wolfgang.slany@tugraz.at

Abstract. Research points at various factors for the low and even decreasing proportion of women in the IT sector in developed countries, e.g., psychological causes, social factors, or structural conditions. These possible explanations all have one thing in common: they recognize adolescence as the essential confidence-building phase in girls. Girls aged 12 to 15 years old seem to lose interest in computer science (CS). Providing mentors and female role models are two key elements to counteract gender stereotypes in CS. "RemoteMentor", a joint Austrian research project brought these two approaches together and expanded them in the form of "remote tutoring": female students aged 14 to 15 received one-on-one human support through smartphones for their coding project during their regular CS and arts lessons. The aim of the one year investigation was to analyse gender aspects in the tutoring process and the output of the collaborative coding project. This was done with group discussions, the evaluation of the online tutoring units and an analysis of the final games in regard to the applied Computational Thinking concepts. Results showed that the project was a promising approach to support and motivate at least a certain group of female students in coding.

Keywords: Remote tutoring · Gender analysis · CT skills · Coding project · Smartphones

1 Introduction

The underrepresentation of women in the field of information technology (IT) has been discussed in interdisciplinary research for decades. A gender-gap occurs

© Springer Nature Switzerland AG 2020
P. Zaphiris and A. Ioannou (Eds.): HCII 2020, LNCS 12205, pp. 547–567, 2020.
https://doi.org/10.1007/978-3-030-50513-4_40

in several STEM disciplines (science, technology, engineering, and mathematics), but it is most evident in the discipline of computer science (CS). The number of women in CS is very low and even declining in most developed countries [27]. Consequently, software engineering jobs are male-dominated, as shown by Eurostat's statistical data [7]. In Europe, 83% of the people working as Information and Communication Technology (ICT) specialists are male. This underrepresentation in terms of participation in the IT sector leads to inequalities and thus to disadvantages for women. Sapna Cheryan et al. [6] describe that stereotypes define the culture of the IT sector. Stereotypes work on two levels: on the one hand, they are descriptive (how is something) and on the other hand, they are prescriptive (how should something be). Examples of such stereotyped ideas of the IT sector would be the "male character" or a "chilly environment". For people working in IT, such stereotyped notions would include nerds or geeks who live socially isolated [6,13]. These ideas are more compatible with typical images of masculinity than femininity. Young people usually engage in areas they feel "compatible" with, which is largely structured by the category of gender. If the profession does not fit the "traditional gender model", one is not as likely to pursue it or feels discriminated against by someone who does. To strengthen girls' confidence and interest, mentoring programs and appropriate role models are two key elements to introduce girls to technical subjects and to awaken their interest for CS [2,3,26]. Researchers are certain that girls' interest in IT changes early in their adolescence between the ages of 12 and 15 years old. For this reason, introducing female mentors from secondary school onwards is described as the most effective [18]. Another option that has proven to be particularly effective in increasing programming interest and motivation is to offer mentoring programs.

We combined these strategies and started the "RemoteMentor" project, a form of online mentoring which works by pairing university students with teenage girls between the ages of 13 and 15 years from two secondary schools in Graz. "RemoteMentor" was a one-year investigation that started in January 2018 with funding from NetIdee (Internet Foundation Austria). For this project, female students used the app Pocket Code and they got immediate help in real time from advanced users (i.e. remote tutoring). A sociological analysis investigated gender aspects in this remote tutoring process by conducting group discussions with 61 girls, analysing the transcripts of the online tutoring sessions. Additionally the final coding projects were evaluated from technical viewpoints and referred to important Computational Thinking (CT) concepts described by Jannette Wing [30]. The aim of the paper is twofold: First, we investigate differences in the teenage girls' tutoring experience by female and male tutors. The developed typology shows how the interactions between attitudes of the girls (i.e. active-passive) and the tutoring orientation (i.e. dictating or supporting) resulted in different tutoring styles (i.e., cooperative, directive, interactive, and authoritative). Second, these results were compared with the evaluations of the coding projects and showed the relationship between girls' types of attitudes and applied CT concepts of their final projects. This paper investigates the following research question: What influence do the following aspects have on the students' attitude towards programming or their final games: the tutoring orientation, the tutoring style of tutors, and the gender of the tutors?

2   Theoretical Background

Gender and technology represent two constructed concepts that influence each other [29], see Sect. 2.1. In addition, stereotypes, social and institutional factors in the context of CS are used to analyse gender aspects, especially those of girls and young women, see Sect. 2.2. Subsequently, theoretical foundations of mentoring and especially of online mentoring, as well as a conceptual definition of mentoring and tutoring, will be discussed in Sect. 2.3. The game creation approach based on visual coding will be presented in Sect. 2.4.

2.1   Gender and Technology

Researchers of the 1980s and 1990s focused on differences in performance (e.g., in school subjects) and preferences (e.g., interests and hobbies) between genders [26]. The underrepresentation of women was connected with gender inequalities in their access, use and attitudes towards computers [1]. Solutions of this time included changing women's attitudes towards computers and technology to more "male" views. Research today does not see the solution in a need to change girls' and women's attitudes towards computers but emphasises the investigation of social influences such as stereotypes, associated power, and domination relationships in the IT sector [1]. Wendy Faulkner [9] states several reasons why it is necessary to include the category of gender in technology research. We would like to mention five reasons that are considered most important for this paper: (1) technology is gendered because the main players in this field are male, (2) there are clear gender differences in the division of labour in technical sectors, (3) technological artefacts have themselves a materially or symbolically gendered character, (4) in Western cultures, notions of the technical sector have predominantly male connotations, and (5) methods of working in the technical field can have a gender aspect. Feminist constructivist technology research argues that technology and gender should be understood as co-constructed and thus as mutually influencing each other [28].

2.2   CS, Stereotypes, Social and Institutional Factors

Stereotypes are among the most influential factors leading to gendered modes of behaviour [3]. Consequently, stereotypes in CS seem incompatible with the self-concept of adolescent girls [23]. This is described by the concept of "interests as identity regulation model" (IIRM) [19,20]. This concept describes the underrepresentation of girls and women in technical areas to this incompatibility of their gendered self-concept and the male connotation of STEM areas—and in particular the area of CS. According to the IIRM, young people choose school subjects and extracurricular activities on the basis of their idea of who they are or what they want to be in the future. Acknowledging or distancing oneself from engagement in certain areas is a way for young people to express and show their identity [19]. According to Kessels et al. [19], the category "gender" plays an important role in such decisions. The IIRM model can help to explain not only commitment but also non-commitment to certain areas. Thus it is well suited to break down gender aspects that have been shown in real-time online-mentoring during the project.

2.3   Mentoring, Online Support, and Tutoring

An established practice to support and encourage interest in programming among teenage girls are mentoring approaches. In regards to CS, girls can receive detailed information about possible professional fields, requirements for applicants, earning opportunities, etc. [10]. If female role models serve as mentors, they can break down stereotypes and girls can learn from their experiences [2,10]. Mentors can also strengthen their mentees with encouragement and confirmation, especially if they doubt their suitability for the IT sector [10]. According to Khare et al. [17], online mentoring offers many possibilities. By eliminating the factor of location, even people who may live in rural areas and for whom a copresent face-to-face meeting would not be feasible can benefit. Compared to analog mentoring, online mentoring is much cheaper, the use of resources is much lower, and it can be used more effectively. Despite these positive aspects, there are also some negative aspects or ethically problematic ones [8]. For instance, misunderstandings in communication, or questions of privacy and confidentiality. Another form of mentoring are tutoring approaches. Tutors help their tutees to achieve a specific goal or skill. This cooperation is usually very limited in time, but can nevertheless have a major impact on the person being supported, for example if a sense of achievement has an influence on later educational or professional ambitions. In the case of the "RemoteMentor" project we are dealing more likely with a tutoring concept. For the presentation of the results we will thus stick to "tutoring".

2.4   Block-Based and Visual Coding

In the last decade, a number of block-based visual programming tools, e.g., the Scratch environment [24], have been introduced with the purpose of helping children and teenagers to have an easier time when first practicing programming. For our project we used the app Pocket Code, an app developed at TU Graz as part of the Open and Free Source Software (FOSS) project Catrobat. Pocket Code is a visual programming language environment that allows the creation of games, stories, animations, and many types of other apps directly on phones or tablets, thereby teaching fundamental programming skills. Drag and drop interfaces particularly make a lot of sense on smartphones, as users prefer using their fingers for dragging and dropping graphical elements on the multi-touch screen in almost all apps, even when entering text on "swipe"-type keyboards. To allow remote sessions via Pocket Code we use a second app with the name "Zoom".

The Zoom app (zoom.us) allows users to host a meeting, invite others, speak and chat with them, share the screen, and use a pen feature for highlighting.

3 Methods

To explore RemoteMentor as an approach to support young girls in their programming we explore the attitudes of the girls in relation to the tutoring style of their tutors and compared them with the CT concepts applied in their final programming projects.

3.1 Participants and Activity Design

The project was conducted at two academic high schools in Graz (Austria) in with a total of 113 students (61 girls, 52 boys). The age of the project participants was between 13 and 15 years. The classes consisted of boys and girls, however, with regard to the research interest, only the data of the girls has been examined for this paper. The students used the app Pocket Code in six to eight double units (=90 min) in a weekly interval. In unit 1 students solved a tutorial which included the basis functionalities of Pocket Code (messages, sensors, etc.). During unit 2 students created their ideas by using storyboards (a framework to support concepts they will need for programming). In units 3 and 4, students received support from a total of 16 (8 female, 10 male) different female and male remote tutors (more experienced users of the app, mostly university students from TU Graz). Tutors were allocated randomly among the students. Every female participant had one session with a male and one with a female tutor to be able to compare tutoring experiences with both male and female tutors. During a 30 to 40-min session, the students called a tutor and shared their screen with them via the app ZOOM to show their scripts and ask for advice, improvements, or further ideas, see Fig. 1.

Fig. 1. Tutoring Session with headphones, Pocket Code, and the Zoom app.

The first survey phase started in May and continued until June 2018. In two secondary schools in Graz, real-time tutoring was offered as part of their regular CS lessons. In this first survey phase, four group discussions were held with 14 teenage girls and 27 transcripts of tutoring units were generated. The second survey phase started in October and continued until November 2018. Tutoring units were offered at the same two schools but this time during arts lessons. Students chose famous paintings and created interactive memes out of them through animations and games. Figure 2 shows some screenshots of the final artefacts. In this second survey, eight group discussions were conducted with 47 female students and 104 transcripts of tutoring units were generated. The research was approved by both universities' institutional ethical review panel prior to commencement. Following permission from the school and teacher to conduct the research, legal guardians of the students were informed of the research. Participants used nicknames in the group discussions and for their games.

Fig. 2. Gaming artefacts during the RemoteMentor project.

3.2   Data Collection Process

Non-participant observations were conducted in both the programming and tutoring phases. The purpose of the observations was merely exploratory and therefore not conducted in a systematic way to develop a guideline for the group discussions. We held a total of 12 group discussions lasting 45 min each with 61 teenage girls. The girls were subdivided into smaller-groups of two to eight students to be able to adequately reconstruct individual stand points and the formation and exchange of opinions within the group setting [11]. The interview guide consisted of 16 questions derived from the literature review on girls/women in computing and from the non-participant observations. The topics included views on programming, their experience of and satisfaction with their work on the project and the tutoring they received, assessment of their own programming skills, and perspectives on female role models in the IT sector. All online tutoring sessions were audio recorded and transcribed into a text file by the tutors themselves for budgetary reasons. There were a total of 131 transcripts, of which 8 had to be excluded for poor quality. The remaining 123 transcripts were included in the evaluation. All completed gaming apps were uploaded to the Catrobat Sharing page (https://share.catrob.at/). A total of 111 games were uploaded, and 60 of them were created by girls. The projects were analysed by using a Computational Thinking (CT) skills matrix, applied by the open source software Dr. Scratch [21]. CT fosters the idea that young people who are introduced to CS, learn more than just programming but apply several higher thinking skills [30]. To successfully implement their own programming solutions, students had to apply different programming concepts, such as loops and conditions, as well as practices, such as abstraction and debugging [16]. Dr. Scratch is an analytical tool that evaluates Scratch projects. Since both, the Scratch environment and Pocket Code uses a very similar visual block-based programming language, these analysis could be easily adopted for our tool. Fundamental CT concepts which are analysed comprise [25]:

- Abstraction and problem decomposition: breaking down a problem into smaller ones (e.g., use more than one script/object)
- Parallelism: focussing the thinking process in more than one direction (e.g., several scripts are triggered by the same events)
- Logical thinking: include decision actions or logical operators (e.g., if-else)
- Synchronization: ability to understand complex information and synchronize code (e.g., by wait actions)
- Flow control: to create plans for known/unknown events (e..g, iterations)
- Interactivity: to include feedback for users or user actions (e.g., mouse click)
- Data representation: e.g., operations on variables and lists.

The redefined matrix for analysing Pocket Code projects is described in the next section.

3.3 Data Analysis

Three kinds of data were the subject of our analysis: (1) the transcripts of the group discussions, (2) the transcripts of the tutoring sessions, and (3) the programmed games. Different methods of data analysis were applied. The transcripts of the group discussions were coded according to constructivist grounded theory [5] and the transcripts of the tutoring sessions were subjected to a summative content analysis [14]. The artefacts of learning, the programmed games, were evaluated according to applied CT concepts following the analysis of the open source software Dr. Scratch [21].

Following the principles of the constructivist grounded theory methodology [5], the use of the different techniques of data analysis and the combination of the different data types followed an iterative logic and resulted in theoretical concepts. We started the process of data analysis by "initial coding", and coded the transcript line-by line in order to identify relevant issues and aspects. In a second step we used the technique of "focused coding" to systematically develop and ground our central categories that had already emerged in the first analysis sessions (different types of girls and tutoring). In the final step of "theoretical coding" we related the codes to our core categories, different types of girl's attitudes to programming as well as the different tutoring orientations, and styles in order to develop our theoretical concept. The development of this theoretical concept was nourished and strengthened by the analysis of the transcripts of the tutoring sessions by a summative content analysis which focused on linguistic and communicative aspects of the tutor and tutee interactions.

The goal of the analysis of the transcripts of the tutoring units was to investigate whether the male and female tutors structured their assistance differently or preferred different linguistic means and also whether the girls' participation would be different depending on their tutor's sex. We conducted a summative content analysis, that combines the counting of frequencies (of words or content) with their contextual interpretation [14]. The context here consisted in linguistic means that we defined, adopting an older method of studying language use in same-sex and mixed-sex dyads developed by Mulac et al. [22]. It allowed us to break the transcripts into coded segments, whose pattern in the given mentoring unit pointed to its overall structure. All transcripts were coded and subsequently assigned to one of four tutoring styles. Subsequently word frequency counts were carried out in order to measure the verbal contribution i.e. the code coverage by type of interaction, language use and learning context of tutors and tutees. The styles could then be mapped onto the corresponding typology of the girls' attitudes to programing resulting from the cooperation between the tutors and tutees.

For analysing the programmed games we made use of the Dr. Scratch coding system [21]. Dr. Scratch maps CT concepts with different competence levels of basic, developing and proficiency. The authors redefined the original mapping of CT concepts to Scratch actions to be suitable to Pocket Code actions. Not all features of Scratch are available in Pocket Code (e.g. definition of block) or make sense on phones (e.g., mouse blocks or key tapped). These are replaced by equivalent actions or additional features of the Pocket Code app. Table 1 shows the matrix of CT concepts to Pocket Code actions based on Dr. Scratch. Adjustment to Pocket Code are highlighted in italic. Note that sprites in Scratch are called objects or actors in Pocket Code and backdrop are called background in Pocket Code.

4   Results and Discussion

We developed three different theoretical concepts in order to describe the tutoring experience in relation to the teenage girls' attitudes to programming and the tutoring orientations and styles and the sex of the tutors. In a second step, these results were compared with the evaluations of the coding projects in order to show the relationship between girls' types of attitudes and the complexity of their final projects.

4.1   The Tutoring Experience

We start by introducing the typology of teenage girls' attitudes toward programming. This is followed by a description of the tutoring orientation by male

Table 1. Mapping of CT concepts to Pocket Code programs based on the analysing system of Dr. Scratch

CT Concept	Basic (1 point)	Developing (2 points)	Proficiency (3 points)
Abstraction and problem decomposition	More than one script and one object	Definition of blocks—Use of functions	*Use of clones—and use of physics bricks*
Parallelism	*Two scripts on green flag—when scene starts*	*Two scripts: key pressed, on sprite clicked—when tapped or when screen is touched*	Two scripts: when I receive message, create clone, when %s is true, background change to
Logical thinking	If	If-else	Logical operations
Synchronization	Wait	Broadcast, when I receive stop scripts	Wait until, when background change to, broadcast and wait
Flow control	Sequence of blocks	Repeat, forever	Repeat until
Interactivity	*Green flag ->Sensor values*	*Key pressed, object clicked, mouse blocks—touches property*	*video, audio, + vibration, pen brick*
Data representation	Modifiers of objects' properties	Operations on variables	Operations on lists

and female tutors. The third concept describes the interaction of teenage girls' attitudes toward programming and the tutoring orientation that could result in four forms of tutoring styles. Finally, the analysis of the games created by girls is presented.

Typology of Teenage Girls' Attitudes Toward Programming: Teenage girls' attitudes toward programming can be differentiated on an activity level to describe the tutees mode of cooperation and participation in the programming activity. Subordinated to this, the interest and the security level have a strengthening (interest, security) or weakening (disinterest, insecurity) effect on the extent of the teenage participants' activities. Teenagers girls' attitudes toward programming represent a continuum with two poles, active and passive. In this model, on the two ends of the active-passive continuum, there are girls with an active attitude on one hand and girls with a passive attitude toward programming on the other. These two characteristics of the typology will be described in more detail to show how teenage girls' attitudes toward programming influence their participation and cooperation in tutoring units, their perception of the tutor, and how these experiences are related to stereotypical opinions and expectations of IT and gender. We further present the numeric distribution of the two characteristics in the conducted tutoring sessions.

Active Girls: Girls with an active attitude toward programming tried to get involved, cooperated and wanted to make decisions about their own games in the tutoring sessions. They were either generally interested in programming or confident in their abilities or both. Usually, at the beginning of the tutoring unit, they clearly presented their developed idea of the game and stuck to their idea even if the tutor proposed another variation, as the following situation shows:

Girl: Exactly and my idea would be, [...] I'm not sure know how to do it [...], but it would be a great idea for a second level. [...] Tutor: Well, I would suggest [...] that there might be an explanation at the very beginning. What to do? Girl: No, no, no. [...] I don't know if it's absolutely necessary. (T36: 64ff.)

These types of girls had thought through the realisation of their ideas in the Pocket Code app and explicitly requested information or explanations from their tutors which they subsequently evaluated. They self confidently corrected their tutors if they did not understand something correctly or rejected his or her proposal if they did not like it. Girls with characteristics of the type active attitude liked to work independently without tutors. This strong desire to be able to work on their own meant that they expected their tutors to listen to them and support them realising their ideas. If tutors did not meet these expectations, active girls were disappointed by the tutoring sessions.

This active type of girls reported strong inhibiting effects of stereotypes on their interest and commitment toward programming in the group discussions: *"[...] people just think programming [...] that's something for boys and not for girls, (...), because if a girl engages in programming but only boys are there then, you feel somehow uncomfortable, because then everyone thinks: yes, she can't do that anyway. And... it's a bit unfair that you think that way, because... that's why there's ah... there are so few girls who are interested in it. And... [...] yeah... I would do it more often." (GD1, 229ff.).*

The girl expressed her general interest in programming but felt limited in following these interests by gendered stereotypes and expectations she described as unfair. The girls were aware of existing stereotypes and reflected on the effect of those and on how they felt in a male dominated field. The impression that others had low expectations in their skills exerted pressure on teenage girls and they consequently might turn away from programming. This is in line with Kessels et al. [19] who describe that the decision for or against the engagement in a certain area serves as a way of identity construction. Consequently it is unlikely that teenage girls develop or cultivate interest for programming, if they experience the field as solely masculine. In about 67.5% of the evaluated tutoring units, the teenage girls showed an active attitude toward programming, i.e. high level of commitment in the tutoring sessions and were characterised by a high degree of independence and intrinsic motivation.

Passive Girls: Girls with a passive attitude toward programming showed little or no effort to develop and realize their own ideas. They did not actively participate in the tutoring sessions and were either uninterested, insecure, or both. They voluntarily handed over the control of their game to their tutors and gladly followed their tutors' suggestions:

Tutor: So what do you want to happen when you tab the "Play"-button?
Girl: Ahm. Maybe I don't know, she could also like... She could like wink (blink?) with the eye or so like or I don't know.
Tutor: Ok. Like add another look.
Girl: Ok so should I go back?
Tutor: No, is this what you want as your game? I mean we can just take the scripts we have for the object [...] and put it into the object of the play button so that she changes her eye shadow colour [...]
Girl: Oh, ok ya. We could do that. [...]

Girls of the passive attitude type prefered to be tutored by those who gave clear commands and decided the next programming steps. If this did not happen from the start, as in the example above, the girls actively asked for help and suggestions. In addition to that they perceived too many questions or too few direct commands unpleasant as they did not feel competent enough to come up with their own ideas. The impression that programming was not for them was likely to be confirmed in such tutoring sessions as the girls had the impression that they were not capable of coping with technical challenges. Gender stereotypes about programming thus nourished their self-doubt and insecurity. In the group discussions, they referred stereotypes to justify and legitimise their refusal to participate actively in the programming sessions: *"I don't know girls sit together often and... talk, gossip, do make-up [...], and boys... play some PlayStation-games together and then maybe the thought comes up that they want to do it themselves, or... kind of just because they are more into computers and stuff"* (GD7, 279ff.).

This teenage girl described dichotomous and opposing characteristics of girls' and boys' interests. She positioned herself in the group as a typical girl and consequently clarifies that programming was incompatible with her self-perception. This is consistent with common gender and IT stereotypes, which tend to attribute natural technical skills to men and social skills and preferences to women [20].

In about 32.5% of the recorded online tutoring sessions, the teenage girls showed a passive attitude toward programming. Depending on the degree of (dis-)interest or (in)security, passive girls did not actively cooperate and showed very little intrinsic motivation to participate in the programming process. This passive attitude was also reflected in the 26.9% share of verbal contribution in the transcripts of the tutoring sessions which was about 10% lower than by teenage participants with an active attitude toward programming. Furthermore, in tutoring sessions with passive girls, the extent of direct commands with 39% (code coverage) was clearly higher than in tutoring sessions with active girls, whose transcripts only showed 21% direct commands.

Tutoring Orientations by Male and Female Tutors: The typology of the tutoring orientation differs the way tutors offered support. On one end of the spectrum, there were tutors who supported their tutees by direct instructions and dictating, and on the other end there were tutors who ensured that their tutees reach their goals independently by giving hints and providing explanations. These two characteristics of the tutoring orientation typology will be described in more detail to show how the tutors' orientation shaped the programming sessions and further affected the tutees' inclinations on how to participate in their programming project as well as their overall learning experience.

Dictating Tutoring Orientation: Tutors of the dicating tutoring orientation were characterized by dictating the programming steps to their tutees. They anticipated most of what was needed instead of trying to motivate their tutees to think and try by themselves. Their focus was on the success of the programming project rather than the learning experience of the teenage girls. Due to this orientation on programming, the tutors took the more active part in the tutorings sessions and their tutees thus had to take the rather passive part of an executor of their tutors' command:

Tutor: Right. And now "if position true ", there "if touched object elephant " and there it should be now, "send to all ", [...] and there we make a new, a new thing and we call it hit, ok and now you go up again.
Girl: But then we don't have to change "if you receive " or something?
Tutor: Yes exactly. I was just about to do that. Very smart (laughs). And it goes up [...] that means 'when program starts', we first have to put an 'if you receive' block over it. (T22, 93ff.).

The sequence shows that tutors of this type did not respond to girls' suggestions or failed to recognize such attempts. Instead of honoring the teenage girls' knowledge, the tutor pointed out that her suggestion would have been the next step he was about to take. Instructions via a dictation mode that were not accompanied by an explanation made it difficult for the tutees to develop an understanding of what happened during their tutoring sessions and subsequently made it hard to continue working on their script independently. Approximately 29% of the recorded tutoring sessions were from tutors with a predominantly dictating orientation. In those sessions about 18% of the tutors' verbal contribution were directives. We observed a slight gender difference as female tutors used 31% more directives while male tutors used 24%, in contrast to Mulac et al. [22] findings. One explanation for this outcome is the (over) adaption of women to the male dominated IT culture [12] that could also become visible in their language use.

Supporting Tutoring Orientation: Tutors with a supporting tutoring orientation intended to realize their tutees ideas and made sure that the tutees understood the programming process. Their focus was on the tutees, their ideas and their learning process rather than the programming output. They actively involved the teenage girls in the programming sessions by letting the tutees come up with their own ideas and solutions, yet guided by their tutors:

Tutor: Yes, you could do a " hide "script with" looks " now, that it will be hidden after 20 s, but you know what could be the problem?
Girl: That you can still type it, right? [...]
Tutor: Yeah, it should. But what happens if you type it at 19.5 s, at 20 s you get a "hide " command, what happens at 20.5 s. Take a look at your script, maybe you will recognize it.
Girl: That it will be shown again, that Leonardo will be shown again, maybe. (T115, 314ff.)

To encourage the girls' involvement, supportive tutors were asking questions about the tutees' own ideas, their knowledge and skills, or the next programming step. Besides their involvement through questions, tutors offered explanations to the programming sequences. Such supporting tutoring orientation allowed tutees to take an active part in the tutoring sessions and their own programming project as they were supported to understand what and how they were programming and subsequently felt encouraged working on their script independently.

Approximately 71% of the recorded tutoring sessions were from tutors with a predominantly supportive orientation. We also detected a gender difference in language use during these tutoring sessions which was in contrast to Mulac et al. [22] findings, as male tutors used more explanations (31%) than the female tutors (22%). However, the verbal share of the teenage girls' active participation (explanations and suggestions) in the recorded tutoring sessions did not significantly differ between male and female tutors.

Tutoring Typology: On the basis of the two topologies of teenage girls' attitudes and the tutoring orientation, we developed a typology of four tutoring styles. These results show that the tutoring experience is shaped by the interplay between tutees' attitudes to programming and the tutors' orientations and that it is necessary to take both parts into account in order to reach the best learning experience and outcome, see Table 2. We will describe these four forms of tutoring styles - authoritative, collaborative, motivating and instructive - in more detail in order to illustrate this interplay.

Authoritative Tutoring: In the authoritative tutoring style, tutors with a dictative orientation met girls of the type active attitude. This combination resulted in step by step instructions by the tutors in imperatives without any explanations. Consequently, there was little or no room for independent work for the teenage girls. In sessions with an authoritative tutoring style there was constant negotiation of the active position in the session and the decisions about the game. On the one hand, the tutors wanted the girls to follow their instructions to program a functioning project. On the other hand the girls repeatedly tried to get involved, to take over control themselves and realise their gaming idea:
Girl: I would like it...
Tutor: Not to this but above so you need the block "When program starts"
Girl: Ah yes...
Tutor: And just do "When program starts" above, one up okey does not matter.

Girl: Yeah. [...] I'd just like to have it underneath but...
Tutor: Then you just take x 0 and y -500. (T80, 115ff.).

The sequence illustrates how the repeating attempts to intervene and participate in the programming process failed as the tutor interrupted the girl with his
commands. For these active girls, who would have liked to understand how to
implement their tasks and prefer to work independently, such tutoring style was
very frustrating. With the result that they stopped participating actively and
ended up in a rather passive position. Consequently, this tutor/tutee constellation was unlikely to provide a positive learning experience or success and did
not meet the purpose of mentoring to offer teenage girls role models, support,
encouragement, and confirmation [10].

Instructive Tutoring: In the instructive tutoring style, tutors with a dictative orientation met girls who were categorized as having a passive attitude. As already
described, these tutors mainly spoke in imperatives, explained little and took
the active role in the programming process, but with the difference that they
met passive types of girls who expected and demanded this kind of instruction:
    Girl: Okay. Should I, what should I do?
Tutor: We have to redo the background.
Girl: Good. How to do it? [...]
Tutor: Go back, once again, and now SLOWLY (laughs) open the backpack,
unpack, select the owl and unpack as object. [...] And now [...], delete or if you
want, you could just disable it.
Girl: Okay. How to disable something? (T1, 111ff.).

Both the tutor and the tutee had their fixed positions in these sessions, the
tutor gave commands while the girl executed them or requested new directions
for each step. Therefore, there was no negotiation for control or participation
in the programming sessions. Although the tutor could follow his interests of
programming a game according to his or her ideas and the girl could hold on
to her passive attitude this instructive tutoring style did not provide a positive
learning experience nor success. Because it did not promote the girls' interests
and ideas or lead to an acquisition of programming skills, it rather reinforced
gender stereotypes than eliminating them and thus clearly failed the purpose of
mentoring in IT [2,10].

Motivating Tutoring: The motivating tutoring style occured when tutors with
a supportive orientation met girls of the type passive attitude to programming.
Tutors with a supporting orientation tried to encourage the girls to think and
work independently. They explained a lot and tried to involve the tutees by
constantly asking questions:
    Girl: And now?
Tutor: When do you want to go the rope, the position from the rope in the picture.
Immediately right?
Girl: Yes, but how do I do that?
Tutor: Now you have to ask yourself when does the program need to do that?

Immediately after start, or when it's tabbed or.
Girl: Ahm, immediately...I think. (T95, 101ff.).

This tutor met a tutee with a passive attitude to programming who preferred to stay passive and did not like questions that require her involvement. If these girls were disinterested, they were annoyed by the constant requests of the tutors for more cooperation. The situation was different if the girl showed a passive attitude due to uncertainty: Here, supporting tutors offered an opportunity to experience a positive programming session. After such sessions the girls were surprised about their abilities and rated themselves as "better than expected". This experience had the potential to correct stereotypes and thus to encourage adolescent girls to engage in programming activities which they were not interested before, one of the central concerns of mentoring in the IT-sector [2]. Consequently, this tutor/tutee constellation could provide a positive learning experience and success when insecure girls were guided by their tutors and thus decide on their projects and understand the programming process in detail.

Collaborative Tutoring: In the collaborative tutoring style, tutors with a supportive orientation met girls of the type active attitude to programming. The kind of support that the supportive type of tutor offered was exactly what active girls preferred by asking questions and offering guiding explanations:
  Tutor: Right, we need to change the place. Where could that be?
Girl: Uhhhh, "motion" right?
Tutor: That's right, try "motion".
Girl: Ok and then you have to change the Y, right?
Tutor: There's... Exactly [...]
Girl: Okay, then... The upper one is better because otherwise you have to do both separately. [...] (T100, 104ff.).

This girl prefered to work independently and asked for support when needed. In the tutoring session she determinedly participated in the programming process by frequently making her own suggestions or asking questions about additional know-how. Therefore, in tutoring sessions with a collaborative tutoring style a lot of negotiations or discussions took place: One side suggests something, the other reacts to it and together they negotiate and decide what the best option was. This tutoring style was ideal for girls with an active attitude to programming and fulfilled the essential functions of mentoring such as support, encouragement, and confirmation [10]. It offered a positive learning experience and success because of the detailed explanations given by the tutors and the constant possibility of thinking and working together. The girls could develop an in-depth understanding of their programming steps and felt in charge of their game. Same as the girls- and tutors typology, the four forms of tutoring could be strengthened by quantitative content analysis. Table 3 shows that in tutoring with a dictating type of tutor (authoritative, instructive) instructions and direct commands occured to a much higher extent than in tutorings with supportive tutors (collaborative, motivating). While in authoritative tutoring 57% of code coverage were instructions and commands, in collaborative tutorings they only cover 20%. Table 3 also shows the role the type of girls' attitude played: while, supportive tutors with passive girls (i.e. motivating tutoring style) explained a lot and gave only a few commands, the girls' participation was lower than sessions with active girls (i.e. collaborative tutoring style). Girls in general engaged more in the style of tutoring they felt most comfortable with: Girls of the active type preferred supportive tutors who let them engage which showed in the highest girls' share in the spoken exchange coverage (36,2%). The second highest share (30,4%) was shown in tutoring sessions with instructive style: the girls had a passive attitude to programming and thus felt comfortable with their tutors' commands.

Table 2. Code coverage in % according to tutoring styles

Code coverage in %	Authoritative tutoring style	Instructive tutoring style	Collaborative tutoring style	Motivating tutoring style
Explanation (girl)	8%	5%	10%	3%
Suggestion (girl)	2%	2%	5%	3%
Directives (tut)	32%	26%	14%	17%
Commands (tut)	25%	16%	6%	9%
Explanation (tut)	24%	23%	26%	34%
Word coverage (girl)	26.05%	30.40%	36.2%	25.04%
Word coverage (girl) with tutor: male/female	20.92%/27.38%	28.39%/31.86%	34.8%/38.2%	24.16%/28.20%
N=	8	27	80	8

4.2 Characteristics of the Programmed Games

In this section we will describe the characteristics of the final games the teenage girls programmed in the course of the RemoteMentor project. The results should provide a decomposition of the programs and show if and how often programming concepts were used. In contrast to the Dr.Scratch suggested analysis we did not count how often these concepts were applied but we counted the use of different concepts, i.e. the variety of concepts in each project. It happened that some concepts were applied very often, e.g. loops or broadcast messages when one had to intercept multiple clones of objects or copies of objects (i.e. separate objects).

In such situations, duplicated objects would give these projects high rates if we would have followed Dr. Scratch's approach here. For our analysis instead the project received points (1, 2 or 3) once per applied concept, according to the Table 3. A percentage of 28.79 of the projects included all three abstraction concepts, 46.07% of the projects had all parallelism concepts included, and 10.61% of the projects had all flow control concepts integrated. Regarding the data representation, 27.27% of the projects made use of basic and developing (properties and variables). The project with the highest score reached 26 points, and used 14 concepts while the lowest rated project had only 6 points with a use of 5 concepts.

4.3   Relationship Between Girls' Attitudes Types and CT Concepts Used in Their Games

Next, we tested the relationship between girls' attitudes types and applied CT concepts. Games made by girls of the active type received at average 18.78 points, games made by girls of the passive type or active/passive type, received at average 17,03 (passive: 18.24, active/passive: 15.33). Table 3 shows the girls' attitudes types correlated with the average values of the different CT concepts. We correlated the average usage of concepts within the different typologies of girls. The results were significant at $\alpha = .05$ at two levels: Girls of type active used significantly more CT concepts in their projects than girls who were once categorized as passive and once as active (p $= .0096$, $\alpha = .05$). Furthermore, girls of type active used significantly more concepts of data representation than girls of type active/passive (p $= .0296$, $\alpha = .05$). The results were significant at $\alpha = .10$: girls of type active used significantly more CT concepts of flow control than girls of type passive (p $= .0731$, $\alpha = .10$) and active/passive (p $= .0901$, $\alpha = .10$). Additionally, girls of type active used significantly more CT concepts of data representation than girls of type passive (p $= .0910$, $\alpha = .10$). Overall, passive girls used more CT concepts of abstraction and problem decomposition (such as clones and physical bricks), more concepts of logical thinking (such as other-if conditions), and more concepts of interactivity (such as sounds or vibration components), but not significantly. One could assume that girls of the passive type received more instructions from their tutors on the use of competence concepts that were not discussed in the class before, such as clones or physical bricks, or that they needed more motivation and were encouraged to use sound or other effects in their projects. So it can be assumed that many CT concepts that were of the "proficiency" type were suggested by tutors. Girls of the active type used the inclination sensor variable very often, which was part of their tutoring game before they started their own project. This shows that they independently made use of the skills acquired in the course of the RemoteMentore project.

Table 3. CT concepts in relation to girls' attitudes types (*significant at $\alpha = 0.05$, **significant at $\alpha = 0.10$)

	Type active	Type passive	Type active/passive	Total
Abstraction and problem decomposition	58.56%	61.76%	45.83%	**57.07**
Parallelism	80.63%	70.83%	73.61%	**76.77%**
Logical thinking	13.96%	20.59%	16.67%	**16.60%**
Synchronization	31.53%	31.37%	25.76%	**30.30%**
Flow control	56.31%	48.04%**	47.22% **	**52.52%**
Interactivity	38.74%	45.10%	25.00%	**37.88%**
Data representation	58.56%	26.47% **	22.22% *	**29.55%**
Total	**46.12%**	**44.89%**	**37.60% ***	**44.25%**

5   Conclusion

The results of the sociological analysis showed that rather than the sex of the tutors itself, it was the nature of their tutoring that framed the introductory programming experiences of the teenage girls. These results show to what extent the tutoring experience depends on the combination of teenage girls' attitudes toward programming and the different tutoring orientations and styles which can lead to both positive and negative outcomes of the learning experience and success. These results further indicated that girls of the type active attitude or insecure passive attitude with persons of supportive tutoring orientations benefit from such one-on-one remote tutoring sessions. Which implies in further projects the deployment of tutors with a supportive orientation and also well educated and sensitizes to gendered aspects in CS and IT. The results of the analysis of the CT concepts showed that throughout girls of the type active applied more CT concepts than girls of mixed types, but overall projects made by girls of the type passive attitude included more CT concepts of abstraction and problem decomposition, logical thinking and interactivity of the type advanced and proficiency. These concepts were not discussed in the first units (before starting their actual game) and were probably proposed by the tutors. This shows that girls of the passive type were more likely to be encouraged to use advanced concepts, while girls of the active type were more likely to independently integrate concepts they had already heard about in the introductory unit and overall used significantly more types of different CT concepts. It remains open whether the girls of the passive type who used these advanced concepts also understood them, as opposed to simply following the instructions of the tutors. This also became visible during the focus group discussions. Gender stereotypes also found its way into the experience of the project. Teenage participants (esp. passive girls) tended to evaluate programming projects such as the RemoteMentor project critically: They stated their impression about a (hidden) agenda behind these kinds of school projects: to get all of them interested in programming regardless of their general interest in IT. Something they evaluated as pointless as they did not believe in someone's willingness to fundamentally change their interests. This resonates with the gender equity discourse [1] that identifies the cause of the low female share in the IT-sector in womens' attitudes and thus aims to change them than the IT-sector or the male dominated environment. The open and probably repeated communication of project goals are thus fundamental in school contexts. The relationship between tutors and tutees was only task-based and could not develop into a deeper relationship due to the short project duration and the nature of online communication. The effect of role models or the dilution of stereotypes was thus limited and short-termed. This short- termed and tasked-based relationships were furthermore problematic, especially for insecure teenage girls who would have prefered to be tutored by more familiar persons or at least female tutors, as Blake-Beard et al. [4] argued, they would have felt more confident with members of their own gender group. However, these teenage girls in our study stated that after their first online programming session they felt more confident about the online tutoring and did not mind about the tutor's gender. In summary, the remote tutoring proved to be a promising approach to support, and motivate at least a certain group of female students when they were supported by adequately skilled tutors in programming.

6 Outlook

In the future, the Catrobat Community Platform will be extended with social communication features which focus more on the principle of helping each other. Currently, our platform is very limited and is only used to upload projects from the app and share them with the world. Other users can download and play them, and further view and modify the source code, and then upload their new version again (i.e., remix). To support social communication features, several improvements are planned. Users will be able to ask questions online and will be connected to other users in chats who can help them. These principles are inspired by online computer games, in which players who do not know each other are automatically connected and can play together [15]. This also removes a hierarchy or barrier that occurs in a tutor/tutee relationship and promotes working in collaborative coding teams, following the principle "teaching is the best learning".

References

1. Abbiss, J.: The need to belong: desire for interpersonal attachments as a fundamental human motivation. Gender Educ. **20**(2), 153–165 (2008)
2. Archard, N.: Rethinking the 'problem' of gender and IT schooling: discourses in literature. Mentoring Tutor. Partnership Learn. **20**(4), 451–472 (2012)

3. Beyer, S.: Why are women underrepresented in computer science? Gender differences in stereotypes, self-efficacy, values, and interests and predictors of future CS course-taking and grades. Comput. Sci. Educ. **24**(2–3), 153–192 (2014)
4. Blake-Beard, S., et al.: Matching by race and gender in mentoring relationships: keeping our eyes on the prize. J. Soc. Issues **67**(3), 622–643 (2011)
5. Charmaz, K.: Den Standpunkt verändern: Methoden der konstruktivistischen Grounded Theory. In: Mey, G., Mruck, K. (Hg.): Grounded theory reader. 2. aktualisierte und erweiterte Auflage Wiesbaden: VS-Verlag. pp. 181–205 (2011). https://doi.org/10.1007/978-3-531-93318-4_9
6. Cheryan, S., Master, A., Meltzoff, N.: Cultural stereotypes as gatekeepers: increasing girls' interest in computer science and engineering by diversifying stereotypes. Gend. Technol. **6**(49), 37–53 (2015)
7. Committee on European Computing Education (CECE): Informatics Education in Europe: Are We All In The Same Boat? Report by The Committee on European Computing Education. Jointly established by Informatics Europe & ACM Europe. https://www.informatics-europe.org/component/phocadownload/category/10-reports.html?download=60:cece-report. Accessed 16 May 2019
8. Ensher, E., Ellen, A., Heun, C., Blanchard, A.: Online mentoring and computer-mediated communication: new directions in research. J. Vocat. Behav. **63**(2), 264–288 (2003). https://doi.org/10.1016/S0001-8791(03)00044-7
9. Faulkner, W.: The technology question in feminism. A view from feminist technology studies. Women's Stud. Int. Forum **24**(1), 79–95 (2001)
10. Finzel, B., Deininger, H., Schmid, U.: From beliefs to intention: mentoring as an approach to motivate female high school students to enrol in computer science studies. In: Marsden, N., Wulf, V., Rode, J. Weibert, A. (eds.) Proceedings of the 4th Conference on Gender & IT - GenderIT 2018, pp. 251–260. ACM Press, New York (2018)
11. Flick, U.: Qualitative Sozialforschung. Eine Einführung. Rowohlt Taschenbuch Verlag, Reinbek bei Hamburg (2009)
12. Guzman, I.R., Stanton, J.M.: Women's adaptation to the IT culture. Women's Stud. **37**(3), 202–228 (2008)
13. Hur, J.W., Andrzejewski, C.E., Marghitu, D.: Girls and computer science: experiences, perceptions, and career aspirations. Comput. Sci. Educ. **27**(2), 100–120 (2017)
14. Hsieh, H.-F., Shannon, S.E.: Three approaches to qualitative content analysis. Qual. Health Res. **15**(9), 1277–1288 (2005)
15. Jaime, S., Ruby, O: Problem Solving and Collaboration Using Mobile Serious Games. Elsevier Ltd. (2011)
16. Kafai, Y., Burke, Q.: Computer programming goes back to school. Phi Delta Kappan **95**(1), 61 (2013)
17. Khare, R., Sahai, E., Pramanick, I.: Remote Mentoring Young Females in STEM through MAGIC. GetMAGIC, Massachusetts Institute of Technology, Google. http://linc.mit.edu/linc2013/proceedings/Session7/Session7Pramanick-Sahai.pdf. Accessed 18 Apr 2019
18. Kerr, B., Robinson, K., Sharon, E.: Encouraging talented girls in math and science: effects of a guidance intervention. High Ability Stud. **15**(1), 85–102 (2004)
19. Kessels, U., Heyder, A., Latsch, M., Hannover, B.: How gender differences in academic engagement relate to students' gender identity. Educ. Res. **56**(2), 220–229 (2014)
20. Kessels, U.: Bridging the gap by enhancing the fit: how stereotypes about STEM clash with stereotypes about girls. Int. J. Gender Sci. Technol. **7**(2), 280–296 (2015)

21. Moreno-Leon, J., Robles, G., Roman-Gonzalez, M.: Examining the relationship between socialization and improved software development skills in the scratch code learning environment. J. UCS **22**(12), 1533–1557 (2016)
22. Mulac, A., et al.: Male/female language differences and effects in same-sex and mixed-sex dyads: the gender-linked language effect. Commun. Monograph. **55**(4), 315–335 (1988)
23. Neuhaus, J., Borowski, A.: Self-to-prototype similarity as a mediator between gender and students' interest in learning to code. Int. J. Gend. Sci. Technol. **10**(2), 233–252 (2018)
24. Resnick, M., et al.: Scratch: programming for all. Commun. ACM **52**(11), 60–67 (2009)
25. Rich, P.J., Hodges, C.B.: Emerging Research, Practice, and Policy on Computational Thinking. Springer, Berlin (2017). https://doi.org/10.1007/978-3-319-52691-1
26. Stoeger, H., et al.: The effectiveness of a one-year online mentoring program for girls in STEM. Comput. Educ. **69**, 408–418 (2013)
27. Vitores, A., Gil-Juarez, A.: The trouble with 'women in computing': a critical examination of the deployment of research on the gender gap in computer science. J. Gend. Stud. **25**(6), 666–680 (2016)
28. Wajcman, J.: From women and technology to gendered technoscience. Inf. Commun. Soc. **10**(3), 287–298 (2007)
29. West, C., Zimmerman, D.H.: Doing Gender. Gend. Soc. **1**(2), 125–151 (1987)
30. Wing, J.: Computational thinking. Commun. ACM **49**(3), 33–35 (2006)

A Holistic Pedagogical Model for STEM Learning and Education Inside and Outside the Classroom

Christian M. Stracke[1(✉)], Guido van Dijk[2], Jan Fasen[2], Fred Lisdat[3],
and Wim Simoens[4]

[1] Open University Netherlands, Heerlen, The Netherlands
christian.stracke@ou.nl
[2] Agora School, Roermond, The Netherlands
[3] Biosystems Technology, Technical University of Applied Science Wildau,
Wildau, Germany
[4] Eekhout Academy, Kortrijk, Belgium

Abstract. This article discusses how to innovate STEM learning and education in- and outside of the classroom. It proposes to use a holistic framework for pupil-centered learning processes called Learn STEM. It was developed by an international research consortium based on the findings from mixed methods research. The research included a literature review, semi-structured interviews and three online surveys with the participation of teachers (n = 217), headmasters (n = 24) and learners (n = 354) from more than ten countries. Furthermore, the findings from the mixed methods research are also informing the international research consortium to design a teacher training programme and to develop an online course. This article provides first summaries of the research results related to the holistic pedagogical model and to the training programme. After a short overview of the final holistic pedagogical model Learn STEM, the paper presents one example how the holistic pedagogical model Learn STEM can be used for improving STEM learning and education outside the classroom. Finally, an outlook for future research is focused.

Keywords: Holistic pedagogical model · Learn STEM · STEM learning · STEM education

1 Background

The whole world is changing in our so called "digital age": Thus, societies and their citizens are confronted with increasing demands (Organisation for Economic Co-operation and Development 2016; Stracke 2011; World Bank 2016). More competitive 21st century work environments require the building and continuous improvement of strong competences and abilities, in particular within science, technologies, engineering and mathematics (STEM) (Stracke 2014, 2019; Weinert 2001). Thus, learner should develop profound knowledge, skills and competences that they can apply in all areas of life, with special focus on transversal competences such as team work, rational thinking

© Springer Nature Switzerland AG 2020
P. Zaphiris and A. Ioannou (Eds.): HCII 2020, LNCS 12205, pp. 568–581, 2020.
https://doi.org/10.1007/978-3-030-50513-4_41

and investigative and creative work (Dewey 1966; European Commission 2007; Piaget 1953; Rousseau 1968; Stracke 2012a, 2012b; Vygotsky 1988; Westera 2001).

To address innovations in STEM education in schools, an international research consortium was established to address and improve the quality and efficiency of STEM learning and teaching (Stracke et al. 2019a). The research consortium designed Mixed Methods research and conducted it with the overall aim of the development of a holistic pedagogical model for learning STEM (Stracke et al. 2019b). To facilitate its introduction and implementation, a teacher training programme and an online course are planned. Therefore, the consortium consists of a combination of research partners, secondary schools and teacher training providers from six European countries.

This article presents briefly the design and methodology of the Mixed Methods research (Sect. 2) and provides an overview of its key findings related to the pedagogical model (Sect. 3) and the teacher training programme (Sect. 4). In the following, the holistic pedagogical model Learn STEM will be introduced (Sect. 5) and its application for STEM learning and education outside the classroom will be discussed through the example of the Tiny House project (Sect. 6). The article concludes with an outlook on the next future activities, challenges and further research demands for innovative STEM education inside and outside the classroom (Sect. 7).

2 Research Design and Methodology

The international research consortium Learn STEM started the Mixed Methods research with a literature review providing an in-depth overview of the current status of STEM education in schools and the needs for its changes and improvements. The research findings were quite homogenous: there is a huge demand for innovative STEM education as well as for related teacher training and it could be summarized that further research on learner-centered and competence-based pedagogies is required (see e.g., Harlen 2015; Organisation for Economic Co-operation and Development 2016; Vasquez 2014; World Bank 2016).

Thus, the research consortium has developed a strategy and plan for a three-year Mixed Methods research that integrates surveys and interviews. The overall objective of Learn STEM was to design a holistic pedagogical model based on informed the results from literature review, surveys and interviews to improve and innovate STEM education in schools in the future.

The pedagogical model was developed and continuously revised and improved in iterative cycles leading to 35 interim versions in total before a final draft was launched (Stracke et al. 2019b). Several interim versions were presented and debated with the audiences in interactive workshops at international conferences: Consequently, the final draft included the feedback from school researchers, teachers and headmasters.

Furthermore, the research partners have generated three surveys on STEM education: one survey for teachers, one for headmasters and one for learners. The surveys asked the three target groups similar sets of questions items with the same clusters and formulations in addition to the demographic questions. Through this design, the comparison of the question was guaranteed. All three surveys were implemented and published at the same time by the Learn STEM coordinator. They were online accessible for all interested persons worldwide opening on Friday, 22nd of February 2019 and closing on Friday, 14th of June 2019 after 16 weeks.

The following sections present the key findings of the Mixed Methods research related to the pedagogical model Learn STEM (Sect. 3) and the teacher training programme (Sect. 4).

3   Research Results on the Pedagogical Model

Teachers, pupils and headmasters have been asked with respect to their beliefs of STEM, their opinion on the main aspects of the pedagogical model for innovative STEM education and the Learn STEM Inquiry Learning packages with some more detailed examples of STEM Teaching. The majority of participants has been pupils (354) with a bias from the Netherlands (111), followed by teachers (217) with a bias from Portugal (111) and 24 headmasters from six participating countries.

The largest group of pupils was in the age from 14–17 (69.4%), whereas the largest group of teachers was between 45–54 (40%) and headmasters between 55 and 64 (45.8%).

A relatively large part of pupils could not decide whether their STEM education is exciting or boring (49%). Only 32.8% found it exciting. This contrasts to 51% of the learners who recognize the importance of STEM since they stated that STEM is important for the future employability and career opportunities. These data may point to the rather large human potential, which can still be explored and developed in order to increase motivation and enthusiasm for STEM. The view is supported by the results of 39% who would like to have more STEM education in their schools and 41% who cannot decide. The latter rather large group of learners seems to correspond to the large number of pupils who are not satisfied with the way STEM is taught nowadays. The present situation in school is good only for 33% and 23% do not like the way how STEM education appears in and outside the lessons.

The approaches how to improve STEM educations in the developed pedagogical model are well received by the learners. Most importantly, 60% of the learners support the idea of practical exercises in order to increase and develop STEM interest and ability. 57% state that real life projects are helpful to learn STEM topics and also 57% are motivated to work in groups with their classmates to search for solutions (and only 9% disagree on that).

The response to the training aspects in STEM education has been more divers since 45% think that repeating tasks and content is helpful to obtain a good learning outcome but 14% disagreed on that. The same picture appears when the learners are asked about self-controlled learning without a prescribed curriculum since 32% like this idea, but 20% dislike it and the majority cannot decide. This indicates that the usage of new approaches in STEM education is not only a challenge for teachers, but also for learners since they need to be become more independent and responsible.

Although 53% of the teachers are not teaching STEM 62% would like to increase the time devoted to STEM education in school and 76% want to see this integrated in the school vision and policy. Interestingly the teachers, who have been asked in the 6 different countries with rather different educational systems, have strongly agreed on the most important aspects of the pedagogical model developed in the Learn STEM project. 85% support the concept of practice during the learning process. Figure 1 illustrates the response of teachers and learners to the question of the usefulness of practical exercises during STEM education. Clearly the high potential of this area for future developments can be seen. But also more than 75% agreed that STEM education should be complex, social and process-oriented. Even 69% support the idea of holistic STEM education.

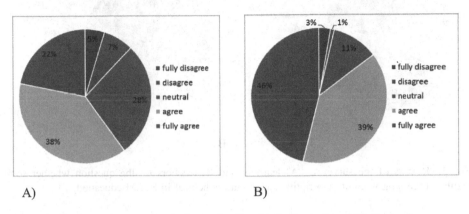

A)   B)

Fig. 1. Responses on practical exercises by A) the learners and B) the teachers.

The overall support of the developed pedagogical model is rather clear with 74% agreement on the usefulness of the approaches for enhancing the quality of school education. However, in few aspects the picture is more divers. 48% think that STEM education should be self-regulated by the learner, whereas 20% disagree and 32% are not decided. Figure 2 compares the response on the question concerning the self-regulation of teachers and learners. It points to the necessity of changing the established roles of teachers and learners or at least modifying them. 57% of the teachers support the concept of repeating tasks and content as essential in the STEM learning process, whereas 19% disagree on that. The opinions on the balance between specialized topics and general knowledge vary significantly since 34% recognize too many specialized topics, 21% disagree and 45% are neutral with this.

Interestingly the group of headmasters – although not very large – is most supportive for the new concepts in STEM teaching. Here 96% would like to increase the time spent for STEM topics and 79% want to increase the quality in STEM education. Here the importance of the STEM area for the future development of the society is very well recognized. Concerning the five aspects of the Learn STEM model: Complex, holistic, process-oriented, practical and social, 88% are supporting these ideas. 92% think that the model is useful for improving STEM education in the schools.

The headmasters are also open to new conceptual ideas in implementing improvements in STEM education and agree with 76% that the process should be self-regulated. They also recognize that repeating tasks and content is helpful to the learning process with 50% agreement. However, with respect to the balance between general overview and many specialized topics the result is also divers as for teachers and learners: 41% state too much focus on specialized topics and 30% disagree.

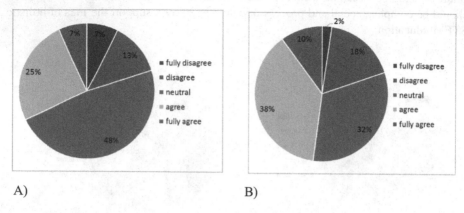

A)   B)

Fig. 2. Results of the survey by A) learners and B) teachers on the question whether self-regulated learning without prescriptive curriculum is helpful in STEM education

In addition to the survey personal interviews have been carried out in the different focus groups. Here there have been 58 participants, with teachers as the largest group (36). In general, the situation of STEM education in school has been reflected and the main ideas of the pedagogical have been discussed. Beside the points, which have already been analysed after the questionnaire, some new aspects have been evolved during these personal discussions. Interestingly the discussions did not question the proposed approaches, but concentrated constructively on the implementation of the model and how potential difficulties can be overcome. Obviously the pedagogical model has met actual demands and wishes of learners and teachers as well. One can group the discussion points accordingly:

a) Aspects which are connected to humans

Teachers are not trained for self-regulated and interdisciplinary STEM teaching. In several countries they need to overcome borders between different disciplines and they need to learn to work together with teachers of other subjects. Teachers will also have to accept to become learners since not all actual subjects will have a backing by the study course they chosen previously.

Learners are also not trained for self-regulated learning and thus, have to learn to work on projects and take responsibility. This might be complicated by the fact that many pupils do not know in which direction the professional career will go after school; thus, it is very important to connect STEM education with everyday life problems.

b) Institutional aspects and regulations

In many countries the aim to have motivated and well-trained pupils is well recognized, but a tight curriculum hinders flexibility in developing new approaches in school. Engaged teachers have to find a compromise between training for exams and the personal development of pupils. For interdisciplinary work several teachers have to work together which also needs organization and planning in the school.

c) Technical and financial aspects

Since practice during the learning process is so important, the technical basis for experiments in the different fields is essential. This is not only connected to computers, but mainly to hands on experiments in physics, chemistry, biology, engineering or interrelated topics. Here new ideas for collaboration of schools or schools with research institutes or companies are necessary. However, also governmental institutions need to be approached.

The mixed method research, which has been performed in the six participating European countries, has clearly shown the necessity for improvements in STEM education. It also verified that a more holistic approach with interdisciplinary focus, aspects of self-regulation, practical experiments and training modules is an attractive way to go. The surveys and the interviews have also allowed a further specification and development of the five basic characteristics of the pedagogical model which will be shortly explained in the following Sect. 5. Before, the Sect. 4 will present an overview of the findings from the Mixed Methods research on the training programme.

4   Research Results on the Teacher Training

In order to define a training programme valid for different European countries and in line with the European policies, based on a common methodology and set of instruments, the partners conducted a survey and interviews during the focus groups with different types of stakeholders: school management, school staff and students. The presence in some interviews and/or focus groups of teacher trainers, curriculum developers and policy makers strengthened the results of the inquiry and attributes a validation to the conclusions and recommendations. The results of these interviews, together with the analysis results, were used for defining the concrete skills and competencies trainers need for being able to successfully teach STEM using the pedagogical model Learn STEM.

An important aspect of the research was to discover what content should be included in the teacher training programme in the view of teachers and principals. The results from the teachers and the principals were very much in line and did not include any contradiction. When we look at the ranking, given in both survey groups, to the content that needed to be included in the teacher training programme, we notice a very similar image (Table 1).

Table 1. Top 7 of the content that needs to be included in the Teacher Training Programme.

	Teachers	Principals
1	Development of interdisciplinary modules	Development of interdisciplinary modules
2	Soft skill enhancement	Soft skill enhancement
3	Open content material	Learner-centred pedagogics
4	Learner-centred pedagogics	Self-regulated competence building
5	Self-regulated competence building	Holistic view on STEM
6	Curriculum design	Curriculum design
7	Holistic view on STEM	Open content material

The only small difference is that teachers attribute a higher importance to the development of open content material then the principals, while principals value more the holistic view on STEM.

In some countries the educational material is provided by Ministries of Education, official Education Authorities, educational publishers or networks of schools. In other countries the teachers have the autonomy to develop their own educational material. As in the participating countries, STEM is recently introduced, there still is no established tradition of providing good examples of STEM content. This can explain the higher need teachers express, to have access to have to open content material.

The society requires every time more that schools prepare the learners to understand general ideas, rather than accumulate specialised knowledge. Also the emphases on the ethical component of STEM and its contribution to the learners' personal development are asked by the society. Principals are responsible for the general policy of the school and that way they tend to have a broader helicopter view on the school. That way they are more sensitive towards demands and thus to a holistic view on STEM.

Based on the analysis of the online survey, interviews and/or focus groups of the teachers and principals, the teacher training programme must at least include aspects of pedagogics, didactics and assessment. A short introduction on the rationale why STEM is needed, can be useful. Teachers and principals ask to develop fresh, sprinkling ideas and examples to implement real life STEM education with research activities and a cyclic approach.

Teachers and principals want to include the development of interdisciplinary modules, soft skill enhancement, learner-centred pedagogics, self-regulated competence building, curriculum design and the holistic view on STEM next items in the teacher training programme. The teachers also favour the development of open content material. This question is addressed through the Inquiry Learning Package that also is a part of the intellectual outcome of the project.

When selecting or presenting examples and exercises in the teacher training programme, one must be aware of gender-related background. The teacher training programme should also prepare teachers to tackle gender in their STEM teaching. This conviction was reported to us during the interviews and focus group with teachers and teacher trainers. While principals didn't bring this up spontaneously, they all agreed when this idea was discussed.

The survey, interviews and focus group with the learners, revealed that the learners believe their teachers could make STEM subjects more interesting by changing or adjusting the pedagogical and didactical approaches. The learners are pointing towards the importance of a modern and challenging learning environment in which real life and practical exercises are included. In a STEM project the different topics should be present and the focus of the project should be oriented to the exploration and research, rather than purely to the end result or end product. The use of activating teaching methods, less frontal teaching, development of the 'investigation skills', stepping away from 'lecture-style' teaching and moving towards more practical exercises, are the most common given examples the learners bring fort worth, to make STEM teaching more attractive. Practical exercises such as experiments, computer work will increase the interest of the learner in STEM (survey results: fully disagree and disagree: 12%).

A second reported set of aspects relates to the education system and the school organisation. Interesting and effective STEM teaching needs a certain degree of autonomy and flexibility. When the curriculum rigidly decides on the content and didactical approaches of every lesson, when the teachers are strictly obliged to follow text books with prescribed exercises, a motivating and qualitative level of STEM teaching cannot be achieved. Learners ask for a flexible school organisation that allows outside activities, study visits to laboratories, research centre or enterprises. A flexibility that empowers their teachers to include also non-formal learning, multi-media, iterative learning, practical work and more experiments into their STEM teaching.

And finally, learners report that the use of traditional assessment methods where only the result is evaluated, isn't consistent with the idea of a process-oriented approach where learners discover STEM in a self-regulated and creative way through exploration and creation. Especially learners from countries with an examination system, based on a very detailed list of content, are afraid that this central assessment doesn't reflect their learning progress, their gained STEM knowledge and their build STEM skills. This is for sure the case when the final evaluation still is composed out of separate subject goals, and not inspired by the interdisciplinary character of STEM-learning. This concern was also brought up during some interviews with teachers and principal.

In summary, the survey results of the teachers and principals are mainly focussed on the improvement of the pedagogical and didactical knowledge and skills. Teachers also emphasise the need of having access to open content material. The analysis of the learner's survey indicate that their motivation can be enhanced by being offered activating, practical and real life teaching in a flexible educational environment with an appropriate assessment. We took this in account when editing the teacher training programme, STEM examples and STEM exercises. This resulted in a proposed structure (Table 2):

Table 2. Learn STEM teacher training programme.

Modules	Structure
1. Introduction: Why STEM learning in schools?	Introduction Presentation of the four subjects of STEM
2. Pedagogical characteristics	Introductory exercise Explanation of the Pedagogical Model and its 5 elements Exploration of the Pedagogical Model using an existing STEM lesson Reflection on the use of Pedagogical Model Reflect about the whole cycle Continuation in peer-cooperation
3. Didactical realizations	Introduction Human Centred Approach Scaffolding Open, problem-based learning Closed methodologies Additional training methodologies
4. Assessment approaches and tools	Why do you assess Who will assess? What to assess? When to assess? Ways to assess?

5   The Holistic Pedagogical Model

The pedagogical model Learn STEM focuses on the learner who shall become the owner of their own learning processes (Stracke et al. 2019b). Thus, the role of teachers needs to change: teachers should facilitate such learning processes and act as coaches. However, teachers may also guide and supervise the learning process. Learn STEM can be combined with other approaches and methodologies to learn and teach STEM.

Learn STEM is based on educational theories and positions and focuses mainly on the following five characteristics of the learning process (Fig. 3):

- Complex
- Process-oriented
- Holistic
- Practical

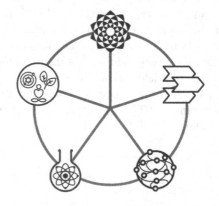

Fig. 3. The pedagogical model Learn STEM.

* Social

Learn STEM addresses three core elements: knowledge, skills and competences. Learners can gain STEM knowledge and build STEM skills. Through their reflection and iterative training, learners can build STEM competences following the principles of assimilation and accommodation. As presented in Learn STEM, the learning process should be interdisciplinary and holistic. Learning is considered as a process with iterative quality improvement cycles. Accordingly, Learn STEM allows flexibility for the teachers who can act more as a coaching mentor or as an instructing tutor depending on the situation in their intended STEM learning and given educational system.

Training modules for teachers help them to support learners solidifying acquired algorithms and knowledge and gaining confidence in using them. Practical courses are valuable tools for the learners during the learning processes as they allow to expand knowledge as well as to develop practical skills. In everyday life tasks, learners can demonstrate and use their knowledge and skills and successfully apply their developed competences in new situations.

Learn STEM incorporates The complexity of STEM learning activities is integrated in Learn STEM and relates them to the diverse STEM disciplines as well as to other (STEM) areas: Learn STEM connects STEM education and learners with our society and offers insights into the complex relationships between STEM and the whole society.

Through that approach, Learn STEM wants to discover and to stimulate the interests of STEM learners and their ability and motivation handling different perspectives of science, technology, engineering and mathematics. As a consequence, Learn STEM may encourage more pupils to select and follow a career in STEM professions. This may help to meet the demands of the society including the search for innovative scientists and engineers who are well educated, motivated and able for critical and design thinking as well as orientated to problem solving.

In order to stimulate the interest in STEM topics STEM education has to take steps out of the class room. This is on the one hand connected to topics which relates STEM topics to everyday life problems, but it also comprises the contact to companies and research institutions. By this the learners will be in a new environment and come in contact with new topics and problems. This can create attention and stimulate the engagement with STEM-related content. Besides that, the contact to persons, who are working in the STEM field, can help to open professional perspectives for the learners and to develop own aims and objectives.

6 Example for Using Learn STEM Outside the Classroom

In this section, we present one example for the usage of the holistic pedagogical model Learn STEM outside the classroom (Stracke et al. 2019a, 2019b). It is used in the Agora school in Roermond located in the south of The Netherlands. The school is following a learner centered approach where pupils learn in small communities on challenges. These challenges are based on the interests of the pupils and most of these challenges are created by themselves. The teachers are called coaches and support the pupils in the learning process by guiding them through the different steps they have to make to solve their solutions for challenges. Experts are also involved in the process. These experts are expert in a specific domain.

In this case we want to explore the case of the Agora "Tiny House" project. This case is a typical case how pupils, experts and coaches learn in realistic challenges. The five pupils are between fourteen and fifteen years old. The team is completed with one coach and two experts in the domain of government and engineering.

The idea of the project Tiny House was born during a workshop on sustainable houses done by a parent of one of the pupils. He asked to help building a sustainable house with him, where he could live with his wife and children (Fig. 4).

Fig. 4. Workshop on sustainable houses.

A Tiny House can be described as a complete home with only the really necessary spaces for easy living but also sustainable. Natural energy sources are used such as sunlight, geothermal heat, etc. They are consciously built and inhabited based on the need to live a simpler life, less focused on consumption and with a smaller ecological footprint. The design and construction of small homes make smart use of space and innovative technologies. A Tiny House is max. 50 m2, ideally (partly) self-sufficient, of good quality and aesthetically built, functioning as a full-time inhabited home. Being mobile is not a condition but often a means, being completely off-the-grid is a possibility but not a requirement.

A big challenge for pupils to build a real product, the tiny house that meets the expectations of the client. The case was complex, because this was not a very easy challenge. A lot of different components are part of this case:

1. The construction and the layout of the tiny house concerning sustainability.
2. Finding solutions for basic needs like collecting energy, water management, heating the house with sustainability in mind.
3. Finding investors to finance the production of the tiny house.
4. Finding a location to place the tiny house.

To solve these problems, the team works in an agile and iterative way working and learning in different sub-teams. Every Wednesday morning the team came together for having a meeting. To guide the process, they have followed the Design Thinking method. Following this method, the pupils had to empathize, define, ideate, prototype, and test their products. Pupils were partly responsible of a part of the project. They have worked and learned from and with their experts. During the period of this project pupils have learned about how to connect to other partners outside the project, how to present their idea to potential investors and how to get in dialog with the government about finding a location. They also have updated or upgraded their knowledge and skills about how to construct a sustainable tiny house with all the requirements and restrictions (Fig. 5).

Fig. 5. Prototype of a tiny house.

The prototype of the tiny house has been realized by the team. The next step is to build the real tiny house and to find a location to live. More about the Tiny House project can be found at their website online: https://www.tinyhouse-agora.nl

7   Conclusions and Outlook

The paper introduces the holistic pedagogical model Learn STEM for innovative STEM education and explains its usage outside of the classroom through the Tiny House project. The pedagogical model Learn STEM was developed based on the findings from Mixed Methods research designed and realized by the international

Learn STEM research consortium. The Mixed Methods research combined an in-depth literature review with interviews in focus groups and three online surveys for teachers (n = 217), headmasters (n = 24) and learners (n = 354). The paper presents first results from the comparison of the surveys for teachers and headmasters: Teachers and headmasters share a similar perspective on the current STEM education with specific interesting differences. Overall, the grading on the usefulness of the pedagogical model Learn STEM was very positive by the teachers (74% fully agreed or agreed) and even better by the headmasters (92% fully agreed or agreed).

Accordingly, the findings from the Mixed Methods research, the international research team designs a training programme and an online course for teachers and headmasters. The objective is to initiate a debate on future innovative STEM education and learning in schools following the five characteristics from the introduced pedagogical model Learn STEM: complex, process-oriented, holistic, practical, and social. Research has analysed the opportunities for (open) online education and the needs and preferences to use it in (STEM education within) schools as well as lifelong learning (Stracke et al. 2017). The design and fulfilment of the appropriate quality is currently the main challenge for (open) online education (Stracke 2019): The re-usage and adaptation of international standards such as first ISO norm for technology-enhanced learning ISO/IEC 40180 (2017) and the Quality Reference Framework (QRF) for online courses and learning support the design of online education (Stracke et al. 2018). These first international quality standards were already applied and used as basis for the holistic pedagogical model Learn STEM presented in this paper. Furthermore, the online course for the teacher training programme of Learn STEM will also benefit from them.

It can be concluded that further research is required to precisely focus the specific requirements of school teachers and headmasters how they can introduce and facilitate pupil-centered STEM education with different approaches of open and closed methodologies inside and outside the classroom that is following the five principles of the pedagogical model Learn STEM.

References

Dewey, J.: Democracy and Education: An Introduction to the Philosophy of Education. The Free Press, New York (1966)

European Commission: Science Education NOW. A Renewed Pedagogy for the Future of Europe [Rocard-Report] (2007). https://ec.europa.eu/research/science-society/document_library/pdf_06/report-rocard-on-science-education_en.pdf

Harlen, W. (ed.): Working with Big Ideas of Science Education. Trieste: Global Network of Science Academics (IAP) Science Education Programme (2015). www.ase.org.uk/bigideas

ISO/IEC 40180: Information Technology - Quality for Learning, Education, and Training—Fundamentals and Reference Framework. Geneva: International Organisation for Standardization (ISO). [developed by international standardization committee ISO/IEC JTC1 SC36] (2017)

Organisation for Economic Co-operation and Development: Education at a glance 2016: OECD indicators. OECD Publishing, Paris (2016)

Piaget, J.: The Origin of Intelligence in the Child. Routledge, London (1953)

Rousseau, J.J.: The Social Contract. Penguin, Harmondsworth (1968)

Stracke, C.M.: Quality frameworks and learning design for open education. Int. Rev. Res. Open Distrib. Learn. **20**(2), 180–203 (2019). https://doi.org/10.19173/irrodl.v20i2.4213, [Open Access]

Stracke, C.M.: How innovations and competence development support quality in lifelong learning. Int. J. Innov. Qual. Learn. **2**(3), 35–44 (2014). http://www.opening-up.education, [Open Access]

Stracke, C.M.: Competences and Skills for the challenges of the Digital Age: Combining Learning-Outcome Orientation with Competence Development and Modelling for Human Resources Development/ЗНАНИЯ И НАВЫКИ ДЛЯ РЕШЕНИЯ ПРОБЛЕМ ЦИФРОВОГО ВЕКА: СОЧЕТАНИЕ ОБУЧЕНИЯ КАК РЕЗУЛЬТАТ ОРИЕНТАЦИИ НА РАЗВИ-ТИЕ КОМ-ПЕТЕНТНОСТИ И МОДЕЛИРОВАНИЕ РАЗВИТИЯ ЛЮДСКИХ РЕСУРСОВ. *Информатизация образования и науки* [= Информике (Informika) **13**(1), 146–160 (2012a). http://www.opening-up.education, ISSN 2073-7572]

Stracke, C.M.: Competences and skills for learning-outcome orientation: competence development, modelling, and standards for human resources development, education and training. 华东师范大学学报 (自然科学版) J. East China Normal Univ. **2**(2012), 115–130 (2012b). https://doi.org/10.3969/j.issn1000-5641.2012.02.012, [CLC number: Q948], http://www.opening-up.education

Stracke, C.M.: Competences and skills in the digital age: competence development, modelling, and standards for human resources development. In: García-Barriocanal, E., Cebeci, Z., Okur, Mehmet C., Öztürk, A. (eds.) MTSR 2011. CCIS, vol. 240, pp. 34–46. Springer, Heidelberg (2011). https://doi.org/10.1007/978-3-642-24731-6_4

Stracke, C.M., et al.: A holistic pedagogical model for stem education in schools: its design and evaluation through mixed methods research with surveys and interviews. In: Proceedings of Learning Innovations and Quality (LINQ) 2019, EPiC Series 2, pp. 40–48 (2019a). https://doi.org/10.29007/t43b

Stracke, C.M., et al.: Learn STEM. The Pedagogical Model for Innovative STEM Learning and Teaching (2019b). http://www.Learn-STEM.org/Model, [Open Access]

Stracke, C.M., et al.: Quality Reference Framework (QRF) for the Quality of Massive Open Online Courses (MOOCs) (2018). http://www.mooc-quality.eu/QRF, [Open Access]

Stracke, C.M., et al.: The quality of open online education: towards a reference framework for MOOCs. In: Proceedings of 2017 IEEE Global Engineering Education Conference (EDUCON), pp. 1712–1715 (2017). https://doi.org/10.1109/educon.2017.7943080, http://www.opening-up.education

Vasquez, J.A.: STEM beyond the acronym. Educ. Leadersh. **72**(4), 10 (2014)

Vygotsky, L.: Thought and Language. MIT Press, Cambridge (1988)

Weinert, F.E.: Concept of competence: a conceptual clarification. In: Rychen, D.S. (ed.) Defining and Selecting Key Competencies, pp. 45–66. Hogrefe & Huber, Seattle (2001)

Westera, W.: Competences in education: a confusion of tongues. J. Curric. Stud. **33**(1), 75–88 (2001). https://doi.org/10.1080/00220270120625

World Bank: World development report 2016: Digital dividends. World Bank, Washington (2016)

Author Index